GIVE ME LIBERTY!

An American History

Second Edition

PROCLAIM LIBERTY

THROUGHOUT ALL THE LAND,

UNTO ALL

THE INHABITANTS THEREOF.

VOLUME 2: FROM 1865

W · W · NORTON & COMPANY · NEW YORK · LONDON

GIVE ME LIBERTY!

AN AMERICAN HISTORY

Second Edition

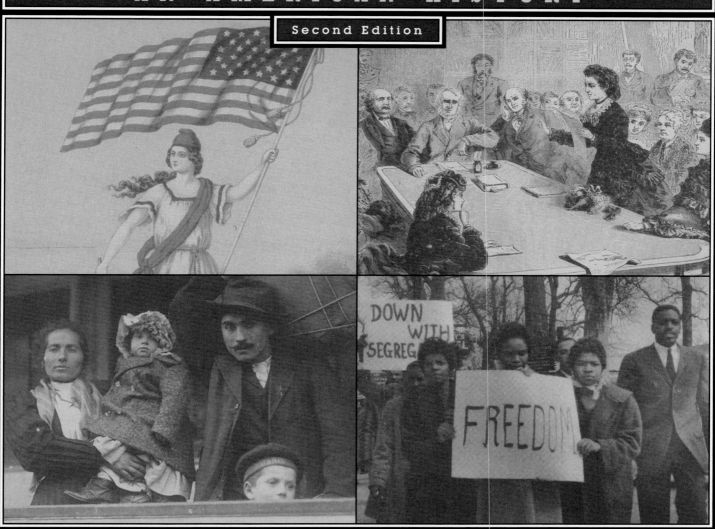

by ERIC FONER

For my mother, Liza Foner (1909–2005), an accom-
plished artist who lived through most of the twentieth
century and into the twenty-first

W. W. Norton & Company has been independent since its founding in 1923, when William Warder Norton and Mary D. Herter Norton first published lectures delivered at the People's Institute, the adult education division of New York City's Cooper Union. The Nortons soon expanded their program beyond the Institute, publishing books by celebrated academics from America and abroad. By mid-century, the two major pillars of Norton's publishing program—trade books and college texts—were firmly established. In the 1950s, the Norton family transferred control of the company to its employees, and today—with a staff of four hundred and a comparable number of trade, college, and professional titles published each year—W. W. Norton & Company stands as the largest and oldest publishing house owned wholly by its employees.

Editor: Steve Forman
Associate Managing Editor, College: Kim Yi
Editorial Assistant: Rebecca Arata
Copy Editor: Alice Vigliani
Managing Editor, College: Marian Johnson
Manufacturing by RR Donnelley, Willard
Composition by Matrix Publishing Services
Book design by Antonina Krass
Production Manager: Chris Granville
Photo Researchers: Rebecca Arata, Stephanie Romeo
Associate Director, Electronic Media: Steven S. Hoge
Cartographer: Martha Bostwick, Maps.com

The Library of Congress has cataloged the one-volume edition as follows:
Foner, Eric.
    Give me liberty! : an American history / by Eric Foner. — 2nd ed.
        p. cm.
    Includes bibliographical references and index.
    ISBN 978-0-393-92944-7 (hardcover)
    1. United States—History. 2. United States—Politics and government. 3. Democracy—United States—History. 4. Liberty—History. I. Title.

E178.F66 2007
973—dc22
                                                                2007001292

ISBN 978-0-393-92944-7 (pbk.)

W. W. Norton & Company, Inc., 500 Fifth Avenue, New York, N. Y. 10110
www.wwnorton.com
W. W. Norton & Company Ltd., Castle House, 75/76 Wells Street, London W1T 3QT
    3 4 5 6 7 8 9 0

Contents

Part 4 Toward a Global Presence, 1870–1920

16. AMERICA'S GILDED AGE, 1870–1890 • 588

Part 5 Depression and Wars, 1920–1953

APPENDIX

DOCUMENTS

TABLES AND FIGURES

List of Maps, Tables, and Figures

ABOUT THE AUTHOR

ERIC FONER is DeWitt Clinton Professor of History at Columbia University, where he earned his B.A. and Ph.D. In his teaching and scholarship, he focuses on the Civil War and Reconstruction, slavery, and nineteenth-century America. Professor Foner's publications include *Free Soil, Free Labor, Free Men: The Ideology of the Republican Party Before the Civil War; Tom Paine and Revolutionary America; Politics and Ideology in the Age of the Civil War; Nothing But Freedom: Emancipation and Its Legacy; Reconstruction: America's Unfinished Revolution, 1863–1877; Freedom's Lawmakers: A Directory of Black Officeholders During Reconstruction; The Story of American Freedom; Who Owns History? Rethinking the Past in a Changing World;* and *Forever Free: The Story of Emancipation and Reconstruction.* His history of Reconstruction won the *Los Angeles Times* Book Award for History, the Bancroft Prize, and the Parkman Prize. He has been co-curator for two historical exhibits, "A House Divided" at the Chicago Historical Society, and "America's Reconstruction" at the Virginia Historical Society. He has served as president of the Organization of American Historians (1993–1994) and the American Historical Association (2000). In 2006 he received the Presidential Award for Outstanding Teaching from Columbia University.

Preface

Give Me Liberty! An American History is a survey of American history from the earliest days of European exploration and conquest of the New World to the first years of the twenty-first century. It offers students a clear, concise narrative whose central theme is the changing contours of American freedom.

I am extremely gratified by the response to the First Edition of *Give Me Liberty!*, which has been used in survey courses at many hundreds of two- and four-year colleges and universities throughout the country. The comments I have received from instructors and students encourage me to think that *Give Me Liberty!* has worked well in their classrooms. Their comments have also included many valuable suggestions for revisions, which I greatly appreciate. These have ranged from corrections of typographical and factual errors that crept into the First Edition (perhaps most embarrassingly, I misstated the year of the sinking of the *Titanic*), to thoughts about subjects that needed more extensive treatment. In making revisions for this Second Edition, I have tried to take these suggestions into account. I have also incorporated the findings and insights of new scholarship that has appeared since the original edition was written.

The most significant changes in the Second Edition are as follows:

Throughout the book, I have revised and added material about the history of Native Americans, an area of American history that has received significant new attention in the past few years. For example, Chapter 1 opens with an expanded treatment of Native American life before European contact; Chapter 4 contains new material on Indian slavery in the colonial era; Chapter 10 devotes increased attention to Supreme Court decisions of the Jacksonian era related to the status of Indians; Chapter 16 includes a new discussion of issues surrounding Indian citizenship in the late nineteenth century, Chapter 18 includes a new examination of Native American Progressivism; and Chapter 25 provides further coverage of the movement for greater rights for American Indians that emerged during the turbulent 1960s.

The history of immigration and the controversies surrounding it receive greater attention throughout this edition. Chapter 9 now includes an expanded section on immigration and nativism in the era before the Civil War; Chapter 18 devotes increased attention to Asian immigration in the early twentieth century; and the final two chapters discuss at length recent shifts in immigration patterns and the way immigration, especially from Latin America, has again become a controversial political issue. The discussion of the evolution of citizenship rights for immigrant groups and racial minorities more broadly has also been expanded, as in discussions of efforts to "colonize" African-Americans outside the United States, in Chapter 12; movements among Chinese and Mexican immigrants for equal rights, in Chapters 17 and 22; and an expanded treatment of the implications of changes in immigration policies in the 1920s, in Chapter 20.

I have strengthened at many points the discussion of the history of the American West, including additional coverage in Chapter 16 of western farming and the role of women in the trans-Mississippi West, a new discussion in Chapter 21 of New Deal agricultural and resource management policies, and a new treatment of the Sagebrush Rebellion as part of the growth of conservatism in the 1970s, in Chapter 26.

Throughout the book, I have strengthened the presentation of American history in a global context. Thus, Chapter 2 examines the impact of the English Civil War of the 1640s on the American colonies, with special attention to how new ideas about English liberty circulated in the New World; Chapter 3 discusses how the colonies participated in an Atlantic world of commerce and ideas; Chapter 6 contains a new section on the fate of the thousands of slaves who left with the British after the War of Independence for new lives in Canada, Britain, and West Africa; Chapter 14 points to changes in world production of cotton stimulated by the cotton embargo during the American Civil War; Chapter 18 places American immigration in the context of worldwide population flows; and Chapter 28 examines the country's relationship with the rest of the world in the aftermath of the terrorist attacks of September 11, 2001 and the war in Iraq.

A number of chapters have been reorganized to achieve greater focus and clarity. Most notably, I have completely restructured Chapters 1–4 covering the colonial period. The first now concentrates on Native American life before European contact and the establishment of the Spanish, French, and Dutch American empires in the New World. Chapter 2 now deals entirely with English America. Chapter 3 explores the making of a distinctive Anglo-American society, culture, and politics, and the diverse ethnic and religious groups that populated the colonies in the eighteenth century. Chapter 4 now includes a more developed treatment of the early history of American slavery, bringing together material previously scattered in the early chapters. In another reorganization, sections on conservative thought and politics in the 1950s and 1960s have been moved from Chapter 26 to their appropriate chronological placement.

The Voices of Freedom sections in each chapter now include two document excerpts instead of one. The excerpts are juxtaposed to suggest differing ideas about American freedom at each historical moment. This pairing allows for the inclusion of a more diverse group of authors, especially a larger number of women than in the first edition. I have also added a series of questions at the end of the sections to further discussion.

This Second Edition also includes a number of new images in each chapter. I have added new photos and figures in order to expand the visual representation of key ideas and personalities in the text.

I have greatly expanded the final chapter, which deals with the momentous events of the early twenty-first century, and especially how ideas and practices concerning freedom have come under strain since the terrorist attacks of September 11, 2001. In addition to adding material on historical developments since the publication of the first edition—the war in Iraq, the reelection of President Bush, the devastation caused by Hurricane Katrina, and the emergence of immigration as a major political issue, for example—I examine current debates over the balance between liberty and security in wartime, whether the United States should be bound by international standards concerning the treatment of prisoners of war, and whether the president, Congress, or the courts has the right to determine the rights of those accused of crimes related to terrorism.

Other improvements in the text intended to make it more accessible to students include an increase in each chapter in the number of subheadings, expanded timelines at the opening of chapters, and a list of key terms in the chapter review pages, with definitions available to students on the companion website and in the Study Guide.

These changes, I believe, enhance the purpose of *Give Me Liberty!*: to offer students a clear, concise, and thematically enriched introduction to American history.

Americans have always had a divided attitude toward history. On the one hand, they tend to be remarkably future-oriented, dismissing events of even the recent past as "ancient history" and sometimes seeing history as a burden to be overcome, a prison from which to escape. On the other hand, like many other peoples, Americans have always looked to history for a sense of personal or group identity and of national cohesiveness. This is why so many Americans devote time and energy to tracing their family trees and why they visit historical museums and National Park Service historical sites in ever-increasing numbers. My hope is that this book will help to convince readers with all degrees of interest that history does matter to them.

The novelist and essayist James Baldwin once observed that history "does not refer merely, or even principally, to the past. On the contrary, the great force of history comes from the fact that we carry it within us, . . . [that] history is literally present in all that we do." As Baldwin recognized, the force of history is evident in our own world. Especially in a political democracy like the United States, whose government is designed to rest on the consent of informed citizens, knowledge of the past is essential—not only for those of us whose profession is the teaching and writing of history, but for everyone. History, to be sure, does not offer simple lessons or immediate answers to current questions. Knowing the history of immigration to the United States, and all of the tensions, turmoil, and aspirations associated with it, for example, does not tell us what current immigration policy ought to be. But without that knowledge, we have no way of understanding which approaches have worked and which have not—essential information for the formulation of future public policy.

History, it has been said, is what the present chooses to remember about the past. Rather than a fixed collection of facts, or a group of interpretations that cannot be challenged, our understanding of history is constantly changing. There is nothing unusual in the fact that each generation rewrites history to meet its own needs, or that scholars disagree among themselves on basic questions like the causes of the Civil War or the reasons for the Great Depression. Precisely because each generation asks different questions of the past, each generation formulates different answers. The past thirty years have witnessed a remarkable expansion of the scope of historical study. The experiences of groups neglected by earlier scholars, including women, African-Americans, working people, and others, have received unprecedented attention from historians. New subfields—social history, cultural history, and family history among them—have taken their place alongside traditional political and diplomatic history.

Give Me Liberty! draws on this voluminous historical literature to present an up-to-date and inclusive account of the American past, paying due attention to the experience of diverse groups of Americans while in no way neglecting the events and processes Americans have experienced in common. It devotes serious attention to political, social, cultural, and economic history, and to their interconnections. The narrative brings together major events and prominent leaders with the many groups of ordinary people who make up American society. *Give Me Liberty!* has a rich cast of characters, from Thomas Jefferson to campaigners for woman suffrage, from Franklin D. Roosevelt to former slaves seeking to breathe meaning into emancipation during and after the Civil War.

Aimed at an audience of undergraduate students with little or no detailed knowledge of American history, *Give Me Liberty!* guides readers through the complexities of the subject without overwhelming them with excessive detail. The unifying theme of freedom that runs through the text gives shape to the narrative and integrates the numerous strands that make up the American experience. This approach builds on that of my earlier book, *The Story of American Freedom* (1998), although *Give Me Liberty!* places events and personalities in the foreground and is more geared to the structure of the introductory survey course.

Freedom, and battles to define its meaning, has long been central to my own scholarship and undergraduate teaching, which focuses on the nineteenth century and especially the era of Civil War and Reconstruction (1850–1877). This was a time when the future of slavery tore the nation apart and emancipation produced a national debate over what rights the former slaves, and all Americans, should enjoy as free citizens. I have found that attention to clashing definitions of freedom and the struggles of different groups to achieve freedom as they understood it offers a way of making sense of the bitter battles and vast transformations of that pivotal era. I believe that the same is true for American history as a whole.

No idea is more fundamental to Americans' sense of themselves as individuals and as a nation than freedom. The central term in our political language, freedom—or liberty, with which it is almost always used interchangeably—is deeply embedded in the record of our history and the language of everyday life. The Declaration of Independence lists liberty among mankind's inalienable rights; the Constitution announces its purpose as securing liberty's blessings. The United States fought the Civil War to bring about a new birth of freedom, World War II for the Four Freedoms, and the Cold War to defend the Free World. Americans' love of liberty has been represented by liberty poles, liberty caps, and statues of liberty, and acted out by burning stamps and burning draft cards, by running away from slavery, and by demonstrating for the right to vote. "Every man in the street, white, black, red, or yellow," wrote the educator and statesman Ralph Bunche in 1940, "knows that this is 'the land of the free' . . . 'the cradle of liberty.'"

The very universality of the idea of freedom, however, can be misleading. Freedom is not a fixed, timeless category with a single unchanging definition. Indeed, the history of the United States is, in part, a story of debates, disagreements, and struggles over freedom. Crises like the American Revolution, the Civil War, and the Cold War have permanently transformed the idea of freedom. So too have demands by various groups of Americans to enjoy greater freedom. The meaning of freedom has been constructed not only in congressional debates and political treatises, but on plantations and picket lines, in parlors and even bedrooms.

Over the course of our history, American freedom has been both a reality and a mythic ideal—a living truth for millions of Americans, a cruel mockery for others. For some, freedom has been what some scholars call a "habit of the heart," an ideal so taken for granted that it is lived out but rarely analyzed. For others, freedom is not a birthright but a distant goal that has inspired great sacrifice.

Give Me Liberty! draws attention to three dimensions of freedom that have been critical in American history: (1) the *meanings* of freedom; (2) the *social conditions* that make freedom possible; and (3) the *boundaries* of freedom that determine who is entitled to enjoy freedom and who is not. All have changed over time.

In the era of the American Revolution, for example, freedom was primarily a set of rights enjoyed in public activity—the right of a community to be governed by laws to which its representatives had consented and of individuals to engage in religious worship without governmental interference. In the nineteenth century, freedom came to be closely identified with each person's opportunity to develop to the fullest his or her innate talents. In the twentieth, the "ability to choose," in both public and private life, became perhaps the dominant understanding of freedom. This development was encouraged by the explosive growth of the consumer marketplace (a development that receives considerable attention in *Give Me Liberty!*), which offered Americans an unprecedented array of goods with which to satisfy their needs and desires. During the 1960s, a crucial chapter in the history of American freedom, the idea of personal freedom was extended into virtually every realm, from attire and "lifestyle" to relations between the sexes. Thus, over time, more and more areas of life have been drawn into Americans' debates about the meaning of freedom.

A second important dimension of freedom focuses on the social conditions necessary to allow freedom to flourish. What kinds of economic institutions and relationships best encourage individual freedom? In the colonial era and for more than a century after independence, the answer centered on economic autonomy, enshrined in the glorification of the independent small producer—the farmer, skilled craftsman, or shopkeeper—

who did not have to depend on another person for his livelihood. As the industrial economy matured, new conceptions of economic freedom came to the fore: "liberty of contract" in the Gilded Age, "industrial freedom" (a say in corporate decision-making) in the Progressive era, economic security during the New Deal, and, more recently, the ability to enjoy mass consumption within a market economy.

The boundaries of freedom, the third dimension of this theme, have inspired some of the most intense struggles in American history. Although founded on the premise that liberty is an entitlement of all humanity, the United States for much of its history deprived many of its own people of freedom. Non-whites have rarely enjoyed the same access to freedom as white Americans. The belief in equal opportunity as the birthright of all Americans has coexisted with persistent efforts to limit freedom by race, gender, class, and in other ways.

Less obvious, perhaps, is the fact that one person's freedom has frequently been linked to another's servitude. In the colonial era and nineteenth century, expanding freedom for many Americans rested on the lack of freedom—slavery, indentured servitude, the subordinate position of women—for others. By the same token, it has been through battles at the boundaries—the efforts of racial minorities, women, and others to secure greater freedom—that the meaning and experience of freedom have been deepened and the concept extended into new realms.

Time and again in American history, freedom has been transformed by the demands of excluded groups for inclusion. The idea of freedom as a universal birthright owes much both to abolitionists who sought to extend the blessings of liberty to blacks and to immigrant groups who insisted on full recognition as American citizens. The principle of equal protection of the law without regard to race, which became a central element of American freedom, arose from the antislavery struggle and Civil War and was reinvigorated by the civil rights revolution of the 1960s, which called itself the "freedom movement." The battle for the right of free speech by labor radicals and birth control advocates in the first part of the twentieth century helped to make civil liberties an essential element of freedom for all Americans.

While concentrating on events within the United States, *Give Me Liberty!* also, as indicated above, situates American history in the context of developments in other parts of the world. Many of the forces that shaped American history, including the international migration of peoples, the development of slavery, the spread of democracy, and the expansion of capitalism, were worldwide processes, not confined to the United States. Today, American ideas, culture, and economic and military power exert unprecedented influence throughout the world. But beginning with the earliest days of settlement, when European empires competed to colonize North America and enrich themselves from its trade, American history cannot be understood in isolation from its global setting.

Readers will find a number of recurring elements in *Give Me Liberty!*, intended to make the book accessible and to highlight the theme of freedom. The book is divided into six parts, each of which opens with a brief introduction and a portfolio of visual images of freedom taken from the chapters of that part. Each chapter begins with a specific historical moment or incident that illuminates some of the major themes that follow.

Each contains two brief documentary excerpts called "Voices of Freedom" that illustrate how Americans at various times have understood the idea of freedom. Many of these excerpts are taken from the companion reader to *Give Me Liberty!*, also called *Voices of Freedom,* a documentary history of American freedom. (A Second Edition of that collection has also been prepared, which considerably increases the number and range of documents included.) All these documents, as well as a selection of documents included in the Appendix to the textbook, are what historians call "primary sources"—that is, they were written or spoken by men and women enmeshed in the events of the past, rather than by later historians. They therefore offer students the opportunity to encounter ideas about freedom in the actual words of participants in the drama of American history. Also included with every chapter is a brief, annotated Suggested Reading list. These lists are meant to direct students to the most important works of historical scholarship on that period.

Freedom is the oldest of clichés and the most modern of aspirations. At various times in our history, it has served as the rallying cry of the powerless and as a justification of the status quo. Freedom helps to bind our culture together and exposes the contradictions between what America claims to be and what it sometimes has been. American history is not a narrative of continual progress toward greater and greater freedom. As the abolitionist Thomas Wentworth Higginson noted after the Civil War, "revolutions may go backward." While freedom can be achieved, it may also be taken away. This happened, for example, when the equal rights granted to former slaves immediately after the Civil War were essentially nullified during the era of segregation. As was said in the eighteenth century, the price of freedom is eternal vigilance.

In the early twenty-first century, freedom continues to play a central role in our political and social life and thought. It is invoked by individuals and groups of all kinds, from critics of economic globalization to those who seek to secure American freedom at home and export it abroad. I hope that *Give Me Liberty!* will offer beginning students a clear account of the course of American history, and of its central theme, freedom, which today remains as varied, contentious, and ever-changing as America itself.

ACKNOWLEDGMENTS

All works of history are, to a considerable extent, collaborative books, in that every writer builds on the research and writing of previous scholars. This is especially true of a textbook that covers the entire American experience over more than five centuries. My greatest debt is to the innumerable historians on whose work I have drawn in preparing this volume. The Suggested Reading list at the end of each chapter offers only a brief introduction to the vast body of historical scholarship that has influenced and informed this book.

More specifically, however, I wish to thank the following scholars, who generously read portions of this work and offered valuable comments, criticisms, and suggestions:

For the First Edition:
  Valerie Adams, Embry-Riddle Aeronautical University
  Terry Alford, Northern Virginia Community College
  Tyler Anbinder, George Washington University
  Eric Arnesen, University of Illinois, Chicago
  Ira Berlin, University of Maryland
  Nikki Brown, Kent State University
  Jon Butler, Yale University
  Diane S. Clemens, University of California, Berkeley
  Paul G. E. Clemens, Rutgers University
  Jane Dailey, Johns Hopkins University
  Douglas Deal, State University of New York, Oswego
  Ricky Dobbs, Texas A&M University, Commerce
  Thomas Dublin, State University of New York, Binghamton
  Joel Franks, San Jose State University
  Kirsten Gardner, University of Texas at San Antonio
  Lawrence B. Glickman, University of South Carolina
  Colin Gordon, University of Iowa
  Sam Haynes, University of Texas at Arlington
  Rebecca Hill, Borough of Manhattan Community College
  Jesse Hingson, Manatee Community College
  Wallace Hutcheon, Northern Virginia Community College
  Kevin Kenny, Boston College
  Peter Kolchin, University of Delaware
  Bruce Laurie, University of Massachusetts, Amherst
  Daniel Letwin, Pennsylvania State University
  Peter Mancall, University of Southern California
  Louis Masur, City College, City University of New York
  Alan McPherson, Howard University
  Don Palm, Sacramento City College
  Larry Peterson, North Dakota State University
  John Recchiuti, Mount Union College
  Scott Sandage, Carnegie-Mellon University
  Bryant Simon, University of Georgia
  Brooks Simpson, Arizona State University
  Judith Stein, City College, City University of New York
  George Stevens, Dutchess Community College
  Thomas Sugrue, University of Pennsylvania
  Alan Taylor, University of California, Davis
  Daniel B. Thorp, Virginia Polytechnic Institute
  Helena Wall, Pomona College
  Jon Wiener, University of California, Irvine.

For the Second Edition:
  Marsha Ackermann, Eastern Michigan University
  Valerie Adams, Embry-Riddle Aeronautical University
  Omar Ali, Towson University
  Ellen Baker, Columbia University
  Ruth Bloch, University of California, Los Angeles

Roger Bromert, Southern Oklahoma State University
Charlotte Brooks, University at Albany, State University of New York
Barbara Calluori, Montclair State University
Robert Cassanello, University of Central Florida
Thomas Clarkin, San Antonio College
Gerard Clock, Pace University
Ronald Dufour, Rhode Island College
Mike Green, Community College of Southern Nevada
Maurine Greenwald, University of Pittsburgh
Evan Haefeli, Columbia University
Sharon A. Roger Hepburn, Radford College
Tam Hoskisson, Northern Arizona University
David Hsiung, Juniata College
Jeanette Keith, Bloomsburg University of Pennsylvania
Daniel Kotzin, Kutztown University
Robert M. S. McDonald, U.S. Military Academy
Stephen L. McIntyre, Missouri State University
Cynthia Northrup, University of Texas at Arlington
Kathleen Banks Nutter, Stony Brook University, State University of
   New York
John Paden, Rappahannock Community College
Sarah Phillips, Columbia University
Charles K. Piehl, Minnesota State University, Mankato
Ann Plane, University of California, Santa Barbara
Charles Postel, California State University, Sacramento
John Recchiuti, Mount Union College
Rob Risko, Trinity Valley Community College, Athens
Wade Shaffer, West Texas A&M University
Silvana R. Siddali, Saint Louis University
Judith Stein, The City College of the City University of New York
George Stevens, Dutchess Community College
Matthew A. Sutton, Oakland University
Timothy Thurber, Virginia Commonwealth University
David Voelker, University of Wisconson—Green Bay
Peter Way, Bowling Green State University
Richard Weiner, Indiana University—Purdue University Fort Wayne
Barbara Welke, University of Minnesota

I am particularly grateful to my colleagues in the Columbia University
Department of History: Even Haefeli and Ellen Baker, who read and made
many suggestions for improvements in their respective areas of expertise
(colonial America, and the history of the West), and Sarah Phillips, who
offered advice on treating the history of the environment.

I am also deeply indebted to graduate students at Columbia University's
Department of History who helped with this project. James Delbourgo conducted research for the chapters on the colonial era. Beverly Gage did the
same for the twentieth century. Daniel Freund provided all-round research
assistance. Victoria Cain did a superb job of locating visual images. And
many thanks to Valerie Adams and Thomas Clarkin for their good and

untiring work on the end-of-chapter materials. I also want to thank my colleagues Elizabeth Blackmar and Alan Brinkley for offering advice and encouragement throughout the writing of this book.

At W. W. Norton & Company, Steve Forman was an ideal editor—patient, encouraging, always ready to offer sage advice, and quick to point out lapses in grammar and logic. His assistant, Rebecca Arata, also did extraordinarily valuable work on this project. Antonina Krass created a beautiful and unobtrusive book design. Debra Morton Hoyt is responsible for the splendid covers. Kim Yi was the center of gravity for the many pieces of this project. She, Chris Granville, and Marian Johnson skillfully guided the project as it moved from final manuscript to bound book. Steve Hoge did the same as *Give Me Liberty!* entered cyberspace.

Many students may have heard stories of how publishing companies alter the language and content of textbooks in an attempt to maximize sales and avoid alienating any potential reader. In this case, I can honestly say that W. W. Norton allowed me a free hand in writing the book and, apart from the usual editorial corrections, did not try to influence its content at all. For this I thank them, while I accept full responsibility for the interpretations presented and for any errors the book may contain. Since no book of this length can be entirely free of mistakes, I welcome readers to send me corrections at ef17@columbia.edu.

My greatest debt, as always, is to my family—my wife, Lynn Garafola, for her good-natured support while I was preoccupied by a project that consumed more than its fair share of my time and energy, and my daughter, Daria, who while a ninth and tenth grader read every chapter as it was written and offered invaluable suggestions about improving the book's clarity, logic, and grammar.

Eric Foner
New York City
July 2007

To the Student, from the Publisher

Eric Foner's *Give Me Liberty! An American History*, Second Edition, provides you with all of the tools you need to succeed in your American history course.

A CONCISE, COHESIVE NARRATIVE

The book itself covers the key events in American history in a concise, clear narrative that is not clogged with dense detail. The narrative is cohesive throughout because it was written entirely by a single author and is driven by a strong theme. That theme—freedom and the continuing efforts of Americans to define it and achieve it—goes to the core of American history. As important today as it has been throughout our history, the theme of American freedom gives you an immediate point of contact with the history you will read in this text. The author, Eric Foner, has earned widespread acclaim for his books on the Civil War and Reconstruction periods and beyond. He has written an authoritative narrative that you can rely on. His narrative also provides you with a fine introduction to the field of history as it is broadly written and taught today. Whether you are a prospective history major or are taking the survey as your only history course, Foner's *Give Me Liberty!* suits your needs.

HELPFUL FEATURES

Give Me Liberty! includes the following features aimed at helping you master the material it presents:

Chapter outlines and chapter chronologies appear in each chapter-opening sequence.

Focus Questions are listed in the chapter openings and then repeated individually above the relevant text in the running heads of right-hand pages. These questions are meant to remind you, at a glance, of the larger issues at stake in the discussion on the page.

Chapter Review page: Each chapter ends with a review page that includes a list of key terms with page references, a series of review questions, and a review table of major events or developments discussed in the chapter.

Voices of Freedom Boxes: Each chapter of the text includes excerpts from two paired primary sources that address the theme of American freedom. (See the Contents for a list of these Voices of Freedom boxes.) Eric Foner chose these excerpts to illustrate key ideas and arguments about American freedom. He has written headnotes and questions for each Voices of Freedom feature.

Part Openers: The book is divided into six chronological Parts, and each one opens with a brief but substantive overview of the major events and developments covered in the section. Don't skip these—they are worth reading!

Suggested Readings: These annotated end-of-chapter lists include sources for the chapter discussions and readings to get you started on projects and research papers.

Appendix with Documents and Tables: The Appendix to *Give Me Liberty* includes a small collection of primary documents ranging from the Declaration of Independence and the Constitution to Frederick Douglass's speech, "What, to the slave, Is the Fourth of July?," the Seneca Falls Declaration and Resolutions, the Omaha Platform of the Populist Party, Martin Luther King Jr.'s "I Have A Dream" speech, and Ronald Reagan's first inaugural address. The tables give you accurate data on broad social and political developments in American history. For a full listing of these documents and the Appendix Tables, see the Contents.

THE WEBSITE

ORGANIZE, LEARN, AND CONNECT WITH STUDYSPACE

wwnorton.com/studyspace
Free and open, the StudySpace website helps you organize, learn, and connect review materials, textbook coverage, and online research. Whether accessing freedom-oriented primary-source documents, reviewing their reading, or interactively testing your grasp of history and geography, you can access a full range of multi-media resources organized within a coherent, assignment-driven study plan.

ORGANIZE

Chapter outlines help you navigate the text as you read.

Eric Foner's brief *Questioning Freedom* **podcasts** provide a thematic context for every chapter. These interview segments are available in both audio and video streaming formats and each question and answer is transcribed and printer-friendly.

LEARN

Interactive maps allow you to explore the geography, historical context, and demographics of specific regions. These iMaps can also be printed without labels for offline re-labeling exercises.

Interactive Chrono-Sequencers challenge students' understanding of the flow of history. These interactive chapter chronologies allow you to reassemble sequences of events and help reinforce your understanding.

Flashcards help you recall and master important events and terms.

CONNECT

Sources of Freedom primary source documents amplify chapter themes. Ideal for brief research projects, the sources are organized by topic, complete with introductions, head notes, and media analysis worksheets, which can be submitted to the instructor via email.

Give Me Liberty! **Soundtrack includes many lasting and controversial freedom songs.** This unique collection of folk and popular songs is sure to spark discussion and provide provocative classroom examples.

PRINT SUPPLEMENTS

Voices of Freedom: A Documentary History

Edited by Eric Foner, this companion reader to *Give Me Liberty!* includes hundreds of primary-source documents touching upon the theme of American freedom. In chapters corresponding to the text chapters, the freedom theme is fleshed out in the words of well-known historical figures and ordinary Americans. Each document is accompanied by an introductory headnote and study questions.

Study Guide in two volumes

Prepared by Daniel Letwin (Pennsylvania State University), John Recchiuti (Mount Union College) and Thomas Clarkin (San Antonio College), the *Study Guide* accompanying *Give Me Liberty!* includes chapter objectives, detailed chapter outlines, chronologies, many study questions in multiple-choice, true/false, and essay form, definitions of the Key Terms in the end-of-chapter review page lists, and suggested readings, film, video, and Web resources.

For more information on Eric Foner's *Give Me Liberty! An American History*, please visit us at www.wwnorton.com/foner.

GIVE ME LIBERTY!

An American History

Second Edition

CHAPTER 15

HON. ROBERT. B. EL
Of South Carolina,
DELIVERING HIS GREAT SPEACH ON CIVIL RIGHTS IN THE HOUSE OF REPRE

AMERICAN SLAVE LABOUR IS OF THE PAST — FREE LABOUR IS OF THE PRESENT —— WE TOIL F

THE SHACKLE BROKEN — BY THE

"What Is Freedom?": Reconstruction, 1865–1877

The Shackle Broken—by the Genius of Freedom, *an 1874 lithograph celebrating the
progress of black freedom during the Civil War and Reconstruction. At the center, Robert
B. Elliott, a black congressman from South Carolina, delivers a celebrated speech
supporting the bill that became the Civil Rights Act of 1875. Elliott is surrounded by
images of black soldiers and sailors, as well as Abraham Lincoln, Senator Charles
Sumner (the bill's author), and a scene of black family life. The print illustrates the
centrality of military service to black claims to citizenship, and the linkage of the ideals of
emancipation, equality, and free labor during the Reconstruction era that followed the
Civil War.*

FOCUS QUESTIONS

• What visions of freedom did the former slaves and slaveholders pursue in the postwar South?

• What were the sources and the significance of radical Reconstruction?

• What were the social and political effects of radical Reconstruction in the South?

• What were the main reasons for the defeat of Reconstruction in the South?

On the evening of January 12, 1865, less than a month after Union forces captured Savannah, Georgia, twenty leaders of the city's black community gathered for a discussion with General William T. Sherman and Secretary of War Edwin M. Stanton. Mostly Baptist and Methodist ministers, the group included several men who within a few years would assume prominent positions during the era of Reconstruction that followed the Civil War. Ulysses S. Houston, pastor of the city's Third African Baptist Church, and James Porter, an episcopal religious leader who had operated a secret school for black children before the war, in a few years would win election to the Georgia legislature. James D. Lynch, who had been born free in Baltimore and educated in New Hampshire, went on to serve as secretary of state of Mississippi.

The conversation revealed that the black leaders brought out of slavery a clear definition of freedom. Asked what he understood by slavery, Garrison Frazier, a Baptist minister chosen as the group's spokesman, responded that it meant one person's "receiving by irresistible power the work of another man, and not by his consent." Freedom he defined as "placing us where we could reap the fruit of our own labor, and take care of ourselves." The way to accomplish this was "to have land, and turn it and till it by our own labor." Frazier insisted that blacks possessed "sufficient intelligence" to maintain themselves in freedom and enjoy the equal protection of the laws.

Sherman's meeting with the black leaders foreshadowed some of the radical changes that would take place during the era known as Reconstruction (meaning, literally, the rebuilding of the shattered nation). In the years following the Civil War, former slaves and their white allies, North and South, would seek to redefine the meaning and boundaries of American freedom. Previously an entitlement of whites, freedom would be expanded to include black Americans. The laws and Constitution would be rewritten to guarantee African-Americans, for the first time in the nation's history, recognition as citizens and equality before the law. Black men would be granted the right to vote, ushering in a period of interracial democracy throughout the South. Black schools, churches, and other institutions would flourish, laying the foundation for the modern African-American community. Many of the advances of Reconstruction would prove temporary, swept away during a campaign of violence in the South, and the North's retreat from the ideal of equality. But Reconstruction laid the foundation for future struggles to extend freedom to all Americans.

All this, however, lay in the future in January 1865. Four days after the meeting, Sherman responded to the black delegation by issuing Special Field Order 15. This set aside the Sea Islands and a large area along the South Carolina and Georgia coasts for the settlement of black families on forty-acre plots of land. He also offered them broken-down mules that the army could no longer use. In Sherman's order lay the origins of the phrase, "forty acres and a mule," that would reverberate across the South in the next few years. By June, some 40,000 freed slaves had been settled on "Sherman land." Among the emancipated slaves, Sherman's order raised hopes that the end of slavery would be accompanied by the economic independence that they, like other Americans, believed essential to genuine freedom.

THE MEANING OF FREEDOM

With the end of the Civil War, declared an Illinois congressman in 1865, the United States was a "new nation," for the first time "wholly free." The destruction of slavery, however, made the definition of freedom the central question on the nation's agenda. "What is freedom?" asked Congressman James A. Garfield in 1865. "Is it the bare privilege of not being chained? If this is all, then freedom is a bitter mockery, a cruel delusion." Did freedom mean simply the absence of slavery, or did it imply other rights for the former slaves, and if so, which ones: equal civil rights, the vote, ownership of property? During Reconstruction, freedom became a terrain of conflict, its substance open to different, often contradictory interpretations. Out of the conflict over the meaning of freedom arose new kinds of relations between black and white southerners, and a new definition of the rights of all Americans.

BLACKS AND THE MEANING OF FREEDOM

African-Americans' understanding of freedom was shaped by their experiences as slaves and their observation of the free society around them. To begin with, freedom meant escaping the numerous injustices of slavery—punishment by the lash, the separation of families, denial of access to education, the sexual exploitation of black women by their owners—and sharing in the rights and opportunities of American citizens. "If I cannot do like a white man," Henry Adams, an emancipated slave in Louisiana, told his former master in 1865, "I am not free."

Blacks relished the opportunity to demonstrate their liberation from the regulations, significant and trivial, associated with slavery. They openly held mass meetings and religious services free of white supervision, and they acquired dogs, guns, and liquor, all barred to them under slavery. No longer required to obtain a pass from their owners to travel, former slaves throughout the South left the plantations in search of better jobs, family members, or simply a taste of personal liberty. Many moved to southern towns and cities, where, it seemed, "freedom was free-er."

Family Record, *a lithograph marketed to former slaves after the Civil War, centers on an idealized portrait of a middle-class black family, with scenes of slavery and freedom.*

A post–Civil War photograph of an unidentified black family, seated before their humble home, possibly a former slave cabin.

Mother and Daughter Reading, Mt. Meigs, Alabama, *an 1890 photograph by Rudolph Eickemeyer. During Reconstruction and for years thereafter, former slaves exhibited a deep desire for education, and learning took place outside of school as well as within.*

FAMILIES IN FREEDOM

With slavery dead, institutions that had existed before the war, like the black family, free blacks' churches and schools, and the secret slave church, were strengthened, expanded, and freed from white supervision. The family was central to the postemancipation black community. Former slaves made remarkable efforts to locate loved ones from whom they had been separated under slavery. One northern reporter in 1865 encountered a freedman who had walked more than 600 miles from Georgia to North Carolina, searching for the wife and children from whom he had been sold away before the war. Meanwhile, widows of black soldiers successfully claimed survivors' pensions, forcing the federal government to acknowledge the validity of prewar relationships that slavery had attempted to deny.

But while Reconstruction witnessed the stabilization of family life, freedom subtly altered relationships within the family. Emancipation increased the power of black men and brought to many black families the nineteenth-century notion that men and women should inhabit separate "spheres." Immediately after the Civil War, planters complained that freedwomen had "withdrawn" from field labor and work as house servants. Many black women preferred to devote more time to their families than had been possible under slavery, and men considered it a badge of honor to see their wives remain at home. Eventually, the dire poverty of the black community would compel a far higher proportion of black women than white women to go to work for wages.

CHURCH AND SCHOOL

At the same time, blacks abandoned white-controlled religious institutions to create churches of their own. On the eve of the Civil War, 42,000 black Methodists worshiped in biracial South Carolina churches; by the end of Reconstruction, only 600 remained. The rise of the independent black church, with Methodists and Baptists commanding the largest followings, redrew the religious map of the South. As the major institution independent of white control, the church played a central role in the black community. A place of worship, it also housed schools, social events, and political gatherings. Black ministers came to play a major role in politics. Some 250 held public office during Reconstruction.

Another striking example of the freedpeople's quest for individual and community improvement was their desire for education. Education, declared a Mississippi freedman, was "the next best thing to liberty." The thirst for learning sprang from many sources—a desire to read the Bible, the need to prepare for the economic marketplace, and the opportunity, which arose in 1867, to take part in politics. Blacks of all ages flocked to the schools established by northern missionary societies, the Freedmen's

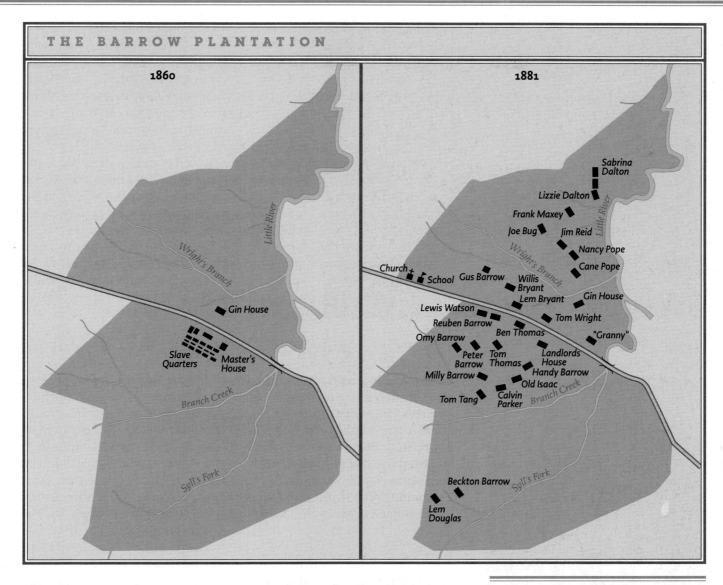

THE BARROW PLANTATION

1860

1881

Two maps of the Barrow plantation illustrate the effects of emancipation on rural life in the South. In 1860, slaves lived in communal quarters near the owner's house. Twenty years later, former slaves working as sharecroppers lived scattered across the plantation and had their own church and school.

Bureau, and groups of ex-slaves themselves. Northern journalist Sidney Andrews, who toured the South in 1865, was impressed by how much education also took place outside of the classroom: "I had occasion very frequently to notice that porters in stores and laboring men in warehouses, and cart drivers on the streets, had spelling books with them, and were studying them during the time they were not occupied with their work." Reconstruction also witnessed the creation of the nation's first black colleges, including Fisk University in Tennessee, Hampton Institute in Virginia, and Howard University in the nation's capital.

POLITICAL FREEDOM

In a society that had made political participation a core element of freedom, the right to vote inevitably became central to the former slaves' desire for empowerment and equality. As Frederick Douglass put it soon after the South's surrender in 1865, "Slavery is not abolished until the black man has the ballot." In a "monarchial government," Douglass explained, no "special" disgrace applied to those denied the right to vote. But in a democracy, "where universal suffrage is the rule," excluding any group meant branding them with "the stigma of inferiority." As soon as the Civil War ended, and in some parts of the South even earlier, free blacks and emancipated slaves claimed a place in the public sphere. They came together in conventions, parades, and petition drives to demand the right to vote and, on occasion, to organize their own "freedom ballots."

Anything less than full citizenship, black spokesmen insisted, would betray the nation's democratic promise and the war's meaning. Speakers at black conventions reminded the nation of Crispus Attucks, who fell at the Boston Massacre, and of black soldiers' contribution to the War of 1812 and during "the bloody struggle through which we have just passed." To demonstrate their patriotism, blacks throughout the South organized Fourth of July celebrations. For years after the Civil War, white southerners would "shut themselves within doors" on Independence Day, as a white resident of Charleston recorded in her diary, while former slaves commemorated the holiday themselves.

LAND, LABOR, AND FREEDOM

Like rural people throughout the world, former slaves' ideas of freedom were directly related to land ownership. Only land, wrote Merrimon Howard, a freedman from Mississippi, would enable "the poor class to enjoy the sweet boon of freedom." On the land they would develop independent communities free of white control. Many former slaves insisted that through their unpaid labor, they had acquired a right to the land. "The property which they hold," declared an Alabama black convention, "was nearly all earned by the sweat of *our* brows." In some parts of the South, blacks in 1865 seized property, insisting that it belonged to them. On one Tennessee plantation, former slaves claimed to be "joint heirs" to the estate and, the owner complained, took up residence "in the rooms of my house."

In its individual elements and much of its language, former slaves' definition of freedom resembled that of white Americans—self-ownership, family stability, religious liberty, political participation, and economic autonomy. But these elements combined to form a vision very much their own. For whites, freedom, no matter how defined, was a given, a birthright to be defended. For African-Americans, it was an open-ended process, a transformation of every aspect of their lives and of the society and culture that had sustained slavery in the first place. Although the freedpeople failed to achieve full freedom as they understood it, their definition did much to shape national debate during the turbulent era of Reconstruction.

MASTERS WITHOUT SLAVES

Most white southerners reacted to military defeat and emancipation with dismay, not only because of the widespread devastation but also because they must now submit to northern demands. "The demoralization is complete," wrote a Georgia girl. "We are whipped, there is no doubt about it." The appalling loss of life, a disaster without parallel in the American expe-

rience, affected all classes of southerners. Nearly 260,000 men died for the
Confederacy—over one-fifth of the
South's adult male white population.
The widespread destruction of work animals, farm buildings, and machinery
ensured that economic revival would be
slow and painful. In 1870, the value of
property in the South, not counting that
represented by slaves, was 30 percent
lower than before the war.

Planter families faced profound
changes in the war's aftermath. Many
lost not only their slaves but their life
savings, which they had patriotically
invested in now-worthless Confederate
bonds. Some, whose slaves departed the
plantation, for the first time found
themselves compelled to do physical
labor. General Braxton Bragg returned to
his "once prosperous" Alabama home to find "*all, all* was lost, except my
debts." Bragg and his wife, a woman "raised in affluence," lived for a time in
a slave cabin.

Southern planters sought to implement an understanding of freedom
quite different from that of the former slaves. As they struggled to accept the
reality of emancipation, most planters defined black freedom in the narrowest manner. As journalist Sidney Andrews discovered late in 1865, "The
whites seem wholly unable to comprehend that freedom for the negro
means the same thing as freedom for them. They readily enough admit that
the government has made him free, but appear to believe that they have the
right to exercise the same old control." Southern leaders sought to revive the
antebellum definition of freedom as if nothing had changed. Freedom still
meant hierarchy and mastery; it was a privilege, not a right, a carefully
defined legal status rather than an open-ended entitlement. Certainly, it
implied neither economic autonomy nor civil and political equality. "A man
may be free and yet not independent," Mississippi planter Samuel Agnew
observed in his diary in 1865. A Kentucky newspaper summed up the stance
of much of the white South: the former slave was "*free*, but free only to labor."

The Great Labor Question from a
Southern Point of View, *a cartoon by the
artist Winslow Homer, published in*
Harper's Weekly, *July 29, 1865. Homer
satirizes the attitudes of many white
southerners. While blacks labor in the
fields, an idle planter warns a former
slave, "My boy, we've toiled and taken
care of you long enough—now you've got
to work!"*

THE FREE LABOR VISION

Along with former slaves and former masters, the victorious Republican
North tried to implement its own vision of freedom. Central to its definition was the antebellum principle of free labor, now further strengthened
as a definition of the good society by the Union's triumph. In the free-labor
vision of a reconstructed South, emancipated blacks, enjoying the same
opportunities for advancement as northern workers, would labor more
productively than they had as slaves. At the same time, northern capital
and migrants would energize the economy. The South would eventually
come to resemble the "free society" of the North, complete with public

schools, small towns, and independent farmers. Unified on the basis of free labor, proclaimed Carl Schurz, a refugee from the failed German revolution of 1848 who rose to become a leader of the Republican Party, America would become "a republic, greater, more populous, freer, more prosperous, and more powerful" than any in history.

With planters seeking to establish a labor system as close to slavery as possible, and former slaves demanding economic autonomy and access to land, a long period of conflict over the organization and control of labor followed on plantations throughout the South. It fell to the Freedmen's Bureau, an agency established by Congress in March 1865, to attempt to establish a working free labor system.

THE FREEDMEN'S BUREAU

Under the direction of O. O. Howard, a graduate of Bowdoin College in Maine and a veteran of the Civil War, the Bureau took on responsibilities that can only be described as daunting. The Bureau was an experiment in government social policy that seems to belong more comfortably to the New Deal of the 1930s or the Great Society of the 1960s (see Chapters 21 and 25, respectively) than to nineteenth-century America. Bureau agents were supposed to establish schools, provide aid to the poor and aged, settle disputes between whites and blacks and among the freedpeople, and secure for former slaves and white Unionists equal treatment before the courts. "It is not . . . in your power to fulfill one-tenth of the expectations of those who framed the Bureau," General William T. Sherman wrote to Howard. "I fear you have Hercules' task."

The Bureau lasted from 1865 to 1870. Even at its peak, there were fewer than 1,000 agents in the entire South. Nonetheless, the Bureau's achieve-

The Freedmen's Bureau, *an engraving from* Harper's Weekly, *July 25, 1868, depicts the Bureau agent as a promoter of racial peace in the violent postwar South.*

ments in some areas, notably education and health care, were striking. While the Bureau did not establish schools itself, it coordinated and helped to finance the activities of northern societies committed to black education. By 1869, nearly 3,000 schools, serving over 150,000 pupils in the South, reported to the Bureau. Bureau agents also assumed control of hospitals established by the army during the war, and expanded the system into new communities. They provided medical care and drugs to both black and white southerners. In economic relations, however, the Bureau's activities proved far more problematic.

THE FAILURE OF LAND REFORM

The idea of free labor, wrote one Bureau agent, was "the noblest principle on earth." All that was required to harmonize race relations in the South was fair wages, good working conditions, and the opportunity to improve the laborer's situation in life. But blacks wanted land of their own, not jobs on plantations. One provision of the law establishing the Bureau gave it the authority to divide abandoned and confiscated land into forty-acre plots for rental and eventual sale to the former slaves.

In the summer of 1865, however, President Andrew Johnson, who had succeeded Lincoln, ordered nearly all land in federal hands returned to its former owners. A series of confrontations followed, notably in South Carolina and Georgia, where the army forcibly evicted blacks who had settled on "Sherman land." When O. O. Howard, head of the Freedmen's Bureau, traveled to the Sea Islands to inform blacks of the new policy, he was greeted with disbelief and protest. A committee of former slaves drew up petitions to Howard and President Johnson. "We want Homesteads," they declared, "we were promised Homesteads by the government." Land, the freedmen insisted, was essential to the meaning of freedom. Without it, they declared, "we have not bettered our condition" from the days of slavery—"you will see, this is not the condition of really free men."

Because no land distribution took place, the vast majority of rural freedpeople remained poor and without property during Reconstruction. They had no alternative but to work on white-owned plantations, often for their former owners. Far from being able to rise in the social scale through hard work, black men were largely confined to farm work, unskilled labor, and service jobs, and black women to positions in private homes as cooks and maids. Their wages remained too low to allow for any accumulation. By the turn of the century, a significant number of southern African-Americans had managed to acquire small parcels of land. But the failure of land reform produced a deep sense of betrayal that survived among the former slaves and their descendants long after the end of Reconstruction. "No sir," Mary Gaffney, an elderly ex-slave, recalled in the 1930s, "we were not given a thing but freedom."

TOWARD A NEW SOUTH

Out of the conflict on the plantations, new systems of labor emerged in the different regions of the South. The task system, under which workers were

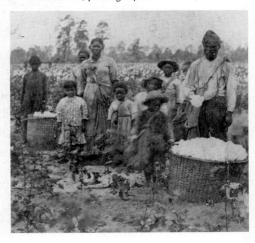

A black family in the cotton fields after the Civil War, photographed in 1867.

VOICES OF FREEDOM

Petition of Committee in Behalf of the Freedmen to Andrew Johnson (1865)

In the summer of 1865, President Andrew Johnson ordered land that had been distributed to freed slaves in South Carolina and Georgia returned to its former owners. A committee of freedmen drafted a petition asking for the right to obtain land. Johnson did not, however, change his policy.

We the freedmen of Edisto Island, South Carolina, have learned from you through Major General O. O. Howard . . . with deep sorrow and painful hearts of the possibility of [the] government restoring these lands to the former owners. We are well aware of the many perplexing and trying questions that burden your mind, and therefore pray to god (the preserver of all, and who has through our late and beloved President [Lincoln's] proclamation and the war made us a free people) that he may guide you in making your decisions and give you that wisdom that cometh from above to settle these great and important questions for the best interests of the country and the colored race.

Here is where secession was born and nurtured.

Here is where we have toiled nearly all our lives as slaves and treated like dumb driven cattle. This is our home, we have made these lands what they were, we are the only true and loyal people that were found in possession of these lands. We have been always ready to strike for liberty and humanity, yea to fight if need be to preserve this glorious Union. Shall not we who are freedmen and have always been true to this Union have the same rights as are enjoyed by others? . . . Are not our rights as a free people and good citizens of these United States to be considered before those who were found in rebellion against this good and just government? . . .

[Are] we who have been abused and oppressed for many long years not to be allowed the privilege of purchasing land but be subject to the will of these large land owners? God forbid. Land monopoly is injurious to the advancement of the course of freedom, and if government does not make some provision by which we as freedmen can obtain a homestead, we have not bettered our condition. . . .

We look to you . . . for protection and equal rights with the privilege of purchasing a homestead—a homestead right here in the heart of South Carolina.

FROM Article by Elizabeth Cady Stanton on Women's Suffrage, *The Revolution* (January 14, 1869)

One of the most prominent leaders of the nineteenth-century women's suffrage movement, Elizabeth Cady Stanton was bitterly disappointed both that the Reconstruction Congress extended the right to vote to black men but not to women, and that many leading abolitionists who had previously supported votes for women proclaimed Reconstruction the "Negro's hour" and supported the congressional policy. In this article, she chastises the abolitionist Gerrit Smith for refusing to sign a women's suffrage petition.

The above is a petition to which our friend Gerrit Smith, as an abolitionist, can not conscientiously put his name. . . . He does not clearly read the signs of the times, or he would see that there is to be no reconstruction of this nation, except on the basis of universal suffrage, as the natural, inalienable right of every citizen. . . . As the aristocracy in this country is the "male sex," and as Mr. Smith belongs to the privileged order, he naturally considers it important for the best interests of the nation, that every type and shade of degraded, ignorant manhood should be enfranchised, before even the higher classes of womanhood should be admitted to the polls. This does not surprise us. Men always judge more wisely of objective wrongs and oppressions, than of those in which they are themselves involved. Tyranny on a Southern plantation is far more easily seen by white men at the North than the wrongs of the women of their own households. . . .

Again; Mr. Smith refuses to sign the petition because he thinks the broader question of "universal suffrage" would defeat the partial one of "manhood suffrage"; in other words, to demand protection for woman against her oppressors, would jeopardize the black men's chance of securing protection against his oppressors. If it is a question of precedence merely, on what principle of justice or courtesy should woman yield her right of enfranchisement to the negro? If men cannot be trusted to legislate for their own sex, how can they legislate for the oppose sex, of whose wants and needs they know nothing? . . .

Mr. Smith . . . would undoubtedly plead the necessity of the ballot for the negro at the south for his protection, and point us to innumerable acts of cruelty he suffers today. But all these things fall as heavily on the women of the black race, yea far more so, for no man can ever know the deep, the damning degradation to which woman is subject in her youth, in helplessness and poverty. The enfranchisement of the men of her race, Mr. Smith would say, is her protection. Our Saxon men have held the ballot in this country for a century, and what honest man can claim that it has been used for woman's protection? . . . Women everywhere are waking up to their own God-given rights, to their true dignity as citizens of a republic, as mothers of the race. . . . End all this talk of class legislation, bury the negro in the citizen, and claim the suffrage for all men and women, as a natural, inalienable right.

QUESTIONS

1. Why do the black petitioners believe that owning land is essential to the enjoyment of freedom?

2. Why does Stanton believe that women need and deserve the right to vote?

3. What do these documents suggest about the boundaries of freedom in the Reconstruction era?

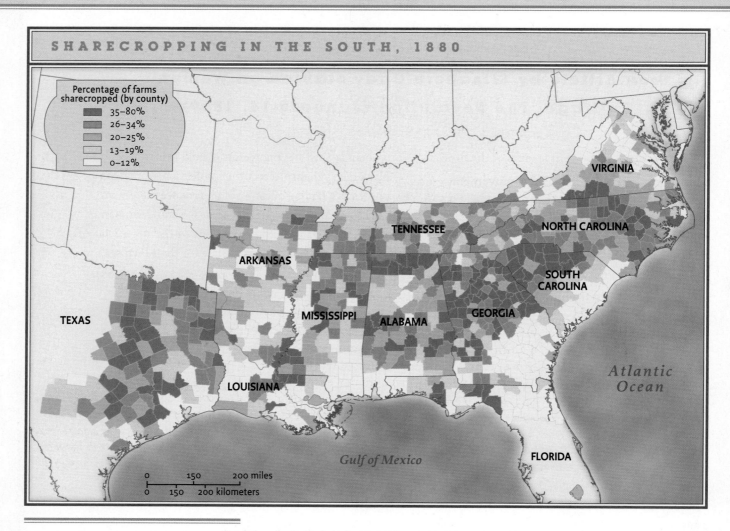

SHARECROPPING IN THE SOUTH, 1880

Percentage of farms
sharecropped (by county)

- 35–80%
- 26–34%
- 20–25%
- 13–19%
- 0–12%

By 1880, sharecropping had become the dominant form of agricultural labor in large parts of the South. The system involved both white and black farmers.

assigned daily tasks, completion of which ended their responsibilities for that day, survived in the rice kingdom of South Carolina and Georgia. Closely supervised wage labor predominated on the sugar plantations of southern Louisiana. Sharecropping came to dominate the Cotton Belt and much of the Tobacco Belt of Virginia and North Carolina.

Sharecropping initially arose as a compromise between blacks' desire for land and planters' demand for labor discipline. The system allowed each black family to rent a part of a plantation, with the crop divided between worker and owner at the end of the year. Sharecropping guaranteed the planters a stable resident labor force. Former slaves preferred it to gang labor because it offered them the prospect of working without day-to-day white supervision. But as the years went on, sharecropping became more and more oppressive. Sharecroppers' economic opportunities were severely limited by a world market in which the price of farm products suffered a prolonged decline.

THE WHITE FARMER

The plight of the small farmer was not confined to blacks in the postwar South. Wartime devastation set in motion a train of events that permanently altered the independent way of life of white yeomen, leading to what they considered a loss of freedom. Before the war, most small farmers had concentrated on raising food for their families and grew little cotton. With much of their property destroyed, many yeomen saw their economic condition worsened by successive crop failures after the war. To obtain supplies from merchants, farmers were forced to take up the growing of cotton and pledge a part of the crop as collateral (property the creditor can seize if a debt is not paid). This system became known as the "crop lien." Since interest rates were extremely high and the price of cotton fell steadily, many farmers found themselves still in debt after marketing their portion of the crop at year's end. They had no choice but to continue to plant cotton to obtain new loans. By the mid-1870s, white farmers, who cultivated only 10 percent of the South's cotton crop in 1860, were growing 40 percent, and many who had owned their land had fallen into dependency as sharecroppers, who now rented land owned by others.

Both black and white farmers found themselves caught in the sharecropping and crop-lien systems. A far higher percentage of black than white farmers in the South rented land rather than owned it. But every census from 1880 to 1940 counted more white than black sharecroppers. The workings of sharecropping and the crop-lien system are illustrated by the case of Matt Brown, a Mississippi farmer who borrowed money each year from a local merchant. He began 1892 with a debt of $226 held over from the previous year. By 1893, although he produced cotton worth $171, Brown's debt had increased to $402, because he had borrowed $33 for food, $29 for clothing, $173 for supplies, and $112 for other items. Brown never succeeded in getting out of debt. He died in 1905; the last entry under his name in the merchant's account book is a coffin.

Farmers with Cotton in the Courthouse Square, *an 1880 photograph from Marietta, Georgia. After the Civil War, more and more white farmers began growing cotton to support their families, permanently altering their formerly self-sufficient way of life.*

THE URBAN SOUTH

Even as the rural South stagnated economically, southern cities experienced remarkable growth after the Civil War. As railroads penetrated the interior, they enabled merchants in market centers like Atlanta to trade directly with the North, bypassing coastal cities that had traditionally monopolized southern commerce. A new urban middle class of merchants, railroad promoters, and bankers reaped the benefits of the spread of cotton production in the postwar South.

Thus, Reconstruction witnessed profound changes in the lives of southerners, black and white, rich and poor. In place of the prewar world of master, slave, and self-sufficient yeoman, the postwar South was peopled by new social classes—landowning employers, black and white sharecroppers, cotton-producing white farmers, wage-earning black laborers, and urban entrepreneurs. Each of these groups turned to Reconstruction politics in an attempt to shape to its own advantage the aftermath of emancipation.

THE MAKING OF RADICAL RECONSTRUCTION

Between 1865 and 1868, the United States confronted one of the greatest political crises of its history—the battle between President Andrew Johnson and Congress over Reconstruction. The struggle resulted in profound changes in the nature of citizenship, the structure of constitutional authority, and the meaning of American freedom.

ANDREW JOHNSON

To Lincoln's successor, Andrew Johnson, fell the task of overseeing the restoration of the Union. Born in poverty in North Carolina, as a youth Johnson worked as a tailor's apprentice. After moving to Tennessee, he achieved success through politics. Beginning as an alderman (a town official), he rose to serve in the state legislature, the U.S. Congress, and for two terms as governor of Tennessee. Johnson identified himself as the champion of his state's "honest yeomen" and a foe of large planters, whom he described as a "bloated, corrupted aristocracy." A strong defender of the Union, he became the only senator from a seceding state to remain at his post in Washington, D.C., when the Civil War began in 1861. When northern forces occupied Tennessee, Abraham Lincoln named him military governor. In 1864, Republicans nominated him to run for vice president as a symbol of the party's hope of extending its organization into the South.

In personality and outlook, Johnson proved unsuited for the responsibilities he shouldered after Lincoln's death. A lonely, stubborn man, he was intolerant of criticism and unable to compromise. He lacked Lincoln's political skills and keen sense of public opinion. A fervent believer in states' rights, Johnson insisted that since secession was illegal, the southern states had never actually left the Union or surrendered the right to govern their own affairs. Moreover, while Johnson had supported emancipation once Lincoln made it a goal of the war effort, he held deeply racist views. African-Americans, Johnson believed, had no role to play in Reconstruction.

THE FAILURE OF PRESIDENTIAL RECONSTRUCTION

A little over a month after Lee's surrender at Appomattox, and with Congress out of session until December, Johnson in May 1865 outlined his plan for reuniting the nation. He issued a series of proclamations that began the period of Presidential Reconstruction (1865–1867). Johnson offered a pardon (which restored political and property rights, except for slaves) to nearly all white southerners who took an oath of allegiance. He excluded Confederate leaders and wealthy planters whose prewar property had been valued at more than $20,000. This exemption suggested at first that Johnson planned a more punitive Reconstruction than Lincoln had intended. Most of those exempted, however, soon received individual pardons from the president. Johnson also appointed provisional governors and ordered them to call state conventions, elected by whites alone, that would establish loyal governments in the South. Apart from the requirement that they abolish slavery, repudiate secession, and refuse to pay the Confederate debt—all unavoidable consequences of southern defeat—he granted the new governments a free hand in managing local affairs.

At first, most northerners believed Johnson's policy deserved a chance to succeed. The conduct of the southern governments elected under his program, however, turned most of the Republican North against the president. By and large, white voters returned prominent Confederates and members of the old elite to power. Reports of violence directed against former slaves and northern visitors in the South further alarmed Republicans.

THE BLACK CODES

But what aroused the most opposition to Johnson's Reconstruction policy were the Black Codes, laws passed by the new southern governments that attempted to regulate the lives of the former slaves. These laws granted blacks certain rights, such as legalized marriage, ownership of property, and limited access to the courts. But they denied them the rights to testify against whites, to serve on juries or in state militias, or to vote. And in response to planters' demands that the freedpeople be required to work on the plantations, the Black Codes declared that those who failed to sign yearly labor contracts could be arrested and hired out to white landowners. Some states limited the occupations open to blacks and barred them from acquiring land, and others provided that judges could assign black children to work for their former owners without the consent of the parents.

Clearly, the death of slavery did not automatically mean the birth of freedom. But the Black Codes so completely violated free labor principles that they called forth a vigorous response from the Republican North. Wars—especially civil wars—often generate hostility and bitterness. But few groups of rebels in history have been treated more leniently than the

Selling a Freeman to Pay His Fine at Monticello, Florida, an engraving from Frank Leslie's Illustrated Newspaper, January 19, 1867. Under the Black Codes enacted by southern legislatures immediately after the Civil War, blacks convicted of "vagrancy"—often because they refused to sign contracts to work on plantations—were fined and, if unable to pay, auctioned off to work for the person who paid the fine.

defeated Confederates. A handful of southern leaders were arrested but most were quickly released. Only one was executed—Henry Wirz, the commander of Andersonville prison, where thousands of Union prisoners of war had died. Most of the Union army was swiftly demobilized. What motivated the North's turn against Johnson's policies was not a desire to "punish" the white South, but the inability of the South's political leaders to accept the reality of emancipation. "We must see to it," announced Republican senator William Stewart of Nevada, "that the man made free by the Constitution of the United States is a freeman indeed."

THE RADICAL REPUBLICANS

When Congress assembled in December 1865, Johnson announced that with loyal governments functioning in all the southern states, the nation had been reunited. In response, Radical Republicans, who had grown increasingly disenchanted with Johnson during the summer and fall, called for the dissolution of these governments and the establishment of new ones with "rebels" excluded from power and black men guaranteed the right to vote. Radicals tended to represent constituencies in New England and the "burned-over" districts of the rural North that had been home to religious revivalism, abolitionism, and other reform movements. Although they differed on many issues, Radicals shared the conviction that Union victory created a golden opportunity to institutionalize the principle of equal rights for all, regardless of race.

The Radicals fully embraced the expanded powers of the federal government born during the Civil War. Traditions of federalism and states' rights, they insisted, must not obstruct a sweeping national effort to protect the rights of all Americans. The most prominent Radicals in Congress were Charles Sumner, a senator from Massachusetts, and Thaddeus Stevens, a lawyer and iron manufacturer who represented Pennsylvania in the House of Representatives. Before the Civil War, both had been outspoken foes of slavery and defenders of black rights. Early in the Civil War, both had urged Lincoln to free and arm the slaves, and both in 1865 favored black suffrage in the South. "The same national authority," declared Sumner, "that destroyed slavery must see that this other pretension [racial inequality] is not permitted to survive."

Thaddeus Stevens's most cherished aim was to confiscate the land of disloyal planters and divide it among former slaves and northern migrants to the South. "The whole fabric of southern society," he declared, "*must* be changed. Without this, this Government can never be, as it has never been, a true republic." But his plan to make "small independent landholders" of the former slaves proved too radical even for many of his Radical colleagues. Congress, to be sure, had already offered free land to settlers in the West in the Homestead Act of 1862. But this land had been in the possession of the federal government, not private individuals (although originally, of course, it had been occupied by Indians). Most congressmen believed too deeply in the sanctity of property rights to be willing to take land from one group of owners and distribute it to others. Stevens's proposal failed to pass.

Thaddeus Stevens, leader of the Radical Republicans in the House of Representatives during Reconstruction.

THE ORIGINS OF CIVIL RIGHTS

With the South unrepresented, Republicans enjoyed an overwhelming majority in Congress. But the party was internally divided. Most Republicans were moderates, not Radicals. Moderates believed that Johnson's plan was flawed, but they desired to work with the president to modify it. They feared that neither northern nor southern whites would accept black suffrage. Moderates and Radicals joined in refusing to seat the southerners recently elected to Congress, but moderates broke with the Radicals by leaving the Johnson governments in place.

Early in 1866, Senator Lyman Trumbull of Illinois proposed two bills, reflecting the moderates' belief that Johnson's policy required modification. The first extended the life of the Freedmen's Bureau, which had been originally established for only one year. The second, the Civil Rights Bill, was described by one congressman as "one of the most important bills ever presented to the House for its action." It defined all persons born in the United States as citizens and spelled out rights they were to enjoy without regard to race. Equality before the law was central to the measure—no longer could states enact laws like the Black Codes discriminating between white and black citizens. So were free labor values. According to the law, no state could deprive any citizen of the right to make contracts, bring lawsuits, or enjoy equal protection of one's person and property. These, said Trumbull, were the "fundamental rights belonging to every man as a free man." The bill made no mention of the right to vote for blacks. In constitutional terms, the Civil Rights Bill represented the first attempt to give concrete meaning to the Thirteenth Amendment, which had abolished slavery, to define in law the essence of freedom.

To the surprise of Congress, Johnson vetoed both bills. Both, he said, would centralize power in the national government and deprive the states of the authority to regulate their own affairs. Moreover, he argued, blacks did not deserve the rights of citizenship. By acting to secure their rights, Congress was discriminating "against the white race." The vetoes made a breach between the president and nearly the entire Republican Party inevitable. Congress failed by a single vote to muster the two-thirds majority necessary to override the veto of the Freedmen's Bureau Bill (although later in 1866, it did extend the Bureau's life to 1870). But in April 1866, the Civil Rights Bill became the first major law in American history to be passed over a presidential veto.

President Andrew Johnson, in an 1868 lithograph by Currier and Ives. Because of Johnson's stubborn opposition to the congressional Reconstruction policy, one disgruntled citizen drew a crown on his head with the words, "I am King."

THE FOURTEENTH AMENDMENT

Congress now proceeded to adopt its own plan of Reconstruction. In June, it approved and sent to the states for ratification the Fourteenth Amendment, which placed in the Constitution the principle of citizenship for all persons born in the United States, and which empowered the federal government to protect the rights of all Americans. The amendment prohibited the states from abridging the "privileges and immunities" of citizens or denying them the "equal protection of the law." This broad language opened the door for future Congresses and the federal courts to breathe meaning into the guarantee of legal equality.

A Democratic Party broadside from the election of 1866 in Pennsylvania uses racist imagery to argue that government assistance aids lazy former slaves at the expense of hardworking whites.

In a compromise between the radical and moderate positions on black suffrage, the amendment did not grant blacks the right to vote. But it did provide that if a state denied the vote to any group of men, that state's representation in Congress would be reduced. (This provision did not apply when states barred women from voting.) The abolition of slavery threatened to increase southern political power, since now all blacks, not merely three-fifths as in the case of slaves, would be counted in determining a state's representation in Congress. The Fourteenth Amendment offered the leaders of the white South a choice—allow black men to vote and keep their state's full representation in the House of Representatives, or limit the vote to whites and sacrifice part of their political power.

The Fourteenth Amendment produced an intense division between the parties. Not a single Democrat in Congress voted in its favor, and only 4 of 175 Republicans were opposed. Radicals, to be sure, expressed their disappointment that the amendment did not guarantee black suffrage. (It was far from perfect, Stevens told the House, but he intended to vote for it, "because I live among men and not among angels.") Nonetheless, by writing into the Constitution the principle that equality before the law regardless of race is a fundamental right of all American citizens, the amendment made the most important change in that document since the adoption of the Bill of Rights.

THE RECONSTRUCTION ACT

The Fourteenth Amendment became the central issue of the political campaign of 1866. Johnson embarked on a speaking tour of the North, called by journalists the "swing around the circle," to urge voters to elect members of Congress committed to his own Reconstruction program. Denouncing his critics, the president made wild accusations that the Radicals were plotting to assassinate him. His behavior further undermined public support for his policies, as did riots that broke out in Memphis and New Orleans, in which white policemen and citizens killed dozens of blacks.

In the northern congressional elections that fall, Republicans opposed to Johnson's policies won a sweeping victory. Nonetheless, at the president's urging, every southern state but Tennessee refused to ratify the Fourteenth Amendment. The intransigence of Johnson and the bulk of the white South pushed moderate Republicans toward the Radicals. In March 1867, over Johnson's veto, Congress adopted the Reconstruction Act, which temporarily divided the South into five military districts and called for the creation of new state governments, with black men given the right to vote. Thus began the period of Radical Reconstruction, which lasted until 1877.

A variety of motives combined to produce Radical Reconstruction—demands by former slaves for the right to vote, the Radicals' commitment to the idea of equality, widespread disgust with Johnson's policies, the desire to fortify the Republican Party in the South, and the determination to keep ex-Confederates from office. But the conflict between President Johnson and Congress did not end with the passage of the Reconstruction Act.

IMPEACHMENT AND THE ELECTION OF GRANT

In March 1867, Congress adopted the Tenure of Office Act, barring the president from removing certain officeholders, including cabinet members, without the consent of the Senate. Johnson considered this an unconstitutional restriction on his authority. In February 1868, he removed Secretary of War Edwin M. Stanton, an ally of the Radicals. The House of Representatives responded by approving articles of impeachment—that is, it presented charges against Johnson to the Senate, which had to decide whether to remove him from office.

That spring, for the first time in American history, a president was placed on trial before the Senate for "high crimes and misdemeanors." By this point, virtually all Republicans considered Johnson a failure as president. But some moderates disliked Benjamin F. Wade, a Radical who, as temporary president of the Senate, would become president if Johnson were removed. Others feared that conviction would damage the constitutional separation of powers between Congress and the executive. Johnson's lawyers assured moderate Republicans that, if acquitted, he would stop interfering with Reconstruction policy. The final tally was 35–19 to convict Johnson, one vote short of the two-thirds necessary to remove him. Seven Republicans had joined the Democrats in voting to acquit the president.

A few days after the vote, Republicans nominated Ulysses S. Grant, the Union's most prominent military hero, as their candidate for president. Grant's Democratic opponent was Horatio Seymour, the former governor of New York. Reconstruction became the central issue of the bitterly fought 1868 campaign. Republicans identified their opponents with secession and treason, a tactic known as "waving the bloody shirt." Democrats denounced Reconstruction as unconstitutional and condemned black suffrage as a violation of America's political traditions. They appealed openly to racism. Seymour's running mate, Francis P. Blair Jr., charged Republicans with placing the South under the rule of "a semi-barbarous race" who longed to "subject the white women to their unbridled lust."

THE FIFTEENTH AMENDMENT

Grant won the election of 1868, although by a margin—300,000 of 6 million votes cast—that many Republicans found uncomfortably slim. The result led Congress to adopt the era's third and final amendment to the Constitution. In February 1869, it approved the Fifteenth Amendment, which prohibited the federal and state governments from denying any citizen the right to vote because of race. Bitterly opposed by the Democratic Party, it was ratified in 1870.

A Democratic ribbon from the election of 1868, with Horatio Seymour and Francis P. Blair Jr., the party's candidates for president and vice president. The ribbon illustrates the explicit appeals to racism that marked the campaign.

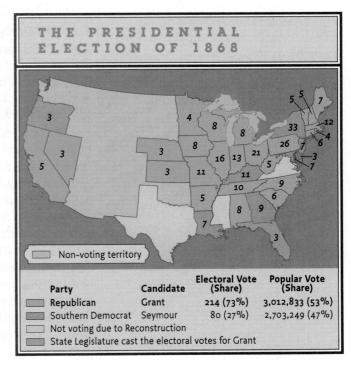

THE PRESIDENTIAL ELECTION OF 1868

Non-voting territory

Party	Candidate	Electoral Vote (Share)	Popular Vote (Share)
Republican	Grant	214 (73%)	3,012,833 (53%)
Southern Democrat	Seymour	80 (27%)	2,703,249 (47%)
Not voting due to Reconstruction			
State Legislature cast the electoral votes for Grant			

The Fifteenth Amendment, *an 1870 lithograph marking the ratification of the constitutional amendment prohibiting states from denying citizens the right to vote because of race. Surrounding an image of a celebration parade are portraits of Abraham Lincoln; President Ulysses S. Grant and his vice president, Schuyler Colfax; abolitionists John Brown, Martin R. Delany, and Frederick Douglass; and Hiram Revels, the first black to serve in the United States Senate. At the bottom are scenes of freedom—education, family, political representation, and church life.*

Although the Fifteenth Amendment opened the door to suffrage restrictions not explicitly based on race—literacy tests, property qualifications, and poll taxes—and did not extend the right to vote to women, it marked the culmination of four decades of abolitionist agitation. As late as 1868, even after Congress had enfranchised black men in the South, only eight northern states allowed African-American men to vote. With the Fifteenth Amendment, the American Anti-Slavery Society disbanded, its work, its members believed, now complete. "Nothing in all history," exclaimed veteran abolitionist William Lloyd Garrison, equaled "this wonderful, quiet, sudden transformation of four millions of human beings from . . . the auction-block to the ballot-box."

THE "GREAT CONSTITUTIONAL REVOLUTION"

The laws and amendments of Reconstruction reflected the intersection of two products of the Civil War era—a newly empowered national state, and the idea of a national citizenry enjoying equality before the law. What Republican leader Carl Schurz called the "great Constitutional revolution" of Reconstruction transformed the federal system and with it, the language of freedom so central to American political culture.

Before the Civil War, American citizenship had been closely linked to race. The first Congress, in 1790, had limited to whites the right to become a naturalized citizen when immigrating from abroad. No black person, free or slave, the Supreme Court had declared in the *Dred Scott* decision of 1857, could be a citizen of the United States. The laws and amendments of Reconstruction repudiated the idea that citizenship was an entitlement of whites alone. The principle of equality before the law, moreover, did not apply only to the South. The Reconstruction amendments voided many northern laws discriminating on the basis of race. And, as one congressman noted, the amendments expanded the liberty of whites as well as blacks, including "the millions of people of foreign birth who will flock to our shores."

The new amendments also transformed the relationship between the federal government and the states. The Bill of Rights had linked civil liberties to the autonomy of the states. Its language—"Congress shall make no law"—reflected the belief that concentrated national power posed the greatest threat to freedom. The authors of the Reconstruction amendments assumed that rights required national power to enforce them. Rather than a threat to liberty, the federal government, in Charles Sumner's words, had become "the custodian of freedom."

The Reconstruction amendments transformed the Constitution from a document primarily concerned with federal-state relations and the rights of property into a vehicle through which members of vulnerable minorities could stake a claim to freedom and seek protection against misconduct by all levels of government. In the twentieth century, many of the Supreme Court's most important decisions expanding the rights of American citizens were based on the Fourteenth Amendment, perhaps most notably the 1954 *Brown* ruling that outlawed school segregation (see Chapter 24).

Uncle Sam's Thanksgiving Dinner, *an engraving by Thomas Nast from* Harper's Weekly, *November 20, 1868, shortly after the election of Ulysses S. Grant, graphically illustrates how the boundaries of freedom had expanded during Reconstruction. The guests include, among others, African-Americans, Asian-Americans, and Native Americans, all enjoying a harmonious feast. The table's centerpiece contains the slogan, "universal suffrage."*

BOUNDARIES OF FREEDOM

Reconstruction redrew the boundaries of American freedom. Lines of exclusion that limited the privileges of citizenship to white men had long been central to the practice of American democracy. Only in an unparalleled crisis could they have been replaced, even temporarily, by the vision of a republic of equals embracing black Americans as well as white. That the United States was a "white man's government" had been a widespread belief before the Civil War. It is not difficult to understand why Andrew Johnson, in one of his veto messages, claimed that federal protection of blacks' civil rights violated "all our experience as a people."

Reconstruction Republicans' belief in universal rights also had its limits. In his remarkable "Composite Nation" speech of 1869, Frederick Douglass condemned prejudice against immigrants from China. America's destiny, he declared, was to transcend race by serving as an asylum for people "gathered here from all corners of the globe by a common aspiration for national liberty." A year later, Charles Sumner moved to strike the word "white" from naturalization requirements. Senators from the western states objected. At their insistence, the naturalization law was amended to make Africans eligible to obtain citizenship when migrating from abroad. But Asians remained ineligible. The racial boundaries of nationality had been redrawn, but not eliminated. The juxtaposition of the amended naturalization law and the Fourteenth Amendment created a significant division in the Asian-American community. Well into the twentieth century, Asian immigrants could not become citizens, but their native-born children automatically did so.

THE RIGHTS OF WOMEN

"The contest with the South that destroyed slavery," wrote the Philadelphia lawyer Sidney George Fisher in his diary, "has caused an immense increase in the popular passion for liberty and equality." But advocates of women's rights encountered the limits of the Reconstruction commitment to equality. Women activists saw Reconstruction as the moment to claim their own emancipation. No less than blacks, proclaimed Elizabeth Cady Stanton, women had arrived at a "transition period, from slavery to freedom." The rewriting of the Constitution, declared suffrage leader Olympia Brown, offered the opportunity to sever the blessings of freedom from sex as well as race and to "bury the black man and the woman in the citizen."

The destruction of slavery led feminists to search for ways to make the promise of free labor real for women. Every issue of the new women's rights journal, *The Agitator*, edited by Mary

A Delegation of Advocates of Women's Suffrage Addressing the House Judiciary Committee, *an engraving from* Frank Leslie's Illustrated Newspaper, *February 4, 1871. The group includes Elizabeth Cady Stanton, seated just to the right of the speaker, and Susan B. Anthony, at the table on the extreme right.*

Livermore, who had led fund-raising efforts for aid to Union soldiers during the war, carried stories complaining of the limited job opportunities and unequal pay for females who entered the labor market. Other feminists debated how to achieve "liberty for married women." Demands for liberalizing divorce laws (which generally required evidence of adultery, desertion, or extreme abuse to terminate a marriage) and for recognizing "woman's control over her own body" (including protection against domestic violence and access to what later generations would call birth control) moved to the center of many feminists' concerns. "Our rotten marriage institution," one Ohio woman wrote, "is the main obstacle in the way of woman's freedom."

FEMINISTS AND RADICALS

Talk of women's suffrage and redesigning marriage found few sympathetic male listeners. Even Radical Republicans insisted that Reconstruction was the "Negro's hour" (the hour, that is, of the black male). The Fourteenth Amendment for the first time introduced the word "male" into the Constitution, in its clause penalizing a state for denying any group of men the right to vote. The Fifteenth Amendment outlawed discrimination in voting based on race but not gender. These measures produced a bitter split both between feminists and Radical Republicans, and within feminist circles.

Some leaders, like Stanton and Susan B. Anthony, opposed the Fifteenth Amendment because it did nothing to enfranchise women. They denounced their former abolitionist allies and moved to sever the women's rights movement from its earlier moorings in the antislavery tradition. On occasion, they appealed to racial and ethnic prejudices, arguing that native-born white women deserved the vote more than non-whites and immigrants. "Patrick and Sambo and Hans and Yung Tung, who do not know the difference between a monarchy and a republic," declared Stanton, had no right to be "making laws for [feminist leader] Lucretia Mott." But other abolitionist-feminists, like Abby Kelley and Lucy Stone, insisted that despite their limitations, the Reconstruction amendments represented steps in the direction of truly universal suffrage and should be supported. The result was a split in the movement and the creation in 1869 of two hostile women's rights organizations—the National Woman Suffrage Association, led by Stanton, and the American Woman Suffrage Association, with Lucy Stone as president. They would not reunite until the 1890s.

Thus, even as it rejected the racial definition of freedom that had emerged in the first half of the nineteenth century, Reconstruction left the gender boundary largely intact. When women tried to use the rewritten legal code and Constitution to claim equal rights, they found the courts unreceptive. Myra Bradwell invoked the idea of free labor in challenging an Illinois statute limiting the practice of law to men, but the Supreme Court in 1873 rebuffed her claim. Free labor principles, the justices declared, did not apply to women, since "the law of the Creator" had assigned them to "the domestic sphere."

Despite their limitations, the Fourteenth and Fifteenth Amendments and the Reconstruction Act of 1867 marked a radical departure in American and world history. Alone among the nations that abolished slavery in the nineteenth century, the United States, within a few years of emancipation, clothed its former slaves with citizenship rights equal to those of whites. "We have cut loose from the whole dead past," wrote Timothy Howe, a Republican senator from Wisconsin, "and have cast our anchor out a hundred years" into the future. The Reconstruction Act of 1867 inaugurated America's first real experiment in interracial democracy.

RADICAL RECONSTRUCTION IN THE SOUTH

"THE TOCSIN OF FREEDOM"

Among the former slaves, the passage of the Reconstruction Act inspired an outburst of political organization. At mass political meetings—community gatherings attended by men, women, and children—African-Americans staked their claim to equal citizenship. Blacks, declared an Alabama meeting, deserved "exactly the same rights, privileges and immunities as are enjoyed by white men. We ask for nothing more and will be content with nothing less."

These gatherings inspired direct action to remedy long-standing grievances. Hundreds took part in sit-ins that integrated horse-drawn public streetcars in cities across the South. Plantation workers organized strikes for higher wages. Speakers, male and female, fanned out across the South. Frances Ellen Watkins Harper, a black veteran of the abolitionist movement, embarked on a two-year tour, lecturing on "Literacy, Land, and Liberation." James D. Lynch, a member of the group that met with General Sherman in 1865, organized Republican meetings. He became known, in the words of a white contemporary, as "a great orator, fluid and graceful," who "stirred the emotions" of his listeners "as no other man could do."

Determined to exercise their new rights as citizens, thousands joined the Union League, an organization closely linked to the Republican Party, and the vast majority of eligible African-Americans registered to vote. James K. Green, a former slave in Hale County, Alabama and a League organizer, went on to serve eight years in the Alabama legislature. In the 1880s, Green looked back on his political career. Before the war, he declared, "I was entirely ignorant; I knew nothing more than to obey my master; and there were thousands of us in the same attitude. . . . But the tocsin [warning bell] of freedom sounded and knocked at the door and we walked out like free men and shouldered the responsibilities."

By 1870, all the former Confederate states had been readmitted to the Union, and in a region where the Republican Party had not existed before the war, nearly all were under Republican control.

Electioneering at the South, *an engraving from* Harper's Weekly, *July 25, 1868, depicts a speaker at a political meeting in the rural South. Women as well as men took part in these grassroots gatherings.*

Their new state constitutions, drafted in 1868 and 1869 by the first public bodies in American history with substantial black representation, marked a considerable improvement over those they replaced. The constitutions greatly expanded public responsibilities. They established the region's first state-funded systems of free public education, and they created new penitentiaries, orphan asylums, and homes for the insane. The constitutions guaranteed equality of civil and political rights and abolished practices of the antebellum era such as whipping as a punishment for crime, property qualifications for officeholding, and imprisonment for debt. A few states initially barred former Confederates from voting, but this policy was quickly abandoned by the new state governments.

THE BLACK OFFICEHOLDER

Throughout Reconstruction, black voters provided the bulk of the Republican Party's support. But African-Americans did not control Reconstruction politics, as their opponents frequently charged. The highest offices remained almost entirely in white hands, and only in South Carolina, where blacks made up 60 percent of the population, did they form a majority of the legislature. Nonetheless, the fact that some 2,000 African-Americans occupied public offices during Reconstruction represented a fundamental shift of power in the South and a radical departure in American government.

African-Americans were represented at every level of government. Fourteen were elected to the national House of Representatives. Two blacks served in the U.S. Senate during Reconstruction, both representing Mississippi. Hiram Revels, who had been born free in North Carolina, was

The First Vote, *an engraving from* Harper's Weekly, *November 16, 1867, depicts the first biracial elections in southern history. The voters represent key sources of the black political leadership that emerged during Reconstruction—the artisan carrying his tools, the well-dressed city person (probably free before the war), and the soldier.*

Black and white members of the Mississippi Senate, 1874–1875, shortly before the end of Reconstruction in the state. The woman in the bottom row is a postmistress.

The Operations of the Registration Laws and Negro Suffrage in the South, *an engraving in* Frank Leslie's Illustrated Newspaper, *November 30, 1867, shows blacks and whites for the first time serving together on a southern jury.*

educated in Illinois, and served as a chaplain in the wartime Union army, in 1870 became the first black senator in American history. The second, Blanche K. Bruce, a former slave, was elected in 1875. Since then, only three African-Americans—Edward W. Brooke of Massachusetts (who served 1967–1978), Carol Moseley Braun of Illinois (1993–1998), and Barack Obama of Illinois (2005–)—have held seats in the Senate.

Pinckney B. S. Pinchback of Louisiana, the Georgia-born son of a white planter and a free black woman, served briefly during the winter of 1872–1873 as America's first black governor. Over a century would pass before L. Douglas Wilder of Virginia, elected in 1989, became the second. Some 700 blacks sat in state legislatures during Reconstruction, and scores held local offices ranging from justice of the peace to sheriff, tax assessor, and policeman. The presence of black officeholders and their white allies made a real difference in southern life, ensuring that blacks accused of crimes would be tried before juries of their peers and enforcing fairness in such aspects of local government as road repair, tax assessment, and poor relief.

In South Carolina and Louisiana, homes of the South's wealthiest and best-educated free black communities, most prominent Reconstruction officeholders had never experienced slavery. In addition, a number of black Reconstruction officials, like Pennsylvania-born Jonathan J. Wright, who served on the South Carolina Supreme Court, had come from the North after the Civil War. The majority, however, were former slaves who had established their leadership in the black community by serving in the Union army, working as ministers, teachers, or skilled craftsmen, or engaging in Union League organizing. Among the most celebrated black officeholders was Robert Smalls, who had worked as a slave on the Charleston docks before the Civil War and who won national fame in 1862 by secretly guiding the *Planter*, a Confederate vessel, out of the harbor and delivering it to Union forces. Smalls became a powerful political leader on the South Carolina Sea Islands and was elected to five terms in Congress.

CARPETBAGGERS AND SCALAWAGS

The new southern governments also brought to power new groups of whites. Many Reconstruction officials were northerners who for one reason or another had made their homes in the South after the war. Their opponents dubbed them "carpetbaggers," implying that they had packed all their belongings in a suitcase and left their homes in order to reap the spoils of office in the South. Some carpetbaggers were undoubtedly corrupt adventurers. The large majority, however, were former Union soldiers who decided to remain in the South when the war ended, before there was any prospect of going into politics. Others were investors in land and railroads who saw in the postwar South an opportunity to combine personal economic advancement with a role in helping to substitute, as one wrote, "the civilization of freedom for that of slavery." Teachers, Freedmen's Bureau officers, and others who came to the region genuinely hoping to assist the former slaves represented another large group of "carpetbaggers."

Most white Republicans, however, had been born in the South. Former Confederates reserved their greatest scorn for these "scalawags," whom they considered traitors to their race and region. Some southern-born Republicans were men of stature and wealth, like James L. Alcorn, the owner of one of Mississippi's largest plantations and the state's first Republican governor.

Most "scalawags," however, were non-slaveholding white farmers from the southern upcountry. Many had been wartime Unionists, and they now cooperated with the Republicans in order to prevent "rebels" from returning to power. Others hoped Reconstruction governments would help them recover from wartime economic losses by suspending the collection of debts and enacting laws protecting small property holders from losing their homes to creditors. In states like North Carolina, Tennessee, and Arkansas, Republicans initially commanded a significant minority of the white vote. Even in the Deep South, the small white Republican vote was important, because the population remained almost evenly divided between blacks (almost all of whom voted for the party of Lincoln) and whites (overwhelmingly Democratic).

SOUTHERN REPUBLICANS IN POWER

In view of the daunting challenges they faced, the remarkable thing is not that Reconstruction governments in many respects failed, but how much they did accomplish. Perhaps their greatest achievement lay in establishing the South's first state-supported public schools. The new educational systems served both black and white children, although generally in schools segregated by race. Only in New Orleans were the public schools integrated during Reconstruction, and only in South Carolina did the state university admit black students (elsewhere, separate colleges were established). By the 1870s, in a region whose prewar leaders had made it illegal for slaves to learn and had done little to provide education for poorer whites, over half the children, black and white, were attending public schools. The new governments also pioneered civil rights legislation. Their laws made it illegal for railroads,

Emancipation, *an 1865 lithograph, is unusual because along with the familiar images of Lincoln and emancipated slaves, it also portrays a poor white family, suggesting that all Americans will benefit from the end of slavery and Reconstruction.*

Black students outside a schoolhouse in a post-Civil War photograph. The teacher is seated at the far right.

hotels, and other institutions to discriminate on the basis of race. Enforcement varied considerably from locality to locality, but Reconstruction established for the first time at the state level a standard of equal citizenship and a recognition of blacks' right to a share of public services.

Republican governments also took steps to strengthen the position of rural laborers and promote the South's economic recovery. They passed laws to ensure that agricultural laborers and sharecroppers had the first claim on harvested crops, rather than merchants to whom the landowner owed money. South Carolina created a state Land Commission, which by 1876 had settled 14,000 black families and a few poor whites on their own farms.

THE QUEST FOR PROSPERITY

Rather than land distribution, however, the Reconstruction governments pinned their hopes for southern economic growth and opportunity for African-Americans and poor whites alike on regional economic development. Railroad construction, they believed, was the key to transforming the South into a society of booming factories, bustling towns, and diversified agriculture. "A free and living republic," declared a Tennessee Republican, would "spring up in the track of the railroad." Every state during Reconstruction helped to finance railroad construction, and through tax reductions and other incentives tried to attract northern manufacturers to invest in the region. The program had mixed results. Economic development in general remained weak. With abundant opportunities existing in the West, few northern investors ventured to the Reconstruction South.

To their supporters, the governments of Radical Reconstruction presented a complex pattern of disappointment and accomplishment. A revitalized southern economy failed to materialize, and most African-Americans remained locked in poverty. On the other hand, biracial democratic government, a thing unknown in American history, for the first time functioned effectively in many parts of the South. Public facilities were rebuilt and expanded, school systems established, and legal codes purged of racism. The conservative elite that had dominated southern government from colonial times to 1867 found itself excluded from political power, while poor whites, newcomers from the North, and former slaves cast ballots, sat on juries, and enacted and administered laws. "We have gone through one of the most remarkable changes in our relations to each other," declared a white South Carolina lawyer in 1871, "that has been known, perhaps, in the history of the world." It is a measure of how far change had progressed that the reaction against Reconstruction proved so extreme.

THE OVERTHROW OF RECONSTRUCTION

RECONSTRUCTION'S OPPONENTS

The South's traditional leaders—planters, merchants, and Democratic politicians—bitterly opposed the new governments. They denounced them as corrupt, inefficient, and examples of "black supremacy." "Intelligence, virtue, and patriotism" in public life, declared a protest by prominent southern Democrats, had given way to "ignorance, stupidity, and vice." Corruption did exist during Reconstruction, but it was confined to no race, region, or party. The rapid growth of state budgets and the benefits to be gained from public aid led in some states to a scramble for influence that produced bribery, insider dealing, and a get-rich-quick atmosphere. Southern frauds, however, were dwarfed by those practiced in these years by the Whiskey Ring, which involved high officials of the Grant administration, and by New York's Tweed Ring, controlled by the Democrats, whose thefts ran into the tens of millions of dollars. (These are discussed in the next chapter.) The rising taxes needed to pay for schools and other new public facilities and to assist railroad development were another cause of opposition to Reconstruction. Many poor whites who had initially supported the Republican Party turned against it when it became clear that their economic situation was not improving.

The most basic reason for opposition to Reconstruction, however, was that most white southerners could not accept the idea of former slaves voting, holding office, and enjoying equality before the law. In order to restore white supremacy in southern public life and to ensure planters a disciplined, reliable labor force, they believed, Reconstruction must be overthrown. Opponents launched a campaign of violence in an

Murder of Louisiana, *an 1873 cartoon, illustrates the intensity of the opposition to Reconstruction. President Ulysses S. Grant, depicted as an emperor advised by Attorney General George H. Williams in the form of the devil, prepares to sacrifice the state on the "altar of radicalism." The victim, held by two black men, has already had her heart cut out by Republican governor William P. Kellogg. The other southern states, with South Carolina kneeling in chains, look on.*

effort to end Republican rule. Their actions posed a fundamental challenge both for Reconstruction governments in the South and for policymakers in Washington, D.C.

"A REIGN OF TERROR"

The Civil War ended in 1865, but violence remained widespread in large parts of the postwar South. In the early years of Reconstruction, violence was mostly local and unorganized. Blacks were assaulted and murdered for refusing to give way to whites on city sidewalks, using "insolent" language, challenging end-of-year contract settlements, and attempting to buy land. The violence that greeted the advent of Republican governments after 1867, however, was far more pervasive and more directly motivated by politics. In wide areas of the South, secret societies sprang up with the aim of preventing blacks from voting and destroying the organization of the Republican Party by assassinating local leaders and public officials.

The most notorious such organization was the Ku Klux Klan, which in effect served as a military arm of the Democratic Party in the South. From its founding in 1866 in Tennessee, the Klan was a terrorist organization. It quickly spread into nearly every southern state. Led by planters, merchants, and Democratic politicians, men who liked to style themselves the South's "respectable citizens," the Klan committed some of the most brutal criminal acts in American history. In many counties, it launched what one victim called a "reign of terror" against Republican leaders, black and white.

The Klan's victims included white Republicans, among them wartime Unionists and local officeholders, teachers, and party organizers. William Luke, an Irish-born teacher in a black school, was lynched in 1870. But African-Americans—local political leaders, those who managed to acquire land, and others who in one way or another defied the norms of white supremacy—bore the brunt of the violence. In York County, South Carolina, where nearly the entire white male population joined the Klan (and women participated by sewing the robes and hoods Klansmen wore as disguises), the organization committed eleven murders and hundreds of whippings.

On occasion, violence escalated from assaults on individuals to mass terrorism and even local insurrections. In Meridian, Mississippi, in 1871, some thirty blacks were murdered in cold blood, along with a white Republican judge. The bloodiest act of violence during Reconstruction took place in Colfax, Louisiana, in 1873, where armed whites assaulted the town with a small cannon. Hundreds of former slaves were murdered, including fifty members of a black militia unit after they had surrendered.

Unable to suppress the Klan, the new southern governments appealed to Washington for help. In 1870 and 1871, Congress adopted three Enforcement Acts, outlawing terrorist societies and allowing the president to use the army against them. These laws continued the expansion of national authority during Reconstruction. They defined crimes that aimed to deprive citizens of their civil and political rights as federal offenses rather than violations of state law. In 1871,

A Prospective Scene in the City of Oaks, a cartoon in the September 1, 1868, issue of the Independent Monitor, *a Democratic newspaper published in Tuscaloosa, Alabama. The cartoon sent a warning to the Reverend A. S. Lakin, who had moved from Ohio to become president of the University of Alabama, and Dr. N. B. Cloud, a southern-born Republican serving as Alabama's superintendent of public education. The Ku Klux Klan forced both men from their positions.*

President Grant dispatched federal marshals, backed up by troops in some areas, to arrest hundreds of accused Klansmen. Many Klan leaders fled the South. After a series of well-publicized trials, the Klan went out of existence. In 1872, for the first time since the Civil War, peace reigned in most of the former Confederacy.

THE LIBERAL REPUBLICANS

Despite the Grant administration's effective response to Klan terrorism, the North's commitment to Reconstruction waned during the 1870s. Many Radicals, including Thaddeus Stevens, who died in 1868, had passed from the scene. Within the Republican Party, their place was taken by politicians less committed to the ideal of equal rights for blacks. Northerners increasingly felt that the South should be able to solve its own problems without constant interference from Washington. The federal government had freed the slaves, made them citizens, and given them the right to vote. Now, blacks should rely on their own resources, not demand further assistance.

In 1872, an influential group of Republicans, alienated by corruption within the Grant administration and believing that the growth of federal power during and after the war needed to be curtailed, formed their own party. They included Republican founders like Lyman Trumbull and prominent editors and journalists such as E. L. Godkin of *The Nation*. Calling themselves Liberal Republicans, they nominated Horace Greeley, editor of the *New York Tribune*, for president.

The Liberals' alienation from the Grant administration initially had little to do with Reconstruction. They claimed that corrupt politicians had come to power in the North by manipulating the votes of immigrants and workingmen, while men of talent and education like themselves had been pushed aside. Democratic criticisms of Reconstruction, however, found a receptive audience among the Liberals. As in the North, they became convinced, the "best men" of the South had been excluded from power while "ignorant" voters controlled politics, producing corruption and misgovernment. Power in the South should be returned to the region's "natural leaders." During the campaign of 1872, Greeley repeatedly called on Americans to "clasp hands across the bloody chasm" by putting the Civil War and Reconstruction behind them.

Greeley had spent most of his career, first as a Whig and then as a Republican, denouncing the Democratic Party. But with the Republican split presenting an opportunity to repair their political fortunes, Democratic leaders endorsed Greeley as their candidate. Many rank and file Democrats, unable to bring themselves to vote for Greeley, stayed at home on election day. As a result, Greeley suffered a devastating defeat by Grant, whose margin of over 700,000 popular votes was the largest in a nineteenth-century presidential contest. But Greeley's campaign placed on the northern agenda the one issue on which the Liberal reformers and the Democrats could agree—a new policy toward the South.

THE NORTH'S RETREAT

The Liberal attack on Reconstruction, which continued after 1872, contributed to a resurgence of racism in the North. Journalist James S. Pike, a

A Mississippi member of the Ku Klux Klan, photographed in his hooded disguise in 1871.

leading Greeley supporter, in 1874 published *The Prostrate State*, an influential account of a visit to South Carolina. The book depicted a state engulfed by political corruption, drained by governmental extravagance, and under the control of "a mass of black barbarism." The South's problems, he insisted, arose from "Negro government." The solution was to restore leading whites to political power. Newspapers that had long supported Reconstruction now began to condemn black participation in southern government. They expressed their views visually as well. Engravings depicting the former slaves as heroic Civil War veterans, upstanding citizens, or victims of violence were increasingly replaced by caricatures presenting them as little more than unbridled animals. Resurgent racism offered a convenient explanation for the alleged "failure" of Reconstruction.

Other factors also weakened northern support for Reconstruction. In 1873, the country plunged into a severe economic depression. Distracted by economic problems, Republicans were in no mood to devote further attention to the South. The depression dealt the South a severe blow and further weakened the prospect that Republicans could revitalize the region's economy. Democrats made substantial gains throughout the nation in the elections of 1874. For the first time since the Civil War, their party took control of the House of Representatives. Before the new Congress met, the old one enacted a final piece of Reconstruction legislation, the Civil Rights Act of 1875. This outlawed racial discrimination in places of public accommodation like hotels and theaters. But it was clear that the northern public was retreating from Reconstruction.

The Supreme Court whittled away at the guarantees of black rights Congress had adopted. In the *Slaughterhouse Cases* (1873), butchers excluded from a state-sponsored monopoly in Louisiana went to court, claiming that their right to equality before the law guaranteed by the Fourteenth Amendment had been violated. The justices rejected their claim, ruling that the amendment had not altered traditional federalism. Most of the rights of cit-

The Old Plantation Home, *a lithograph from 1872 produced by the prominent firm of Currier and Ives in New York City, illustrates how a nostalgic image of slavery as a time of carefree happiness for African-Americans was being promoted even as Reconstruction took place.*

Changes in graphic artist Thomas Nast's depiction of blacks in Harper's Weekly *mirrored the evolution of Republican sentiment in the North.* And Not This Man, *August 5, 1865, shows the black soldier as an upstanding citizen deserving of the vote.* Colored Rule in a Reconstructed (?) State, *March 14, 1874, suggests that Reconstruction legislatures had become travesties of democratic government.*

izens, it declared, remained under state control. Three years later, in *U.S. v. Cruikshank*, the Court gutted the Enforcement Acts by throwing out the convictions of some of those responsible for the Colfax Massacre of 1873.

THE TRIUMPH OF THE REDEEMERS

By the mid-1870s, Reconstruction was clearly on the defensive. Democrats had already regained control of states with substantial white voting majorities such as Tennessee, North Carolina, and Texas. The victorious Democrats called themselves Redeemers, since they claimed to have "redeemed" the white South from corruption, misgovernment, and northern and black control.

In those states where Reconstruction governments survived, violence again erupted. This time, the Grant administration showed no desire to intervene. In contrast to the Klan's activities—conducted at night by disguised men—the violence of 1875 and 1876 took place in broad daylight, as if to underscore Democrats' conviction that they had nothing to fear from Washington. In Mississippi, in 1875, white rifle clubs drilled in public and openly assaulted and murdered Republicans. When Governor Adelbert Ames, a Maine-born Union general, frantically appealed to the federal government for assistance, President Grant responded that the northern

Of Course He Wants to Vote the Democratic Ticket, *a cartoon from* Harper's Weekly, *October 21, 1876, comments on the campaign of terror launched by South Carolina Democrats in an attempt to carry the election of 1876.*

public was "tired out" by southern problems. On election day, armed Democrats destroyed ballot boxes and drove former slaves from the polls. The result was a Democratic landslide and the end of Reconstruction in Mississippi. "A revolution has taken place," wrote Ames, "and a race are disfranchised—they are to be returned to . . . an era of second slavery."

Similar events took place in South Carolina in 1876. Democrats nominated for governor former Confederate general Wade Hampton. Hampton promised to respect the rights of all citizens of the state, but his supporters, inspired by Democratic tactics in Mississippi, launched a wave of intimidation. Democrats intended to carry the election, one planter told a black official, "if we have to wade in blood knee-deep."

THE DISPUTED ELECTION AND BARGAIN OF 1877

Events in South Carolina directly affected the outcome of the presidential campaign of 1876. To succeed Grant, the Republicans nominated Governor Rutherford B. Hayes of Ohio. Democrats chose as his opponent New York's governor, Samuel J. Tilden. By this time, only South Carolina, Florida, and Louisiana remained under Republican control. The election turned out to be so close that whoever captured these states—which both parties claimed to have carried—would become the next president.

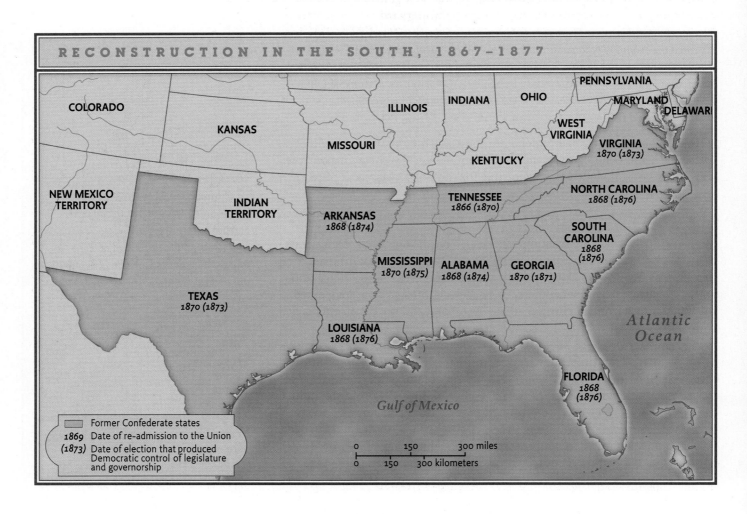

RECONSTRUCTION IN THE SOUTH, 1867–1877

Legend:
- Former Confederate states
- 1869 Date of re-admission to the Union
- (1873) Date of election that produced Democratic control of legislature and governorship

Unable to resolve the impasse on its own, Congress in January 1877 appointed a fifteen-member Electoral Commission, composed of senators, representatives, and Supreme Court justices. Republicans enjoyed an 8–7 majority on the commission, and to no one's surprise, the members decided by that margin that Hayes had carried the disputed southern states and had been elected president. Even as the commission deliberated, however, behind-the-scenes negotiations took place between leaders of the two parties. Hayes's representatives agreed to recognize Democratic control of the entire South and to avoid further intervention in local affairs. They also pledged that Hayes would place a southerner in the cabinet position of postmaster general and that he would work for federal aid to the Texas and Pacific railroad, a transcontinental line projected to follow a southern route. For their part, Democrats promised not to dispute Hayes's right to office and to respect the civil and political rights of blacks.

Thus was concluded the Bargain of 1877. Not all of its parts were fulfilled. But Hayes became president, and he did appoint David M. Key of Tennessee as postmaster general. Hayes quickly ordered federal troops to stop guarding the state houses in Louisiana and South Carolina, allowing Democratic claimants to become governor. (Contrary to legend, Hayes did not remove the last soldiers from the South—he simply ordered them to return to their barracks.) But the Texas and Pacific never did get its land grant. Of far more significance, the triumphant southern Democrats failed to live up to their pledge to recognize blacks as equal citizens.

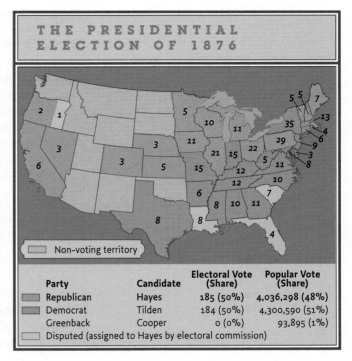

THE PRESIDENTIAL ELECTION OF 1876

Non-voting territory

Party	Candidate	Electoral Vote (Share)	Popular Vote (Share)
Republican	Hayes	185 (50%)	4,036,298 (48%)
Democrat	Tilden	184 (50%)	4,300,590 (51%)
Greenback	Cooper	0 (0%)	93,895 (1%)
Disputed (assigned to Hayes by electoral commission)			

THE END OF RECONSTRUCTION

As a historical process—the nation's adjustment to the destruction of slavery—Reconstruction continued well after 1877. Blacks continued to vote and, in some states, hold office into the 1890s. But as a distinct era of national history—when Republicans controlled much of the South, blacks exercised significant political power, and the federal government accepted the responsibility for protecting the fundamental rights of all American citizens—Reconstruction had come to an end. Despite its limitations, Reconstruction was a remarkable chapter in the story of American freedom. Nearly a century would pass before the nation again tried to bring equal rights to the descendants of slaves. The civil rights era of the 1950s and 1960s would sometimes be called the Second Reconstruction.

Even while it lasted, however, Reconstruction revealed some of the tensions inherent in nineteenth-century discussions of freedom. The policy of granting black men the vote while denying them the benefits of land ownership strengthened the idea that the free citizen could be a poor, dependent laborer. Reconstruction placed on the national agenda a problem that would dominate political discussion for the next half-century—how, in a modern society, to define the economic essence of freedom.

Is This a Republican Form of Government?, *a cartoon by Thomas Nast in* Harper's Weekly, *September 2, 1876, illustrates his conviction that the overthrow of Reconstruction meant that the United States was not prepared to live up to its democratic ideals or protect the rights of black citizens threatened by violence.*

SUGGESTED READING

Carter, Dan T. *When the War Was Over: The Failure of Self-Reconstruction in the South, 1865–1867* (1985). A careful study of the South during the period of presidential Reconstruction.

Du Bois, W. E. B. *Black Reconstruction in America* (1935). The first comprehensive refutation of the "traditional" view of Reconstruction as an era of misgovernment, which originated with opponents of black rights, and of racism in historical writing on the era.

DuBois, Ellen C. *Feminism and Suffrage: The Emergence of an Independent Women's Movement in America, 1848–1869* (1978). Explores how the split over the exclusion of women from the Fourteenth and Fifteenth Amendments gave rise to a movement for women's suffrage no longer tied to the abolitionist tradition.

Edwards, Laura. *Gendered Strife and Confusion: The Political Culture of Reconstruction* (1997). Considers how issues relating to gender relations affected the course of southern Reconstruction.

Fields, Barbara J. *Slavery and Freedom on the Middle Ground: Maryland during the Nineteenth Century* (1985). A study of slavery and emancipation in a key border state.

Foner, Eric. *Reconstruction: America's Unfinished Revolution, 1863–1877* (1988). The most comprehensive recent account of the Reconstruction era.

Hahn, Steven. *A Nation under Our Feet: Black Political Struggles in the Rural South from Slavery to the Great Migration* (2003). A detailed study of black political activism, stressing nationalist consciousness and emigration movements.

Hyman, Harold M. *A More Perfect Union: The Impact of the Civil War and Reconstruction on the Constitution* (1973). Analyzes how the laws and constitutional amendments of Reconstruction changed the Constitution and the rights of all Americans.

Litwack, Leon F. *Been in the Storm So Long: The Aftermath of Slavery* (1979). A detailed look at the immediate aftermath of the end of slavery and the variety of black and white responses to emancipation.

Rable, George C. *But There Was No Peace: The Role of Violence in the Politics of Reconstruction* (1984). The only full-scale study of violence in the Reconstruction South.

Ransom, Roger L., and Richard Sutch. *One Kind of Freedom: The Economic Consequences of Emancipation* (1977). Two economic historians examine the transition from slavery to sharecropping in the cotton South.

Richardson, Heather C. *The Death of Reconstruction: Race, Labor, and Politics in the Post–Civil War North* (2001). An examination of the numerous causes of the North's retreat from Reconstruction.

Rodrigue, John C. *Reconstruction in the Cane Fields: From Slavery to Free Labor in Louisiana's Sugar Parishes, 1862–1880* (2001). A study of how an often-neglected part of the South experienced the aftermath of slavery.

Summers, Mark W. *Railroads, Reconstruction, and the Gospel of Prosperity: Aid under the Radical Republicans, 1865–1877* (1984). A detailed look at southern governments' efforts to promote economic development, and the political corruption that sometimes accompanied it.

Trefousse, Hans L. *The Radical Republicans: Lincoln's Vanguard for Racial Justice* (1969). An account of the political history of the Radical Republicans, from the pre–Civil War period through the end of Reconstruction.

REVIEW QUESTIONS

1. Frederick Douglass insisted that "slavery is not abolished until the black man has the ballot." What did Douglass mean by this?

2. The women's movement split into two separate national organizations in part because the Fifteenth Amendment did not give women the vote. Explain why the two groups split.

3. What meanings of freedom were most important to the freed slaves?

4. What were the arguments for and against land distribution for the freed slaves?

5. Why was Reconstruction brought to an end in 1877?

KEY TERMS

black families (p. 550)

presidential pardons (p. 561)

"swing around the circle" (p. 564)

literacy tests (p. 566)

Bradwell v. Illinois (p. 569)

Enforcement Acts (p. 576)

Civil Rights Act of 1875 (p. 578)

Slaughterhouse Cases (p. 578)

REVIEW TABLE

Reconstruction Constitutional Amendments

Amendment	Date Ratified	Provisions
Thirteenth	1865	Ends slavery
Fourteenth	1868	Guarantees federal protection of citizenship
Fifteenth	1870	Prohibits voting restrictions based on race, color, or previous conditions of servitude

Part 4

TOWARD A GLOBAL PRESENCE, 1870–1920

Between the era of Reconstruction and the end of World War I, the United States underwent a profound social and economic revolution that affected all aspects of Americans' lives. By 1900, the country had emerged as the world's major industrial power and, thanks to the Spanish-American War of 1898, the possessor of a small overseas empire. Giant new corporations now dominated the economy. They introduced new forms of labor control and new methods of mass production, manufacturing a seemingly endless array of industrial and consumer goods. Immigrants arrived from abroad in unprecedented numbers, providing labor for the expanding economy and fueling the growth of the nation's cities. In 1920, residents of cities for the first time outnumbered those living in rural areas.

In the first two decades of the twentieth century, the United States became a major participant in world affairs. It repeatedly sent troops to direct the affairs of Caribbean and Central American countries. During World War I, President Woodrow Wilson not only dispatched American soldiers, for the first time, to fight in Europe but also called for continuous American involvement in the creation and preservation of a peaceful, economically interconnected world order.

These changes increased the economic opportunities of many Americans. The middle class of clerks, managers, and other white-collar workers expanded significantly. Economic growth drew large numbers of women into the workforce. When the outbreak of World War I cut off immigration from Europe, hundreds of thousands of blacks moved from southern farms to jobs in northern cities, gaining access to the industrial economy and changing the country's racial configuration.

What is sometimes called "the second industrial revolution" also led to an era of persistent and often violent labor conflict. To many Americans, social life seemed increasingly polarized between those at the top, who reaped most of the benefits of economic expansion, and workers struggling to make ends meet on low wages and living in desperate conditions in city slums. Democracy itself seemed threatened by the political influence of the large corporations and the corrupt activities of city bosses. In the early twentieth century, increasing numbers of Americans concluded that only the reform of politics and increased government intervention in economic life could curb the powers of the new corporations, ensure safe working conditions, and provide economic security for ordinary men and women.

Throughout these years, divergent views of the country's course of development, and the proper role of government in shaping and reshaping it, found expression in debates over American freedom. Many Americans held to a traditional understanding of freedom as the absence of external restraints on free individuals operating in a competitive marketplace. In this view, known as "liberty of contract," any government interference with economic relationships represented an infringement on property rights and, therefore, on freedom.

Others turned to collective action, economic and political, to try to reverse what they considered a decline of traditional freedoms. Workers flocked into unions that promised not only higher wages but also "industrial freedom"—a share in basic economic decision making. During the 1890s, millions of farmers joined the Populist movement in an attempt to reverse their declining economic prospects and rescue the government from what they saw as control by powerful corporate interests. In the Progressive era of the early twentieth century, urban reformers sought to expand economic and political freedom by increasing workers' rights, weakening the power of city bosses, and using the power of the state and national governments to regulate corporate behavior.

In many cities and states, and at the national level under Presidents Theodore Roosevelt, William Howard Taft, and Woodrow Wilson, government took on new roles in Progressive America. It sought to protect workers, especially women and children, from economic hardship, established agencies to determine rules for corporate behavior, and set aside parks and forests to preserve them from commercial exploitation. To Progressives, freedom was a positive idea, the effective power to achieve personal and social goals. At the same time, the expansion of the consumer economy and the new freedoms for women offered by city life encouraged the growth of an idea of personal freedom based on individual fulfillment, including self-determination in the most intimate areas of life.

Even as definitions of freedom expanded, the number of Americans who enjoyed genuine freedom contracted. In the 1890s and the early twentieth century, the political leaders of the white South imposed on the region's African-Americans a comprehensive system of second-class citizenship that rested on racial segregation, denial of the right to vote, lack of economic opportunities, and the ever-present threat of violence. Many native-born Americans considered immigrants, especially the large numbers arriving from southern and eastern Europe, as unfit for American citizenship. They sought to restrict their numbers and to force those already here to "Americanize" themselves by abandoning traditional cultures for mainstream values.

The country's emergence as a world power intensified these debates over freedom. To its supporters, the new American empire represented a continuation of the country's traditional self-image of promoting liberty and democracy throughout the world. President Wilson envisioned American involvement in World War I as a crusade not for national aggrandizement, but to "make the world safe for democracy." Yet critics of the acquisition of foreign colonies questioned whether an empire could still be considered a democracy. This question gained new urgency during World War I. On the one hand, the war ushered in the final success of the long struggle for women's suffrage, the greatest expansion of democracy in American history. On the other, the federal government and private patriotic organizations embarked on the most extensive campaign in American history to stifle criticism of administration policies and the economic status quo. By 1920, the United States was the world's foremost economic and military power. But the role it would play in world affairs in the future, and the fate of freedom at home, remained unresolved.

CHAPTER 16

America's Gilded Age, 1870–1890

The Ironworkers' Noontime, painted in 1880–1881 by Thomas Anshutz, an artist born in West Virginia, whose family owned iron factories. Unlike artists who depicted factories and workers earlier in the century, Anshutz does not try to reconcile nature and industry (there are no reminders of the natural environment). Nor does he emphasize the dignity of labor. The workers seem dwarfed by the factory, and some seem exhausted.

FOCUS QUESTIONS

• How did the United States become a mature industrial society in the decades after the Civil War?

• How was the West transformed economically and socially in this period?

• How effective was the political system of the Gilded Age?

• How was American freedom transformed by the economic development of the Gilded Age?

• How did reformers of the period approach the problems of an industrial society?

An immense crowd gathered in New York Harbor on October 28, 1886, for the dedication of *Liberty Enlightening the World*, a fitting symbol for a nation now wholly free. The idea for the statue originated in 1865 with Édouard de Laboulaye, a French educator and the author of several books on the United States, as a response to the assassination of Abraham Lincoln. The statue, de Laboulaye hoped, would celebrate both the historic friendship between France and the United States and the triumph, through the Union's victory in the Civil War, of American freedom. Measuring over 150 feet from torch to toe and standing atop a huge pedestal, the edifice was the tallest man-made structure in the Western Hemisphere. It exceeded in height, newspapers noted with pride, the Colossus of Rhodes, a wonder of the ancient world.

In time, the Statue of Liberty, as it came to be called, would become Americans' most revered national icon. For over a century it has stood as a symbol of freedom. The statue has offered welcome to millions of immigrants—the "huddled masses yearning to breathe free" celebrated in a poem by Emma Lazarus inscribed on its base in 1903. In the years since its dedication, the statue's familiar image has been reproduced by folk artists in every conceivable medium and has been used by advertisers to promote everything from cigarettes and lawn mowers to war bonds. As its use by Chinese students demanding democracy in the Tiananmen Square protests of 1989 showed, it has become a powerful international symbol as well.

The year of the statue's dedication, 1886, also witnessed the "great upheaval," a wave of strikes and labor protests that touched every part of the nation. Six months before the unveiling of the Statue of Liberty, police had killed four striking workers who attempted to prevent strikebreakers

The dedication of the Statue of Liberty, October 18, 1886.

from entering a Chicago factory. This was only one of many violent clashes that accompanied labor unrest between the end of Reconstruction in 1877 and the turn of the twentieth century. The 600 dignitaries (598 of them men) who gathered on what is now called Liberty Island for the dedication hoped the Statue of Liberty would·inspire renewed devotion to the nation's political and economic system. But for all its grandeur, the statue could not conceal the deep social divisions and fears about the future of American freedom that accompanied the country's emergence as the world's leading industrial power. Nor did the celebrations address the crucial questions that moved to the center stage of American public life during the 1870s and 1880s and remained there for decades to come: What are the social conditions that make freedom possible, and what role should the national government play in defining and protecting the liberty of its citizens?

The Strike, *an 1886 painting by the German-born artist Robert Koehler, who had grown up in a working-class family in Milwaukee. Koehler depicts a confrontation between a factory owner, dressed in a silk top hat, and angry workers. A woman and her children, presumably members of a striker's family, watch from the side while another woman, at the center, appears to plead for restraint. The threat of violence hangs in the air, and a striker in the lower right-hand corner reaches for a stone. The painting was inspired by events in Pittsburgh during the Great Railroad Strike of 1877, although Koehler was living in New York City at the time.*

THE SECOND INDUSTRIAL REVOLUTION

Between the end of the Civil War and the early twentieth century, the United States underwent one of the most rapid and profound economic revolutions any country has ever experienced. There were numerous causes for this explosive economic growth. The country enjoyed abundant natural resources, a growing supply of labor, an expanding market for manufactured goods, and the availability of capital for investment. In addition, the federal

Permanent and Temporary Bridge at Green River, Wyoming, *by Andrew J. Russell, who took hundreds of photographs in 1868 and 1869 of the construction of the Union Pacific portion of the transcontinental railroad. In the background is Citadel Rock.*

government actively promoted industrial and agricultural development. It enacted high tariffs that protected American industry from foreign competition, granted land to railroad companies to encourage construction, and used the army to remove Indians from western lands desired by farmers and mining companies.

THE INDUSTRIAL ECONOMY

The rapid expansion of factory production, mining, and railroad construction in all parts of the country except the South signaled the transition from Lincoln's America—a world centered on the small farm and artisan workshop—to a mature industrial society. Americans of the late nineteenth century marveled at the triumph of the new economy. "One can hardly believe," wrote the philosopher John Dewey, "there has been a revolution in history so rapid, so extensive, so complete."

By 1913, the United States produced one-third of the world's industrial output—more than the total of Great Britain, France, and Germany combined. Small-scale craft production still flourished in many trades, and armies of urban workers, male and female, toiled in their own homes or in the households of others as outworkers and domestics. But half of all industrial workers now labored in plants with over 250 employees. On the eve of the Civil War, the first industrial revolution, centered on the textile industry, had transformed New England into a center of manufacturing. But otherwise, the United States was still primarily an agricultural nation. By 1880, for the first time, the Census Bureau found a majority of the workforce engaged in non-farming jobs. The traditional dream of economic independence seemed obsolete. By 1890, two-thirds of Americans worked for wages, rather than owning a farm, business, or

Table 16.1 INDICATORS OF ECONOMIC CHANGE, 1870–1920			
	1870	*1900*	*1920*
Farms (millions)	2.7	5.7	6.4
Land in farms (million acres)	408	841	956
Wheat grown (million bushels)	254	599	843
Employment (millions)	14	28.5	44.5
In manufacturing (millions)	2.5	5.9	11.2
Percentage in workforce[a]			
Agricultural	52		27
Industry[b]	29		44
Trade, service, administration[c]	20		27
Railroad track (thousands of miles)	53	258	407
Steel produced (thousands of tons)	.8	11.2	46
CNP (billions of dollars)	7.4	18.7	91.5
Per capita (in 1958 dollars)	531	1,011	1,315
Life expectancy at birth (years)	42	47	54

a. Percentages are rounded and do not total 100.
b. Includes manufacturing, transportation, mining, construction.
c. Includes trade, finance, public administration.

craft shop. Drawn to factories by the promise of employment, a new working class emerged in these years. Between 1870 and 1920, almost 11 million Americans moved from farm to city, and another 25 million immigrants arrived from overseas.

Most manufacturing now took place in industrial cities. New York, with its new skyscrapers and hundreds of thousands of workers in all sorts of manufacturing establishments, symbolized dynamic urban growth. After merging with Brooklyn in 1898, its population exceeded 3.4 million. The city financed industrialization and westward expansion, its banks and stock exchange funneling capital to railroads, mines, and factories. But the heartland of the second industrial revolution was the region around the Great Lakes, with its factories producing iron and steel, machinery, chemicals, and packaged foods. Pittsburgh had become the world's center of iron and steel manufacturing. Chicago, by 1900 the nation's second-largest city, with 1.7 million inhabitants, was home to factories producing steel and farm machinery and giant stockyards where cattle were processed into meat products for shipment east in refrigerated cars. Smaller industrial cities also proliferated, often concentrating on a single industry—cast-iron stoves in Troy, New York, silk in Paterson, New Jersey, furniture in Grand Rapids, Michigan.

RAILROADS AND THE NATIONAL MARKET

The railroad made possible what is sometimes called the "second industrial revolution." Spurred by private investment and massive grants of land and

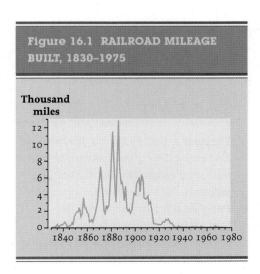

Figure 16.1 RAILROAD MILEAGE BUILT, 1830–1975

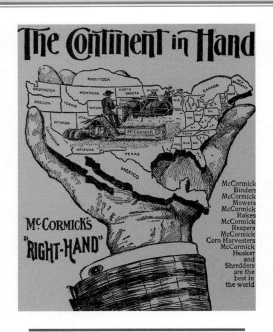

An advertisement for agricultural machinery produced by the Chicago-based McCormick Company illustrates the continental reach of the new national market.

money by federal, state, and local governments, the number of miles of railroad track in the United States tripled between 1860 and 1880 and tripled again by 1920, opening vast new areas to commercial farming and creating a truly national market for manufactured goods. In 1886, the railroads adopted a standard national gauge (the distance separating the two tracks), making it possible for the first time for trains of one company to travel on any other company's track. By the 1890s, five transcontinental lines transported the products of western mines, farms, ranches, and forests to eastern markets and carried manufactured goods to the West. The railroads reorganized time itself. In 1883, the major companies divided the nation into the four time zones still in use today. Indeed, the centrality of railroads to the national market meant that when railroads experienced financial crises, the entire economy suffered.

The growing population formed an ever-expanding market for the mass production, mass distribution, and mass marketing of goods, essential elements of a modern industrial economy. The spread of national brands like Ivory soap and Quaker Oats symbolized the continuing integration of the economy. So did the growth of national chains, most prominently the Atlantic and Pacific Tea Company, better known as A & P grocery stores. Based in Chicago, the national mail-order firms Montgomery Ward and Sears, Roebuck & Co. sold clothing, jewelry, farm equipment, and numerous other goods to rural families throughout the country.

The cover of the 1897 Sears, Roebuck, and Co. catalog. One of the country's largest mail-order companies, Sears, Roebuck processed 100,000 orders per day at the end of the nineteenth century. The cornucopia at the center suggests the variety of items one could order by mail: furniture, a piano, a bicycle, and farm tools.

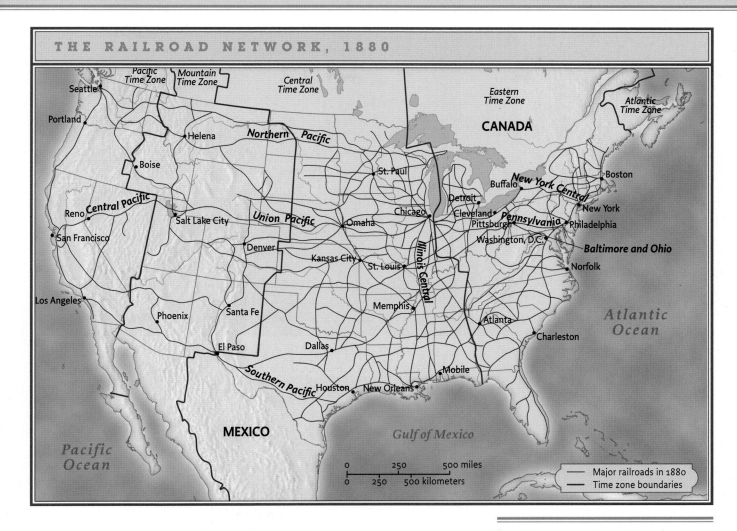

THE RAILROAD NETWORK, 1880

By 1880, the completion of the national rail network made possible the creation of a truly national market for goods.

THE SPIRIT OF INNOVATION

A remarkable series of technological innovations spurred rapid communication and economic growth. The opening of the Atlantic cable in 1866 made it possible to send electronic telegraph messages instantaneously between the United States and Europe. During the 1870s and 1880s, the telephone, typewriter, and handheld camera came into use.

Scientific breakthroughs poured forth from research laboratories in Menlo Park and Orange, New Jersey, created by the era's greatest inventor, Thomas A. Edison. Born in Ohio in 1847, Edison had little formal education, but as a teenager he read popular books on science and began doing chemistry experiments. During the course of his life, Edison helped to establish entirely new industries that transformed private life, public entertainment, and economic activity, including the phonograph, light bulb, motion picture, and a system for generating and distributing electric power. He opened the first electric generating station in Manhattan in 1882 to provide power to streetcars, factories, and private homes, and he established, among other companies, the forerunner of General Electric to market electrical equipment. The spread of electricity was essential to

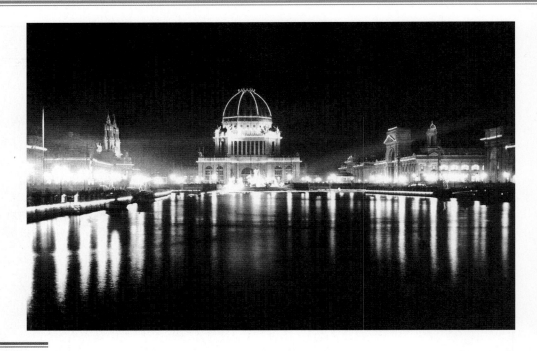

A photograph of buildings at the Chicago World's Fair of 1893, by the exposition's official photographer, C. D. Arnold. The elaborate lighting at the fair illustrated how electricity was changing the visual landscape.

industrial and urban growth, providing a more reliable and flexible source of power than water or steam.

COMPETITION AND CONSOLIDATION

Economic growth was dramatic but highly volatile. The combination of a market flooded with goods and federal monetary policies (discussed later) that removed money from the national economy led to a relentless fall in prices. The world economy suffered prolonged downturns in the 1870s and 1890s. Indeed, before the 1930s, the years from 1873 to 1897 were known throughout the world as the Great Depression.

Businesses engaged in ruthless competition. Railroads and other companies tried various means of bringing order to the chaotic marketplace. They formed "pools" that divided up markets between supposedly competing firms and fixed prices. They established "trusts"—legal devices whereby the affairs of several rival companies were managed by a single director. Such efforts to coordinate the economic activities of independent companies generally proved short-lived, disintegrating as individual firms continued their intense pursuit of profits.

To avoid cutthroat competition, more and more corporations battled to control entire industries. Many companies fell by the wayside or were gobbled up by others. The process of economic concentration culminated between 1897 and 1904, when some 4,000 firms vanished into larger corporations that served national markets and exercised an unprecedented degree of control over the marketplace. By the time the wave of mergers had been completed, giant corporations like U.S. Steel (created by financier J. P. Morgan in 1901 by combining eight large steel companies into the first billion-dollar economic enterprise), Standard Oil, and International Harvester (a manufacturer of agricultural machinery) dominated major parts of the economy.

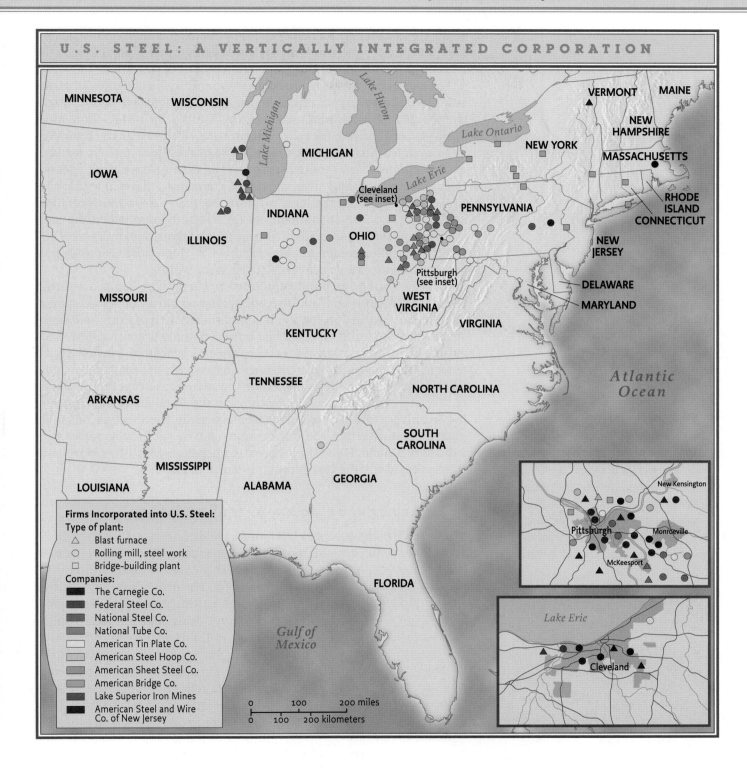

U.S. STEEL: A VERTICALLY INTEGRATED CORPORATION

Firms Incorporated into U.S. Steel:

Type of plant:
- △ Blast furnace
- ○ Rolling mill, steel work
- □ Bridge-building plant

Companies:
- The Carnegie Co.
- Federal Steel Co.
- National Steel Co.
- National Tube Co.
- American Tin Plate Co.
- American Steel Hoop Co.
- American Sheet Steel Co.
- American Bridge Co.
- Lake Superior Iron Mines
- American Steel and Wire Co. of New Jersey

THE RISE OF ANDREW CARNEGIE

In an era without personal or corporate income taxes, some business leaders accumulated enormous fortunes and economic power. Under the aggressive leadership of Thomas A. Scott, the Pennsylvania Railroad—for a time the nation's largest corporation—forged an economic empire that stretched across the continent and included coal mines and oceangoing steamships. With an army of professional managers to oversee its far-flung activities, the railroad pioneered modern techniques of business organization.

Another industrial giant was Andrew Carnegie, who emigrated with his family from his native Scotland at the age of thirteen and as a teenager worked in a Pennsylvania textile factory. During the 1850s, Scott hired Carnegie as his private telegraph operator and, by the eve of the Civil War, had promoted him to one of the Pennsylvania Railroad's major management positions. During the depression that began in 1873, Carnegie set out to establish a "vertically integrated" steel company—that is, one that controlled every phase of the business from raw materials to transportation, manufacturing, and distribution. By the 1890s, he dominated the steel industry and had accumulated a fortune worth hundreds of millions of dollars. Carnegie's complex of steel factories at Homestead, Pennsylvania, were the most technologically advanced in the world.

Carnegie's father, an immigrant Scottish weaver who had taken part in popular efforts to open the British political system to working-class participation, had instilled in his son a commitment to democracy and social equality. From his mother, Carnegie learned that life was a ceaseless struggle in which one must strive to get ahead or sink beneath the waves. His life reflected the tension between these elements of his upbringing. Believing that the rich had a moral obligation to promote the advancement of society, Carnegie denounced the "worship of money" and distributed much of his wealth to various philanthropies, especially the creation of public libraries in towns throughout the country. But he ran his companies with a dictatorial hand. His factories operated nonstop, with two twelve-hour shifts every day of the year except the Fourth of July.

THE TRIUMPH OF JOHN D. ROCKEFELLER

If any single name became a byword for enormous wealth, it was John D. Rockefeller, who began his working career as a clerk for a Cleveland merchant and rose to dominate the oil industry. He drove out rival firms through cutthroat competition, arranging secret deals with railroad companies, and fixing prices and production quotas. Rockefeller began with "horizontal" expansion—buying out competing oil refineries. But like Carnegie, he soon established a vertically integrated monopoly, which controlled the drilling, refining, storage, and distribution of oil. By the 1880s, his Standard Oil Company controlled 90 percent of the nation's oil industry. Like Carnegie, Rockefeller gave much of his fortune away, establishing foundations to promote education and medical research.

Next!, *a cartoon from the magazine* Puck, *September 7, 1904, depicts the Standard Oil Company as an octopus with tentacles wrapped around the copper, steel, and shipping industries, as well as a state house and Congress. One tentacle reaches for the White House.*

And like Carnegie, he bitterly fought his employees' efforts to organize unions.

These and other industrial leaders inspired among ordinary Americans a combination of awe, admiration, and hostility. Depending on one's point of view, they were "captains of industry," whose energy and vision pushed the economy forward, or "robber barons," who wielded power without any accountability in an unregulated marketplace. Most rose from modest backgrounds and seemed examples of how inventive genius and business sense enabled Americans to seize opportunities for success. But their dictatorial attitudes, unscrupulous methods, repressive labor policies, and exercise of power without any democratic control led to fears that they were undermining political and economic freedom. Concentrated wealth degraded the political process, declared Henry Demarest Lloyd in *Wealth Against Commonwealth* (1894), an exposé of how Rockefeller's Standard Oil Company made a mockery of economic competition and political democracy by manipulating the market and bribing legislators. "Liberty and monopoly," Lloyd concluded, "cannot live together."

WORKERS' FREEDOM IN AN INDUSTRIAL AGE

Striking as it was, the country's economic growth distributed its benefits very unevenly. For a minority of workers, the rapidly expanding industrial system created new forms of freedom. In some industries, skilled workers commanded high wages and exercised considerable control over the production process. A worker's economic independence now rested on technical skill rather than ownership of one's own shop and tools as in earlier times. What was known as "the miner's freedom" consisted of elaborate work rules that left skilled underground workers free of managerial supervision on the job. Through their union, skilled iron- and steelworkers fixed output quotas and controlled the training of apprentices in the technique of iron rolling. These workers often knew more about the details of production than their employers did.

Such "freedom," however, applied only to a tiny portion of the industrial labor force and had little bearing on the lives of the growing army of semi-skilled workers who tended machines in the new factories. For most workers, economic insecurity remained a basic fact of life. During the depressions of the 1870s and 1890s, millions of workers lost their jobs or were forced to accept reductions of pay. The "tramp" became a familiar figure on the social landscape as thousands of men took to the roads in search of work. Many industrial workers labored sixty-hour weeks with no pensions, compensation for injuries, or protections against unemployment. Although American workers received higher wages than their counterparts in Europe, they also experienced more dangerous working conditions. Between 1880 and 1900, an average of 35,000 workers perished each year in factory and mine accidents, the highest rate in the industrial world. Most strikes for higher wages failed, as employers found it easy to call on the unemployed to take the strikers' jobs, and to bring in public and private police forces to intimidate workers.

A turn-of-the-century photograph of the Casino Grounds, Newport, Rhode Island, an exclusive country club for rich socialites of the Gilded Age.

Much of the working class remained desperately poor and to survive needed income from all family members. In 1888, the Chicago *Times* published a series of articles by reporter Nell Cusack under the title "City Slave Girls," exposing wretched conditions among the growing number of women working for wages in the city's homes, factories, and sweatshops. The articles unleashed a flood of letters to the editor from women workers. One woman singled out domestic service—still the largest employment category for women—as "a slave's life," with "long hours, late and early, seven days in the week, bossed and ordered about as before the war."

SUNSHINE AND SHADOW: INCREASING WEALTH AND POVERTY

An engraving from Harper's Weekly *showing the Bradley Martin ball, in which guests dressed as members of the court of Louis XIV, February 20, 1897.*

At the other end of the economic spectrum, the era witnessed an unprecedented accumulation of wealth. Class divisions became more and more visible. In frontier days, all classes in San Francisco, for example, lived near the waterfront. In the late nineteenth century, upper-class families built mansions on Nob Hill and Van Ness Avenue (known as "millionaire's row"). In eastern cities as well, the rich increasingly resided in their own exclusive neighborhoods and vacationed among members of their own class at exclusive resorts like Newport, Rhode Island. The growing urban middle class of professionals, office workers, and small businessmen moved to new urban and suburban neighborhoods linked to central business districts by streetcars and commuter railways. "Passion for money," wrote the novelist Edith Wharton in *The House of Mirth* (1905) dominated society. Wharton's book traced the difficulties of

Lily Bart, a young woman of modest means pressured by her mother and New York high society to "barter" her beauty for marriage to a rich husband in a world where "to be poor . . . amounted to disgrace."

By 1890, the richest 1 percent of Americans received the same total income as the bottom half of the population and owned more property than the remaining 99 percent. Many of the wealthiest Americans consciously pursued an aristocratic lifestyle, building palatial homes, attending exclusive social clubs, schools, and colleges, holding fancy-dress balls, and marrying into each other's families. In 1899, the economist and social historian Thorstein Veblen published *The Theory of the Leisure Class*, a devastating critique of an upper-class culture focused on "conspicuous consumption"—that is, spending money not on needed or even desired goods, but simply to demonstrate the possession of wealth. One of the era's most widely publicized spectacles was an elaborate costume ball organized in 1897 by Mrs. Bradley Martin, the daughter of a New York railroad financier. The theme was the court of the prerevolutionary French monarch Louis XIV. The Waldorf-Astoria Hotel was decorated to look like the palace of Versailles, the guests wore the dress of the French nobility, and the hostess bedecked herself with the actual jewels of Queen Marie Antoinette.

Not that far from the Waldorf, much of the working class lived in desperate conditions. Matthew Smith's 1868 best-seller *Sunshine and Shadow in New York* opened with an engraving that contrasted department store magnate Alexander T. Stewart's two-million-dollar mansion with housing in the city's slums. Two decades later, Jacob Riis, in *How the Other Half Lives* (1890), offered a shocking account of living conditions among the urban poor, complete with photographs of apartments in dark, airless, overcrowded tenement houses.

The opening image in Matthew Smith's book, Sunshine and Shadow in New York *(1868), contrasts the living conditions of the city's rich and poor.*

Baxter Street Court, 1890, one of numerous photographs by Jacob Riis depicting living conditions in New York City's slums.

THE TRANSFORMATION OF THE WEST

Nowhere did capitalism penetrate more rapidly or dramatically than in the trans-Mississippi West, whose "vast, trackless spaces," as the poet Walt Whitman called them, were now absorbed into the expanding economy. At the close of the Civil War, the frontier of settlement did not extend far beyond the Mississippi River. To the west lay millions of acres of fertile and mineral-rich land roamed by giant herds of buffalo whose meat and hides provided food, clothing, and shelter for a population of more than 250,000 Indians.

In 1893, the historian Frederick Jackson Turner gave a celebrated lecture, "The Significance of the Frontier in American History," in which he argued that on the western frontier the distinctive qualities of American culture were forged: individual freedom, political democracy, and economic mobility. The West, he added acted as a "safety valve," drawing off those dissatisfied with their situation in the East and therefore counteracting the threat of social unrest. Turner's was one of the most influential interpretations of American history ever developed. But his lecture summarized attitudes toward the West that had been widely shared among Americans long before 1893. Ever since the beginning of colonial settlement in British North America, the West—a region whose definition shifted as the population expanded—had been seen as a place of opportunity for those seeking to improve their condition in life.

Many Americans did indeed experience the westward movement in the way Turner described it. From farmers moving into Ohio, Indiana, and Illinois in the decades after the American Revolution to prospectors who struck it rich in the California gold rush of the mid-nineteenth century,

Ole Johnson, a Norwegian immigrant, posed in 1886 with his family in front of their Nebraska sod house, a typical dwelling for pioneers on the Great Plains. The photographer who recorded this image returned in 1904 to find the same family living in a white clapboard farm house.

millions of Americans and immigrants from abroad found in the westward movement a path to economic opportunity. But Turner offered only a partial account of western history. Most settlers moved west in family groups or as members of immigrant communities, not as lone pioneers. Turner seemed to portray the West as an empty space before the coming of white settlers. In fact, of course, it was already inhabited by Native Americans, whose dispossession was essential to the opening of land for settlement by others. Moreover, the West was hardly a uniform paradise of small, independent farmers. Beginning in the eighteenth century, for example, California was the site of forced Indian labor on missions established by members of religious orders, a system that helped establish the pattern of large agricultural land holdings in that region. Landlords, railroads, and mining companies in the West also utilized Mexican migrant and indentured labor, Chinese working on long-term contracts, and, until the the end of the Civil War, African-American slaves.

A DIVERSE REGION

The West, of course, was hardly a single area. West of the Mississippi River lay a variety of regions, all marked by remarkable physical beauty—the "vast, trackless" Great Plains, the Rocky Mountains, the desert of the Southwest, the Sierra Nevada and the valleys and coastline of California and Pacific Northwest. It would take many decades before individual settlers and corporate business enterprises penetrated all these areas. But the process was far advanced by the end of the nineteenth century.

The political and economic incorporation of the American West was part of a global process. In many parts of the world, indigenous inhabitants—the Mapuche in Chile, the Zulu in South Africa, aboriginal peoples in Australia, American Indians—were pushed aside (often after fierce resistance) as centralizing governments brought large interior regions under their control. In the United States, it required the active intervention of the federal government—which acquired Indian land by war and treaty, administered land sales, regulated territorial politics, and distributed land and money to farmers, railroads, and mining companies—to incorporate the West.

In the twentieth century, the construction of federally financed irrigation systems and dams would open large areas to commercial farming. Ironically, the West would become known (not least to its own inhabitants) as a place of rugged individualism and sturdy independence. But without active governmental assistance, the region could never have been settled and developed.

FARMING ON THE MIDDLE BORDER

Even as sporadic Indian wars raged, settlers poured into the West. Territorial and state governments eager for population, and railroad companies anxious to sell land they had acquired from the government, flooded European countries and eastern cities with promotional literature promising easy access to land. More land came into cultivation in the thirty years after the Civil War than in the previous two and a half centuries of American

RES. & RANCH OF H. P. GRAY, EAST OF LEMORE, TULARE CO. CAL.

An engraving from the early 1880s of a California farm adjacent to the Southern Pacific Railroad. Having been granted vast tracts of land by the federal government, the railroad encouraged settlement along its lines.

history. Hundreds of thousands of families acquired farms under the Homestead Act, and even more purchased land from speculators and from railroad companies that had been granted immense tracts of public land by the federal government. A new agricultural empire producing wheat and corn for national and international markets arose on the Middle Border (Minnesota, the Dakotas, Nebraska, and Kansas), whose population rose from 300,000 in 1860 to 5 million in 1900. The farmers were a diverse group, including native-born easterners, blacks escaping the post-Reconstruction South, and immigrants from Canada, Germany, Scandinavia, and Great Britain. Although ethnic diversity is generally associated with eastern cities, in the late nineteenth century the most multicultural state in the Union was North Dakota.

Despite the promises of promotional pamphlets, farming on the Great Plains was not an easy task. Difficulties came in many forms—from the poisonous rattlesnakes that lived in the tall prairie grass to the blizzards and droughts that periodically afflicted the region. Much of the burden fell on women. Farm families generally invested in the kinds of labor-saving machinery that would bring in cash, not machines that would ease women's burdens in the household (like the back-breaking task of doing laundry). While husbands and sons tended to devote their labor to cash crops, farm wives cared for animals, grew crops for food, and cooked and cleaned. A farm woman in Arizona described her morning chores in her diary: "Get up, turn out my chickens, draw a pail of water . . . make a fire, put potatoes to cook, brush and sweep half inch of dust off floor, feed three litters of chickens, then mix biscuits, get breakfast, milk, besides work in the house, and this morning had to go half mile after calves." On far-flung homesteads, many miles from schools, medical care, and sources of entertainment, farm families suffered from loneliness and isolation—a problem especially severe for women when their husbands left, sometimes for weeks at a time, to market their crops.

BONANZA FARMS

John Wesley Powell, the explorer and geologist who surveyed the Middle Border in the 1870s, warned that because of the region's arid land and limited rainfall, development there required large-scale irrigation projects. The model of family farming envisioned by the Homestead Act of 1862 could not apply: no single family could do all the work required on irrigated farms—only cooperative, communal farming could succeed, Powell maintained.

Despite the emergence of a few "bonanza farms" that covered thousands of acres and employed large numbers of agricultural wage workers, family

A combined reaper-thresher harvests wheat on a western "bonanza" farm, in a photograph from around 1890.

farms still dominated the trans-Mississippi West. Even small farmers, however, became increasingly oriented to national and international markets, specializing in the production of single crops for sale in faraway places. At the same time, railroads brought factory-made goods to rural people, replacing items previously produced in farmers' homes. Farm families became more and more dependent on loans to purchase land, machinery, and industrial products, and more and more vulnerable to the ups and downs of prices for agricultural goods in the world market. Agriculture reflected how the international economy was becoming more integrated. The combination of economic depressions and expanding agricultural production in places like Argentina, Australia, and the American West pushed prices of farm products steadily downward. From Italy and Ireland to China, India, and the American South, small farmers throughout the world suffered severe difficulties in the last quarter of the nineteenth century. Many joined the migration to cities within their countries or the increasing international migration of labor.

LARGE-SCALE AGRICULTURE IN CALIFORNIA

The future of western farming ultimately lay with giant agricultural enterprises relying heavily on irrigation, chemicals, and machinery—investments far beyond the means of family farmers. A preview of the agricultural future was already evident in California, where, as far back as Spanish and Mexican days, landownership had been concentrated in large units. In the late nineteenth century, California's giant fruit and vegetable farms, owned by corporations like the Southern Pacific Railroad, were tilled not by agricultural laborers who could expect to acquire land of their own, but by migrant laborers from China, the Philippines, Japan, and

In the late 1800s, California tried to attract immigrants by advertising its pleasant climate and the availability of land, although large-scale corporate farms were coming to dominate the state's agriculture.

Mexico, who tramped from place to place following the ripening crops. "California is not a country of farms, but . . . of plantations and estates," wrote the young journalist Henry George in 1871, urging the government to take action against "land monopoly" and to "give all men an equal chance" to achieve economic independence.

THE COWBOY AND THE CORPORATE WEST

The two decades following the Civil War also witnessed the golden age of the cattle kingdom. The Kansas Pacific Railroad's stations at Abilene, Dodge City, and Wichita, Kansas, became destinations for the fabled drives of millions of cattle from Texas. A collection of white, Mexican, and black men who conducted the cattle drives, the cowboys became symbols of a life of freedom on the open range. Their exploits would later serve as the theme of many a Hollywood movie, and their clothing inspired fashions that remain popular today. But there was nothing romantic about the life of the cowboys, most of whom were low-paid wage workers. (Texas cowboys even went on strike for higher pay in 1883.) The days of the long-distance cattle drive ended in the mid-1880s, as farmers enclosed more and more of the open range with barbed-wire fences, making it difficult to graze cattle on the grasslands of the Great Plains, and two terrible winters destroyed millions of cattle. When the industry recuperated, it was reorganized in large, enclosed ranches close to rail connections.

The West was more than a farming empire. By 1890, a higher percentage of its population lived in cities than was the case in other regions. The economic focus of California's economy remained San Francisco, a major manufacturing and trading center. The explosive growth of southern California began in the 1880s, first with tourism, heavily promoted by railroad companies, followed by the discovery of oil in Los Angeles in 1892. Large corporate enterprises appeared throughout the West. The lumber industry, dominated by small-scale producers in 1860, came under the control of corporations that acquired large tracts of forest and employed armies of loggers. Western mining, from Michigan iron ore and copper to gold and silver in California, Nevada, and Colorado, fell under the sway of companies that mobilized eastern and European investment to introduce advanced technology. Gold and silver rushes took place in the Dakotas in 1876, Idaho in 1883, and Alaska at the end of the century. But as in California after 1848, the independent prospector, working a surface mine with his pick and shovel, quickly gave way to deep-shaft corporate mining employing wage workers.

A similar process occurred in New Mexico, where traditional life based on sheep farming on land owned in common by Mexican villagers had continued more or less unchanged after the United States acquired the area in the Mexican War. Railroads reached the area in the 1870s, bringing with them eastern mining companies and commercial ranchers and farmers. Because courts only recognized Mexican-era land titles to individual plots of land, communal landholdings were increasingly made available for sale to newcomers. By 1880, three-quarters of New Mexico's sheep belonged to just twenty families. Unable to continue as sheep raisers, more and more Hispanic residents went to work for the new mines and railroads.

THE SUBJUGATION OF THE PLAINS INDIANS

The incorporation of the West into the national economy spelled the doom of the Plains Indians and their world. Their lives had already undergone profound transformations. In the eighteenth century, the spread of horses, originally introduced by the Spanish, led to a wholesale shift from farming and hunting on foot to mounted hunting of buffalo. New Indian groups migrated to the Great Plains to take advantage of the horse, coalescing into the great tribes of the nineteenth century—the Cheyenne, Comanche, Crow, Kiowa, and Sioux. Persistent warfare took place between the more established tribes and newcomers, including Indians removed from the East, who sought access to their hunting grounds.

Most migrants on the Oregon and California Trails before the Civil War encountered little hostility from Indians, often trading with them for food and supplies. But as settlers encroached on Indian lands, bloody conflict between the army and Plains tribes began in the 1850s and continued for decades. During the Civil War, the Sioux killed hundreds of white farmers in Minnesota before being subdued by the army. After a military court sentenced over 300 Indians to death, President Lincoln commuted the sentences of all but 38. But their hanging in December 1862 remains the largest official execution in American history.

Some tribes that owned slaves sided with the Confederacy. After 1865, they were forced to cede much of their land to the government and give land to some of their former slaves (the only slaveowners required to do so).

Albert Bierstadt's 1863 painting, The Rocky Mountains, Lander's Peak, *depicts Indians as an integral part of the majestic landscape of the West.*

Hunters shooting buffalo as the Kansas-Pacific Railroad cuts across the West, 1870s.

The Union army also launched a campaign against the Navajo in the Southwest, destroying their orchards and sheep and forcing 8,000 people to move to a reservation set aside by the government. The Navajos' Long Walk became as central to their historical experience as the Trail of Tears of the Cherokee (see Chapter 10). Unlike the eastern Indians, however, the Navajo were eventually allowed to return to a portion of their lands.

In 1869, President Ulysses S. Grant announced a new "peace policy" in the West, but warfare soon resumed. Drawing on methods used to defeat the Confederacy, Civil War generals like Philip H. Sheridan set out to destroy the foundations of the Indian economy—villages, horses, and especially the buffalo. Hunting by mounted Indians had already reduced the buffalo population—estimated at 30 million in 1800—but it was army campaigns and the depredations of hunters seeking buffalo hides that rendered the vast herds all but extinct. By 1886, an expedition from the Smithsonian Institution in Washington had difficulty finding twenty-five "good specimens." "A cold wind blew across the prairie when the last buffalo fell," said the Sioux leader Sitting Bull, "a death-wind for my people."

"LET ME BE A FREE MAN"

The army's relentless attacks broke the power of one tribe after another. In 1877, troops commanded by former Freedmen's Bureau commissioner O. O. Howard pursued the Nez Percé Indians on a 1,700-mile chase across the Far West. The Nez Percé (whose name was given them by Lewis and Clark in 1805 and means "pierced noses" in French) were seeking to escape to Canada after fights with settlers who had encroached on tribal lands in Oregon and Idaho. After four months, Howard forced the Indians to surrender, and they were removed to Oklahoma.

Two years later, the Nez Percé leader, Chief Joseph, delivered a speech in Washington to a distinguished audience including President Rutherford B. Hayes. Condemning the policy of confining Indians to reservations, Joseph adopted the language of freedom and equal rights before the law so powerfully reinforced by the Civil War and Reconstruction. "Treat all men alike," he pleaded. "Give them the same law. . . . Let me be a free man—free to travel, free to stop, free to work, free to trade where I choose, free to . . . think and talk and act for myself." The government eventually transported the surviving Nez Percé to another reservation in Washington Territory. Until his death in 1904, Joseph would unsuccessfully petition successive presidents for his people's right to return to their beloved Oregon homeland.

Indians occasionally managed to inflict costly delay and even defeat on army units. The most famous Indian victory took place in June 1876 at Little Bighorn, when General George A. Custer and his entire command of 250 men perished. The Sioux and Cheyenne warriors, led by Sitting Bull and Crazy Horse, were defending tribal land in the Black Hills of the Dakota Territory. Reserved for them in an 1868 treaty "for as long as the grass shall grow," their lands had been invaded by whites after the discovery of gold. In the Southwest, Cochise, Geronimo, and other leaders of the Apache, who had been relocated by the government a number of times, led bands that crossed and recrossed the border with Mexico, evading the army and occasionally killing civilians. They would not surrender until the mid-1880s.

These events delayed only temporarily the onward march of white soldiers, settlers, and prospectors. Between the end of the Civil War and 1890, eight new western states entered the Union (Nebraska, Colorado, North and South Dakota, Montana, Washington, Idaho, and Wyoming). Railroads now crisscrossed the Great Plains, farmers and cattlemen exploited land formerly owned by Indians, and the Plains tribes had been concentrated on reservations, where they lived in poverty, preyed upon by unscrupulous traders and government agents. A strong opponent of the reservation

The Battle of the Little Bighorn, June 25–26, 1876, in which General George A. Custer and his entire command were killed, as drawn by Red Horse, a Sioux chief.

VOICES OF FREEDOM

From Chief Joseph of the Nez Percé Indians,
Speech in Washington, D.C. (1879)

Chief Joseph, leader of the Nez Percé Indians, led his people on a 1,700-mile trek from their homes in Oregon and Idaho through the Far West in 1877 in an unsuccessful effort to escape to Canada. Two years later, he addressed an audience in Washington, D.C., that included President Rutherford B. Hayes, appealing for the freedom and equal rights enshrined in the law after the Civil War.

My friends, I have been asked to show you my heart. I am glad to have a chance to do so. I want the white people to understand my people. Some of you think an Indian is like a wild animal. This is a great mistake. I will tell you all about our people, and then you can judge whether an Indian is a man or not.... I will tell you in my way how the Indian sees things. The white man has more words to tell you how they look to him, but it does not require many words to speak the truth....

I have heard talk and talk, but nothing is done. Good words do not last long unless they amount to something. Words do not pay for my dead people. They do not pay for my country, now overrun by white men.... Good words will not get my people a home where they can live in peace and take care of themselves. I am tired of talk that comes to nothing. It makes my heart sick when I remember all the ... broken promises....

If the white man wants to live in peace with the Indian he can live in peace. There need be no trouble. Treat all men alike. Give them the same law. Give them all an even chance to live and grow. All men were made by the same Great Spirit Chief. They are all brothers. The earth is the mother of all people, and all people should have equal rights upon it. You might as well expect the rivers to run backward as that any man who was born a free man should be contented when penned up and denied liberty to go where he pleases....

When I think of our condition my heart is heavy. I see men of my race treated as outlaws and driven from country to country, or shot down like animals. I know that my race must change. We cannot hold our own with the white men as we are. We only ask an even chance to live as other men live....

Let me be a free man—free to travel, free to stop, free to work, free to trade where I choose, free to choose my own teachers, free to follow the religion of my fathers, free to think and talk and act for myself— and I will obey every law, or submit to the penalty.

FROM HENRY GEORGE,
Progress and Poverty (1879)

Among the most influential writers on social issues during the Gilded Age, Henry George identified the monopolization of land as the cause of social inequality. His best-selling book, *Progress and Poverty*, offered a critique of the expansion of poverty amid material abundance.

———————————

The evils arising from the unjust and unequal distribution of wealth, which are becoming more and more apparent as modern civilization goes on . . . will not cure themselves, but, on the contrary, must, unless their cause is removed, grow greater and greater, until they sweep us back into barbarism by the road every previous civilization had trod. . . . These evils are not imposed by natural laws; . . . they spring solely from social mal-adjustments which ignore natural laws, and . . . in removing their cause we shall be giving an enormous impetus to progress.

The poverty which in the midst of abundance, pinches and embrutes me, and all the manifold evils which flow from it, spring from a denial of justice. . . . Rights are denied when the equal right to land, on which and by which men alone can live, is denied. Equality of political rights will not compensate for the denial of the equal right to the bounty of nature. Political liberty, when the equal right to land is denied, becomes, as population increases and invention goes on, merely the liberty to compete for employment at starvation wages. This is the truth that we have ignored. . . .

We honor Liberty in name and in form. We set up her statues and sound her praises. But we have not fully trusted her. . . . For Liberty means Justice, and Justice is the natural law—the law of health and symmetry and strength, of fraternity and cooperation.

They who look upon Liberty as having accomplished her mission when she has abolished hereditary privileges and given men the ballot, who think of her as having no further relations to the everyday affairs of life, have not seen her real grandeur. . . . We speak of Liberty as one thing, and virtue, wealth, knowledge, invention, national strength and national independence as other things. But, of all these, Liberty is the source, the mother, the necessary condition. . . .

With steam and electricity, and the new powers born of progress, forces have entered the world that will either compel us to a higher plane or overwhelm us, as nation after nation, as civilization after civilization, have been overwhelmed before. . . . Between democratic ideas and the aristocratic adjustments of society there is an irreconcilable conflict. . . . We cannot go on prating of the inalienable rights of man and then denying the inalienable right to the bounty of the Creator.

═══════════════

QUESTIONS

1. What are Chief Joseph's complaints about the treatment of his people?

2. How does Henry George describe the relationship between political liberty and economic liberty?

3. In what ways do the definitions of freedom in the two documents agree and differ?

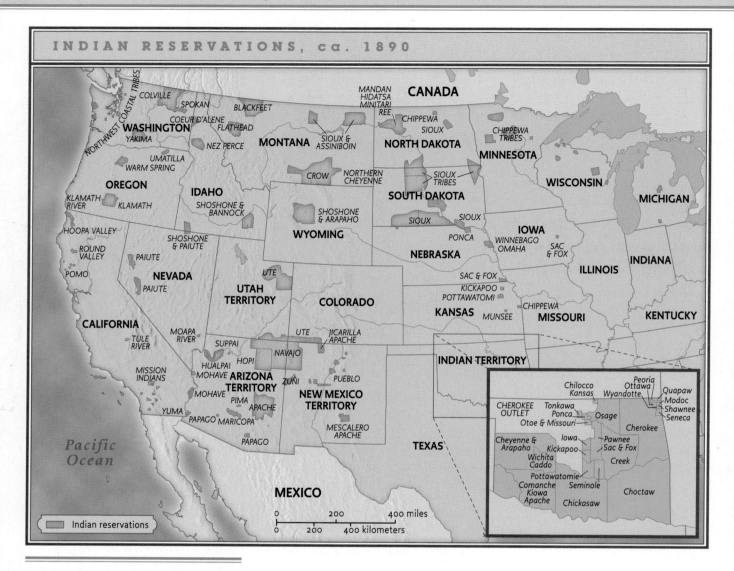

INDIAN RESERVATIONS, ca. 1890

By 1890, the vast majority of the remaining Indian population had been removed to reservations scattered across the western states.

system, Sitting Bull escaped to Canada after the army defeated the Sioux, but he returned and was imprisoned in 1881. He was released in 1883 and for a time became part of Buffalo Bill's Wild West Show, a popular traveling extravaganza complete with mock Indian attacks and shooting and riding exhibitions. For most Americans, Indians were now simply objects of curiosity or entertainment.

REMAKING INDIAN LIFE

"The life my people want is a life of freedom," Sitting Bull declared. The Indian idea of freedom, however, which centered on preserving their cultural and political autonomy and control of ancestral lands, conflicted with the interests and values of most white Americans. Nearly all officials believed that the federal government should persuade or force the Plains Indians to surrender most of their land and to exchange their religion, communal property, nomadic way of life, and gender relations for Christian

Boys from the Lakota tribe on their arrival (left) *and during their stay at Carlisle, a boarding school that aimed to "civilize" Indians, by J. N. Choate, a local photographer.*

worship, private ownership, and small farming on reservations with men tilling the fields and women working in the home.

In 1871, Congress eliminated the treaty system that dated back to the revolutionary era, by which the federal government negotiated agreements with Indians as if they were independent nations. This step was supported by railroad companies that found tribal sovereignty an obstacle to construction and by Republicans who believed that it contradicted the national unity born of the Civil War. The federal government pressed forward with its assault on Indian culture. The Bureau of Indian Affairs established boarding schools where Indian children, removed from the "negative" influences of their parents and tribes, were dressed in non-Indian clothes, given new names, and educated in white ways.

THE DAWES ACT

The crucial step in attacking "tribalism" came in 1887 with the passage of the Dawes Act, named for Senator Henry L. Dawes of Massachusetts, chair of the Senate's Indian Affairs Committee. The act broke up the land of nearly all tribes into small parcels to be distributed to Indian families, with the remainder auctioned off to white purchasers. Indians who accepted the farms and "adopted the habits of civilized life" would become full-fledged American citizens. The policy proved to be a disaster, leading to the loss of much tribal land and the erosion of Indian cultural traditions. Whites, however, benefited enormously. On the Nez Percé reservation, for example, 172,000 acres were divided into farms for

An 1893 photograph depicts the land rush when a portion of Cherokee land in the Oklahoma Territory was opened to white settlement under the provisions of the Dawes Act.

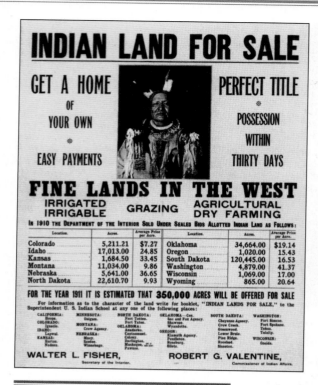

INDIAN LAND FOR SALE

GET A HOME
OF
YOUR OWN
*
EASY PAYMENTS

PERFECT TITLE
*
POSSESSION
WITHIN
THIRTY DAYS

FINE LANDS IN THE WEST
IRRIGATED   GRAZING   AGRICULTURAL
IRRIGABLE   DRY FARMING

IN 1910 THE DEPARTMENT OF THE INTERIOR SOLD UNDER SEALED BIDS ALLOTTED INDIAN LAND AS FOLLOWS:

Location	Acres	Average Price per Acre	Location	Acres	Average Price per Acre
Colorado	5,211.21	$7.27	Oklahoma	34,664.00	$19.14
Idaho	17,013.00	24.85	Oregon	1,020.00	15.43
Kansas	1,684.50	33.45	South Dakota	120,445.00	16.53
Montana	11,034.00	9.86	Washington	4,879.00	41.37
Nebraska	5,641.00	36.65	Wisconsin	1,069.00	17.00
North Dakota	22,610.70	9.93	Wyoming	865.00	20.64

FOR THE YEAR 1911 IT IS ESTIMATED THAT **350,000** ACRES WILL BE OFFERED FOR SALE

For information as to the character of the land write for booklet, "INDIAN LANDS FOR SALE," to the
Superintendent U. S. Indian School at any one of the following places:

CALIFORNIA: MINNESOTA: NORTH DAKOTA: OKLAHOMA—Con.   SOUTH DAKOTA: WASHINGTON:

WALTER L. FISHER,
Secretary of the Interior.

ROBERT G. VALENTINE,
Commissioner of Indian Affairs.

A 1911 poster advertising the federal government's sale of land formerly possessed by Indians. Under the Dawes Act of 1887, Indian families were allotted individual farms and the remaining land on reservations, so-called surplus land, was made available to whites.

Indians, but white ranchers and land speculators purchased 500,000 acres. When the government made 2 million acres of Indian land available in Oklahoma, 50,000 white settlers poured into the territory to claim farms on the single day of April 22, 1889. Further land rushes followed in the 1890s. In the half century after the passage of the Dawes Act, Indians lost 86 million of the 138 million acres of land in their possession in 1887.

INDIAN CITIZENSHIP

Many laws and treaties in the nineteenth century offered Indians the right to become American citizen if they left the tribal setting and assimilated into American society. But tribal identity was the one thing nearly every Indian wished to maintain, and very few took advantage of these offers. Thus, few Indians were recognized as American citizens. Western courts ruled that the citizenship rights guaranteed by the Fourteenth and Fifteenth Amendments did not apply to them, and in *Elk v. Wilkins* (1884) the U.S. Supreme Court agreed, even though John Elk had left his tribe in Oklahoma and lived among white settlers in Nebraska. The Court questioned whether any Indian had achieved the degree of "civilization" required of American citizens.

By 1900, roughly 53,000 Indians had become American citizens by accepting land allotments under the Dawes Act. The following year, Congress granted citizenship to 100,000 residents of Indian Territory (in present-day Oklahoma). The remainder would have to wait until 1919 (for those who fought in World War I) and 1924, when Congress made all Indians American citizens.

THE GHOST DANCE AND WOUNDED KNEE

Some Indians sought solace in the Ghost Dance, a religious revitalization campaign reminiscent of the pan-Indian movements led by earlier prophets like Neolin and Tenskwatawa (discussed in Chapters 4 and 8). Its leaders foretold a day when whites had disappeared, the buffalo returned, and Indians again practiced their ancestral customs "free from misery, death, and disease." Large numbers of Indians gathered for days of singing, dancing, and religious observances. Fearing a general uprising, the government sent troops to the reservations. On December 29, 1890, soldiers opened fire on Ghost Dancers encamped near Wounded Knee Creek in South Dakota, killing between 150 and 200 Indians, mostly women and children.

The Wounded Knee massacre marked the end of four centuries of armed conflict between the continent's native population and European settlers and their descendants. By 1900, the Indian population had fallen to 250,000, the lowest point in American history. A children's book about Indians published around this time stated flatly, "the Indian pictured in these pages no longer exists." Yet despite everything, Indians survived, and in the twentieth century their numbers once again would begin to grow.

A quilt created by a Sioux woman who lived on a reservation in South Dakota around 1900, possibly as a gift for a nearby white family. It depicts scenes of traditional daily life among the Indians, including hunting buffalo and cooking game. The bird's eggs at the top left corner have hatched at the bottom right.

POLITICS IN A GILDED AGE

The era from 1870 to 1890 is the only period of American history commonly known by a derogatory name—the Gilded Age, after the title of an 1873 novel by Mark Twain and Charles Dudley Warner. "Gilded" means covered with a layer of gold, but it also suggests that the glittering surface covers a core of little real value and is therefore deceptive. Twain and Warner were referring not only to the remarkable expansion of the economy in this period but also to the corruption caused by corporate dominance of politics and to the oppressive treatment of those left behind in the scramble for wealth. "Get rich, dishonestly if we can, honestly if we must," was the era's slogan, according to *The Gilded Age*.

THE CORRUPTION OF POLITICS

As they had earlier in the nineteenth century, Americans during the Gilded Age saw their nation as an island of political democracy in a world still dominated by undemocratic governments. In Europe, only France and Switzerland enjoyed universal male suffrage. Even in Britain, which prided itself on its tradition of political liberty, most of the working class could not

The Bosses of the Senate, *a cartoon from Puck, January 23, 1889, shows well-fed monopolists towering over the obedient senators. Above them, a sign rewrites the closing words of Lincoln's Gettysburg Address: "This is the Senate of the Monopolists, by the Monopolists, and for the Monopolists."*

vote until the passage of the Reform Act of 1884. As late as the eve of World War I, the House of Lords, an unelected body of hereditary aristocrats, could veto any legislation passed by the House of Commons.

Nonetheless, the power of the new corporations, seemingly immune to democratic control, raised disturbing questions for the American understanding of political freedom as popular self-government. Political corruption was rife. "The galleries and lobbies of every legislature," observed an Illinois Republican leader, "are thronged with men seeking to procure an advantage" for one corporation or another. In Pennsylvania's legislature, the "third house" of railroad lobbyists supposedly exerted as much influence as the elected chambers. In the West, many lawmakers held stock or directorships in lumber companies and railroads that received public aid.

Urban politics fell under the sway of corrupt political machines like New York's Tweed Ring, which plundered the city of tens of millions of dollars. "Boss" William M. Tweed's organization reached into every neighborhood. He forged close ties with railroad men and labor unions, and he won support from the city's immigrant poor by fashioning a kind of private welfare system that provided food, fuel, and jobs in hard times. A combination of political reformers and businessmen tired of paying tribute to the ring ousted Tweed in the early 1870s, although he remained popular among the city's poor, who considered him an urban Robin Hood.

At the national level, many lawmakers supported bills aiding companies in which they had invested money or from which they received stock or salaries. The most notorious example of corruption came to light during Grant's presidency. This was Crédit Mobilier, a corporation formed by an inner ring of Union Pacific Railroad stockholders to oversee the line's government-assisted construction. Essentially, it enabled the participants to sign contracts with themselves, at an exorbitant profit, to build the new line. The arrangement was protected by the distribution of stock to influential politicians, including Speaker of the House Schuyler Colfax, who was elected vice president in 1868. In another example of corruption, the Whiskey Ring of the Grant administration united Republican officials, tax collectors, and whiskey manufacturers in a massive scheme that defrauded the federal government of millions of tax dollars.

THE POLITICS OF DEAD CENTER

In national elections, party politics bore the powerful imprint of the Civil War. Republicans controlled the industrial North and Midwest and the agrarian West and were particularly strong among members of revivalist churches, Protestant immigrants, and blacks. Organizations of Union veterans formed a bulwark of Republican support. Every Republican candidate for president from 1868 to 1900 had fought in the Union army. (In the 1880 campaign, all four candidates—Republican James A. Garfield, Democrat Winfield Scott Hancock, Prohibitionist Neal Dow, and James B. Weaver of the Greenback-Labor Party, discussed later—had been Union generals during the war.) By 1893, a lavish system of pensions for Union soldiers and their widows and children consumed more than 40 percent of the federal budget. Democrats, after 1877, dominated the South and did well among Catholic voters, especially Irish-Americans, in the nation's cities.

The parties were closely divided. In three of the five presidential elections between 1876 and 1892, the margin separating the major candidates was less than 1 percent of the popular vote. Twice, in 1876 and 1888, the candidate with an electoral-college majority trailed in the popular vote. The congressional elections of 1874, when Democrats won control of the House of Representatives, ushered in two decades of political stalemate. A succession of one-term presidencies followed: Rutherford B. Hayes (elected in 1876), James A. Garfield (succeeded after his assassination in 1881 by Chester A. Arthur), Grover Cleveland in 1884, Benjamin Harrison in 1888, and Cleveland, elected for the second time, in 1892. Only for brief periods did the same party control the White House and both houses of Congress. More than once, Congress found itself paralyzed as important bills shuttled back and forth between House and Senate and special sessions to complete legislation became necessary. Gilded Age presidents made little effort to mobilize public opinion or exert executive leadership. Their staffs were quite small. Grover Cleveland himself answered the White House doorbell.

In some ways, American democracy in the Gilded Age seemed remarkably healthy. Elections were closely contested, party loyalty was intense, and 80 percent or more of eligible voters turned out to cast ballots. It was an era of massive party rallies and spellbinding political oratory. James G. Blaine was among the members of Congress tainted by the Crédit Mobilier scandal, but Robert G. Ingersoll's speech before the Republican national convention of 1876 nearly secured Blaine's nomination for president by depicting him as a "plumed knight" who had raised his "shining lance" against the country's enemies.

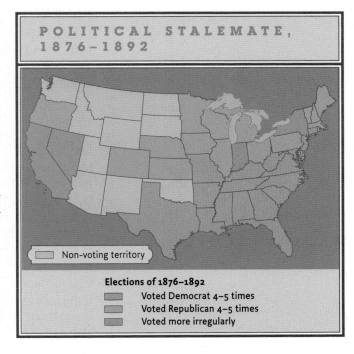

POLITICAL STALEMATE, 1876–1892

Non-voting territory

Elections of 1876–1892
Voted Democrat 4–5 times
Voted Republican 4–5 times
Voted more irregularly

GOVERNMENT AND THE ECONOMY

The nation's political structure, however, proved ill equipped to deal with the problems created by the economy's rapid growth. Despite its expanded scope and powers arising from the Civil War, the federal government remained remarkably small by modern standards. Activities from education to medical care, business regulation, civil and criminal prosecutions, and many others were almost entirely under the control of local and state governments or private institutions. The federal workforce in 1880 numbered 100,000 (today, it exceeds 2.5 million).

Nationally, both parties came under the control of powerful political managers with close ties to business interests. Republicans strongly supported a high tariff to protect American industry, and throughout the 1870s they pursued a fiscal policy based on reducing federal spending, repaying much of the national debt, and withdrawing greenbacks—the paper money issued by the Union during the Civil War—from circulation. Democrats opposed the high tariff, but the party's national leadership remained closely linked to New York bankers and financiers and resisted demands from debt-ridden agricultural areas for an increase in the money supply. In 1879, for the first time since the war, the United States returned to the gold standard—that is, paper currency became exchangeable for gold at a fixed rate.

By reducing competition from foreign manufactured goods and leaving the banks, not the government, in control of issuing money, Republican economic policies strongly favored the interests of eastern industrialists and bankers. These policies worked to the disadvantage of southern and western farmers, who had to pay a premium for manufactured goods while the prices they received for their produce steadily declined.

REFORM LEGISLATION

Gilded Age national politics did not entirely lack accomplishments. Inspired in part by President Garfield's assassination by a disappointed office seeker, the Civil Service Act of 1883 created a merit system for federal employees, with appointment via competitive examinations rather than political influence. Although it applied at first to only 10 percent of the over 100,000 government workers, the act marked the first step in establishing a professional civil service and removing officeholding from the hands of political machines. (However, since funds raised from political appointees had helped to finance the political parties, civil service reform had the unintended result of increasing politicians' dependence on donations from business interests.)

In 1887, in response to public outcries against railroad practices, Congress established the Interstate Commerce Commission (ICC) to ensure that the rates railroads charged farmers and merchants to transport their goods were "reasonable" and did not offer more favorable treatment to some shippers over others. The ICC was the first federal agency intended to regulate economic activity, but since it lacked the power to establish rates on its own—it could only sue companies in court—it had little impact on railroad practices. Three years later, Congress passed the Sherman

Antitrust Act, which banned combinations and practices that restrained free trade. But the language was so vague that the act proved almost impossible to enforce. Weak as they were, these laws helped to establish the precedent that the national government could regulate the economy to promote the public good.

POLITICAL CONFLICT IN THE STATES

The nation had to weather the effects of drastic economic change and periodic economic crises without leadership from Washington. At the state and local level, however, the Gilded Age was an era of political ferment and conflict over the proper uses of governmental authority. In the immediate aftermath of the Civil War, state governments in the North, like those in the Reconstruction South, greatly expanded their responsibility for public health, welfare, and education, and cities invested heavily in public works such as park construction and improved water and gas services. Those who suffered from economic change called on the activist state created by the war to redress their own grievances.

Third parties enjoyed significant if short-lived success in local elections. The Greenback-Labor Party proposed that the federal government stop taking "greenback" money out of circulation. This, it argued, would make more funds available for investment and give the government, not private bankers, control of the money supply. It also condemned the use of militias and private police against strikes. In the late 1870s, the party controlled local government in a number of industrial and mining communities and contributed to the election of twenty-one members of Congress independent of the two major parties.

The policies of railroad companies produced a growing chorus of protest, especially in the West. Farmers and local merchants complained of excessively high freight rates, discrimination in favor of large producers and shippers, and high fees charged by railroad-controlled grain warehouses. Critics of the railroads came together in the Patrons of Husbandry, or Grange, which moved to establish cooperatives for storing and marketing farm output in the hope of forcing the carriers "to take our produce at a fair price." Founded in 1867, the Grange claimed over 700,000 members by the mid-1870s. Its members called on state governments to establish fair freight rates and warehouse charges. In several states, the Grange succeeded in having commissions established to investigate—and, in some cases, regulate—railroad practices.

The labor movement, revitalized during the Civil War, simultaneously demanded laws establishing eight hours as a legal day's work. Seven northern legislatures passed such laws, but since

Laying Tracks at Union Square for a Railroad, *an 1890 painting, depicts one of the era's many public works assisted by state and local governments.*

most lacked strong means of enforcement they remained dead letters. But the efforts of farmers and workers to use the power of the state to counteract the inequalities of the Gilded Age inspired a far-reaching debate on the relationship between political and economic freedom in an industrial society.

FREEDOM IN THE GILDED AGE

THE SOCIAL PROBLEM

As the United States matured into an industrial economy, Americans struggled to make sense of the new social order. Debates over political economy engaged the attention of millions of Americans, reaching far beyond the tiny academic world into the public sphere inhabited by self-educated workingmen and farmers, reformers of all kinds, newspaper editors, and politicians. This broad public discussion produced thousands of books, pamphlets, and articles on such technical issues as land taxation and currency reform, as well as widespread debate over the social and ethical implications of economic change.

Many Americans sensed that something had gone wrong in the nation's social development. Talk of "better classes," "respectable classes," and "dangerous classes" dominated public discussion, and bitter labor strife seemed to have become the rule. During the Gilded Age, Congress and a number of states established investigating committees to inquire into the relations between labor and capital. Their hearings produced powerful evidence of distrust between employees and employers. In 1881, the Massachusetts Bureau of Labor Statistics reported that virtually every worker it interviewed in Fall River, the nation's largest center of textile production, complained of overwork, poor housing, and tyrannical employers. For their part, manufacturers claimed their workingmen were "the scum of the English and Irish," whose complaints reflected nothing more than a "hereditary feeling of discontent."

FREEDOM, INEQUALITY, AND DEMOCRACY

The appearance of what Massachusetts cotton manufacturer Edward Atkinson called "a permanent factory population" living on the edge of poverty alongside a growing class of millionaires posed a sharp challenge to traditional definitions of freedom. Did America's promise still lie in the opportunity it offered ordinary citizens to achieve economic autonomy? "The great curse of the Old World—the division of society into classes," declared *The Nation*, had come to America. It became increasingly difficult to view wage labor as a temporary resting place on the road to economic independence, or the West as a haven for the dispossessed small producers of the East.

Given the vast expansion of the nation's productive capacity, many Americans viewed the concentration of wealth as inevitable, natural, and justified by progress. By the turn of the century, advanced economics taught that wages were determined by the iron law of supply and demand and that wealth rightly flowed not to those who worked the hardest but to men with business skills and access to money. The close link between freedom and equality, forged in the Revolution and reinforced during the Civil War, appeared increasingly out of date. The task of social science, wrote iron manufacturer Abram Hewitt, was to devise ways of making "men who are equal in liberty" content with the "inequality in . . . distribution" inevitable in modern society.

Among the first to take up this challenge were the self-styled "liberal" reformers. (Their beliefs were quite different from those called liberals in modern America, who advocate that an activist government try to address social needs.) This group of editors and professionals broke with the Republican Party in 1872 and helped to bring about a change in northern opinion regarding Reconstruction. But their program was not confined to the South. Like the men who led the movement for a new constitution in the 1780s, Gilded Age reformers feared that with lower-class groups seeking to use government to advance their own interests, democracy was becoming a threat to individual liberty and the rights of property. Some urged a return to the long-abandoned principle that voting should be limited to property owners. During the 1830s, Alexis de Tocqueville had reported that opponents of democracy "hide their heads." By the 1870s, wrote one observer, "expressions of doubt and distrust in regard to universal suffrage are heard constantly . . . [at] the top of our society."

SOCIAL DARWINISM IN AMERICA

The idea of the natural superiority of some groups to others, which before the Civil War had been invoked to justify slavery in an otherwise free society, now reemerged in the vocabulary of modern science to explain the success and failure of individuals and social classes. In 1859, the British scientist Charles Darwin published *On the Origin of Species*. One of the most influential works of science ever to appear, it expounded the theory of evolution whereby plant and animal species best suited to their environment took the place of those less able to adapt.

In a highly oversimplified form, language borrowed from Darwin, such as "natural selection," "the struggle for existence," and "the survival of the fittest," entered public discussion of social problems in the Gilded Age. According to what came to be called Social Darwinism, evolution was as natural a process in human society as in nature, and government must not interfere. Especially misguided, in this view, were efforts to uplift those at the bottom of the social order, such as laws regulating conditions of work or public assistance to the poor. The giant industrial corporation, Social Darwinists believed, had emerged because it was better adapted to its environment than earlier forms of enterprise. To restrict its operations by legislation would reduce society to a more primitive level.

Even the depressions of the 1870s and 1890s did not shake the widespread view that the poor were essentially responsible for their own fate. Charity workers and local governments spent much time and energy distinguishing the "deserving" poor (those, like widows and orphans, destitute through no fault of their own) from the "undeserving," a far larger number. Failure to advance in society was widely thought to indicate a lack of character, an absence of self-reliance and determination in the face of adversity. As late as 1900, half the nation's largest cities offered virtually no public relief, except to persons living in poorhouses. To improve their lot, according to the philosophy of Social Darwinism, workers should practice personal economy, keep out of debt, and educate their children in the principles of the marketplace, not look to the government for aid.

The era's most influential Social Darwinist was Yale professor William Graham Sumner. For Sumner, freedom meant "the security given to each man" that he can acquire, enjoy, and dispose of property "exclusively as he chooses," without interference from other persons or from government. Freedom thus defined required frank acceptance of inequality. Society faced two and only two alternatives: "liberty, inequality, survival of the fittest; not-liberty, equality, survival of the unfittest." In 1883, Sumner published *What Social Classes Owe to Each Other*. His answer, essentially, was nothing: "In a free state," no one was entitled to claim "help from, and cannot be charged to [offer] help to, another." Government, Sumner believed, existed only to protect "the property of men and the honor of women," not to upset social arrangements decreed by nature.

A detail from Capital and Labor, *a cotton textile from around 1870, illustrates the free labor ideal, with an employer and employee shaking hands and laborers enjoying dignity at work and a "happy home." During the Gilded Age, many worried that this vision of harmony no longer described American life.*

LIBERTY OF CONTRACT

The growing influence of Social Darwinism helped to popularize an idea that would be embraced by the business and professional classes in the last quarter of the nineteenth century—a "negative" definition of freedom as limited government and an unrestrained free market. Central to this social vision was the idea of contract. "The laws of contract," wrote one reformer, "are the foundation of civilization." Labor contracts reconciled freedom and authority in the workplace. So long as labor relations were governed by contracts freely arrived at by independent individuals, neither the government nor unions had a right to interfere with working conditions, and Americans had no grounds to complain of a loss of freedom.

Demands by workers that the government enforce an eight-hour day, provide relief to the unemployed, or in other ways intervene in the economy struck liberals as an example of how the misuse of political power posed a threat to liberty. "The right of each man to labor as much or as little as he chooses, and to enjoy his own earnings, is the very foundation stone of . . . freedom," wrote Chicago newspaper editor Horace White. The principle of free labor, which originated as a celebration of the independent small producer in a society of broad equality and social harmony, was transformed into a defense of the unrestrained operations of the capitalist marketplace.

THE COURTS AND FREEDOM

In elevating liberty of contract from one element of freedom to its very essence, the courts played a significant role. The Fourteenth Amendment had empowered the federal government to overturn state laws that violated citizens' rights. By the 1880s, liberty of contract, not equality before the law for former slaves, came to be defined as the amendment's true meaning. State and federal courts regularly struck down state laws regulating economic enterprise as an interference with the right of the free laborer to choose his employment and working conditions, and of the entrepreneur to utilize his property as he saw fit. For decades, the courts viewed state regulation of business—especially laws establishing maximum hours of work and safe working conditions—as an insult to free labor.

At first, the Supreme Court was willing to accept laws regulating enterprises that represented a significant "public interest." In *Munn v. Illinois*, an 1877 decision, it upheld the constitutionality of an Illinois law that established a state board empowered to eliminate railroad rate discrimination and set maximum charges. Nine years later, however, in *Wabash v. Illinois*, the Court essentially reversed itself, ruling that only the federal government, not the states, could regulate railroads engaged in interstate commerce, as all important lines were. The decision led directly to the passage of the Interstate Commerce Act of 1887. But on virtually every occasion when cases brought by the ICC against railroads made their way to the Supreme Court, the company emerged victorious.

The courts generally sided with business enterprises that complained of a loss of economic freedom. In 1885, the New York Court of Appeals invalidated a state law that prohibited the manufacture of cigars in tenement dwellings on the grounds that such legislation deprived the worker of the "liberty" to work "where he will." Although women still lacked political rights, they were increasingly understood to possess the same economic "liberty," defined in this way, as men. On the grounds that it violated women's freedom, the Illinois Supreme Court in 1895 declared unconstitutional a state law that outlawed the production of garments in sweatshops and established a forty-eight-hour working week for women and children. In the same year, in *U.S. v. E. C. Knight Co.*, the United States Supreme Court ruled that the Sherman Antitrust Act of 1890, which barred combinations in restraint of trade, could not be used to break up a sugar refining monopoly, since the Constitution empowered Congress to regulate commerce, but not manufacturing. Their unwillingness to allow regulation of the economy, however, did not prevent the courts from acting to impede labor organization. The Sherman Act, intended to prevent business mergers that stifled competition, was used by judges primarily to issue injunctions prohibiting strikes on the grounds that they illegally interfered with the freedom of trade.

In a 1905 case that became almost as notorious as *Dred Scott* and gave the name "Lochnerism" to the entire body of liberty of contract decisions, the Supreme Court in *Lochner v. New York* voided a state law establishing ten hours per day or sixty per week as the maximum hours of work for bakers. The law, wrote Associate Justice Rufus Peckham for the 5-4 majority, "interfered with the right of contract between employer and employee" and therefore infringed upon individual freedom. By this time, the Court was invoking "liberty" in ways that could easily seem absurd. In one case, it overturned as a violation of "personal liberty" a Kansas law prohibiting "yellow-dog" contracts, which made nonmembership in a union a condition of employment. In another, it struck down state laws requiring payment of coal miners in money rather than paper usable only at company-owned stores. Workers, observed mine union leader John P. Mitchell, could not but feel that "they are being guaranteed the liberties they do not want and denied the liberty that is of real value to them."

LABOR AND THE REPUBLIC

"THE OVERWHELMING LABOR QUESTION"

Ruins of the Pittsburgh Round House, *a photograph published in the July 1895 issue of* Scribner's Magazine, *shows the widespread destruction of property during the Great Railroad Strike of July 1877.*

As Mitchell's remark suggests, public debate in the late nineteenth century more than at almost any other moment in American history divided along class lines. The shift from the slavery controversy to what one politician called "the overwhelming labor question" was dramatically illustrated in 1877, the year of both the end of Reconstruction and also the first national labor walkout—the Great Railroad Strike. When workers protesting a pay cut paralyzed rail traffic in much of the country, militia units tried to force them back to work. After troops fired on strikers in Pittsburgh, killing twenty people, workers responded by burning the city's railroad yards, destroying millions of dollars in property. General strikes paralyzed Chicago and St. Louis. The strike revealed both a strong sense of solidarity among workers and the close ties between the Republican Party and the new class of industrialists. President Rutherford B. Hayes, who a few months earlier had ordered federal troops in the South to end their involvement in local politics, ordered the army into the North. The workers, the president wrote in his diary, were "put down by force."

"The days are over," declared the *New York Times*, "in which this country could rejoice in its freedom from the elements of social strife which have long abounded in the old countries." In the aftermath of 1877, the federal government constructed armories in major cities to ensure that troops would be on hand in the event of further labor difficulties. Henceforth, national power would be used not to protect beleaguered former slaves, but to guarantee the rights of property.

THE KNIGHTS OF LABOR AND THE "CONDITIONS ESSENTIAL TO LIBERTY"

The 1880s witnessed a new wave of labor organizing. At its center stood the Knights of Labor. The Knights were the first group to try to organize unskilled workers as well as skilled, women alongside men, and blacks as well as whites (although even the Knights excluded the despised Asian immigrants on the West Coast). It reached a peak membership of nearly 800,000 in 1886 and involved millions of workers in strikes, boycotts, political action, and educational and social activities.

Caught between nostalgia for the era of small production and acknowledgment of the factory's triumph, labor reformers of the Gilded Age put forward a wide array of programs, from the eight-hour day to public employment in hard times, currency reform, anarchism, socialism, and the creation of a vaguely defined "cooperative commonwealth." All these ideas arose from the conviction that the social conditions of the 1880s needed drastic change. Americans, declared Terence V. Powderly, head of the Knights of Labor, were not "the free people that we imagine we are."

The labor movement launched a sustained assault on the understanding of freedom grounded in Social Darwinism and liberty of contract. Because of unrestrained economic growth and political corruption, the Knights charged, ordinary Americans had lost control of their economic livelihoods and their own government. Reaching back across the divide of the Civil War, labor defined employers as a new "slave power." Concentrated capital, warned George E. McNeill, a shoemaker and factory worker who became one of the movement's most eloquent writers, had become "a greater power than that of the state." "Extremes of wealth and poverty," he warned, threatened the very existence of democratic government. The remedy was to "engraft republican principles into our

An engraving from Frank Leslie's Illustrated Newspaper, *October 16, 1886, shows black delegate Frank J. Farrell introducing Terrence V. Powderly, leader of the Knights of Labor, at the labor organization's national convention in Richmond, Virginia. The Knights were among the few nineteenth-century labor groups to recruit black members.*

The Great Labor Parade of September 1, *from* Frank Leslie's Illustrated Newspaper, *September 13, 1884. A placard illustrates how the labor movement identified Gilded Age employers with the Slave Power of the pre–Civil War era.*

industrial system" by guaranteeing a basic set of economic rights for all Americans.

Labor raised the question whether meaningful freedom could exist in a situation of extreme economic inequality. On July 4, 1886, the Federated Trades of the Pacific Coast rewrote the Declaration of Independence. Workers, the new Declaration claimed, had been subjected not to oppressive government, but to "the unjust domination of a special class." It went on to list among mankind's inalienable rights, "Life and the means of living, Liberty and the conditions essential to liberty."

MIDDLE-CLASS REFORMERS

Dissatisfaction with social conditions in the Gilded Age extended well beyond aggrieved workers. Supreme Court justice John Marshall Harlan in the late 1880s spoke of a "deep feeling of unease," a widespread fear that the country "was in real danger of another kind of slavery that would result from the aggregation of capital in the hands of a few individuals." Alarmed by fear of class warfare and the growing power of concentrated capital, social thinkers offered numerous plans for change. In the last quarter of the century, over 150 utopian or cataclysmic novels appeared, predicting that social conflict would end either in a new, harmonious social order or in total catastrophe. One popular novel of the era, *Caesar's Column* (1891) by Ignatius Donnelly, ended with civilized society destroyed in a savage civil war between labor and capital.

Of the many books proposing more optimistic remedies for the unequal distribution of wealth, the most popular were *Progress and Poverty* (1879) by Henry George, *The Cooperative Commonwealth* (1884) by Laurence Gronlund, and Edward Bellamy's *Looking Backward* (1888). All three were among the century's greatest best-sellers, their extraordinary success testifying to what George called "a wide-spread consciousness . . . that there is something *radically* wrong in the present social organization." All three writers, though in very different ways, sought to reclaim an imagined golden age of social harmony and American freedom.

PROGRESS AND POVERTY

Although it had no direct impact on government policy, *Progress and Poverty* probably commanded more public attention than any book on economics in American history. An antislavery newspaper editor in California in the 1850s and 1860s, Henry George had witnessed firsthand the rapid monopolization of land in the state. His book began with a famous statement of "the problem" suggested by its title—the growth of "squalor and misery" alongside material progress. His solution was the "single tax," which would replace other taxes with a levy on increases in the value of real estate. The single tax would be so high that it would prevent speculation in both urban and rural land. No one knows how many of Henry George's readers actually believed in this way of solving the nation's ills. But millions responded to his clear explanation of economic relationships and his stirring account of how the "social distress" long thought to be confined to the Old World had made its appearance in the New.

Freedom lay at the heart of George's analysis. The "proper name" for the political movement spawned by his book, he once wrote, was "freedom men," who would "do for the question of industrial slavery" what the Republican Party had done for the slavery of blacks. George rejected the traditional equation of liberty with ownership of land (since the single tax in effect made land the "common property" of the entire society). In other ways, however, his definition of freedom was thoroughly in keeping with mainstream thought. Despite calling for a single massive public intervention in the economy, George saw government as a "repressive power," whose functions in the "co-operative society" of the future would be limited to enhancing the quality of life—building "public baths, museums, libraries, gardens," and the like.

Quite different in outlook was *The Cooperative Commonwealth*, the first book to popularize socialist ideas for an American audience. Its author, Laurence Gronlund, was a lawyer who had emigrated from Denmark in 1867. Socialism—the belief that private control of economic enterprises should be replaced by government ownership in order to ensure a fairer distribution of the benefits of the wealth produced—became a major political force in western Europe in the late nineteenth century. In the United States, however, where access to private property was widely considered essential to individual freedom, socialist beliefs were largely confined to immigrants, whose writings, frequently in foreign languages, attracted little attention.

Gronlund began the process of socialism's Americanization. While Karl Marx, the nineteenth century's most influential socialist theorist, had predicted that socialism would come into being via a working-class revolution, Gronlund portrayed it as the end result of a process of peaceful evolution, not violent upheaval. He thus made socialism seem more acceptable to middle-class Americans who desired an end to class conflict and the restoration of social harmony.

BELLAMY'S UTOPIA

Not until the early twentieth century would socialism become a significant presence in American public life. As Gronlund himself noted, the most important result of *The Cooperative Commonwealth* was to prepare an audience for Edward Bellamy's *Looking Backward*, which promoted socialist ideas while "ignoring that name" (Bellamy wrote of nationalism, not socialism). Bellamy lived virtually his entire life in the small industrial city of Chicopee Falls, Massachusetts. In *Looking Backward*, his main character falls asleep in the late nineteenth century only to awaken in the year 2000, in a world where cooperation has replaced class strife, "excessive individualism," and cutthroat competition. Inequality has been banished and with it the idea of liberty as a condition to be achieved through individual striving free of governmental restraint. Freedom, Bellamy insisted, was a social condition, resting on interdependence, not autonomy.

From today's vantage point, Bellamy's utopia—with citizens obligated to labor for years in an Industrial Army controlled by a single Great Trust—seems a chilling social blueprint. Yet the book inspired the creation of hundreds of nationalist clubs devoted to bringing into existence the world of

Edward Bellamy, author of the utopian novel Looking Backward.

2000 and left a profound mark on a generation of reformers and intellectuals. Bellamy held out the hope of retaining the material abundance made possible by industrial capitalism while eliminating inequality. In proposing that the state guarantee economic security to all, Bellamy offered a far-reaching expansion of the idea of freedom. "I am aware that you called yourself free in the nineteenth century," a resident of the year 2000 tells Bellamy's Rip Van Winkle. But "the meaning of the word could not then have been at all what it is at present," or it could not have been applied to a society in which so many lived in a state of "galling personal dependence upon others as to the very means of life."

A SOCIAL GOSPEL

By 1888, when *Looking Backward* appeared, Social Darwinism and the laissez-faire definition of freedom were under attack from many quarters, including the labor movement and middle-class writers like George and Bellamy, as well as clergymen shocked by the inequities in the emerging industrial order. Most of the era's Protestant preachers concentrated on attacking individual sins like drinking and Sabbath-breaking and saw nothing immoral about the pursuit of riches. Their Gospel of Wealth gave a moral underpinning to the "liberty of contract" outlook. But the outlines of what came to be called the Social Gospel were taking shape in the writings of Walter Rauschenbusch, a Baptist minister in New York City, and others. They insisted that freedom and spiritual self-development required an equalization of wealth and power and that unbridled competition mocked the Christian ideal of brotherhood.

The Social Gospel movement originated as an effort to reform Protestant churches by expanding their appeal in poor urban neighborhoods and making them more attentive to the era's social ills. The movement's adherents established missions and relief programs in urban areas that attempted to alleviate poverty, combat child labor, and encourage the construction of better working-class housing. They worked with the Knights of Labor and other groups demanding health and safety laws. Some suggested that a more cooperative organization of the economy should replace competitive capitalism. Within American Catholicism, as well, a group of priests and bishops emerged who attempted to alter the church's traditional hostility to movements for social reform and its isolation from contemporary currents of social thought. With most of its parishioners working men and women, they argued, the church should lend its support to the labor movement. These developments suggested the existence of widespread dissatisfaction with the "liberty of contract" understanding of freedom.

THE HAYMARKET AFFAIR

The year of the dedication of the Statue of Liberty, 1886, also witnessed an unprecedented upsurge in labor activity. Inspired by a successful strike by western railroad unions against lines controlled by the powerful financier Jay Gould, workers flooded into the Knights of Labor. Its membership, only

A cartoon from the 1880s depicts radicals as foreigners attempting to destroy the foundations of American society. A caterpillar labeled "comunism" [sic] gnaws at the leaf "capital" beneath which are the fruits of American society—among them education, industry, business, law, order, and peace.

100,000 in 1885, rose more than sevenfold in the following year. On May 1, 1886, some 350,000 workers in cities across the country demonstrated for an eight-hour day. Having originated in the United States, May 1, or May Day as it came to be called, soon became an annual date of parades, picnics, and protests, celebrated around the world by organized labor.

The most dramatic events of 1886 took place in Chicago, a city with a large and vibrant labor movement that brought together native-born and immigrant workers, whose outlooks ranged from immigrant socialism and anarchism to American traditions of equality and antimonopoly. In 1885, the iron moulders union—one of the most powerful organizations of skilled industrial workers in the country—had organized a strike against a wage reduction at the great McCormick plant that produced agricultural machinery. The company brought in strikebreakers and private police, who battled in the streets with the strikers. Fearing chaos, the mayor and prominent business leaders persuaded the company to settle on the union's terms. But in February 1886, after the company installed new machinery that reduced its dependence on the iron moulders' traditional skills, it announced that henceforth the factory would operate on a nonunion basis. The result was a bitter, prolonged strike.

This time, Chicago's city government sided with the company. On May 3, 1886, four strikers were killed by police when they attempted to prevent strikebreakers from entering the factory. The next day, a rally was held in Haymarket Square to protest the killings. Near the end of the speeches, someone—whose identity has never been determined—threw a bomb into the crowd, killing a policeman. The panicked police opened fire, shooting several bystanders and a number of their own force. There quickly followed police raids on the offices of labor and radical groups and the arrest of their leaders. Employers took the opportunity to paint the labor movement as a dangerous and un-American force, prone to violence and controlled by foreign-born radicals. The McCormick strike was defeated and the union local destroyed. Eight anarchists were charged with plotting and carrying out the bombing. Even though the evidence against them was extremely weak, a jury convicted the "Haymarket martyrs." Four were hanged, one committed suicide in prison, and the remaining three were imprisoned until John Peter Altgeld, a pro-labor governor of Illinois, commuted their sentences in 1893.

Seven of the eight men accused of plotting the Haymarket bombing were foreign-born—six Germans and an English immigrant. The last was Albert Parsons, a native of Alabama who had served in the Confederate army in the Civil War and edited a Republican newspaper in Texas during Reconstruction. Fearing violence because of his political views and the fact that his wife, Lucy Parsons, was black, Albert Parsons moved to Chicago during the 1870s. Having survived the Ku Klux Klan in Reconstruction Texas, Parsons perished on the Illinois gallows for a crime that he, like the other "Haymarket martyrs," did not commit.

LABOR AND POLITICS

Haymarket took place amid an outburst of independent labor political activity. One study has identified over 100 local political tickets associated with the Knights of Labor between 1886 and 1888, from Anniston, Alabama, to Whitewater, Wisconsin. Their major aim was to end the use of public and private police forces and court injunctions against strikes and labor organizations. At least sixty achieved some kind of electoral success. In Kansas City, a coalition of black and Irish-American workers and middle-class voters elected Tom Hanna as mayor. He proceeded to side with unions rather than employers in industrial disputes.

The most celebrated labor campaign took place in New York City, where in 1886, somewhat to his own surprise, Henry George found himself thrust into the role of labor's candidate for mayor. George's aim in running was to bring attention to the single tax on land. The labor leaders who organized the United Labor Party had more immediate goals in mind, especially stopping the courts from barring strikes and jailing unionists for conspiracy. George ran a spirited campaign, speaking at factories, immigrant associations, and labor parades and rallies. A few days after the dedication of the Statue of Liberty, New Yorkers flocked to the polls to elect their mayor. Nearly 70,000 voted for George, who finished second, eclipsing the total of the Republican candidate, Theodore Roosevelt, and coming close to defeating Democrat Abram Hewitt.

In a political system that within living memory had witnessed the disappearance of the Whig Party, the rise and fall of the Know-Nothings, and the emergence of the Republicans, the events of 1886 suggested that labor might be on the verge of establishing itself as a permanent political force. In fact, that year marked the high point of the Knights of Labor. Facing

In this pro-labor cartoon from 1888, a workingman rescues liberty from the stranglehold of monopolies and the pro-business major parties.

increasing employer hostility and with a poorly organized structure that could not assimilate the great spurt in new members, the Knights soon declined. The major parties, moreover, proved remarkably resourceful in appealing to labor voters.

Thus, America's Gilded Age witnessed deep and sometimes violent divisions over the definition of freedom in a rapidly industrializing society. The battle between upholders of Social Darwinism and laissez-faire, who saw freedom as the right of individuals to pursue their economic interests without outside restraint, and those who believed in collective efforts to create "industrial freedom" for ordinary Americans, would continue for many decades. In the early twentieth century, reformers would turn to new ways of addressing the social conditions of freedom and new means of increasing ordinary Americans' political and economic liberty. But before this, in the 1890s, the nation would face its gravest crisis since the Civil War, and the boundaries of freedom would once again be redrawn.

SUGGESTED READING

Bensel, Richard F. *The Political Economy of American Industrialization, 1877–1900* (2000). A study of the policies and political divisions that contributed to and resulted from the second industrial revolution.

Brown, Dee. *Bury My Heart at Wounded Knee: An Indian History of the American West* (1970). A classic account of the conquest of the West from the Indian point of view.

Chandler, Alfred. *The Visible Hand: The Managerial Revolution in American Business* (1977). Examines how railroads pioneered techniques of modern business management that other corporations then adopted.

De Leon, Arnoldo. *Racial Frontiers: Africans, Chinese, and Mexicans in Western America, 1848–1890* (2002). Emphasizes the diversity of the West's population and the different experiences of its racial minorities.

Deutsch, Sarah. *No Separate Refuge: Culture, Class, and Gender on the Anglo-Hispanic Frontier in the American Southwest, 1880–1940* (1987). A careful analysis of the changing experience of people of Hispanic origin in the Southwest during these years.

Fink, Leon. *Workingmen's Democracy: The Knights of Labor and American Politics* (1983). Examines the rise of the Knights of Labor and their forays into local politics in the mid-1880s.

Hofstadter, Richard. *Social Darwinism in American Thought* (1944). A classic study of a major tendency in American thought during the Gilded Age.

Isenberg, Andrew C. *The Destruction of the Bison: An Environmental History, 1750–1920* (2000). Examines the numerous causes for the decimation of buffalo herds, from climate change to commercial hunting.

Jeffrey, Julie R. *Frontier Women: "Civilizing" the West? 1840–1880* (rev. ed., 1998). A study, based on letters and diaries, of the experience of women on the western frontier.

Keller, Morton. *Affairs of State: Public Life in Late Nineteenth-Century America* (1977). A comprehensive account of the activities of government during the Gilded Age.

Morgan, H. Wayne. *From Hayes to McKinley: National Party Politics, 1877–1896* (1969). The standard narrative of national politics during these years.

Shannon, Fred A. *The Farmer's Last Frontier: Agriculture 1860–1897* (1945). Remains an excellent introduction to the experience of farmers in the last four decades of the nineteenth century.

Sproat, John G. *"The Best Men": Liberal Reformers in the Gilded Age* (1968). Traces the origins, outlook, and political impact of reformers dissatisfied with the corruption of national politics.

Thomas, John L. *Alternative Americas: Henry George, Edward Bellamy, Henry Demarest Lloyd and the Adversary Tradition* (1983). A thorough exposition of the thought of three critics of Gilded Age society.

Trachtenberg, Alan. *The Incorporation of America: Culture and Society in the Gilded Age* (1982). An influential survey of how economic change affected American life during the Gilded Age.

REVIEW QUESTIONS

1. Describe the importance of the railroad to the successful development of America's Second Industrial Revolution.

2. Explain what was required for Indians to attain citizenship and evaluate the advantages and disadvantages of citizenship to the Indian.

3. Analyze how the shift from an agricultural society to an urban society changed the American social order.

4. Compare William Sumner's words in *What Social Classes Owe to Each Other* to that of the Federated Trades of the Pacific Coast's "rewrite" of the Declaration of Independence. What two positions are laid out?

5. In what ways did Americans respond to the overwhelming labor question that arose after the Great Railroad Strike of 1877?

KEY TERMS

standard gauge (p. 594)

Standard Oil (p. 598)

bonanza farming (p. 604)

Cowboy Strike of 1883 (p. 606)

Ghost Dance (p. 614)

greenbacks (p. 618)

civil service (p. 618)

Sherman Antitrust Act (p. 619)

Lochner v. New York (p. 624)

REVIEW TABLE

Landmarks in Indian Relations, 1876–1890

Event	Date	Outcome
Battle at Little Bighorn	1876	General Custer's army is massacred
Chief Joseph's trek toward freedom	1877	Nez Percé tribe is captured and placed on a reservation
Dawes Act	1887	Indian lands are divided into small family plots, and the rest is sold off
Battle at Wounded Knee	1890	Final defeat, ending the Indian Wars

CHAPTER 17

Freedom's Boundaries, at Home and Abroad, 1890–1900

Charge of the Rough Riders at San Juan Hill, *a painting by Frederic Remington, depicts the celebrated unit, commanded by Theodore Roosevelt, in action in Cuba during the Spanish-American War of 1898. Roosevelt, on horseback, leads the troops. Remington had been sent to the island the previous year by publisher William Randolph Hearst to provide pictures of Spanish atrocities during the Cuban war for independence in the hope of boosting the* New York Journal's *circulation.*

☞ FOCUS QUESTIONS

• What were the sources and the significance of Populism?

• How was a system of racial segregation established in the South?

• In what ways did the boundaries of American freedom grow narrower in this period?

• How did the United States emerge as an imperial power in the 1890s?

One of the most popular songs of 1892 bore the title "Father Was Killed by a Pinkerton Man." It was inspired by an incident during a bitter strike at Andrew Carnegie's steelworks at Homestead, Pennsylvania, the nineteenth century's most widely publicized confrontation between labor and capital. The strike pitted one of the nation's leading industrial corporations against a powerful union, the Amalgamated Association, which represented the skilled iron- and steelworkers among the complex's 3,800 employees.

Homestead's twelve steel mills were the most profitable and technologically advanced in the world. The union contract gave the Amalgamated Association a considerable say in their operation, including the right to approve the hiring of new workers and to regulate the pace of work. To Carnegie and Henry Clay Frick, his local supervisor, the union's power increasingly seemed an intolerable infringement on management's rights. In 1892, they decided to operate the plant on a nonunion basis. Frick surrounded the factory with a fence topped by barbed wire, constructed barracks to house strikebreakers, and fired the entire workforce. Henceforth, only workers who agreed not to join the union could work at Homestead. In response, the workers, including the unskilled laborers not included in the Amalgamated Association, blockaded the steelworks and mobilized support from the local community. The battle memorialized in song took place on July 6, 1892, when armed strikers confronted 300 private policemen from the Pinkerton Detective Agency. Seven workers and three Pinkerton agents were killed, and the Pinkertons were forced to retreat. Four days later, the governor of Pennsylvania dispatched 8,000 militiamen to open the complex on management's terms. The strikers held out until November, but the union's defeat was now inevitable. In the end, the Amalgamated Association was destroyed.

The Carnegie corporation's tactics and the workers' solidarity won the strikers widespread national sympathy. "Ten thousand Carnegie libraries," declared the *St. Louis Post-Dispatch*, "would not compensate the country for the evils resulting from Homestead." The strike became an international cause célèbre as well. British newspapers pointed out that their country restricted the use of private police forces far more severely than the United States. Britons, they claimed, understood economic liberty better than Americans.

Homestead demonstrated that neither a powerful union nor public opinion could influence the conduct of the largest corporations. The writer Hamlin Garland, who visited Homestead two years after the strike, found the workforce sullen and bitter. He described a town "as squalid and unlovely as could be imagined," with dingy houses over which hung dense clouds of black smoke. It was "American," he wrote, "only in the sense in which [it] represents the American idea of business."

In fact, two American ideas of freedom collided at Homestead—the employers' definition, based on the idea that property rights, unrestrained by union rules or public regulation, sustained the public good, and the workers' conception, which stressed economic security and independence from what they considered the "tyranny" of employers. The strife at Homestead also reflected broader battles over American freedom during the 1890s. Like the Homestead workers, many Americans came to believe that they were being denied economic independence and democratic self-government, long central to the popular understanding of freedom.

Andrew Carnegie's ironworks at Homestead, Pennsylvania.

During the 1890s, millions of farmers joined the Populist movement in an attempt to reverse their declining economic prospects and to rescue the government from what they saw as control by powerful corporate interests. The 1890s witnessed the imposition of a new racial system in the South that locked African-Americans into the status of second-class citizenship, denying them many of the freedoms white Americans took for granted. Increasing immigration produced heated debates over whether the country should reconsider its traditional self-definition as a refuge for foreigners seeking greater freedom on American shores. At the end of the 1890s, in the Spanish-American War, the United States for the first time acquired overseas possessions and found itself ruling over subject peoples from Puerto Rico to the Philippines. Was the democratic republic, many Americans wondered, becoming an empire like those of Europe? Rarely has the country experienced at one time so many debates over both the meaning of freedom and freedom's boundaries.

THE POPULIST CHALLENGE

THE FARMERS' REVOLT

Even as labor unrest crested, a different kind of uprising was ripening in the South and the trans-Mississippi West, a response to falling agricultural prices and growing economic dependency in rural areas. Like industrial workers, small farmers faced increasing economic insecurity. In the South, the sharecropping system, discussed in Chapter 15, locked millions of tenant farmers, white and black, into perpetual poverty. The interruption of cotton exports during the Civil War had led to the rapid expansion of production in India, Egypt, and Brazil. The glut of cotton on the world market led to declining *ᵃA group of Kansas Populists, perhaps on their way to a political gathering, in a photograph from the 1890s.*

prices (from 11 cents a pound in 1881 to 4.6 cents in 1894), throwing millions of small farmers deep into debt and threatening them with the loss of their land. In the West, farmers who had mortgaged their property to purchase seed, fertilizer, and equipment faced the prospect of losing their farms when unable to repay their bank loans. Farmers increasingly believed that their plight derived from the high freight rates charged by railroad companies, excessive interest rates for loans from merchants and bankers, and the fiscal policies of the federal government (discussed in the previous chapter) that reduced the supply of money and helped to push down farm prices.

Through the Farmers' Alliance, the largest citizens' movement of the nineteenth century, farmers sought to remedy their condition. Founded in Texas in the late 1870s, the Alliance spread to forty-three states by 1890. The farmers' alternatives, said J. D. Fields, a Texas Alliance leader, were "success and freedom, or failure and servitude." At first, the Alliance remained aloof from politics, attempting to improve rural conditions by the cooperative financing and marketing of crops. Alliance "exchanges" would loan money to farmers and sell their produce. But it soon became clear that farmers on their own could not finance this plan, and banks refused to extend loans to the exchanges. The Alliance therefore proposed that the federal government establish warehouses where farmers could store their crops until they were sold. Using the crops as collateral, the government would then issue loans to farmers at low interest rates, thereby ending their dependence on bankers and merchants. Since it would have to be enacted by Congress, the "subtreasury plan," as this proposal was called, led the Alliance into politics.

THE PEOPLE'S PARTY

In the early 1890s, the Alliance evolved into the People's Party (or Populists), the era's greatest political insurgency. The party did not just attract farmers. It sought to speak for all the "producing classes" and achieved some of its greatest successes in states like Colorado and Idaho, where it won the support of miners and industrial workers. It attracted veterans of the Knights of Labor by condemning the use of court injunctions and private police forces against strikers. But its major base lay in the cotton and wheat belts of the South and West.

Building on the Farmers' Alliance network of local institutions, the Populists embarked on a remarkable effort of community organization and education. To spread their message they published numerous pamphlets on political and economic questions, established over 1,000 local newspapers, and sent traveling speakers throughout rural America. Wearing "a huge black sombrero and a black Prince Albert coat," Texas Populist orator "Cyclone" Davis traveled the Great Plains accompanied by the writings of Thomas Jefferson, which he quoted to demonstrate the evils of banks and large corporations. At great gatherings on the western plains, similar in some ways to religious revival meetings, and in small-town southern country stores, one observer wrote, "people commenced to think who had never thought before, and people talked who had seldom spoken.... Little by little they commenced to theorize upon their condition."

Here was the last great political expression of the nineteenth-century vision of America as a commonwealth of small producers whose freedom rested on the ownership of productive property and respect for the dignity of labor. "Day by day," declared the *People's Party Paper* of Georgia in 1893, "the power of the individual sinks. Day by day the power of the classes, or the corporations, rises.... In all essential respects, the republic of our fathers is dead."

THE POPULIST PLATFORM

The Populist platform of 1892, adopted at the party's Omaha convention, remains a classic document of American reform (see the Appendix for the full text). Written by Ignatius Donnelly, a Minnesota editor and former Radical Republican congressman during Reconstruction, it spoke of a nation "brought to the verge of moral, political, and material ruin" by political corruption and economic inequality. "The fruits of the toil of millions," the platform declared, "are boldly stolen to build up colossal fortunes ... while their possessors despise the republic and endanger liberty." The platform put forth a long list of proposals to restore democracy and economic opportunity, many of which would be adopted during the next half-century: the direct election of U.S. senators, government control of the currency, a graduated income tax, a system of low-cost public financing to enable farmers to market their crops, and recognition of the right of workers to form labor unions. In addition, Populists called for public ownership of the railroads to guarantee farmers inexpensive access to markets for their crops.

Convinced that only the national government could curb the power of the corporations and make American society a "united brotherhood of free men," Populists sought to rethink the relationship between freedom and government to address the economic plight of farmers and laborers. "The power of government—in other words, of the people—should be expanded," declared the Omaha platform, to eliminate "oppression, injustice, and poverty" from American life. A generation would pass before a major party offered so sweeping a plan for political action to create the social conditions of freedom.

THE POPULIST COALITION

In some southern states, the Populists made remarkable efforts to unite black and white small farmers on a common political and economic program. The obstacles to such an alliance were immense—not merely the heritage of racism and the political legacy of the Civil War, but the fact that many white Populists were landowning farmers while most blacks were tenants and agricultural laborers. Unwelcome in the southern branches of the Farmers' Alliance, black farmers formed their own organization, the Colored Farmers' Alliance. In 1891, it tried to organize a strike of cotton pickers on plantations in South Carolina, Arkansas, and Texas. The action was violently suppressed by local authorities and landowners, some of them sympathetic to the white Alliance but unwilling to pay higher wages to their own laborers.

Tom Watson, the Georgia Populist leader, on the cover of the party's "campaign book" for 1892.

In a cartoon from Tom Watson's People's Party Paper, *February 25, 1892, northern and southern Civil War veterans bury their past antagonism and unite in the Populist campaign.*

In general, southern white Populists' racial attitudes did not differ significantly from those of their non-Populist neighbors. Nonetheless, recognizing the need for allies to break the Democratic Party's stranglehold on power in the South, some white Populists insisted that black and white farmers shared common grievances and could unite for common goals. Tom Watson, Georgia's leading Populist, worked the hardest to forge a black-white alliance. "You are kept apart," he told interracial audiences, "that you may be separately fleeced of your earnings. . . . This race antagonism perpetuates a monetary system which beggars both." While many blacks refused to abandon the party of Lincoln, others were attracted by the Populist appeal. In 1894, a coalition of white Populists and black Republicans won control of North Carolina, bringing to the state a "second Reconstruction" complete with increased spending on public education and a revival of black officeholding. In most of the South, however, Democrats fended off the Populist challenge by resorting to the tactics they had used to retain power since the 1870s—mobilizing whites with warnings about "Negro supremacy," intimidating black voters, and stuffing ballot boxes on election day.

The Populist movement also engaged the energies of thousands of reform-minded women from farm and labor backgrounds. Some, like Mary Elizabeth Lease, a former homesteader and one of the first female lawyers in Kansas, became prominent organizers, campaigners, and strategists. Lease was famous for her speeches urging farmers to "raise less corn and more hell" (although she apparently never actually uttered those exact words, which would have been considered inappropriate for a woman in pub-

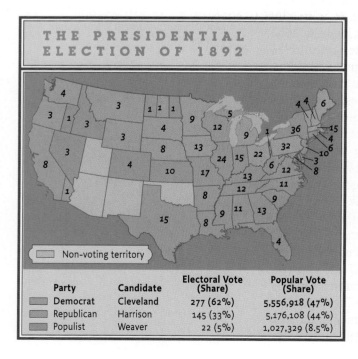

THE PRESIDENTIAL
ELECTION OF 1892

Non-voting territory

Party	Candidate	Electoral Vote (Share)	Popular Vote (Share)
Democrat	Cleveland	277 (62%)	5,556,918 (47%)
Republican	Harrison	145 (33%)	5,176,108 (44%)
Populist	Weaver	22 (5%)	1,027,329 (8.5%)

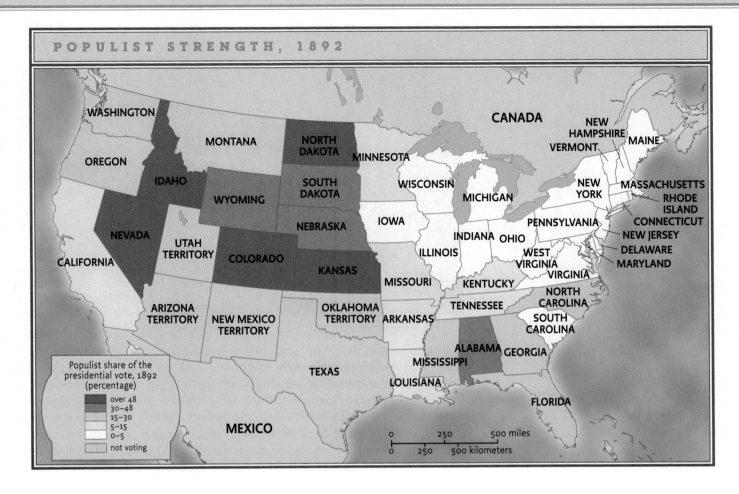

POPULIST STRENGTH, 1892

Populist share of the presidential vote, 1892 (percentage)

- over 48
- 30–48
- 15–30
- 5–15
- 0–5
- not voting

lic). "We fought England for our liberty," Lease declared, "and put chains on four million blacks. We wiped out slavery and . . . began a system of white wage slavery worse than the first." During the 1890s, referendums in Colorado and Idaho approved extending the vote to women, while in Kansas and California the proposal went down in defeat. Populists in all these states endorsed women's suffrage.

Populist presidential candidate James Weaver received over 1 million votes in 1892. The party carried five western states, with twenty-two electoral votes, and elected three governors and fifteen members of Congress. In his inaugural address in 1893, Lorenzo Lewelling, the new Populist governor of Kansas, anticipated a phrase made famous seventy years later by Martin Luther King Jr.: "I have a dream. . . . In the beautiful vision of a coming time I behold the abolition of poverty. A time is foreshadowed when . . . liberty, equality, and justice shall have permanent abiding places in the republic."

THE GOVERNMENT AND LABOR

Were the Populists on the verge of replacing one of the two major parties? The severe depression that began in 1893 led to increased conflict between capital and labor and seemed to create an opportunity for expanding the Populist vote. Time and again, employers brought state or federal authority

Coxey's Army on the march in 1894.

to bear to protect their own economic power or put down threats to public order. Even before the economic downturn, in 1892, the governor of Idaho declared martial law and sent militia units and federal troops into the mining region of Coeur d'Alene to break a strike. In May 1894, the federal government deployed soldiers to disperse Coxey's Army—a band of several hundred unemployed men led by Ohio businessman Jacob Coxey, who marched to Washington demanding economic relief.

DEBS AND THE PULLMAN STRIKE

Also in 1894, workers in the company-owned town of Pullman, Illinois, where railroad sleeping cars were manufactured, called a strike to protest a reduction in wages. The American Railway Union, whose 150,000 members included both skilled and unskilled railroad laborers, announced that its members would refuse to handle trains with Pullman cars. When the boycott crippled national rail service, President Grover Cleveland's attorney general, Richard Olney (himself on the board of several railroad companies), obtained a federal court injunction ordering the strikers back to work. Federal troops and United States marshals soon occupied railroad centers like Chicago and Sacramento. Violent clashes between troops and workers erupted from Maine to California, leaving thirty-four persons dead.

The strike collapsed when the union's leaders, including its charismatic president, Eugene V. Debs, were jailed for contempt of court for violating the judicial order. In the case of *In re Debs*, the Supreme Court unanimously confirmed the sentences and approved the use of injunctions against striking labor unions. On his release from prison in November 1895, over 100,000 persons greeted Debs at a Chicago railroad depot. Hailing the crowd of well-wishers as "lovers of liberty," Debs charged that concentrated economic power, now aligned with state and national governments, was attempting to "wrest from the weak" their birthright of freedom.

Federal troops pose atop a railroad engine after being sent to Chicago to help suppress the Pullman Strike of 1894.

POPULISM AND LABOR

In 1894, Populists made determined efforts to appeal to industrial workers. Populist senators supported the demand of Coxey's Army for federal unemployment relief, and Governor Davis Waite of Colorado, who had edited a labor newspaper before his election, sent the militia to protect striking miners against company police. In the state and congressional elections of that year, as the economic depression deepened, voters by the millions abandoned the Democratic Party of President Cleveland.

In rural areas, the Populist vote increased in 1894. But urban workers did not rally to the Populists, whose core issues—the subtreasury plan and lower mortgage interest rates—had little meaning for them and whose demand for higher prices for farm goods would raise the cost of food and reduce the value of workers' wages. Moreover, the revivalist atmosphere of many Populist gatherings and the biblical cadences of Populist speeches were alien to the largely immigrant and Catholic industrial working class. Urban working-class voters in 1894 instead shifted en masse to the Republicans, who claimed that raising tariff rates (which Democrats had recently reduced) would restore prosperity by protecting manufacturers and industrial workers from the competition of imported goods and cheap foreign labor. In one of the most decisive shifts in congressional power in American history, the Republicans gained 117 seats in the House of Representatives.

BRYAN AND FREE SILVER

In 1896, Democrats and Populists joined to support William Jennings Bryan for the presidency. A thirty-six-year-old congressman from Nebraska, Bryan won the Democratic nomination after delivering to the national convention an electrifying speech that crystallized the farmers' pride and grievances. "Burn down your cities and leave our farms," Bryan proclaimed, "and your cities will spring up again as if by magic; but destroy our farms and grass will grow in the streets of every city in the country." Bryan called

THE SACRILEGIOUS CANDIDATE.

A cartoon from the magazine Judge, *September 14, 1896, condemns William Jennings Bryan and his "cross of gold" speech for defiling the symbols of Christianity. Bryan tramples on the Bible while holding his golden cross; a vandalized church is visible in the background.*

for the "free coinage" of silver—the unrestricted minting of silver money. In language ringing with biblical imagery, Bryan condemned the gold standard: "You shall not press down upon the brow of labor this crown of thorns. You shall not crucify mankind upon a cross of gold."

At various points in the nineteenth century, from debates over "hard" versus "soft" money in the Jacksonian era to the greenback movement after the Civil War, the "money question" had played a central role in American politics. Bryan's demand for "free silver" was the latest expression of the view that increasing the amount of currency in circulation would raise the prices farmers received for their crops and make it easier to pay off their debts. His nomination wrested control of the Democratic Party from long-dominant leaders like President Grover Cleveland, who were closely tied to eastern businessmen.

There was more to Bryan's appeal, however, than simply free silver. A devoutly religious man, he was strongly influenced by the Social Gospel movement (discussed in the previous chapter) and tried to apply the teachings of Jesus Christ to uplifting the "little people" of the United States. He championed a vision of the government helping ordinary Americans that anticipated provisions of the New Deal of the 1930s, including a progressive income tax, banking regulation, and the right of workers to form unions.

Many Populists were initially cool to Bryan's campaign. Their party had been defrauded time and again by Democrats in the South. Veteran Populists feared that their broad program was in danger of being reduced to "free silver." But realizing that they could not secure victory alone, the party's leaders endorsed Bryan's candidacy. Bryan broke with tradition and embarked on a nationwide speaking tour, seeking to rally farmers and workers to his cause.

THE CAMPAIGN OF 1896

Republicans met the silverite challenge head on, insisting that gold was the only "honest" currency. Abandoning the gold standard, they insisted, would destroy business confidence and prevent recovery from the depression by making creditors unwilling to extend loans, since they could not be certain of the value of the money in which they would be repaid. The party nominated for president Ohio governor William McKinley, who as a congressman in 1890 had shepherded to passage the strongly protectionist McKinley Tariff.

The election of 1896 is sometimes called the first modern presidential campaign because of the amount of money spent by the Republicans and the efficiency of their national organization. Eastern bankers and industrialists, thoroughly alarmed by Bryan's call for monetary inflation and his fiery speeches denouncing corporate arrogance, poured millions of dollars into Republican coffers. (McKinley's campaign raised some $10 million; Bryan's around $300,000.) While McKinley remained at his Ohio home, where he addressed crowds of supporters from his front porch, his political manager Mark Hanna created a powerful national political machine that flooded the country with pamphlets, posters, and campaign buttons.

The results revealed a nation as divided along regional lines as in 1860. Bryan carried the South and West and received 6.5 million votes. McKinley

A Republican cartoon, entitled Dubious, *from the 1896 campaign, suggests that Bryan's platform would reduce the United States to the status of poor countries that utilized silver money.*

swept the more populous industrial states of the Northeast and Midwest, attracting 7.1 million. The Republican candidate's electoral margin was even greater: 271 to 176. The era's bitter labor strife did not carry over into the electoral arena; indeed, party politics seemed to mute class conflict rather than to reinforce it. Industrial America, from financiers and managers to workers, now voted solidly Republican, a loyalty reinforced when prosperity returned after 1897.

According to some later critics, the popular children's classic *The Wonderful Wizard of Oz*, published by L. Frank Baum in 1900, offered a commentary on the election of 1896 and its aftermath. In this interpretation, the Emerald City (where everything is colored green, for money) represents Washington, D.C., and the Wizard of Oz, who remains invisible in his palace and rules by illusion, is President McKinley. The only way to get to the city is via a Yellow Brick Road (the color of gold). The Wicked Witches of the East and West represent oppressive industrialists and mine owners. In the much-beloved film version made in the 1930s, Dorothy, the all-American girl from the heartland state of Kansas, wears ruby slippers. But in the book her shoes are silver, supposedly representing the money preferred by ordinary people.

Whatever Baum's symbolism, one thing was clear. McKinley's victory shattered the political stalemate that had persisted since 1876 and created one of the most enduring political majorities in American history. During McKinley's presidency, Republicans placed their stamp on economic policy by passing the Dingley Tariff of 1897, raising rates to the highest level in history, and the Gold Standard Act of 1900. Not until 1932, in the midst of another economic depression, would the Democrats become the nation's majority party. The election of 1896 also proved to

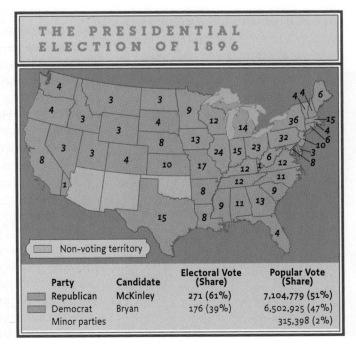

THE PRESIDENTIAL ELECTION OF 1896

Non-voting territory

Party	Candidate	Electoral Vote (Share)	Popular Vote (Share)
Republican	McKinley	271 (61%)	7,104,779 (51%)
Democrat	Bryan	176 (39%)	6,502,925 (47%)
Minor parties			315,398 (2%)

be the last presidential election with extremely high voter turnout (in some states, over 90 percent of those eligible). From then on, with the South solidly Democratic and the North overwhelmingly Republican, few states witnessed vigorous two-party campaigns. Voter participation began a steady downhill trend that continues to this day, when less than half the electorate casts ballots.

THE SEGREGATED SOUTH

THE REDEEMERS IN POWER

The failure of Populism in the South opened the door for the full imposition of a new racial order. The coalition of merchants, planters, and business entrepreneurs who dominated the region's politics after 1877 called themselves Redeemers, since they claimed to have redeemed the region from the alleged horrors of misgovernment and "black rule." On achieving power, they had moved to undo as much as possible of Reconstruction. State budgets were slashed, taxes, especially on landed property, reduced, and public facilities like hospitals and asylums closed. Hardest hit were the new public school systems. Louisiana spent so little on education that it became the only state in the Union in which the percentage of whites unable to read and write actually increased between 1880 and 1900. Black schools, however, suffered the most, as the gap between expenditures for black and white pupils widened steadily. "What I want here is Negroes who can make cotton," declared one planter, "and they don't need education to help them make cotton."

New laws authorized the arrest of virtually any person without employment and greatly increased the penalties for petty crimes. "They send [a man] to the penitentiary if he steals a chicken," complained a former slave in North Carolina. As the South's prison population rose, the renting out of convicts became a profitable business. Every southern state placed at least a portion of its convicted criminals, the majority of them blacks imprisoned for minor offenses, in the hands of private businessmen. Railroads, mines, and lumber companies competed for this new form of cheap, involuntary labor. Conditions in labor camps were often barbaric, with disease rife and the death rates high. "One dies, get another" was the motto of the system's architects. The Knights of Labor made convict labor a major issue in the South. In 1892, miners in Tennessee burned the stockade where convict workers were housed and shipped them out of the region. Tennessee abolished the convict lease system three years later but replaced it with a state-owned coal mine using prison labor that reaped handsome profits for decades.

THE FAILURE OF THE NEW SOUTH DREAM

During the 1880s, Atlanta editor Henry Grady tirelessly promoted the promise of a New South, an era of prosperity based on industrial expansion and agricultural diversification. In fact, while planters, merchants, and industrialists prospered, the region as a whole sank deeper and deeper into poverty. Some industry did develop, including mining in the Appalachians, textile production in the Carolinas and Georgia, and furniture and ciga-

A group of Florida convict laborers. Southern states notoriously used convicts for public labor, or leased them out to work in dire conditions for private employers.

rette manufacturing in certain southern cities. The new upcountry cotton factories offered jobs to entire families of poor whites from the surrounding countryside. But since the main attractions for investors were the South's low wages and taxes and the availability of convict labor, these enterprises made little contribution to regional economic development. With the exception of Birmingham, Alabama, which by 1900 had developed into an important center for the manufacture of iron and steel, southern cities were mainly export centers for cotton, tobacco, and rice, with little industry or skilled labor. Overall, the region remained dependent on the North for capital and manufactured goods. In 1900, southern per capita income amounted to only 60 percent of the national average. As late as the 1930s, President Franklin D. Roosevelt would declare the South the nation's "number one" economic problem.

BLACK LIFE IN THE SOUTH

As the most disadvantaged rural southerners, black farmers suffered the most from the region's condition. In the Upper South, economic development offered some opportunities—mines, iron furnaces, and tobacco factories employed black laborers, and a good number of black farmers managed to acquire land. In the rice kingdom of coastal South Carolina and Georgia, planters found themselves unable to acquire the capital necessary to repair irrigation systems and machinery destroyed by the war. By the turn of the century, most of the great plantations had fallen to pieces, and many blacks acquired land and took up self-sufficient farming. In most of the Deep South, however, African-Americans owned a smaller percentage of the land in 1900 than they had at the end of Reconstruction.

Coal miners, in a photograph by Lewis Hine. Mining was one occupation in which blacks and whites often worked side by side.

In southern cities, the network of institutions created after the Civil War—schools and colleges, churches, businesses, women's clubs, and the like—served as the foundation for increasingly diverse black urban communities. They supported the growth of a black middle class, mostly professionals like teachers and physicians, or businessmen like undertakers and shopkeepers serving the needs of black customers. But the labor market was rigidly divided along racial lines. Black men were excluded from supervisory positions in factories and workshops and white-collar jobs such as clerks in offices. A higher percentage of black women than white worked for wages, but mainly as domestic servants. They could not find employment among the growing numbers of secretaries, typists, and department store clerks.

Even after the demise of the Knights of Labor, some local unions, mainly of dockworkers and mine laborers, had significant numbers of black members. (One reason workers in these jobs could cooperate across racial lines was their almost exclusively male work situations, which undercut fears that allowing black men into unions would encourage them to seek sexual relations with white women.) But in most

Black women washing laundry, one of the few jobs open to them in the New South.

occupations, the few unions that existed in the South excluded blacks, forming yet another barrier to their economic advancement.

THE KANSAS EXODUS

Overall, one historian has written, the New South was "a miserable landscape dotted only by a few rich enclaves that cast little or no light upon the poverty surrounding them." Trapped at the bottom of a stagnant economy, some blacks sought a way out through emigration from the South. In 1879 and 1880, an estimated 40,000 to 60,000 African-Americans migrated to Kansas, seeking political equality, freedom from violence, access to education, and economic opportunity. The name participants gave to this migration, the Exodus, derived from the biblical account of the Jews escaping slavery in Egypt, indicated that its roots lay in deep longings for the substance of freedom. Those promoting the Exodus, including former fugitive slave Benjamin "Pap" Singleton, the organizer of a real estate company, distributed flyers and lithographs picturing Kansas as an idyllic land of rural plenty. Lacking the capital to take up farming, however, most black migrants ended up as unskilled laborers in towns and cities. But few chose to return to the South. In the words of one minister active in the movement, "We had rather suffer and be free."

Despite deteriorating prospects in the South, most African-Americans had little alternative but to stay in the region. The real expansion of job opportunities was taking place in northern cities. But most northern employers refused to offer jobs to blacks in the expanding industrial economy, preferring to hire white migrants from rural areas and immigrants from Europe. Not until the outbreak of World War I in Europe in 1914 cut off immigration did northern employers open industrial jobs to blacks, setting in motion the Great Migration discussed in Chapter 19. Until then, the vast majority of African-Americans remained in the South.

An 1878 poster seeking recruits for the Kansas Exodus.

Benjamin "Pap" Singleton (on the left), who helped to organize the "Exodus" of 1879, superimposed on a photograph of a boat carrying African-Americans emigrating from the South to Kansas.

THE DECLINE OF BLACK POLITICS

Neither black voting nor black officeholding came to an abrupt end in 1877. Blacks continued to cast ballots in large numbers, although Democrats solidified their control of state and local affairs by redrawing district lines and substituting appointive for elective officials in counties with black majorities. A few blacks even served in Congress in the 1880s and 1890s. Nonetheless, political opportunities became more and more restricted. Not until the 1990s would the number of black legislators in the South approach the level seen during Reconstruction.

For black men of talent and ambition, other avenues—business, the law, the church—increasingly seemed to offer greater opportunities for personal advancement and community service than politics. The banner of political leadership passed to black women activists. The National Association of Colored Women, founded in 1896, brought together local and regional women's clubs to press for both women's rights and racial uplift. Most female activists emerged from the small urban black middle class and preached the necessity of "respectable" behavior as part and parcel of the struggle for equal rights. They aided poor families, offered lessons in home life and child rearing, and battled gambling and drinking in black communities. Some poor blacks resented middle-class efforts to instruct them in proper behavior. But by insisting on the right of black women to be considered as "respectable" as their white counterparts, the women reformers challenged the racial ideology that consigned all blacks to the status of degraded second-class citizens.

For nearly a generation after the end of Reconstruction, despite fraud and violence, black southerners continued to cast ballots. In some states, the Republican Party remained competitive. In Virginia, a coalition of mostly black Republicans and anti-Redeemer Democrats formed an alliance known as the Readjuster movement (the name derived from their plan to scale back, or "readjust," the state debt). They governed the state between 1879 and 1883. Tennessee and Arkansas also witnessed the formation of biracial political coalitions that challenged Democratic Party rule. Despite the limits of the Populists' interracial alliance, the threat of a biracial political insurgency frightened the ruling Democrats and contributed greatly to the disenfranchisement movement. In North Carolina, for example, the end of the Populist-Republican coalition government in 1898—accomplished by a violent campaign that culminated in a riot in Wilmington in which scores of blacks were killed—was quickly followed by the elimination of black voting.

THE ELIMINATION OF BLACK VOTING

Between 1890 and 1906, every southern state enacted laws or constitutional provisions meant to eliminate the black vote. Since the Fifteenth Amendment prohibited the use of race as a qualification for the suffrage, how were such measures even possible? Southern legislatures drafted laws that on paper appeared color-blind, but that were actually designed to end black voting. The most popular devices were the poll tax (a fee that each citizen had to pay in order to retain the right to vote), literacy tests, and the requirement that a prospective voter demonstrate to election officials an "understanding" of the state constitution. Six southern states also adopted a "grandfather clause," exempting from the new requirements descendants of persons eligible to vote before the Civil War (when only whites, of course, could cast ballots in the South). The racial intent of the grandfather clause was so clear that the Supreme Court in 1915 invalidated such laws for violating the Fifteenth Amendment. The other methods of limiting black voting, however, remained on the books.

Some white leaders presented disenfranchisement as a "good government" measure—a means of purifying politics by ending the fraud, violence, and manipulation of voting returns regularly used against Republicans and Populists. But ultimately, as a Charleston newspaper declared, the aim was to make clear that the white South "does not desire or intend ever to include black men among its citizens." Democrats persistently raised the threat of "Negro domination" to justify the denial of the right to vote. Although election officials often allowed whites who did not meet the new qualifications to register, numerous poor and illiterate whites also lost the right to vote, a result welcomed by many planters and urban reformers. Louisiana, for example, reduced the number of blacks registered to vote from 130,000 in 1894 to 1,342 a decade later. But 80,000 white voters also lost the right. Disenfranchisement led directly to the rise of a generation of southern "demagogues," who mobilized white voters by extreme appeals to racism. Tom Watson, who as noted before had tried to forge an interracial Populist coalition in the 1890s, reemerged early in the twentieth century as a power in Georgia public life through vicious speeches whipping up prejudice against blacks, Jews, and Catholics.

As late as 1940, only 3 percent of adult black southerners were registered to vote. The elimination of black and many white voters, which reversed the nineteenth-century trend toward more inclusive suffrage, could not have been accomplished without the approval of the North. In 1891, the Senate defeated a proposal for federal protection of black voting rights in the South. Apart from the grandfather clause, the Supreme Court gave its approval to disenfranchisement laws. According to the Fourteenth Amendment, any state that deprived male citizens of the franchise was supposed to lose part of its representation in Congress. But like much of the Constitution, this provision was consistently violated so far as African-Americans were concerned. As a result, southern congressmen wielded far greater power on the national scene than their tiny electorates warranted. As for blacks, for decades thereafter, they would regard "the loss of suffrage as being the loss of freedom."

THE LAW OF SEGREGATION

Along with disenfranchisement, the 1890s saw the widespread imposition of segregation in the South. Laws and local customs requiring the separation of the races had numerous precedents. They had existed in many parts of the pre–Civil War North. Southern schools and many other institutions had been segregated during Reconstruction. In the 1880s, however, southern race relations remained unsettled. Some railroads, theaters, and hotels admitted blacks and whites on an equal basis while others separated them by race or excluded blacks altogether.

In 1883, in the *Civil Rights Cases*, the Supreme Court invalidated the Civil Rights Act of 1875, which had outlawed racial discrimination by hotels, theaters, railroads, and other public facilities. The Fourteenth Amendment, the Court insisted, prohibited unequal treatment by state authorities, not private businesses. In 1896, in the landmark decision in *Plessy v. Ferguson*, the Court gave its approval to state laws requiring separate facilities for blacks and whites. The case arose in Louisiana, where the legislature had required railroad companies to maintain a separate car or section for black passengers. A Citizens Committee of black residents of New Orleans came together to challenge the law. To create a test case, Homer Plessy, a light-skinned African-American, refused a conductor's order to move to the "colored only" part of his railroad car and was arrested.

To argue the case before the Supreme Court, the Citizens Committee hired Albion W. Tourgée, who as a judge in North Carolina during Reconstruction had waged a courageous battle against the Ku Klux Klan. "Citizenship is national and knows no color," he insisted, and racial segregation violated the Fourteenth Amendment's guarantee of equal protection before the law. But in an 8-1 decision, the Court upheld the Louisiana law, arguing that segregated facilities did not discriminate so long as they were "separate but equal." The lone dissenter, John Marshall Harlan, reprimanded the majority with an oft-quoted comment: "Our constitution is color-blind." Segregation, he insisted, sprang from whites' conviction that they were the "dominant race" (a phrase used by the Court's majority), and it violated the principle of equal liberty. To Harlan, freedom for the former slaves meant the right to participate fully and equally in American society.

SEGREGATION AND WHITE DOMINATION

As Harlan predicted, states reacted to the *Plessy* decision by passing laws mandating racial segregation in every aspect of southern life, from schools to hospitals, waiting rooms, toilets, and cemeteries. Some states forbade taxi drivers to carry members of different races at the same time. Despite the "thin disguise" (Harlan's phrase) of equality required by the Court's "separate but equal" doctrine, facilities for blacks were either nonexistent or markedly inferior. In 1900, no public high school for blacks existed in the entire South. Black elementary schools, one observer reported, occupied buildings "as bad as stables."

More than a form of racial separation, segregation was one part of an all-encompassing system of white domination, in which each component—disenfranchisement, unequal economic status, inferior education—reinforced the others. The point was not so much to keep the races apart as to ensure that when they came into contact with each other, whether in politics, labor relations, or social life, whites held the upper hand. For example, many blacks could be found in "whites-only" railroad cars. But they entered as servants and nurses, not as paying customers entitled to equal treatment.

An elaborate social etiquette developed, with proper behavior differentiated by race. One sociologist who studied the turn-of-the-century South reported that in places of business, blacks had to stand back and wait until whites had been served. They could not raise their voices or in other ways act assertively in the presence of whites, and they had to "give way" on the streets. In shops, whites but not blacks were allowed to try on clothing.

Segregation affected other groups as well as blacks. In some parts of Mississippi where Chinese laborers had been brought in to work the fields after the Civil War, three separate school systems—white, black, and Chinese—were established. In California, black, Hispanic, and American Indian children were frequently educated alongside whites, but state law required separate schools for those of "mongolian or Chinese descent." In Texas and California, although Mexicans were legally considered "white," they found themselves barred from many restaurants, places of entertainment, and other public facilities.

THE RISE OF LYNCHING

Those blacks who sought to challenge the system, or who refused to accept the demeaning behavior that was a daily feature of southern life, faced not only overwhelming political and legal power but also the threat of violent reprisal. In every year between 1883 and 1905, more than fifty persons, the vast majority of them black men, were lynched in the South—that is, murdered by a mob. Lynching continued well into the twentieth century. By mid-century, the total number of victims since 1880 had reached nearly 5,000. Some lynchings occurred secretly at night; others were advertised in advance and attracted large crowds of onlookers. Mobs engaged in activities that shocked the civilized world. In 1899, Sam Hose, a plantation laborer who killed his employer in self-defense, was brutally murdered near Newman, Georgia, before 2,000 onlookers, some of whom arrived on a special excursion train from Atlanta. A crowd including young children watched as his executioners cut off Hose's ears, fingers, and genitals, burned him alive, and then fought over pieces of his bones as souvenirs. Law enforcement authorities made no effort to prevent the lynching or to bring those who committed the crime to justice.

Table 17.1 STATES WITH OVER 200 LYNCHINGS, 1889–1918	
State	Number of Lynchings
Georgia	386
Mississippi	373
Texas	335
Louisiana	313
Alabama	276
Arkansas	214

Part of the crowd of 10,000 that watched the 1893 lynching of Henry Smith in Paris, Texas. Smith was accused of raping and murdering a four-year-old girl. The word "justice" was painted on the platform.

Like many victims of lynchings, Hose was accused after his death of having raped a white woman. Many white southerners considered preserving the purity of white womanhood a justification for extralegal vengeance. Yet in nearly all cases, as activist Ida B. Wells argued in a newspaper editorial after a Memphis lynching in 1892, the charge of rape was a "bare lie." Born a slave in Mississippi in 1862, Wells had become a schoolteacher and editor. Her essay condemning the lynching of three black men in Memphis led a mob to destroy her newspaper, the *Memphis Free Press*, while she was out of the city. Wells moved to the North, where she became the nation's leading antilynching crusader. She bluntly insisted that given the conditions of southern blacks, the United States had no right to call itself the "land of the free."

Widespread lynching was a phenomenon unknown in other countries. Canada, for example, has experienced only one lynching in its history—in 1884, when a mob from the United States crossed the border into British Columbia to lynch an Indian teenager who had fled after being accused of murder.

Years later, black writer Blyden Jackson recalled growing up in early-twentieth-century Louisville, Kentucky, a city in many ways typical of the New South. It was a divided society. There was the world "where white folks lived . . . the Louisville of the downtown hotels, the lower floors of the big movie houses . . . the inner sanctums of offices where I could go only as a humble client or a menial custodian." Then there was the black world, "the homes, the people, the churches, and the schools," where "everything was black." "I knew," Jackson later recalled, "that there were two Louisvilles and . . . two Americas."

THE POLITICS OF MEMORY

As the white North and South moved toward reconciliation in the 1880s and 1890s, one cost was the abandonment of the dream of racial equality spawned by the Civil War and written into the laws and Constitution during Reconstruction. In popular literature and memoirs by participants, at veterans' reunions and in public memorials, the Civil War came to be remembered as a tragic family quarrel among white Americans in which blacks had played no significant part. It was a war of "brother against brother" in which both sides fought gallantly for noble causes—local rights on the part of the South, preservation of the Union for the North. Slavery increasingly came to be viewed as a minor issue, not the war's fundamental cause, and Reconstruction as a regrettable period of "Negro rule" when former slaves had power thrust upon them by a vindictive North. This outlook gave legitimacy to southern efforts to eliminate black voting, lest the region once again suffer the alleged "horrors" of Reconstruction.

Southern governments erected monuments to the Lost Cause, school history texts emphasized happy slaves and the evils of Reconstruction, and the role of black soldiers in winning the war was all but forgotten. In fact, when a group of black veterans attempted to participate in a Florida ceremony commemorating the fiftieth anniversary of the outbreak of the Civil War in 1911, a white mob tore the military insignias off their jackets and drove them away.

REDRAWING THE BOUNDARIES

The effective nullification of the laws and amendments of Reconstruction and the reduction of blacks to the position of second-class citizens reflected nationwide patterns of thought and policy. As the nineteenth century drew to a close, American society seemed to be fracturing along lines of both class and race. The result, commented economist Simon Patten, was a widespread obsession with redrawing the boundary of freedom by identifying and excluding those unworthy of the blessings of liberty. "The South," he wrote, "has its negro, the city has its slums. . . . The friends of American institutions fear the ignorant immigrant, and the workingman dislikes the

A cartoon from the magazine Judge *illustrates anti-immigrant sentiment. A tide of newcomers representing the criminal element of other countries washes up on American shores, to the consternation of Uncle Sam.*

THE HIGH TIDE OF IMMIGRATION—A NATIONAL MENACE.

Chinese." As Patten suggested, many Americans embraced a more and more restricted definition of nationhood. The new exclusiveness was evident in the pages of popular periodicals, filled with derogatory imagery depicting blacks and other "lesser" groups as little more than savages and criminals incapable of partaking in American freedom.

THE NEW IMMIGRATION AND THE NEW NATIVISM

The 1890s witnessed a major shift in the sources of immigration to the United States. Despite the prolonged depression, 3.5 million newcomers entered the United States during the decade, seeking jobs in the industrial centers of the North and Midwest. Over half arrived not from Ireland, England, Germany, and Scandinavia, the traditional sources of immigration, but from southern and eastern Europe, especially Italy and the Russian and Austro-Hungarian empires. The "new immigrants" were widely described by native-born Americans as members of distinct "races," whose lower level of civilization explained everything from their willingness to work for substandard wages to their supposed inborn tendency toward criminal behavior. They were "beaten men from beaten races," wrote economist Francis Amasa Walker, representing "the worst failures in the struggle for existence." American cities, said an Ohio newspaper, were being overrun by foreigners who "have no true appreciation of the meaning of liberty" and therefore posed a danger to democratic government.

Founded in 1894 by a group of Boston professionals, the Immigration Restriction League called for reducing immigration by barring the illiterate from entering the United States. Such a measure was adopted by Congress early in 1897 but was vetoed by President Cleveland. Like the South, northern and western states experimented with ways of eliminating undesirable voters. Nearly all the states during the 1890s adopted the secret or "Australian" ballot, meant both to protect voters' privacy and to limit the participation of illiterates (who could no longer receive help from party officials at polling places). Several states ended the nineteenth-century practice of allowing immigrants to vote before becoming citizens and adopted stringent new residency and literacy requirements. None of these measures approached the scope of black disenfranchisement in the South or the continued denial of voting rights to women. But suffrage throughout the country was increasingly becoming a privilege, not a right.

CHINESE EXCLUSION AND CHINESE RIGHTS

The boundaries of nationhood, expanded so dramatically in the aftermath of the Civil War, slowly contracted. Leaders of both parties expressed vicious opinions regarding immigrants from China—they were "odious, abominable, dangerous, revolting," declared Republican leader James G. Blaine. Between 1850 and 1870, nearly all Chinese immigrants had been unattached men, brought in by labor contractors to work in western gold fields, railroad construction, and factories. In the early 1870s, entire Chinese families began to immigrate, leading Congress in 1875 to exclude Chinese women from entering the country. California congressman Horace Page, the bill's author, insisted that it was intended to preserve the health of white citizens by

Chinese agricultural laborers in southern California around 1880.

VOICES OF FREEDOM

FROM SAUM SONG BO,
Letter in *American Missionary* (October 1885)

During the 1880s, Chinese-Americans were subjected to discrimination in every phase of their lives. In 1882, Congress barred further immigration from China. In 1885, when funds were being raised to build a pedestal for the Statue of Liberty, Saum Song Bo, a Chinese-American writer, contrasted the celebration of liberty with the treatment of the Chinese.

A paper was presented to me yesterday for inspection, and I found it to be specially drawn up for subscription among my countrymen toward the Pedestal Fund of the . . . Statue of Liberty. . . . But the word liberty makes me think of the fact that this country is the land of liberty for men of all nations except the Chinese. I consider it as an insult to us Chinese to call on us to contribute toward building in this land a pedestal for a statue of Liberty. That statue represents Liberty holding a torch which lights the passage of those of all nations who come into this country. But are the Chinese allowed to come? As for the Chinese who are here, are they allowed to enjoy liberty as men of all other nationalities enjoy it? Are they allowed to go about everywhere free from the insults, abuses, assaults, wrongs, and injuries from which men of other nationalities are free?

If there be a Chinaman who came to this country when a lad, who has passed through an American institution of learning of the highest grade, who has so fallen in love with American manners and ideas that he desires to make his home in this land, and who, seeing that his countrymen demand one of their own number to be their legal adviser, representative, advocate, and protector, desires to study law, can he be a lawyer? By the law of this nation, he, being a Chinaman, cannot become a citizen, and consequently cannot be a lawyer.

And this statue of Liberty is a gift from another people who do not love liberty for the Chinese. [To] the Annamese and Tonquinese Chinese [colonial subjects of the French empire in Indochina], . . . liberty is as dear as to the French. What right have the French to deprive them of their liberty?

Whether this statute against the Chinese or the statue to Liberty will be the most lasting monument to tell future ages of the liberty and greatness of this country, will be known only to future generations.

From The Reverend Charles G. Ames, Address to Anti-Imperialism Meeting in Boston (1898)

The emergence of the United States as an imperial power as a result of the Spanish-American War sparked an intense debate over the relationship among political democracy, race, and citizenship. Anti-imperialists like Ames warned that acquiring an overseas empire threatened to undermine democracy at home.

We are told that it is "our duty" to extend to the struggling people of the Philippines the same help and protection we have pledged to Cuba. . . . Almost before we have lifted a finger to deliver Cuba, we set up a claim to Spanish possessions on the other side of the globe! . . . Is there a man in America who wishes those seven millions of Malays, Negritos and Chinamen for fellow citizens and joint rulers of this Republic? But if we govern them without their consent, it must be by military occupation,—by force; that is by the Spanish method. . . .

But the scheme of conquest does not end with the acquisition of the Philippines; it only begins there. The imperial program includes a chain of island possessions. The European powers are dividing the Asiatic, African and Polynesian world among themselves; we are to go in for a share of the booty. . . . And we are to do it by war; the right of might. Can we not show the world a more excellent way?

What will be the effect on our domestic policy? How can we undertake to rule subject provinces in distant parts of the globe without trampling on the principles of free government? Once accepting this way of dealing with other people, how long will it be before some occasion will arise for applying it at home? In committing ourselves to permanent military methods of government anywhere, we give up the republic, for we abandon its fundamental principle, even while boasting of the name. . . .

The imperial scheme requires us to go very deeply into military and naval expenditure, that we may be ever on fighting footing. We must girdle the earth with strategic possessions, every one of which must be fortified and garrisoned. . . . We are to be a great military nation! Our industry is to foot the bills. If you object, you are no patriot! But where will be the republic? . . .

The policy of imperialism threatens to change the temper of our people, and to put us into a permanent attitude of arrogance, testiness and defiance toward other nations. . . . If once we enter the field of international conflict as a great military and naval power, we shall be one more bully among bullies: we shall only add one more to the list of oppressors of mankind. . . . The programme of imperialism reads to me like a declaration of war for the new century.

QUESTIONS

1. Why does Bo believe that the Chinese do not enjoy liberty in the United States?

2. Why does Ames see imperialism as undermining "free government"?

3. How do the views of race and its relationship to democracy differ in the two documents?

Result of an anti-Chinese riot in Seattle, Washington.

barring Chinese prostitutes. But immigration authorities enforced the Page law so as to keep out as well the wives and daughters of arriving men and of those already in the country.

Beginning in 1882, Congress temporarily excluded immigrants from China from entering the country altogether. Although non-whites had long been barred from becoming naturalized citizens, this was the first time that race had been used to exclude an entire group of people from entering the United States. Congress renewed the restriction ten years later and made it permanent in 1902. Whether America would truly achieve "liberty and greatness," observed Saum Song Bo, a Chinese-American writer, would in the future depend on "whether this statute against the Chinese or the statue to Liberty will be the more lasting monument."

At the time of exclusion, 105,000 persons of Chinese descent lived in the United States. Nearly all of them resided on the West Coast, where they suffered intense discrimination and periodic mob violence. Their demands for equal rights forced the state and federal courts to define the reach of the Fourteenth Amendment. For example, between 1871 and 1885, San Francisco provided no public education for Chinese children. In 1885, the California Supreme Court, in *Tape v. Hurley*, ordered the city to admit Chinese students to public schools. The state legislature responded by passing a law authorizing segregated education, and the city established a school for Chinese. But Joseph and Mary Tape, who had lived in the United States since the 1860s, insisted that their daughter be allowed to attend her neighborhood school like other children. "Is it a disgrace to be born a Chinese?" Mary Tape wrote. "Didn't God make us all!" But her protest failed. Not until the 1947 did California repeal the law authorizing separate schools for the Chinese.

The United States Supreme Court also considered the status of Chinese-Americans. In *Yick Wo v. Hopkins* (1886), the Court unanimously ordered San Francisco to grant licenses to Chinese-operated laundries, which the city government had refused to do. To deny a person the opportunity to earn a living, the Court declared, was "intolerable in any country where freedom prevails." Twelve years later, in *United States v. Wong Kim Ark*, the Court ruled that the Fourteenth Amendment awarded citizenship to children of Chinese immigrants born on American soil.

Yet the Justices also affirmed the right of Congress to set racial restrictions on immigration. And in its decision in *Fong Yue Ting* (1893), the Court authorized the federal government to expel Chinese aliens without due process of law. In his dissent, Justice David J. Brewer acknowledged that the power was now directed against a people many Americans found "obnoxious." But "who shall say," he continued, "it will not be exercised tomorrow against other classes and other people?" Brewer proved to be an accurate prophet. In 1904, the Court cited *Fong Yue Ting* in upholding a law barring anarchists from entering the United States, demonstrating how restrictions on the rights of one group can become a precedent for infringing on the rights of others.

Exclusion profoundly shaped the experience of Chinese-Americans, long stigmatizing them as incapable of assimilation and justifying their isolation from mainstream society. Congress for the first time also barred groups of whites from entering the country, beginning in 1875 with prostitutes and convicted felons, and in 1882 adding "lunatics" and those likely to become a "public charge." "Are we still a [place of refuge] for the oppressed of all nations?" wondered James B. Weaver, the Populist candidate for president in 1892.

THE EMERGENCE OF BOOKER T. WASHINGTON

The social movements that had helped to expand the nineteenth-century boundaries of freedom now redefined their objectives so that they might be realized within the new economic and intellectual framework. Prominent black leaders, for example, took to emphasizing economic self-help and individual advancement into the middle class as an alternative to political agitation.

Symbolizing the change was the juxtaposition, in 1895, of the death of Frederick Douglass with Booker T. Washington's widely praised speech at the Atlanta Cotton Exposition that urged blacks to adjust to segregation and abandon agitation for civil and political rights. Born a slave in 1856, Washington had studied as a young man at Hampton Institute, Virginia. He adopted the outlook of Hampton's founder, General Samuel Armstrong, who emphasized that obtaining farms or skilled jobs was far more important to African-Americans emerging from slavery than the rights of citizenship. Washington put this view into practice when he became head of Tuskegee Institute in Alabama, a center for vocational education (education focused on training for a job rather than broad learning).

In his Atlanta speech, Washington repudiated the abolitionist tradition that stressed ceaseless agitation for full equality. He urged blacks not to try to combat segregation: "In all the things that are purely social we can be as separate as the fingers, yet one as the hand in all things essential to mutual progress." Washington advised his people to seek the assistance of white employers who, in a land racked by labor turmoil, would prefer a docile, dependable black labor force to unionized whites. Washington's ascendancy rested in large part on his success in channeling aid from wealthy northern whites to Tuskegee and to black politicians and newspapers who backed his program. But his support in the black community also arose from a widespread sense that in the world of the late nineteenth century, frontal assaults on white power were impossible and that blacks should concentrate on building up their segregated communities.

THE RISE OF THE AFL

Within the labor movement, the demise of the Knights of Labor and the ascendancy of the American Federation of Labor (AFL) during the 1890s reflected a similar shift away from a broadly reformist past to more limited

Booker T. Washington, advocate of industrial education and economic self-help.

goals. As the Homestead and Pullman strikes demonstrated, direct confrontations with the large corporations were likely to prove suicidal. Unions, declared Samuel Gompers, the AFL's founder and longtime president, should not seek economic independence, pursue the Knights' utopian dream of creating a "cooperative commonwealth," or form independent parties with the aim of achieving power in government. Rather, the labor movement should devote itself to negotiating with employers for higher wages and better working conditions for its members. Like Washington, Gompers spoke the language of the era's business culture. Indeed, the AFL policies he pioneered were known as "business unionism." Gompers embraced the idea of "freedom of contract," shrewdly turning it into an argument against interference by judges with workers' right to organize unions.

During the 1890s, union membership rebounded from its decline in the late 1880s. But at the same time, the labor movement became less and less inclusive. Abandoning the Knights' ideal of labor solidarity, the AFL restricted membership to skilled workers—a small minority of the labor force—effectively excluding the vast majority of unskilled workers and, therefore, nearly all blacks, women, and new European immigrants. AFL membership centered on sectors of the economy like printing and building construction that were dominated by small competitive businesses where workers frequently were united by craft skill and ethnic background. AFL unions had little presence in basic industries like steel and rubber, or in the large-scale factories that now dominated the economy.

THE WOMEN'S ERA

Changes in the women's movement reflected the same combination of expanding activities and narrowing boundaries. The 1890s launched what would later be called the "women's era"—three decades during which women, although still denied the vote, enjoyed larger opportunities than in the past for economic independence and played a greater and greater role in public life. By now, nearly every state had adopted laws giving married women control over their own wages and property and the right to sign separate contracts and make separate wills. Nearly 5 million women worked for wages in 1900. Although most were young, unmarried, and concentrated in traditional jobs such as domestic service and the garment industry, a generation of college-educated women was beginning to take its place in better-paying clerical and professional positions.

Through a network of women's clubs, temperance associations, and social reform organizations, women exerted a growing influence on public affairs. Founded in 1874, the Women's Christian Temperance Union (WCTU) grew to become the era's largest female organization, with a membership by 1890 of 150,000. Under the banner of Home Protection, it moved from demanding the prohibition of alcoholic beverages (blamed for leading men to squander their wages on drink and treat their wives abusively) to a comprehensive program of economic and political reform including the right to vote. Women, insisted Frances Willard, the group's president, must abandon the idea that "weakness" and dependence were their nature and join assertively in movements to change society. "A wider freedom is coming to the women of America," she declared in a 1895 speech to male and female strikers in a Massachusetts shoe factory. "Too long has it been held that woman has no right to enter these movements. So much for the movements. Politics is the place for woman."

At the same time, the center of gravity of feminism shifted toward an outlook more in keeping with prevailing racial and ethnic norms. The earlier "feminism of equal rights," which claimed the ballot as part of a larger transformation of women's status, was never fully repudiated. The movement continued to argue for women's equality in employment, education, and politics. But with increasing frequency, the native-born, middle-class women who dominated the suffrage movement claimed the vote as educated members of a "superior race."

A new generation of suffrage leaders suggested that educational and other voting qualifications did not conflict with the movement's aims, so long as they applied equally to men and women. Immigrants and former slaves had been enfranchised with "ill-advised haste," declared Carrie Chapman Catt, president of the National American Woman Suffrage Association (created in 1890 to reunite the rival suffrage organizations formed after the Civil War). Indeed, Catt suggested, extending the vote to native-born white women would help to counteract the growing power of the "ignorant foreign vote" in the North and the dangerous potential for a second Reconstruction in the South. Elitism within the movement was reinforced when many advocates of suffrage blamed the "slum vote" for the defeat of a women's suffrage referendum in California. In 1895, the same year that Booker T. Washington delivered his Atlanta address, the National American Woman Suffrage Association held its annual convention in that segregated city. Like other American institutions, the organized movement for women's suffrage had made its peace with nativism and racism.

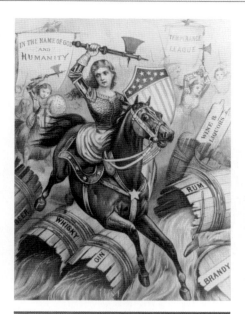

Woman's Holy War, *a lithograph from 1874, the year the Women's Christian Temperance Union was founded, portrays an advocate of prohibition as an armed crusader against hard liquor.*

BECOMING A WORLD POWER

THE NEW IMPERIALISM

In the last years of the 1890s, the narrowed definition of nationhood was projected abroad, as the United States took its place as an imperial power on the international stage. In world history, the last quarter of the nineteenth century is known as the age of imperialism, when rival European empires carved up large parts of the world among themselves. For most of this period, the United States remained a second-rate power. In 1880, the sultan of Turkey decided to close three foreign embassies to reduce expenses. He chose those in Sweden, Belgium, and the United States. In that year, the American navy was smaller than Denmark's or Chile's. When European powers met at the Berlin Congress of 1884–1885 to divide most of Africa among themselves, the United States attended because of its relationship with Liberia but did not sign the final agreement.

Throughout the nineteenth century, large empires dominated much of the globe. Some were land-based, like the Russian, Ottoman, and Chinese empires, and others included territories on several continents linked by sea, such as the British, French, and Spanish. After 1870, a "new imperialism" arose, dominated by European powers and Japan. Belgium, Great Britain, and France consolidated their hold on colonies in Africa, and newly unified Germany acquired colonies there as well. The British and Russians sought to increase their influence in Central Asia, and all the European powers struggled to dominate parts of China. By the early twentieth century, most of Asia, Africa, the Middle East, and the Pacific had been divided among these empires. The justification for this expansion of imperial power was that it would bring modern "civilization" to the supposedly backward peoples of the non-European world. The natives, according to their colonial occupiers, would be instructed in Western values, labor practices, and the Christian religion. Eventually, they would be accorded the right of self-government, although no one could be sure how long this would take. In the meantime, "empire" was another word for "exploitation."

AMERICAN EXPANSIONISM

Until the 1890s, American expansion had taken place on the North American continent. Ever since the Monroe Doctrine (see Chapter 10), to be sure, many Americans had considered the Western Hemisphere an American sphere of influence. There was persistent talk of acquiring Cuba, and President Grant had sought to annex the Dominican Republic, only to see the Senate reject the idea. The last territorial acquisition before the 1890s had been Alaska, purchased from Russia by Secretary of State William H. Seward in 1867, to much derision from those who could not see the purpose of American ownership of "Seward's icebox." Seward, however, was mostly interested in the Aleutian Islands, a part of Alaska that stretched much of the way to Asia and that, he believed, could be the site of coaling stations for merchant ships plying the Pacific.

Most Americans who looked overseas were interested in expanded trade, not territorial possessions. The country's agricultural and industrial production could no longer be entirely absorbed at home. By 1890, companies like Singer Sewing Machines and John D. Rockefeller's Standard Oil Company aggressively marketed their products abroad. Especially during economic downturns, business leaders insisted on the necessity of greater access to foreign customers.

THE LURE OF EMPIRE

A small group of late-nineteenth-century thinkers actively promoted American expansionism, warning that the country must not allow itself to be shut out of the scramble for empire. In *Our Country* (1885), Josiah Strong, a prominent Congregationalist clergyman, sought to update the idea of manifest destiny. Having demonstrated their special aptitude for liberty and self-government on the North American continent, Strong announced, Anglo-Saxons should now spread their institutions and values to "inferior races" throughout the world. The economy would benefit, he insisted, since one means of civilizing "savages" was to turn them into consumers of American goods.

Naval officer Alfred T. Mahan, in *The Influence of Sea Power Upon History* (1890), argued that no nation could prosper without a large fleet of ships engaged in international trade, protected by a powerful navy operating from overseas bases. Mahan published his book in the same year that the census bureau announced that there was no longer a clear line separating settled from unsettled land. Thus, the frontier no longer existed. "Americans," wrote Mahan, "must now begin to look outward." His arguments influenced the outlook of James G. Blaine, who served as secretary of state during Benjamin Harrison's presidency (1889–1893). Harrison persuaded Congress to fund the building of four new battleships. Blaine urged the president to try to acquire Hawaii, Puerto Rico, and Cuba as strategic naval bases.

Although independent, Hawaii was already closely tied to the United States through treaties that exempted imports of its sugar from tariff duties and provided for the establishment of an American naval base at Pearl Harbor. Hawaii's economy was dominated by American-owned sugar plantations that employed a workforce of native islanders and Chinese, Japanese, and Filipino laborers under long-term contracts. Early in 1893, a group of American planters organized a rebellion that overthrew the Hawaii government of Queen Liliuokalani. On the eve of leaving office, Harrison submitted a treaty of annexation to the Senate. After determining that a majority of Hawaiians did not favor the treaty, Harrison's successor, Grover Cleveland, withdrew it.

The depression that began in 1893 heightened the belief that a more aggressive foreign policy was necessary to stimulate American exports. Fears of economic and ethnic disunity fueled an assertive nationalism. In the face of social conflict and the new immigration, government and private organizations in the 1890s promoted a unifying patriotism. These were the years when rituals like the Pledge of Allegiance and the practice of standing for the playing of "The Star-Spangled Banner" came into existence. Americans had long honored the Stars and Stripes, but the "cult of the flag," including an official Flag Day, dates to the 1890s. New, mass-circulation newspapers also promoted nationalistic sentiments. By the late 1890s, papers like William Randolph Hearst's *New York Journal* and Joseph Pulitzer's *New York World*—dubbed the "yellow press" by their critics after the color in which Hearst printed a popular comic strip—were selling a million copies each day by mixing sensational accounts of crime and political corruption with aggressive appeals to patriotic sentiments.

THE "SPLENDID LITTLE WAR"

All these factors contributed to America's emergence as a world power in the Spanish-American War of 1898. But the immediate origins of the war lay not at home but in the long Cuban struggle for independence from Spain. Ten years of guerrilla war had followed a Cuban revolt in 1868. The movement for independence resumed in 1895. As reports circulated of widespread suffering caused by the Spanish policy of rounding up civilians and moving them into detention camps, the Cuban struggle won growing support in the United States.

Demands for intervention escalated after February 15, 1898, when an explosion—probably accidental, a later investigation concluded—destroyed the American battleship *Maine* in Havana Harbor, with the loss of nearly 270 lives. The yellow press blamed Spain and insisted on retribution. After Spain rejected an American demand for a cease-fire on the island

A cartoon in Puck, *December 1, 1897, imagines the annexation of Hawaii by the United States as a shotgun wedding. The minister, President McKinley, reads from a book entitled* Annexation Policy. *The Hawaiian bride appears to be looking for a way to escape. Most Hawaiians did not support annexation.*

The destruction of the battleship Maine *in Havana Harbor (later found to have been an accident) provided the occasion for patriotic pageants like "Remember the* Maine," *by William H. West's Big Minstrel Jubilee.*

and eventual Cuban independence, President McKinley in April asked Congress for a declaration of war. The purpose, declared Senator Henry Teller of Colorado, was to aid Cuban patriots in their struggle for "liberty and freedom." To underscore the government's humanitarian intentions, Congress adopted the Teller Amendment, stating that the United States had no intention of annexing or dominating the island.

Secretary of State John Hay called the Spanish-American conflict a "splendid little war." It lasted only four months and resulted in fewer than 400 American combat deaths. Having shown little interest in imperial expansion before 1898, McKinley now embraced the idea. The war's most decisive engagement, in fact, took place not in Cuba but at Manila Bay, a strategic harbor in the Philippine Islands in the distant Pacific Ocean. Here, on May 1, the American navy under Admiral George Dewey defeated a Spanish fleet. Soon afterwards, soldiers went ashore, becoming the first American army units to engage in combat outside the Western Hemisphere. July witnessed another naval victory off Santiago, Cuba, and the landing of American troops on Cuba and Puerto Rico.

ROOSEVELT AT SAN JUAN HILL

The most highly publicized land battle of the war took place in Cuba. This was the charge up San Juan Hill, outside Santiago, by Theodore Roosevelt's Rough Riders. An ardent expansionist, Roosevelt had long believed that a war would reinvigorate the nation's unity and sense of manhood, which had suffered, he felt, during the 1890s. A few months shy of his fortieth birthday when war broke out, Roosevelt resigned his post as assistant secretary of the navy to raise a volunteer cavalry unit, which rushed to Cuba to participate in the fighting. Roosevelt envisioned his unit as a cross section of American society and enrolled athletes from Ivy League colleges, western cowboys, representatives of various immigrant groups, and even some American Indians. But with the army still segregated, he excluded blacks from his regiment. Ironically, when the Rough Riders reached the top of San Juan Hill, they found that black units had preceded them—a fact Roosevelt omitted in his reports of the battle, which were widely reproduced in the popular press. His heroic exploits made Roosevelt a national hero. He was elected governor of New York that fall and in 1900 became McKinley's vice president.

AN AMERICAN EMPIRE

With the backing of the yellow press, the war quickly escalated from a crusade to aid the suffering Cubans to an imperial venture that ended with the United States in possession of a small overseas empire. In July 1898, the United States annexed the Hawaiian Islands. McKinley also became convinced that the United States could neither return the Philippines to Spain

In both the Caribbean and the Pacific, the United States achieved swift victories over Spain in the Spanish-American War.

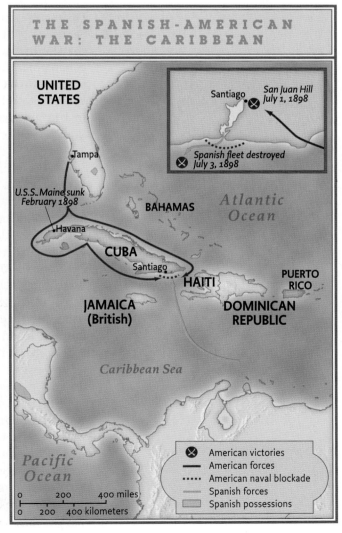

nor grant them independence, for which he believed the inhabitants unprepared. In an interview with a group of Methodist ministers, the president spoke of receiving a divine revelation that Americans had a duty to "uplift and civilize" the Filipino people and to train them for self-government. In the treaty with Spain ending the war, the United States acquired the Philippines, Puerto Rico, and the Pacific island of Guam. As for Cuba, before recognizing its independence, McKinley forced the island's new government to approve the Platt Amendment to the new Cuban constitution (drafted by Senator Orville H. Platt of Connecticut), which authorized the United States to intervene militarily whenever it saw fit. The United States also acquired a permanent lease on naval stations in Cuba, including what is now the facility at Guantánamo Bay.

American interest in its new possessions had more to do with trade than gaining wealth from natural resources or large-scale American settlement. Puerto Rico and Cuba (where the United States retained a naval base at Guantánamo Bay even after recognizing the island's independence) were gateways to Latin America, strategic outposts from which American naval and commercial power could be projected throughout the hemisphere. The Philippines, Guam, and Hawaii lay astride shipping routes to the markets of Japan and China. In 1899, soon after the end of the Spanish-American War, Secretary of State John Hay announced the Open Door policy, demanding that European powers that had recently divided China into commercial spheres of influence grant equal access to American exports. The Open Door referred to the free movement of goods and money, not people. Even as the United States banned the immigration of Chinese into this country, it insisted on access to the markets and investment opportunities of Asia.

THE PHILIPPINE WAR

Many Cubans, Filipinos, and Puerto Ricans had welcomed American intervention as a way of breaking Spain's long hold on these colonies. Large planters looked forward to greater access to American markets, and local elites hoped that the American presence would fend off radical changes proposed by rebellious nationalist movements. Nationalists and labor leaders admired America's democratic ideals and believed that American participation in the destruction of Spanish rule would lead to social reform and political self-government.

But the American determination to exercise continued control, direct or indirect, led to a rapid change in local opinion, nowhere more so than the Philippines. Filipinos had been fighting a war against Spain since 1896. After Dewey's victory at Manila Bay, their leader, Emilio Aguinaldo, established a provisional government with a constitution modeled on that of the United States. But once McKinley decided to retain possession of the islands, the Filipino movement turned against the United States. The result was a second war, far longer (it lasted from 1899 to 1903) and bloodier (it cost the lives of well over 100,000 Filipinos and 4,200 Americans) than the Spanish-American conflict. Today, this is perhaps the least remembered of all American wars. At the time, however, it was closely followed and widely debated in the United States. Press reports of atrocities committed by Amer-

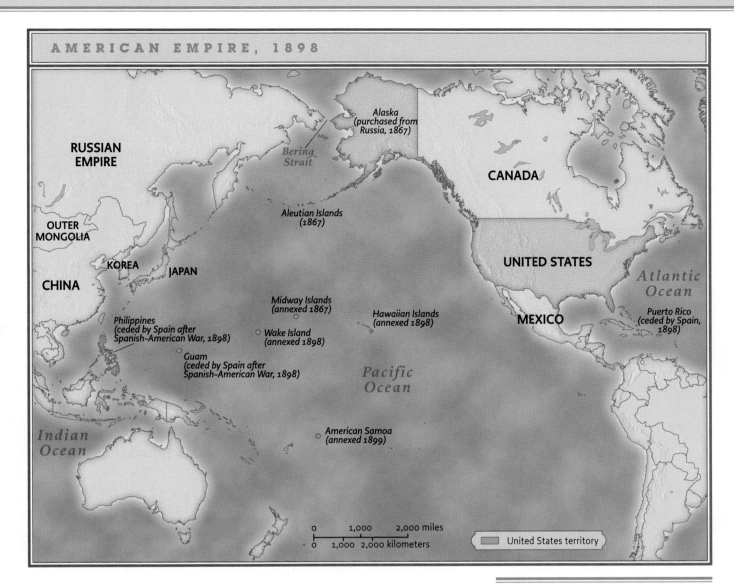

AMERICAN EMPIRE, 1898

RUSSIAN EMPIRE

Alaska (purchased from Russia, 1867)

Bering Strait

CANADA

OUTER MONGOLIA

Aleutian Islands (1867)

KOREA   JAPAN

UNITED STATES

Atlantic Ocean

CHINA

Midway Islands (annexed 1867)

Hawaiian Islands (annexed 1898)

MEXICO

Puerto Rico (ceded by Spain, 1898)

Philippines (ceded by Spain after Spanish-American War, 1898)

Wake Island (annexed 1898)

Guam (ceded by Spain after Spanish-American War, 1898)

Pacific Ocean

Indian Ocean

American Samoa (annexed 1899)

0   1,000   2,000 miles
0   1,000   2,000 kilometers

United States territory

---

ican troops—the burning of villages, torture of prisoners of war, and rape and execution of civilians—tarnished the nation's self-image as liberators. "We do not intend to free the people of the Philippines," complained Mark Twain. "We have gone there to conquer."

The McKinley administration justified its policies on the grounds that its aim was to "uplift and civilize and Christianize" the Filipinos (although most residents of the islands were already Roman Catholics). William Howard Taft, who became governor of the Philippines in 1901, believed it might take a century to raise Filipinos to the condition where they could appreciate "what Anglo-Saxon liberty is."

Once in control of the Philippines, American authorities embarked on programs of economic modernization. The colonial administration expanded the islands' harbors and railroads and brought in American schoolteachers and public health officials. Yet in all the new possessions, American policies tended to serve the interests of land-based local elites—

As a result of the Spanish-American War, the United States became the ruler of a far-flung overseas empire.

Some of the 1,200 Filipinos exhibited at the 1904 Louisiana Purchase Exposition in St. Louis. The federal government displayed the Filipinos in a "native" setting in order to win public support for the annexation of the Philippines.

native-born landowners in the Philippines, American sugar planters in Hawaii and Puerto Rico—and such policies bequeathed enduring poverty to the mass of the rural population. Under American rule, Puerto Rico, previously an island of diversified small farmers, became a low-wage plantation economy controlled by absentee corporations. By the 1920s, its residents were among the poorest in the entire Caribbean.

CITIZENS OR SUBJECTS?

American rule also brought with it American racial attitudes. In an 1899 poem, the British writer Rudyard Kipling urged the United States to take up the "white man's burden" of imperialism. American proponents of empire agreed that the domination of non-white peoples by whites formed part of the progress of civilization. Among the soldiers sent to the Philippines to fight Aguinaldo were a number of black regiments. Their letters from the front suggested that American atrocities arose from white troops applying to the Filipino population the same "treatment for colored peoples" practiced at home. "Is America any better than Spain?" wondered George W. Prioleau, a black cavalryman who had fought at San Juan Hill.

America's triumphant entry into the ranks of imperial powers sparked an intense debate over the relationship among political democracy, race, and American citizenship. The American system of government had no provision for permanent colonies. The right of every people to self-government was one of the main principles of the Declaration of Independence. The idea of an "empire of liberty" assumed that new territories would eventually be admitted as equal states and their residents would be American citizens. In the aftermath of the Spanish-American War, however, nationalism, democracy, and American freedom emerged more closely identified than ever with notions of Anglo-Saxon superiority.

Leaders of both parties, while determined to retain the new overseas possessions, feared that people of what one congressman called "an alien race and foreign tongue" could not be incorporated into the Union. The Foraker Act of 1900 declared Puerto Rico an "insular territory," different from previous territories in the West. Its 1 million inhabitants were defined as citizens of Puerto Rico, not the United States, and denied a future path to statehood. Filipinos occupied a similar status. In a series of cases decided between 1901 and 1904 and known collectively as the Insular Cases, the Supreme Court held that the Constitution did not fully apply to the territories recently acquired by the United States—a significant limitation of the scope of American freedom. Congress, the Court declared, must recognize the "fundamental" personal rights of residents of the Philippines and Puerto Rico. But otherwise it could govern them as it saw fit for an indefinite period of time. Thus, two principles central to American freedom since the War of Independence—no taxation without representation, and government based on the consent of the governed—were abandoned when it came to the nation's new possessions.

In the twentieth century, the territories acquired in 1898 would follow different paths. Hawaii, which had a sizable population of American missionaries and planters, became a traditional territory. Its population, except for Asian immigrant laborers, became American citizens. Hawaii would be admitted as a state in 1959. After nearly a half-century of American rule, the Philippines achieved independence in 1946. Until 1950, the U.S. Navy administered Guam, which remains today an "unincorporated" territory. As for Puerto Rico, it is sometimes called "the world's oldest colony," because ever since the Spanish conquered the island in 1493 it has lacked full self-government. Congress extended American citizenship to Puerto Ricans in 1917. Puerto Rico today remains in a kind of political limbo, poised on the brink of statehood or independence. The island has the status of a commonwealth. It elects its own government but lacks a voice in Congress and in the election of the U.S. president, and key issues such as defense and environmental policy are controlled by the United States.

School Begins, *an 1899 cartoon from* Puck, *suggests doubts about the project of "civilizing" non-whites in new American possessions. Uncle Sam lectures four unkempt black children, labeled "Philippines," "Hawaii," "Porto Rico," and "Cuba," while neatly dressed white pupils representing various states study quietly. In the background, an American Indian holds a book upside down, while a black child washes the window.*

"REPUBLIC OR EMPIRE?"

The emergence of the United States as an imperial power sparked intense debate. Opponents formed the Anti-Imperialist League. It united writers and social reformers who believed American energies should be directed at home, businessmen fearful of the cost of maintaining overseas outposts, and racists who did not wish to bring non-white populations into the United States. Among its prominent members were E. L. Godkin, the editor of *The Nation*, the novelist William Dean Howells, and the labor leader George E. McNeill. The League held meetings throughout the country and published pamphlets called Liberty Tracts, warning that empire was incompatible with democracy. America's historic mission, the League declared, was to "help the world by an example of successful self-government," not to conquer other peoples. A "republic of free men," anti-imperialists proclaimed, should assist the people of Puerto Rico and the Philippines in their own "struggles for liberty," rather than subjecting them to colonial rule.

In 1900, Democrats again nominated William Jennings Bryan to run against McKinley. The Democratic platform opposed the Philippine War for placing the United States in the "un-American" position of "crushing with military force" another people's desire for "liberty and self-government." George S. Boutwell, president of the Anti-Imperialist League, declared that the most pressing question in the election was the nation's future character—"republic or empire?"

But without any sense of contradiction, proponents of an imperial foreign policy also adopted the language of freedom. Anti-imperialists were the real "infidels to the gospel of liberty," claimed Senator Albert Beveridge of Indiana, because America ventured abroad not for material gain or national power, but to bring "a new day of freedom" to the peoples of the world. America's was a "benevolent" imperialism, rooted in a national mission to uplift backward cultures and spread liberty across the globe. Beveridge did not, however, neglect more practical considerations. American trade, he insisted, "henceforth must be with Asia. The Pacific is our ocean. . . . Where shall we turn for consumers of our surplus? Geography answers the question. China is our natural customer." And the Philippines held the key to "the commercial situation of the entire East." Riding the wave of patriotic sentiment inspired by the war, and with the economy having recovered from the depression of 1893–1897, McKinley in 1900 repeated his 1896 triumph.

At the dawn of the twentieth century, the United States seemed poised to take its place among the world's great powers. Writers at home and overseas confidently predicted that American influence would soon span the globe. In his 1902 book *The New Empire*, Brooks Adams, a grandson of John Quincy Adams, predicted that because of its economic power, the United States would soon "outweigh any single empire, if not all empires combined." Years would pass before this prediction was fulfilled. But in 1900, many features that would mark American life for much of the twentieth century were already apparent. The United States had surpassed Britain, France, and Germany in industrial production. The merger movement of 1897–1904 (discussed in the previous chapter) left broad sections of the economy under the control of giant corporations. The political system had stabilized. The

Civilization Begins at Home, a cartoon from the New York World, *depicts a figure representing justice urging President McKinley to turn his attention from the Philippines to racial violence in the United States.*

A Republican campaign poster from the election of 1900 links prosperity at home and benevolent imperialism abroad as achievements of William McKinley's first term in office.

white North and South had achieved reconciliation, while rigid lines of racial exclusion—the segregation of blacks, Chinese exclusion, Indian reservations—limited the boundaries of freedom and citizenship.

Yet the questions central to nineteenth-century debates over freedom— the relationship between political and economic liberty, the role of government in creating the conditions of freedom, and the definition of those entitled to enjoy the rights of citizens—had not been permanently answered. Nor had the dilemma of how to reconcile America's role as an empire with traditional ideas of freedom. These were the challenges bequeathed by the nineteenth century to the first generation of the twentieth.

SUGGESTED READING

Aleinikoff, Alexander. *Semblances of Sovereignty: The Constitution, the State, and American Citizenship* (2002). Includes a careful discussion of the citizenship status of American minorities and residents of overseas possessions.

Blight, David. *Race and Reunion: The Civil War in American Memory* (2001). Examines how a memory of the Civil War that downplayed the issue of slavery played a part in sectional reconciliation and the rise of segregation.

Brands, H. W. *The Reckless Decade: America in the 1890s* (2002). A lively account of the decade.

Factor, Robert L. *The Black Response to America: Men, Ideals, and Organization from Frederick Douglass to the NAACP* (1970). Discusses black social and political thought, including that of Booker T. Washington and his critics.

Goodwyn, Lawrence. *The Populist Moment: A Short History of the Agrarian Revolt in America* (1978). A sympathetic account of the rise and fall of Populism.

Higginbotham, Evelyn. *Righteous Discontent: The Women's Movement in the Black Baptist Church, 1880–1920* (1993). Explains how black women developed ways of exerting their influence in public life even as black men were losing the right to vote.

Kraditor, Aileen S. *The Ideas of the Woman Suffrage Movement, 1890–1920* (1962). A careful examination of various tendencies in the movement for the right to vote for women.

Krause, Paul. *The Battle for Homestead, 1880–1892: Politics, Culture, and Steel* (1992). An account of the era's most celebrated conflict between capital and labor.

LaFeber, Walter. *The New Empire: An Interpretation of American Expansion, 1860–1898* (1963). A classic examination of the forces that led the United States to acquire an overseas empire.

Linn, Brian M. *The Philippine War, 1899–1902* (2000). A detailed history of America's "forgotten war."

McClain, Charles J. *In Search of Equality: The Chinese Struggle against Discrimination in Nineteenth-Century America* (1994). Explores how Chinese-Americans worked to combat the discrimination to which they were subjected and to assert their rights.

McMillen, Neil R. *Dark Journey: Black Mississippians in the Age of Jim Crow* (1989). A powerful account of black life in the segregation era and the boundaries within which it operated.

Perez, Louis A. *The War of 1898: The United States and Cuba in History and Historiography* (1998). Presents the Cuban side of the Spanish-American War, including a detailed discussion of the Cuban movement for independence and how American intervention affected it.

Sanders, Elizabeth. *Roots of Reform: Farmers, Workers, and the American State, 1877–1917* (1999). Emphasizes the role of farmers' movements in putting forth many of the proposals associated with political reform in the late nineteenth and early twentieth centuries.

Woodward, C. Vann. *Origins of the New South, 1877–1913* (1951). A classic treatment of the New South, emphasizing how its rulers failed to meet the needs of most southerners, white as well as black.

REVIEW QUESTIONS

1. Why were the Populists unable to get the mass support of the urban worker?

2. Describe the society of the New South. What changed after the Civil War and what remained constant?

3. Describe the debate sparked by the Spanish-American War over the relationship between political democracy, race, and citizenship.

4. What were the main characteristics of the new immigrants, and how were their freedoms limited by nativists?

5. How did blacks, women, and labor respond to the limitations placed on them in the Gilded Age?

KEY TERMS

agricultural expansion and decline (p. 632)

Coxey's Army (p. 642)

black voting (p. 650)

Yick Wo v. Hopkins (p. 658)

The U.S. Navy (p. 661)

sinking of the U.S.S. *Maine* (p. 663)

the press and war (p. 666)

REVIEW TABLE

Facing the Limits of Freedom

Group Affected	Challenge Faced	Response	Explanation
Blacks	Jim Crow laws; lynching	Booker T. Washington's "Atlanta Compromise"	Advocated a policy of accommodation and vocational education
Labor	Viewed as radical	Samuel Gompers's "business unionism"	Concentrated only on wages, hours, and working not conditions, social reform
Women	Denied the right to vote	Clubs like the Women's Christian Temperance Union	Allowed women to exert more influence on public affairs
Chinese	1882 Chinese Exclusion Act	*United States v. Wong Kim Ark*	Decision held that the Fourteenth Amendment awarded citizenship to American-born children of Chinese immigrants

CHAPTER 18

The Progressive Era, 1900–1916

A rare color photograph from around 1900 shows the teeming street life of Mulberry Street, on New York City's densely populated Lower East Side. The massive immigration of the early twentieth century transformed the life of urban centers throughout the country and helped to spark the Progressive movement.

FOCUS QUESTIONS

- Why was the city such a central element in Progressive America?

- How did the labor and women's movements change the meanings of American freedom?

- In what ways did Progressivism include both democratic and anti-democratic impulses?

- How did the Progressive presidents foster the rise of the nation-state?

It was late afternoon on March 25, 1911, when fire broke out at the Triangle Shirtwaist Company. The factory occupied the top three floors of a ten-story building in the Greenwich Village neighborhood of New York City. Here some 500 workers, mostly young Jewish and Italian immigrant women, toiled at sewing machines producing ladies' blouses, some earning as little as three dollars per week. Those who tried to escape the blaze discovered that the doors to the stairwell had been locked—the owners' way, it was later charged, of discouraging theft and unauthorized bathroom breaks. The fire department rushed to the scene with high-pressure hoses. But their ladders reached only to the sixth floor. As the fire raged, onlookers watched in horror as girls leapt from the upper stories. By the time the blaze had been put out, 46 bodies lay on the street and 100 more were found inside the building.

The Triangle Shirtwaist Company was typical of manufacturing in the nation's largest city, a beehive of industrial production in small, crowded factories. New York was home to 30,000 manufacturing establishments with over 600,000 employees—more industrial workers than the entire state of Massachusetts. Triangle had already played a key role in the era's labor history. When 200 of its workers tried to join the International Ladies' Garment Workers Union (ILGWU), the owners responded by firing them. This incident helped to spark a general walkout of female garment workers in 1909—the Uprising of the 20,000. Among the strikers' demands was better safety in clothing factories. The impoverished immigrants forged an alliance with middle- and upper-class female supporters, including members of the Women's Trade Union League, which had been founded in 1903 to help bring women workers into unions. Alva Belmont, the ex-wife of railroad magnate William Vanderbilt, contributed several of her cars to a parade in support of the striking workers. By the time the walkout ended early in 1911, the ILGWU had won union contracts with over 300 firms. But the Triangle Shirtwaist Company was not among them.

The Triangle fire was not the worst fire disaster in American history (seven years earlier, over 1,000 people had died in a blaze on the *General Slocum* excursion boat in New York Harbor). But it had an unrivaled impact on public consciousness. Over twenty years later, Franklin D. Roosevelt would refer to it in a press conference as an example of why the government needed to regulate industry. In its wake, efforts to organize the city's workers accelerated, and the legislature passed new factory inspection laws and fire safety codes.

Triangle focused attention on the social divisions that plagued American society during the first two decades of the twentieth century, a period known as the Progressive era. These were years when economic expansion produced millions of new jobs and brought an unprecedented array of goods within reach of American consumers. Cities expanded rapidly—by 1920, for

Policemen stare up as the Triangle fire of 1911 rages, while the bodies of factory workers who plunged to their deaths to escape the blaze lie on the sidewalk.

the first time, more Americans lived in towns and cities than rural areas. Yet severe inequality remained the most visible feature of the urban landscape, and persistent labor strife raised anew the question of government's role in combating social inequality. The fire and its aftermath also highlighted how traditional gender roles were changing as women took on new responsibilities in the workplace and in the making of public policy.

The word "Progressive" came into common use around 1910, as a way of describing a broad, loosely defined political movement of individuals and groups who hoped to bring about significant change in American social and political life. Progressives included forward-looking businessmen who realized that workers must be accorded a voice in economic decision making and labor activists bent on empowering industrial workers. Other major contributors to Progressivism were members of female reform organizations who hoped to protect women and children from exploitation, social scientists who believed that academic research would help to solve social problems, and members of an anxious middle class who feared that their status was threatened by the rise of big business.

Everywhere in early-twentieth-century America the signs of economic and political consolidation were apparent—in the power of a small directorate of Wall Street bankers and corporate executives, the manipulation of democracy by corrupt political machines, the rise of new systems of managerial control in workplaces. In these circumstances, wrote Benjamin P. DeWitt, in his 1915 book *The Progressive Movement*, "the individual could not hope to compete. . . . Slowly, Americans realized that they were not free."

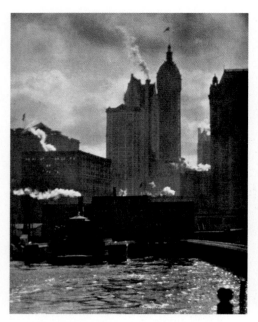

City of Ambition, *1910, by the photographer Alfred Stieglitz, captures the stark beauty of New York City's new skyscrapers.*

As this and the following chapter will discuss, Progressive reformers responded to the perception of declining freedom in varied, contradictory ways. The era saw the expansion of political and economic freedom through the reinvigoration of the movement for women's suffrage, the use of political power to expand workers' rights, and efforts to improve democratic government by weakening the power of city bosses and giving ordinary citizens more influence on legislation. It witnessed the flowering of understandings of freedom based on individual fulfillment and personal self-determination—the ability to participate fully in the ever-expanding consumer marketplace and, especially for women, to enjoy economic and sexual freedoms long considered the province of men. At the same time, many Progressives supported efforts to limit the full enjoyment of freedom to those deemed fit to exercise it properly. The new system of white supremacy born in the 1890s became fully consolidated in the South. Growing numbers of native-born Americans demanded that immigrants abandon their traditional cultures and become fully "Americanized." And efforts were made at the local and national levels to place political decision making in the hands of experts who did not have to answer to the electorate. Even as the idea of freedom expanded, freedom's boundaries contracted in Progressive America.

AN URBAN AGE AND A CONSUMER SOCIETY

FARMS AND CITIES

The Progressive era was a period of explosive economic growth, fueled by increasing industrial production, a rapid rise in population, and the continued expansion of the consumer marketplace. In the first decade of the twentieth century, the economy's total output rose by about 85 percent. For the last time in American history, farms and cities grew together. As farm prices recovered from their low point during the depression of the 1890s, American agriculture entered what would later be remembered as its "golden age." The expansion of urban areas stimulated demand for farm goods. Farm families poured into the western Great Plains. Over 1 million claims for free government land were filed under the Homestead Act of 1862—more than in the previous forty years combined. Between 1900 and 1910, the combined population of Texas and Oklahoma rose by nearly 2 million people, and Kansas, Nebraska, and the Dakotas added 800,000. Irrigation transformed the Imperial Valley of California and parts of Arizona into major areas of commercial farming.

Table 18.1 RISE OF THE CITY, 1880–1920		
Year	**Urban Population (Percentage)**	**Number of Cities with 100,000+ Population**
1880	20%	12
1890	28	15
1900	38	18
1910	50	21
1920	68	26

But it was the city that became the focus of Progressive politics and of a new mass-consumer society. Throughout the industrialized world, the number of great cities multiplied. The United States counted fifty cities whose population exceeded 100,000, the largest of them New York, with 4.7 million residents in 1910. The twenty-three square miles of Manhattan Island were home to over 2 million people, more than lived in thirty-three of the states. Fully a quarter of them inhabited the Lower East Side, an immigrant neighborhood more densely populated than Bombay or Calcutta in India.

The mansion of Cornelius Vanderbilt II on New York City's Fifth Avenue, in a 1920 photograph. Designed in the style of a French château, it took up the entire block. Today, the Bergdorf Goodman department store occupies the site.

The stark urban inequalities of the 1890s continued into the Progressive era. Immigrant families in New York's downtown tenements often had no electricity or indoor toilets. Three miles to the north stood the mansions of Fifth Avenue's Millionaire's Row. According to one estimate, J. P. Morgan's financial firm directly or indirectly controlled 40 percent of all financial and industrial capital in the United States. Alongside such wealth, reported the Commission on Industrial Relations, established by Congress in 1912, over one-third of the country's mining and manufacturing workers lived in "actual poverty."

Six O'Clock, Winter, *a 1912 painting by John Sloan, depicts a busy city street with an elevated railroad overhead. Sloan was one of a group of painters dubbed the Ashcan School because of their focus on everyday city life.*

The city captured the imagination of artists, writers, and reformers. The glories of the American landscape had been the focal point of nineteenth-century painters (exemplified by the Hudson River school, which produced canvases celebrating the wonders of nature). The city and its daily life now became their preoccupation. Painters like George W. Bellows and John Sloan and photographers such as Alfred Stieglitz and Edward Steichen captured the electric lights, crowded bars and theaters, and soaring skyscrapers of the urban landscape. With its youthful, exuberant energies, the city seemed an expression of modernity itself.

THE MUCKRAKERS

Others saw the city as a place where corporate greed undermined traditional American values. At a time when over 2 million children under the age of fifteen worked for wages, Lewis Hine photographed child laborers to draw attention to persistent social inequality. A new generation of journalists writing for mass-circulation national magazines exposed the ills of industrial and urban life. *The Shame of the Cities* by Lincoln Steffens (published as a series in *McClure's Magazine* in 1901–1902 and in book form in 1904) showed how party bosses and business leaders profited from political corruption. *McClure's* also hired Ida Tarbell to expose the arrogance and economic machinations of John D. Rockefeller's Standard Oil Company. Published in two volumes in 1904, her *History of the Standard Oil Company* was the most substantial product of what Theodore Roosevelt disparaged as "muckraking"—the use of journalistic skills to expose the underside of American life.

Major novelists of the era took a similar unsparing approach to social ills. Theodore Dreiser's *Sister Carrie* (1900) traced a hopeful young woman's descent into prostitution in Chicago's harsh urban environment. Perhaps the era's most influential novel was Upton Sinclair's *The Jungle* (1906), whose description of unsanitary slaughterhouses and the sale of rotten meat stirred public outrage and led directly to the passage of the Pure Food and Drug Act and the Meat Inspection Act of 1906.

Two photographs by Lewis Hine, who used his camera to chronicle the plight of child laborers: a young spinner in a southern cotton factory and "breaker" boys who worked in a Pennsylvania coal mine.

IMMIGRATION AS A GLOBAL PROCESS

If one thing characterized early-twentieth-century cities, it was their immigrant character. The "new immigration" from southern and eastern Europe (discussed in Chapter 17) had begun around 1890 but reached its peak during the Progressive era. Between 1901 and the outbreak of World War I in Europe in 1914, some 13 million immigrants came to the United States, the majority from Italy, Russia, and the Austro-Hungarian empire. In fact, Progressive-era immigration formed part of a larger process of worldwide migration set in motion by industrial expansion and the decline of traditional agriculture. Poles emigrated not only to Pittsburgh and Chicago but to work in German factories and Scottish mines. Italians sought jobs in Belgium, France, and Argentina as well as the United States. As many as 750,000 Chinese migrated to other countries each year.

During the years from 1840 to 1924 (when immigration to the United States would be virtually cut off), perhaps 40 million persons emigrated to the United States and another 20 million to other parts of the Western Hemisphere, including Canada, Argentina, Brazil, and the Caribbean.

The century between 1815, when the Napoleonic Wars in Europe and the War of 1812 in the United States ended, and the outbreak of World War I in 1914, witnessed a series of massive shifts in the world's population. The 35 million people who crossed the Atlantic to North America formed the largest migration stream, but millions of migrants also moved to South America, eastern Russia, and various parts of Asia.

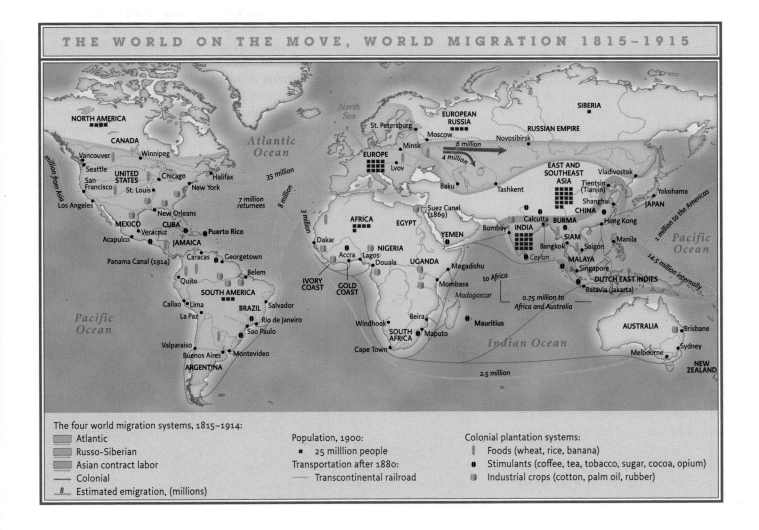

THE WORLD ON THE MOVE, WORLD MIGRATION 1815–1915

The four world migration systems, 1815–1914:
- Atlantic
- Russo-Siberian
- Asian contract labor
- — Colonial
- 8 Estimated emigration, (millions)

Population, 1900:
- ■ 25 milllion people

Transportation after 1880:
- ┈┈┈ Transcontinental railroad

Colonial plantation systems:
- Foods (wheat, rice, banana)
- Stimulants (coffee, tea, tobacco, sugar, cocoa, opium)
- Industrial crops (cotton, palm oil, rubber)

The cover of the New York World's *Sunday magazine, April 29, 1906, depicts some of the European immigrants who came to the United States. During the previous week, 45,000 immigrants had entered New York City through Ellis Island, pictured in the background.*

This population flow formed one part of a massive shifting of peoples throughout the world, much of which took place in Asia. Millions of persons migrated to Southeast Asia and the South Pacific, mainly from India and China. Millions more moved from Russia and northern Asia to Manchuria, Siberia, and Central Asia.

Numerous causes inspired this massive uprooting of population. Rural southern and eastern Europe and large parts of Asia were regions marked by widespread poverty and illiteracy, burdensome taxation, and declining economies. Political turmoil at home, like the revolution that engulfed Mexico after 1911, also inspired emigration. Not all of these immigrants could be classified as "free laborers," however. Large numbers of Chinese, Mexican, and Italian migrants, including many who came to the United States, were bound to long-term labor contracts. These contracts were signed with labor agents, who then provided the workers to American employers. But all the areas attracting immi-grants were frontiers of one kind or another—agricultural, mining, or industrial—with expanding job opportunities.

Most European immigrants to the United States entered through Ellis Island. Located in New York Harbor, this became in 1892 the nation's main facility for processing immigrants. Millions of Americans today trace their ancestry to an immigrant who passed through Ellis Island. The less fortunate, who failed a medical examination or were judged to be anarchists, prostitutes, or in other ways undesirable, were sent home.

At the same time, an influx of Asian and Mexican newcomers was taking place in the West. After the exclusion of immigrants from China in the late nineteenth century, a small number of Japanese arrived, primarily to work as agricultural laborers in California's fruit and vegetable fields and on Hawaii's sugar plantations. By 1910, the population of Japanese origin had grown to 72,000. Between 1910 and 1940, Angel Island in San Francisco Bay—the "Ellis Island of the West"—served as the main entry point for immigrants from Asia.

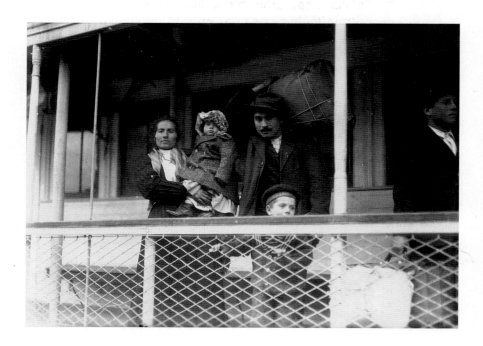

Italian Family on Ferry Boat, Leaving Ellis Island, *a 1905 photograph by Lewis Hine. The family of immigrants has just passed through the inspection process at the gateway to the United States.*

Far larger was Mexican immigration. Between 1900 and 1930, some 1 million Mexicans (over 10 percent of that country's population) entered the United States—a number exceeded by only a few European countries. Many Mexicans entered through El Paso, Texas, the main southern gateway into the United States. Many ended up in the San Gabriel Valley of California, where citrus growers searching for cheap labor had earlier experimented with Native American, South Asian, Chinese, and Filipino migrant workers.

By 1910, one-seventh of the American population was foreign-born, the highest percentage in the country's history. Over 40 percent of New York City's population had been born abroad. In Chicago and smaller industrial cities like Providence, Milwaukee, and San Francisco, the figure exceeded 30 percent. Although many newcomers moved west to take part in the expansion of farming, most clustered in industrial centers. By 1910, nearly three-fifths of the workers in the twenty leading manufacturing and mining industries were foreign-born.

THE IMMIGRANT QUEST FOR FREEDOM

Like their nineteenth-century predecessors, the new immigrants arrived imagining the United States as a land of freedom, where all persons enjoyed equality before the law, could worship as they pleased, enjoyed economic opportunity, and had been emancipated from the oppressive social hierarchies of their homelands. "America is a free country," one Polish immigrant wrote home. "You don't have to be a serf to anyone." Agents sent abroad by the American government to investigate the reasons for large-scale immigration reported that the main impetus was a desire to share in the "freedom and prosperity enjoyed by the people of the United States." Freedom, they added, was largely an economic ambition—a desire to escape from "hopeless poverty" and achieve a standard of living impossible at home. While some of the new immigrants, especially Jews fleeing religious persecution in the Russian empire, thought of themselves as permanent emigrants, the majority initially planned to earn enough money to return home and purchase land. Groups like Mexicans and Italians included many "birds of passage," who remained only temporarily in the United States. In 1908, a year of economic downturn in the United States, more Italians left the country than entered.

The new immigrants clustered in close-knit "ethnic" neighborhoods with their own shops, theaters, and community organizations, and often continued to speak their native tongues. As early as 1900, over 1,000 foreign-language newspapers were published in the United States. Churches were pillars of these immigrant communities. In New York's East Harlem, even anti-clerical Italian immigrants, who resented the close alliance in Italy between the Catholic Church and the oppressive state, participated eagerly in the annual festival of the Madonna of Mt. Carmel. After Italian-Americans scattered to the suburbs, they continued to return each year to reenact the festival.

Although most immigrants earned more than was possible in the impoverished regions from which they came, they endured low wages, long hours, and dangerous working conditions. In the mines and factories of Pennsylvania and the Midwest, eastern European immigrants performed

Table 18.2 IMMIGRANTS AND THEIR CHILDREN AS PERCENTAGE OF POPULATION, TEN MAJOR CITIES, 1920

City	Percentage
New York City	76%
Cleveland	72
Boston	72
Chicago	71
Detroit	65
San Francisco	64
Minneapolis	63
Pittsburgh	59
Seattle	55
Los Angeles	45

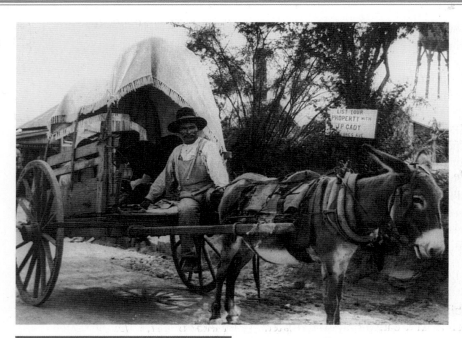

An immigrant from Mexico, arriving around 1912 in a cart drawn by a donkey.

low-wage unskilled labor, while native-born workers dominated skilled and supervisory jobs. The vast majority of Mexican immigrants became poorly paid agricultural, mine, and railroad laborers, with little prospect of upward economic mobility. "My people are not in America," remarked one Slavic priest, "they are under it."

CONSUMER FREEDOM

Cities, however, were also the birthplace of a mass-consumption society that added new meaning to American freedom. There was, of course, nothing unusual in the idea that the promise of American life lay, in part, in the enjoyment by the masses of citizens of goods available in other countries only to the well-to-do. Not until the Progressive era, however, did the advent of large downtown department stores, chain stores in urban neighborhoods, and retail mail-order houses for farmers and small-town residents, make available to consumers throughout the country the vast array of goods now pouring from the nation's factories. By 1910, Americans could purchase, among many other items, electric sewing machines, washing machines, vacuum cleaners, and record players. Low wages, the unequal distribution of income, and the South's persistent poverty limited the consumer economy, which would not fully come into its own until after World War II. But it was in Progressive America

In Hester Street, *painted in 1905, George Luks, a member of the Ashcan School of urban artists, captures the colorful street life of an immigrant neighborhood in New York City.*

that the promise of mass consumption became the foundation for a new understanding of freedom as access to the cornucopia of goods made available by modern capitalism.

Leisure activities also took on the characteristics of mass consumption. Amusement parks, dance halls, and theaters attracted large crowds of city dwellers. The most popular form of mass entertainment at the turn of the century was vaudeville, a live theatrical entertainment consisting of numerous short acts typically including song and dance, comedy, acrobats, magicians, and trained animals. In the 1890s, brief motion pictures were already being introduced into vaudeville shows. As the movies became longer and involved more sophisticated plot narratives, separate theaters developed. By 1910, 25 million Americans per week, mostly working-class urban residents, were attending "nickelodeons"—motion-picture theaters whose five-cents admission charge was far lower than at vaudeville shows.

THE WORKING WOMAN

The new visibility of women in urban public places—at work, as shoppers, and in places of entertainment like cinemas and dance halls—indicated that traditional gender roles were changing dramatically in Progressive America. As the Triangle fire revealed, more and more women were working for wages. Black women still worked primarily as domestics or in southern cotton fields. Immigrant women were largely confined to low-paying factory employment. But for native-born white women, the kinds of jobs available expanded enormously. By 1920, around 25 percent of employed women were office workers or telephone operators, and only 15 percent worked in domestic service, the largest female job category of the nineteenth century. Female work was no longer confined to young, unmarried white women and adult black women. In 1920, of 8 million women working for wages, one-quarter were married and living with their husbands.

The working woman—immigrant and native, working-class and professional—became a symbol of female emancipation. Women faced special limitations on their economic freedom, including wage discrimination and exclusion from many jobs. Yet almost in spite of themselves, union leader Abraham Bisno remarked, young immigrant working women developed a sense of independence: "They acquired the *right to a personality*,"

Theatre Unique, a New York City vaudeville house, photographed in 1908.

Year	All Women	Married Women	Women As % of Labor Force
1900	20.4%	5.6%	18%
1910	25.2	10.7	24
1920	23.3	9.0	24
1930	24.3	11.7	25

Table 18.3 PERCENTAGE OF WOMEN 14 YEARS AND OLDER IN THE LABOR FORCE

Women at work in a shoe factory, 1908.

Table 18.4 PERCENTAGE OF WOMEN WORKERS IN VARIOUS OCCUPATIONS

Occupation	1900	1920
Professional, technical	8.2%	11.7%
Clerical	4.0	18.7
Sales workers	4.3	6.2
Unskilled and semiskilled manufacturing	23.7	20.2
Household workers	28.7	15.7

The Return from Toil, *a drawing by John Sloan for the radical magazine* The Masses, *pictures working women not as downtrodden but as independent-minded, stylish, and self-confident.*

something alien to the highly patriarchal family structures of the old country. "We enjoy our independence and freedom" was the assertive statement of the Bachelor Girls Social Club, a group of female mail-order clerks in New York.

The growing number of younger women who desired a lifelong career, wrote Charlotte Perkins Gilman in her influential book *Women and Economics* (1898), offered evidence of a "spirit of personal independence" that pointed to a coming transformation of both economic and family life. Gilman's writings reinforced the claim that the road to woman's freedom lay through the workplace. In the home, she argued, women experienced not fulfillment but oppression, and the housewife was an unproductive parasite, little more than a servant to her husband and children. By condemning women to a life of domestic drudgery, prevailing gender norms made them incapable of contributing to society or enjoying freedom in any meaningful sense of the word.

The desire to participate in the consumer society produced remarkably similar battles within immigrant families of all nationalities between parents and their self-consciously "free" children, especially daughters. Contemporaries, native and immigrant, noted how "the novelties and frivolities of fashion" appealed to young working women, who spent part of their meager wages on clothing and makeup and at places of entertainment. Daughters considered parents who tried to impose curfews or to prevent them from going out alone to dances or movies as old-fashioned and not sufficiently "American." Immigrant parents found it very difficult to adapt to what one Mexican mother called "this terrible freedom in this United States." "The Mexican girls," she told a sociologist studying immigrant life in Los Angeles, "seeing American girls with freedom, they want it too."

THE RISE OF FORDISM

If any individual exemplified the new consumer society, it was Henry Ford. The son of an immigrant Irish farmer, Ford had worked as an apprentice in Michigan machine shops and later as an engineer for the Edison Illuminating Company. Ford did not invent the automobile, but he developed the techniques of production and marketing that brought it within the reach of ordinary Americans. In 1905, he established the Ford Motor Company, one of dozens of small automobile manufacturing firms that emerged in these years. Three years later, he introduced the Model T, a simple, light vehicle sturdy enough to navigate the country's poorly maintained roads. While early European models like the Mercedes aimed at an elite market and were superior in craftsmanship, Ford concentrated on standardizing output and lowering prices.

In 1913, Ford's factory in Highland Park, Michigan, adopted the method of production known as the moving assembly line, in which car frames were brought to workers on a continuously moving conveyor belt. The process enabled Ford to expand output by greatly reducing the time it took to produce each car. In 1914, he raised wages at his factory to the unheard of level of five dollars per day (more than double the pay of most industrial workers), enabling him to attract a steady stream of skilled laborers. Labor

The assembly line at the Ford Motor Company factory in Highland Park, Michigan, around 1915.

conditions in the Ford plant were not as appealing as the wages, however: assembly-line work was monotonous (the worker repeated the same basic motions for the entire day), and Ford used spies and armed detectives to prevent unionization. When other businessmen criticized him for endangering profits by paying high wages, Ford replied that workers must be able to afford the goods being turned out by American factories. Ford's output rose from 34,000 cars, priced at $700 each, in 1910, to 730,000 Model T's that sold at a price of $316 (well within the reach of many workers) in 1916. The economic system based on mass production and mass consumption came to be called Fordism.

THE PROMISE OF ABUNDANCE

As economic production shifted from capital goods (steel, railroad equipment, etc.) to consumer products, the new advertising industry perfected ways of increasing sales, often by linking goods with the idea of freedom. Numerous products took "liberty" as a brand name or used an image of the Statue of Liberty as a sales device. The department-store magnate Edward Filene called consumerism a "school of freedom," since shoppers made individual choices on basic questions of living. Economic abundance would eventually come to define the "American way of life," in which personal fulfillment was to be found through acquiring material goods.

The promise of abundance shifted the quest for freedom to the realm of private life, but it also inspired political activism. Exclusion from the world of mass consumption would come to seem almost as great a denial of the rights of citizenship as being barred from voting once had been. The desire for consumer goods led many workers to join unions and fight for higher

Table 18.5 SALES OF PASSENGER CARS	
Year	**Number of Cars (in thousands)**
1900	4.1
1905	24.2
1910	181.0
1915	895.9
1920	1,905.5
1925	3,735.1

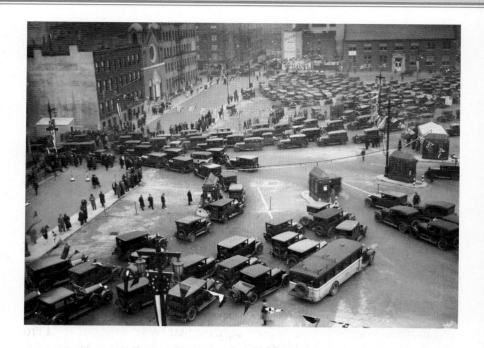

Cars entering the Holland Tunnel, which links New York City with New Jersey, in 1927. Most of the cars appear to be standardized Fords.

One of the numerous advertisements of the early twentieth century that invoked the Statue of Liberty to market consumer goods, in this case a brand of crackers.

wages. The argument that monopolistic corporations artificially raised prices at the expense of consumers became a weapon against the trusts. "Consumers' consciousness," wrote Walter Lippmann, who emerged in these years as one of the nation's most influential social commentators, was growing rapidly, with the "high cost of living" as its rallying cry.

AN AMERICAN STANDARD OF LIVING

The maturation of the consumer economy gave rise to concepts—a "living wage" and an "American standard of living"—that offered a new language for criticizing the inequalities of wealth and power in Progressive America. Father John A. Ryan's influential book *A Living Wage* (1906) described a decent standard of living (one that enabled a person to participate in the consumer economy) as a "natural and absolute" right of citizenship. Ryan had grown up in Minnesota in a family sympathetic to Henry George, the Knights of Labor, and the Populists. His book sought to translate into American terms Pope Leo XIII's powerful statement of 1894, *Rerum Novarum*, which criticized the divorce of economic life from ethical considerations, endorsed the right of workers to organize unions, and repudiated competitive individualism in favor of a more cooperative vision of the good society. Ryan's insistence that economic relationships should be governed by moral standards had a powerful influence on social thought among American Catholics.

The popularity of the idea of an American standard of living reflected, in part, the emergence of a mass-consumption society during the Progressive era. For the first time in the nation's history, mass consumption came to occupy a central place in descriptions of American society and its future. In the Gilded Age, social theorists like Henry George had wondered why economic progress produced both increased wealth and abject misery. The Progressive generation was strongly influenced by the more optimistic writings of Simon W. Patten, a prophet of prosperity. Patten announced the end of the "reign of want" and the advent of a society of abundance and leisure. In the dawning "new civilization," he proclaimed, Americans would enjoy economic equality in a world in which "every one is independent and free."

VARIETIES OF PROGRESSIVISM

For most Americans, however, Patten's "new civilization" lay far in the future. The more immediate task, in the Progressives' view, was to humanize industrial capitalism and find common ground in a society still racked by labor conflict and experiencing massive immigration from abroad. Some Progressives proposed to return to a competitive marketplace populated by small producers. Others accepted the permanence of the large corporation and looked to the government to reverse the growing concentration of wealth and to ensure social justice. Still others would relocate freedom from the economic and political worlds to a private realm of personal fulfillment and unimpeded self-expression. But nearly all Progressives agreed that freedom must be infused with new meaning to deal with the economic and social conditions of the early twentieth century. The "old democracy," wrote Walter Weyl, associate editor of *The New Republic*, a weekly magazine that became the "bible" of Progressive intellectuals, provided no answer to the problems of a world in which the "chief restrictions upon liberty" were economic, not political.

INDUSTRIAL FREEDOM

In Progressive America, complaints of a loss of freedom came not only from the most poorly paid factory workers but from better-off employees as well. Large firms in the automobile, electrical, steel, and other industries sought to implement greater control over the work process. Efficiency expert Frederick W. Taylor pioneered what he called "scientific management"—a program that sought to streamline production and boost profits by systematically controlling costs and work practices. Through scientific study, the "one best way" of producing goods could be determined and implemented. The role of workers was to obey the detailed instructions of supervisors. Not surprisingly, many skilled workers saw the erosion of their traditional influence over the work process as a loss of freedom. "Men and women," complained Samuel Gompers, whose American Federation of Labor (AFL) represented such skilled workers, "cannot live during working hours under autocratic conditions, and instantly become sons and daughters of freedom as they step outside the shop gates."

The great increase in the number of white-collar workers—the army of salespeople, bookkeepers, salaried professionals, and corporate managers that sprang up with the new system of management—also undermined the experience of personal autonomy. For although they enjoyed far higher social status and incomes than manual workers, many, wrote one commentator, were the kind of individuals who "under former conditions, would have been . . . managing their own businesses," not working for someone else.

These developments helped to place the ideas of "industrial freedom" and "industrial democracy," which had entered the political vocabulary in the Gilded Age, at the center of political discussion during the Progressive era. Lack of "industrial freedom" was widely believed to lie at the root of the much-discussed "labor problem." Since in an industrial age the prospect of managing one's own business seemed increasingly remote, many Progressives believed that the key to increasing industrial freedom lay in empowering workers to participate in economic decision making via strong unions. Louis D. Brandeis, an active ally of the labor movement whom President Woodrow Wilson appointed to the Supreme Court in 1916, maintained that unions embodied an essential principle of freedom—the right of people to govern themselves. The contradiction between "political liberty" and "industrial slavery," Brandeis insisted, was America's foremost social problem. Workers deserved a voice not only in establishing wages and working conditions but also in making such managerial decisions as the relocation of factories, layoffs, and the distribution of profits.

THE SOCIALIST PRESENCE

Economic freedom was also a rallying cry of American socialism, which reached its greatest influence during the Progressive era. Founded in 1901, the Socialist Party brought together surviving late-nineteenth-century radicals such as Populists and followers of Edward Bellamy, with a portion of the labor movement. The party called for immediate reforms such as free college education, legislation to improve the condition of laborers, and, as an ultimate goal, democratic control over the economy through public ownership of railroads and factories. It was the task of socialism, said western labor leader John O'Neill, to "gather together the shards of liberty"—the fragments of the American heritage of freedom—scattered by a government controlled by capitalist millionaires.

By 1912, the Socialist Party claimed 150,000 dues-paying members, published hundreds of newspapers, enjoyed substantial support in the American Federation of Labor, and had elected scores of local officials. Socialism flourished in diverse communities throughout the country. On the Lower East Side of New York City, it arose from the economic exploitation of immigrant workers and Judaism's tradition of social reform. Here, a vibrant socialist culture developed, complete with Yiddish-language newspapers and theaters, as well as large public meetings and street demonstrations. In 1914, the district elected socialist Meyer London to Congress. Another center of socialist strength was Milwaukee, where Victor Berger, a German-born teacher and newspaper editor, mobilized local AFL unions into a potent political force that elected Emil Seidel mayor in 1910. Seidel's administration provided aid to the unemployed, forced the police to recognize the rights of strikers, and won the respect of middle-class residents for its honesty and freedom from machine domination. Socialism also made inroads among tenant farmers in old Populist areas like Oklahoma, and in the mining regions of Idaho and Montana.

THE GOSPEL OF DEBS

No one was more important in spreading the socialist gospel or linking it to ideals of equality, self-government, and freedom than Eugene V. Debs, the railroad union leader who, as noted in the previous chapter, had been jailed during the Pullman Strike of 1894. For two decades, Debs criss-

Roller skaters with socialist leaflets during a New York City strike in 1916. A "scab" is a worker who crosses the picket line during a strike.

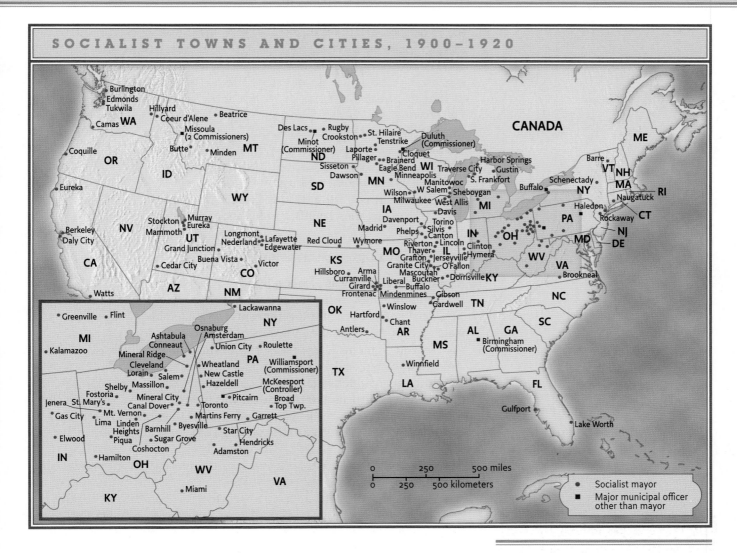

SOCIALIST TOWNS AND CITIES, 1900–1920

crossed the country preaching that control of the economy by a democratic government held out the hope of uniting "political equality and economic freedom." As a champion of the downtrodden, Debs managed to bridge the cultural divide among New York's Jewish immigrants, prairie socialists of the West, and native-born intellectuals attracted to the socialist ideal. "While there is a lower class," proclaimed Debs, "I am in it, . . . while there is a soul in prison, I am not free."

Throughout the Atlantic world of the early twentieth century, socialism was a rising presence. Debs would receive over 900,000 votes for president (6 percent of the total) in 1912. In that year, the socialist *Appeal to Reason*, published in Girard, Kansas, with a circulation of 700,000, was the largest weekly newspaper in the country, and socialist Max Hayes polled one-third of the vote when he challenged Samuel Gompers for the presidency of the AFL. In western Europe, socialism experienced even more pronounced growth. In the last elections before the outbreak of World War I in 1914, socialists in France, Germany, and Scandinavia won between one-sixth and one-third of the vote. "Socialism is coming," declared the *Appeal to Reason*. "It is coming like a prairie fire and nothing can stop it."

Although the Socialist Party never won more than 6 percent of the vote nationally, it gained control of numerous small and medium-sized cities between 1900 and 1920.

VOICES OF FREEDOM

FROM CHARLOTTE PERKINS GILMAN, Women and Economics (1898)

Women and Economics, by the prolific feminist social critic and novelist Charlotte Perkins Gilman, influenced the new generation of women aspiring to greater independence. It insisted that how people earned a living shaped their entire lives, and that therefore women must free themselves from the home to achieve genuine freedom.

It is not motherhood that keeps the housewife on her feet from dawn till dark; it is house service, not child service. Women work longer and harder than most men.... A truer spirit is the increasing desire of young girls to be independent, to have a career of their own, at least for a while, and the growing objection of countless wives to the pitiful asking for money, to the beggary of their position. More and more do fathers give their daughters, and husbands their wives, a definite allowance,—a separate bank account,—something ... all their own.

The spirit of personal independence in the women of today is sure proof that a change has come.... The radical change in the economic position of women is advancing upon us.... The growing individualization of democratic life brings inevitable change to our daughters as well as to our sons.... One of its most noticeable features is the demand in women not only for their own money, but for their own work for the sake of personal expression. Few girls today fail to manifest some signs of this desire for individual expression....

Economic independence for women necessarily involves a change in the home and family relation. But, if that change is for the advantage of individual and race, we need not fear it. It does not involve a change in the marriage relation except in withdrawing the element of economic dependence, nor in the relation of mother to child save to improve it. But it does involve the exercise of human faculty in women, in social service and exchange rather than in domestic service solely.... [Today], when our still developing social needs call for an ever-increasing ... freedom, the woman in marrying becomes the house-servant, or at least the housekeeper, of the man.... When women stand free as economic agents, they will [achieve a] much better fulfilment of their duties as wives and mothers and [contribute] to the vast improvement in health and happiness of the human race.

From John Mitchell, "The Workingman's Conception of Industrial Liberty" (1910)

During the Progressive era, the idea of "industrial liberty" moved to the center of political discussion. Progressive reformers and labor leaders like John Mitchell, head of the United Mine Workers, condemned the prevailing idea of liberty of contract in favor of a broader definition of economic freedom.

While the Declaration of Independence established civil and political liberty, it did not, as you all know, establish industrial liberty. . . . Liberty means more than the right to choose the field of one's employment. He is not a free man whose family must buy food today with the money that is earned tomorrow. He is not really free who is forced to work unduly long hours and for wages so low that he can not provide the necessities of life for himself and his family; who must live in a crowded tenement and see his children go to work in the mills, the mines, and the factories before their bodies are developed and their minds trained. To have freedom a man must be free from the harrowing fear of hunger and want; he must be in such a position that by the exercise of reasonable frugality he can provide his family with all of the necessities and the reasonable comforts of life. He must be able to educate his children and to provide against sickness, accident, and old age. . . .

A number of years ago the legislatures of several coal producing States enacted laws requiring employers to pay the wages of their workmen in lawful money of the United States and to cease the practice of paying wages in merchandise. From time immemorial it had been the custom of coal companies to conduct general supply stores, and the workingmen were required, as a condition of employment, to accept products in lieu of money in return for services rendered. This system was a great hardship to the workmen. . . . The question of the constitutionality of this legislation was carried into the courts and by the highest tribunal it was declared to be an invasion of the workman's liberty to deny him the right to accept merchandise in lieu of money as payment of his wages. . . . [This is] typical of hundreds of instances in which laws that have been enacted for the protection of the workingmen have been declared by the courts to be unconstitutional, on the grounds that they invaded the liberty of the working people. . . . Is it not natural that the workingmen should feel that they are being guaranteed the liberties they do not want and denied the liberty that is of real value to them? May they not exclaim, with Madame Roland [of the French Revolution], "O Liberty! Liberty! How many crimes are committed in thy name!"

QUESTIONS

1. What does Gilman see as the main obstacles to freedom for women?

2. What does Mitchell believe will be necessary to establish "industrial liberty"?

3. How do the authors differ in their view of the relationship of the family to individual freedom?

One Big Union, *the emblem of the Industrial Workers of the World.*

AFL AND IWW

Socialism was only one example of widespread discontent in Progressive America. The labor strife of the Gilded Age continued into the early twentieth century. Having survived the depression of the 1890s, the American Federation of Labor saw its membership triple to 1.6 million between 1900 and 1904. At the same time, it sought to forge closer ties with forward-looking corporate leaders willing to deal with unions as a way to stabilize employee relations. AFL president Gompers joined with George Perkins of the J. P. Morgan financial empire and Mark Hanna, who had engineered McKinley's election, in the National Civic Federation, which accepted the right of collective bargaining for "responsible" unions. It helped to settle hundreds of industrial disputes and encouraged improvements in factory safety and the establishment of pension plans for long-term workers. Most employers nonetheless continued to view unions as an intolerable interference with their authority, and resisted them stubbornly.

The AFL mainly represented the most privileged American workers—skilled industrial and craft laborers, nearly all of them white, male, and native-born. In 1905, a group of unionists who rejected the AFL's exclusionary policies formed the Industrial Workers of the World (IWW). Part trade union, part advocate of a workers' revolution that would seize the means of production and abolish the state, the IWW made solidarity its guiding principle, extending "a fraternal hand to every wage-worker, no matter what his religion, fatherland, or trade." The organization sought to mobilize those excluded from the AFL—the immigrant factory-labor force, migrant timber and agricultural workers, women, blacks, and even the despised Chinese on the West Coast. The IWW's most prominent leader was William "Big Bill" Haywood, who had worked in western mines as a youth. Dubbed by critics "the most dangerous man in America," Haywood became a national figure in 1906 when he was kidnapped and spirited off to Idaho, accused of instigating the murder of a former anti-union governor. Defended by labor lawyer Clarence Darrow, Haywood was found not guilty.

THE NEW IMMIGRANTS ON STRIKE

The Uprising of the 20,000 in New York's garment industry, mentioned earlier, was one of a series of mass strikes among immigrant workers that placed labor's demand for the right to bargain collectively at the forefront of the reform agenda. These strikes demonstrated that while ethnic divisions among workers impeded labor solidarity, ethnic cohesiveness could also be a basis of unity, so long as strikes were organized on a democratic basis. The IWW did not originate these confrontations but was sometimes called in by local unionists to solidify the strikers. IWW organizers printed leaflets, posters, and banners in multiple languages and insisted that each nationality enjoy representation on the committee coordinating a walkout. It drew on the sense of solidarity within immigrant communities to persuade local religious leaders, shopkeepers, and officeholders to support the strikes.

The labor conflict that had the greatest impact on public consciousness took place in Lawrence, Massachusetts. The city's huge woolen mills employed 32,000 men, women and children representing twenty-five nationalities. They worked six days per week and earned an average of six-

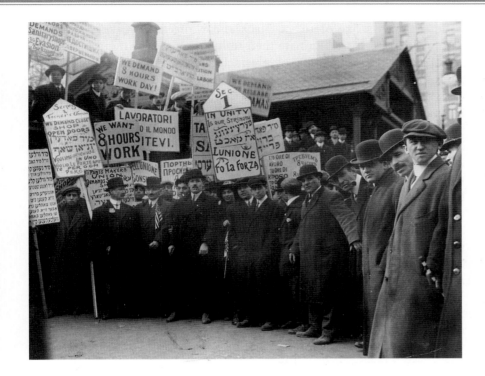

Striking New York City garment workers carrying signs in multiple languages, 1913.

teen cents per hour. When the state legislature in January 1912 enacted a fifty-four-hour limit to the workweek, employers reduced the weekly take-home pay of those who had been laboring longer hours. Workers spontaneously went on strike, and called on the IWW for assistance.

In February, Haywood and a group of women strikers devised the idea of sending strikers' children out of the city for the duration of the walkout. Socialist families in New York City agreed to take them in. The sight of the children, many of whom appeared pale and half-starved, marching up Fifth Avenue from the train station led to a wave of sympathy for the strikers. "I have worked in the slums of New York," wrote one observer, "but I have never found children who were so uniformly ill-nourished, ill-fed, and ill-

Striking textile workers at Lawrence, Massachusetts, in 1912, carrying American flags, were confronted by the state militia.

clothed." A few days later, city officials ordered that no more youngsters could leave Lawrence. When a group of mothers and children gathered at the railroad station in defiance of the order, club-wielding police drove them away, producing outraged headlines around the world. The governor of Massachusetts soon intervened, and the strike was settled on the workers' terms. A banner carried by the Lawrence strikers gave a new slogan to the labor movement: "We want bread and roses, too"—a declaration that workers sought not only higher wages but the opportunity to enjoy the finer things of life.

Another highly publicized labor uprising took place in New Orleans, where a 1907 strike of 10,000 black and white dockworkers prevented employers' efforts to eliminate their unions and reduce their wages. This was a remarkable expression of interracial solidarity at a time when segregation had become the norm throughout the South. Other strikes proved less successful. A six-month walkout of 25,000 silk workers in Paterson, New Jersey, in 1913 failed despite publicity generated by the Paterson pageant, in which the strikers reenacted highlights of their struggle before a sympathetic audience at New York's Madison Square Garden.

A strike against the Rockefeller-owned Colorado Fuel and Iron Company was also unsuccessful. Mostly recent immigrants from Europe and Mexico, the strikers demanded recognition of the United Mine Workers of America, wage increases, an eight-hour workday, and the right to shop and live in places not owned by the company. When the walkout began, in September 1913, the mine owners evicted 11,000 strikers and their families from company housing. They moved into tent colonies, which armed militia units soon surrounded. On April 20, 1914, the militia attacked the largest tent city, at Ludlow, and burned it to the ground, killing an estimated twenty to thirty men, women, and children. Seven months after the Ludlow Massacre, the strike was called off.

LABOR AND CIVIL LIBERTIES

The fiery organizer Mary "Mother" Jones, who at the age of eighty-three had been jailed after addressing the Colorado strikers, later told a New York audience that the union "had only the Constitution; the other side had the bayonets." Yet the struggle of workers for the right to strike and of labor radicals against restraints on open-air speaking made free speech a significant public issue in the early twentieth century. By and large, the courts rejected their claims. But these battles laid the foundation for the rise of civil liberties as a central component of freedom in twentieth-century America.

State courts in the Progressive era regularly issued injunctions prohibiting strikers from speaking, picketing, or distributing literature during labor disputes. Like the abolitionists before them, the labor movement, in the name of freedom, demanded the right to assemble, organize, and spread their views. The investigations of the Commission on Industrial Relations revealed the absence of free speech in many factory communities, with labor organizers prohibited from speaking freely under threat of either violence from private police or suppression by local authorities. "I don't think we live in a free country or enjoy civil liberties," Clarence Darrow told the commission.

The IWW's battle for civil liberties breathed new meaning into the idea of freedom of expression. Lacking union halls, its organizers relied on songs, street theater, impromptu organizing meetings, and street corner gatherings to spread their message and attract support. In response to IWW activities, officials in Los Angeles, Spokane, Denver, and more than a dozen other cities limited or prohibited outdoor meetings. To arouse popular support, the IWW filled the jails with members who defied local law by speaking in public. Sometimes, prisoners were brutally treated, as in Spokane, where three died and hundreds were hospitalized after being jailed for violating a local law requiring prior approval of the content of public speeches. In nearly all the free-speech fights, however, the IWW eventually forced local officials to give way. "Whether they agree or disagree with its methods or aims," wrote one journalist, "all lovers of liberty everywhere owe a debt to this organization for . . . [keeping] alight the fires of freedom."

THE NEW FEMINISM

During the Progressive era, the word "feminism" first entered the political vocabulary. One organization, the Feminist Alliance, constructed apartment houses with communal kitchens, cafeterias, and daycare centers, to free women from the constraints of the home. In 1914, a mass meeting at New York's Cooper Union debated the question "What is Feminism?" The meeting was sponsored by Heterodoxy, a women's club located in Greenwich Village that brought together female professionals, academics, and reformers. Feminism, said one speaker, meant women's emancipation "both as a human being and a sex-being." Feminists' forthright attack on traditional rules of sexual behavior added a new dimension to the discussion of personal freedom.

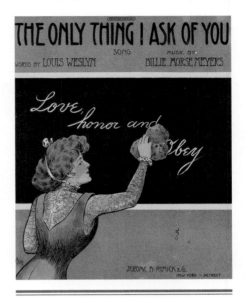

A sheet music cover, with a modern woman erasing the word "obey" from marriage vows.

Heterodoxy was part of a new radical "bohemia" (a social circle of artists, writers, and others who reject conventional rules and practices). Its definition of feminism merged issues like the vote and greater economic opportunities with open discussion of sexuality. In New York's Greenwich Village and counterparts in Chicago, San Francisco, and other cities, a "lyrical left" came into being in the prewar years. Its members formed discussion clubs, attended experimental theaters, and published magazines. They confidently expected to preside over the emancipation of the human spirit from the prejudices of the nineteenth century.

One symbol of the new era was Isadora Duncan, who brought from California a new, expressive dance based on the free movement of a body liberated from the constraints of traditional technique and costume. "I beheld the dance I had always dreamed of," wrote the novelist Edith Wharton on seeing a Duncan performance, "satisfying every sense as a flower does, or a phrase of Mozart's." Another sign of artistic revolution was the Armory Show of 1913, an exhibition that exposed New Yorkers to new cubist paintings from Europe by artists previously unknown in the United States, like Pablo Picasso.

The lyrical left made freedom the key to its vision of society. At the famed salon in heiress Mabel Dodge's New York living room, a remarkable array of talented radicals gathered to discuss with equal passion labor unrest, modern trends in the arts, and sexual liberation. Although many Progressives frequented the Dodge salon, there was a world of difference between the exuberant individualism of the lyrical left and most Progressives' preoccupation with order and efficiency. "What [women] are really after," explained Crystal Eastman, is *freedom.*" A graduate of New York University Law School, Eastman had taken a leading role both in the suffrage movement and in investigating industrial accidents. But her definition of freedom went beyond the vote, beyond "industrial democracy," to encompass emotional and sexual self-determination.

Isadora Duncan brought a new freedom to an old art form.

Modern ideas on War, Labor and the Sex Question are revolutionizing thought. If you believe in learning things yourself, it will pay you to hear

Emma Goldman

Who will deliver a Series of Lectures in Portland on Vital Subjects at

Portland, Subject and Dates:

Sunday, August 1st, 3 P. M.
THE PHILOSOPHY OF ANARCHISM

Sunday, August 1st, 8 P. M.
THE "POWER" OF BILLY SUNDAY

Monday, August 2nd, 8 P. M.
MISCONCEPTIONS OF FREE LOVE

Tuesday, August 3rd, 8 P. M.
FRIEDRICH NIETZSCHE—The Intellectual Storm Center of Europe

Wednesday, August 4th, 8 P. M.
JEALOUSY—Its Cause and Possible Cure

Thursday, August 5th, 8 P. M.
ANARCHISM AND LITERATURE

Friday, August 6th, 8 P. M.
THE BIRTH CONTROL (Why and How Small Families Are Desirable)

Saturday, August 7th, 8 P. M.
THE INTERMEDIATE SEX (A Discussion of Homosexuality)

Sunday, August 8th, 3 P. M.
WAR AND THE SACRED RIGHT OF PROPERTY

Sunday, August 8th, 8 P. M.
VARIETY OR MONOGAMY—WHICH?

ADMISSION 25 CENTS
8 Lectures With MOTHER EARTH, Subscription $2.50
OVER
Scandinavian Socialist Hall, 4th and Yamhill

The much-beloved and much-feared Emma Goldman, with a poster advertising a series of her lectures, illustrating the remarkable variety of topics on which she spoke.

THE RISE OF PERSONAL FREEDOM

During the Progressive era, as journalist William M. Reedy jested, it struck "sex o'clock" in America. The founder of psychiatry, Sigmund Freud, lectured at Clark University in Worcester, Massachusetts, in 1909, and discovered that his writings on infantile sexuality, repression, and the irrational sources of human behavior were widely known "even in prudish America." Issues of intimate personal relations previously confined to private discussion blazed forth in popular magazines and public debates.

For the generation of women who adopted the word "feminism" to express their demand for greater liberty, free sexual expression and reproductive choice emerged as critical definitions of women's emancipation. Greenwich Village became a center of sexual experimentation. The aura of tolerance attracted many homosexuals to the area, and although organized demands for gay rights lay far in the future, the gay community became an important element of the Village's lifestyle. But new sexual attitudes spread far beyond bohemia; they flourished among the young, unmarried, self-supporting women who made sexual freedom a hallmark of their oft-proclaimed personal independence.

THE BIRTH-CONTROL MOVEMENT

The growing presence of women in the labor market reinforced demands for access to birth control, an issue that gave political expression to changing sexual behavior. In the nineteenth century, the right to "control one's body" generally meant the ability to refuse sexual advances, including those of a woman's husband. Now, it suggested the ability to enjoy an active sexual life without necessarily bearing children. Emma Goldman, who had emigrated to the United States from Lithuania at the age of sixteen, toured the country lecturing on subjects from anarchism to the need for more enlightened attitudes toward homosexuality. She regularly included the right to birth control in her speeches and distributed pamphlets with detailed information about various contraceptive devices. "I demand freedom for both sexes," she proclaimed, "freedom of action, freedom in love and freedom in motherhood." Goldman constantly ran afoul of the law. By one count, she was arrested more than forty times for dangerous or "obscene" statements or simply to keep her from speaking.

By forthrightly challenging the laws banning contraceptive information and devices, Margaret Sanger, one of eleven children of an Irish-American working-class family, placed the issue of birth control at the heart of the new feminism. In 1911, she began a column on sex education, "What Every Girl Should Know," for *The Call*, a New York socialist newspaper. Postal officials barred one issue, containing a column on venereal disease, from the mails. The next issue of *The Call* included a blank page with the headline: "What Every Girl Should Know—Nothing; by order of the U. S. Post Office."

By 1914, the intrepid Sanger was openly advertising birth-control devices in her own journal, *The Woman Rebel.* "No woman can call herself free," she proclaimed, "who does not own and control her own body [and] can choose consciously whether she will or will not be a mother." In 1916, Sanger opened a clinic in a working-class neighborhood of Brooklyn and began distributing contraceptive devices to poor Jewish and Italian women, an action for which

Mothers with baby carriages wait outside Margaret Sanger's birth-control clinic in Brownsville, Brooklyn, 1916.

she was sentenced to a month in prison. Few Progressives rallied to her defense. But for a time, the birth-control issue became a crossroads where the paths of labor radicals, cultural modernists, and feminists intersected. The IWW and Socialist Party distributed Sanger's writings. Like the IWW free-speech fights and Goldman's persistent battle for the right to lecture, Sanger's travail was part of a rich history of dissent in the Progressive era that helped to focus enlightened opinion on the ways local authorities and national obscenity legislation set rigid limits to Americans' freedom of expression.

NATIVE-AMERICAN PROGRESSIVISM

Many groups participated in the Progressive impulse. Founded in 1911, the Society of American Indians was a reform organization typical of the era. It brought together Indian intellectuals to promote discussion of the plight of Native Americans in the hope that public exposure would be the first step toward remedying injustice. Because many of the Society's leaders had been educated at government-sponsored boarding schools, the Society united Indians of many tribal backgrounds. It created a pan-Indian public space independent of white control.

Many of these Indian intellectuals were not unsympathetic to the basic goals of federal Indian policy, including the transformation of communal landholdings on reservations into family farms. But Carlos Montezuma, a founder of the Society of American Indians, became an outspoken critic. Born in Arizona, he had been captured as a child by members of a neighboring tribe and sold to a traveling photographer, who brought him to Chicago. There Montezuma attended school and eventually obtained a medical degree.

In 1916, Montezuma established a newsletter, *Wassaja* (meaning "signaling"), that condemned federal paternalism toward the Indians and called for the abolition of the Bureau of Indian Affairs. Convinced that outsiders exerted too much power over life on the reservations, he insisted that self-determination was the only way for Indians to escape poverty and marginalization: "We must free ourselves. . . . We must be independent." But he also demanded that Indians be granted full citizenship and all the constitutional rights of other Americans. Montezuma's writings had little influence at the time on government policy, but Indian activists would later rediscover him as a forerunner of Indian radicalism.

THE POLITICS OF PROGRESSIVISM

EFFECTIVE FREEDOM

Progressivism was an international movement. In the early twentieth century, cities throughout the world experienced similar social strains arising from rapid industrialization and urban growth. In 1850, London and Paris were the only cities whose population exceeded 1 million. By 1900, there were twelve—New York, Chicago, and Philadelphia in the United States, and others in Europe, Latin America, and Asia. Facing similar social problems, reformers across the globe exchanged ideas and envisioned new social policies. Sun Yat-Sen, the Chinese leader, was influenced by the writings of Henry George and Edward Bellamy. The mayor of Osaka, Japan, called for a new "social economy" that replaced competition with cooperation.

As governments in Britain, France, and Germany instituted old age pensions, minimum wage laws, unemployment insurance, and the regulation of workplace safety, American reformers came to believe they had much to learn from the Old World. The term "social legislation," meaning governmental action to address urban problems and the insecurities of working-class life, originated in Germany but soon entered the political vocabulary of the United States.

Progressives believed that the modern era required a fundamental rethinking of the functions of political authority, whether the aim was to combat the power of the giant corporations, protect consumers, civilize the marketplace, or guarantee industrial freedom at the workplace. Drawing on the reform programs of the Gilded Age and the example of European legislation, Progressives sought to reinvigorate the idea of an activist, socially conscious government. Even in South Carolina, with its strong tradition of belief in local autonomy, Governor Richard I. Manning urged his constituents to modify their view of government as "a threat to individual liberty," to see it instead as "a means for solving the ills of the body politic."

Progressives could reject the traditional assumption that powerful government posed a threat to freedom, because their understanding of freedom was itself in flux. "Effective freedom," wrote the philosopher John Dewey, was far different from the "highly formal and limited concept of liberty" as protection from outside restraint. Freedom was a positive, not a negative, concept—the "power to do specific things." As such, it depended on "the *distribution* of powers that exists at a given time." Thus, freedom inevitably became a political question. "Freedom," wrote Dewey's brilliant young admirer, the writer Randolph Bourne, "means a democratic cooperation in determining the ideals and purposes and industrial and social institutions of a country."

STATE AND LOCAL REFORMS

Throughout the western world, social legislation proliferated in the early twentieth century. In the United States, with a political structure more decentralized than in European countries, state and local governments enacted most of the era's reform measures. In cities, Progressives worked to reform the structure of government to reduce the power of political bosses, establish public control of "natural monopolies" like gas and water works, and improve public transportation. They raised property taxes in order to spend more money on schools, parks, and other public facilities.

Gilded Age mayors Hazen Pingree and Samuel "Golden Rule" Jones pioneered urban Progressivism. A former factory worker who became a successful shoe manufacturer, Pingree served as mayor of Detroit from 1889 to 1897. He battled the business interests that had dominated city government, forcing gas and telephone companies to lower their rates, and established a municipal power plant. Jones had instituted an eight-hour day and paid vacations at his factory that produced oil drilling equipment. As mayor of Toledo, Ohio, from 1897 to 1905, he founded night schools and free kindergartens, built new parks, and supported the right of workers to unionize.

Children at play at the Hudson-Bank Gymnasium, built in 1898 in a New York immigrant neighborhood by the Outdoor Recreation League, one of many Progressive- era groups that sought to improve life in urban centers.

Since state legislatures defined the powers of city government, urban Progressives often carried their campaigns to the state level. Pingree became governor of Michigan in 1896, in which post he continued his battle against railroads and other corporate interests. Hiram Johnson, who as public prosecutor had secured the conviction for bribery of San Francisco political boss Abraham Ruef, was elected governor of California in 1910. Having promised to "kick the Southern Pacific [Railroad] out of politics," he secured passage of the Public Utilities Act, one of the country's strongest railroad-regulation measures, as well as laws banning child labor and limiting the working hours of women.

The most influential Progressive administration at the state level was that of Robert M. La Follette, who made Wisconsin a "laboratory for democracy." After serving as a Republican member of Congress, La Follette became convinced that an alliance of railroad and lumber companies controlled state politics. Elected governor in 1900, he instituted a series of measures known as the Wisconsin Idea, including nominations of candidates for office through primary elections rather than by political bosses, the taxation of corporate wealth, and state regulation of railroads and public utilities. To staff his administration, he drew on nonpartisan faculty members from the University of Wisconsin.

PROGRESSIVE DEMOCRACY

"We are far from free," wrote Randolph Bourne in 1913, "but the new spirit of democracy is the angel that will free us." Progressives hoped to reinvigorate democracy by restoring political power to the citizenry and civic harmony to a divided society. Alarmed by the upsurge in violent class conflict and the unrestricted power of corporations, they believed that political reforms could help to create a unified "people" devoted to greater democracy and social reconciliation. Yet increasing the responsibilities of government made it all the more important to identify who was entitled to political participation and who was not.

The Progressive era saw a host of changes implemented in the political process, many seemingly contradictory in purpose. The electorate was simultaneously expanded and contracted, empowered and removed from direct influence on many functions of government. Democracy was enhanced by the Seventeenth Amendment—which provided that United States senators be chosen by popular vote rather than by state legislatures—by widespread adoption of the popular election of judges, and by the use of primary elections among party members to select candidates for office. Several states, including California under Hiram Johnson, adopted the initiative and referendum (the former allowed voters to propose legislation, the latter to vote directly on it) and the recall, by which officials could be removed from office by popular vote. The era culminated with a constitutional amendment enfranchising women—the largest expansion of democracy in American history.

But the Progressive era also witnessed numerous restrictions on democratic participation, most strikingly the disenfranchisement of blacks in the South, a process, as noted in Chapter 17, supported by many white southern Progressives as a way of ending election fraud. To make city government more honest and efficient, many localities replaced elected mayors with appointed nonpartisan commissions or city managers—a change that insulated officials from machine domination but also from popular control. New literacy tests and residency and registration requirements, common in northern as well as southern states, limited the right to vote among the poor. Taken as a whole, the electoral changes of the Progressive era represented a significant reversal of the idea that voting was an inherent right of American citizenship. And, as will be noted in the next chapter, most white Progressives proved remarkably indifferent to the plight of African-Americans. The "fitness" of voters, not their absolute numbers, defined a functioning democracy.

GOVERNMENT BY EXPERT

"He didn't believe in democracy; he believed simply in government." The writer H. L. Mencken's quip about Theodore Roosevelt came uncomfortably close to the mark for many Progressive advocates of an empowered state. Most Progressive thinkers were highly uncomfortable with the real world of politics, which seemed to revolve around the pursuit of narrow class, ethnic, and regional interests. Robert M. La Follette's reliance on college professors to staff important posts in his administration reflected a larger Progressive faith in expertise. The government could best exercise intelligent control over society through a democracy run by impartial experts and in many respects unaccountable to the citizenry.

This impulse toward order, efficiency, and centralized management—all in the name of social justice—was an important theme of Progressive reform. The title of Walter Lippmann's influential 1914 work of social commentary, *Drift and Mastery*, posed the stark alternatives facing the nation. "Drift" meant continuing to operate according to the outmoded belief in individual autonomy. "Mastery" required applying scientific inquiry to modern social problems. The new generation of educated professionals, Lippmann believed, could be trusted more fully than ordinary citizens to solve America's deep social problems. Political freedom was less a matter of direct participation in government than of qualified persons devising the best public policies.

JANE ADDAMS AND HULL HOUSE

But alongside this elitist politics, Progressivism also included a more democratic vision of the activist state. As much as any other group, organized women reformers spoke for the more democratic side of Progressivism. Still barred from voting and holding office in most states, women nonetheless became central to the political history of the Progressive era. Women challenged the barriers that excluded them from formal political participation and developed a democratic, grassroots vision of Progressive government. In so doing, they placed on the political agenda new understandings of female freedom. The immediate catalyst was a growing awareness among women reformers of the plight of poor immigrant communities and the emergence of the condition of women and child laborers as a major focus of public concern.

A staff member greets an immigrant family at Hull House, the settlement house established in Chicago by Jane Addams.

The era's most prominent female reformer was Jane Addams, who had been born in 1860, the daughter of an Illinois businessman. After graduating from college, Addams, who never married, resented the prevailing expectation that a woman's life should be governed by what she called the "family claim"—the obligation to devote herself to parents, husband, and children. In 1889, she founded Hull House in Chicago, a "settlement house" devoted to improving the lives of the immigrant poor. Hull House was modeled on Toynbee Hall, which Addams had visited after its establishment in a working-class neighborhood of London in 1884. Unlike previous reformers, who had aided the poor from afar, settlement house workers moved into poor neighborhoods. They built kindergartens and playgrounds for children, established employment bureaus and health clinics, and showed female victims of domestic abuse how to gain legal protection. By 1910, over 400 settlement houses had been established in cities throughout the country.

SPEARHEADS FOR REFORM

Addams was typical of the Progressive era's "new woman." By 1900, there were over 80,000 college-educated women in the United States. Many found a calling in providing social services, nursing, and education to poor families in the growing cities. The effort of middle-class women to uplift the poor, and of laboring women to uplift themselves, helped to shift the center of gravity of politics toward activist government. Women like Addams discovered that even well-organized social work was not enough to alleviate the problems of inadequate housing, income, and health. Government action was essential. Hull House instigated an array of reforms in Chicago, soon adopted elsewhere, including stronger building and sanitation codes, shorter working hours and safer labor conditions, and the right of labor to organize.

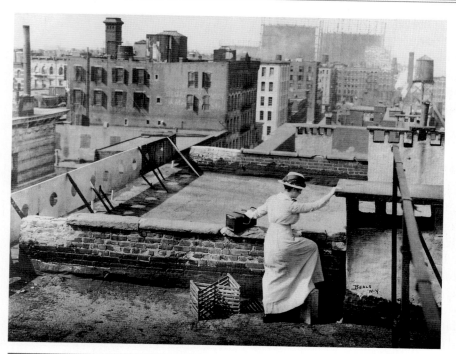

Visiting nurse on a New York city rooftop, 1908. Efforts to uplift the immigrant poor offered new opportunities for professional employment to many women during the Progressive era.

Female activism spread throughout the country. Ironically, the exclusion of blacks from jobs in southern textile mills strengthened the region's movement against child labor. Reformers portrayed child labor as a menace to white supremacy, depriving white children of educations they would need as adult members of the dominant race. These reformers devoted little attention to the condition of black children. Women's groups in Alabama were instrumental in the passage of a 1903 state law restricting child labor. By 1915, every southern state had followed suit. But with textile mill owners determined to employ children and many poor families dependent on their earnings, these laws were enforced only sporadically.

The settlement houses have been called "spearheads for reform." They produced prominent Progressive figures like Julia Lathrop, the first woman to head a federal agency (the Children's Bureau, established in 1912 to investigate the conditions of mothers and children and advocate their interests). Florence Kelley, the daughter of Civil War–era Radical Republican congressman William D. Kelley and a veteran of Hull House, went on to mobilize women's power as consumers as a force for social change. In the Gilded Age, the writer Helen Campbell had brilliantly exposed the contradiction of a market economy in which fashionable women wore clothing produced by poor women in wretched sweatshops. "Emancipation on the one side," she pointedly observed, "has meant no corresponding emancipation for the other." A generation later, under Kelley's leadership, the National Consumers' League became the nation's leading advocate of laws governing the working conditions of women and children. Freedom of choice in the marketplace, Kelley insisted, enabled socially conscious consumers to "unite with wage earners" by refusing to purchase goods produced under exploitative conditions.

THE CAMPAIGN FOR WOMEN'S SUFFRAGE

After 1900, the campaign for women's suffrage moved beyond the elitism of the 1890s to engage a broad coalition ranging from middle-class members of women's clubs to unionists, socialists, and settlement house workers. For the first time, it became a mass movement. Membership in the National American Woman Suffrage Association grew from 13,000 in 1893 to over 2 million by 1917. The group campaigned throughout the country for the right to vote and began to enjoy some success. By 1900, over half the states allowed women to vote in local elections dealing with school issues, and Wyoming, Colorado, Idaho, and Utah had adopted full women's suffrage.

Cynics charged that Wyoming legislators used suffrage to attract more female migrants to their predominantly male state, while Utah hoped to

In this 1912 women's suffrage parade in New York City, a mother wheels a baby carriage to counteract the charge that allowing women to vote would undermine the family.

enhance the political power of husbands in polygamous marriages banned by law but still practiced by some Mormons. In Colorado and Idaho, however, the success of referendums in the 1890s reflected the power of the Populist Party, a strong supporter of votes for women. Between 1910 and 1914, seven more western states enfranchised women. In 1913, Illinois became the first state east of the Mississippi River to allow women to vote in presidential elections.

These campaigns, which brought women aggressively into public space, were conducted with a new spirit of militancy. They also made effective use of the techniques of advertising, publicity, and mass entertainment characteristic of modern consumer society. California's successful 1911 campaign utilized automobile parades, numerous billboards and electric signs, and countless suffrage buttons and badges. Nonetheless, state campaigns were difficult, expensive, and usually unsuccessful. The movement increasingly focused its attention on securing a national constitutional amendment giving women the right to vote.

Two well-dressed Cincinnati women putting up a poster for women's suffrage, 1912.

MATERNALIST REFORM

Ironically, the desire to exalt women's role within the home did much to inspire the reinvigoration of the suffrage movement. Many of the era's experiments in public policy arose from the conviction that the state had an obligation to protect women and children. Female reformers helped to launch a mass movement for direct government action to improve the living standards of poor mothers and children. Laws providing for mothers' pensions (state aid to mothers of young children who lacked male support) spread rapidly after 1910. The pensions tended to be less than generous, and local eligibility requirements opened the door to unequal treatment (white widows benefited the most, single mothers were widely discriminated against, and black women were almost entirely excluded). "Maternalist" reforms like mothers' pensions rested on the assumption that the

*Louis D. Brandeis, Progressive reformer
and advocate of the labor movement,
appointed to the Supreme Court in 1916
by President Woodrow Wilson.*

government should encourage women's capacity for bearing and raising children and enable them to be economically independent at the same time. Both feminists and believers in conventional domestic roles supported such measures. The former hoped that these laws would subvert women's dependence on men, the latter that they would strengthen traditional families and the mother-child bond.

Other Progressive legislation recognized that large numbers of women did in fact work outside the home, but defined them as a dependent group (like children) in need of state protection in ways male workers were not. In 1908, in the landmark case of *Muller v. Oregon*, Louis D. Brandeis filed a famous brief citing scientific and sociological studies to demonstrate that because they had less strength and endurance than men, long hours of labor were dangerous for women, while their unique ability to bear children gave the government a legitimate interest in their working conditions. Persuaded by Brandeis's argument, the Supreme Court unanimously upheld the constitutionality of an Oregon law setting maximum working hours for women.

Thus, three years after the notorious *Lochner* decision invalidating a New York law limiting the working hours of male bakers (discussed in Chapter 16), the Court created the first large breach in "liberty of contract" doctrine. But the cost was high: at the very time that women in unprecedented numbers were entering the labor market and earning college degrees, Brandeis's brief and the Court's opinion solidified the view of women workers as weak, dependent, and incapable of enjoying the same economic rights as men. By 1917, thirty states had enacted laws limiting the hours of labor of female workers. Many women derived great benefit from these laws; others saw them as an infringement on their freedom.

While the maternalist agenda built gender inequality into the early foundations of the welfare state, the very use of government to regulate working conditions called into question basic assumptions concerning liberty of contract. Although not all reformers were willing to take the step, it was easy to extend the idea of protecting women and children to demand that government better the living and working conditions of men as well, by insuring them against the impact of unemployment, old age, ill health, and disability. Brandeis himself insisted that government should concern itself with the health, income, and future prospects of all its citizens.

THE IDEA OF ECONOMIC CITIZENSHIP

Brandeis envisioned a different welfare state from that of the maternalist reformers, one rooted less in the idea of healthy motherhood than in the notion of universal economic entitlements, including the right to a decent income and protection against unemployment and work-related accidents. For him, the right to assistance derived from citizenship itself, not some special service to the nation (as in the case of mothers) or upstanding character (which had long differentiated the "deserving" from the "undeserving" poor).

This vision, too, enjoyed considerable support in the Progressive era. By 1913, twenty-two states had enacted workmen's compensation laws to benefit workers, male or female, injured on the job, the entering wedge for broader programs of social insurance. To avoid the stigma of depending on governmental assistance, contributions from workers' own wages funded these programs in part, thus distinguishing them from charity dispensed by local authorities to the poor. But state minimum wage laws and most laws regulating working hours applied only to women. Women and children may have needed protection, but interference with the freedom of contract of adult male workers was still widely seen as degrading. The establishment of a standard of living and working conditions beneath which no American should be allowed to fall would await the coming of the New Deal.

THE PROGRESSIVE PRESIDENTS

Despite the ferment of Progressivism on the city and state levels, the most striking political development of the early twentieth century was the rise of the national state. The process of nationalization was occurring throughout American life. National corporations dominated the economy; national organizations like the American Medical Association came into being to raise the incomes and respect of professions. The process was even reflected in the consolidation of local baseball teams into the American and National Leagues and the advent in 1903 of the World Series. Only energetic national government, Progressives believed, could create the social conditions of freedom.

Despite creative experiments in social policy at the city and state levels, the tradition of localism seemed to most Progressives an impediment to a renewed sense of national purpose. Poverty, economic insecurity, and lack of industrial democracy were national problems that demanded national solutions. The democratic national state, wrote *New Republic* editor Herbert Croly, offered an alternative to control of Americans' lives by narrow interests that manipulated politics or by the all-powerful corporations. Croly proposed a new synthesis of American political traditions. To achieve the "Jeffersonian ends" of democratic self-determination and individual freedom, he insisted, the country needed to employ the "Hamiltonian means" of government intervention in the economy. Each in his own way, the Progressive presidents—Theodore Roosevelt, William Howard Taft, and Woodrow Wilson—tried to address this challenge.

THEODORE ROOSEVELT

In September 1901, the anarchist Leon Czolgosz assassinated William McKinley while the president visited the Pan-American Exposition in Buffalo, New York. At the age of forty-two, Vice President Theodore Roosevelt became the youngest man ever to hold the office of president. Roosevelt was an impetuous, energetic individual with a penchant for what he called the "strenuous life" of manly adventure. In many ways, he became the model for the twentieth-century president, an official actively and continuously engaged in domestic and foreign affairs. (The foreign policies of the Progressive presidents will be discussed in the next chapter.) Roosevelt regarded the president as "the steward of the public welfare." He moved aggressively to set the political agenda.

When the British writer H. G. Wells visited the United States soon after the turn of the century, he found that "the steady trend towards concentration" had become "the cardinal topic of thought and discussion in the American mind." Roosevelt's program, which he called the Square Deal, attempted to confront the problems caused by economic consolidation by distinguishing between "good" and "bad" corporations. The former, among which he included U.S. Steel and Standard Oil, served the public interest. The latter were run by greedy financiers interested only in profit, and had no right to exist.

Soon after assuming office, Roosevelt shocked the corporate world by announcing his intention to prosecute under the Sherman Antitrust Act the Northern Securities Company. Created by financier J. P. Morgan, this "holding company" owned the stock and directed the affairs of three major western railroads. It monopolized transportation between the Great Lakes and the Pacific. Morgan was outraged. "Wall Street is paralyzed," quipped one newspaper, "at the thought that a President of the United States should sink to enforce the law." In 1904, the Supreme Court ordered Northern Securities dissolved, a major victory for the antitrust movement.

ROOSEVELT AND ECONOMIC REGULATION

Roosevelt also believed that the president should be an honest broker in labor disputes, rather than automatically siding with employers as his predecessors had done. When a strike paralyzed the West Virginia and Pennsylvania coalfields in 1902, he summoned union and management leaders to the White House. By threatening a federal takeover of the mines, he persuaded the owners to allow the dispute to be settled by a commission he himself would appoint.

Reelected in 1904, Roosevelt pushed for more direct federal regulation of the economy. Appealing to the public for support, he condemned the misuse of the "vast power conferred by vast wealth." He proposed to strengthen the Interstate Commerce Commission, which the Supreme Court had essentially limited to collecting economic statistics. By this time, journalistic exposés, labor unrest, and the agitation of Progressive reformers had created significant public support for Roosevelt's regulatory program. In 1906, Congress passed the Hepburn Act, giving the ICC the power to examine railroads' business records and to set reasonable rates, a significant step in the development of federal intervention in the corporate economy. That year, as has been noted, also saw the Pure Food and Drug Act, which established a federal agency to police the quality and labeling of food and drugs, and the Meat Inspection Act. Many businessmen supported these measures, recognizing that they would benefit from greater public confidence in the quality and safety of their products. But they were alarmed by Roosevelt's calls for federal inheritance and income taxes and the regulation of all interstate businesses.

THE CONSERVATION MOVEMENT

A dedicated outdoorsman who built a ranch in North Dakota in the 1880s, Roosevelt also moved to preserve parts of the natural environment from

President Theodore Roosevelt addressing a crowd in Evanston, Illinois, in 1902.

economic exploitation. If the United States lagged behind Europe in many areas of social policy, it led the way in the conservation of national resources. The first national park, Yellowstone in Wyoming, had been created in 1872—partly to preserve an area of remarkable natural beauty, and partly at the urging of the Northern Pacific Railroad, which was anxious to promote western tourism. In the 1890s, the Scottish-born naturalist John Muir organized the Sierra Club to help preserve forests, which he called "God's first temples," from uncontrolled logging by timber companies and other intrusions of civilization. Congress in that decade authorized the president to withdraw "forest reserves" from economic development.

It was under Roosevelt that conservation became a concerted federal policy. Relying for advice on Gifford Pinchot, the head of the U.S. Forest Service, he ordered that millions of acres be set aside as wildlife preserves and encouraged Congress to create new national parks. The creation of parks like Yellowstone, Yosemite, and Glacier required the removal of Indians who hunted and fished there as well as the reintroduction of animals that had previously disappeared. City dwellers who visited the national parks did not realize that these were to a considerable extent artificially created and managed environments, not primordial nature.

In some ways, conservation was a typical Progressive reform. Manned by experts, the government could stand above political and economic battles, serving the public good while preventing "special interests" from causing irreparable damage to the environment. The aim was less to end the economic utilization of natural resources than to develop responsible, scientific plans for their use. Pinchot halted timber companies' reckless assault on the nation's forests. But unlike Muir, he believed that development and conservation could go hand in hand and that logging, mining, and grazing on public lands should be controlled, not eliminated. Conservation also reflected the Progressive thrust toward efficiency and control—in this case, control of nature itself.

In the view of Progressive conservationists, the West's scarcest resource—water—cried out for regulation. Governments at all levels moved to control the power of western rivers, building dams and irrigation projects to regularize their flow, prevent waste, and provide water for large-scale agriculture and urban development. With such projects came political conflict, as cities like Los Angeles and San Francisco battled with rural areas for access to water. After secretly buying up large tracts of land in the Owens Valley east of the city, for example, the City of Los Angeles constructed a major aqueduct between 1908 and 1913, over the vigorous objections of the valley's residents. By the 1920s, so much water had been diverted to the city that the once thriving farming and ranching businesses of Owens Valley could no longer operate.

Theodore Roosevelt and the conservationist John Muir at Glacier Point, Yosemite Valley, California, in 1906. Yosemite was set aside as a national park in 1890.

TAFT IN OFFICE

Having served nearly eight years as president, Roosevelt did not run again in 1908. His chosen successor was William Howard Taft, a federal judge from Ohio who had served as governor of the Philippines after the Spanish-American War. Taft defeated William Jennings Bryan, making his third unsuccessful race for the White House. Taft's inaugural address expressed the Progressive view of the state: "The scope of a modern government . . . has been widened far beyond the principles laid down by the old 'laissez-faire' school of political writers."

Although temperamentally more conservative than Roosevelt, Taft pursued antitrust policy even more aggressively. He persuaded the Supreme Court in 1911 to declare John D. Rockefeller's Standard Oil Company (one of Roosevelt's "good" trusts) in violation of the Sherman Antitrust Act and to order its breakup into separate marketing, producing, and refining companies. The government also won a case against American Tobacco, which the Court ordered to end pricing policies that were driving smaller firms out of business. In these decisions, the justices announced a new standard for judging large corporations—the "rule of reason"—which in effect implemented Roosevelt's old distinction between good and bad trusts. Big businesses were not, in and of themselves, antitrust violators, unless they engaged in policies that stifled competition.

Taft supported the Sixteenth Amendment to the Constitution, which authorized Congress to enact a graduated income tax (one whose rate of taxation is higher for wealthier citizens). It was ratified shortly before he left office. A 2 percent tax on incomes over $4,000 had been included in a tariff enacted in 1894 but had been quickly declared unconstitutional by the Supreme Court as a "communistic threat to property." The movement to resurrect the income tax united southern and western farmers who wished to reduce government dependence on revenue from the tariff, which they believed discriminated against nonindustrial states, and Progressives who believed that taxation should be based on the ability to pay. A key step in the modernization of the federal government, the income tax provided a reliable and flexible source of revenue for a national state whose powers, responsibilities, and expenditures were growing rapidly.

Despite these accomplishments, Taft seemed to gravitate toward the more conservative wing of the Republican Party. Only a few months after taking office, he signed the Payne-Aldrich Tariff, which reduced rates on imported goods but not nearly as much as reformers wished. Taft's rift with Progressives grew deeper when Richard A. Ballinger, the new secretary of the interior, concluded that Roosevelt had exceeded his authority in placing land in forest reserves. Ballinger decided to return some of this land to the public domain, where mining and lumber companies would have access to it. Gifford Pinchot accused Ballinger of colluding with business interests and repudiating the environmental goals of the Roosevelt administration. When Taft fired Pinchot in 1910, the breach with party Progressives became irreparable. In 1912, Roosevelt challenged Taft for the Republican nomination. Defeated, Roosevelt launched an independent campaign at the head of the new Progressive Party.

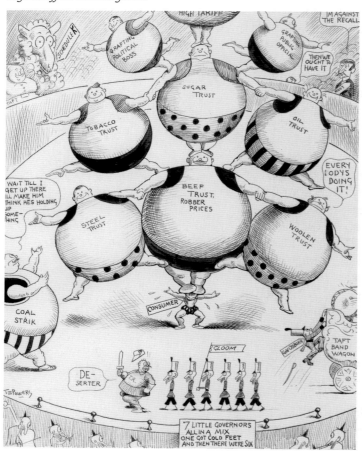

The Monopoly Brothers Supported by the Little Consumer, a cartoon from the New York American, April 2, 1912, shows the consumer supporting bloated monopolies and political bosses. Theodore Roosevelt marches by with a group of governors who had urged him to run for a third term, one of whom has abandoned him to support President Taft. Taft himself watches the performance on the upper left, seated next to a sheep representing the high tariff on woolen goods.

THE ELECTION OF 1912

All the crosscurrents of Progressive era thinking about what *McClure's Magazine* called "the problem of the relation of the State and the corporation" came together in the presidential campaign of 1912. The four-way contest between Taft, Roosevelt, Democrat Woodrow Wilson, and Socialist Eugene V. Debs became a national debate on the relationship between political and economic freedom in the age of big business. At one end of the political spectrum stood Taft, who stressed that economic individualism could remain the foundation of the social order so long as government and private entrepreneurs cooperated in addressing social ills. At the other end was Debs. Relatively few Americans supported the Socialist Party's goal of abolishing the "capitalistic system" altogether, but its immediate demands—including public ownership of the railroads and banking system, government aid to the unemployed, and laws establishing shorter working hours and a minimum wage—summarized forward-looking Progressive thought.

Eugene V. Debs, the Socialist Party candidate, speaking in Chicago during the 1912 presidential campaign.

But it was the battle between Wilson and Roosevelt over the role of the federal government in securing economic freedom that galvanized public attention in 1912. The two represented competing strands of Progressivism. Both believed government action necessary to preserve individual freedom, but they differed about the dangers of increasing the government's power and the inevitability of economic concentration. Though representing a party thoroughly steeped in states' rights and laissez-faire ideology, Wilson was deeply imbued with Progressive ideas. "Freedom today," he declared, "is something more than being let alone. The program of a government of freedom must in these days be positive, not negative merely." As governor of New Jersey, Wilson had presided over the implementation of a system of workmen's compensation and state regulation of utilities and railroads.

NEW FREEDOM AND NEW NATIONALISM

Strongly influenced by Louis D. Brandeis, with whom he consulted frequently during the campaign, Wilson insisted that democracy must be reinvigorated by restoring market competition and freeing government from domination by big business. Wilson feared big government as much as he feared the power of the corporations. The New Freedom, as he called his program, envisioned the federal government strengthening antitrust laws, protecting the right of workers to unionize, and actively encouraging small businesses—creating, in other words, the conditions for the renewal of economic competition without increasing government regulation of the economy. Wilson warned that corporations were as likely to corrupt government as to be managed by it, a forecast that proved remarkably accurate.

To Roosevelt's supporters, Wilson seemed a relic of a bygone era; his program, they argued, served the needs of small businessmen but ignored the inevitability of economic concentration and the interests of professionals,

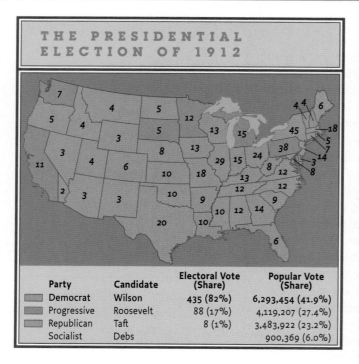

THE PRESIDENTIAL ELECTION OF 1912

Party	Candidate	Electoral Vote (Share)	Popular Vote (Share)
Democrat	Wilson	435 (82%)	6,293,454 (41.9%)
Progressive	Roosevelt	88 (17%)	4,119,207 (27.4%)
Republican	Taft	8 (1%)	3,483,922 (23.2%)
Socialist	Debs		900,369 (6.0%)

consumers, and labor. Wilson and Brandeis spoke of the "curse of bigness." What the nation actually needed, Walter Lippmann countered, was frank acceptance of the benefits of bigness, coupled with the intervention of government to counteract its abuses. Lippmann was expressing the core of the New Nationalism, Roosevelt's program of 1912. Only the "controlling and directing power of the government," Roosevelt insisted, could restore "the liberty of the oppressed." He called for heavy taxes on personal and corporate fortunes and federal regulation of industries, including railroads, mining, and oil.

The Progressive Party platform offered numerous proposals to promote social justice. Drafted by a group of settlement-house activists, labor reformers, and social scientists, the platform laid out a blueprint for a modern, democratic welfare state, complete with women's suffrage, federal supervision of corporate enterprise, national labor and health legislation for women and children, an eight-hour day and "living wage" for all workers, and a national system of social insurance covering unemployment, medical care, and old age. Described by Roosevelt as the "most important document" since the end of the Civil War, the platform brought together many of the streams of thought and political experiences that flowed into Progressivism. Roosevelt's campaign helped to give freedom a modern social and economic content and established an agenda that would define political liberalism for much of the twentieth century.

WILSON'S FIRST TERM

The Republican split ensured a sweeping victory for Wilson, who won about 42 percent of the popular vote, although Roosevelt humiliated Taft by winning about 27 percent to the president's 23 percent. In office, Wilson proved himself a strong executive leader. He established an office at the Capitol so that he could confer regularly with members of Congress about pending legislation, and he was the first president to hold regular press conferences in order to influence public opinion directly and continuously. He delivered messages personally to Congress rather than sending them in written form like all his predecessors since John Adams.

With Democrats in control of Congress, Wilson moved aggressively to implement his version of Progressivism. The first significant measure of his presidency was the Underwood Tariff, which substantially reduced duties on imports and, to make up for lost revenue, imposed a graduated income tax on the richest 5 percent of Americans. There followed the Clayton Act of 1914, which exempted labor unions from antitrust laws and barred courts from issuing injunctions curtailing the right to strike. In 1916 came the Keating-Owen Act outlawing child labor in the manufacture of goods sold in interstate commerce, the Adamson Act establishing an eight-hour workday on the nation's railroads, and the Warehouse Act, reminiscent of the Populist subtreasury plan, which extended credit to farmers when they stored their crops in federally licensed warehouses.

THE EXPANDING ROLE OF GOVERNMENT

Some of Wilson's policies seemed more in tune with Roosevelt's New Nationalism than the New Freedom of 1912. He abandoned the idea of aggressive trust-busting in favor of greater government supervision of the economy. Wilson presided over the creation of two powerful new public agencies. In 1913, Congress created the Federal Reserve System, consisting of twelve regional banks. They were overseen by a central board appointed by the president and empowered to handle the issuance of currency, aid banks in danger of failing, and influence interest rates so as to promote economic growth. The law was a delayed response to the Panic of 1907, when the failure of several financial companies threatened a general collapse of the banking system. With the federal government lacking a modern central bank, it had been left to J. P. Morgan to assemble the funds to prop up threatened financial institutions. Morgan's actions highlighted the fact that in the absence of federal regulation of banking, power over finance rested entirely in private hands.

A second expansion of national power occurred in 1914, when Congress established the Federal Trade Commission (FTC) to investigate and prohibit "unfair" business activities such as price-fixing and monopolistic practices. Both the Federal Reserve and FTC were welcomed by many business leaders as a means of restoring order to the economic marketplace and warding off more radical measures for curbing corporate power. But they reflected the remarkable expansion of the federal role in the economy during the Progressive era.

By 1916, the social ferment and political mobilizations of the Progressive era had given birth to a new American state. With new laws, administrative agencies, and independent commissions, government at the local, state, and national levels had assumed the authority to protect and advance "industrial freedom." Government had established rules for labor relations, business behavior, and financial policy, protected citizens from market abuses, and acted as a broker among the groups whose conflicts threatened to destroy social harmony. But a storm was already engulfing Europe that would test the Progressive faith in empowered government as the protector of American freedom.

SUGGESTED READING

Bodnar, John. *The Transplanted: A History of Immigrants in Urban America* (1985). A comprehensive account of American immigration.

Cameron, Ardis. *Radicals of the Worst Sort: Laboring Women in Lawrence, Massachusetts, 1860–1912* (1993). Describes the lives of working women in Lawrence and their role in the strike of 1912.

Cott, Nancy F. *The Grounding of Modern Feminism* (1987). A careful study of feminist ideas in the Progressive era.

Dawley, Alan. *Struggles for Justice: Social Responsibility and the Liberal State* (1991). Examines the varieties of Progressive reform and various efforts to use the power of government for social betterment.

Diner, Steven. *A Very Different Age: Americans of the Progressive Era* (1998). A survey of the main trends of the Progressive period.

Glickman, Lawrence B. *A Living Wage: Workers and the Making of American Consumer Society* (1997). Traces the origins and development of the idea that workers are entitled to a "living wage."

Hofstadter, Richard. *The Age of Reform: From Bryan to F. D. R.* (1955). A classic account of the ideas of reformers from Populism to the New Deal.

Johnston, Robert D. *The Radical Middle Class: Populist Democracy and the Question of Capitalism in Progressive Era Portland* (2003). Analyzes how Progressivism operated in one important city.

Maddox, Lucy. *Citizen Indians: Native American Intellectuals, Race, and Reform* (2005). A study of the Society of American Indians and other manifestations of Indian Progressivism.

Montgomery, David. *The Fall of the House of Labor: The Workplace, the State, and American Labor Activism, 1865–1925* (1987). An account of the labor battles of the era and the gradual decline of labor's power, especially at the workplace.

Orsi, Robert A. *The Madonna of 115th Street: Faith and Community in Italian Harlem, 1880–1950* (1985). An influential study of a single immigrant community and the role of religion in binding it together.

Peiss, Kathy. *Cheap Amusements: Working Women and Leisure in Turn-of-the-Century New York* (1986). Explores the rise of mass entertainment and how it affected women's lives in Progressive America.

Rodgers, Daniel T. *Atlantic Crossings: Social Politics in a Progressive Age* (1998). A comprehensive study of the flow of Progressive ideas and policies back and forth across the Atlantic.

Stansell, Christine. *American Moderns: Bohemian New York and the Creation of a New Century* (2000). A colorful account of the Greenwich Village radicals who expanded the idea of personal freedom in the Progressive era.

Stromquist, Shelton. *Re-Inventing "The People": The Progressive Movement, the Class Problem, and the Origins of Modern Liberalism* (2006). Discusses how the desire to re-create social harmony in an age of labor conflict shaped Progressivism.

CHAPTER REVIEW

REVIEW QUESTIONS

1. Describe how traditional gender roles were changing in the work place and the public sphere during the Progressive era.

2. Explain how and why Progressivism was an international movement.

3. Illustrate how Native Americans took part in the Progressive movement.

4. What were the main characteristics of the Progressive era?

5. How did each president of the Progressive era view the role of the federal government?

KEY TERMS

population growth (p. 678)

child labor (p. 680)

Mexican immigration (p. 683)

commission form of city government (p. 684)

censoring the movies (p. 685)

Seventeenth Amendment (p. 702)

Muller v. Oregon (p. 706)

coal miners' strike of 1902 (p. 708)

Roosevelt and conservation (p. 709)

REVIEW TABLE

Key Federal Legislation

Act	Date	Purpose
Hepburn Act	1906	To give the Interstate Commerce Commission the power to oversee railroad practices and rates
Pure Food and Drug Act	1906	To police the quality and labeling of food and drugs
Federal Reserve System	1913	To regulate interest rates and promote national economic growth
Federal Trade Commission	1914	To investigate and prohibit "unfair" business activities
Clayton Act	1914	To exempt labor unions from antitrust laws and allow unions the right to strike
Keating-Owen Act	1916	To outlaw child labor in manufacturing goods sold in interstate commerce
Adamson Act	1916	To establish an eight-hour work day on the nation's railroads

CHAPTER 19

Safe for Democracy: The United States and World War I, 1916–1920

The Greatest Department Store on Earth, a cartoon from Puck, *November 29, 1899, depicting Uncle Sam selling goods, mostly manufactured products, to the nations of the world. The search for markets overseas would be a recurring theme of twentieth-century American foreign policy.*

- In what ways did the Progressive presidents project American power abroad?

- How did the United States get involved in World War I?

- How did the United States mobilize resources and opinion for the war effort?

- How did the war accentuate Progressive attitudes toward race and ethnicity?

- Why was 1919 such a watershed year for the United States and the world?

In 1902, W. T. Stead published a short volume with the arresting title *The Americanization of the World; or, the Trend of the Twentieth Century.* Stead was an English editor whose sensational writings included an exposé of London prostitution, *Maiden Tribute of Modern Babylon.* He would meet his death in 1912 as a passenger on the *Titanic,* the ocean liner that foundered after striking an iceberg in the North Atlantic. Impressed by Americans' "exuberant energies," Stead predicted that the United States would soon emerge as "the greatest of world-powers." But what was most striking about his work was that Stead located the source of American power less in the realm of military might or territorial acquisition than in the country's single-minded commitment to the "pursuit of wealth" and the relentless international spread of American culture—art, music, journalism, even ideas about religion and gender relations. He foresaw a future in which the United States promoted its interests and values through an unending involvement in the affairs of other nations. Stead proved to be an accurate prophet.

The Spanish-American War had established the United States as an international empire. Despite the conquest of the Philippines and Puerto Rico, however, the country's overseas holdings remained tiny compared to those of Britain, France, and Germany. And no more were added, except for a strip of land surrounding the Panama Canal, acquired in 1903, and the Virgin Islands, purchased from Denmark in 1917. In 1900, Great Britain ruled over more than 300 million people in possessions scattered across the globe, and France had nearly 50 million subjects in Asia and Africa. Compared with these, the American presence in the world seemed very small. As Stead suggested, America's empire differed significantly from those of European countries—it was economic, cultural, and intellectual, rather than territorial.

The world economy at the dawn of the twentieth century was already highly globalized. An ever-increasing stream of goods, investments, and people flowed from country to country. Although Britain still dominated world banking and the British pound remained the major currency of international trade, the United States had become the leading industrial power. By 1914, it produced over one-third of the world's manufactured goods. Already, Europeans complained of an "American invasion" of steel, oil, agricultural equipment, and consumer goods. Spearheads of American culture like movies and popular music were not far behind.

America's growing economic connections with the outside world led to increasing military and political involvement. In the two decades after 1900, many of the basic principles that would guide American foreign policy for the rest of the century were formulated. The "open door"—the free flow of trade, investment, information, and culture—emerged as a key principle of American foreign relations. "Since the manufacturer insists on having the world as a market," wrote Woodrow Wilson, "the flag of his nation must follow him and the doors of nations which are closed against him must be battered down."

Americans in the twentieth century often discussed foreign policy in the language of freedom. At least in rhetoric, the United States ventured abroad—including intervening militarily in the affairs of other nations—not to pursue strategic goals or to make the world safe for American economic interests, but to promote liberty and democracy. A supreme faith in America's historic destiny and in the righteousness of its ideals enabled the country's leaders to think of the United States simultaneously as an emerging great power and as the worldwide embodiment of freedom.

More than any other individual, Woodrow Wilson articulated this vision of America's relationship to the rest of the world. His foreign policy, called by historians "liberal internationalism," rested on the conviction that economic and political progress went hand in hand. Thus, greater worldwide freedom would follow inevitably from increased American investment and trade abroad. Frequently during the twentieth century, this conviction would serve as a mask for American power and self-interest. It would also inspire sincere efforts to bring freedom to other peoples. In either case, liberal internationalism represented a shift from the nineteenth-century tradition of promoting freedom primarily by example, to active intervention to remake the world in the American image.

American involvement in World War I provided the first great test of Wilson's belief that American power could "make the world safe for democracy." Most Progressives embraced the country's participation in the war, believing that the United States could help to spread Progressive values throughout the world. But rather than bringing Progressivism to other peoples, the war destroyed it at home. The government quickly came to view critics of American involvement not simply as citizens with a different set of opinions, but as enemies of the very ideas of democracy and freedom. As a result, the war produced one of the most sweeping repressions of the right to dissent in all of American history.

A 1906 pamphlet published by the United Fruit Company, seeking to encourage consumption of bananas grown on its plantations in Central America. United Fruit was a major beneficiary of American interventions in the region.

AN ERA OF INTERVENTION

Just as they expanded the powers of the federal government in domestic affairs, the Progressive presidents were not reluctant to project American power outside the country's borders. At first, their interventions were confined to the Western Hemisphere, whose affairs the United States had claimed a special right to oversee ever since the Monroe Doctrine of 1823. Between 1901 and 1920, U.S. marines landed in Caribbean countries more

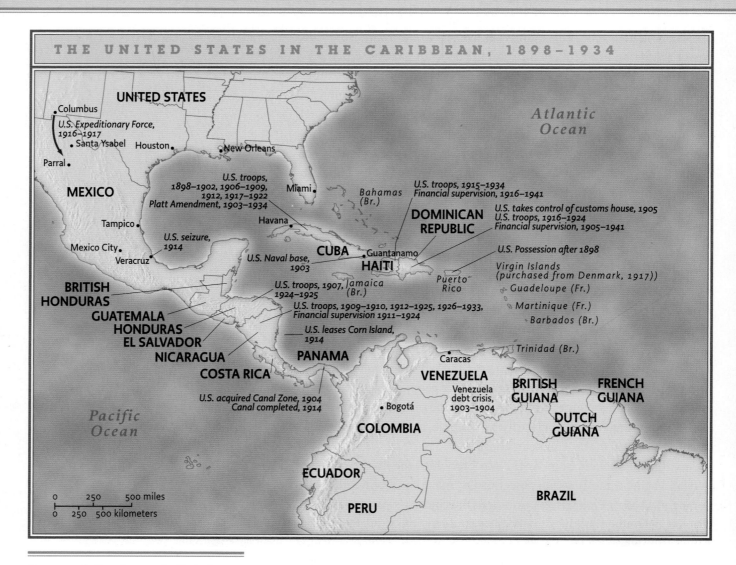

THE UNITED STATES IN THE CARIBBEAN, 1898–1934

UNITED STATES

Columbus

U.S. Expeditionary Force, 1916–1917

Santa Ysabel   Houston

New Orleans

Parral

Atlantic Ocean

MEXICO

Tampico

Mexico City
Veracruz

U.S. seizure, 1914

BRITISH HONDURAS

GUATEMALA
HONDURAS
EL SALVADOR
NICARAGUA

COSTA RICA

Pacific Ocean

Miami

U.S. troops, 1898–1902, 1906–1909, 1912, 1917–1922
Platt Amendment, 1903–1934

Havana

CUBA

U.S. Naval base, 1903

Guantanamo

HAITI

U.S. troops, 1907,
1924–1925

Jamaica
(Br.)

U.S. troops, 1909–1910, 1912–1925, 1926–1933,
Financial supervision 1911–1924

U.S. leases Corn Island,
1914

PANAMA

U.S. acquired Canal Zone, 1904
Canal completed, 1914

Bahamas
(Br.)

DOMINICAN
REPUBLIC

U.S. troops, 1915–1934
Financial supervision, 1916–1941

U.S. takes control of customs house, 1905
U.S. troops, 1916–1924
Financial supervision, 1905–1941

U.S. Possession after 1898

Puerto
Rico

Virgin Islands
(purchased from Denmark, 1917))

Guadeloupe (Fr.)

Martinique (Fr.)

Barbados (Br.)

Trinidad (Br.)

Caracas

VENEZUELA

Venezuela
debt crisis,
1903–1904

BRITISH
GUIANA

FRENCH
GUIANA

DUTCH
GUIANA

Bogotá

COLOMBIA

ECUADOR

PERU

BRAZIL

0   250   500 miles
0   250   500 kilometers

Between 1898 and 1934, the United States intervened militarily numerous times in Caribbean countries, generally to protect the economic interests of American banks and investors.

than twenty times. Usually, they were dispatched to create a welcoming economic environment for American companies that wanted stable access to raw materials like bananas and sugar, and for bankers nervous that their loans to local governments might not be repaid.

"I TOOK THE CANAL ZONE"

Just as he distinguished between good and bad trusts, Theodore Roosevelt divided the world into "civilized" and "uncivilized" nations. The former, he believed, had an obligation to establish order in an unruly world. Roosevelt became far more active in international diplomacy than most of his predecessors, helping, for example, to negotiate a settlement of the Russo-Japanese War of 1905, a feat for which he was awarded the Nobel Peace Prize. Closer to home, his policies were more aggressive. "I have always been fond of the West African proverb," he wrote, " 'Speak softly and carry a big stick.' " And although he declared that the United States "has not the slightest desire for territorial aggrandizement at the expense of its southern neighbors," Roosevelt pursued a policy of intervention in Central America.

In his first major action in the region, Roosevelt engineered the separation of Panama from Colombia in order to facilitate the construction of a canal linking the Atlantic and Pacific Oceans. The idea of a canal across the fifty-one-mile-wide Isthmus of Panama had a long history. In 1879–1881, the French engineer Ferdinand de Lesseps attempted to construct such a waterway but failed because of inadequate funding and the toll exacted on his workers by yellow fever and malaria. Roosevelt had long been a proponent of American naval development. He was convinced that a canal would facilitate the movement of naval and commercial vessels between the two oceans. In 1903, when Colombia, of which Panama was a part, refused to cede land for the project, Roosevelt helped to set in motion an uprising by conspirators led by Philippe Bunau-Varilla, a representative of the Panama Canal Company. An American gunboat prevented the Colombian army from suppressing the rebellion.

Upon establishing Panama's independence, Bunau-Varilla signed a treaty giving the United States both the right to construct and operate a canal and sovereignty over the Canal Zone, a ten-mile-wide strip of land through which the route would run. The largest construction project in history to that date, the building of the canal involved nearly 50,000 workers, the largest number brought in from Barbados. It also required a massive effort to eradicate the mosquitoes that carried the tropical diseases responsible, in part, for the failure of earlier French efforts. When completed in 1914, the canal reduced the sea voyage between the East and West Coasts of the United States by 8,000 miles. "I took the Canal Zone," Roosevelt exulted. But the manner in which the canal had been initiated and continued American rule over the Canal Zone would long remain a source of tension. In 1977, President Jimmy Carter negotiated treaties that led to turning over the canal's operation and control of the Canal Zone to Panama in the year 2000 (see Chapter 26).

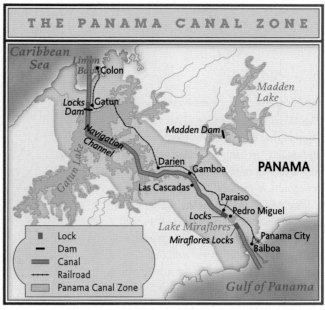

Constructed in the first years of the twentieth century, after Theodore Roosevelt helped engineer Panama's independence from Colombia, the Panama Canal drastically reduced the time it took for commercial and naval vessels to sail from the Atlantic to the Pacific Oceans.

THE ROOSEVELT COROLLARY

Roosevelt's actions in Panama reflected a principle that came to be called the Roosevelt Corollary to the Monroe Doctrine. This held that the United States had the right to exercise "an international police power" in the Western Hemisphere—a significant expansion of Monroe's pledge to defend the hemisphere against European intervention. Early in Roosevelt's administration, British, Italian, and German naval forces blockaded Venezuela to ensure the payment of debts to European bankers. Roosevelt persuaded them to withdraw, but the incident convinced him that financial instability in the New World would invite intervention from the Old. In 1904, Roosevelt ordered American forces to seize the customs houses of the Dominican Republic to ensure payment of its debts to European and American investors. He soon arranged an "executive agreement" giving a group of American banks control over Dominican finances. In 1906, he dispatched troops to Cuba to oversee a disputed election; they remained in the country until 1909. Roosevelt also encouraged

The World's Constable, *a cartoon commenting on Theodore Roosevelt's "new diplomacy," in* Judge, *January 14, 1905, portrays Roosevelt as an impartial policeman, holding in one hand the threat of force and in the other the promise of the peaceful settlement of disputes. Roosevelt stands between the undisciplined non-white peoples of the world and the imperialist powers of Europe and Japan.*

The White Man's Burden, *a 1916 political cartoon depicting Woodrow Wilson attempting to carry Mexico over a difficult landscape.*

investment by American corporations like the United Fruit Company, whose huge banana plantations soon dominated the economies of Honduras and Costa Rica.

Roosevelt's successor, William Howard Taft, landed marines in Nicaragua to protect a government friendly to American economic interests. In general, however, Taft emphasized economic investment and loans from American banks, rather than direct military intervention, as the best way to spread American influence. As a result, his foreign policy became known as Dollar Diplomacy. In Honduras, Nicaragua, the Dominican Republic, and even Liberia—the West African nation established in 1816 as a home for freed American slaves—Taft pressed for more efficient revenue collection, stable government, and access to land and labor by American companies.

MORAL IMPERIALISM

The son of a Presbyterian minister, Woodrow Wilson brought to the presidency a missionary zeal and a sense of his own and the nation's moral righteousness. He appointed as secretary of state William Jennings Bryan, a strong anti-imperialist. Wilson repudiated Dollar Diplomacy and promised a new foreign policy that would respect Latin America's independence and free it from foreign economic domination. But Wilson could not abandon the conviction that the United States had a responsibility to teach other peoples the lessons of democracy. Moreover, he believed, the export of American manufactured goods and investments went hand in hand with the spread of democratic ideals. To Wilson, expanding American economic influence served a higher purpose than mere profit. Americans, he told a group of businessmen in 1916, were "meant to carry liberty and justice" throughout the world. "Go out and sell goods," he urged them, "that will make the world more comfortable and happy, and convert them to the principles of America."

Wilson's "moral imperialism" produced more military interventions in Latin America than any president before or since. In 1915, he sent marines to occupy Haiti after the government refused to allow American banks to oversee its financial dealings. In 1916, he established a military government in the Dominican Republic, with the United States controlling the country's customs collections and paying its debts. American soldiers remained in the Dominican Republic until 1924 and in Haiti until 1934. They built roads and schools, but did little or nothing to promote democracy. Wilson's foreign policy underscored a paradox of modern American history: the presidents who spoke the most about freedom were likely to intervene most frequently in the affairs of other countries.

WILSON AND MEXICO

Wilson's major preoccupation in Latin America was Mexico, where in 1911 a revolution led by Francisco Madero overthrew the government of dictator Porfirio Díaz. Two years later, without Wilson's knowledge but with the backing of the U.S. ambassador and of American companies that controlled Mexico's oil and mining industries, military commander Victoriano Huerta assassinated Madero and seized power.

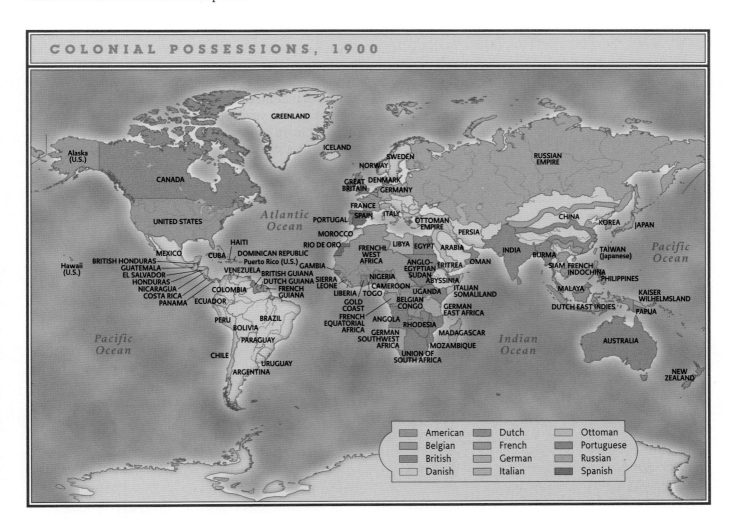

COLONIAL POSSESSIONS, 1900

Wilson was appalled. The United States, he announced, would not extend recognition to a "government of butchers." He would "teach" Latin Americans, he added, "to elect good men." When civil war broke out in Mexico, Wilson ordered American troops to land at Vera Cruz to prevent the arrival of weapons meant for Huerta's forces. But to Wilson's surprise, Mexicans greeted the marines as invaders rather than liberators. Vera Cruz, after all, was where the forces of the conquistador Hernán Cortés had landed in the sixteenth century and those of Winfield Scott during the Mexican War. Over 100 Mexicans and 19 Americans died in the fighting that followed. Huerta left the presidency in 1914, but civil war continued, and neither side seemed grateful for Wilson's interference.

In 1916, the war spilled over into the United States when "Pancho" Villa, the leader of one faction, attacked Columbus, New Mexico, where he killed seventeen Americans. Wilson ordered over 10,000 troops into northern Mexico on an expedition that unsuccessfully sought to arrest Villa. Mexico was a warning that it might be more difficult than Wilson assumed to use American might to reorder the internal affairs of other nations, or to apply moral certainty to foreign policy.

AMERICA AND THE GREAT WAR

In June 1914, a Serbian nationalist assassinated Archduke Franz Ferdinand, heir to the throne of the Austro-Hungarian empire, in Sarajevo, Serbia. (Today, Sarajevo is the capital of Bosnia-Herzegovina.) This deed set in motion a chain of events that plunged Europe into the most devastating war the world had ever seen. In the years before 1914, European nations had engaged in a scramble to obtain colonial possessions overseas and had constructed a shifting series of alliances seeking military domination within Europe. In the aftermath of the assassination, Austria-Hungary, the major power in eastern Europe, declared war on Serbia. Within a little over a

An airplane flies over Washington, D.C., in 1910. World War I would reveal the military uses for this new technology.

PEACE·HAS·HER·CONQUESTS·GREATER·FAR·THAN·WAR

R.M.S. LUSITANIA
QUEEN OF THE SEAS

The liner Lusitania, *pictured on a "peace" postcard. Its sinking by a German submarine in 1915 strengthened those who wished to see the United States enter the European war.*

month, because of European powers' interlocking military alliances, Britain, France, Russia, and Japan, called the Allies, found themselves at war with the Central Powers—Germany, Austria-Hungary, and the Ottoman empire, whose holdings included modern-day Turkey and much of the Middle East.

German forces quickly overran Belgium and part of northern France. The war then settled into a prolonged stalemate, with bloody, indecisive battles succeeding one another. New military technologies—submarines, airplanes, machine guns, tanks, and poison gas—produced unprecedented slaughter. In one five-month battle at Verdun, in 1916, 600,000 French and German soldiers perished—nearly as many combatants as in the entire American Civil War. By the time the war ended, an estimated 10 million soldiers, and uncounted millions of civilians, had perished. And the war was followed by widespread famine and a worldwide epidemic of influenza that killed an estimated 21 million people more.

The Great War, or World War I as it came to be called, dealt a severe blow to the optimism and self-confidence of Western civilization. For decades, philosophers, reformers, and politicians had hailed the triumph of reason and human progress. Despite increasingly bitter rivalries between European powers, especially Germany and Britain, as they competed for political and military dominance at home and carved up Asia and Africa into rival empires, mankind seemed to have moved beyond the time when disputes were settled by war. The conflict was also a shock to European socialist and labor movements. Of the two great ideologies that had arisen in the nineteenth century, nationalism and socialism, the former proved more powerful. Karl Marx had called on the "workers of the world" to unite against their oppressors. Instead, they marched off to kill each other.

NEUTRALITY AND PREPAREDNESS

As war engulfed Europe, Americans found themselves sharply divided. British-Americans sided with their nation of origin, as did many other Americans who associated Great Britain with liberty and democracy and

Germany with repressive government. On the other hand, German-Americans identified with Germany. Irish-Americans bitterly opposed any aid to the British, a sentiment reinforced in 1916 when authorities in London suppressed the Easter Rebellion, an uprising demanding Irish independence, and executed several of its leaders. Immigrants from the Russian empire, especially Jews, had no desire to see the United States aid the czar's regime. Indeed, the presence of Russia, the world's largest despotic state, as an ally of Britain and France made it difficult to see the war as a clear-cut battle between democracy and autocracy. Many feminists, pacifists, and social reformers, moreover, had become convinced that peace was essential to further efforts to enhance social justice at home. They lobbied vigorously against American involvement.

When war broke out in 1914, President Wilson proclaimed American neutrality. But as in the years preceding the War of 1812, naval warfare in Europe reverberated in the United States. Britain declared a naval blockade of Germany and began to stop American merchant vessels. Germany launched submarine warfare against ships entering and leaving British ports. In May 1915, a German submarine sank the British liner *Lusitania* (which was carrying a large cache of arms) off the coast of Ireland, causing the death of 1,198 passengers, including 124 Americans. Wilson composed a note of protest so strong that Bryan resigned as secretary of state, fearing that the president was laying the foundation for military intervention. Bryan had advocated warning Americans not to travel on the ships of belligerents, but Wilson felt this would represent a retreat from the principle of freedom of the seas.

The sinking of the *Lusitania* out-raged American public opinion and strengthened the hand of those who believed that the United States must prepare for possible entry into the war. These included longtime advocates of a stronger military establishment, like Theodore Roosevelt, and businessmen with close economic ties to Britain, the country's leading trading partner and the recipient of over 2 billion dollars in wartime loans from American banks.

Wilson himself had strong pro-British sympathies and viewed Germany as "the natural foe of liberty." By the end of 1915, he had embarked on a policy of "preparedness"—a crash program to expand the American army and navy.

THE ROAD TO WAR

In May 1916, Germany announced the suspension of submarine warfare against noncombatants. Wilson's preparedness program seemed to have succeeded in securing the right of Americans to travel freely on the high seas without committing American forces to the conflict. "He kept us out of war" became the slogan of his campaign for reelection. With the Republican

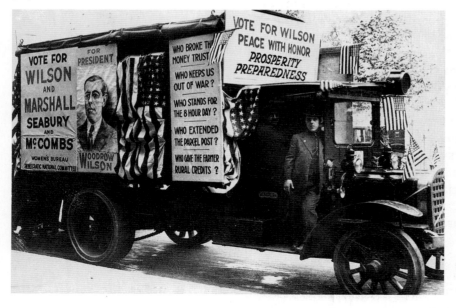

A 1916 Wilson campaign truck (a new development in political campaigning), promising peace, prosperity, and preparedness.

Party reunited after its split in 1912, the election proved to be one of the closest in American history. Wilson defeated Republican candidate Charles Evans Hughes by only twenty-three electoral votes and about 600,000 popular votes out of over 18 million cast. Partly because he seemed to promise not to send American soldiers to Europe, Wilson carried ten of the twelve states that had adopted women's suffrage. Without the votes of women, Wilson would not have been reelected.

On January 22, 1917, Wilson called for a "peace without victory" in Europe and outlined his vision for a world order including freedom of the seas, restrictions on armaments, and self-determination for nations great and small. Almost immediately, however, Germany announced its intention to resume submarine warfare against ships sailing to or from the British Isles, and several American merchant vessels were sunk. The German government realized that its actions would probably lead Wilson to intervene, but German strategists gambled that the blockade would strangle Britain economically before the arrival of American troops.

In March 1917, British spies intercepted and made public the Zimmerman Telegram, a message by German foreign secretary Arthur Zimmerman calling on Mexico to join in a coming war against the United States and promising to help it recover territory lost in the Mexican War of 1846–1848. A revolution in Russia that same month overthrew the czar and established a constitutional government, making it more plausible to believe that the United States would be fighting on the side of democracy. On April 2, Wilson went before Congress to ask for a declaration of war against Germany. "The world," he proclaimed, "must be made safe for democracy. Its peace must be planted upon the tested foundation of political liberty." The war resolution passed the Senate 82–6 and the House 373–50.

THE FOURTEEN POINTS

Not until the spring of 1918 did American forces arrive in Europe in large numbers. By then, the world situation had taken a dramatic turn. In November 1917, a communist revolution headed by Vladimir Lenin overthrew the Russian government that had come to power the previous spring. Shortly thereafter, Lenin withdrew Russia from the war and published the secret treaties by which the Allies had agreed to divide up conquered territory after the war—an embarrassment for Wilson, who had promised a just peace.

Partly to assure the country that the war was being fought for a moral cause, Wilson in January 1918 issued the Fourteen Points, the clearest statement of American war aims and of his vision of a new international order. Among the key principles were self-determination for all nations, freedom of the seas, free trade, open diplomacy (an end to secret treaties), the readjustment of colonial claims with colonized people given "equal weight" in deciding their futures, and the creation of a "general association of nations" to preserve the peace. Wilson envisioned this last provision, which led to the establishment after the war of the League of Nations, as a kind of global counterpart to the regulatory commissions Progressives had created at home to maintain social harmony and prevent the powerful

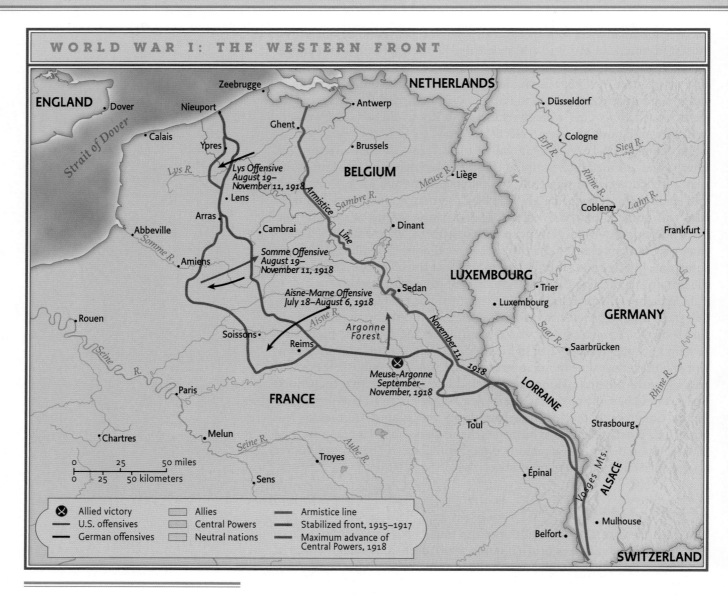

WORLD WAR I: THE WESTERN FRONT

After years of stalemate on the western front in World War I, the arrival of American troops in 1917 and 1918 shifted the balance of power and made possible Allied victory.

from exploiting the weak. Although purely an American program, not endorsed by the other Allies, the Fourteen Points established the agenda for the peace conference that followed the war.

The United States threw its economic resources and manpower into the war—although its army acted under its own leadership, not as part of a unified command. When American troops finally arrived in Europe, they turned the tide of battle. In the spring of 1918, they helped to repulse a German advance near Paris and by July were participating in a major Allied counteroffensive. In September, in the Meuse-Argonne campaign, over 1 million American soldiers under General John J. Pershing helped to push back the outnumbered and exhausted German army. With his forces in full retreat, the German kaiser abdicated on November 9. Two days later, Germany sued for peace. Over 100,000 Americans had died, a substantial number, but only 1 percent of the 10 million soldiers killed in the Great War.

THE WAR AT HOME

THE PROGRESSIVES' WAR

Looking back on American participation in the European conflict, Randolph Bourne summed up one of its lessons: "War is the health of the state." Bourne saw the expansion of government power as a danger, but it struck most Progressives as a golden opportunity. To them, the war offered the possibility of reforming American society along scientific lines, instilling a sense of national unity and self-sacrifice, and expanding social justice. That American power could now disseminate Progressive values around the globe heightened the war's appeal.

Almost without exception, Progressive intellectuals and reformers, joined by prominent labor leaders and native-born socialists, rallied to Wilson's support. The roster included intellectuals like John Dewey, journalists such as Walter Lippmann and Herbert Croly, AFL head Samuel Gompers, socialist writers like Upton Sinclair, and prominent reformers including Florence Kelley and Charlotte Perkins Gilman. In *The New Republic*, Dewey urged Progressives to recognize the "social possibilities of war." The crisis, he wrote, offered the prospect of "the more conscious and extensive use of science for communal purposes," and of attacking the "immense inequality of power" within the United States, thus laying the foundation for Americans to enjoy "effective freedom."

THE WARTIME STATE

Like the Civil War, World War I created, albeit temporarily, a national state with unprecedented powers and a sharply increased presence in Americans' everyday lives. Under the Selective Service Act of May 1917, 24 million men were required to register with the draft, and the army soon swelled from 120,000 to 5 million men. The war seemed to bring into being the New Nationalist state Theodore Roosevelt and so many Progressives had desired. New federal agencies moved to regulate industry, transportation, labor relations, and agriculture. Headed by Wall Street financier Bernard Baruch, the War Industries Board presided over all elements of war production from the distribution of raw materials to the prices of manufactured goods. To spur efficiency, it established standardized specifications for everything from automobile tires to shoe colors (three were permitted—black, brown, and white). The Railroad Administration took control of the nation's transportation system, and the Fuel Agency rationed coal and oil. The Food Administration instructed farmers on modern methods of cultivation and promoted the more efficient preparation of meals. Its director, Herbert Hoover, mobilized the shipment of American food to the war-devastated Allies, popularizing the slogan "Food will win the war."

These agencies generally saw themselves as partners of business as much as regulators. They guaranteed government suppliers a high rate of profit and encouraged cooperation among former business rivals by suspending antitrust laws. At the same time, however, the War Labor Board, which included representatives of government, industry, and the

American Federation of Labor, pressed for the establishment of a minimum wage, eight-hour workday, and the right to form unions. During the war, wages rose substantially, working conditions in many industries improved, and union membership doubled. To finance the war, corporate and individual income taxes rose enormously. By 1918, the wealthiest Americans were paying 60 percent of their income in taxes. Tens of millions of Americans answered the call to demonstrate their patriotism by purchasing Liberty bonds. Once peace arrived, the wartime state quickly withered away. But for a time, the federal government seemed well on its way to fulfilling the Progressive task of promoting economic rationalization, industrial justice, and a sense of common national purpose.

THE PROPAGANDA WAR

During the Civil War, it had been left to private agencies—Union Leagues, the Loyal Publication Society, and others—to mobilize prowar public opinion. But the Wilson administration decided that patriotism was too important to leave to the private sector. Many Americans were skeptical about whether democratic America should enter a struggle between rival empires. Some vehemently opposed American participation, notably the Industrial Workers of the World (IWW) and the bulk of the Socialist Party, which in 1917 condemned the declaration of war as "a crime against the people of the United States" and called on "the workers of all countries" to refuse to fight. As the major national organization to oppose Wilson's policy, the Socialist Party became a rallying point for antiwar sentiment. In mayoral elections across the country in the fall of 1917, the Socialist vote averaged 20 percent, far above the party's previous total.

In April 1917, the Wilson administration created the Committee on Public Information (CPI) to explain to Americans and the world, as its director, George Creel, put it, "the cause that compelled America to take arms in defense of its liberties and free institutions." Enlisting academics, journalists, artists, and advertising men, the CPI flooded the country with prowar propaganda, using every available medium from pamphlets (of which it issued 75 million) to posters, newspaper advertisements, and motion pictures. It trained and dispatched across the country 75,000 Four-Minute Men, who delivered brief standardized talks (sometimes in Italian, Yiddish, and other immigrant languages) to audiences in movie theaters, schools, and other public venues.

Never before had an agency of the federal government attempted the "conscious and intelligent manipulation of the organized habits and opinions of the masses," in the words of young Edward Bernays, a member of Creel's staff who would later create the modern profession of public relations. In fact, the fledgling advertising industry followed the CPI's activities closely. They proved, one adman wrote, that it was possible to "sway the ideas of whole populations, change their habits of life, create belief, practically universal in any policy or idea." In the 1920s, advertisers would use what they had learned to sell goods. But the CPI also set a precedent for active governmental efforts to shape public opinion in later international conflicts, from World War II to the Cold War and Iraq.

A poster addressed to Jewish immigrants by the U.S. Food Administration proclaims, "Food Will Win the War." It adds, "You came here seeking freedom, now you must help preserve it." Copies were also printed in other European languages.

A female figure wearing a cap of liberty rings the liberty bell in this patriotic illustration from 1918.

"THE GREAT CAUSE OF FREEDOM"

The CPI couched its appeal in the Progressive language of social cooperation and expanded democracy. Abroad, this meant a peace based on the principle of national self-determination. At home, it meant improving "industrial democracy." A Progressive journalist, Creel believed the war would accelerate the movement toward solving the "age-old problems of poverty, inequality, oppression, and unhappiness." He took to heart a warning from historian Carl Becker that a simple contrast between German tyranny and American democracy would not seem plausible to the average worker: "You talk to him of our ideals of liberty and he thinks of the shameless exploitation of labor and of the ridiculous gulf between wealth and poverty." The CPI distributed pamphlets foreseeing a postwar society complete with a "universal eight-hour day" and a living wage for all.

While "democracy" served as the key term of wartime mobilization, "freedom" also took on new significance. The war, a CPI advertisement proclaimed, was being fought in "the great cause of freedom." Thousands of persons, often draftees, were enlisted to pose in giant human tableaus representing symbols of liberty. One living representation of the Liberty Bell at Fort Dix, New Jersey, included 25,000 people. The most common visual image in wartime propaganda was the Statue of Liberty, employed especially to rally support among immigrants. "You came here seeking Freedom," stated a caption on one Statue of Liberty poster. "You must now help preserve it." Buying Liberty bonds became a demonstration of patriotism. Wilson's speeches cast the United States as a land of liberty, fighting alongside a "concert of free people" to secure self-determination for the oppressed peoples of the world. The idea of freedom, it seems, requires an antithesis, and the CPI found one in the German kaiser and, more generally, the German nation and people. Government propaganda whipped up hatred of the wartime foe by portraying it as a nation of barbaric Huns.

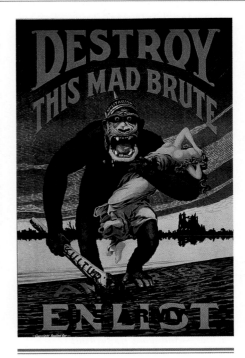

A vivid example of the anti-German propaganda produced by the federal government to encourage prowar sentiment during World War I.

THE COMING OF WOMEN'S SUFFRAGE

The enlistment of "democracy" and "freedom" as ideological war weapons inevitably inspired demands for their expansion at home. In 1916, Wilson had cautiously endorsed votes for women. America's entry into the war threatened to tear the suffrage movement apart, since many advocates had been associated with opposition to American involvement. Indeed, among those who voted against the declaration of war was the first woman member of Congress, the staunch pacifist Jeannette Rankin of Montana. "I want to stand by my country, but I cannot vote for war," she said. Although she was defeated in her reelection bid in 1918, Rankin would return to Congress in 1940. She became the only member to oppose the declaration of war against Japan in 1941, ending her political career. In 1968, at the age of eighty-five, Rankin took part in a giant march on Washington to protest the war in Vietnam.

As during the Civil War, however, most leaders of women's suffrage organizations enthusiastically enlisted in the effort. Women sold war bonds, organized patriotic rallies, and went to work in war production jobs. Some 22,000 served as clerical workers and nurses with American forces in Europe. Many believed wartime service would earn them equal rights at home.

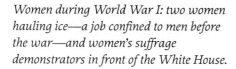

Women during World War I: two women hauling ice—a job confined to men before the war—and women's suffrage demonstrators in front of the White House.

At the same time, a new generation of college-educated activists, organized in the National Women's Party, pressed for the right to vote with militant tactics many older suffrage advocates found scandalous. The party's leader, Alice Paul, had studied in England between 1907 and 1910 when the British suffrage movement adopted a strategy that included arrests, imprisonments, and vigorous denunciations of a male-dominated political system. How could the country fight for democracy abroad, Paul asked, while denying it to women at home? She compared Wilson to the kaiser and with a group of followers chained herself to the White House fence, resulting in a seven-month prison sentence. When they began a hunger strike, the prisoners were force-fed.

The combination of women's patriotic service and widespread outrage over the mistreatment of Paul and her fellow prisoners pushed the administration toward full-fledged support for women's suffrage. "We have made partners of the women in this war," Wilson proclaimed. "Shall we admit

A 1915 cartoon showing the western states where women had won the right to vote. Women in the East reach out to a western woman carrying a torch of liberty.

them only to a partnership of suffering and sacrifice and toil and not to a partnership of privilege and right?" In 1920, the long struggle ended with the ratification of the Nineteenth Amendment barring states from using sex as a qualification for the suffrage. The United States became the twenty-seventh country to allow women to vote.

PROHIBITION

The war gave a powerful impulse to other campaigns that had engaged the energies of many women in the Progressive era. Ironically, efforts to stamp out prostitution and protect soldiers from venereal disease led the government to distribute birth-control information and devices—the very action for which Margaret Sanger had recently been jailed, as noted in the previous chapter.

Prohibition, a movement inherited from the nineteenth century that had gained new strength and militancy in Progressive America, finally achieved national success during the war. Numerous impulses flowed into the renewed campaign to ban intoxicating liquor. Employers hoped it would create a more disciplined labor force. Urban reformers believed that it

In the early years of the twentieth century, many states and localities in the South and West banned the manufacture and sale of alcoholic beverages. ("Wet" counties allowed alcoholic beverages, "dry" counties banned them.) Prohibition became national with the adoption of the Eighteenth Amendment in 1919.

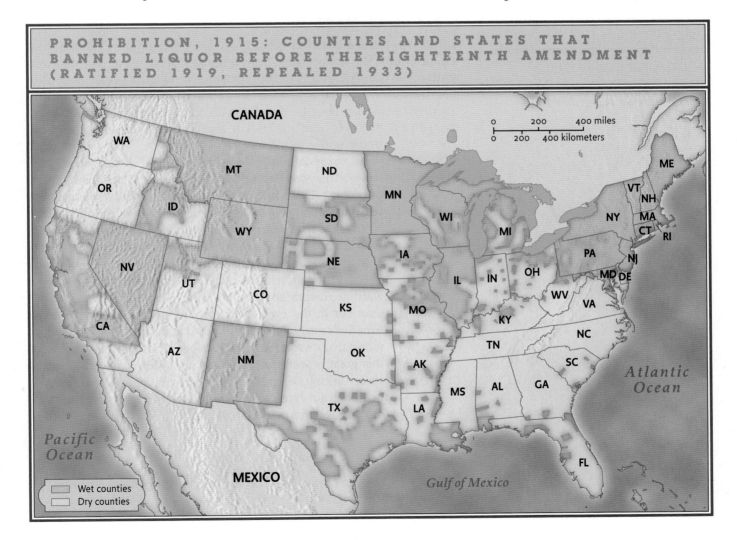

PROHIBITION, 1915: COUNTIES AND STATES THAT BANNED LIQUOR BEFORE THE EIGHTEENTH AMENDMENT (RATIFIED 1919, REPEALED 1933)

would promote a more orderly city environment and undermine urban machines that used saloons as places of political organization. Women reformers hoped Prohibition would protect wives and children from husbands who engaged in domestic violence when drunk or who squandered their wages at saloons. Many native-born Protestants saw Prohibition as a way of imposing "American" values on immigrants.

Like the suffrage movement, Prohibitionists first concentrated on state campaigns. By 1915, they had won victories in eighteen southern and midwestern states where the immigrant population was small and Protestant denominations like Baptists and Methodists strongly opposed drinking. But like the suffrage movement, Prohibitionists came to see national legislation as their best strategy. The war gave them added ammunition. Many prominent breweries were owned by German-Americans, making beer seem unpatriotic. The Food Administration insisted that grain must be used to produce food, not distilled into beer and liquor. In December 1917, Congress passed the Eighteenth Amendment, prohibiting the manufacture and sale of intoxicating liquor. It was ratified by the states in 1919 and went into effect at the beginning of 1920.

The Liberty Bell, formed by 25,000 soldiers at Camp Dix, New Jersey in 1918, another example of the use of an image of liberty to inspire patriotic sentiment during World War I.

LIBERTY IN WARTIME

World War I raised questions already glimpsed during the Civil War that would trouble the nation again during the McCarthy era and in the aftermath of the terrorist attacks of 2001: What is the balance between security and freedom? Does the Constitution protect citizens' rights during wartime? Should dissent be equated with lack of patriotism? It demonstrated that during a war, traditional civil liberties are likely to come under severe pressure.

In 1917, Randolph Bourne ridiculed Progressives who believed they could mold the war according to their own "liberal purposes." The conflict, he predicted, would empower not reformers but the "least democratic forces in American life." The accuracy of Bourne's prediction soon become apparent. Despite the administration's idealistic language of democracy and freedom, the war inaugurated the most intense repression of civil liberties the nation has ever known. Perhaps the very nobility of wartime rhetoric contributed to the massive suppression of dissent. For in the eyes of Wilson and many of his supporters, America's goals were so virtuous that disagreement could only reflect treason to the country's values. "It is a fearful thing to lead this great peaceful people into war," Wilson remarked in his speech asking Congress to bring America into the conflict. Even he could not have predicted how fearful an impact the war would have on American freedom.

THE ESPIONAGE ACT

For the first time since the Alien and Sedition Acts of 1798, the federal government enacted laws to restrict freedom of speech. The Espionage Act of 1917 prohibited not only spying and interfering with the draft but also "false statements" that might impede military success. The postmaster general barred from the mails numerous newspapers and magazines critical of the administration. The victims ranged from virtually the entire socialist press and many foreign-language publications to *The Jeffersonian*, a newspaper owned by ex-Populist leader Tom Watson, which criticized the draft as a violation of states' rights. In 1918, the Sedition Act made it a crime to make spoken or printed statements that intended to cast "contempt, scorn, or disrepute" on the "form of government," or that advocated interference with the war effort. The government charged over 2,000 persons with violating these laws. Over half were convicted. A court sentenced Ohio farmer John White to twenty-one months in prison for saying that the murder of innocent women and children by German soldiers was no worse than what the United States had done in the Philippines in the war of 1899–1903.

The most prominent victim was Eugene V. Debs, convicted in 1918 under the Espionage Act for delivering an antiwar speech. Before his sentencing, Debs gave the court a lesson in the history of American freedom, tracing the tradition of dissent from Thomas Paine to the abolitionists, and pointing out that the nation had never engaged in a war without internal opposition. Germany sent socialist leader Karl Liebknecht to prison for four years for opposing the war; in the United States, Debs's sentence was ten years. After the war's end, Wilson rejected the advice of his attorney general that he commute Debs's sentence. Debs ran for president while still in prison in 1920 and received 900,000 votes. It was left to Wilson's successor, Warren G. Harding, to release Debs from prison in 1921.

COERCIVE PATRIOTISM

Even more extreme repression took place at the hands of state governments and private groups. Americans had long displayed the flag (and used it in advertisements for everything from tobacco products to variety shows). But during World War I, attitudes toward the American flag became a test of patriotism. Persons suspected of disloyalty were forced to kiss the flag in public; those who made statements critical of the flag could be imprisoned. During the war, thirty-three states outlawed the possession or display of red or black flags (symbols, respectively, of communism and anarchism), and twenty-three outlawed a newly created offense, "criminal syndicalism," the advocacy of unlawful acts to accomplish political change or "a change in industrial ownership."

"Who is the real patriot?" Emma Goldman asked when the United States entered the war. She answered, those who "love America with open eyes," who were not blind to "the wrongs committed in the name of patriotism." But from the federal government to local authorities and private groups, patriotism came to be equated with support for the government, the war, and the American economic system, while antiwar sentiment, labor radicalism, and sympathy for the Russian Revolution became "un-American." Minnesota established a Commission of Public Safety to root out disloyalty from the state. Local authorities formally investigated residents who failed to subscribe to Liberty Loans. Throughout the country, schools revised their course offerings to ensure their patriotism and required teachers to sign loyalty oaths.

VOICES OF FREEDOM

From Eugene V. Debs,
Speech to the Jury before Sentencing under the Espionage Act (1918)

The most prominent spokesman for American socialism and a fervent opponent of American participation in World War I, Eugene V. Debs was arrested for delivering an antiwar speech and convicted of violating the Espionage Act. In his speech to the jury, he defended the right of dissent in wartime.

I wish to admit the truth of all that has been testified to in this proceeding. . . . Gentlemen, you have heard the report of my speech at Canton on June 16, and I submit that there is not a word in that speech to warrant the charges set out in the indictment. . . . In what I had to say there my purpose was to have the people understand something about the social system in which we live and to prepare them to change this system by perfectly peaceable and orderly means into what I, as a Socialist, conceive to be a real democracy. . . . I have never advocated violence in any form. I have always believed in education, in intelligence, in enlightenment; and I have always made my appeal to the reason and to the conscience of the people.

In every age there have been a few heroic souls who have been in advance of their time, who have been misunderstood, maligned, persecuted, sometimes put to death. . . . Washington, Jefferson, Franklin, Paine, and their compeers were the rebels of their day. . . . But they had the moral courage to be true to their convictions. . . .

William Lloyd Garrison, Wendell Phillips, Elizabeth Cady Stanton . . . and other leaders of the abolition movement who were regarded as public enemies and treated accordingly, were true to their faith and stood their ground. . . . You are now teaching your children to revere their memories, while all of their detractors are in oblivion.

This country has been engaged in a number of wars and every one of them has been condemned by some of the people. The war of 1812 was opposed and condemned by some of the most influential citizens; the Mexican War was vehemently opposed and bitterly denounced, even after the war had been declared and was in progress, by Abraham Lincoln, Charles Sumner, Daniel Webster. . . . They were not indicted; they were not charged with treason. . . .

I believe in the Constitution. Isn't it strange that we Socialists stand almost alone today in upholding and defending the Constitution of the United States? The revolutionary fathers . . . understood that free speech, a free press and the right of free assemblage by the people were fundamental principles in democratic government. . . . I believe in the right of free speech, in war as well as in peace.

From W. E. B. Du Bois, "Returning Soldiers," *The Crisis* (1919)

Scholar, poet, activist, founder of the National Association for the Advancement of Colored People and editor of its magazine, *The Crisis*, W. E. B. Du Bois was the most prominent black leader of the first half of the twentieth century. He supported black participation in World War I, but he insisted that black soldiers must now join in the struggle for freedom at home.

We are returning from war! *The Crisis* and tens of thousands of black men were drafted into a great struggle. For bleeding France and what she means and has meant and will mean to us and humanity and against the threat of German race arrogance, we fought gladly and to the last drop of blood; for America and her highest ideals, we fought in far-off hope; for the dominant southern oligarchy entrenched in Washington, we fought in bitter resignation. For the America that represents and gloats in lynching, disfranchisement, caste, brutality and devilish insult—for this, in the hateful upturning and mixing of things, we were forced by vindictive fate to fight, also.

But today we return! . . . We sing: This country of ours, despite all its better souls have done and dreamed, is yet a shameful land.

It *lynches*.

And lynching is barbarism of a degree of contemptible nastiness unparalleled in human history. Yet for fifty years we have lynched two Negroes a week, and we have kept this up right through the war.

It *disfranchises* its own citizens.

Disfranchisement is the deliberate theft and robbery of the only protection of poor against rich and black against white. The land that disfranchises its citizens and calls itself a democracy lies and knows it lies.

It encourages *ignorance*.

It has never really tried to educate the Negro. A dominate minority does not want Negroes educated. It wants servants. . . .

It *insults* us.

It has organized a nationwide and latterly a worldwide propaganda of deliberate and continuous insult and defamation of black blood wherever found. . . .

This is the country to which we Soldiers of Democracy return. This is the fatherland for which we fought! But it is *our* fatherland. It was right for us to fight. . . .

We *return fighting*.

Make way for Democracy!

QUESTIONS

1. Why does Debs relate the history of wartime dissent in America?

2. What connections does Du Bois draw between blacks fighting abroad in the war and returning to fight at home?

3. In what ways does each author point up the contradiction between America's professed values and its actual conduct?

Fighting in France for Freedom!--Are YOU Helping at Home?

Civilians apprehended in a 1918 "slacker raid." In a three-day drive in New York City, government agents stopped and questioned 61,000 men. About 1,500 were arrested for failing to carry draft cards.

The 250,000 members of the newly formed American Protective League (APL) helped the Justice Department identify radicals and critics of the war by spying on their neighbors and carrying out "slacker raids" in which thousands of men were stopped on the streets of major cities and required to produce draft registration cards. Many private groups seized upon the atmosphere of repression as a weapon against domestic opponents. Employers cooperated with the government in crushing the Industrial Workers of the World (IWW), a move long demanded by business interests. In July 1917, vigilantes in Bisbee, Arizona, rounded up some 1,200 striking copper miners and their sympathizers, herded them into railroad boxcars, and transported them into the desert, where they were abandoned. In August, a crowd in Butte, Montana, lynched IWW leader Frank Little. The following month, operating under one of the broadest warrants in American history, federal agents swooped down on IWW offices throughout the country, arresting hundreds of leaders and seizing files and publications.

The war experience, commented Walter Lippmann, demonstrated "that the traditional liberties of speech and opinion rest on no solid foundation." Yet while some Progressives protested individual excesses, most failed to speak out against the broad suppression of freedom of expression. Civil liberties, by and large, had never been a major concern of Progressives, who had always viewed the national state as the embodiment of democratic purpose and insisted that freedom flowed from participating in the life of society, not standing in opposition. Strong believers in the use of national power to improve social conditions, Progressives found themselves ill prepared to develop a defense of minority rights against majority or governmental tyranny. From the AFL to *New Republic* intellectuals, moreover, supporters of the war saw the elimination of socialists and alien radicals as a necessary prelude to the integration of labor and immigrants into an ordered society, an outcome they hoped would emerge from the war.

WHO IS AN AMERICAN?

In many respects, Progressivism was a precursor to major developments of the twentieth century—the New Deal, the Great Society, the socially active state. But in accepting the idea of "race" as a permanent, defining characteristic of individuals and social groups, Progressives bore more resemblance to nineteenth-century thinkers than to later twentieth-century liberals, with whom they are sometimes compared.

THE "RACE PROBLEM"

Even before American participation in World War I, what contemporaries called the "race problem"—the tensions that arose from the country's increasing ethnic diversity—had become a major subject of public concern. "Race" referred to far more than black-white relations. The *Dictionary of Races of Peoples*, published in 1911 by the U.S. Immigration Commission, listed no fewer than forty-five immigrant "races," each supposedly with its own inborn characteristics. They ranged from Anglo-Saxons at the top down to Hebrews, Northern Italians, and, lowest of all, Southern Italians— supposedly violent, undisciplined, and incapable of assimilation.

In 1907, Congress had decreed that an American woman who married an alien automatically forfeited her American citizenship. Popular best-sellers like *The Passing of the Great Race*, published in 1916 by Madison Grant, president of the New York Zoological Society, warned that the influx of new immigrants and the low birthrate of native white women threatened the foundations of American civilization. The new science of eugenics, which studied the alleged mental characteristics of different races, gave anti-immigrant sentiment an air of professional expertise. If democracy could not flourish in the face of vast inequalities of economic power, neither, most Progressives believed, could it survive in a nation permanently divided along racial and ethnic lines.

The Lion's Club of Trenton, New Jersey, displayed this billboard in 1922, urging native-born Americans to help immigrants assimilate.

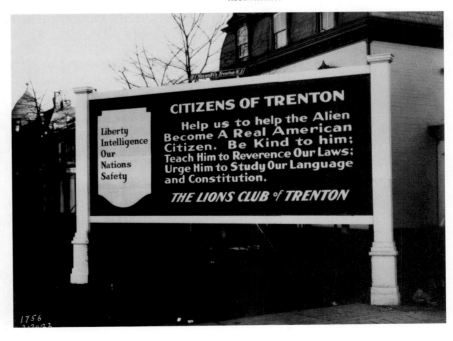

AMERICANIZATION AND PLURALISM

Somehow, the very nationalization of politics and economic life served to heighten awareness of ethnic and racial difference and spurred demands for "Americanization"—the creation of a more homogeneous national culture. A 1908 play by the Jewish immigrant writer Israel Zangwill, *The Melting Pot*, gave a popular name to the process by which newcomers were supposed to merge their identity into existing American nationality. Public and private groups of all kinds—including educators, employers, labor leaders, social reformers, and public officials—took up the task of Americanizing new immigrants. The Ford Motor Company's famed sociological department entered the homes of immigrant workers to evaluate their clothing, furniture, and food preferences and enrolled them in English-language courses. Ford fired those who failed to adapt to American standards after a reasonable period of time. Americanization programs often targeted women as the bearers and transmitters of culture. In Los Angeles, teachers and religious missionaries worked to teach English to Mexican-American women so that they could then assimilate American values. Fearful that adult newcomers remained too stuck in their Old World ways, public schools paid great attention to Americanizing immigrants' children. The challenge facing schools, wrote one educator, was "to implant in their children, so far as can be done, the Anglo-Saxon conception of righteousness, law and order, and popular government."

A minority of Progressives questioned Americanization efforts and insisted on respect for immigrant subcultures. At Hull House, teachers offered English-language instruction but also encouraged immigrants to value their European heritage. Probably the most penetrating critique issued from the pen of Randolph Bourne, whose 1916 essay, "Trans-National America," exposed the fundamental flaw in the Americanization model. "There is no distinctive American culture," Bourne pointed out. Interaction between individuals and groups had produced the nation's music, poetry, and other cultural expressions. Bourne envisioned a democratic, cosmopolitan society in which immigrants and natives alike submerged their group identities in a new "trans-national" culture.

Even before the war, some Progressives had advocated universal military training so that newcomers, thrown together with "real Americans," would cease to be "hyphenated" (Italian-Americans, Polish-Americans, and so on). Once the immigrant had served in the army, wrote Assistant Secretary of War Henry Breckenridge, "no matter from what race stock he may come—Teuton, Slav, Czech, Italian—out goes the hyphen, up goes the Stars and Stripes." Until the United States entered World War I, however, efforts at

Graduates of the Ford English School at the conclusion of their 1916 graduation ceremony. Dressed in their traditional national costumes, they disembarked from an immigrant ship into a giant melting pot. After teachers stirred the pot with ladles, the Ford workers emerged in American clothing, carrying American flags.

assimilation were largely conducted by private organizations like the National Americanization Committee, whose mottos included "100 Percent Americanism" and "English First." The war transformed Americanization into a government-sponsored campaign in which compulsory assimilation triumphed over Bourne's vision of pluralism.

With President Wilson declaring that some Americans "born under foreign flags" were guilty of "disloyalty . . . and must be absolutely crushed," the federal and state governments demanded that immigrants demonstrate their unwavering devotion to the United States. The Committee on Public Information renamed the Fourth of July, 1918, Loyalty Day and asked ethnic groups to participate in patriotic pageants. New York City's celebration included a procession of 75,000 persons with dozens of floats and presentations linking immigrants with the war effort and highlighting their contributions to American society. Leaders of ethnic groups that had suffered discrimination saw the war as an opportunity to gain greater rights. Prominent Jewish leaders promoted enlistment and expressions of loyalty. The Chinese-American press insisted that even those born abroad and barred from citizenship should register for the draft, to "bring honor to the people of our race."

A 1919 Americanization pageant in Milwaukee, in which immigrants encounter Abraham Lincoln and the Statue of Liberty.

THE ANTI-GERMAN CRUSADE

German-Americans bore the brunt of forced Americanization. The first wave of German immigrants had arrived before the Civil War. By 1914, German-Americans numbered nearly 9 million, including immigrants and persons of German parentage. They had created thriving ethnic institutions including clubs, sports associations, schools, and theaters. On the eve of the war, many Americans admired German traditions in literature, music, and philosophy, and one-quarter of all the high school students in the country studied the German language. But after American entry into the war, the use of German and expressions of German culture became a target of prowar organizations. In Iowa, Governor William L. Harding issued a proclamation requiring that all oral communication in schools, public places, and over the telephone be conducted in English. Freedom of speech, he declared, did not include "the right to use a language other than the language of the country."

By 1919, the vast majority of the states had enacted laws restricting the teaching of foreign languages. Popular words of German origin were changed: "hamburger" became "liberty sandwich," and "sauerkraut" was renamed "liberty cabbage." Many communities banned the playing of German music. The government jailed Karl Müch, the director of the Boston

Symphony and a Swiss citizen, as an enemy alien after he insisted on including the works of German composers like Beethoven in his concerts. The war dealt a crushing blow to German-American culture. By 1920, the number of German-language newspapers had been reduced to 276 (one-third the number twenty years earlier), and only 1 percent of high school pupils still studied German. The Census of 1920 reported a 25 percent drop in the number of Americans admitting to having being born in Germany.

TOWARD IMMIGRATION RESTRICTION

Even as Americanization programs sought to assimilate immigrants into American society, the war strengthened the conviction that certain kinds of undesirable persons ought to be excluded altogether. The new immigrants, one advocate of restriction declared, appreciated the values of democracy and freedom far less than "the Anglo-Saxon," as evidenced by their attraction to "extreme political doctrines" like anarchism and socialism. Stanford University psychologist Lewis Terman introduced the term "IQ" (intelligence quotient) in 1916, claiming that this single number could measure an individual's mental capacity. Intelligence tests administered to recruits by the army seemed to confirm scientifically that blacks and the new immigrants stood far below native white Protestants on the IQ scale, further spurring demands for immigration restriction.

In 1917, over Wilson's veto, Congress required that immigrants be literate in English or another language. The war accelerated other efforts to upgrade the American population. Some were inspired by the idea of improving the human race by discouraging reproduction among less "desirable" persons. Indiana in 1907 had passed a law authorizing doctors to sterilize insane and "feeble-minded" inmates in mental institutions so that they would not pass their "defective" genes on to children. Numerous other states now followed suit. In *Buck v. Bell* (1927), the Supreme Court upheld the constitutionality of these laws. Justice Oliver Wendell Holmes's opinion included the famous statement, "three generations of imbeciles are enough." By the time the practice ended in the 1960s, some 63,000 persons had been involuntarily sterilized.

GROUPS APART: MEXICANS, PUERTO RICANS, AND ASIAN-AMERICANS

No matter how coercive, Americanization programs assumed that European immigrants and especially their children could eventually adjust to the conditions of American life, embrace American ideals, and become productive citizens enjoying the full blessings of American freedom. This assumption did not apply to non-white immigrants or to blacks. Although the melting-pot idea envisioned that newcomers from Europe would leave their ethnic enclaves and join the American mainstream, non-whites confronted ever-present boundaries of exclusion.

The war led to further growth of the Southwest's Mexican population. Wartime demand for labor from the area's mine owners and large farmers led the government to exempt Mexicans temporarily from the literacy test enacted in 1917. Mexicans were legally classified as white, and many Progressive reformers viewed the growing Mexican population as candidates for Americanization. Teachers and religious missionaries sought to instruct them in English, convert them to Protestantism, and in other ways promote their assimilation into the mainstream culture. Yet public officials in the Southwest treated them as a group apart. Segregation, by law and custom, was common in schools, hospitals, theaters, and other institutions in states with significant Mexican populations. By 1920, nearly all Mexican children in California and the Southwest were educated in their own schools or class-rooms. Phoenix, Arizona, established separate public schools for Indians, Mexicans, blacks, and whites.

Puerto Ricans also occupied an ambiguous position within American society. On the eve of American entry into World War I, Congress termi-nated the status "citizen of Puerto Rico" and conferred American citizen-ship on residents of the island. The aim was to dampen support for Puerto Rican independence and to strengthen the American hold on a strategic outpost in the Caribbean. The change did not grant islanders the right to vote for president, or representation in Congress. Puerto Rican men, nonetheless, were subject to the draft and fought overseas. José de Diego, the Speaker of the House of the island's legislature, wrote the president in 1917 asking that Puerto Rico be granted the democracy the United States was fighting for in Europe.

Even more restrictive were policies toward Asian-Americans. In 1906, the San Francisco school board ordered all Asian students confined to a sin-gle public school. When the Japanese government protested, president Theodore Roosevelt persuaded the city to rescind the order. He then nego-tiated the Gentlemen's Agreement of 1907 whereby Japan agreed to end migration to the United States except for the wives and children of men already in the country. In 1913, California barred all aliens incapable of becoming naturalized citizens (that is, Asians) from owning or leasing land.

THE COLOR LINE

By far the largest non-white group, African-Americans, were excluded from nearly every Progressive definition of freedom described in Chapter 18. After their disenfranchisement in the South, few could participate in Amer-ican democracy. Barred from joining most unions and from skilled employ-ment, black workers had little access to "industrial freedom." A majority of adult black women worked outside the home, but for wages that offered no hope of independence. Predominantly domestic and agricultural workers, they remained unaffected by the era's laws regulating the hours and condi-tions of female labor. Nor could blacks, the majority desperately poor, par-ticipate fully in the emerging consumer economy, either as employees in the new department stores (except as janitors and cleaning women) or as purchasers of the consumer goods now flooding the marketplace.

Progressive intellectuals, social scientists, labor reformers, and suffrage advocates displayed a remarkable indifference to the black condition. Israel Zangwill did not include blacks in the melting-pot idea popularized by his Broadway play. Walter Weyl waited until the last fifteen pages of *The New Democracy* to introduce the "race problem." His comment, quoted in the previous chapter, that the chief obstacles to freedom were economic, not political, revealed little appreciation of how the denial of voting rights underpinned the comprehensive system of inequality to which southern blacks were subjected.

Most settlement house reformers accepted segregation as natural and equitable, assuming there should be white settlements for white neighborhoods and black settlements for black. White leaders of the women's suffrage movement said little about black disenfranchisement. In the South, upper-class white club women sometimes raised funds for black schools and community centers. But suffrage leaders insisted that the vote was a racial entitlement, a "badge and synonym of freedom," in the words of Rebecca Felton of Georgia, that should not be denied to "free-born white women." During Reconstruction, women had been denied constitutional recognition because it was "the Negro's hour." Now, World War I's "woman's hour" excluded blacks. The amendment that achieved women's suffrage left the states free to limit voting by poll taxes and literacy tests. Living in the South, the vast majority of the country's black women did not enjoy its benefits.

ROOSEVELT, WILSON, AND RACE

The Progressive presidents shared prevailing attitudes concerning blacks. Theodore Roosevelt shocked white opinion by inviting Booker T. Washington to dine with him in the White House and by appointing a number of blacks to federal offices. But in 1906, when a small group of black soldiers shot off their guns in Brownsville, Texas, killing one resident, and none of their fellows would name them, Roosevelt ordered the dishonorable discharge of three black companies—156 men in all, including six winners of the Congressional Medal of Honor. Roosevelt's ingrained belief in Anglo-Saxon racial destiny (he called Indians "savages" and blacks "wholly unfit for the suffrage") did nothing to lessen Progressive intellectuals' enthusiasm for his New Nationalism. Even Jane Addams, one of the few Progressives to take a strong interest in black rights and a founder of the National Association for the Advancement of Colored People (NAACP), went along when the Progressive Party convention of 1912 rejected a civil rights plank in its platform and barred black delegates from the South.

Woodrow Wilson, a native of Virginia, could speak without irony of the South's "genuine representative government" and its exalted "standards of liberty." His administration imposed racial segregation in federal departments in Washington, D.C., and dismissed numerous black federal employees. Wilson allowed D. W. Griffith's film *Birth of a Nation*, which glorified the Ku Klux Klan as the defender of white civilization during Reconstruction, to have its premiere at the White House in 1915. "Have you a 'new freedom' for white Americans and a new slavery for your African-American fellow citizens?" William Monroe Trotter, the militant black editor of the *Boston Guardian* and founder of the all-black National Equal Rights League, asked the president.

Blacks subject to disenfranchisement and segregation were understandably skeptical of the nation's claim to embody freedom and fully appreciated the ways the symbols of liberty could coexist with brutal racial violence. In one of hundreds of lynchings during the Progressive era, a white mob in Springfield, Missouri, in 1906 falsely accused three black men of rape,

A cartoon from the St. Louis Post-Dispatch, *April 17, 1906, commenting on the lynching of three black men in Springfield, Missouri. The shadow cast by the Statue of Liberty forms a gallows on the ground.*

hanged them from an electric light pole, and burned their bodies in a public orgy of violence. Atop the pole stood a replica of the Statue of Liberty.

W. E. B. DU BOIS AND THE REVIVAL OF BLACK PROTEST

Black leaders struggled to find a strategy to rekindle the national commitment to equality that had flickered brightly, if briefly, during Reconstruction. No one thought more deeply, or over so long a period, about the black condition and the challenge it posed to American democracy than the scholar and activist W. E. B. Du Bois. Born in Great Barrington, Massachusetts, in 1868, and educated at Fisk and Harvard universities, Du Bois lived to his ninety-fifth year. The unifying theme of his career was Du Bois's effort to reconcile the contradiction between what he called "American freedom for whites and the continuing subjection of Negroes." His book *The Souls of Black Folk* (1903) issued a clarion call for blacks dissatisfied with the accommodationist policies of Booker T. Washington to press for equal rights. Du Bois believed that educated African-Americans like himself—the "talented tenth" of the black community—must use their education and training to challenge inequality.

In some ways, Du Bois was a typical Progressive who believed that investigation, exposure, and education would lead to solutions for social problems. As a professor at Atlanta University, he projected a grandiose plan for decades of scholarly study of black life in order to make the country aware of racism and point the way toward its elimination. But he also understood the necessity of political action.

In 1905, Du Bois gathered a group of black leaders at Niagara Falls (meeting on the Canadian side since no American hotel would provide accommodations) and organized the Niagara movement, which sought to reinvigorate the abolitionist tradition. "We claim for ourselves," Du Bois wrote in the group's manifesto, "every single right that belongs to a freeborn American, political, civil, and social; and until we get these rights we will never cease to protest and assail the ears of America." The Declaration of Principles adopted at Niagara Falls called for restoring to blacks the right to vote, an end to racial segregation, and complete equality in economic and educational opportunity. These would remain the cornerstones of the black struggle for racial justice for decades to come. Four years later, Du Bois joined with a group of mostly white reformers shocked by a lynching in Springfield, Illinois (Lincoln's adult home), to create the National Association for the Advancement of Colored People. The NAACP, as it was known, launched a long struggle for the enforcement of the Fourteenth and Fifteenth Amendments.

W. E. B. Du Bois, founder of the NAACP and editor of its magazine, The Crisis, *in his New York office.*

The NAACP's legal strategy won a few victories. In *Bailey v. Alabama* (1911), the Supreme Court overturned southern "peonage" laws that made it a crime for sharecroppers to break their labor contracts. Six years later, it ruled unconstitutional a Louisville zoning regulation excluding blacks from living in certain parts of the city (primarily because it interfered with whites' right to sell their property as they saw fit). Overall, however, the Progressive era witnessed virtually no progress toward racial justice. At a time when Americans' rights were being reformulated, blacks, said Moorfield Story, the NAACP's president, enjoyed a "curious citizenship." They shared obligations like military service, but not "the fundamental rights to which all men are entitled unless we repudiate . . . the Declaration of Independence."

CLOSING RANKS

Among black Americans, the wartime language of freedom inspired hopes for a radical change in the country's racial system. With the notable exception of William Monroe Trotter, most black leaders saw American participation in the war as an opportunity to make real the promise of freedom. To Trotter, much-publicized German atrocities were no worse than American lynchings; rather than making the world safe for democracy, the government should worry about "making the South safe for the Negroes." Yet the black press rallied to the war. Du Bois himself, in a widely reprinted editorial in the NAACP's monthly magazine, *The Crisis*, called on African-Americans to "close ranks" and enlist in the army, to help "make our own America a real land of the free."

Black participation in the Civil War had helped to secure the destruction of slavery and the achievement of citizenship. But during World War I, closing ranks did not bring significant gains. The navy barred blacks entirely, and the segregated army confined most of the 400,000 blacks who served in the war to supply units rather than combat. Contact with African colonial soldiers fighting alongside the British and French widened the horizons of black American soldiers. But while colonial troops marched in the victory parade in Paris, the Wilson administration did not allow black Americans to participate.

THE GREAT MIGRATION AND THE "PROMISED LAND"

Nonetheless, the war unleashed social changes that altered the contours of American race relations. The combination of increased wartime production and a drastic falloff in immigration from Europe once war broke out opened thousands of industrial jobs to black laborers for the first time, inspiring a large-scale migration from South to North. On the eve of World War I, 90 percent of the African-American population still lived in the South. Most northern cities had tiny black populations, and domestic and service work still predominated among both black men and women in the North. But between 1910 and 1920, half a million blacks left the South. The black population of Chicago more than doubled, New York City's rose 66 percent, and smaller industrial cities like Akron, Buffalo, and Trenton showed similar gains.

Many motives sustained the Great Migration—higher wages in northern factories than were available in the South (even if blacks remained confined to menial and unskilled positions), opportunities for educating their children, escape from the threat of lynching, and the prospect of exercising

A black veteran watches his regiment parade in New York City after the end of the war.

the right to vote. Migrants spoke of a Second Emancipation, of "crossing over Jordan," and of leaving the realm of pharaoh for the Promised Land. One group from Mississippi stopped to sing, "I am bound for the land of Canaan," after their train crossed the Ohio River into the North.

The black migrants, mostly young men and women, carried with them "a new vision of opportunity, of social and economic freedom," as Alain Locke explained in the preface to his influential book, *The New Negro* (1925). Yet the migrants encountered vast disappointments—severely restricted employment opportunities, exclusion from unions, rigid housing segregation, and outbreaks of violence that made it clear that no region of the country was free from racial hostility. More white southerners than blacks moved north during the war, often with similar economic aspirations. But the new black presence, coupled with demands for change inspired by the war, created a racial tinderbox that needed only an incident to trigger an explosion.

Table 19.1 THE GREAT MIGRATION			
City	Black Population, 1910	Black Population, 1920	Percent Increase
New York	91,709	152,467	66.3%
Philadelphia	84,459	134,229	58.9
Chicago	44,103	109,458	148.2
St. Louis	43,960	69,854	58.9
Detroit	5,741	40,838	611.3
Pittsburgh	25,623	37,725	47.2
Cleveland	8,448	34,451	307.8

RACIAL VIOLENCE, NORTH AND SOUTH

Dozens of blacks were killed during a 1917 riot in East St. Louis, Illinois, where employers had recruited black workers in an attempt to weaken unions (most of which excluded blacks from membership). In 1919, more than 250 persons died in riots in the urban North. Most notable was the violence in Chicago, touched off by the drowning by white bathers of a black teenager who accidentally crossed the unofficial dividing line between black and white beaches on Lake Michigan. The riot that followed raged for five days and involved pitched battles between the races throughout the city. By the time the National Guard restored order, 38 persons had been killed and over 500 injured.

Violence was not confined to the North. In the year after the war ended, seventy-six persons were lynched in the South, including several returning black veterans wearing their uniforms. In Phillips County, Arkansas, attacks on striking black sharecroppers by armed white vigilantes left as many as 200 persons dead and required the intervention of the army to restore order. The worst race riot in American history occurred in Tulsa, Oklahoma, in 1921, when more than 300 blacks were killed and over 10,000 left homeless after a white mob, including police and National Guardsmen, burned an all-black section of the city to the ground. The violence erupted after a group of black veterans tried to prevent the lynching of a youth who had accidently tripped and fallen on a white female elevator operator, causing rumors of rape to sweep the city.

THE RISE OF GARVEYISM

World War I kindled a new spirit of militancy. The East St. Louis riot of 1917 inspired a widely publicized Silent Protest Parade on New York's Fifth Avenue

The silent parade down Fifth Avenue, July 28, 1917, in which 10,000 black marchers protested the East St. Louis race riot.

in which 10,000 blacks silently carried placards reading, "Mr. President, Why Not Make America Safe for Democracy?" In the new densely populated black ghettos of the North, widespread support emerged for the Universal Negro Improvement Association, a movement for African independence and black self-reliance launched by Marcus Garvey, a recent immigrant from Jamaica. Freedom for Garveyites meant national self-determination. Blacks, they insisted, should enjoy the same internationally recognized identity enjoyed by other peoples in the aftermath of the war. "Everywhere we hear the cry of freedom," Garvey proclaimed in 1921. "We desire a freedom that will lift us to the common standard of all men, . . . freedom that will give us a chance and opportunity to rise to the fullest of our ambition and that we cannot get in countries where other men rule and dominate." Du Bois and other established black leaders viewed Garvey as little more than a demagogue. They applauded when the government deported him after a conviction for mail fraud. But the massive following his movement achieved testified to the sense of betrayal that had been kindled in black communities during and after the war.

1919

A WORLDWIDE UPSURGE

The combination of militant hopes for social change and disappointment with the war's outcome was evident far beyond the black community. In the Union of Soviet Socialist Republics (or Soviet Union), as Russia had been renamed after the revolution, Lenin's government had nationalized landholdings, banks, and factories and proclaimed the socialist dream of a workers' government. The Russian Revolution and the democratic aspirations unleashed by World War I sent tremors of hope and fear throughout the world. Like 1848 and, in the future, 1968, 1919 was a year of worldwide social and political upheaval. Inspired by Lenin's call for revolution, communist-led governments came to power in Bavaria (a part of Germany) and Hungary. General strikes demanding the fulfillment of wartime promises of "industrial democracy" took place in Belfast, Glasgow, and Winnipeg. In Spain, anarchist peasants began seizing land. Crowds in India challenged British rule, and nationalist movements in other colonies demanded independence. "We are living and shall live all our lives in a revolutionary world," wrote Walter Lippmann.

The worldwide revolutionary upsurge produced a countervailing mobilization by opponents of radical change. Even as they fought the Germans, the Allies viewed the Soviet government as a dire threat and attempted to overturn it. In the summer of 1918, Allied expeditionary forces—British, French, Japanese, and Americans—landed in Russia to aid Lenin's opponents in the civil war that had engulfed the country. The last of them did not leave until 1920.

Wilson's policies toward the Soviet Union revealed the contradictions within the liberal internationalist vision. On the one hand, in keeping with the principles of the Fourteen Points and its goal of a worldwide economic open door, Wilson hoped to foster trade with the new government. On the other, fear of communism as a source of international instability and a threat to private property inspired military intervention in Russia. The Allies did not invite the Soviet Union to the Versailles peace conference, and Wilson refused to extend diplomatic recognition to Lenin's government. The Soviet regime survived, but in the rest of the world the tide of change receded. By the fall, the mass strikes had been suppressed and conservative governments had been installed in central Europe. Anticommunism would remain a pillar of twentieth-century American foreign policy.

UPHEAVAL IN AMERICA

In the United States, 1919 also brought unprecedented turmoil. It seemed all the more disorienting for occurring in the midst of a worldwide flu epidemic that killed between 20 and 40 million persons, including nearly 700,000 Americans. Racial violence, as noted above, was widespread. In June, bombs exploded at the homes of prominent Americans including the attorney general, A. Mitchell Palmer, who escaped uninjured. Among aggrieved American workers, wartime language linking patriotism with democracy and freedom inspired hopes that an era of social justice and economic empowerment was at hand. In 1917, Wilson had told the AFL, "While we are fighting for freedom, we must see to it among other things that labor is free." Labor took him seriously—more seriously, it seems, than Wilson intended. The government, as one machinist put it, had "proclaimed to the World that the freedom and democracy we are fighting for shall be practiced in the industries of America."

By the war's end, many Americans believed that the country stood on the verge of what Herbert Hoover called " a new industrial order." Sidney Hillman, leader of the garment workers' union, was one of those caught up in the utopian dreams inspired by the war and reinforced by the Russian Revolution. "One can hear the footsteps of the Deliverer," he wrote. "Labor will rule and the World will be free." In 1919, over 4 million workers engaged in strikes—the greatest wave of labor unrest in American history. There were walkouts, among many others, by textile workers, telephone operators, and Broadway actors. Throughout the country, workers appropriated the imagery and rhetoric of the war, parading in army uniforms with Liberty buttons, denouncing their employers as "kaisers," and demanding "freedom in the workplace." They were met by an unprecedented mobilization of employers, government, and private patriotic organizations.

The strike wave began in January 1919 in Seattle, where a walkout of shipyard workers mushroomed into a general strike that for once united AFL unions and the IWW. For five days, a committee of labor leaders oversaw city services, until federal troops arrived to end the strike. In

An advertisement placed by a steel company in a Pittsburgh newspaper announces, in several languages, that the steel strike of 1919 "has failed." The use of the figure of Uncle Sam illustrates how the companies clothed their anti-union stance in the language of patriotism.

Local police with literature seized from a Communist Party office in Cambridge, Massachusetts, November 1919.

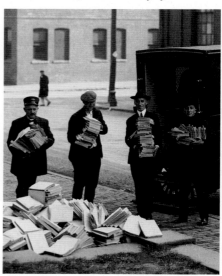

September, Boston policemen struck for higher wages and shorter working hours. Declaring "there is no right to strike against the public safety," Massachusetts governor Calvin Coolidge called out the National Guard to patrol the city and fired the entire police force. In the nation's coalfields, a company manager observed, wartime propaganda had raised unrealistic expectations among workers, who took the promise of "an actual emancipation" too "literally." When the war ended, miners demanded an end to company absolutism. Their strike was ended by a court injunction obtained by Attorney General Palmer.

THE GREAT STEEL STRIKE

The wartime rhetoric of economic democracy and freedom helped to inspire the era's greatest labor uprising, the 1919 steel strike. Centered in Chicago, it united some 365,000 mostly immigrant workers in demands for union recognition, higher wages, and an eight-hour workday. Before 1917, the steel mills were little autocracies where managers arbitrarily established wages and working conditions and suppressed all efforts at union organizing. During the war, workers flooded into the Amalgamated Association, the union that had been nearly destroyed by its defeat at Homestead a generation earlier. By the end of 1918, they had won an eight-hour day. Employers' anti-union activities resumed following the armistice that ended the fighting. "For why this war?" asked one Polish immigrant steelworker at a union meeting. "For why we buy Liberty bonds? For the mills? No, for freedom and America—for everybody. No more [work like a] horse and wagon. For eight-hour day."

In response to the strike, steel magnates launched a concerted counterattack. Employers appealed to anti-immigrant sentiment among native-born workers, many of whom returned to work, and conducted a propaganda campaign that associated the strikers with the IWW, communism, and disloyalty. "Americanism vs. Alienism" was the issue of the strike, declared the *New York Tribune*. With middle-class opinion having turned against the labor movement and police in Pittsburgh assaulting workers on the streets, the strike collapsed in early 1920.

THE RED SCARE

Many Progressives hoped to see the wartime apparatus of economic planning continue after 1918. The Wilson administration, however, quickly dismantled the agencies that had established controls over industrial production and the labor market, although during the 1930s they would serve as models for some policies of Franklin D. Roosevelt's New Deal. Wartime repression of dissent, however, continued. It reached its peak with the Red Scare of 1919–1920, a short-lived but intense period of political intolerance inspired by the postwar strike wave and the social tensions and fears generated by the Russian Revolution.

Convinced that episodes like the steel strike were part of a worldwide communist conspiracy, Attorney General A. Mitchell Palmer in November 1919 and January 1920 dispatched federal agents to raid the offices of radical and labor organizations throughout the country. They carried search warrants so broad that they reminded those with a sense of history of the writs of assistance against which James Otis had eloquently protested as being destructive of liberty in 1761. The Palmer Raids were overseen by the twenty-four-year-old director of the Radical Division of the Justice Department, J. Edgar Hoover. Over 5,000 persons were arrested, most of them without warrants, and held for months without charge. The government deported hundreds of immigrant radicals, including Emma Goldman, the prominent radical speaker mentioned in the previous chapter. Hoover also began compiling files on thousands of Americans suspected of holding radical political ideas, a practice he would later continue as head of the Federal Bureau of Investigation.

The abuse of civil liberties in early 1920 was so severe that Palmer came under heavy criticism from Congress and much of the press. Secretary of Labor Louis Post began releasing imprisoned immigrants, and the Red Scare collapsed. Even the explosion of a bomb outside the New York Stock Exchange in September 1920, which killed forty persons, failed to rekindle it. (The perpetrators of this terrorist explosion, the worst on American soil until the Oklahoma City bombing of 1995, were never identified.) The reaction to the Palmer Raids planted the seeds for a new appreciation of the importance of civil liberties that would begin to flourish during the 1920s. But in their immediate impact, the events of 1919 and 1920 dealt a devastating setback to radical and labor organizations of all kinds and kindled an intense identification of patriotic Americanism with support for the political and economic status quo. The IWW had been effectively destroyed, and many moderate unions lay in disarray. The Socialist Party crumbled under the weight of governmental repression (the New York legislature expelled five Socialist members, and Congress denied Victor Berger the seat to which he had been elected from Wisconsin) and internal differences over the Russian Revolution.

WILSON AT VERSAILLES

The beating back of demands for fundamental social change was a severe rebuke to the hopes with which so many Progressives had enlisted in the war effort. Wilson's inability to achieve a just peace based on the Fourteen Points compounded the sense of failure. Late in 1918, the president traveled to France to attend the Versailles peace conference. Greeted by ecstatic Paris crowds, he declared that American soldiers had come to Europe "as crusaders, not merely to win a war, but to win a cause . . . to lead the world on the way of liberty." But he proved a less adept negotiator than his British and French counterparts, David Lloyd George and Georges Clemenceau.

Part of the crowd that greeted President Wilson in November 1918 when he traveled to Paris to take part in the peace conference. An electric sign proclaims "Long Live Wilson."

While the Fourteen Points had called for "open covenants openly arrived at," the negotiations were conducted in secret. The Versailles Treaty did accomplish some of Wilson's goals. It established the League of Nations, the body central to his vision of a new international order. It applied the principle of self-determination to eastern Europe and redrew the map of that region. From the ruins of the Austro-Hungarian empire and parts of Germany and czarist Russia, new European nations emerged from the war—Finland, Poland, Czechoslovakia, Austria, Hungary, Latvia, Lithuania, Estonia, and Yugoslavia. Some enjoyed ethno-linguistic unity, while others comprised unstable combinations of diverse nationalities.

Despite Wilson's pledge of a peace without territorial acquisitions or vengeance, the Versailles Treaty was a harsh document that all but guaranteed future conflict in Europe. Clemenceau won for France the right to occupy the Saar Basin and Rhineland—iron- and coal-rich parts of Germany. The treaty placed strict limits on the size of Germany's future army and navy. Lloyd George persuaded Wilson to agree to a clause declaring Germany morally responsible for the war and setting astronomical repara-

World War I and the Versailles Treaty redrew the map of Europe and the Middle East. The Austro-Hungarian and Ottoman empires ceased to exist, and Germany and Russia were reduced in size. A group of new states emerged in eastern Europe, embodying the principle of self-determination, one of Woodrow Wilson's Fourteen Points.

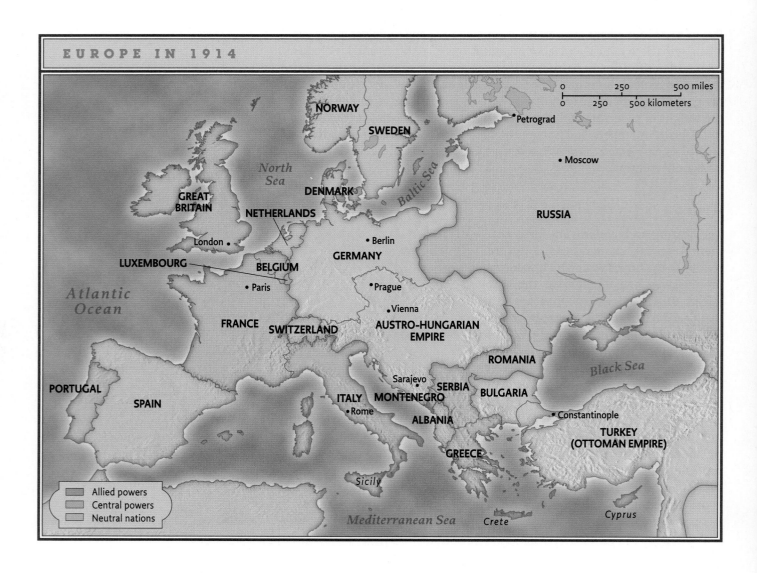

EUROPE IN 1914

- Allied powers
- Central powers
- Neutral nations

tions payments (they were variously estimated at between $33 billion and $56 billion), which crippled the German economy.

IMPOSSIBLE DEMANDS

Outside of Europe, the idea of "self-determination" was stillborn. When the peace conference opened, Secretary of State Robert Lansing warned that the phrase was "loaded with dynamite" and would "raise hopes which can never be realized." Wilson's language, he feared, had put "dangerous" ideas "into the minds of certain races" and would inspire "impossible demands, and cause trouble in many lands." As Lansing anticipated, advocates of colonial independence descended on Paris to lobby the peace negotiators. Arabs demanded that a unified independent state be carved from the old Ottoman empire in the Middle East. Nguyen That Thanh, a young Vietnamese patriot working in Paris, pressed his people's claim for greater rights within the French empire. W. E. B. Du Bois organized a Pan-African Congress in Paris that put forward the idea of a self-governing nation to be

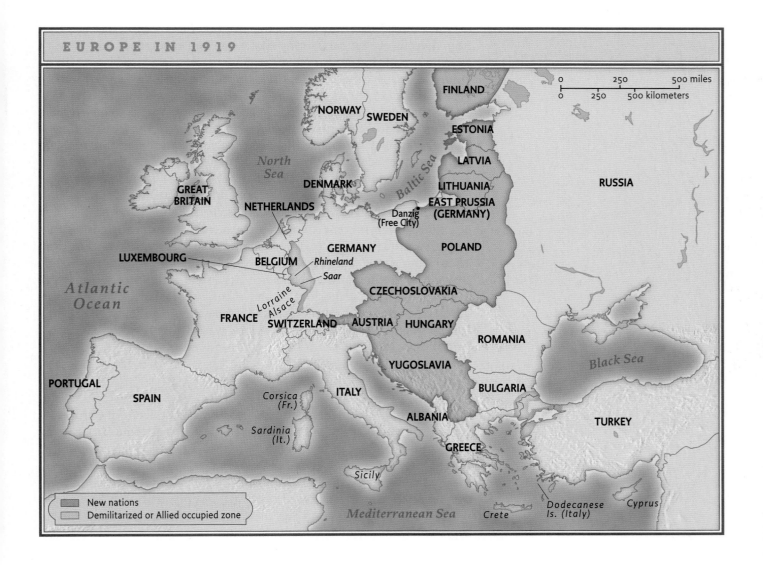

EUROPE IN 1919

New nations
Demilitarized or Allied occupied zone

carved out of Germany's African colonies. Koreans, Indians, Irish, and others also pressed claims for self-determination.

The British and French, however, had no intention of applying this principle to their own empires. They rebuffed the pleas of colonial peoples for self-rule. During the war, the British had encouraged Arab nationalism as a weapon against the Ottoman empire and had also pledged to create a homeland in Palestine for the persecuted Jews of Europe. In fact, the victors of World War I divided Ottoman territory into a series of new territories, including Syria, Lebanon, Iraq, and Palestine, controlled by the victorious Allies under League of Nations "mandates." South Africa, Australia, and Japan acquired former German colonies in Africa and Asia. Nor did Ireland achieve its independence at Versailles. Only at the end of 1921 did Britain finally agree to the creation of the Irish Free State, while continuing to rule the northeastern corner of the island.

THE SEEDS OF WARS TO COME

Du Bois, as noted above, had hoped that black participation in the war effort would promote racial justice at home and self-government for colonies abroad. "We return," he wrote in *The Crisis* in May 1919, "we return from fighting, we return fighting. Make way for Democracy!" But the war's aftermath both in the United States and overseas left him bitterly disappointed. Du Bois concluded that Wilson had "never at any single moment meant to include in his democracy" black Americans or the colonial peoples of the world. "Most men today," he complained, "cannot conceive of a freedom that does not involve somebody's slavery." In 1903, in *The Souls of Black Folk*, Du Bois had made the memorable prediction that "the problem of the twentieth century is the problem of the color-line." He now forecast a "fight for freedom" that would pit "black and brown and yellow men" throughout the world against racism and imperialism.

As Du Bois recognized, World War I sowed the seeds not of a lasting peace but of wars to come. German resentment over the peace terms would help to fuel the rise of Adolf Hitler and the coming of World War II. Nguyen That Thanh would take the name Ho Chi Minh and lead a long and bloody struggle for Vietnamese independence. At the end of the twentieth century, in the breakup of Czechoslovakia and Yugoslavia, violence over the status of Northern Ireland, and the seemingly unending conflict in the Middle East between Arabs and Israelis, the world was still haunted by the ghost of Versailles.

THE TREATY DEBATE

One final disappointment awaited Wilson on his return from Europe. He viewed the new League of Nations as the war's finest legacy. But many Americans feared that membership in the League would commit the United States to an open-ended involvement in the affairs of other countries. Wilson asserted that the United States could not save the world without being continually involved with it. His opponents, led by Senator Henry Cabot Lodge of Massachusetts, argued that the League threatened to deprive the country of its freedom of action.

A considerable majority of senators would have accepted the treaty with "reservations" ensuring that the obligation to assist League members against attack did not supercede the power of Congress to declare war. As governor of New Jersey and as president, Wilson had proved himself to be a skilled politician, capable of compromising with opponents. In this case, however, convinced that the treaty reflected "the hand of God," Wilson refused to negotiate with congressional leaders. In October 1919, in the midst of the League debate, Wilson suffered a serious stroke. Although the extent of his illness was kept secret, he remained incapacitated for the rest of his term. In effect, his wife, Edith, headed the government for the next seventeen months. In November 1919 and again in March 1920, the Senate rejected the Versailles Treaty.

American involvement in World War I lasted barely nineteen months, but it cast a long shadow over the following decade—and, indeed, the rest of the century. In its immediate aftermath, the country retreated from international involvements. But in the long run, Wilson's combination of idealism and power politics had an enduring impact. His appeals to democracy, open markets, and a special American mission to instruct the world in freedom coupled with a willingness to intervene abroad militarily to promote American interests and values would create the model for twentieth-century American international relations.

On its own terms, the war to make the world safe for democracy failed. Even great powers cannot always bend the world to their purposes. The war brought neither stability nor democracy to most of the world, and it undermined freedom in the United States. It also led to the eclipse of Progressivism. Republican candidate Warren G. Harding, who had no connection with the party's Progressive wing, swept to victory in the presidential election of 1920. Harding's campaign centered on a "return to normalcy" and a repudiation of what he called "Wilsonism." He received 60 percent of the popular vote. Begun with idealistic goals and grand hopes for social change, American involvement in the Great War laid the foundation for one of the most conservative decades in the nation's history.

Interrupting the Ceremony, *a 1918 cartoon from the* Chicago Tribune, *depicts Senate opponents of the Versailles Treaty arriving just in time to prevent the United States from becoming permanently ensnared in "foreign entanglements" through the League of Nations.*

SUGGESTED READING

Bederman, Gail. *Manliness and Civilization: A Cultural History of Race and Gender in the United States, 1880–1917* (1995). Explores how ideas concerning civilization and gender affected American foreign policy.

Dawley, Alan. *Changing the World: American Progressives in War and Revolution* (2003). Presents the war as a fulfillment and betrayal of the Progressive impulse.

Gilmore, Glenda E. *Gender and Jim Crow: Women and the Politics of White Supremacy in North Carolina, 1896–1920* (1996). A careful study of how black and white women negotiated the boundaries of segregation in a southern state.

Green, Elna C. *Southern Strategies: Southern Women and the Woman Suffrage Question* (1997). Describes how southern women campaigned for the vote without challenging the subordinate status of African-Americans.

Grossman, James R. *Land of Hope: Chicago, Black Southerners, and the Great Migration* (1989). An in-depth study of the migration of blacks to one American city.

Healy, David. *Drive to Hegemony: The United States in the Caribbean, 1898–1917* (1988). Examines American foreign policy in the Caribbean from McKinley to Wilson.

Kennedy, David M. *Over Here: The First World War and American Society* (1980). A comprehensive account of how the war affected domestic life in the United States.

Knock, Thomas J. *To End All Wars: Woodrow Wilson and the Quest for a New World Order* (1992). Discusses Wilson's internationalist vision and how it led the United States into a successful war and a failed peace.

Meier, August. *Negro Thought in America, 1880–1915* (1966). A pioneering study of the ideas of black leaders, including W. E. B. Du Bois.

Mitchell, David J. *1919: Red Mirage* (1970). A global account of the upheavals of 1919.

Preston, William, Jr. *Aliens and Dissenters: Federal Suppression of Radicals, 1903–1933* (1963). An influential study of the federal government's efforts to suppress dissenting ideas, especially during and immediately after World War I.

Renda, Mary A. *Taking Haiti: Military Occupation and the Culture of U.S. Imperialism, 1915–1940* (2001). Examines the causes and consequences of the American occupation of Haiti.

Stein, Judith. *The World of Marcus Garvey: Race and Class in Modern Society* (1986). Places the Garvey movement in an Atlantic perspective linking Africa, the United States, and the West Indies.

Tuttle, William. *Race Riot: Chicago in the Red Summer of 1919* (1970). A vivid account of the most violent racial upheaval of the era.

Weinstein, James. *The Decline of Socialism in America, 1912–1925* (1967). Explores how World War I and the Russian Revolution contributed to the demise of the American Socialist Party.

REVIEW QUESTIONS

1. Explain the role of the Committee on Public Information (CPI) during the war and what admen (advertisers) were able to gain from the CPI.

2. Illustrate some wartime examples of coercive patriotism.

3. In what ways did the United States intervene in world affairs, aside from World War I, in the first two decades of the twentieth century?

4. What were the major arguments made by W .E. B. Du Bois in furthering civil rights in America?

5. What were the major causes of the Red Scare?

KEY TERMS

yellow fever (p. 721)

Vera Cruz incident (p. 724)

Sinking of the *Lusitania* (p. 726)

Selective Service Act (p. 729)

state sedition acts (p. 735)

Brownsville Affair (p. 744)

Bailey v. Alabama (p. 746)

Garvey and African nationalism (p. 748)

The United States in Russia (p. 749)

Red Scare bombings (p. 751)

REVIEW TABLE

Wartime and Freedom

Event	Date	Consequences
Espionage Act	1917	Restricted freedom of speech by prohibiting "false statements" that might impede military success
American Protective League	1917–1919	Members spied on their neighbors in order to identify radicals and critics of the war to the federal government
Anti-German Crusade	1917–1919	Prowar organizations targeted the use of German and expressions of German culture, banning German music and changing German names
Red Scare	1919–1920	Over five thousand persons are arrested without warrants and held without charge, while hundreds of others are deported

Part 5

DEPRESSION AND WARS, 1920–1953

For the United States and the world at large, the decades between the end of World War I and the middle of the twentieth century marked one of the most painful eras in modern history. These years witnessed the Great Depression (1929–1939), World War II (1939–1945), and the advent of a Cold War that pitted the United States and the Soviet Union, former wartime allies, against each other in a global contest for power. These epochal events produced the deaths of tens of millions of people and wreaked economic havoc on hundreds of millions of others. By the end of this period, the United States and the world lived with the anxiety caused by the constant threat of nuclear war.

These developments could not have been anticipated in the immediate aftermath of World War I. After that conflict, the United States withdrew from active involvement in international affairs and enjoyed a decade of economic prosperity. During the 1920s, conservatism dominated the political arena. The labor movement suffered setback after setback, the government turned its back on many of the reforms of the Progressive era, and organized feminism faded from the public sphere. A nineteenth-century understanding of freedom based on liberty of contract in an unregulated marketplace, much criticized in the years before World War I, gained a new lease on life during the administrations of Warren G. Harding and Calvin Coolidge.

If political dissent faded during the 1920s, cultural differences seemed stronger than ever. In the name of personal freedom, many Americans embraced a new culture, centered in the nation's cities, based on consumption and enjoyment of new mass forms of leisure and entertainment, including radio and motion pictures. Other Americans, living in rural areas of the

South and West where traditional religion still held sway, saw the new urban culture not as an expansion of freedom, but as a threat to an understanding of freedom rooted in long-established moral values. During the 1920s, debates over immigration, Prohibition, the teaching of Darwin's theory of evolution in public schools, and the behavior of young, sexually liberated women in the nation's cities reflected the tension between older and newer cultures, each with its own definition of freedom.

The heady days of the 1920s came to an abrupt end with the stock market crash of 1929, which ushered in the Great Depression, the greatest economic crisis in American history. With the federal government unable to reverse the economic decline or relieve widespread distress, the election of 1932 brought to the presidency Franklin D. Roosevelt, who promised a New Deal for the American people. Roosevelt presided over a profound political and social transformation in government, society, and understandings of freedom. During his presidency, the federal government undertook unprecedented initiatives in an attempt to stimulate economic recovery and expand Americans' economic liberties. The government determined what farmers could plant, required employers to deal with unions, insured bank deposits, regulated the stock market, loaned money to home owners, and provided payments to a majority of the elderly and unemployed. It transformed the physical environment through hydroelectric dams, reforestation projects, and rural electrification. Under Roosevelt's leadership, the Democratic Party was transformed into a coalition of farmers, white southerners, urban working-class voters representing numerous ethnic groups, and northern African-Americans. It dominated national politics for many years. The New Deal helped to inspire, and was powerfully influenced by, a popular upsurge that redefined the idea of freedom to include a public guarantee of economic security for ordinary citizens.

Even as the United States struggled with the economic crisis, events abroad drew the country into the largest war in human history. The rise of powerful dictatorships bent on military expansion—Germany in Europe and Japan in Asia—led inexorably to World War II. Most Americans hoped to remain aloof from the crisis. This "isolationism" restrained

Roosevelt's efforts to aid those fighting Germany, even though he saw Hitler's conquests in Europe as a threat to American security. When the Japanese attacked the American naval base at Pearl Harbor, Hawaii, on December 7, 1941, the United States became part of the war.

World War II expanded even further the size and power of the national government. War production finally ended the Depression and drew millions of Americans from rural areas into the army or to industrial centers in the North and West. The Four Freedoms—Roosevelt's statement of Allied war aims—became the wartime rallying cry. Unlike during World War I, the federal government promoted group equality as central to American freedom—although the internment of over 100,000 Japanese-Americans revealed the limits of racial tolerance. The war also placed on the national agenda, for the first time since Reconstruction, the contradiction between the nation's rhetoric of freedom and the condition of its black population. It inspired an upsurge of black militancy, expressed in the slogan "double-V"—victory over enemies overseas, and over racial inequality at home.

No retreat into isolationism followed World War II. The United States had refused to join the League of Nations, but it became the leading member of the United Nations, which was established in 1945. But the wartime alliance among the United States, Britain, and the Soviet Union soon shattered, replaced by the worldwide contest known as the Cold War. By the 1950s, through a series of global anticommunist alliances, the United States had taken on a permanent military presence throughout the world. As in previous wars, freedom both helped to mobilize public support for the Cold War and was subtly changed in the process. The defense of freedom—increasingly equated with "free enterprise"—became the rationale for the doctrine of "containment," or global opposition to the spread of communism. The Cold War also inspired an anticommunist crusade within the United States. In the late 1940s and early 1950s, thousands of Americans accused of holding "subversive" beliefs lost their jobs, and an atmosphere of political conformity dominated public life. The battle to defend the "free world" abroad produced severe infringements on freedom at home.

CHAPTER 20

From Business Culture to Great Depression: The Twenties, 1920–1932

Blues, *a 1929 painting by Archibald Motley Jr., depicts one side of the 1920s: dance halls, jazz bands, and drinking despite the advent of Prohibition.*

FOCUS QUESTIONS

• What were the main features of the new society of the 1920s?

• In what ways did government policy become pro-business in the 1920s?

• Why did the protection of civil liberties gain importance in the 1920s?

• What were the main expressions of fundamentalism and pluralism in the 1920s?

• What brought about the Great Depression?

In May 1920, at the height of the postwar Red Scare, police arrested two Italian immigrants accused of participating in a robbery at a South Braintree, Massachusetts, factory in which a security guard was killed. Nicola Sacco, a shoemaker, and Bartolomeo Vanzetti, an itinerant unskilled laborer, were anarchists who dreamed of a society in which government, churches, and private property had been abolished. They saw violence as an appropriate weapon of class warfare. But very little evidence linked them to this particular crime. One man claimed to have seen Vanzetti at the wheel of the getaway car, but all the other eyewitnesses described the driver quite differently. Disputed tests on one of the six bullets in the dead man's body suggested that it might have been fired from a gun owned by Sacco. Neither fingerprints nor possession of stolen money linked either to the crime. In the atmosphere of anti-radical and anti-immigrant fervor, however, their conviction was a certainty. "I have suffered," Vanzetti wrote from prison, "for things that I am guilty of. I am suffering because I am a radical and indeed I am a radical; I have suffered because I was an Italian, and indeed I am an Italian."

Although their 1921 trial had aroused little public interest outside the Italian-American community, the case of Sacco and Vanzetti attracted international attention during the lengthy appeals that followed. There were mass protests in Europe against their impending execution. In the United States, the movement to save their lives attracted the support of an impressive array of intellectuals, including the novelist John Dos Passos, the poet Edna St. Vincent Millay, and Felix Frankfurter, a professor at Harvard Law School and a future justice of the Supreme Court. In response to the mounting clamor, the governor of Massachusetts appointed a three-member commission to review the case, headed by Abbott Lawrence Lowell, the president of Harvard University (and for many years an official of the Immigration Restriction League). The commission upheld the verdict and death sentences, and on August 23, 1927, Sacco and Vanzetti died in the electric chair. "It is not every prisoner," remarked the journalist Heywood Broun, "who has a president of Harvard throw the switch for him."

The Sacco-Vanzetti case laid bare some of the fault lines beneath the surface of American society during the 1920s. The case, the writer Edmund Wilson commented, "revealed the whole anatomy of American life, with all its classes, professions and points of view and . . . it raised almost every fundamental question of our political and social system." It demonstrated how long the Red Scare extended into the 1920s and how powerfully it undermined basic American freedoms. It reflected the fierce cultural battles that raged in many communities during the decade. To many native-born Americans, the two men symbolized an alien threat to their way of life. To Italian-Americans, including respectable middle-class organizations like the Sons of Italy that raised money for the defense, the outcome symbolized the nativist prejudices and stereotypes that haunted immigrant communities. To Dos

A 1927 photograph shows Nicola Sacco and Bartolomeo Vanzetti outside the courthouse in Dedham, Massachusetts, surrounded by security agents and onlookers. They are about to enter the courthouse, where the judge will pronounce their death sentence.

Passos, the executions underscored the success of the anti-radical crusade: "They are stronger. They are rich. They hire and fire the politicians, the old judges, . . . the college presidents." Dos Passos's lament was a bitter comment on the triumph of pro-business conservatism during the 1920s.

In popular memory, the decade that followed World War I is recalled as the Jazz Age or the Roaring Twenties. With its flappers (young, sexually liberated women), speakeasies (nightclubs that sold liquor in violation of Prohibition), and a soaring stock market fueled by easy credit and a get-rich-quick outlook, it was a time of revolt against moral rules inherited from the nineteenth century. Observers from Europe, where class divisions were starkly visible in work, politics, and social relations, marveled at the uniformity of American life. Factories poured out standardized consumer goods, their sale promoted by national advertising campaigns. Conservatism dominated a political system from which radical alternatives seemed to have been purged. Radio and the movies spread mass culture throughout the nation. Americans seemed to dress alike, think alike, go to the same movies, and admire the same larger-than-life national celebrities.

Many Americans, however, did not welcome the new secular, commercial culture. They resented and feared the ethnic and racial diversity of America's cities and what they considered the lax moral standards of urban life. The 1920s was a decade of profound social tensions—between rural and urban Americans, traditional and "modern" Christianity, participants in the burgeoning consumer culture and those who did not fully share in the new prosperity.

Advertisements, like this one for a refrigerator, promised that consumer goods would enable Americans to fulfill their hearts' desires.

The spread of the telephone network hastened the nation's integration and opened further job opportunities for women. Lewis Hine photographed this telephone operator in the 1920s.

THE BUSINESS OF AMERICA

A DECADE OF PROSPERITY

The chief business of the American people," said Calvin Coolidge, who became president after Warren G. Harding's sudden death from a heart attack in 1923, "is business." Rarely in American history had economic growth seemed more dramatic, cooperation between business and government so close, and business values so widely shared. After a sharp postwar recession that lasted into 1922, the 1920s was a decade of prosperity. Productivity and economic output rose dramatically as new industries—chemicals, aviation, electronics—flourished and older ones like food processing and the manufacture of household appliances adopted Henry Ford's moving assembly line. By 1929, the United States produced over 40 percent of the world's manufactured goods.

The automobile was the backbone of economic growth. The most celebrated American factories now turned out cars, not textiles and steel as in the nineteenth century. Annual automobile production tripled during the 1920s, from 1.5 to 4.8 million. General Motors, which learned the secret of marketing numerous individual models and stylish designs, surpassed Ford with its cheap, standardized Model T (replaced in 1927 by the Model A). By 1929, the United States produced 85 percent of the world's cars and half of all American families owned one (a figure not reached in England until 1980). The automobile industry stimulated the expansion of steel, rubber, and oil production, road construction, and other sectors of the economy. It promoted tourism and the growth of suburbs (already, some commuters were driving to work) and helped to reduce rural isolation.

A NEW SOCIETY

During the 1920s, consumer goods of all kinds proliferated, marketed by salesmen and advertisers who promoted them as ways of satisfying Americans' psychological desires and everyday needs. Frequently purchased on credit through new installment buying plans, they rapidly altered daily life. Telephones made communication easier. Vacuum cleaners, washing machines, and refrigerators transformed work in the home and reduced the demand for domestic servants. Boosted by Prohibition and an aggressive advertising campaign that, according to the company's sales director, made it "impossible for the consumer to *escape*" the product, Coca-Cola became a symbol of American life.

Americans spent more and more of their income on leisure activities like vacations, movies, and sporting events. By 1929, weekly movie attendance had reached 80 million, double the figure of 1922. Hollywood films now dominated the world movie market. Movies had been produced early in the century in several American cities, but shortly before World War I filmmakers gravitated to Hollywood, a district of Los Angeles, attracted by the open space, year-round sunshine for outdoor filming, and varied scenery. In 1910, two French companies, Pathé and Gaumont, had been the world's leading film producers. By 1925, American releases outnumbered French by eight to one. In the 1920s, both companies abandoned film production for the more profitable business of distributing American films in Europe.

Radios and phonographs brought mass entertainment into Americans' living rooms. The number of radios in Americans' homes rose from 190,000 in 1923 to just under 5 million in 1929. These developments helped to create and spread a new celebrity culture, in which recording, film, and sports stars moved to the top of the list of American heroes. During the 1920s, over 100 million records were sold each year. RCA Victor sold so many recordings of the great opera tenor Enrico Caruso that he is sometimes called the first modern celebrity. He was soon joined by the film actor Charlie Chaplin, baseball player Babe Ruth, and boxer Jack Dempsey. Ordinary Americans followed every detail of their lives. Perhaps the decade's greatest celebrity, in terms of intensive press coverage, was the aviator Charles Lindbergh, who in 1927 made the first solo nonstop flight across the Atlantic.

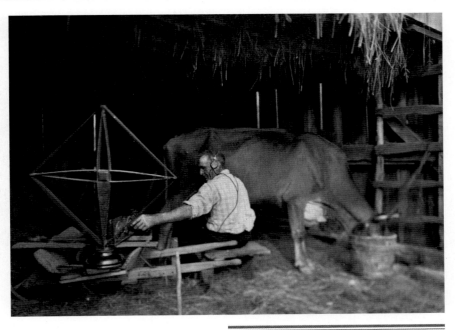

During the 1920s, radio penetrated virtually the entire country. In this photograph, a farmer tunes in to a program while milking his cow.

André Siegfried, a Frenchman who had visited the United States four times since the beginning of the century, commented in 1928 that a "new society" had come into being, in which Americans considered their "standard of living" a "sacred acquisition, which they will defend at any price." In this new "mass civilization," widespread acceptance of going into debt to purchase consumer goods had replaced the values of thrift and self-denial, central to nineteenth-century notions of upstanding character. Work, once seen as a source of pride in craft skill or collective empowerment via trade unions, now came to be valued as a path to individual fulfillment through consumption and entertainment.

THE LIMITS OF PROSPERITY

"Big business in America," remarked the journalist Lincoln Steffens, "is producing what the socialists held up as their goal—food, shelter, and clothing for all." But signs of future trouble could be seen beneath the prosperity of the 1920s. The fruits of increased production were very unequally distributed. Real wages for industrial workers (wages adjusted to take account of inflation) rose by one-quarter between 1922 and 1929, but corporate profits rose at more than twice that rate. The process of economic concentration continued unabated. A handful of firms dominated numerous sectors of the economy. In 1929, 1 percent of the nation's banks controlled half of its financial resources. Most of the small auto companies that had existed earlier in the century had fallen by the wayside. General Motors, Ford, and Chrysler now controlled four-fifths of the industry.

At the beginning of 1929, the share of national income of the wealthiest 5 percent of American families exceeded that of the bottom 60 percent. A majority of families had no savings, and an estimated 40 percent of the population remained in poverty, unable to participate in the flourishing

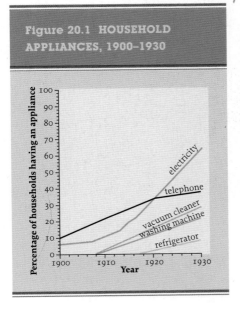

Figure 20.1 HOUSEHOLD APPLIANCES, 1900–1930

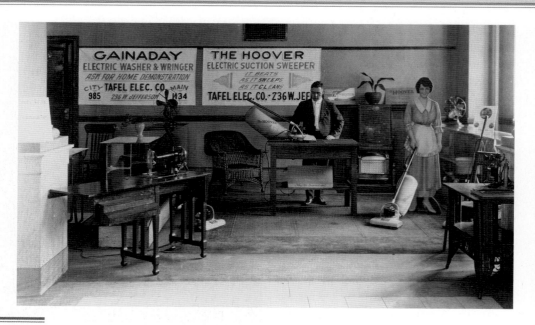

Electric washing machines and Hoover vacuum cleaners (demonstrated by a salesman) were two of the home appliances that found their way into many American homes during the 1920s. The woman on the right is a cardboard cutout.

consumer economy. Improved productivity meant that goods could be produced with fewer workers. During the 1920s, more Americans worked in the professions, retailing, finance, and education, but the number of manufacturing workers declined by 5 percent, the first such drop in the nation's history. Parts of New England were already experiencing the chronic unemployment caused by deindustrialization. Many of the region's textile companies failed in the face of low-wage competition from southern factories, or shifted production to take advantage of the South's cheap labor. Most advertisers directed their messages at businessmen and the middle class. At the end of the decade, 75 percent of American households still did not own a washing machine, and 60 percent had no radio.

THE FARMERS' PLIGHT

Nor did farmers share in the decade's prosperity. The "golden age" of American farming had reached its peak during World War I, when the need to feed war-torn Europe and government efforts to maintain high farm prices had raised farmers' incomes and promoted the purchase of more land on credit. Thanks to mechanization and the increased use of fertilizer and insecticides, agricultural production continued to rise even when government subsidies ended and world demand stagnated. As a result, farm incomes declined steadily and banks foreclosed tens of thousands of farms whose owners were unable to meet mortgage payments.

For the first time in the nation's history, the number of farms and farmers declined during the 1920s. For example, half the farmers in Montana lost their land to foreclosure between 1921 and 1925. Extractive industries, like mining and lumber, also suffered as their products faced a glut on the world market. During the decade, some 3 million persons migrated out of rural areas. Many headed for southern California, whose rapidly growing economy needed new labor. The population of Los Angeles, the West's leading industrial center, a producer of oil, automobiles, aircraft, and, of course, Hollywood movies, rose from 575,000 to 2.2 million during the decade, largely because of an influx of displaced farmers from the Midwest. Well before the 1930s, rural America was in an economic depression.

THE IMAGE OF BUSINESS

Even as unemployment remained high in Britain throughout the 1920s, and inflation and war reparations payments crippled the German economy, Hollywood films spread images of "the American way of life" across the globe. America, wrote the historian Charles Beard, was "boring its way" into the world's consciousness. In high wages, efficient factories, and the mass production of consumer goods, Americans seemed to have discovered the secret of permanent prosperity. Businessmen like Henry Ford and engineers like Herbert Hoover were cultural heroes. Photographers like Lewis Hine and Margaret Bourke-White and painters like Charles Sheeler celebrated the beauty of machines and factories. *The Man Nobody Knows*, a 1925 bestseller by advertising executive Bruce Barton, portrayed Jesus Christ as "the greatest advertiser of his day, . . . a virile go-getting he-man of business,"

Farmers, like this family of potato growers in rural Minnesota, did not share in the prosperity of the 1920s.

River Rouge Plant, *by the artist Charles Sheeler, exemplifies the "machine-age aesthetic" of the 1920s. Sheeler found artistic beauty in Henry Ford's giant automobile assembly factory.*

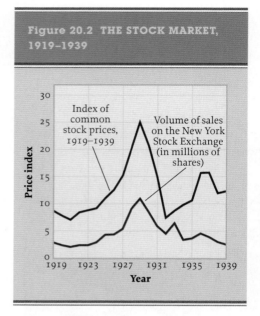

Figure 20.2 THE STOCK MARKET, 1919–1939

This graph illustrates the rapid rise and dramatic collapse of stock prices and the number of shares traded during the late 1920s.

who "picked twelve men from the bottom ranks and forged a great organization."

After the Ludlow Massacre of 1914, discussed in Chapter 18, John D. Rockefeller himself had hired a public relations firm to repair his tarnished image. Now, persuaded by the success of World War I's Committee on Public Information that it was possible, as an advertising magazine put it, to "sway the minds of whole populations," numerous firms established public relations departments. They aimed to justify corporate practices to the public and counteract its longstanding distrust of big business.

They succeeded in changing popular attitudes toward Wall Street. Congressional hearings of 1912–1914 headed by Louisiana congressman Arsène Pujo had laid bare the manipulation of stock prices by a Wall Street "money trust." The Pujo investigation had reinforced the widespread view of the stock market as a place where insiders fleeced small investors—as, indeed, they frequently did. But in the 1920s, as the steadily rising price of stocks made front-page news, the market attracted more investors. Many assumed that stock values would rise forever. By 1928, an estimated 1.5 million Americans owned stock—still a small minority of the country's 28 million families, but far more than in the past.

THE DECLINE OF LABOR

With the defeat of the labor upsurge of 1919 and the dismantling of the wartime regulatory state, business appropriated the rhetoric of Americanism and "industrial freedom" as weapons against labor unions. Some corporations during the 1920s implemented a new style of management. They provided their employees with private pensions and medical insurance plans, job security, and greater workplace safety. They established sports programs to occupy their employees' leisure time. They spoke of "welfare capitalism," a more socially conscious kind of business leadership, and trumpeted the fact that they now paid more attention to the "human factor" in employment.

At the same time, however, employers in the 1920s embraced the American Plan, at whose core stood the open shop—a workplace free of both government regulation and unions, except, in some cases, "company unions" created and controlled by management. Collective bargaining, declared one group of employers, represented "an infringement of personal liberty and a menace to the institutions of a free people." Prosperity, they insisted, depended on giving business complete freedom of action. This message was reinforced in a propaganda campaign that linked unionism and socialism as examples of the sinister influence of foreigners on American life. Even the most forward-looking companies continued to employ strikebreakers, private detectives, and the blacklisting of union organizers to prevent or defeat strikes.

During the 1920s, organized labor lost over 2 million members and unions agreed to demand after demand by employers in an effort to stave off complete elimination. In cities like Minneapolis, New Orleans, and Seattle, once centers of thriving labor movements, unions all but disappeared. Uprisings by the most downtrodden workers did occur sporadically throughout the decade. Southern textile mills witnessed desperate strikes by workers who charged employers with "making slaves out of the men and women" who labored there. Facing the combined opposition of business, local politicians, and the courts, as well as the threat of violence, such strikes were doomed to defeat.

THE EQUAL RIGHTS AMENDMENT

The idealistic goals of World War I, wrote the young minister Reinhold Niebuhr, seemingly had been abandoned: "We are rapidly becoming the most conservative nation on earth." Like the labor movement, feminists struggled to adapt to the new political situation. The achievement of suffrage in 1920 eliminated the bond of unity between various activists, each "struggling for her own conception of freedom," in the words of labor reformer Juliet Stuart Poyntz. Black feminists insisted that the movement must now demand enforcement of the Fifteenth Amendment in the South, but they won little support from white counterparts. A few prominent feminists, including Elizabeth Cady Stanton's daughter Harriot Stanton Blatch, joined the rapidly diminishing Socialist Party, convinced that women should support an independent electoral force that promoted governmental protection of vulnerable workers.

The long-standing division between two competing conceptions of woman's freedom—one based on motherhood, the other on individual autonomy and the right to work—now crystallized in the debate over an Equal Rights Amendment (ERA) to the Constitution promoted by Alice Paul and the National Women's Party. This amendment proposed to eliminate all legal distinctions "on account of sex." In Paul's opinion, the ERA followed logically from winning the right to vote. Having gained political equality, she insisted, women no longer required special legal protection—they needed equal access to employment, education, and all the other opportunities of citizens. To supporters of mothers' pensions and laws limiting women's hours of labor, which the ERA would sweep away, the proposal represented a giant step backward. Apart from the National Women's Party, every major female organization, from the League of Women Voters to the Women's Trade Union League, opposed the ERA.

In the end, none of these groups achieved success in the 1920s. The ERA campaign failed, and only six states ratified a proposed constitutional amendment giving Congress the power to prohibit child labor, which farm groups and business organizations opposed. In 1929, Congress repealed the Sheppard-Towner Act of 1921, a major achievement of the maternalist reformers that had provided federal assistance to programs for infant and child health.

WOMEN'S FREEDOM

If political feminism faded, the prewar feminist demand for personal freedom survived in the vast consumer marketplace and in the actual behavior of the decade's much-publicized liberated young women. Female liberation resurfaced as a lifestyle, the stuff of advertising and mass entertainment, stripped of any connection to political or economic radicalism. No longer one element in a broader program of social reform, sexual freedom now

Advertisers in the 1920s urged older women, as well as younger, to partake in new freedoms. In this ad for Modess sanitary napkins, part of a sales campaign entitled "Modernizing Mother," a woman tries to teach her mother an up-to-date dance. The ad's accompanying text urges women to abandon "old-fashioned ideas" and adopt "the new thought of not growing old."

The August 27, 1925, cover of Life *magazine shows a young man and a young woman dressed identically at the beach in revealing bathing suits (by 1920s standards) and enjoying cigarettes—symbols of female independence.*

meant individual autonomy or personal rebellion. With her bobbed hair, short skirts, public smoking and drinking, and unapologetic use of birth-control methods such as the diaphragm, the young, single "flapper" epitomized the change in standards of sexual behavior, at least in large cities. She frequented dance halls and music clubs where white people now performed "wild" dances like the Charleston that had long been popular in black communities. She attended sexually charged Hollywood films featuring stars like Clara Bow, the provocative " 'It' Girl," and Rudolph Valentino, the original onscreen "Latin Lover." When Valentino died of a sudden illness in 1926, crowds of grieving women tried to storm the funeral home.

What had been scandalous a generation earlier—women's self-conscious pursuit of personal pleasure—became a device to market goods from automobiles to cigarettes. In 1904, a woman had been arrested for smoking in public in New York City. Two decades later, Edward Bernays, the "father" of modern public relations, masterminded a campaign to persuade women to smoke, dubbing cigarettes women's "torches of freedom." The new freedom, however, was available only during one phase of a woman's life. Once she married, what Jane Addams had called the "family claim" still ruled. And marriage, according to one advertisement, remained "the one pursuit that stands foremost in the mind of every girl and woman." Having found a husband, women were expected to seek freedom within the confines of the home, finding "liberation," according to the advertisements, in the use of new labor-saving appliances.

BUSINESS AND GOVERNMENT

THE RETREAT FROM PROGRESSIVISM

In 1924, a social scientist remarked that the United States had just passed through "one of the most critical ten-year periods" in its history. Among the changes was the disintegration of Progressivism as a political movement and body of thought. The government's success in whipping up mass hysteria during the war seemed to undermine the very foundation of democratic thought—the idea of the rational, self-directed citizen. Followers of Sigmund Freud emphasized the unconscious, instinctual motivations of human behavior; scientists pointed to wartime IQ tests allegedly demonstrating that many Americans were mentally unfit for self-government. "The great bulk of people are stupid," declared one advertising executive, explaining why advertisements played on the emotions rather than providing actual information.

During the 1920s, Walter Lippmann published two of the most penetrating indictments of democracy ever written, *Public Opinion* and *The Phantom Public*, which repudiated the Progressive hope of applying "intelligence" to social problems in a mass democracy. Instead of acting out of careful consideration of the issues or even individual self-interest, Lippmann claimed, the American voter was ill-informed and prone to fits of enthusiasm. Not only were modern problems beyond the understanding of ordinary men and women (a sentiment that had earlier led Lippmann to favor administration by experts), but the independent citizen was nothing but a myth.

Like advertising copywriters and journalists, he continued, the government had perfected the art of creating and manipulating public opinion—a process Lippmann called the "manufacture of consent."

In 1929, the sociologists Robert and Helen Lynd published *Middletown*, a classic study of life in Muncie, Indiana, a typical community in the American heartland. The Lynds found that new leisure activities and a new emphasis on consumption had replaced politics as the focus of public concern. Elections were no longer "lively centers" of public attention as in the nineteenth century, and voter participation had fallen dramatically. National statistics bore out their point; the turnout of eligible voters, over 80 percent in 1896, had dropped to less than 50 percent in 1924. Many factors helped to explain this decline, including the consolidation of one-party politics in the South, the long period of Republican dominance in national elections, and the enfranchisement of women, who for many years voted in lower numbers than men. But the shift from public to private concerns also played a part. "The American citizen's first importance to his country," declared a Muncie newspaper, "is no longer that of a citizen but that of a consumer."

THE REPUBLICAN ERA

Government policies reflected the pro-business ethos of the 1920s. Recalling the era's prosperity, one stockbroker later remarked, "God, J. P. Morgan and the Republican Party were going to keep everything going forever." Business lobbyists dominated national conventions of the Republican Party. They called on the federal government to lower taxes on personal incomes and business profits, maintain high tariffs, and support employers' continuing campaign against unions. The administrations of Warren G. Harding and Calvin Coolidge obliged. "Never before, here or anywhere else," declared the *Wall Street Journal*, "has a government been so completely fused with business." The two presidents appointed so many pro-business members of the Federal Reserve Board, the Federal Trade Commission, and other Progressive era agencies that, complained Nebraska senator George W. Norris, they in effect repealed the regulatory system. The Harding administration did support Secretary of Commerce Herbert Hoover's successful effort to persuade the steel industry to reduce the workday from twelve to eight hours. But it resumed the practice of obtaining court injunctions to suppress strikes, as in a 1922 walkout of 250,000 railroad workers protesting a wage cut.

Under William Howard Taft, appointed chief justice in 1921, the Supreme Court remained strongly conservative. A resurgence of laissez-faire jurisprudence eclipsed the Progressive ideal of a socially active national state. The Court struck down a federal law that barred goods produced by child labor from interstate commerce. It even repudiated *Muller v. Oregon* (see Chapter 18) in a 1923 decision overturning a minimum wage law for women in Washington, D.C. Now that women enjoyed the vote, the justices declared, they were entitled to the same workplace freedom as men. "This," lamented Florence Kelley, "is a new Dred Scott decision," which, in the name of liberty of contract, "fills those words with the bitterest and most cruel mockery."

The policies of President Calvin Coolidge were music to the ears of big business, according to one 1920s cartoonist.

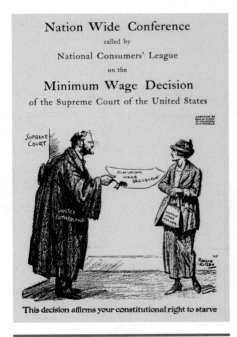

A 1923 cartoon criticizes the Supreme Court decision declaring unconstitutional a Washington, D.C., law establishing a minimum wage for women. Justice George Sutherland, appointed to the Court the previous year by President Harding, wrote the majority decision.

VOICES OF FREEDOM

FROM ANDRÉ SIEGFRIED,
"The Gulf Between," *Atlantic Monthly* (March 1928)

The French writer André Siegfried in 1928 commented on the rise of an industrial economy and consumer culture and the changes they produced in American society.

Never has Europe more eagerly observed, studied, discussed America; and never . . . have the two continents been wider apart in their aspirations and ideals. . . . Europe, after all, is not very different from what it was a generation ago; but there has been born since then a new America. . . .

The conquest of the continent has been completed, and—all recent American historians have noted the significance of the event—the western frontier has disappeared; the pioneer is no longer needed, and, with him, the mystic dream of the West . . . has faded away. Thus came the beginning of the era of organization: the new problem was not to conquer adventurously but to produce methodically. The great man of the new generation was no longer a pioneer like Lincoln . . . but . . . Henry Ford. From this time on, America has been no more an unlimited prairie with pure and infinite horizons, in

which free men may sport like wild horses, but a huge factory of prodigious efficiency. . . .

In the last twenty-five or thirty years America has produced a new civilization. . . . From a *moral point of view*, it is obvious that Americans have come to consider their standard of living as a somewhat sacred acquisition, which they will defend at any price. This means that they would be ready to make many an intellectual or even moral concession in order to maintain that standard.

From a *political point of view*, it seems that the notion of efficiency of production is on the way to taking [precedence over] the very notion of liberty. In the name of efficiency, one can obtain, from the American, all sorts of sacrifices in relation to his personal and even to certain of his political liberties. . . .

Mass production and mass civilization, its natural consequence, are the true characteristics of the new American society. . . . Lincoln, with his Bible and classical tradition, was easier for Europe to understand than Ford, with his total absence of tradition and his proud creation of new methods and new standards, especially conceived for a world entirely different from our own.

From Majority Opinion, Justice James C. McReynolds, in *Meyer v. Nebraska* (1923)

A landmark in the development of civil liberties, the Supreme Court's decision in *Meyer v. Nebraska* rebuked the coercive Americanization impulse of World War I, overturning a Nebraska law that required all school instruction to take place in English.

The problem for our determination is whether the statute [prohibiting instruction in a language other than English] as construed and applied unreasonably infringes the liberty guaranteed . . . by the Fourteenth Amendment. . . .

The American people have always regarded education and acquisition of knowledge as matters of supreme importance which should be diligently promoted. . . . The calling always has been regarded as useful and honorable, essential, indeed, to the public welfare. Mere knowledge of the German language cannot reasonably be regarded as harmful. Heretofore it has been commonly looked upon as helpful and desirable. [Meyer] taught this language in school as part of his occupation. His right to teach and the right of parents to engage him so to instruct their children, we think, are within the liberty of the Amendment.

It is said the purpose of the legislation was to promote civil development by inhibiting training and education of the immature in foreign tongues and ideals before they could learn English and acquire American ideals. . . . It is also affirmed that the foreign born population is very large, that certain communities commonly use foreign words, follow foreign leaders, move in a foreign atmosphere, and that the children are therefore hindered from becoming citizens of the most useful type and the public safety is impaired.

That the State may do much, go very far, indeed, in order to improve the quality of its citizens, physically, mentally, and morally, is clear; but the individual has certain fundamental rights which must be respected. The protection of the Constitution extends to all, to those who speak other languages as well as to those born with English on the tongue. Perhaps it would be highly advantageous if all had ready understanding of our ordinary speech, but this cannot be coerced by methods which conflict with the Constitution. . . . No emergency has arisen which rendered knowledge by a child of some language other than English so clearly harmful as to justify its inhibition with the consequent infringement of rights long freely enjoyed.

QUESTIONS

1. Why does Siegfried feel Europeans no longer find America understandable?

2. How does the decision in *Meyer v. Nebraska* expand the definition of liberty protected by the Fourteenth Amendment?

3. How do the two excerpts reflect the changes American society experienced in the 1910s and 1920s?

A 1924 cartoon commenting on the scandals of the Harding administration. The White House, Capitol, and Washington Monument have been sold to the highest bidder.

CORRUPTION IN GOVERNMENT

Warren G. Harding took office as president in 1921 promising a return to "normalcy" after an era of Progressive reform and world war. Reflecting the prevailing get-rich-quick ethos, his administration quickly became one of the most corrupt in American history. A likeable, somewhat ineffectual individual—he called himself "a man of limited talents from a small town"—Harding seemed to have little regard for either governmental issues or the dignity of the presidency. Prohibition did not cause him to curb his appetite for liquor. He continued a previous illicit affair with a young Ohio woman, Nan Britton. The relationship did not become known until 1927, when Britton published *The President's Daughter*, about their child to whom Harding had left nothing in his will.

Although his cabinet included men of integrity and talent, like Secretary of State Charles Evans Hughes and Secretary of Commerce Herbert Hoover, Harding also surrounded himself with cronies who used their offices for private gain. Attorney General Harry Daugherty accepted payments not to prosecute accused criminals. The head of the Veterans' Bureau, Charles Forbes, received kickbacks from the sale of government supplies. The most notorious scandal involved Secretary of the Interior Albert Fall, who accepted nearly $500,000 from private businessmen to whom he leased government oil reserves at Teapot Dome, Wyoming. Fall became the first cabinet member in history to be convicted of a felony.

THE ELECTION OF 1924

Harding's successor, Calvin Coolidge, who as governor of Massachusetts had won national fame for using state troops against striking Boston policemen in 1919, was a dour man of few words. But in contrast to his predecessor he seemed to exemplify Yankee honesty. The scandals subsided, but otherwise Coolidge continued his predecessor's policies. He twice vetoed the McNary-Haugen Bill, the top legislative priority of congressmen from farm states. This bill sought to have the government purchase agricultural products for sale overseas in order to raise farm prices. Coolidge denounced it as an unwarranted interference with the free market. In 1924, Coolidge was reelected in a landslide, defeating John W. Davis, a Wall Street lawyer nominated on the 103rd ballot by a badly divided Democratic convention. (This was when the comedian Will Rogers made the quip, often repeated in future years, "I am a member of no organized political party; I am a Democrat.")

One-sixth of the electorate in 1924 voted for Robert La Follette, running as the candidate of a new Progressive Party, which called for greater taxation of wealth, the conservation of natural resources, public ownership of the railroads, farm relief, and the end of child labor. Although such ideas had been proposed many times before World War I, Coolidge described the platform as a blueprint for a "communistic and socialistic" America. Despite endorsements from veteran Progressives like Jane Addams and John Dewey and the American Federation of Labor, La Follette could raise no more than $250,000 for his campaign. He carried only his native Wisconsin. But his candidacy demonstrated the survival of some currents of dissent in a highly conservative decade.

ECONOMIC DIPLOMACY

Foreign affairs also reflected the close working relationship between business and government. "Any student of modern diplomacy," declared Huntington Wilson, a State Department official, "knows that in these days of competition, capital, trade, agriculture, labor and statecraft all go hand in hand if a country is to profit." The 1920s marked a retreat from Wilson's goal of internationalism in favor of unilateral American actions mainly designed to increase exports and investment opportunities overseas. Indeed, what is sometimes called the "isolationism" of the 1920s represented a reaction against the disappointing results of Wilson's military and diplomatic pursuit of freedom and democracy abroad. The United States did play host to the Washington Naval Arms Conference of 1922 that negotiated reductions in the navies of Britain, France, Japan, Italy, and the United States. But the country remained outside the League of Nations. Even as American diplomats continued to press for access to markets overseas, the Fordney-McCumber Tariff of 1922 raised taxes on imported goods to their highest levels in history, a repudiation of Wilson's principle of promoting free trade.

Much foreign policy was conducted through private economic relationships rather than governmental action. The United States emerged from World War I as both the world's foremost center of manufacturing and the major financial power, thanks to British and French debts for American loans that had funded their war efforts. During the 1920s, New York bankers, sometimes acting on their own and sometimes with the cooperation of the Harding and Coolidge administrations, solidified their international position by extending loans to European and Latin American governments. They advanced billions of dollars to Germany to enable the country to meet its World War I reparations payments. American industrial firms, especially in auto, agricultural machinery, and electrical

A German cartoon inspired by President Coolidge's dispatch of American troops to Nicaragua. While Coolidge insisted that the United States acted in the interest of preserving international order, residents of other countries often saw the United States as a grasping imperial power.

equipment manufacturing, established plants overseas to supply the world market and take advantage of inexpensive labor. American investors gained control over raw materials such as copper in Chile and oil in Venezuela. In 1928, in the so-called Red Line Agreement, British, French, and American oil companies divided oil-producing regions in the Middle East and Latin America among themselves.

As before World War I, the government dispatched soldiers when a change in government in the Caribbean threatened American economic interests. Having been stationed in Nicaragua since 1912, American marines withdrew in 1925. But the troops soon returned in an effort to suppress a nationalist revolt headed by General Augusto César Sandino. Having created a National Guard headed by General Anastasio Somoza, the marines finally departed in 1933. A year later, Somoza assassinated Sandino and seized power. For the next forty-five years, he and his family ruled and plundered Nicaragua. Somoza was overthrown in 1978 by a popular movement calling itself the Sandinistas (see Chapter 26).

THE BIRTH OF CIVIL LIBERTIES

Among the casualties of World War I and the 1920s was Progressivism's faith that an active federal government embodied the national purpose and enhanced the enjoyment of freedom. Wartime and postwar repression, Prohibition, and the pro-business policies of the 1920s all illustrated, in the eyes of many Progressives, how public power could go grievously wrong.

This lesson opened the door to a new appreciation of civil liberties—rights an individual may assert even against democratic majorities—as essential elements of American freedom. Building on prewar struggles for freedom of expression by labor unions, socialists, and birth-control advocates, some reformers now developed a greater appreciation of the necessity of vibrant, unrestricted political debate. In the name of a "new freedom for the individual," the 1920s saw the birth of a coherent concept of civil liberties and the beginnings of significant legal protection for freedom of speech against the government.

THE "FREE MOB"

Wartime repression continued into the 1920s. Under the heading "Sweet Land of Liberty," *The Nation* magazine in 1923 detailed recent examples of the degradation of American freedom—lynchings in Alabama, Arkansas, and Florida; the beating by Columbia University students of an undergraduate who had written a letter defending freedom of speech and the press; the arrest of a union leader in New Jersey and 400 members of the IWW in California; refusal to allow a socialist to speak in Pennsylvania. Throughout the 1920s, artistic works with sexual themes were subjected to rigorous censorship. The Postal Service removed from the mails books it deemed obscene. The Customs Service barred works by the sixteenth-century French satirist Rabelais, the modern novelist James Joyce, and many others from entering the country. A local crusade against indecency made the phrase "Banned in Boston" a term of ridicule among upholders of artistic freedom. Boston's Watch and Ward Committee excluded sixty-five books from the city's bookstores, including works by the novelists Upton Sinclair, Theodore Dreiser, and Ernest Hemingway.

Hollywood producers feared that publicity over actress Mary Pickford's divorce, actor Wallace Reid's death from a drug overdose, and a murder trial involving actor Fatty Arbuckle would reinforce the belief that movies promoted immorality. In 1922, the film industry adopted the Hays code, a sporadically enforced set of guidelines that prohibited movies from depicting nudity, long kisses, and adultery, and barred scripts that portrayed clergymen in a negative light or criminals sympathetically. (The code in some ways anticipated recent efforts by television networks, music companies, and video game producers to adopt self-imposed guidelines to fend off governmental regulation.) Filmmakers hoped that self-censorship would prevent censorship by local governments, a not uncommon occurrence since the courts deemed movies a business subject to regulation, not a form of expression. Not until 1951, in a case involving *The Miracle*, a film many Catholics found offensive, would the Supreme Court declare movies an artistic form protected by the First Amendment.

Even as Europeans turned in increasing numbers to American popular culture and consumer goods, some came to view the country as a repressive cultural wasteland. Americans, commented the British novelist D. H. Lawrence, who lived for a time in the United States, prided themselves on being the "land of the free," but "the free mob" had destroyed the right to dissent. "I have never been in any country," he wrote, "where the individual has such an abject fear of his fellow countrymen." Disillusionment with the conservatism of American politics and the materialism of the culture inspired some American artists and writers to emigrate to Paris. The Lost Generation of cultural exiles included novelists and poets like Ernest Hemingway, Gertrude Stein, and F. Scott Fitzgerald. Europe, they felt, valued art and culture, and appreciated unrestrained freedom of expression (and, of course, allowed individuals to drink legally).

A "CLEAR AND PRESENT DANGER"

During World War I, the minister John Haynes Holmes later recalled, "there suddenly came to the fore in our nation's life the new issue of civil liberties." The arrest of antiwar dissenters under the Espionage and Sedition Acts inspired the formation in 1917 of the Civil Liberties Bureau, which in 1920 became the American Civil Liberties Union (ACLU). For the rest of the century, the ACLU would take part in most of the landmark cases that helped to bring about a "rights revolution." Its efforts helped to give meaning to traditional civil liberties like freedom of speech and invented new ones, like the right to privacy. When it began, however, the ACLU was a small, beleaguered organization. A coalition of pacifists, Progressives shocked by wartime repression, and lawyers outraged at what they considered violations of Americans' legal rights, it saw its own pamphlets defending free speech barred from the mails by postal inspectors.

Prior to World War I, the Supreme Court had done almost nothing to protect the rights of unpopular minorities. Now, it was forced to address the question of the permissible limits on political and economic dissent. In its initial decisions, it dealt the concept of civil liberties a series of devastating blows. In 1919, the Court upheld the constitutionality of the Espionage Act and the conviction of Charles T. Schenck, a socialist who had distributed antidraft leaflets through the mails. Speaking for the Court, Justice Oliver Wendell Holmes declared that the First Amendment did not prevent Congress from prohibiting speech that presented a "clear and present danger" of inspiring illegal actions. Free speech, he observed, "would not protect a man in falsely shouting fire in a theater and causing a panic."

For the next half-century, Holmes's doctrine would remain the basic test in First Amendment cases. Since the Court usually allowed public officials to decide what speech was in fact "dangerous," it hardly provided a stable basis for the defense of free expression in times of crisis. A week after *Schenck v. United States*, the Court unanimously upheld the conviction of Eugene V. Debs for a speech condemning the war. It also affirmed the wartime jailing of the editor of a German-language newspaper whose editorials had questioned the draft's constitutionality.

THE COURT AND CIVIL LIBERTIES

Also in 1919, the Court upheld the conviction of Jacob Abrams and five other men for distributing pamphlets critical of American intervention in Russia after the Bolshevik revolution. This time, however, Holmes and Louis Brandeis dissented, marking the emergence of a court minority committed to a broader defense of free speech. Six years after *Abrams*, the two again dissented when the majority upheld the conviction of Benjamin Gitlow, a communist whose *Left-wing Manifesto* calling for revolution led to his conviction under a New York law prohibiting "criminal anarchy." "The only meaning of free speech," Holmes now declared, was that advocates of every set of beliefs, even "proletarian dictatorship," should have the right to convert the public to their views in the great "marketplace of ideas" (an apt metaphor for a consumer society). In approving Gitlow's conviction, the Court majority observed that the Fourteenth Amendment obligated the states to refrain from unreasonable restraints on freedom of speech and the press. The comment marked a major step in the long process by which the Bill of Rights was transformed from an ineffective statement of principle into a significant protection of Americans' freedoms.

The tide of civil-liberties decision making slowly began to turn. By the end of the 1920s, the Supreme Court had voided a Kansas law that made it a crime to advocate unlawful acts to change the political or economic system, and one from Minnesota authorizing censorship of the press. The new regard for free speech went beyond political expression. In 1930, the Court threw out the conviction of Mary Ware Dennett for sending a sex-education pamphlet, *The Sex Side of Life*, through the mails. Three years later, a federal court overturned the Customs Service's ban on James Joyce's novel *Ulysses*, a turning point in the battle against the censorship of works of literature.

Meanwhile, Brandeis was crafting an intellectual defense of civil liberties on grounds somewhat different from Holmes's model of a competitive market in ideas. In 1927, the Court upheld the conviction of the prominent California socialist and women's rights activist Anita Whitney for attending a convention of the Communist Labor Party where speakers advocated violent revolution. Brandeis voted with the majority on technical grounds.

But he issued a powerful defense of freedom of speech as essential to active citizenship in a democracy: "Those who won our independence believed . . . that freedom to think as you will and to speak as you think are indispensable to the discovery and spread of political truth. . . . The greatest menace to freedom is an inert people." A month after the decision, the governor of California pardoned Whitney, terming freedom of speech the "indispensable birthright of every free American." The intrepid Mrs. Whitney was soon back in court for violating a California law making it a crime to display a red flag. In 1931, the Supreme Court overturned the law as "repugnant to the guaranty of liberty contained in the Fourteenth Amendment." A judicial defense of civil liberties was slowly being born.

THE CULTURE WARS

THE FUNDAMENTALIST REVOLT

Although many Americans embraced modern urban culture with its religious and ethnic pluralism, mass entertainment, and liberated sexual rules, others found it alarming. Many evangelical Protestants felt threatened by the decline of traditional values and the increased visibility of Catholicism and Judaism because of immigration. They also resented the growing presence within mainstream Protestant denominations of "modernists" who sought to integrate science and religion and adapt Christianity to the new secular culture. "The day is past," declared Harry Emerson Fosdick, pastor of New York's First Presbyterian Church and a prominent modernist, "when you can ask thoughtful men to hold religion in one compartment of their minds and their modern world view in another."

Convinced that the literal truth of the Bible formed the basis of Christian belief, fundamentalists launched a campaign to rid Protestant denominations of modernism and to combat the new individual freedoms that seemed to contradict traditional morality. Their most flamboyant apostle

City Activities with Dance Hall, *a mural painted in 1930 by Thomas Hart Benton for the New School for Social Research in New York City, portrays aspects of 1920s urban culture that alarmed many moral traditionalists, including dance halls, movies, and independent women.*

A 1923 lithograph by George Bellows captures the dynamic style of the most prominent evangelical preacher of the 1920s, Billy Sunday.

Federal agents pour confiscated liquor into a sewer in 1920, shortly after the advent of Prohibition.

was Billy Sunday, a talented professional baseball player who became a revivalist preacher. Between 1900 and 1930, Sunday drew huge crowds with a highly theatrical preaching style and a message denouncing sins ranging from Darwinism to alcohol. He was said to have preached to 100 million people during his lifetime—more than any other individual in history.

Much of the press portrayed fundamentalism as a movement of backwoods bigots. In fact, it was a national phenomenon. Even in New York City, the center of the new modern culture, Fosdick was removed from his ministry in 1924 (whereupon John D. Rockefeller Jr. built the interdenominational Riverside Church for him). Fundamentalism remained an important strain of 1920s culture and politics. Prohibition, which fundamentalists strongly supported, succeeded in reducing the consumption of alcohol as well as public drunkenness and drink-related diseases. Not until 1975 would per capita consumption of alcohol reach its pre-Prohibition level of 2.6 gallons per person each year.

Too many Americans, however, deemed Prohibition a violation of individual freedom for the flow of illegal liquor to stop. In urban areas, Prohibition led to large profits for the owners of illegal speakeasies and the "bootleggers" who supplied them. It produced widespread corruption as police and public officials accepted bribes to turn a blind eye to violations of the law. These developments reinforced fundamentalists' identification of urban life and modern notions of freedom with immorality and a decline of Christian liberty.

THE SCOPES TRIAL

In 1925, a trial in Tennessee threw into sharp relief the division between traditional values and modern, secular culture. John Scopes, a teacher in a Tennessee public school, was arrested for violating a state law that prohibited the teaching of Charles Darwin's theory of evolution. His trial became a national sensation. The proceedings were even carried live on national radio.

The Scopes trial reflected the enduring tension between two American definitions of freedom. Fundamentalist Christians, strongest in rural areas of the South and West, clung to the traditional idea of "moral" liberty—voluntary adherence to time-honored religious beliefs. The theory that man had evolved over millions of years from ancestors like apes contradicted the biblical account of creation. Those who upheld the Tennessee law identified evolutionists with feminists, socialists, and religious modernists, all of whom, they claimed, substituted human judgment for the word of God. To Scopes's defenders, including the American Civil Liberties Union, which had persuaded him to violate the law in order to test its constitutionality, freedom meant above all the right to independent thought and individual self-expression. To them, the Tennessee law offered a lesson in the dangers of religious intolerance and the merger of church and state.

The renowned labor lawyer Clarence Darrow defended Scopes. The trial's highlight came when Darrow called William Jennings Bryan to the stand as an "expert witness" on the Bible. Viewing the trial as a "duel to the death" between science and Christianity, he accepted Darrow's challenge. But Bryan revealed an almost complete ignorance of modern science and proved unable to respond effectively to Darrow's sarcastic questioning. Does the serpent really crawl on its belly as punishment for having tempted Eve in the Garden of Evil? When Bryan answered "yes," Darrow

The Anti-Evolution League selling its publications outside the Tennessee courthouse where the Scopes trial was taking place.

Because of extreme heat, some sessions of the Scopes Trial were held outdoors, in front of the courthouse in Dayton, Tennessee. A photographer snapped this picture of the trial's climactic moment, when Clarence Darrow (standing at the center) questioned William Jennings Bryan (seated) about interpretation of the Bible.

inquired how it got around before being cursed—on its tail? Asked whether God had actually created the world in six days, Bryan replied that these should be understood as ages, "not six days of twenty-four hours"— thus opening the door to the very nonliteral interpretation of the Bible fundamentalists rejected.

The jury found Scopes guilty, although the Tennessee supreme court later overturned the decision on a technicality. Shortly after the trial ended, Bryan died and the movement for anti-evolution laws disintegrated. Fundamentalists retreated for many years from battles over public education, preferring to build their own schools and colleges where teaching could be done as they saw fit and preachers were trained to spread their interpretation of Christianity. The battle would be rejoined, however, toward the end of the twentieth century, when fundamentalism reemerged as an important force in politics. To this day, the teaching of the theory of evolution in public schools arouses intense debate in parts of the United States.

THE SECOND KLAN

Few features of urban life seemed more alien to rural and small-town native-born Protestants than their immigrant populations and cultures. The wartime obsession with "100 percent Americanism" continued into the 1920s, a decade of citizenship education programs in public schools, legally sanctioned visits to immigrants' homes to investigate their household arrangements, and vigorous efforts by employers to instill appreciation for "American values." Only "an agile and determined immigrant," commented the *Chicago Tribune*, could "hope to escape Americanization by at least one of the many processes now being prepared for his special benefit." In 1922, Oregon became the only state ever to require all students to attend public schools—a measure aimed, said the state's attorney general, at abolishing parochial education and preventing "bolshevists, syndicalists and communists" from organizing their own schools.

The Ku Klux Klan brought 40,000 members to Washington, D.C., for a 1925 parade.

Perhaps the most menacing expression of the idea that enjoyment of American freedom should be limited on religious and ethnic grounds was the resurgence of the Ku Klux Klan in the early 1920s. The Klan had been reborn in Atlanta in 1915 after the lynching of Leo Frank, a Jewish factory manager accused of killing a teenage girl. By the mid-1920s, it claimed over 3 million members, nearly all white, native-born Protestants, many of whom held respected positions in their communities. Unlike the Klan of Reconstruction, the organization now sank deep roots in parts of the North and West. It became the largest private organization in Indiana and for a time controlled the state Republican Party. It was partly responsible for the Oregon law banning private schools. In southern California, its large marches and auto parades made the Klan a visible presence. The new Klan attacked a far broader array of targets than during Reconstruction. American civilization, it insisted, was endangered not only by blacks but by immigrants (especially Jews and Catholics) and all the forces (feminism, unions, immorality, even, on occasion, the giant corporations) that endangered "individual liberty."

CLOSING THE GOLDEN DOOR

The Klan's influence faded after 1925, when its leader in Indiana was convicted of assaulting a young woman. But the Klan's attacks on modern secular culture and political radicalism and its demand that control of the nation be returned to "citizens of the old stock" reflected sentiments widely shared in the 1920s. The decade witnessed a flurry of legislation that offered a new answer to the venerable question "Who is an American?" Some new laws redrew the boundary of citizenship to include groups previously outside it. With women now recognized as part of the political nation, Congress in the Cable Act of 1922 overturned the 1907 law requiring American women who married foreigners to assume the citizenship of the husband—except in the case of those who married Asians, who still forfeited their nationality. Two years later, it declared all Indians born in the United States to be American citizens, although many western states continued to deny the vote to those living on reservations.

Far more sweeping was a fundamental change in immigration policy. Immigration restriction had a long history. The Naturalization Act of 1790 had barred blacks and Asians from naturalization, with the ban lifted for the former in 1870. Beginning in 1875, various classes of immigrants had been excluded, among them prostitutes, the mentally retarded, and those with contagious diseases. Nonetheless, prior to World War I virtually all the white persons who wished to pass through the "golden door" into the United States and become citizens were able to do so. During the 1920s, however, the pressure for wholesale immigration restriction became irresistible. One index of the changing political climate was that large employers dropped their traditional opposition. Fears of immigrant radicalism now outweighed the desire for cheap unskilled labor, especially since mechanization had halted the growth of the industrial labor force and the Great Migration of World War I had accustomed industrialists to employing African-Americans.

In 1921, a temporary measure restricted immigration from Europe to 357,000 per year (one-third of the annual average before the war). Three years later, Congress permanently limited European immigration to 150,000 per year, distributed according to a series of national quotas that severely restricted the numbers from southern and eastern Europe. The law aimed to ensure that descendants of the old immigrants forever outnumbered the children of the new. However, to satisfy the demands of large farmers in California who relied heavily on seasonal Mexican labor, the 1924 law established no limits on immigration from the Western Hemisphere.

The 1924 law did bar the entry of all those ineligible for naturalized citizenship—that is, the entire population of Asia, even though Japan had

The Only Way to Handle It, *a cartoon endorsing immigration restriction.*

fought on the American side in World War I. The only Asians still able to enter the United States were residents of the Philippines, who were deemed to be "American nationals" (although not citizens) because the islands had been U.S. territory since the Spanish-American War. Largely to bar further Philippine immigration, Congress in 1934 established a timetable for the islands' independence, which was finally achieved in 1946. The 1934 law established an immigration quota of fifty Filipinos a year to the mainland United States, but allowed their continued entry into the Hawaiian Islands to work as plantation laborers.

Although a few Chinese had tried to enter the country in the past in spite of exclusion legislation, the law of 1924 established in effect, for the first time a new category—the "illegal alien." With it came a new enforcement mechanism, the Border Patrol, charged with policing the land boundaries of the United States and empowered to arrest and deport persons who entered the country in violation of the new nationality quotas or other restrictions. Later associated almost exclusively with Latinos, "illegal aliens" at first referred mainly to southern and eastern Europeans who tried to sneak across the border from Mexico or Canada.

RACE AND THE LAW

The new immigration law reflected the heightened emphasis on "race" as a determinant of public policy. By the early 1920s, political leaders of both North and South agreed upon the relegation of blacks to second-class citizenship. In a speech in Alabama in 1921, President Harding unconsciously echoed W. E. B. Du Bois by affirming that the "problem" of race was a global one, not confined to the South. Unlike Du Bois, he believed the South showed the way to the problem's solution. "It would be helpful," he added, "to have that word 'equality' eliminated from this consideration." Clearly, the Republican Party of the Civil War era was dead.

But "race policy" meant far more than black-white relations. "America must be kept American," declared President Coolidge in signing the 1924 immigration law. His secretary of labor, James J. Davis, commented that immigration policy, once based on the need for labor and the notion of the United States as an asylum of liberty, must now rest on a biological definition of the ideal population. Although enacted by a highly conservative Congress strongly influenced by nativism, the 1924 immigration law also reflected the Progressive desire to improve the "quality" of democratic citizenship and to employ scientific methods to set public policy. It revealed how these aims were overlaid with pseudo-scientific assumptions about the superiority and inferiority of particular "races."

The seemingly "scientific" calculation of the new quotas—based on the "national origins" of the American population dating back to 1790— involved a highly speculative analysis of past census returns, with the results altered to increase allowable immigration by politically influential groups like Irish-Americans. Non-whites (one-fifth of the population in 1790) were excluded altogether when calculating quotas—otherwise, Africa would have received a far higher quota than the tiny number allotted to it. But then, the entire concept of race as a basis of public policy lacked any rational foundation. The Supreme Court admitted as much in

Table 20.1 SELECTED ANNUAL IMMIGRATION QUOTAS UNDER 1924 IMMIGRATION ACT

Country	Quota	Immigrants in 1914
Northern and Western Europe:		
Great Britain and Northern Ireland	65,721	48,729 (Great Britain only)
Germany	25,957	35,734
Ireland	17,853	24,688 (includes Northern Ireland)
Scandinavia (Sweden, Norway, Denmark, Finland)	7,241	29,391
Southern and Eastern Europe:		
Poland	6,524	(Not an independent state; included in Germany, Russia, and Austria-Hungary)
Italy	5,802	283,738
Russia	2,784	255,660
Other:		
Africa (total of various colonies and countries)	1,000	1,539
Western Hemisphere	No quota limit	122,695
Asia (China, India, Japan, Korea)	0	11,652

1923 when it rejected the claim of Bhagat Singh Thind, an Indian-born World War I veteran, who asserted that as a "pure Aryan," he was actually white and could therefore become an American citizen. "White," the Court declared, was not a scientific concept at all, but part of "common speech, to be interpreted with the understanding of the common man" (a forthright statement of what later scholars would call the "social construction" of race).

PLURALISM AND LIBERTY

During the 1920s, some Americans challenged the idea that southern and eastern Europeans were unfit to become citizens, or could only do so by abandoning their traditions in favor of Anglo-Saxon ways. Horace Kallen, himself of German-Jewish origin, in 1924 coined the phrase "cultural pluralism" to describe a society that gloried in ethnic diversity rather than attempting to suppress it. Toleration of difference was part of the "American Idea," Kallen wrote. Anthropologists like Franz Boas, Alfred Kroeber, and Ruth Benedict insisted that no scientific basis existed for theories of racial superiority or for the notion that societies and races could be ranked on a fixed scale running from "primitive" to "civilized."

These writings, however, had little immediate impact on public policy. In the 1920s, the most potent defense of a pluralist vision of American society came from the new immigrants themselves. Every major city still contained ethnic enclaves with their own civic institutions, theaters, churches, and foreign-language newspapers. Their sense of separate identity had been heightened by the emergence of independent nation-states in eastern Europe after the war. It would be wrong, to be sure, to view ethnic communities as united in opposition to Americanization. In a society increasingly knit together by mass culture and a consumer economy, few could escape the pull of assimilation. The department store, dance hall, and motion picture theater were as much agents of Americanization as the school and workplace. From the perspective of many immigrant women, moreover, assimilation often seemed not so much the loss of an inherited culture as a loosening of patriarchal bonds and an expansion of freedom. But most immigrants resented the coercive aspects of Americanization programs, so often based on the idea of the superiority of Protestant mainstream culture.

PROMOTING TOLERANCE

In the face of immigration restriction, Prohibition, a revived Ku Klux Klan, and widespread anti-Semitism and anti-Catholicism, immigrant groups asserted the validity of cultural diversity and identified toleration of difference—religious, cultural, and individual—as the essence of American freedom. In effect, they reinvented themselves as "ethnic" Americans, claiming an equal share in the nation's life but, in addition, the right to remain in many respects culturally distinct. The Roman Catholic Church urged immigrants to learn English and embrace "American principles," but it continued to maintain separate schools and other institutions. In 1924, the Catholic Holy Name Society brought 10,000 marchers to Washington to challenge the Klan and to affirm Catholics' loyalty to the nation. Throughout the country, organizations like the Anti-Defamation League of B'nai B'rith (founded in 1916 to combat anti-Semitism) and the National Catholic Welfare Council lobbied, in the name of "personal liberty," for laws prohibiting discrimination against immigrants by employers, colleges, and government agencies. The Americanization movement, declared a Polish newspaper in Chicago, had "not the smallest particle of the true American spirit, the spirit of freedom, the brightest virtue of which is the broadest possible tolerance."

The efforts of immigrant communities to resist coerced Americanization and of the Catholic Church to defend its school system broadened the definition of liberty for all Americans. In landmark decisions, the Supreme Court struck down Oregon's law, mentioned earlier, requiring all students to attend public schools and Nebraska's prohibiting teaching in a language other than English—one of the anti-German measures of World War I. "The protection of the Constitution," the decision in *Meyer v. Nebraska* (1923) declared, "extends to all, to those who speak other languages as well as to those born with English on the tongue," a startling rebuke to enforced Americanization. The decision expanded the freedom of all immigrant groups. In its aftermath, federal courts overturned various Hawaii laws imposing special taxes and regulations on private Japanese-language schools. In these cases, the Court also interpreted the Fourteenth Amendment's guarantee of equal liberty to include the right to "marry, establish a home and bring up children" and to practice religion as one chose, "without interference from the state." The decisions gave pluralism a constitutional foundation and paved the way for the Court's elaboration, two generations later, of a constitutional right to privacy.

THE EMERGENCE OF HARLEM

The 1920s also witnessed an upsurge of self-consciousness among black Americans, especially in the North's urban ghettos. With European immigration all but halted, the Great Migration of World War I continued apace. Nearly 1 million blacks left the South during the 1920s, and the black population of New York, Chicago, and other urban centers more than doubled. New York's Harlem gained an international reputation as the "capital" of black America, a mecca for migrants from the South and immigrants

A black family arriving in Chicago in 1922, as part of the Great Migration from the rural South.

from the West Indies, 150,000 of whom entered the United States between 1900 and 1930. Unlike the southern newcomers, most of whom had been agricultural workers, the West Indians included a large number of well-educated professional and white-collar workers. Their encounter with American racism appalled them. "I had heard of prejudice in America," wrote the poet and novelist Claude McKay, who emigrated from Jamaica in 1912, "but never dreamed of it being so intensely bitter."

The 1920s became famous for "slumming," as groups of whites visited Harlem's dance halls, jazz clubs, and speakeasies in search of exotic adventure. The Harlem of the white imagination was a place of primitive passions, free from the puritanical restraints of mainstream American culture. The real Harlem was a community of widespread poverty, its residents confined to low-wage jobs and, because housing discrimination barred them from other neighborhoods, forced to pay exorbitant rents. Most Harlem businesses were owned by whites; even the famed Cotton Club excluded black customers and employed only light-skinned dancers in its renowned chorus line. Few blacks, North or South, shared in the prosperity of the 1920s.

THE HARLEM RENAISSANCE

But Harlem also contained a vibrant black cultural community that established links with New York's artistic mainstream. Poets and novelists like Countee Cullen, Langston Hughes, and Claude McKay were befriended and sponsored by white intellectuals and published by white presses. Broadway for the first time presented black actors in serious dramatic roles, as well as shows like *Dixie to Broadway* and *Blackbirds* that featured great entertainers like the singers Florence Mills and Ethel Waters and the tap dancer Bill Robinson. At the same time, the theater flourished in Harlem, freeing black writers and actors from the constraints imposed by white producers.

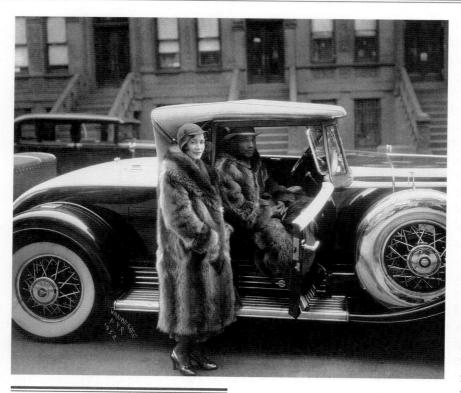

James VanDerZee was the most prominent photographer during the Harlem Renaissance. Most residents of Harlem were desperately poor, but not all, as VanDerZee's 1932 image of a well-off black couple in raccoon coats suggests.

The term "New Negro," associated in politics with pan-Africanism and the militancy of the Garvey movement, in art meant the rejection of established stereotypes and a search for black values to put in their place. This quest led the writers of what came to be called the Harlem Renaissance to the roots of the black experience—Africa, the rural South's folk traditions, and the life of the urban ghetto. Claude McKay made the major character of his novel *Home to Harlem* (1928) a free spirit who wandered from one scene of exotic life to another in search of a beautiful girl he had known. W. E. B. Du Bois feared that a novel like McKay's, with its graphic sex and violence, actually reinforced white prejudices about black life. Harlem Renaissance writings, however, also contained a strong element of protest. This mood was exemplified by McKay's poem "If We Must Die," a response to the race riots of 1919. The poem affirmed that blacks would no longer allow themselves to be murdered defenselessly by whites:

> If we must die, let it not be like hogs
> Hunted and penned in an inglorious spot,
> While round us bark the mad and hungry dogs,
> Making their mock at our accursed lot....
> Like men we'll face the murderous, cowardly pack,
> Pressed to the wall, dying, but fighting back!

Winston Churchill would invoke McKay's words to inspire the British public during World War II. The celebrated case of Ossian Sweet, a black physician who moved into a previously all-white Detroit neighborhood in 1925, reflected the new spirit of assertiveness among many African-Americans. When a white mob attacked his home, Sweet fired into the crowd, killing a man. Indicted for murder along with his two brothers, Sweet was defended by Clarence Darrow, fresh from his participation in the Scopes trial. The jury proved unable to agree on a verdict. A second prosecution, of Sweet's brother, ended in acquittal.

THE GREAT DEPRESSION

THE ELECTION OF 1928

Few men elected as president have seemed destined for a more successful term in office than Herbert Hoover. Born in Iowa in 1874, the son of a blacksmith and his schoolteacher wife, Hoover accumulated a fortune as a mining engineer working for firms in Asia, Africa, and Europe. During and immediately after World War I, he gained international fame by coordinating overseas food relief. The British economist John Maynard Keynes, a severe critic of the 1919 Versailles Treaty, called Hoover "the only man" to emerge from the peace conference "with an enhanced reputation." He "had never known failure," wrote the novelist Sherwood Anderson. Hoover seemed to exemplify what was widely called the "new era" of American capitalism. In 1922, while serving as secretary of commerce, he published *American Individualism*, which condemned government regulation as an interference with the economic opportunities of ordinary Americans, but also insisted that self-interest should be subordinated to public service. Hoover considered himself a Progressive, although he preferred what he called "associational action," in which private agencies directed regulatory and welfare policies, to government intervention in the economy.

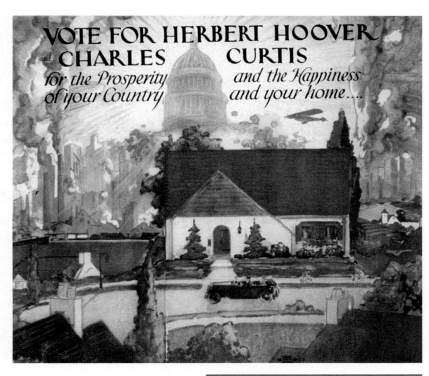

A 1928 campaign poster for the Republican ticket of Herbert Hoover and Charles Curtis.

After "silent Cal" Coolidge in 1927 handed a piece of paper to a group of reporters that stated, "I do not choose to run for president in 1928," Hoover quickly emerged as his successor. Accepting the Republican nomination, Hoover celebrated the decade's prosperity and promised that poverty would "soon be banished from this earth." His Democratic opponent was Alfred E. Smith, the first Catholic to be nominated by a major party. Born into poverty on New York's Lower East Side, Smith had become a fixture in Tammany Hall politics. Although he had no family connection with the new immigrants from southern and eastern Europe (his grandparents had emigrated from Ireland), Smith emerged as their symbolic spokesman. The Triangle fire of 1911 made him an advocate of Progressive social legislation. He served three terms as governor of New York, securing passage of laws limiting the hours of working women and children and establishing widows' pensions. Smith denounced the Red Scare and called for the repeal of Prohibition. His bid for the Democratic nomination in 1924 had been blocked by delegates beholden to nativists and Klansmen, but he secured the nod four years later.

Given the prevailing prosperity and his own sterling reputation, Hoover's victory was inevitable. Other than on Prohibition, moreover, the Democratic platform did not differ much from the Republican one, leaving little to discuss except the candidates' personalities and religions. Smith's Catholicism became the focus of the race. Many Protestant ministers and religious publications denounced him for his faith. For the first time since Reconstruction, Republicans carried several southern states, reflecting the

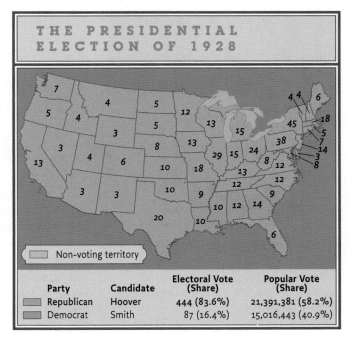

THE PRESIDENTIAL ELECTION OF 1928

Non-voting territory

Party	Candidate	Electoral Vote (Share)	Popular Vote (Share)
Republican	Hoover	444 (83.6%)	21,391,381 (58.2%)
Democrat	Smith	87 (16.4%)	15,016,443 (40.9%)

strength of anti-Catholicism and nativism among religious fundamentalists. "Hoover," wrote one previously Democratic southern newspaper editor, "is sprung from American soil and stock," while Smith represented "the aliens." On the other hand, Smith carried the nation's twelve largest cities and won significant support in economically struggling farm areas. With over 58 percent of the vote, Hoover was elected by a landslide. But Smith's campaign helped to lay the foundation for the triumphant Democratic coalition of the 1930s, based on urban ethnic voters, farmers, and the South.

THE COMING OF THE DEPRESSION

On October 21, 1929, President Hoover traveled to Michigan to take part in the Golden Anniversary of the Festival of Light, organized by Henry Ford to commemorate the invention of the light bulb by Thomas Edison fifty years earlier. Hoover's speech was a tribute to progress, and especially to the businessmen and scientists from whose efforts "we gain constantly in better standards of living, more stability of employment . . . and decreased suffering." Three days later, on Black Thursday, the stock market crashed. As panic selling set in, more than $10 billion in market value (equivalent to over ten times that amount in today's money) vanished in five hours. Soon the United States and, indeed, the entire world, found itself in the grip of the Great Depression, the greatest economic disaster in modern history.

The stock market crash did not, by itself, cause the Depression. Even before 1929, signs of economic trouble had become evident. Southern California and Florida experienced frenzied real-estate speculation and then spectacular busts, with banks failing, land remaining undeveloped, and mortgages foreclosed. The highly unequal distribution of income and the prolonged depression in farm regions reduced American purchasing power. Sales of new autos and household consumer goods stagnated after 1926. European demand for American goods also declined, partly because industry there had recovered from wartime destruction.

A fall in the bloated stock market, driven ever higher during the 1920s by speculators, was inevitable. But it came with such severity that it destroyed many of the investment companies that had been created to buy and sell stock, wiping out thousands of investors, and it greatly reduced business and consumer confidence. Around 26,000 businesses failed in 1930. Those that survived cut back on further investment and began laying off workers. The global financial system, which was based on the gold standard, was ill-equipped to deal with the downturn. Germany defaulted on reparations payments to France and Britain, leading these governments to stop repaying debts to American banks. Throughout the industrial world, banks failed as depositors withdrew money, fearful that they could no longer count on the promise to redeem paper money in gold. Millions of families lost their life savings.

Although stocks recovered somewhat in 1930, they soon resumed their relentless downward slide. Between 1929 and 1932, the price of a share of U.S. Steel fell from $262 to $22, and General Motors from $73 to $8. Four-fifths of the Rockefeller family fortune disappeared. William C. Durant, one of the founders of General Motors, lost all his money and ended up

Oct. 29—Dies Irae, *a 1929 lithograph by James N. Rosenberg, depicts skyscrapers tottering, stockbrokers jumping from windows, and crowds panicking as the stock market crashes. The title means "Day of Wrath."*

running a bowling alley in Flint, Michigan. In 1932, the economy hit rock bottom. Since 1929, the gross national product (the value of all the goods and services in the country) had fallen by one-third, prices by nearly 40 percent, and over 11 million Americans—25 percent of the labor force—could not find work. U.S. Steel, which had employed 225,000 full-time workers in 1929, had none at the end of 1932, when it was operating at only 12 percent of capacity. Those who retained their jobs confronted reduced hours and dramatically reduced wages. Every industrial economy suffered, but the United States, which had led the way in prosperity in the 1920s, was hit hardest of all.

AMERICANS AND THE DEPRESSION

The Depression transformed American life. Hundreds of thousands of people took to the road in search of work. Hungry men and women lined the streets of major cities. In Detroit, 4,000 children stood in bread lines each day seeking food. Thousands of families, evicted from their homes, moved into ramshackle shanty towns, dubbed Hoovervilles, that sprang up in parks and on abandoned land. Cities quickly spent the little money they had available for poor relief. In Chicago, where half the working population was unemployed at the beginning of 1932, Mayor Anton Cermak telephoned people individually, begging them to pay their taxes. "We saw want and despair walking the streets," wrote a Chicago social worker, "and our friends, sensible, thrifty families, reduced to poverty." When the Soviet Union advertised its need for skilled workers, it received over 100,000 applications from the United States.

The Depression actually reversed the long-standing movement of population from farms to cities. Many Americans left cities to try to grow food for their families. In 1935, 33 million people lived on farms—more than at any previous point in American history. But rural areas, already poor, saw families reduce the number of meals per day and children go barefoot.

Unemployed men, lined up at the New York Municipal Lodging House in 1930. Established in 1909 to provide food and shelter for the homeless, the Lodging House was overwhelmed by the advent of the Great Depression.

A Hooverville—a shantytown created by homeless squatters—outside Seattle, Washington, in 1933.

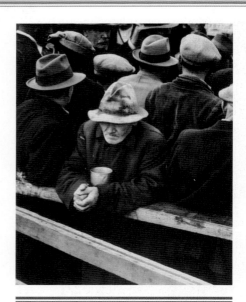

The celebrated photographer Dorothea Lange took this photograph of an unemployed man on a San Francisco breadline in 1933.

With the future shrouded in uncertainty, the American suicide rate rose to the highest level in the nation's history, and the birthrate fell to the lowest.

"The American way of life," the confident slogan of the consumer culture, and common sayings like "safe as a bank" took on a hollow ring. The image of big business, carefully cultivated during the 1920s, collapsed as congressional investigations revealed massive irregularities committed by bankers and stockbrokers. Banks had knowingly sold worthless bonds. Prominent Wall Streeters had unloaded their own portfolios while advising small investors to maintain their holdings. Richard Whitney, the president of the New York Stock Exchange, was convicted of stealing funds from customers, including from a fund to aid widows and orphans. He ended up in jail.

RESIGNATION AND PROTEST

Many Americans reacted to the Depression with resignation or blamed themselves for economic misfortune. Others responded with protests that were at first spontaneous and uncoordinated, since unions, socialist organizations, and other groups that might have provided disciplined leadership had been decimated during the 1920s. In the spring of 1932, 20,000 unemployed World War I veterans descended on Washington to demand early payment of a bonus due in 1945, only to be driven away by federal soldiers led by the army's chief of staff, Douglas MacArthur. Throughout the country, the unemployed demonstrated for jobs and public relief. That summer, led by the charismatic Milo Reno, a former Iowa Populist, the National Farmers' Holiday Association protested low prices by temporarily blocking roads in the Midwest to prevent farm goods from getting to market.

Only the minuscule Communist Party seemed able to give a political focus to the anger and despair. "The most fully employed persons I met during the Depression," one labor leader later recalled, "were the Communists." They "brought misery out of hiding," forming unemployed councils, sponsoring marches and demonstrations for public assistance, and protesting the eviction of unemployed families from their homes. The press discussed the idea that the United States was on the verge of a revolution. The

Police battling "bonus marchers" in Washington, D.C., July 1932. Soon afterwards, President Hoover sent federal troops to evict the marchers.

insurance firm Lloyd's of London reported an upsurge in American requests for riot insurance. The Hoover administration in 1931 opposed efforts to save money by reducing the size of the army, warning that this would "lessen our means of maintaining domestic peace and order."

HOOVER'S RESPONSE

In the eyes of many Americans, President Hoover's response to the Depression seemed inadequate and uncaring. Leading advisers, including Andrew Mellon, the wealthy secretary of the treasury, told Hoover that economic downturns were a normal part of capitalism, which weeded out unproductive firms and encouraged moral virtue among the less fortunate. Businessmen strongly opposed federal aid to the unemployed, and many publications called for individual "belt-tightening" as the road to recovery. Some initially saw a silver lining in the Depression. Wages had fallen so sharply, reported *Fortune* magazine, that "you can have your garden taken care of in Los Angeles for $1 a week" or hire an "affable Negro to fry your chicken and do your washing for $8 a month in Virginia."

Communist Party headquarters in New York City, 1932. The banners illustrate the variety of activities the party organized in the early 1930s.

The federal government had never faced an economic crisis as severe as the Great Depression. Few political leaders understood how important consumer spending had become in the American economy. Most held to the conventional view that government intervention to aid those who had lost their jobs would do little to spur economic recovery and would encourage Americans to rely on government charity to address misfortune. In 1931, Hoover quoted former president Grover Cleveland from four decades earlier: "The Government should not support the people.... Federal aid ... weakens the sturdiness of our national character."

Strongly opposed on principle to direct federal intervention in the economy, Hoover remained committed to "associational action." He put his faith in voluntary steps by business to maintain investment and employment—something few found it possible to do—and efforts by local charity organizations to assist needy neighbors. He called numerous conferences of business and labor leaders and established commissions to encourage firms to cooperate in maintaining prices and wages without governmental dictation. Hoover attempted to restore public confidence, making frequent public statements that "the tide had turned." But these made him increasingly seem out of touch with reality. About the unemployed men who appeared on city streets offering apples at five cents apiece, Hoover would later write, "Many persons left their jobs for the more profitable one of selling apples."

An unemployed man and woman selling apples on a city street during the Great Depression.

THE WORSENING ECONOMIC OUTLOOK

Some administration remedies, like the Hawley-Smoot Tariff, which Hoover signed with some reluctance in 1930, made the economic situation worse. Raising the already high taxes on imported goods, it inspired similar increases abroad, further reducing international trade. A tax increase Hoover pushed through Congress in 1932 in an attempt to balance the federal budget further reduced Americans' purchasing power. Other initiatives inspired ridicule. When he approved funds to provide food for livestock, one observer remarked that the president would feed "jackasses but . . . not starving babies."

By 1932, Hoover had to admit that voluntary action had failed to stem the Depression. He signed laws creating the Reconstruction Finance Corporation, which loaned money to failing banks, railroads, and other businesses, and the Federal Home Loan Bank System, which offered aid to home owners threatened with foreclosure. Having vetoed previous bills to create employment through public-works projects like road and bridge construction, he now approved a measure appropriating nearly $2 billion for such initiatives and helping to fund local relief efforts. These were dramatic departures from previous federal economic policy. But further than this, Hoover would not go. He adamantly opposed offering direct relief to the unemployed—it would do them a "disservice," he told Congress.

FREEDOM IN THE MODERN WORLD

In 1927, the New School for Social Research in New York City organized a series of lectures on the theme of Freedom in the Modern World. Founded eight years earlier as a place where "free thought and intellectual integrity" could flourish in the wake of wartime repression, the School's distinguished faculty included the philosopher John Dewey and historian Charles Beard (who had resigned from Columbia University in 1917 to protest the dismissal of antiwar professors). The lectures painted a depressing portrait of American freedom on the eve of the Great Depression. "The idea of freedom, declared economist Walton H. Hamilton, had become "an intellectual instrument for looking backward. . . . Liberty of contract has been made the be-all and end-all of personal freedom; . . . the domain of business has been defended against control from without in the name of freedom." The free exchange of ideas, moreover, had not recovered from the crisis of World War I. The "sacred dogmas of patriotism and Big Business," said the educator Horace Kallen, dominated teaching, the press, and public debate. A definition of freedom reigned supreme that celebrated the unimpeded reign of economic enterprise yet tolerated the surveillance of private life and individual conscience.

The prosperity of the 1920s had reinforced this definition of freedom. With the economic crash, compounded by the ineffectiveness of the Hoover administration's response, it would be discredited. By 1932, the seeds had already been planted for a new conception of freedom that combined two different elements in a sometimes uneasy synthesis. One was the Progressive belief in a socially conscious state making what Dewey called "positive and constructive changes" in economic arrangements. The other, which arose in the 1920s, centered on respect for civil liberties and cultural pluralism and declared that realms of life like group identity, personal behavior, and the free expression of ideas lay outside legitimate state concern. These two principles would become the hallmarks of modern liberalism, which during the 1930s would redefine American freedom.

SUGGESTED READING

Boyle, Kevin. *Arc of Justice: A Saga of Race, Civil Rights, and Murder in the Jazz Age* (2004). A history of the Sweet case, placing it in the context of postwar Detroit and the nation.

Cohen, Warren I. *Empire without Tears: America's Foreign Relations, 1921–1933* (1987). A careful examination of American foreign policy between the presidencies of Wilson and Roosevelt.

Dumenil, Lynn. *The Modern Temper: America in the Twenties* (1995). A brief survey of the main political and cultural trends of the decade.

Garraty, John A. *The Great Depression* (1986). Places the Depression in a global context and compares various governments' responses to it.

Gerstle, Gary. *American Crucible: Race and Nation in the Twentieth Century* (2002). A sweeping survey of how changing ideas of race have affected the concept of American nationality, with a strong account of the debates of the 1920s.

Gordon, Colin. *New Deals: Business, Labor, and Politics in America, 1920–1935* (1994). Examines how the federal government dealt with business and labor from the Republican era to the early New Deal.

Higham, John. *Strangers in the Land: Patterns of American Nativism, 1860–1925* (1955). A classic account of American hostility to immigrants, concluding with the immigration restriction of 1924.

Larson, Edward. *Summer for the Gods: The Scopes Trial and America's Continuing Debate over Science and Religion* (1998). A history of the famous trial and the enduring debate over evolution.

Lewis, David L. *When Harlem Was in Vogue* (1981). A lively account of the Harlem Renaissance of the 1920s.

Maclean, Nancy. *Behind the Mask of Chivalry: The Making of the Second Ku Klux Klan* (1994). A careful analysis of the membership and motivations of the Ku Klux Klan of the 1920s.

Marchand, Roland. *Advertising the American Dream: Making Way for Modernity, 1920–1940* (1985). Examines how advertisers responded to and helped to shape changes in American life between the two world wars.

Marsden, George M. *Fundamentalism and American Culture: The Shaping of Twentieth-Century Evangelicism, 1870–1925* (1980). Traces the ups and downs of American fundamentalism, culminating in the Scopes trial.

Murphy, Paul L. *World War I and the Origin of Civil Liberties in the United States* (1979). An analysis of how the repression of free speech during World War I paved the way for a heightened awareness of the importance of civil liberties.

Ngai, Mae. *Impossible Subjects: Illegal Aliens and the Making of Modern America* (2004). An influential examination of immigration policy toward Mexicans and Asians, and the development of the legal category of "illegal alien."

Ross, William G. *Forging New Freedoms: Nativism, Education, and the Constitution, 1917–1927* (1994). Discusses battles over cultural pluralism in the 1920s and how they laid the groundwork for an expanded definition of personal liberty.

REVIEW QUESTIONS

1. Explain how the questions raised by the public and the Supreme Court over free speech and the First Amendment redefined the meaning of freedom in the 1920s.

2. Do you think U.S. society in the 1920s reflected the concept of cultural pluralism as explained by Horace Kallen? Why or why not?

3. Explain how and why many saw race as a global issue in the 1920s.

4. In what ways was it true that the business of America in the 1920s was business?

5. In what ways did women define freedom in the 1920s?

KEY TERMS

productivity and wage gap (p. 768)

farming in the 1920s (p. 768)

rise of the stock market (p.770)

Teapot Dome Scandal (p. 776)

McNary-Haugen Bill (p. 777)

Tennessee and the teaching of evolution (p. 782)

American Indians and citizenship (p. 785)

defining whiteness (p. 787)

Bonus Army (p. 794)

Hawley-Smoot Tariff (p. 796)

REVIEW TABLE

The Fear of Modernization

Event	Date	Historical Significance
Reemergence of the Ku Klux Klan	1915, with the release of *Birth of a Nation* and the lynching of Leo Frank	Included anti-black, anti-immigrant, anti-Catholic, and anti-Prohibition elements
Immigration Act	1924	Severely limited immigration from eastern and southern Europe and excluded all Asians
Scopes Trial	1925	Fundamentalists fought against teaching Darwin's theory of evolution in schools

Chapter 21

The New Deal, 1932–1940

This panel depicting the construction of a dam was painted in 1939 by William Gropper as part of a mural for the new Department of Interior building in Washington, D.C. Born on New York City's Lower East Side to a Jewish immigrant family, Gropper became a prominent "social realist" artist, whose works depicting scenes of American life included satirical cartoons of political and business leaders and paintings of labor struggles of the 1930s. Like other artists who found it difficult to obtain work during the Depression, he was hired by the Works Projects Administration, a New Deal agency, to paint murals for government buildings. This one was inspired by the construction of the Grand Coulee Dam on the Columbia River and the Davis Dam on the Colorado River, two of the many New Deal projects that expanded the nation's infrastructure and provided employment to victims of the Depression.

FOCUS QUESTIONS

- What were the major policy initiatives of the New Deal in the Hundred Days?

- Who were the main proponents of economic justice in the mid-1930s?

- What were the major initiatives of the Second New Deal?

- How did the New Deal recast the meaning of American freedom?

- How did the New Deal affect women and minorities?

- What were the characteristics of Popular Front culture in the 1930s?

Early in 1941, the unemployed Woody Guthrie, soon to become one of the country's most popular songwriters and folk singers, brought his family to Portland, Oregon. He hoped to star in a film about the great public-works projects under way on the Columbia River. Given a temporary job by the Bonneville Power Authority, the public agency that controlled the Columbia dams, Guthrie produced a song every day for the next month. One, "Roll on, Columbia," became a popular statement of the benefits that resulted when government took the lead in economic planning and in improving the lot of ordinary citizens:

> And on up the river is the Grand Coulee Dam,
> The biggest thing built by the hand of a man,
> To run the great factories and water the land,
> So, roll on, Columbia, roll on....
> Your power is turning our darkness to dawn.
> So, roll on, Columbia, roll on. ©

The Columbia River winds its way on a 1,200-mile course from Canada through Washington and Oregon to the Pacific Ocean. Because of its steep descent from uplands to sea level, it produces an immense amount of energy. Residents of the economically underdeveloped Pacific Northwest had long dreamed of tapping this unused energy for electricity and irrigation. But not until the 1930s did the federal government launch the program of dam construction that transformed the region. The project created thousands of jobs for the unemployed, and the network of dams produced abundant cheap power.

When the Grand Coulee Dam went into operation in 1941, it was the largest man-made structure in world history. It eventually produced over 40 percent of the nation's hydroelectric power. The dam provided the cheapest electricity in the country for towns that sprang up out of nowhere, farms on what had once been deserts in eastern Washington and Oregon, and factories that would soon be producing aluminum for World War II airplanes. The project also had less appealing consequences. From time immemorial, the Columbia River had been filled with salmon. But the Grand Coulee Dam made no provision for the passage of fish, and the salmon all but vanished. This caused little concern during the Depression but became a source of controversy later in the century as Americans became more concerned about preserving the natural environment.

The Grand Coulee Dam was part of what one scholar has called a "public works revolution" that transformed the American economy and landscape during the 1930s. The Roosevelt administration spent far more money on building roads, dams, airports, bridges, and housing than any other activity.

Franklin D. Roosevelt believed regional economic planning like that in the Northwest would promote economic growth, ease the domestic and working lives of ordinary Americans, and keep control of key natural resources in public rather than private hands. "It promises," one supporter wrote, "a world replete with more freedom and happiness than mankind has ever known."

The Columbia River project reflected broader changes in American life and thought during the New Deal of the 1930s. Roosevelt oversaw the transformation of the Democratic Party into a coalition of farmers, industrial workers, the reform-minded urban middle class, liberal intellectuals, northern African-Americans, and, somewhat incongruously, the white supremacist South, united by the belief that the federal government must provide Americans with protection against the dislocations caused by modern capitalism. "Liberalism," traditionally understood as limited government and free market economics, took on its modern meaning. Thanks to the New Deal, it now referred to active efforts by the national government to uplift less fortunate members of society.

Freedom, too, underwent a transformation during the 1930s. The Depression had discredited the ideas that social progress rests on the unrestrained pursuit of wealth and that, apart from unfortunates like widows and orphans, most poverty is self-inflicted. The New Deal elevated a public guarantee of economic security to the forefront of American discussions of freedom. The 1930s were a decade of dramatic social upheaval. Social and political activists, most notably a revitalized labor movement, placed new issues on the political agenda. When one writer in 1941 published a survey of democratic thought beginning in the ancient world, he concluded that what distinguished his own time was its awareness of "the social conditions of freedom." Thanks to the New Deal, he wrote, "economic security" had "at last been recognized as a political condition of personal freedom." Regional economic planning like that in the Northwest reflected this understanding of freedom. So did other New Deal measures, including the Social Security Act, which offered aid to the unemployed and aged, and the Fair Labor Standards Act, which established a national minimum wage.

Yet while the New Deal significantly expanded the meaning of freedom, it did not erase freedom's boundaries. Its benefits flowed to industrial workers but not tenant farmers, to men far more fully than women, and to white Americans but not blacks, who still were deprived of the basic rights of citizenship.

Hydroelectric generators at the Grand Coulee Dam.

THE FIRST NEW DEAL

FDR AND THE ELECTION OF 1932

It is indeed paradoxical that Franklin D. Roosevelt, who had been raised in privilege on a New York country estate, came to be beloved as the symbolic representative of ordinary citizens. But like Lincoln, with whom he is often

COLUMBIA RIVER BASIN PROJECT, 1949

CANADA

Chief Joseph Dam
(building)

WASHINGTON

Grand Coulee
Dam

Spokane

Albeni Falls Dam
(proposed)

Pend Oreille R.

Kootenai R.

Glacier View Dam
(proposed)

Libby Dam
(proposed)

Hungry Horse Dam
(building)

R O C K Y

Seattle

Rock Island Dam

Tacoma

Priest Rapids Dam
(proposed)

Yakima R.

Snake R.

Lewiston

MONTANA

Helena

B I T T E R R O O T   R A N G E

Missouri R.

M O U N T A I N S

Madison R.

Pacific
Ocean

Astoria

Columbia R.

Portland

John Day Dam
(proposed)

Bonneville
Dam

The Dalles Dam
(proposed)

McNary Dam
(building)

Four Navigation
Dams (authorized)

Hells Canyon Dam
(proposed)

Salmon R.

Coast Range

Willamette R.

Deschutes R.

C A S C A D E

John Day R.

M O U N T A I N S

OREGON

Payette R.

IDAHO

Boise

Snake R.

Pocatello

0   50   100 miles
0   50   100 kilometers

*A 1949 map of the Columbia River
project, showing its numerous dams,
including the Grand Coulee, the largest
man-made structure in the world at the
time of its opening in 1941.*

compared, Roosevelt's greatness lay in his willingness to throw off the "dogmas of the quiet past" (Lincoln's words) to confront an unprecedented national crisis. FDR, as he liked to be called, was born in 1882, a fifth cousin of Theodore Roosevelt. He graduated from Harvard in 1904 and six years later won election to the New York legislature from Duchess County, site of his family's home at Hyde Park. After serving as undersecretary of the navy during World War I, he ran for vice president on the ill-fated Democratic ticket of 1920 headed by James M. Cox. In 1921, he contracted polio and lost the use of his legs, a fact carefully concealed from the public in that pre-television era. Very few Americans realized that the president who projected an image of vigorous leadership during the 1930s and World War II was confined to a wheelchair.

In his speech accepting the Democratic nomination for president in 1932, Roosevelt promised a "new deal" for the American people. But his campaign offered only vague hints of what this might entail. Roosevelt spoke of the government's responsibility to guarantee "every man . . . a right to make a comfortable living." But he also advocated a balanced federal budget and criticized his opponent, President Hoover, for excessive government spending. The biggest difference between the parties during the campaign was the Democrats' call for the repeal of Prohibition. Battered by the economic crisis, Americans in 1932 were desperate for new leadership, and Roosevelt won a resounding victory. He received 57 percent of the popular vote, and Democrats swept to a commanding majority in Congress.

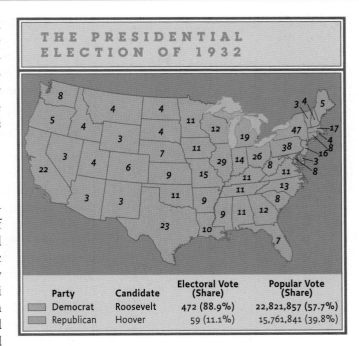

Party	Candidate	Electoral Vote (Share)	Popular Vote (Share)
Democrat	Roosevelt	472 (88.9%)	22,821,857 (57.7%)
Republican	Hoover	59 (11.1%)	15,761,841 (39.8%)

THE COMING OF THE NEW DEAL

The Depression did not produce a single pattern of international public response. For nearly the entire decade of the 1930s, conservative governments ruled Britain and France. They were more interested in preserving public order than relieving suffering or embarking on policy innovations. In Germany, Adolf Hitler, leader of the Nazi Party, established one of the most brutal dictatorships in human history. Hitler banned all political opposition and launched a reign of terror against Jews and others deemed to be "un-German." In the Soviet Union, another tyrant, Joseph Stalin, embarked on successive five-year plans that at great social cost produced rapid industrialization and claimed to have eliminated unemployment.

Roosevelt conceived of the New Deal as an alternative to socialism on the left, Nazism on the right, and the inaction of upholders of unregulated capitalism. He hoped to reconcile democracy, individual liberty, and economic planning. "You have made yourself," the British economist John Maynard Keynes wrote to FDR, "the trustee for those in every country who seek to mend the evils of our condition by reasoned experiment within the framework of the existing social system." If Roosevelt failed, Keynes added, the only remaining choices would be "orthodoxy" (that is, doing nothing), or "revolution."

Roosevelt did not enter office with a blueprint for dealing with the Depression. At first, he relied heavily for advice on a group of intellectuals and social workers who took up key positions in his administration. They included Secretary of Labor Frances Perkins, a veteran of Hull House and the New York Consumers' League who had been among the eyewitnesses to the Triangle fire of 1911; Harry Hopkins, who had headed emergency relief efforts during Roosevelt's term as governor of New York; Secretary of the Interior Harold Ickes, a veteran of Theodore Roosevelt's Progressive campaign of 1912; and Louis Brandeis, who had advised Woodrow Wilson during the 1912 campaign and now offered political advice to FDR while serving on the Supreme Court.

The presence of these individuals reflected how Roosevelt drew on the reform traditions of the Progressive era. But Progressivism, as noted in Chapter 18, was hardly a unified movement, and Roosevelt's advisers did not speak with one voice. Brandeis believed that large corporations not only wielded excessive power but had contributed to the Depression by keeping prices artificially high and failing to increase workers' purchasing power. They should be broken up, he insisted, not regulated. But the "brains trust"—a group of academics including a number of Columbia University professors—saw bigness as inevitable in a modern economy. The competitive marketplace, they argued, was a thing of the past, and large firms needed to be managed and directed by the government, not dismantled. Their view prevailed during what came to be called the First New Deal.

THE BANKING CRISIS

"This nation asks for action and action now," Roosevelt announced on taking office on March 4, 1933. The country, wrote the journalist and political commentator Walter Lippmann, "was in such a state of confused desperation that it would have followed almost any leader anywhere he chose to go." FDR spent much of 1933 trying to reassure the public. In his inaugural address, he declared that "the only thing we have to fear is fear itself." (See the Appendix for the full text.)

Roosevelt confronted a banking system on the verge of collapse. As bank funds invested in the stock market lost their value and panicked depositors withdrew their savings, bank after bank had closed its doors. By March 1933, banking had been suspended in a majority of the states—that is, people could not gain access to money in their bank accounts. Roosevelt declared a "bank holiday," temporarily halting all bank operations, and called Congress into special session. On March 9, it rushed to pass the Emergency Banking Act, which provided funds to shore up threatened institutions.

Further measures soon followed that transformed the American financial system. The Glass-Steagall Act barred commercial banks from becom-

A "run" on a bank: crowds of people wait outside a New York City bank, hoping to withdraw their money.

ing involved in the buying and selling of stocks. Until its repeal in the 1990s, the law prevented many of the irresponsible practices that had contributed to the stock market crash. The same law established the Federal Deposit Insurance Corporation (FDIC), a government system that insured the accounts of individual depositors. And Roosevelt took the United States off the gold standard—that is, he severed the link between the country's currency and its gold reserves, thus making possible the issuance of more money in the hope of stimulating business activity. Together, these measures rescued the financial system and greatly increased the government's power over it. About 5,000 banks—one-third of the nation's total—had failed between 1929 and 1933, representing a loss of tens of millions of dollars to depositors. In 1936, not a single bank failed in the United States.

THE NRA

The Emergency Banking Act was the first of an unprecedented flurry of legislation during the first three months of Roosevelt's administration, a period known as the "Hundred Days." Seizing on the sense of crisis and the momentum of his electoral victory, Roosevelt won rapid passage of laws he hoped would promote economic recovery. He persuaded Congress to create a host of new agencies, whose initials soon became part of the language of politics—NRA, AAA, CCC. Never in American history had a president exercised such power or so rapidly expanded the role of the federal government in people's lives.

The centerpiece of Roosevelt's plan for combating the Depression, the National Industrial Recovery Act, was to a large extent modeled on the government–business partnership established by the War Industries Board of World War I. Roosevelt called it "the most important and far-reaching legislation ever enacted by the American Congress." The act established the National Recovery Administration (NRA), which would work with groups of business leaders to establish industry codes setting standards for output, prices, and working conditions. Thus, "cutthroat" competition (in which companies took losses to drive competitors out of business) would be ended. These industry-wide arrangements would be exempt from antitrust laws.

The NRA reflected how even in its early days, the New Deal reshaped understandings of freedom. In effect, FDR had repudiated the older idea of liberty based on the idea that the best way to encourage economic activity and ensure a fair distribution of wealth was to allow market competition to operate, unrestrained by the government. And to win support from labor, section 7a of the new law recognized the workers' right to organize unions—a departure from the "open shop" policies of the 1920s and a step toward government support for what workers called "industrial freedom."

Headed by Hugh S. Johnson, a retired general and businessman, the NRA quickly established codes

The Spirit of the New Deal, *a cartoon in the* Washington Star, *1933, depicts the federal government, through the National Recovery Administration, promoting peace between workers and employers.*

that set standards for production, prices, and wages in the textile, steel, mining, and auto industries. Johnson launched a publicity campaign to promote the NRA and its symbol, the Blue Eagle, which stores and factories that abided by the codes displayed. But after initial public enthusiasm, the NRA became mired in controversy. Large companies dominated the code-writing process. An inquiry conducted by the labor lawyer Clarence Darrow in 1934 concluded that they used the NRA to drive up prices, limit production, lay off workers, and divide markets among themselves at the expense of smaller competitors. Many anti-union employers ignored section 7a. The government lacked the manpower to police the 750 codes in effect by 1935. The NRA produced neither economic recovery nor peace between employers and workers.

GOVERNMENT JOBS

The Hundred Days also brought the government into providing relief to those in need. Roosevelt and most of his advisers shared the widespread fear that direct government payments to the unemployed would undermine individual self-reliance. Indeed, one of the first measures of the Hundred Days had been the Economy Act, which reduced federal spending in an attempt to win the confidence of the business community. But with nearly a quarter of the workforce unemployed, spending on relief was unavoidable. In May 1933, Congress created the Federal Emergency Relief Administration, to make grants to local agencies that aided those impoverished by the Depression. FDR, however, much preferred to create temporary jobs, thereby combating unemployment while improving the nation's infrastructure of roads, bridges, public buildings, and parks.

In March 1933, Congress established the Civilian Conservation Corps (CCC), which set unemployed young men to work on projects like forest preservation, flood control, and the improvement of national parks and wildlife preserves. By the time the program ended in 1942, over 3 million persons had passed through CCC camps, where they received government wages of $30 per month.

A Civilian Conservation Corps workforce in Yosemite National Park, 1935.

PUBLIC-WORKS PROJECTS

One section of the National Industrial Recovery Act created the Public Works Administration (PWA), with an appropriation of $3.3 billion. Directed by Secretary of the Interior Harold Ickes, it built roads, schools, hospitals, and other public facilities, including New York City's Triborough Bridge and the Overseas Highway between Miami and Key West, Florida. In November, yet another agency, the Civil Works Administration (CWA), was launched. By January 1934, it employed over 4 million persons in the construction of highways, tunnels, courthouses, and airports. But as the cost spiraled upward and complaints multiplied that the New Deal was creating a class of Americans permanently dependent on government jobs, Roosevelt ordered the CWA dissolved.

Some New Deal public-works initiatives looked to government-planned economic transformation as much as economic relief. The Tennessee Valley Authority (TVA), another product of the Hundred Days, built a series of dams to prevent floods and deforestation along the Tennessee River and to provide cheap electric power for homes and factories in a seven-state region where many families still lived in isolated log cabins. The TVA put the federal government for the first time in the business of selling electricity in competition with private companies. It was a preview of the program of regional planning that spurred the economic development of the West.

THE NEW DEAL AND AGRICULTURE

Another policy initiative of the Hundred Days addressed the disastrous plight of American farmers. The Agricultural Adjustment Act (AAA) authorized the federal government to try to raise farm prices by setting production quotas for major crops and paying farmers not to plant more. Many crops already in the field were destroyed. In 1933, the government ordered over 6 million pigs slaughtered as part of the policy, a step critics found strange at a time of widespread hunger.

The AAA succeeded in significantly raising farm prices and incomes. But not all farmers benefited. Benefits flowed to property-owning farmers, ignoring the large number who worked on land owned by others. The AAA policy of paying landowning farmers not to grow crops encouraged the eviction of thousands of poor tenants and sharecroppers. Many joined the rural exodus to cities or to the farms of the West Coast.

Sharecroppers evicted from the farms on which they had been working in New Madrid County, Missouri, as a result of government subsidies to farm owners to reduce crop production.

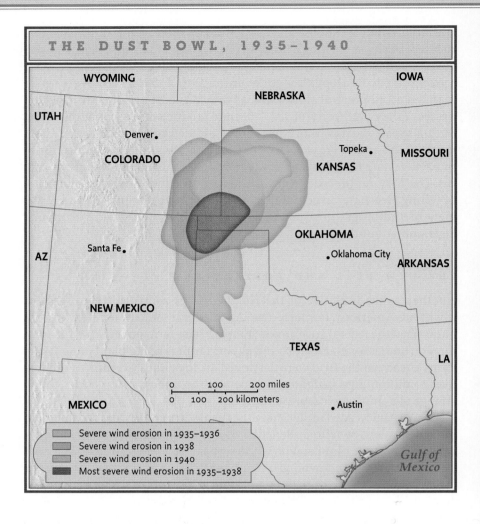

THE DUST BOWL, 1935–1940

Severe wind erosion in 1935–1936
Severe wind erosion in 1938
Severe wind erosion in 1940
Most severe wind erosion in 1935–1938

The onset in 1930 of a period of unusually dry weather in the nation's heartland worsened the Depression's impact on rural America. By mid-decade, the region suffered from the century's most severe drought. Mechanized agriculture in this semiarid region had pulverized the topsoil and killed native grasses that prevented erosion. Winds now blew much of the soil away, creating the Dust Bowl, as the affected areas of Oklahoma, Texas, Kansas, and Colorado were called. A local newspaper described the situation in Cimarron County, Oklahoma: "Not a blade of wheat; cattle dying on the range, ninety percent of the poultry dead because of the sand storms, milk cows gone dry." One storm in 1934 carried dust as far as Washington, D.C. The drought and dust storms displaced more than 1 million farmers. John Steinbeck's novel *The Grapes of Wrath* (1939) and a popular film based on the book captured their plight, tracing a dispossessed family's trek from Oklahoma to California.

THE NEW DEAL AND HOUSING

Owning one's home had long been a widely shared American ambition. "A man is not a whole and complete man," Walt Whitman had written in the 1850s, "unless he owns a house and the ground it stands on." For many

A giant dust storm engulfs a town in western Kansas on April 14, 1935, known as Black Sunday in the American West.

members of the middle class, home ownership had become a mark of respectability. For workers, it offered economic security at a time of low wages, erratic employment, and limited occupational mobility. On the eve of World War I, a considerably higher percentage of immigrant workers than the native-born middle class owned their homes.

The Depression devastated the American housing industry. The construction of new residences all but ceased, and banks and savings and loan associations that had financed home ownership collapsed or, to remain afloat, foreclosed on many homes (a quarter of a million in 1932 alone). In 1931, President Hoover convened a Conference on Home Building and Home Ownership to review the housing crisis. The president called owning a home an American "birthright," the embodiment of the spirit of "enterprise, of independence, and of . . . freedom." Rented apartments, he pointed out, did not inspire "immortal ballads" like *Home, Sweet Home* or *The Little Gray Home in the West.* Papers presented at the conference revealed

Russell Lee's 1939 photograph of a migrant family saying grace before eating by the side of the road near Fort Gibson, Oklahoma, shows how, even in the most difficult circumstances, families struggled to maintain elements of their normal lives.

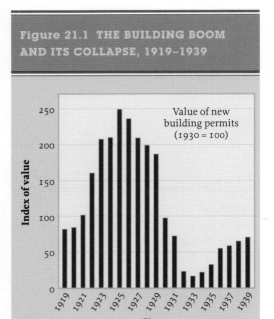

Figure 21.1 THE BUILDING BOOM AND ITS COLLAPSE, 1919–1939

Value of new building permits (1930 = 100)

As it did in other sectors of the economy, the Great Depression led to a collapse in the construction industry.

The Illegal Act, *a cartoon critical of the Supreme Court's decision declaring the NRA unconstitutional. FDR tells a drowning Uncle Sam, "I'm sorry, but the Supreme Court says I must chuck you back in."*

that millions of Americans lived in overcrowded, unhealthy urban slums or in ramshackle rural dwellings. Private enterprise alone, it seemed clear, was unlikely to solve the nation's housing crisis.

Hoover's administration established a federally sponsored bank to issue home loans. Not until the New Deal, however, did the government systematically enter the housing market. Roosevelt spoke of "the security of the home" as a fundamental right akin to "the security of livelihood, and the security of social insurance." In 1933 and 1934, his administration moved energetically to protect homeowners from foreclosure and to stimulate new construction. The Home Owners Loan Corporation and Federal Housing Administration (FHA) insured millions of long-term mortgages issued by private banks. At the same time, the federal government itself built thousands of units of low-rent housing. New Deal housing policy represented a remarkable departure from previous government practice. Thanks to the FHA and, later, the Veterans' Administration, home ownership came within the reach of tens of millions of families. It became cheaper for most Americans to buy single-family homes than to rent apartments.

Other important measures of Roosevelt's first two years in office included the ratification of the Twenty-first Amendment to the Constitution, which repealed Prohibition; the establishment of the Federal Communications Commission to oversee the nation's broadcast airwaves and telephone communications; and the creation of the Securities and Exchange Commission to regulate the stock and bond markets. Taken together, the First New Deal was a series of experiments some of which succeeded and some of which did not. They transformed the role of the federal government, constructed numerous public facilities, and provided relief to millions of needy persons. But they did not end the Depression. Some 10 million Americans, over 20 percent of the workforce, remained unemployed when 1934 came to an end.

THE COURT AND THE NEW DEAL

In 1935, the Supreme Court, still controlled by conservative Republican judges who held to the nineteenth-century understanding of freedom as liberty of contract, began to invalidate key New Deal laws. First came the NRA, declared unconstitutional in May in a case brought by the Schechter Poultry Company of Brooklyn, which had been charged with violating the code adopted by the chicken industry. In a unanimous decision, the Court declared the NRA unlawful because in its codes and other regulations it delegated legislative powers to the president and attempted to regulate local businesses that did not engage in interstate commerce. In January 1936, the AAA fell in *United States v. Butler*, which declared it an unconstitutional exercise of congressional power over local economic activities. In June, by a 5–4 vote, the justices ruled that New York could not establish a minimum wage for women and children.

Having failed to end the Depression or win judicial approval, the First New Deal ground to a halt. Meanwhile, pressures were mounting outside Washington that propelled the administration toward more radical departures in policy.

THE GRASSROOTS REVOLT

LABOR'S GREAT UPHEAVAL

The most striking development of the mid-1930s was the mobilization of millions of workers in mass-production industries that had successfully resisted unionization. "Labor's great upheaval," as this era of unprecedented militancy was called, came as a great surprise. Previous depressions, like those of the 1870s and 1890s, had devastated the labor movement. Unlike in the past, however, the federal government now seemed to be on the side of labor, a commitment embodied in the National Industrial Recovery Act and in the Wagner Act (discussed later) of 1935, which granted workers the legal right to form unions. With the severe reduction of European immigration, ethnic differences among workers had diminished in importance. American-born children of the new immigrants now dominated the industrial labor force, and organizers no longer had to distribute materials in numerous languages as the IWW had done. And a cadre of militant labor leaders, many of them socialists and communists with long experience in organization, had survived the repression of the 1920s. They provided leadership to the labor upsurge.

American factories at the outset of the New Deal were miniature dictatorships in which unions were rare, workers could be beaten by supervisors and fired at will, and management determined the length of the workday and speed of the assembly line. In industrial communities scattered across the country, local government firmly supported the companies. "Jesus Christ couldn't speak in Duquesne for the union," declared the mayor of that Pennsylvania steel town. Workers' demands during the 1930s went beyond better wages. They included an end to employers' arbitrary power in the workplace, and basic civil liberties for workers, including the right to picket, distribute literature, and meet to discuss their grievances. All these goals required union recognition.

Roosevelt's election as president did much to rekindle hope among those who called themselves, in the words of a worker writing to Secretary of Labor Frances Perkins, "slaves of the depression." His inauguration unleashed a flood of poignant letters to the federal government describing what a Louisiana sugar laborer called the "terrible and inhuman condition" of many workers. Labor organizers spread the message that the "political liberty for which our forefathers fought" had been "made meaningless by economic inequality" and "industrial despotism." "We are free Americans," declared the Steel Workers Organizing Committee. "We shall exercise our inalienable rights to organize into a great industrial union."

Labor's great upheaval exploded in 1934, a year that witnessed no fewer than 2,000 strikes. Many produced violent confrontations between workers and the local police. In Toledo, Ohio, 10,000 striking auto workers surrounded the Electric Auto-Lite factory, where managers had brought strikebreakers to take their jobs, leading to a seven-hour fight with police and the National Guard. In Minneapolis, where an organization of businessmen known as the Citizens Alliance controlled the city government, a four-month strike by truck drivers led to pitched battles in the streets and the governor declaring martial law. San Francisco experienced the

Pennsylvania Steelworkers outside the Local Headquarters of the Steel Workers Organizing Committee, *a 1938 photograph by Arnold Rothstein.*

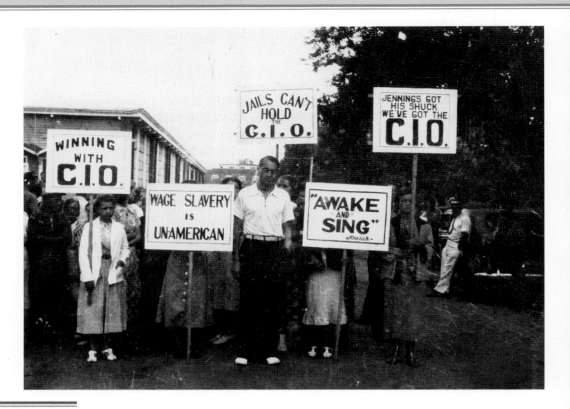

Signs carried by striking cotton mill workers in Lumberton, North Carolina in 1937 illustrate how the labor movement revived the nineteenth-century language of "wage slavery" to demand union recognition.

country's first general strike since 1919. It began with a walkout of dock-workers led by the fiery communist Harry Bridges. Workers demanded recognition of the International Longshoremen's Association and an end to the hated "shape up" system in which they had to gather en masse each day to wait for work assignments. The year 1934 also witnessed a strike of 400,000 textile workers in states from New England to the Deep South, demanding recognition of the United Textile Workers. Many of these walkouts, including those in Toledo, Minneapolis, and San Francisco, won at least some of the workers' demands. But the textile strike failed.

THE RISE OF THE CIO

The labor upheaval posed a challenge to the American Federation of Labor's traditional policy of organizing workers by craft—welders or machine repairers, for example—rather than seeking to mobilize all the workers in a given industry, such as steel manufacturing. In 1934, thirty AFL leaders called for the creation of unions of industrial workers. When the AFL convention of 1935 refused, the head of the United Mine Workers, John L. Lewis, led a walkout that produced a new labor organization, the Congress of Industrial Organizations (CIO). It set out to create unions in the main bastions of the American economy. It aimed, said Lewis, at nothing less than to secure "economic freedom and industrial democracy" for American workers—a fair share in the wealth produced by their labor, and a voice in determining the conditions under which they worked.

In December 1936, the United Auto Workers (UAW), a fledgling CIO union, unveiled the sit-down, a strikingly effective tactic that the IWW had pioneered three decades earlier. Rather than walking out of a plant, thus enabling management to bring in strikebreakers, workers halted production but remained inside. In the UAW's first sit-down strike, 7,000 General Motors workers seized control of the Fisher Body Plant in Cleveland. Sit-downs soon spread to GM plants in Flint, Michigan, the nerve center of automobile production. When local police tried to storm the Flint plants, workers fought them off. Democratic governor Frank Murphy, who had been elected with strong support from the CIO, declared his unwillingness to use force to dislodge the strikers. The strikers demonstrated a remarkable spirit of unity. They cleaned the plant, oiled the idle machinery, settled disputes among themselves, prepared meals, and held concerts of labor songs. Workers' wives shuttled food into the plant. "They made a palace out of what had been their prison," wrote one reporter. On February 11, General Motors agreed to negotiate with the UAW. Not until 1941 would the bitterly anti-union Henry Ford sign a labor contract. But by the end of 1937, the UAW claimed 400,000 members.

The victory in the auto industry reverberated throughout industrial America. Steelworkers had suffered memorable defeats in the struggle for unionization, notably at Homestead in 1892 and in the Great Steel Strike of 1919. U.S. Steel, the country's single most important business firm, owner of an industrial empire that stretched across several states and employed over 200,000 workers, had been among the strongest opponents of unionization. But in March 1937, fearing a sit-down campaign and aware that it could no longer count on the aid of state and federal authorities, the company agreed to recognize the Steel Workers Organizing Committee (forerunner of the United Steelworkers of America). Smaller steel firms, however, refused to follow suit. On Memorial Day, 1937, company guards and Chicago police fired on a picnic of striking Republic Steel workers, killing ten persons. Not until 1942 would Republic sign a labor contract.

Sit-down strike at a General Motors factory in Flint, Michigan, 1937.

Union membership nonetheless reached 9 million by 1940, more than double the number in 1930. The coming of the union, said a member of New York City's transit workers' organization, enabled workers "to go to our bosses and talk to them like men, instead of . . . like slaves." Unions frequently demanded and won a say in workplace management, including the right to contest the amount and pace of work and the introduction of new technology. They gained new grievance procedures and seniority systems governing hiring, firing, and promotions. The CIO unions helped to stabilize a chaotic employment situation and offered members a sense of dignity and freedom.

LABOR AND POLITICS

Throughout the industrial heartland, the labor upsurge altered the balance of economic power and propelled to the forefront of politics labor's goal of a fairer, freer, more equal America. Unlike the AFL, traditionally hostile to government intervention in labor-management relations, the CIO put forward an ambitious program for federal action to shield Americans from economic and social insecurity, including public housing, universal health care, and unemployment and old age insurance.

Building on the idea, so prominent in the 1920s, that the key to prosperity lay in an American standard of living based on mass consumption, CIO leaders explained the Depression as the result of an imbalance of wealth and income. The role of unions, in cooperation with the government, they argued, was to "create a consumer's demand" by raising wages and redistributing wealth. Only in this way could society absorb the products that rolled off modern assembly lines. The pathbreaking 1937 agreement between the UAW and General Motors spoke of a "rate of pay commensurate with an American standard of living." By mid-decade, many New Dealers accepted the "underconsumptionist" explanation of the Depression, which saw lack of sufficient consumer demand as its underlying cause. They concluded that the government must act to raise dramatically wage earners' share of the national income.

VOICES OF PROTEST

Other popular movements of the mid-1930s also placed the question of economic justice on the political agenda. In California, the novelist Upton Sinclair won the Democratic nomination for governor in 1934 as the head of the End Poverty in California movement. Sinclair called for the state to use idle factories and land in cooperative ventures that would provide jobs for the unemployed. He lost the election after being subjected to one of the first modern "negative" media campaigns. Sinclair's opponents circulated false newsreels showing armies of unemployed men marching to California to support his candidacy and a fake endorsement from the Communist Party.

The rise to national prominence of Huey Long offered another sign of popular dissatisfaction with the slow pace of economic recovery. Long's career embodied both Louisiana's Populist and Socialist traditions (Winn Parish, his home, had voted for both these third parties) and the state's heritage of undemocratic politics. Driven by intense ambition and the desire to help uplift the state's "common people," Long won election as governor in 1928 and in 1930 took a seat in the U.S. Senate. From Washington, he dominated every branch of state government. He used his dictatorial power to build roads, schools, and hospitals and to increase the tax burden on Louisiana's oil companies.

One of the most colorful characters in twentieth-century American politics, Long was referred to by both admirers and critics as the "Kingfish." In 1934, he launched the Share Our Wealth movement, with the slogan "Every Man a King." He called for the confiscation of most of the wealth of the richest Americans in order to finance an immediate grant of $5,000 and a guaranteed job and annual income for all citizens. In his inimitable style, Long explained his goal: "Let's pull down these huge piles of gold until there shall be a real job, not a little old sow-belly, black-eyed pea job but a real spending money, beefsteak and gravy . . . Ford in the garage . . . red, white, and blue job for every man." Long claimed a following of 5 million. He was on the verge of announcing a run for president when the son of a defeated political rival assassinated him in 1935.

Also in the mid-1930s, the "radio priest," Father Charles E. Coughlin, attracted millions of listeners with weekly broadcasts attacking Wall Street bankers and greedy capitalists, and calling for government ownership of key industries as a way of combating the Depression. Initially a strong supporter of FDR, Coughlin became increasingly critical of the president for what he considered the failure of the New Deal to promote social justice. His crusade would later shift to anti-Semitism and support for European fascism. Dr. Francis Townsend, a California physician, meanwhile won wide support for a plan by which the government would make a monthly payment of $200 to older Americans, with the requirement that they spend it immediately. This, he argued, would boost the economy. By the end of 1934, Townsend Clubs claimed over 2 million members. Along with the rise of the CIO, these signs of popular discontent helped to spark the Second New Deal.

A portrait of Huey Long, the "Kingfish" of Louisiana politics, towers over the inauguration of his supporter, Richard Leche, as governor in 1936.

THE SECOND NEW DEAL

Spurred by the failure of his initial policies to pull the country out of the Depression and the growing popular clamor for greater economic equality, and buoyed by Democratic gains in the midterm elections of 1934, Roosevelt in 1935 launched the Second New Deal. The First had focused on economic recovery. The emphasis of the Second was economic security—a guarantee that Americans would be protected against unemployment and poverty. "Boys," Roosevelt's relief administrator, Harry Hopkins, told his staff, "this is our hour. We've got to get everything we want—a [public] works program, social security, wages and hours, everything—now or never."

The idea that lack of consumer demand caused the Depression had been popularized by Huey Long, Francis Townsend, and the CIO. By 1935, more and more New Dealers had concluded that the government should no longer try to plan business recovery but should try to redistribute the national income so as to sustain mass purchasing power in the consumer economy. A series of measures in 1935 attacked head-on the problem of weak demand and economic inequality. Congress levied a highly publicized tax on large fortunes and corporate profits—a direct response to the popularity of Huey Long's Share Our Wealth campaign. It created the Rural Electrification Agency (REA) to bring electric power to homes that lacked it—80 percent of farms were still without electricity in 1934—in part to enable more Americans to purchase household appliances.

The REA proved to be one of the Second New Deal's most successful programs. By 1950, 90 percent of the nation's farms had been wired for electricity, and almost all now possessed radios, electric stoves, refrigerators, and mechanical equipment to milk cows. In addition, the federal government under the Second New Deal tried to promote soil conservation and family farming. This effort resulted from the belief that the country would never achieve prosperity so long as farmers' standard of living lagged well behind that of city dwellers, and that rural poverty resulted mainly from the poor use of natural resources. Thus, farmers received federal assistance in reducing soil loss in their fields. The federal government also purchased significant amounts of marginal and eroded land and converted these areas from farms into national grasslands and parks. It encouraged more environmentally conscious agricultural techniques. These measures (like those of the AAA) mainly benefited landowners, not sharecroppers, tenants, or migrant workers. In the long run, the Second New Deal failed to arrest the trend toward larger farms and fewer farmers.

THE WPA AND THE WAGNER ACT

In 1934, Roosevelt had severely curtailed federal employment for those in need. Now, he approved the establishment of the Works Progress Administration (WPA), which hired some 3 million Americans in virtually every walk of life each year until it ended in 1943. Under Harry Hopkins's direction, the WPA changed the physical face of the United States. It constructed thousands of public buildings and bridges, over 500,000 miles of roads, and 600 airports. It built stadiums, swimming pools, and sewage treatment plants. Unlike previous work relief programs, the WPA employed many out-of-work white-collar workers and professionals, even doctors and dentists.

Perhaps the most famous WPA projects were in the arts. The WPA set hundreds of artists to work decorating public buildings with murals. It hired writers to produce local histories and guidebooks to the forty-eight states and to record the recollections of ordinary Americans, including hundreds of former slaves. Its Federal Theater Project put on plays, including an all-black production of *Macbeth* and Sinclair Lewis's drama *It Can't Happen Here*, about fascism coming to the United States. The Federal Music Project established orchestras and choral groups, and the Federal Dance Project sponsored ballet and modern dance programs. Thanks to the WPA, audiences across the country enjoyed their first glimpse of live musical and theatrical performances and their first opportunity to view exhibitions of American art. Also in 1935, Congress created the National Youth Administration to provide relief to American teenagers and young adults.

A poster by the artist Vera Bock for the Federal Art Project of the Works Progress Administration depicts farmers and laborers joining hands to produce prosperity.

Another major initiative of the Second New Deal, the Wagner Act, was known at the time as "Labor's Magna Carta" (a reference to an early landmark in the history of freedom). This brought democracy into the American workplace by empowering the National Labor Relations Board to supervise elections in which employees voted on union representation. It also outlawed "unfair labor practices," including the firing and blacklisting of union organizers. The bill's main sponsor, Robert Wagner of New York, told the Senate that the ability of workers to pool their strength through collective bargaining represented the "next step" in "the evolution of American freedom." He also promised that unionization and higher wages would aid economic recovery by boosting the purchasing power of ordinary Americans.

THE AMERICAN WELFARE STATE

The centerpiece of the Second New Deal was the Social Security Act of 1935. It embodied Roosevelt's conviction that the national government had a responsibility to ensure the material well-being of ordinary Americans. It created a system of unemployment insurance, old age pensions, and aid to the disabled, the elderly poor, and families with dependent children.

None of these were original ideas. The Progressive platform of 1912 had called for old age pensions. Assistance to poor families with dependent children descended from the mothers' pensions promoted by maternalist reformers. Many European countries had already adopted national unemployment insurance plans. What was new, however, was that in the name of economic security, the American government would now supervise not simply temporary relief but a permanent system of social insurance.

The Social Security Act launched the American version of the welfare state—a term that originated in Britain during World War II to refer to a system of income assistance, health coverage, and social services for all citizens. The act illustrated both the extent and the limits of the changes ushered in by the Second New Deal. The American welfare state marked a radical departure from previous government policies, but compared with similar programs in Europe, it has always been far more decentralized, involved lower levels of public spending, and covered fewer citizens. The original Social Security Bill, for example, envisioned a national system of health insurance. But Congress dropped this after ferocious opposition from the American Medical Association, which feared government regulation of doctors' activities and incomes.

THE SOCIAL SECURITY SYSTEM

Some New Dealers desired a program funded by the federal government's general tax revenues, and with a single set of eligibility standards administered by national officials. But Secretary of Labor Frances Perkins, along with powerful members of Congress, wished to keep relief in the hands of state and local authorities and believed that workers should contribute directly to the cost of their own benefits. Roosevelt himself preferred to fund Social Security by taxes on employers and workers, rather than out of general government revenues. He believed that paying such taxes gave contributors

A 1935 poster promoting the new Social Security system.

"a legal, moral, and political right" to collect their old age pensions and unemployment benefits, which no future Congress could rescind.

As a result, Social Security emerged as a hybrid of national and local funding, control, and eligibility standards. Old age pensions were administered nationally but paid for by taxes on employers and employees. Such taxes also paid for payments to the unemployed, but this program was highly decentralized, with the states retaining considerable control over the level of benefits. The states paid most of the cost of direct poor relief, under the program called Aid to Dependent Children, and eligibility and the level of payments varied enormously from place to place. As will be discussed later, the combination of local administration and the fact that domestic and agricultural workers were not covered by unemployment and old age benefits meant that Social Security excluded large numbers of Americans, especially women and non-whites.

Nonetheless, Social Security represented a dramatic departure from the traditional functions of government. The Second New Deal transformed the relationship between the federal government and American citizens. Before the 1930s, national political debate often revolved around the question of *whether* the federal government should intervene in the economy. After the New Deal, debate rested on *how* it should intervene. In addition, the government assumed a responsibility, which it has never wholly relinquished, for guaranteeing Americans a living wage and protecting them against economic and personal misfortune. "Laissez-faire is dead," wrote Walter Lippmann, "and the modern state has become responsible for the modern economy [and] the task of insuring . . . the standard of life for its people."

A RECKONING WITH LIBERTY

The Depression made inevitable, in the words of one writer, a "reckoning with liberty." For too many Americans, Roosevelt proclaimed, "life was no longer free; liberty no longer real; men could no longer follow the pursuit of happiness." The 1930s produced an outpouring of books and essays on freedom. The large majority took for granted the need for a new definition. In a volume entitled *Land of the Free* (1938), the poet Archibald MacLeish used photographs of impoverished migrants and sharecroppers to question the reality of freedom in desperate times. "We told ourselves we were free," he wrote. Now, "we wonder if the liberty is done . . . or if there's something different men can mean by Liberty."

Like the Civil War, the New Deal recast the idea of freedom by linking it to the expanding power of the national state. "Our democracy," wrote Father John A. Ryan, a prominent Catholic social critic, "finds itself . . . in a new age where not political freedom but social and industrial freedom is the most insistent cry." Influenced by Ryan, the National Catholic Welfare Conference in 1935 declared that "social justice" required a government guarantee of continuous employment and a "decent livelihood and adequate security" for all Americans. A 1935 survey by *Fortune* magazine found that among poor respondents, 90 percent believed that the government should guarantee that "every man who wants work has a job."

FDR AND THE IDEA OF FREEDOM

Along with being a superb politician, Roosevelt was a master of political communication. At a time when his political opponents controlled most newspapers, he harnessed radio's power to bring his message directly into American homes. By the mid-1930s, over two-thirds of American families owned radios. They listened avidly to Roosevelt's radio addresses, known as "fireside chats."

Roosevelt adeptly appealed to traditional values in support of new policies. He gave the term "liberalism" its modern meaning. In the nineteenth century, liberalism had been a shorthand for limited government and free-market economics. Roosevelt consciously chose to employ it to describe a large, active, socially conscious state. He reclaimed the word "freedom" from conservatives and made it a rallying cry for the New Deal. In his second fireside chat, Roosevelt juxtaposed his own definition of liberty as "greater security for the average man" to the older notion of liberty of contract, which served the interests of "the privileged few." Henceforth, he would consistently link freedom with economic security and identify entrenched economic inequality as its greatest enemy. "The liberty of a democracy," he declared in 1938, was not safe if citizens could not "sustain an acceptable standard of living."

Even as Roosevelt invoked the word to uphold the New Deal, "liberty"—in the sense of freedom from powerful government—became the fighting slogan of his opponents. Their principal critique of the New Deal was that its "reckless spending" undermined fiscal responsibility and its new government regulations restricted American freedom. When conservative

FDR delivering one of his "fireside chats" in 1938. Roosevelt was the first president to make effective use of the radio to promote his policies.

This 1935 cartoon by William Gropper portrays Uncle Sam as Gulliver tied down by Lilliputians in the famous eighteenth-century novel Gulliver's Travels *by Jonathan Swift. In this case, the bonds are the numerous agencies and laws created by the New Deal, which, Gropper suggests, are inhibiting the country from getting back on its feet during the Great Depression.*

VOICES OF FREEDOM

From Franklin D. Roosevelt,
Speech Accepting Renomination for President (1936)

The Democratic Party nominated Roosevelt for a second term as president in 1936. Roosevelt traveled to the convention to accept the nomination, and he used the occasion to outline his definition of freedom.

Philadelphia is a good city in which to write American history. This is a fitting ground on which to reaffirm the faith of our fathers; to pledge ourselves to restore to the people a wider freedom; to give to 1936 as the founders gave to 1776—an American way of life.

That very word freedom, in itself and of necessity, suggests freedom from some restraining power. In 1776 we sought freedom from the tyranny of a political autocracy—from the eighteenth century royalists who held special privileges from the crown. It was to perpetuate their privilege that they governed without the consent of the governed; that they denied the right of free assembly and free speech.... It was to win freedom from the tyranny of political autocracy that the American Revolution was fought....

Out of modern civilization economic royalists carved new dynasties. New kingdoms were built upon concentration of control over material things.

Through new uses of corporations, banks and securities, new machinery of industry and agriculture, of labor and capital—all undreamed of by the fathers—the whole structure of modern life was impressed into this royal service....

It was natural and perhaps human that the privileged princes of these new economic dynasties, thirsting for power, reached out for control over Government itself. They created a new despotism and wrapped it in the robes of legal sanction. In its service new mercenaries sought to regiment the people, their labor, and their property. And as a result the average man once more confronts the problem that faced the Minute Men.

The hours men and women worked, the wages they received, the conditions of their labor—these had passed beyond the control of the people.... Those who tilled the soil no longer reaped the rewards which were their right.... Throughout the Nation, opportunity was limited by monopoly....

An old English judge once said: "Necessitous men are not free men." Liberty requires opportunity to make a living—a living decent according to the standard of the time, a living which gives man not only enough to live by, but something to live for.... Here in America we are waging a great and successful war. ... It is a war for the survival of democracy.

FROM JOHN STEINBECK, *The Harvest Gypsies:*
On the Road to the Grapes of Wrath (1938)

John Steinbeck's popular novel *The Grapes of Wrath* (1939), and the film version that followed shortly thereafter, focused national attention on the plight of homeless migrants displaced from their farms as a result of the Great Depression. Before that book appeared, Steinbeck had published a series of newspaper articles based on eyewitness accounts of the migrants, which became the basis for his novel.

In California, we find a curious attitude toward a group that makes our agriculture successful. The migrants are needed, and they are hated. . . . The migrants are hated for the following reasons, that they are ignorant and dirty people, that they are carriers of disease, that they increase the necessity for police and the tax bill for schooling in a community, and that if they are allowed to organize they can, simply by refusing to work, wipe out the season's crops. . . .

Let us see what kind of people they are, where they come from, and the routes of their wanderings. In the past they have been of several races, encouraged to come and often imported as cheap labor. Chinese in the early period, then Filipinos, Japanese and Mexicans. These were foreigners, and as such they were ostracized and segregated and herded about. . . . But in recent years the foreign migrants have begun to organize, and at this danger they have been deported in great numbers, for there was a new reservoir from which a great quantity of cheap labor could be obtained.

The drought in the middle west has driven the agricultural populations of Oklahoma, Nebraska and parts of Kansas and Texas westward. . . . Thousands of them are crossing the borders in ancient rattling automobiles, destitute and hungry and homeless, ready to accept any pay so that they may eat and feed their children. . . .

The earlier foreign migrants have invariably been drawn from a peon class. This is not the case with the new migrants. They are small farmers who have lost their farms, or farm hands who have lived with the family in the old American way. . . . They have come from the little farm districts where democracy was not only possible but inevitable, where popular government, whether practiced in the Grange, in church organization or in local government, was the responsibility of every man. And they have come into the country where, because of the movement necessary to make a living, they are not allowed any vote whatever, but are rather considered a properly unprivileged class. . . .

As one little boy in a squatter's camp said, "When they need us they call us migrants, and when we've picked their crop, we're bums and we got to get out."

===

QUESTIONS

1. What does Roosevelt consider the main threat to American freedom?

2. According to Steinbeck, how do Depression-era migrant workers differ from those in earlier periods?

3. Do the migrant workers described by Steinbeck enjoy economic liberty as Roosevelt defines it?

businessmen and politicians in 1934 formed an organization to mobilize opposition to Roosevelt's policies, they called it the American Liberty League. Robert Taft of Ohio, leader of the Republicans in Congress, accused Roosevelt of sacrificing "individual freedom" in a misguided effort to "improve the conditions of the poor."

As the 1930s progressed, opponents of the New Deal invoked the language of liberty with greater and greater passion. The United States Chamber of Commerce charged FDR with attempting to "Sovietize" America. Even though his own administration had abandoned laissez-faire in the face of economic disaster, former president Hoover launched strident attacks on his successor for endangering "fundamental American liberties." In *The Challenge to Liberty* (1934), Hoover called the New Deal "the most stupendous invasion of the whole spirit of liberty" the nation had ever seen.

THE ELECTION OF 1936

By 1936, with working-class voters providing massive majorities for the Democratic Party and businesses large and small bitterly estranged from the New Deal, politics reflected class divisions more completely than at any other time in American history. Conceptions of freedom divided sharply as well. Americans, wrote George Soule, editor of *The New Republic*, confronted "two opposing systems of concepts about liberty," reflecting "the needs and purposes of two opposing [parts] of the population." One was the idea of "freedom for private enterprise," the other "socialized liberty" based on "an equitably shared abundance."

A fight for the possession of "the ideal of freedom," reported the *New York Times*, emerged as the central issue of the presidential campaign of 1936. The Democratic platform insisted that in a modern economy the government has an obligation to establish a "democracy of opportunity for all the people." In his speech accepting renomination, Roosevelt launched a blistering attack against "economic royalists" who, he charged, sought to establish a new tyranny over the "average man." Economic rights, he went on, were the precondition of liberty—poor men "are not free men." Throughout the campaign, FDR would insist that the threat posed to economic freedom by the "new despotism" of large corporations was the main issue of the election.

As Roosevelt's opponent, Republicans chose Kansas governor Alfred Landon, a former Theodore Roosevelt Progressive. Landon denounced Social Security and other measures as threats to individual liberty. Opposition to the New Deal planted the seeds for the later flowering of an antigovernment conservatism bent on upholding the free market and dismantling the welfare state. But in 1936 Roosevelt won a landslide reelection, with over 60 percent of the popular vote. He carried every state except Maine and Vermont. Roosevelt's victory was all the more remarkable in view of the heavy support most of the nation's newspapers and nearly the entire business community gave to the Republicans. His success stemmed from strong backing from organized labor and his ability to unite southern white and northern black voters, Protestant farmers and urban Catholic and Jewish ethnics, industrial workers and middle-class home owners. These groups made up the so-called New Deal coalition, which would dominate American politics for nearly half a century.

THE COURT FIGHT

Roosevelt's second inaugural address was the first to be delivered on January 20. In order to lessen a newly elected president's wait before taking office, the recently ratified Twentieth Amendment had moved inauguration day from March 4. FDR called on the nation to redouble its efforts to aid those "who have too little." The Depression, he admitted, had not been conquered: "I see one-third of a nation ill-housed, ill-clad, and ill-nourished." Emboldened by his electoral triumph, Roosevelt now made what many considered a serious political miscalculation. On the pretense that several members of the Supreme Court were too old to perform their functions, he proposed that the president be allowed to appoint a new justice for each one who remained on the Court past age seventy (an age that six of the nine had already surpassed). FDR's aim, of course, was to change the balance of power on a Court that, he feared, might well invalidate Social Security, the Wagner Act, and other measures of the Second New Deal.

The plan aroused cries that the president was an aspiring dictator. Congress rejected it. But Roosevelt accomplished his underlying purpose. The Supreme Court, it is sometimes said, follows the election returns. Coming soon after Roosevelt's landslide victory of 1936, the threat of "court packing" inspired an astonishing about-face on the part of key justices. Beginning in March 1937, the Court suddenly revealed a new willingness to support economic regulation by both the federal government and the states. It upheld a minimum wage law of the state of Washington similar to the New York measure it had declared unconstitutional a year earlier. It turned aside challenges to Social Security and the Wagner Act. In subsequent cases, the Court affirmed federal power to regulate wages, hours, child labor, agricultural production, and numerous other aspects of economic life.

Announcing a new judicial definition of freedom, Chief Justice Charles Evans Hughes pointed out that the words "freedom of contract" did not appear in the Constitution. "Liberty," however, did, and this, Hughes continued, required "the protection of law against the evils which menace the health, safety, morals, and welfare of the people." The Court's new willingness to accept the New Deal marked a permanent change in judicial policy. Having declared dozens of economic laws unconstitutional in the decades leading up to 1937, the justices have rarely done so since.

THE END OF THE SECOND NEW DEAL

Even as the Court made its peace with Roosevelt's policies, the momentum of the Second New Deal slowed. The landmark United States Housing Act did pass in 1937, initiating the first major national effort to build homes for the poorest Americans. But the Fair Labor Standards Bill failed to reach the floor for over a year. When it finally passed in 1938, it banned goods produced by child labor from interstate commerce, set forty cents as the minimum hourly wage, and required overtime pay for hours of work exceeding forty per week. This last major piece of New Deal legislation established

Fall In!, *a cartoon commenting on Roosevelt's proposal to "pack" the Supreme Court, from the* Richmond Times-Dispatch, *January 8, 1937.*

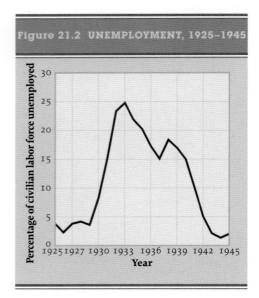

Figure 21.2 UNEMPLOYMENT, 1925–1945

The New Deal did not really solve the problem of unemployment, which fell below 10 percent only in 1941, as the United States prepared to enter World War II.

the practice of federal regulation of wages and working conditions, another radical departure from pre-Depression policies.

The year 1937 also witnessed a sharp downturn of the economy. With economic conditions improving in 1936, Roosevelt had reduced federal funding for farm subsidies and WPA work relief. The result was disastrous. As government spending fell, so did business investment, industrial production, and the stock market. Unemployment, still 14 percent at the beginning of 1937, rose to nearly 20 percent by year's end.

In 1936, in *The General Theory of Employment, Interest, and Money*, John Maynard Keynes had challenged economists' traditional belief in the sanctity of balanced budgets. Large-scale government spending, he insisted, was necessary to sustain purchasing power and stimulate economic activity during downturns. Such spending should be enacted even at the cost of a budget deficit (a situation in which the government spends more money than it takes in). By 1938, Roosevelt was ready to follow this prescription, which would later be known as Keynesian economics. In April, he asked Congress for billions more for work relief and farm aid. By the end of the year, the immediate crisis had passed. But the events of 1937–1938 marked a major shift in New Deal philosophy. Rather than economic planning, as in 1933–1934, or economic redistribution, as in 1935–1936, public spending would now be the government's major tool for combating unemployment and stimulating economic growth. The Second New Deal had come to an end.

THE LIMITS OF CHANGE

Roosevelt conceived of the Second New Deal, and especially Social Security, as expanding the meaning of freedom by extending assistance to broad groups of needy Americans—the unemployed, elderly, and dependent—as a right of citizenship, not charity or special privilege. But political realities, especially the power of inherited ideas about gender and black disenfranchisement in the South, powerfully affected the drafting of legislation. Different groups of Americans experienced the New Deal in radically different ways.

THE NEW DEAL AND AMERICAN WOMEN

The New Deal brought more women into government than ever before in American history. A number of talented women, including Secretary of Labor Frances Perkins, advised the president and shaped public policy. Most prominent of all was Eleanor Roosevelt, FDR's distant cousin whom he had married in 1905. She transformed the role of "first lady," turning a position with no formal responsibilities into a base for political action. She traveled widely, spoke out on public issues, wrote a regular newspaper column that sometimes disagreed openly with her husband's policies, and worked to enlarge the scope of the New Deal in areas like civil rights, labor legislation, and work relief.

But even as the New Deal increased women's visibility in national politics, organized feminism, already in disarray during the 1920s, disappeared as a political force. Indeed, the Depression inspired widespread demands for women to remove themselves from the labor market to make room for unem-

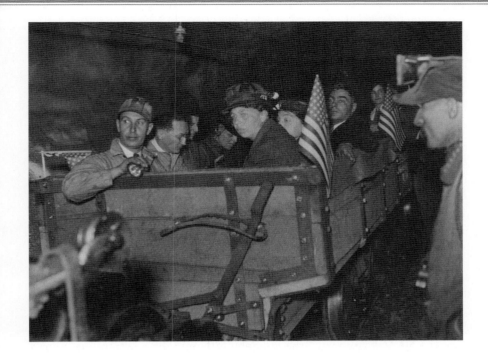

Eleanor Roosevelt transformed the role of First Lady by taking an active and visible part in public life. Here, she visits a West Virginia coal mine in 1933.

ployed men. Because the Depression hit industrial employment harder than low-wage clerical and service jobs where women predominated, the proportion of the workforce made up of women rose. The government tried to reverse this trend. The Economy Act of 1932 prohibited both members of a married couple from holding federal jobs. Until its repeal in 1937, it led to the dismissal of numerous female civil service employees whose husbands worked for the government. Many states and localities prohibited the hiring of women whose husbands earned a "living wage," and employers from banks to public school systems barred married women from jobs. Although the CIO organized female workers, it, too, adhered to the idea that women should be supported by men. "The working wife whose husband is employed," said a vice president of the United Auto Workers, "should be barred from industry."

Most New Deal programs did not exclude women from benefits (although the CCC restricted its camps to men). But the ideal of the male-headed household powerfully shaped social policy. Since paying taxes on one's wages made one eligible for the most generous Social Security programs—old age pensions and unemployment insurance—they left most women uncovered, since they did not work outside the home. The program excluded the 3 million mostly female domestic workers altogether. "Those who need protection most are completely overlooked," the sister of a household worker complained to Secretary of Labor Perkins. "What about the poor domestics, both in private homes and private institutions. What have you done for them? Nothing."

THE SOUTHERN VETO

Roosevelt made the federal government the symbolic representative of all the people, including racial and ethnic groups generally ignored by previous administrations. Yet the power of the Solid South helped to mold the

New Deal welfare state into an entitlement of white Americans. After the South's blacks lost the right to vote around the turn of the century, Democrats enjoyed a political monopoly in the region. Democratic members of Congress were elected again and again. With results predetermined, many whites did not bother to vote (only about 20 percent of eligible southern voters cast ballots in the election of 1920). But this tiny electorate had an enormous impact on national policy. Committee chairmanships in Congress rest on seniority—how many years a member has served in office. Beginning in 1933, when Democrats took control of Congress, southerners took the key leadership positions. Despite his personal popularity, Roosevelt felt he could not challenge the power of southern Democrats if he wished legislation to pass. At their insistence, the Social Security law excluded agricultural and domestic workers, the largest categories of black employment.

Roosevelt spoke of Social Security's universality, but the demand for truly comprehensive coverage came from the political left and black organizations. Congressman Ernest Lundeen of Minnesota in 1935 introduced a bill establishing a federally controlled system of old age, unemployment, and health benefits for all wage workers, plus support for female heads of households with dependents. Black organizations like the Urban League and the NAACP supported the Lundeen bill and lobbied strenuously for a system that enabled agricultural and domestic workers to receive unemployment and old age benefits and that established national relief standards. The Social Security Act, however, not Lundeen's proposal, became law. Its limitations, complained the *Pittsburgh Courier*, a black newspaper, reflected the power of "reactionary elements in the South who cannot bear the thought of Negroes getting pensions and compensations" and who feared that the inclusion of black workers would disrupt the region's low-wage, racially divided labor system.

THE STIGMA OF WELFARE

Because of the "southern veto," the majority of black workers found themselves confined to the least generous and most vulnerable wing of the new welfare state. The public assistance programs established by Social Security, notably aid to dependent children and to the poor elderly, were open to all Americans who could demonstrate financial need. But they set benefits at extremely low levels and authorized the states to determine eligibility standards, including "moral" behavior as defined by local authorities. As a result, public assistance programs allowed for widespread discrimination in the distribution of benefits. Because recipients did not pay Social Security taxes, they soon came to bear the humiliating stigma of dependency on government handouts, which would soon come to be known as "welfare."

In 1942, the National Resources Planning Board noted that because of their exclusion from programs "which give aid under relatively favorable conditions," blacks were becoming disproportionately dependent on welfare, a program widely viewed with popular disfavor. The situation, the report concluded, seemed certain to stigmatize blacks as recipients of unearned government assistance, and welfare as a program for minorities, thus dooming it forever to inadequate "standards of aid." Over time, this is precisely what happened, until the federal government abolished its responsibility for welfare in 1996, during the presidency of Bill Clinton.

THE INDIAN NEW DEAL

Overall, the Depression and New Deal had a contradictory impact on America's racial minorities. Under Commissioner of Indian Affairs John Collier, the administration launched an "Indian New Deal." Collier ended the policy of forced assimilation and allowed Indians unprecedented cultural autonomy. He replaced boarding schools meant to eradicate the tribal heritage of Indian children with schools on reservations, and dramatically increased spending on Indian health. He secured passage of the Indian Reorganization Act of 1934, ending the policy, dating back to the Dawes Act of 1887, of dividing Indian lands into small plots for individual families and selling off the rest. Federal authorities once again recognized Indians' right to govern their own affairs, except where specifically limited by national laws. Such limitations, however, could weigh heavily on Indian tribes. The Navajos, the nation's largest tribe, refused to cooperate with the Reorganization Act as a protest against a federal soil conservation program that required them to reduce their herds of livestock.

The New Deal marked the most radical shift in Indian policy in the nation's history. But living conditions on the desperately poor reservations did not significantly improve, and New Deal programs often ignored Indians' interests. The building of the Grand Coulee Dam on the Columbia River flooded thousands of acres where Indians had hunted and fished for centuries. But the government did not make any of the irrigation water available to the region's reservations.

Most Mexican-Americans during the 1930s worked in agriculture or in farm-related industries. In this photograph, Mexican-American women shell pecans in a San Antonio factory in 1939.

THE NEW DEAL AND MEXICAN-AMERICANS

For Mexican-Americans, the Depression was a wrenching experience. With demand for their labor plummeting, over 400,000 (one-fifth of the population of Mexican origin) returned to Mexico, some voluntarily, others at the strong urging of local authorities in the Southwest. A majority of those "encouraged" to leave the country were recent immigrants, but they included perhaps 200,000 Mexican-American children who had been born in the United States and were therefore citizens. Those who remained mostly worked in grim conditions in California's vegetable and fruit fields, whose corporate farms benefited enormously from New Deal dam construction that provided them with cheap electricity and water for irrigation. The Wagner and Social Security Acts did not apply to agricultural laborers. When the workers tried to organize a union as part of the decade's labor upsurge, they were brutally suppressed. In his 1939 book *Factories in the Field*, the writer Carey McWilliams exposed the low wages, inadequate housing, and political repression under which the migrant laborers suffered, which the New Deal did nothing to alleviate.

LAST HIRED, FIRST FIRED

As the "last hired and first fired," African-Americans were hit hardest by the Depression. Even those who retained their jobs now faced competition from unemployed whites who had previously considered positions like waiter and porter beneath them. With an unemployment rate double that of whites, blacks benefited disproportionately from direct government relief and, especially in northern cities, jobs on New Deal public-works projects. Half of the families in Harlem received public assistance during the 1930s.

The Depression propelled economic survival to the top of the black agenda. Demonstrations in Harlem demanded jobs in the neighborhood's white-owned stores, with the slogan "Don't Buy Where You Can't Work." W. E. B. Du Bois abandoned his earlier goal of racial integration as unrealistic for the foreseeable future. Blacks, he wrote, must recognize themselves as "a nation within a nation." He called on blacks to organize for economic survival by building an independent, cooperative economy within their segregated communities, and to gain control of their own separate schools (a position reminiscent of that of Booker T. Washington, whom he had earlier condemned).

A NEW DEAL FOR BLACKS

Although Roosevelt seems to have had little personal interest in race relations or civil rights, he appointed Mary McLeod Bethune, a prominent black educator, as a special adviser on minority affairs and a number of other blacks to important federal positions. Key members of his administration, including his wife, Eleanor, and Secretary of the Interior Harold Ickes, a former president of the Chicago chapter of the NAACP, directed national attention to the injustices of segregation, disenfranchisement, and lynching. In 1939, Eleanor Roosevelt resigned from the Daughters of the American Revolution when the organization refused to allow the black singer Marian Anderson to present a concert at Constitution Hall in Washington. The president's wife arranged for Anderson to sing on the steps of the Lincoln Memorial and for the concert to be broadcast nationally on the radio.

Thanks to the New Deal, Bethune proclaimed, a "new day" had dawned when blacks would finally reach "the promised land of liberty." The decade witnessed a historic shift in black voting patterns. In the North and West, where they enjoyed the right to vote, blacks in 1934 and 1936 abandoned their allegiance to the party of Lincoln and emancipation in favor of Democrats and the New Deal. But their hopes for broad changes in the nation's race system were disappointed. Despite a massive lobbying campaign, southern congressmen prevented passage of a federal antilynching law. FDR offered little sup-

Marian Anderson performing at the Lincoln Memorial in 1939, after the Daughters of the American Revolution barred her from singing at Constitution Hall.

port. "I did not choose the tools with which I must work," he told Walter White of the NAACP; he could not jeopardize his economic programs by alienating powerful members of Congress. The CCC established segregated work camps. Because of the exclusion of agricultural and domestic workers, Social Security's old age pensions and unemployment benefits and the minimum wages established by the Fair Labor Standards Act left uncovered 60 percent of all employed blacks and 85 percent of black women.

FEDERAL DISCRIMINATION

Federal housing policy, which powerfully reinforced residential segregation, revealed the limits of New Deal freedom. As in the case of Social Security, local officials put national housing policy into practice in a way that reinforced existing racial boundaries. Nearly all municipalities, North as well as South, insisted that housing built or financially aided by the federal government be racially segregated. (In Texas, some communities financed three sets of housing projects—for whites, blacks, and Mexicans.) The Federal Housing Administration, moreover, had no hesitation about insuring mortgages that contained clauses barring future sales to non-white buyers, and it refused to channel money into integrated neighborhoods. In some cases, the presence of a single black family led the agency to declare an entire block off-limits for federal mortgage insurance. Along with discriminatory practices by private banks and real estate companies, federal policy became a major factor in further entrenching housing segregation in the United States.

Federal employment practices also discriminated on the basis of race. As late as 1940, of the 150,000 blacks holding federal jobs, only 2 percent occupied positions other than clerk or custodian. In the South, many New Deal construction projects refused to hire blacks at all. "They give all the work to white people and give us nothing," a black resident of Mississippi wrote to FDR in 1935. The New Deal began the process of modernizing southern agriculture, but tenants, black and white, footed much of the bill. Tens of thousands of sharecroppers, as noted earlier, were driven off the land as a result of the AAA policy of raising crop prices by paying landowners to reduce cotton acreage.

Support for civil rights would eventually become a test of liberal credentials. But in the 1930s, one could advocate Roosevelt's economic program and oppose antilynching legislation and moves to incorporate black workers within Social Security. Theodore Bilbo, the notoriously racist senator from Mississippi, was one of the New Deal's most loyal backers. Not until the Great Society of the 1960s would those left out of Social Security and other New Deal programs—racial minorities, many women, migrants and other less privileged workers—win inclusion in the American welfare state.

A map of Charlotte, North Carolina, prepared by the Home Owners' Loan Corporation, illustrates how federal agencies engaged in "redlining" of neighborhoods containing blue-collar and black residents. Wealthy areas, coded green, were given the best credit ratings, white-collar districts, in blue, the second best. Residents of red districts found it almost impossible to obtain government housing loans.

A NEW CONCEPTION OF AMERICA

But if the New Deal failed to dismantle the barriers that barred non-whites from full participation in American life, the 1930s witnessed the absorption of other groups into the social mainstream. With Catholics and Jews occupying prominent posts in the Roosevelt administration and new immigrant voters forming an important part of its electoral support, the New Deal made ethnic pluralism a living reality in American politics. The election of the Italian-American Fiorello La Guardia as mayor of New York City in 1933 symbolized the coming to power of the new immigrants. Although elected as a Republican, La Guardia worked closely with FDR and launched his own program of spending on housing, parks, and public works. La Guardia's was one of numerous "little New Deals" that brought ethnic working-class voters to power in communities throughout the industrial heartland.

Thanks to the virtual cutoff of southern and eastern European immigration in 1924, the increasing penetration of movies, chain stores, and mass advertising into ethnic communities, and the common experience of economic crisis, the 1930s witnessed an acceleration of cultural assimilation. But the process had a different content from the corporate-sponsored Americanization plans of the preceding years. For the children of the new immigrants, labor and political activism became agents of a new kind of Americanization. One could participate fully in the broader society without surrendering one's ideals and ethnic identity. "Unionism is Americanism" became a CIO rallying cry. "The Mesabi Range," a Minnesota miner wrote to Secretary of Labor Perkins, complaining of low wages and management hostility to unions in the iron-rich region, "isn't Americanized yet."

THE HEYDAY OF AMERICAN COMMUNISM

In the mid-1930s, for the first time in American history, the left—an umbrella term for socialists, communists, labor radicals, and many New Deal liberals—enjoyed a shaping influence on the nation's politics and culture. The CIO and Communist Party became focal points for a broad social

A card issued by the Communist Party during the 1936 campaign illustrates the party's attempt at "Americanization" (note the images of the American Revolution and Abraham Lincoln), as well as its emphasis on interracialism. James Ford, an African-American, was the party's vice-presidential candidate.

and intellectual impulse that helped to redraw the boundaries of American freedom. An obscure, faction-ridden organization when the Depression began, the Communist Party experienced remarkable growth during the 1930s. The party's membership never exceeded 100,000, but several times that number passed through its ranks.

The party's commitment to socialism resonated with a widespread belief that the Depression had demonstrated the bankruptcy of capitalism. But it was not so much the party's ideology as its vitality—its involvement in a mind-boggling array of activities including demonstrations of the unemployed, struggles for industrial unionism, and a renewed movement for black civil rights—that for a time made it the center of gravity for a broad democratic upsurge. At the height of the Popular Front—a period during the mid-1930s when the Communist Party sought to ally itself with socialists and New Dealers in movements for social change, urging reform of the capitalist system rather than revolution—Communists gained an unprecedented respectability. Earl Browder, the party's leader, even appeared on the cover of *Time* magazine. It is one of the era's ironies that an organization with an undemocratic structure and closely tied to Stalin's dictatorial regime in Russia should have contributed to the expansion of freedom in the United States. But the Communist Party helped to imbue New Deal liberalism with a militant spirit and a more pluralistic understanding of Americanism.

Arts of the West painted in 1932 by Thomas Hart Benton as part of his series of Life in America, *illustrates the widespread fascination during the 1930s with expressions of American folk culture. The son of a Populist Congressman from Missouri, Benton was part of a generation of artists who sought to produce socially meaningful works that depicted ordinary Americans in scenes of everyday life and in a style accessible to a broad audience.*

REDEFINING THE PEOPLE

In theater, film, and dance, the Popular Front vision of American society sank deep roots and survived much longer than the political moment from which it sprang. In this broad left-wing culture, social and economic radicalism, not support for the status quo, defined true Americanism, ethnic and racial diversity was the glory of American society, and the "American

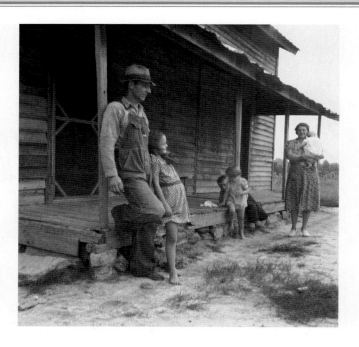

A Dorothea Lange photograph of a sharecropper and his family outside their modest home.

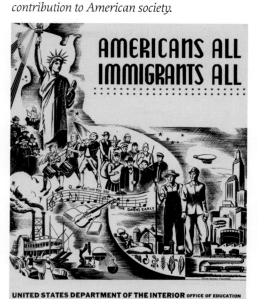

A brochure for the government-sponsored radio series Americans All, Immigrants All, *a celebration of immigrants' contribution to American society.*

way of life" meant unionism and social citizenship, not the unbridled pursuit of wealth. The American "people," viewed by many intellectuals in the 1920s as representing mean-spirited fundamentalism and crass commercialism, were suddenly rediscovered as embodiments of democratic virtue.

The "common man," Roosevelt proclaimed, embodied "the heart and soul of our country." During the 1930s, artists and writers who strove to create socially meaningful works eagerly took up the task of depicting the daily lives of ordinary farmers and city dwellers. Art about the people—such as Dorothea Lange's photographs of migrant workers and sharecroppers— and art created by the people—such as black spirituals—came to be seen as expressions of genuine Americanism. The Federal Music Project dispatched collectors with tape recorders to help preserve American folk music. Films celebrated populist figures who challenged and defeated corrupt businessmen and politicians, as in *Mr. Deeds Goes to Town* (1936) and *Mr. Smith Goes to Washington* (1939). New immigrants, especially Jews and Italians, played a prominent role in producing and directing Hollywood films of the 1930s. Their movies, however, glorified not urban ethnic communities but ordinary small-town middle-class Americans.

PROMOTING DIVERSITY

"A new conception of America is necessary," wrote the immigrant labor radical Louis Adamic in 1938. Despite bringing ethnic and northern black voters into its political coalition, the Democratic Party said little about ethno-cultural issues, fearful of rekindling the divisive battles of the 1920s. But the Popular Front forthrightly sought to promote the idea that the country's strength lay in diversity, tolerance, and the rejection of ethnic prejudice and class privilege. The CIO avidly promoted the idea of ethnic and racial inclusiveness. It broke decisively with the AFL's tradition of

A scene from the Emancipation episode of Martha Graham's American Document, *photographed by Barbara Morgan. The dancers are Martha Graham and Eric Hawkins.*

exclusionary unionism. The CIO embraced cultural pluralism—an idea, as noted in Chapter 20, previously associated with intellectuals like Horace Kallen and the self-defense of ethnic and Catholic communities against enforced Americanization. "We are the only Americans who take them into our organization as equals," wrote labor organizer Rose Pesotta, referring to the Mexican-Americans who flocked to the Cannery and Agricultural Workers union.

Popular Front culture presented a heroic but not uncritical picture of the country's past. Martha Graham's modern dance masterpiece *American Document* (1938), an embodiment of Popular Front aesthetics with its emphasis on America's folk traditions and multi-ethnic heritage, centered its account of history on the Declaration of Independence and the Gettysburg Address. Yet Graham did not neglect what her narrator called "things we are ashamed of," including the dispossession of the Indians and the plight of the unemployed. Graham's answer to Hector St. John de Crèvecoeur's old question, "What, then, is the American, this new man?" was that Americans were not only middle-class Anglo-Saxons but also blacks, immigrants, and the working class. Earl Robinson's song "Ballad for Americans," a typical expression of Popular Front culture that celebrated the religious, racial, and ethnic diversity of American society, became a national hit and was performed in 1940 at the Republican national convention.

CHALLENGING THE COLOR LINE

It was fitting that "Ballad for Americans" reached the top of the charts in a version performed by the magnificent black singer Paul Robeson. Popular Front culture moved well beyond New Deal liberalism in condemning

The "Scottsboro boys," flanked by two prison guards, with their lawyer, Samuel Liebowitz.

racism as incompatible with true Americanism. In the 1930s, groups like the American Jewish Committee and the National Conference of Christians and Jews actively promoted ethnic and religious tolerance, defining pluralism as "the American way." But whether in Harlem or East Los Angeles, the Communist Party was the era's only predominantly white organization to make fighting racism a top priority. "The communists," declared Charles H. Houston, the NAACP's chief lawyer, "made it impossible for any aspirant to Negro leadership to advocate less than full economic, political and social equality."

Communist influence spread even to the South. The Communist-dominated International Labor Defense mobilized popular support for black defendants victimized by a racist criminal justice system. It helped to make the Scottsboro case an international cause célèbre. The case revolved around nine young black men arrested for the rape of two white women in Alabama in 1931. Despite the weakness of the evidence against the "Scottsboro boys" and the fact that one of the two accusers recanted, Alabama authorities three times put them on trial and three times won convictions. Landmark Supreme Court decisions overturned the first two verdicts and established legal principles that greatly expanded the definition of civil liberties—that defendants have a constitutional right to effective legal representation, and that states cannot systematically exclude blacks from juries. But the Court allowed the third set of convictions to stand, which led to prison sentences for five of the defendants. In 1937, a defense lawyer worked out a deal whereby Alabama authorities released nearly all the defendants on parole, although the last of the Scottsboro boys did not leave prison until thirteen years had passed.

Despite considerable resistance from white workers determined to preserve their monopoly of skilled positions and access to promotions, the CIO welcomed black members and advocated the passage of antilynching laws and the return of voting rights to southern blacks. The CIO brought large numbers of black industrial workers into the labor movement for the first time and ran extensive educational campaigns to persuade white workers to recognize the interests they shared with their black counterparts. Black workers, many of them traditionally hostile to unions because of their long experience of exclusion, responded with enthusiasm to CIO organizing efforts. The union offered the promise of higher wages, dignity in the workplace, and an end to the arbitrary power of often racist foremen. Ed McRea, a white CIO organizer in Memphis, Tennessee, reported that he had little difficulty persuading black workers of the value of unionization: "You didn't have any trouble explaining this to blacks, with the kinds of oppression and conditions they had. It was a question of freedom."

LABOR AND CIVIL LIBERTIES

Another central element of Popular Front public culture was its mobilization for civil liberties, especially the right of labor to organize. The struggle to launch industrial unions encountered sweeping local restrictions on freedom of speech as well as repression by private and public police forces. Nationwide publicity about the wave of violence directed against the

Southern Tenant Farmers Union in the South and the CIO in industrial communities in the North elevated the rights of labor to a central place in discussions of civil liberties. The American Civil Liberties Union, primarily concerned in the 1920s with governmental repression, by 1934 concluded that "the masters of property" posed as great a danger to freedom of speech and assembly as political authorities.

Beginning in 1936, a Senate subcommittee headed by Robert M. La Follette Jr. exposed the methods employers used to combat unionization, including spies and private police forces. Workers had "no liberties at all," an employee of General Motors wrote to the committee from Saginaw, Michigan. The extensive violence unleashed against strikers in California's cotton and lettuce fields made that state, the committee report concluded, seem more like a "European dictatorship" than part of the United States.

Labor militancy helped to produce an important shift in the understanding of civil liberties. Previously conceived of as individual rights that must be protected against infringement by the government, the concept now expanded to include violations of free speech and assembly by powerful private groups. As a result, just as the federal government emerged as a guarantor of economic security, it also became a protector of freedom of expression.

By the eve of World War II, civil liberties had assumed a central place in the New Deal understanding of freedom. In 1939, Attorney General Frank Murphy established a Civil Liberties Unit in the Department of Justice. "For the first time in our history," Murphy wrote the president, "the full weight of the Department will be thrown behind the effort to preserve in this country the blessings of liberty." Meanwhile, the same Supreme Court that in 1937 relinquished its role as a judge of economic legislation moved to expand its authority over civil liberties. The justices insisted that constitutional guarantees of free thought and expression were essential to "nearly every other form of freedom" and therefore deserved special protection by the courts. Thus, civil liberties replaced liberty of contract as the judicial foundation of freedom. In 1937, the Court overturned on free speech grounds the conviction of Angelo Herndon, a Communist organizer jailed in Georgia for "inciting insurrection." Three years later, it invalidated an Alabama law that prohibited picketing in labor disputes. Since 1937, the large majority of state and national laws overturned by the courts have been those that infringe on civil liberties, not the property rights of business.

The new appreciation of free expression was hardly universal. In 1938, the House of Representatives established an Un-American Activities Committee to investigate disloyalty. Its expansive definition of "un-American" included communists, labor radicals, and the left of the Democratic Party, and its hearings led to the dismissal of dozens of federal employees on charges of subversion. Two years later, Congress enacted the Smith Act, which made it a federal crime to "teach, advocate, or encourage" the overthrow of the government. A similar pursuit of radical views took place at the state level. The New York legislature's Rapp-Coudert Committee held sweeping hearings investigating "subversive" influences in New York City's public colleges, resulting in the firing in 1941 of some sixty faculty members charged with communist sympathies.

THE END OF THE NEW DEAL

By then the New Deal, as an era of far-reaching social reform, had already begun to recede. One reason was that more and more southern Democrats were finding themselves at odds with Roosevelt's policies. In 1938, the administration released a "Report on Economic Conditions in the South," along with a letter by the president referring to the region as "the nation's No. 1 economic problem." The document revealed that the South lagged far behind other parts of the country in industrialization and investment in education and public health. Its per capita income stood at half that of the rest of the nation. Also in 1938, a new generation of homegrown radicals—southern New Dealers, black activists, labor leaders, communists, even a few elected officials—founded the Southern Conference for Human Welfare to work for unionization, unemployment relief, and racial justice.

Until the late 1930s, prominent southern Democrats had been strong supporters of the New Deal, while at the same time working to shape legislation to allow for the local administration of relief and the exclusion of most black workers. Now, southern business and political leaders feared that continuing federal intervention in their region would encourage unionization and upset race relations. Roosevelt concluded that the enactment of future New Deal measures required a liberalization of the southern Democratic Party. In 1938, he tried to persuade the region's voters to replace conservative congressmen with ones who would support his policies. The South's small electorate dealt him a stinging rebuke. In the North, where the economic downturn, the "Court-packing" plan, and the upsurge of CIO militancy alarmed many middle-class voters, Republicans increased their congressional representation.

A period of political stalemate followed the congressional election of 1938. For many years, a conservative coalition of southern Democrats and northern Republicans dominated Congress. Further reform initiatives became almost impossible, and Congress moved to abolish existing ones, beginning with the Federal Theater Project, which had alarmed conservatives because of the presence of radicals and homosexuals on its payroll. Congress repealed an earlier tax on corporate profits and rejected a proposed program of national medical insurance. The administration, moreover, increasingly focused its attention on the storm gathering in Europe. Even before December 1941, when the United States entered World War II, "Dr. Win the War," as Roosevelt put it, had replaced "Dr. New Deal."

THE NEW DEAL IN AMERICAN HISTORY

Given the scope of the economic calamity it tried to counter, the New Deal seems in many ways quite limited. Compared to later European welfare states, Social Security remained restricted in scope and modest in cost. The New Deal failed to address the problem of racial inequality, which in some ways it actually worsened.

Yet even as the New Deal receded, its substantial accomplishments remained. It greatly expanded the federal government's role in the American economy and made it an independent force in relations between industry and labor. The government told farmers what they could and could not plant, required employers to deal with unions, insured bank deposits, regulated the stock market, loaned money to home owners, and provided payments to a majority of the elderly and unemployed. It transformed the physical environment through hydroelectric dams, reforestation projects, rural electrification, and the construction of innumerable public facilities. It restored faith in democracy and made the government an institution directly experienced in Americans' daily lives and directly concerned with their welfare. It redrew the map of American politics. It helped to inspire, and was powerfully influenced by, a popular upsurge that recast the idea of freedom to include a public guarantee of economic security for ordinary citizens and that identified economic inequality as the greatest threat to American freedom.

One thing the New Deal failed to do was generate prosperity. Over 15 percent of the workforce remained unemployed in 1940. Only the mobilization of the nation's resources to fight World War II would finally end the Great Depression.

SUGGESTED READING

Brinkley, Alan. *Voices of Protest: Huey Long, Father Coughlin, and the Great Depression* (1982). An account of the political careers of two key figures of the New Deal era and their influence on national events.

Cohen, Lizabeth. *Making a New Deal: Industrial Workers in Chicago, 1919–1939* (1990). Describes how the assimilation of immigrants and their children paved the way for the creation of the New Deal political coalition.

Denning, Michael. *The Cultural Front: The Laboring of American Culture in the Twentieth Century* (1996). A comprehensive account of the rise of cultural activity associated with the political left and the New Deal.

Goodman, James. *Stories of Scottsboro* (1994). Discusses how different participants viewed one of the most notorious legal cases of the 1930s.

Hawley, Ellis W. *The New Deal and the Problem of Monopoly: A Study in Economic Ambivalence* (1966). Explores the changing approach toward concentrated economic power adopted by the Roosevelt administration.

Kessler-Harris, Alice. *In Pursuit of Equity: Men, Women, and the Quest for Economic Citizenship in 20th-Century America* (2001). Explores how assumptions regarding the proper roles of men and women helped to shape New Deal measures such as Social Security.

Kirby, Jack T. *Rural Worlds Lost: The American South, 1920–1960* (1987). Traces the transformation of the South in these four decades, with emphasis on how the New Deal affected the southern states.

Leuchtenberg, William E. *Franklin D. Roosevelt and the New Deal, 1932–1940* (1963). Still the standard one-volume account of Roosevelt's first two terms as president.

Naison, Mark. *Communists in Harlem during the Depression* (1983). Examines the rise and decline of the Communist Party in a center of black life, and its impact on the movement for racial justice.

Phillips, Sarah T. *The Land, This Nation: Conservation, Rural America, and the New Deal* (2007). Examines New Deal policies regarding agricultural development, rural conservation, and land use, and its attempt to modernize and uplift rural life.

Sanchez, George. *Becoming Mexican American: Ethnicity, Culture, and Identity in Chicano Los Angeles, 1900–1945* (1995). A careful study of Mexican-Americans in Los Angeles, including their participation in the social unrest of the 1930s and the movement for deporting them during that decade.

Sitkoff, Harvard. *A New Deal for Blacks: The Emergence of Civil Rights as a National Issue* (1978). Discusses the changing approach of the Roosevelt administration toward black Americans.

Sullivan, Patricia. *Days of Hope: Race and Democracy in the New Deal Era* (1996). Analyzes how the New Deal inspired the emergence of a biracial movement for civil rights in the South.

Worster, Donald. *Dust Bowl: The Southern Plains in the 1930s* (1979). A social and environmental history of one of the key episodes in rural America during the 1930s.

Zieger, Robert H. *The CIO, 1935–1955* (1995). A comprehensive history of the Congress of Industrial Organizations, the major labor group to emerge during the New Deal.

REVIEW QUESTIONS

1. Illustrate how the Columbia River project reflected broader changes in American life during the New Deal.

2. How did the Second New Deal reflect some of the ideas put forth by Franklin D. Roosevelt's critics such as Huey Long and Francis Townsend?

3. Analyze the effects on Indians of the Indian Reorganization Act of 1934.

4. What were the major characteristics of "liberalism" by 1939?

5. How did the Popular Front define freedom in America?

KEY TERMS

bank holiday (p. 806)

Agricultural Adjustment Act (p. 809)

Townsend Plan (p. 817)

court packing (p. 825)

minimum wage law (p. 825)

recession of 1937 (p. 826)

Indian New Deal (p. 829)

antilynching laws (p. 836)

Scottsboro boys (p. 836)

Smith Act (p. 837)

REVIEW TABLE

Landmark New Deal Legislation

Legislation	Date	Purpose
Federal Deposit Insurance Corporation	1933	To insure deposits, protecting customers against bank failures
National Recovery Administration	1933	To bring business and labor together to establish standards for output, prices, and working conditions
Agricultural Adjustment Act	1933	To authorize the federal government to raise farm prices by setting production quotas
Civilian Conservation Corps	1933	To employ young men to work on conservation projects
Tennessee Valley Authority	1933	To supply hydroelectric power to the Tennessee Valley
Works Project Administration	1935	To employ a significant number of blacks, white-collar workers, professionals, and artists
Social Security	1935	To create a system of unemployment insurance, old-age pensions, and aid to the disabled, the elderly poor, and families with dependent children
Wagner Act	1935	To protect the rights of unions
Fair Labor	1938	To set a minimum hourly wage and maximum hours of work

Chapter 22

1778

1943

Fighting for the Four Freedoms: World War II, 1941–1945

FIGHTING WORLD WAR II

Good Neighbors
The Road to War
Isolationism
War in Europe
Toward Intervention
Pearl Harbor
The War in the Pacific
The War in Europe

THE HOME FRONT

Mobilizing for War
Business and the War
Labor in Wartime
Fighting for the Four Freedoms
Freedom from Want
The Office of War Information
The Fifth Freedom
Women at War
Women at Work

VISIONS OF POSTWAR FREEDOM

Toward an American Century
"The Way of Life of Free Men"
An Economic Bill of Rights
The Road to Serfdom

THE AMERICAN DILEMMA

Patriotic Assimilation
The Bracero Program
Mexican-American Rights
Indians during the War
Asian-Americans in Wartime
Japanese-American Internment
Blacks and the War
Blacks and Military Service
Birth of the Civil Rights
   Movement
The Double-V
What the Negro Wants
Progress Comes Slowly
An American Dilemma

THE END OF THE WAR

"The Most Terrible Weapon"
The Dawn of the Atomic Age
The Nature of the War
Planning the Postwar World
Yalta and Bretton Woods
The United Nations
Peace, but not Harmony

One of the patriotic war posters issued by the Office of War Information during World War II, it links modern-day soldiers with patriots of the American Revolution as fighters for freedom, a major theme of government efforts to mobilize support for the war.

> ☞ FOCUS QUESTIONS

• What steps led to American intervention in World War II?

• How did the United States mobilize resources and opinion for the war effort?

• What visions of America's postwar role began to emerge during the war?

• How did African-Americans and other minorities experience the war at home and abroad?

• How did the end of the war begin to shape the postwar world?

By far the most popular works of art produced during World War II were paintings of the Four Freedoms by the magazine illustrator Norman Rockwell. In his State of the Union Address, delivered before Congress on January 6, 1941, President Roosevelt spoke eloquently of a future world order founded on the "essential human freedoms": freedom of speech, freedom of worship, freedom from want, and freedom from fear. The Four Freedoms became Roosevelt's favorite statement of Allied aims. At various times, he compared them with the Ten Commandments, the Magna Carta, and the Emancipation Proclamation. They embodied, Roosevelt declared in a 1942 radio address, the "rights of men of every creed and every race, wherever they live," and made clear "the crucial difference between ourselves and the enemies we face today."

Rockwell's paintings succeeded in linking the Four Freedoms with the defense of traditional American values. "Words like *freedom* or *liberty*," declared one wartime advertisement, "draw close to us only when we break them down into the homely fragments of daily life." This insight helps to explain Rockwell's astonishing popularity. Born in New York City in 1894, Rockwell had lived in the New York area until 1939, when he and his family moved to Arlington, Vermont, where they could enjoy, as he put it, "the clean, simple country life, as opposed to the complicated world of the city." Drawing on the lives of his Vermont neighbors, Rockwell translated the Four Freedoms into images of real people situated in small-town America. Each of the paintings focuses on an instantly recognizable situation. An ordinary citizen rises to speak at a town meeting; members of different religious groups are seen at prayer; a family enjoys a Thanksgiving dinner; a mother and father stand over a sleeping child.

The Four Freedoms paintings first appeared in the *Saturday Evening Post* early in 1943. Letters of praise poured in to the magazine's editors. The government produced and sold millions of reprints. The paintings toured the country as the centerpiece of the Four Freedoms Show, which included theatrical presentations, parades, and other events aimed at persuading Americans to purchase war bonds. By the end of its tour, the Four Freedoms Show had raised $133 million.

Even as Rockwell invoked images of small-town life to rally Americans to the war effort, however, the country experienced changes as deep as at any time in its history. Many of the economic trends and social movements that we associate with the last half of the twentieth century had their roots in the war years. As during World War I, but on a far larger scale, wartime mobilization expanded the size and scope of government and energized the economy. The gross national product more than doubled and unemployment disappeared as war production finally conquered the Depression. The demand for labor drew millions of women into the workforce and sent a tide of migrants from rural America to the industrial cities of the North and West, permanently altering the nation's social geography. Some 30 million Americans moved during the war, half going into military service and half taking up new jobs.

World War II gave the country a new and lasting international role and greatly strengthened the idea that American security was global in scope and could only be protected by the worldwide triumph of core American values. Government military spending sparked the economic development of the South and West, laying the foundation for the rise of the modern Sunbelt. The war created a close link between big business and a militarized federal government—a "military-industrial complex," as President Dwight D. Eisenhower would later call it—that long survived the end of fighting.

World War II also redrew the boundaries of American nationality. In contrast to World War I, the government recognized the "new immigrants" of the early twentieth century and their children as loyal Americans. Black Americans' second-class status assumed, for the first time

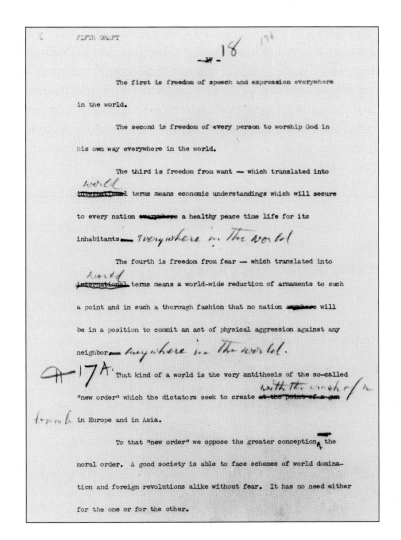

A draft of FDR's Four Freedoms speech of 1941 shows how he added the words "everywhere in the world," indicating that the Four Freedoms should be truly international ideals.

OURS... to fight for

Freedom of Speech   *Freedom of Worship*

Freedom from Want   *Freedom from Fear*

The immensely popular Office of War Information poster reproducing Norman Rockwell's paintings of the Four Freedoms, President Roosevelt's shorthand for American purposes in World War II.

since Reconstruction, a prominent place on the nation's political agenda. But toleration had its limits. With the United States at war with Japan, the federal government removed over 100,000 Japanese-Americans, the majority of them American citizens, from their homes and placed them in internment camps.

As a means of generating support for the struggle, the Four Freedoms provided a crucial language of national unity. But this unity obscured divisions within American society that the war in some ways intensified, divisions reflected in debates over freedom. While some Americans looked forward to a worldwide New Deal, others envisioned "free enterprise" replacing government intervention in the economy. The war gave birth to the modern civil rights movement but strengthened the commitment of many white Americans to maintain the existing racial order. The movement of women into the labor force challenged traditional gender relations, but most men and not a few women longed for the restoration of family life with a male breadwinner and a wife responsible for the home.

Even Rockwell's popular paintings suggested some of the ambiguities within the idea of freedom. With the exception of *Freedom of Speech*, which depicts civic democracy in action, the paintings emphasized private situations. The message seemed to be that Americans were fighting to preserve freedoms enjoyed individually or within the family rather than in the larger public world. This emphasis on freedom as an element of private life would become more and more prominent in postwar America.

FIGHTING WORLD WAR II

GOOD NEIGHBORS

During the 1930s, with Americans preoccupied by the economic crisis, international relations played only a minor role in public affairs. From the outset of his administration, nonetheless, FDR embarked on a number of departures in foreign policy. In 1933, hoping to stimulate American trade, he exchanged ambassadors with the Soviet Union, whose government his Republican predecessors had stubbornly refused to recognize.

Roosevelt also formalized a policy initiated by Herbert Hoover by which the United States repudiated the right to intervene militarily in the internal affairs of Latin American countries. This Good Neighbor Policy, as it was called, had mixed results. During the 1930s, the United States withdrew its troops from Haiti and Nicaragua. FDR accepted Cuba's repeal of the Platt Amendment (discussed in Chapter 17), which had authorized American military interventions on that island. These steps offered a belated recognition of the sovereignty of America's neighbors. But while Roosevelt condemned "economic royalists" (wealthy businessmen) at home, like previous presidents he felt comfortable dealing with undemocratic governments friendly to American business interests abroad. The United States lent its support to dictators like Anastasio Somoza in Nicaragua, Rafael Trujillo Molina in the Dominican Republic, and Fulgencio Batista in Cuba. "He may be a son of a bitch, but he's *our* son of a bitch," FDR said of Somoza.

THE ROAD TO WAR

Ominous developments in Asia and Europe quickly overshadowed events in Latin America. By the mid-1930s, it seemed clear that the rule of law was disintegrating in international relations and that war was on the horizon. In 1931, seeking to expand its military and economic power in Asia, Japan invaded Manchuria, a province of northern China. Six years later, its troops moved farther into China. When the Japanese overran the city of Nanjing, they massacred an estimated 300,000 Chinese prisoners of war and civilians.

An aggressive power threatened Europe as well. After brutally consolidating his rule in Germany, Adolf Hitler embarked on a campaign to control the entire continent. In violation of the Versailles Treaty, he feverishly pursued German rearmament. In 1936, he sent troops to occupy the Rhineland, a demilitarized zone between France and Germany established after World War I. The failure of Britain, France, and the United States to oppose this action convinced Hitler that the democracies could not muster the will to halt his aggressive plans. Italian leader Benito Mussolini, the founder of fascism, a movement similar to Hitler's Nazism, invaded and conquered Ethiopia. When General Francisco Franco in 1936 led an uprising against the democratically elected government of Spain, Hitler poured in arms, seeing the conflict as a testing ground for new weaponry. In 1939, Franco emerged victorious from a bitter civil war, establishing yet another fascist government in Europe. As part of a campaign to unite all Europeans of German origin in a single empire, Hitler in 1938 annexed Austria and the Sudetenland, an ethnically German part of Czechoslovakia. Shortly thereafter, he gobbled up all of that country.

As the 1930s progressed, Roosevelt became more and more alarmed at Hitler's aggression as well as his accelerating campaign against Germany's Jews, whom the Nazis stripped of citizenship and property and began to deport to concentration camps. In a 1937 speech in Chicago, FDR called for international action to "quarantine" aggressors. But no further steps followed. Roosevelt had little choice but to follow the policy of "appeasement" adopted by Britain and France, who hoped that agreeing to Hitler's demands would prevent war. British prime minister Neville Chamberlain returned from the Munich conference of 1938, which awarded Hitler the Sudetenland, proclaiming that he had guaranteed "peace in our time."

ISOLATIONISM

To most Americans, the threat arising from Japanese and German aggression seemed very distant. Moreover, Hitler had more than a few admirers in the United States. Obsessed with the threat of communism, some

This Hand Guides the Reich, *a Nazi propaganda poster from 1930s Germany. The bottom text reads: "German youth follow it in the ranks of Hitler youth."*

In a 1940 cartoon, war clouds engulf Europe, while Uncle Sam observes that the Atlantic Ocean no longer seems to shield the United States from involvement.

Americans approved his expansion of German power as a counterweight to the Soviet Union. Businessmen did not wish to give up profitable overseas markets. Henry Ford did business with Nazi Germany throughout the 1930s. Indeed, Ford plants there employed slave labor provided by the German government. Trade with Japan also continued, including shipments of American trucks and aircraft and considerable amounts of oil. Until 1941, 80 percent of Japan's oil supply came from the United States.

Many Americans remained convinced that involvement in World War I had been a mistake. Senate hearings in 1934–1935 headed by Gerald P. Nye of North Dakota revealed that international bankers and arms exporters had pressed the Wilson administration to enter that war and had profited handsomely from it. Pacifism spread on college campuses, where tens of thousands of students took part in a "strike for peace" in 1935. Ethnic allegiances reinforced Americans' traditional reluctance to enter foreign conflicts. Many Americans of German and Italian descent celebrated the expansion of national power in their countries of origin, even when they disdained their dictatorial governments. Irish-Americans remained strongly anti-British.

Isolationism—the 1930s version of Americans' long-standing desire to avoid foreign entanglements—dominated Congress. Beginning in 1935, lawmakers passed a series of Neutrality Acts that banned travel on belligerents' ships and the sale of arms to countries at war. These policies, Congress hoped, would allow the United States to avoid the conflicts over freedom of the seas that had contributed to involvement in World War I. Despite the fact that the Spanish Civil War pitted a democratic government against an aspiring fascist dictator, the western democracies, including the United States, imposed an embargo on arms shipments to both sides. Some 3,000 Americans volunteered to fight in the Abraham Lincoln Brigade on the side of the Spanish republic. But with Germany supplying the forces of Franco, the decision by democratic countries to abide by the arms embargo contributed substantially to his victory.

WAR IN EUROPE

In the Munich agreement of 1938, Britain and France had caved in to Hitler's aggression. In 1939, the Soviet Union proposed an international agreement to oppose further German demands for territory. Britain and France, who distrusted Stalin and saw Germany as a bulwark against the spread of communist influence in Europe, refused. Stalin then astonished the world by signing a nonaggression pact with Hitler, his former sworn enemy. On September 1, immediately after the signing of the Nazi–Soviet pact, Germany invaded Poland. This time, Britain and France, who had pledged to protect Poland against aggression, declared war. But Germany appeared unstoppable. Within a year, the Nazi *blitzkrieg* (lightning war) had overrun Poland, much of Scandinavia, Belgium, and the Netherlands.

On June 14, 1940, German troops occupied Paris. Hitler now dominated nearly all of Europe, as well as North Africa. In September 1940, Germany, Italy, and Japan created a military alliance known as the Axis.

For nearly two years, Britain stood virtually alone in fighting Germany. Winston Churchill, who became prime minister in 1940, vowed to resist a threatened Nazi invasion. In the Battle of Britain of 1940–1941, the German air force launched devastating attacks on London and other cities. The Royal Air Force eventually turned back the air assault. But Churchill pointedly called on the "new world, with all its power and might," to step forward to rescue the old.

TOWARD INTERVENTION

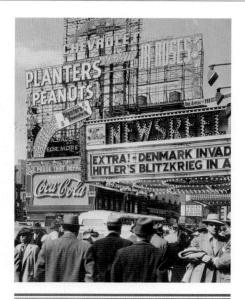

A newsreel theater in New York's Times Square announces Hitler's blitzkrieg *in Europe in the spring of 1940.*

Roosevelt viewed Hitler as a mad gangster whose victories posed a direct threat to the United States. But most Americans remained desperate to remain out of the conflict. "What worries me, especially," FDR wrote to Kansas editor William Allen White, "is that public opinion over here is patting itself on the back every morning and thanking God for the Atlantic Ocean and the Pacific Ocean." After a tumultuous debate, Congress in 1940 agreed to allow the sale of arms to Britain on a "cash and carry" basis—that is, they had to be paid for in cash and transported in British ships. It also approved plans for military rearmament. But with a presidential election looming, Roosevelt was reluctant to go further. Opponents of involvement in Europe organized the America First Committee, with hundreds of thousands of members and a leadership that included well-known figures like Henry Ford, Father Coughlin, and Charles A. Lindbergh.

In 1940, breaking with a tradition that dated back to George Washington, Roosevelt announced his candidacy for a third term as president. The international situation was too dangerous and domestic recovery too fragile, he insisted, for him to leave office. Republicans chose as his opponent a political amateur, Wall Street businessman and lawyer Wendell Willkie. Differences between the candidates were far more muted than in 1936. Both supported the law, enacted in September 1940, that established the nation's first peacetime draft. Willkie endorsed New Deal social legislation. He captured more votes than Roosevelt's previous opponents, but FDR still emerged with a decisive victory.

During 1941, the United States became more and more closely allied with those fighting Germany and Japan. America, FDR declared, would be the "great arsenal of democracy." But with Britain virtually bankrupt, it could no longer pay for supplies. At Roosevelt's urging, Congress passed the Lend-Lease Act, which authorized military aid so long as countries promised somehow to return it all after the war. Under the law's provisions, the United States funneled billions of dollars worth of arms to Britain and China, as well as the Soviet Union, after Hitler renounced his nonaggression pact and invaded that country in June 1941. FDR also froze Japanese assets in the United States, halting virtually all trade between the countries, including the sale of oil vital to Japan.

Those who believed that the United States must intervene to stem the rising tide of fascism tried to awaken a reluctant country to prepare for war. Interventionists popularized slogans that would become central to

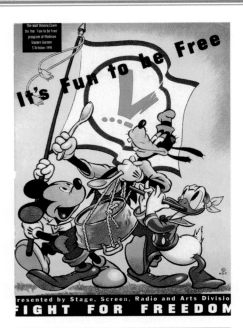

Walt Disney's program cover for the October 1941 "Fight for Freedom" rally at New York's Madison Square Garden, which demanded American intervention in the European war.

wartime mobilization. In June 1941, refugees from Germany and the occupied countries of Europe joined with Americans to form the Free World Association, which sought to bring the United States into the war against Hitler. The same year saw the formation of Freedom House. With a prestigious membership that included university presidents, ministers, businessmen, and labor leaders, Freedom House described the war raging in Europe as an ideological struggle between dictatorship and the "free world." In October 1941, it sponsored a "Fight for Freedom" rally at New York's Madison Square Garden, complete with a patriotic variety show entitled "It's Fun to Be Free." The rally ended by demanding an immediate declaration of war against Germany.

PEARL HARBOR

Until November 1941, the administration's attention focused on Europe. But at the end of that month, intercepted Japanese messages revealed that an assault in the Pacific was imminent. No one, however, knew where it would come. On December 7, 1941, Japanese planes, launched from aircraft carriers, bombed the naval base at Pearl Harbor in Hawaii, the first attack by a foreign power on American soil since the War of 1812. Pearl Harbor was a complete and devastating surprise. In a few hours, over 2,000 American servicemen were killed, and 187 aircraft and 18 naval vessels, including 8 battleships, had been destroyed or damaged. By a stroke of fortune, no aircraft carriers—which would prove decisive in the Pacific war—happened to be docked at Pearl Harbor on December 7.

To this day, conspiracy theories abound suggesting that FDR knew of the attack and did nothing to prevent it so as to bring the United States into the war. No credible evidence supports this charge. Indeed, with the country drawing ever closer to intervention in Europe, Roosevelt hoped to keep the peace in the Pacific. But Secretary of Labor Frances Perkins, who saw the president after the attack, remarked that he seemed calm—"his terrible

The battleships West Virginia *and* Tennessee *in flames during the Japanese attack on Pearl Harbor. Both were repaired and later took part in the Pacific war.*

Some of the 13,000 American troops forced to surrender to the Japanese on Corregidor Island in the Philippines in May 1942.

moral problem had been resolved." Terming December 7 "a date which will live in infamy," Roosevelt asked Congress for a declaration of war against Japan. The combined vote in Congress was 477 in favor and 1 against—pacifist Jeanette Rankin of Montana, who had also voted against American entry into World War I. The next day, Germany declared war on the United States. America had finally joined the largest war in human history.

THE WAR IN THE PACIFIC

World War II has been called a "gross national product war," meaning that its outcome turned on which coalition of combatants could outproduce the other. In retrospect, it appears inevitable that the entry of the United States, with its superior industrial might, would ensure the defeat of the Axis powers. But the first few months of American involvement witnessed an unbroken string of military disasters. Having earlier occupied substantial portions of French Indochina (now Vietnam, Laos, and Cambodia), Japan in early 1942 conquered Burma (Myanmar) and Siam (Thailand). Japan also took control of the Dutch East Indies (Indonesia), whose extensive oil fields could replace supplies from the United States. And it occupied Guam, the Philippines, and other Pacific islands. At Bataan, in the Philippines, the Japanese forced 78,000 American and Filipino troops to lay down their arms—the largest surrender in American military history. Thousands perished on the ensuing "death march" to a prisoner-of-war camp, and thousands more of disease and starvation after they arrived. At the same time, German submarines sank hundreds of Allied merchant and naval vessels during the Battle of the Atlantic.

Soon, however, the tide of battle began to turn. In May 1942, in the Battle of the Coral Sea, the American navy turned back a Japanese fleet intent on attacking Australia. The following month, it inflicted devastating losses on the Japanese navy in the Battle of Midway Island. These victories

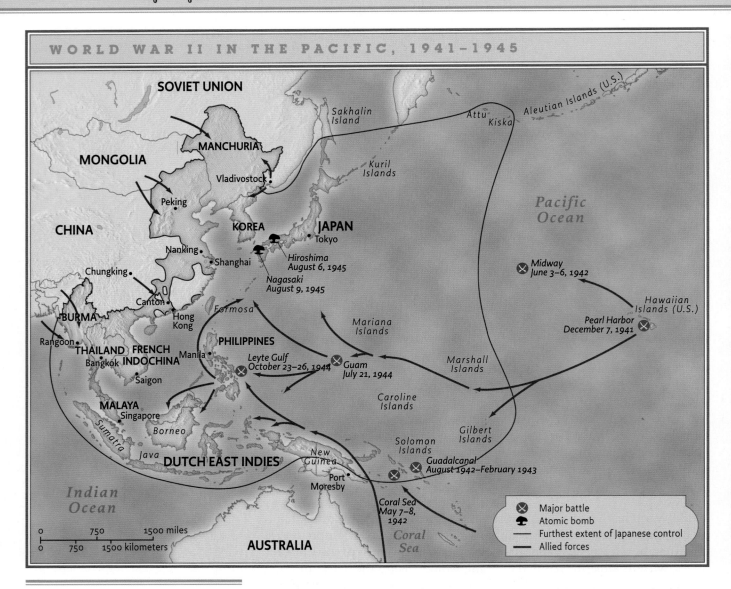

WORLD WAR II IN THE PACIFIC, 1941–1945

Although the Japanese navy never fully recovered from its defeats at the Coral Sea and Midway in 1942, it took three more years for American forces to near the Japanese homeland.

allowed American forces to launch the bloody campaigns that one by one drove the Japanese from fortified islands like Guadalcanal and the Solomons in the western Pacific and brought American troops ever closer to Japan.

THE WAR IN EUROPE

In November 1942, British and American forces invaded North Africa and by May 1943 forced the surrender of the German army commanded by General Erwin Rommel. By the spring of 1943, the Allies also gained the upper hand in the Atlantic, as British and American destroyers and planes devastated the German submarine fleet. But even though Roosevelt was committed to liberating Europe from Nazi control, American troops did not immediately become involved on the European continent. As late as the end of 1944, more American military personnel were deployed in the Pacific than against Germany. In July 1943, American and British forces invaded Sicily, beginning the liberation of Italy. A popular uprising in Rome overthrew the Mussolini government, whereupon Germany occupied most of the country. Fighting there raged throughout 1944.

The major involvement of American troops in Europe did not begin until June 6, 1944. On that date, known as D-Day, nearly 200,000 American, British, and Canadian soldiers under the command of General Dwight D. Eisenhower landed in Normandy in northwestern France. More than a million troops followed them ashore in the next few weeks, in the most massive sea–land operation in history. After fierce fighting, German armies retreated eastward. By August, Paris had been liberated.

Ben Hurwitz, a soldier from New York City who fought in North Africa and Italy during World War II, made numerous sketches of his experiences. Here, American troops pass a wrecked German tank in southern Italy in June 1944.

The crucial fighting in Europe, however, took place on the eastern front, the scene of an epic struggle between Germany and the Soviet Union. Over 3 million German soldiers took part in the 1941 invasion. After sweeping through western Russia, German armies in August 1942 launched a siege of Stalingrad, a city located deep inside Russia on the Volga River. This proved to be a catastrophic mistake. Bolstered by an influx of military supplies from the United States, the Russians surrounded the German troops and forced them to surrender. Some 800,000 Germans and 1.2 million Russians perished in the fighting. The German surrender at Stalingrad in January 1943 marked the turning point of the European war. Combined with a Russian victory at Kursk six months later in the greatest tank battle in history, the campaign in the east devastated Hitler's forces and sent surviving units on a long retreat back toward Germany.

Allied troops wade ashore on D-Day, June 6, 1944, the largest land-sea military operation in history. The photographer, Robert F. Sargent, named this image Taxi to Hell—and Back.

Most of the land fighting in Europe during World War II took place on the eastern front between the German and Soviet armies.

Of 13.6 million German casualties in World War II, 10 million came on the Russian front. They represented only part of the war's vast toll in human lives. Millions of Poles and at least 20 million Russians, probably many more, perished—not only soldiers but civilian victims of starvation, disease, and massacres by German soldiers. After his armies had penetrated eastern Europe in 1941, moreover, Hitler embarked on the "final solution"—the

WORLD WAR II IN EUROPE, 1942–1945

D-DAY

GREAT BRITAIN
London
Calais
English Channel
Assembly Area
Cherbourg
Le Havre
Caen
Rouen
FRANCE

Major battles
Allied offensives
Allied countries
Neutral countries
Axis countries
Extent of Axis control
Vichy France (controlled by Axis)

SWEDEN
NORWAY
FINLAND
1944
Leningrad
ESTONIA
1944
LATVIA
Moscow
1944
SOVIET UNION
IRELAND
DENMARK
LITHUANIA
GREAT BRITAIN
NETHERLANDS
EAST PRUSSIA
London
1945 Berlin 1945
Warsaw
Kursk July 1943
BELGIUM
GERMANY
1944
POLAND
1943
Stalingrad August 1942– February 1943
D-Day June 1944
Battle of the Bulge December 1944
1944
Paris
1945
1945
CZECHOSLOVAKIA
1943
LUXEMBOURG
FRANCE
AUSTRIA HUNGARY
1944
SWITZERLAND
Vichy
1944
ROMANIA
1944
1945
YUGOSLAVIA
PORTUGAL
BULGARIA
SPAIN
ITALY
Rome
ALBANIA (It.)
1944
1943
GREECE
TURKEY
1942
SPANISH MOROCCO
Algiers
Oran
Casablanca
1942
1943
Kasserine Pass February 1943
Mediterranean Sea
SYRIA (Fr.)
IRAQ (Br.)
LEBANON (Fr.)
MOROCCO
ALGERIA
TUNISIA
PALESTINE (Br.)
1943
El Alamein October– November 1942
TRANSJORDAN (Br.)
FRENCH NORTH AFRICA (Vichy France)
1943
1942
SAUDI ARABIA
LIBYA (Italy)
EGYPT

0   250   500 miles
0   250   500 kilometers

mass extermination of "undesirable" peoples—Slavs, gypsies, homosexuals, and, above all, Jews. By 1945, 6 million Jewish men, women, and children had died in Nazi death camps. What came to be called the Holocaust was the horrifying culmination of the Nazi belief that Germans constituted a "master race" destined to rule the world.

Prisoners at a German concentration camp liberated by Allied troops in 1945.

THE HOME FRONT

MOBILIZING FOR WAR

At home, World War II transformed the role of the national government. FDR created federal agencies like the War Production Board, the War Manpower Commission, and the Office of Price Administration to regulate the allocation of labor, control the shipping industry, establish manufacturing quotas, and fix wages, prices, and rents. The number of federal workers rose from 1 million to 4 million, part of a tremendous growth in new jobs that pushed the unemployment rate down from 14 percent in 1940 to 2 percent three years later.

The government built housing for war workers and forced civilian industries to retool for war production. Michigan's auto factories now turned out trucks, tanks, and jeeps for the army. By 1944, American factories produced a ship every day and a plane every five minutes. The gross national product rose from $91 billion to $214 billion during the war, and the federal government's expenditures amounted to twice the combined total of the previous 150 years. The government marketed billions of dollars worth of war bonds, increased taxes, and began the practice of withholding income tax directly from weekly paychecks. Before the war,

War-related production essentially ended the Great Depression. In this photograph from 1942, workers wait to be paid at a Maryland shipyard.

only the 4 million wealthiest Americans paid income taxes; by 1945, over 40 million did so. The government, one historian writes, moved during the war from "class taxation" to "mass taxation."

BUSINESS AND THE WAR

The relationship between the federal government and big business changed dramatically from the days of the Second New Deal. "If you are going to go to war in a capitalist country," observed Secretary of War Henry Stimson, "you had better let business make money out of the process." As corporate executives flooded into federal agencies concerned with war production, Roosevelt offered incentives to spur production—low-interest loans, tax concessions, and contracts with guaranteed profits. The great bulk of federal spending went to the largest corporations, furthering the long-term trend toward economic concentration. By the end of the war, the 200 biggest industrial companies accounted for almost half of all corporate assets in the United States.

Americans marveled at the achievements of wartime manufacturing. Thousands of aircraft, 100,000 armored vehicles, and 2.5 million trucks rolled off American assembly lines, and entirely new products like synthetic rubber replaced natural resources now controlled by Japan. Government-sponsored scientific research perfected inventions like radar, jet engines, and early computers that helped to win the war and would have a large impact on postwar life. These accomplishments not only made it possible to win a two-front war but also helped to restore the reputation of business and businessmen, which had reached a low point during the Depression.

Federal funds reinvigorated established manufacturing areas and created entirely new industrial centers. World War II saw the West Coast emerge as a focus of military-industrial production. The government invested billions of dollars in the shipyards of Seattle, Portland, and San Francisco and in the steel plants and aircraft factories of southern California. By the war's end, California had received one-tenth of all federal spending, and Los Angeles had become the nation's second largest manufacturing center. Nearly 2 million Americans moved to California for jobs in defense-related industries, and millions more passed through for military training and embarkation to the Pacific war.

In the South, the combination of rural out-migration and government investment in military-related factories and shipyards hastened a shift from agricultural to industrial employment. During the war, southern per capita income rose from 60 percent to 70 percent of the national average. But the South remained very poor when the war

M-5 tanks on the assembly line at a Detroit Cadillac plant, in a 1942 photograph. During the war, General Motors and other automakers produced vehicles for the armed forces rather than cars for consumers.

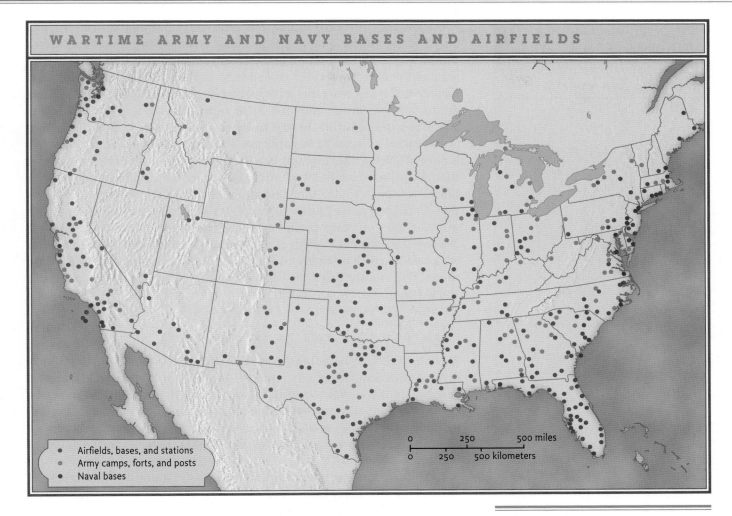

WARTIME ARMY AND NAVY BASES AND AIRFIELDS

- Airfields, bases, and stations
- Army camps, forts, and posts
- Naval bases

ended. Much of its rural population still lived in small wooden shacks with no indoor plumbing. The region had only two cities—Houston and New Orleans—with populations exceeding 500,000. Despite the expansion of war production, the South's economy still relied on agriculture and extractive industries—mining, lumber, oil—or manufacturing linked to farming, like the production of cotton textiles.

As this map indicates, the military and naval facilities built by the federal government during World War II were concentrated in the South and West, sparking the economic development of these regions.

LABOR IN WARTIME

Organized labor repeatedly described World War II as a crusade for freedom that would expand economic and political democracy at home and abroad and win for unions a major voice in politics and industrial management. During the war, labor entered a three-sided arrangement with government and business that allowed union membership to soar to unprecedented levels. In order to secure industrial peace and stabilize war production, the federal government forced reluctant employers to recognize unions. In 1944, when Montgomery Ward, the large mail-order company, defied a pro-union order, the army seized its headquarters and physically evicted its president. For their part, union leaders agreed not to strike and conceded employers' right to "managerial prerogatives" and a "fair profit."

Table 22.1 LABOR UNION MEMBERSHIP	
Year	**Number of Members**
1933	2,857,000
1934	3,728,000
1935	3,753,000
1936	4,107,000
1937	5,780,000
1938	8,265,000
1939	8,980,000
1940	8,944,000
1941	10,489,000
1942	10,762,000
1943	13,642,000
1944	14,621,000
1945	14,796,000

Despite the gains produced by labor militancy during the 1930s, unions only became firmly established in many sectors of the economy during World War II. By 1945, union membership stood at nearly 15 million, one-third of the non-farm labor force and the highest proportion in American history. But if labor became a partner in government, it was very much a junior partner. The decline of the New Deal, already evident in the late 1930s, proceeded during the war. Congress continued to be dominated by a conservative alliance of Republicans and southern Democrats. They left intact core New Deal programs like Social Security but eliminated agencies thought to be controlled by leftists, including the Civilian Conservation Corps, National Youth Administration, and Works Progress Administration. Congress rejected Roosevelt's call for a cap on personal incomes and set taxes on corporate profits at a level far lower than FDR requested. Despite the "no-strike" pledge, 1943 and 1944 witnessed numerous brief walkouts in which workers protested the increasing speed of assembly-line production and the disparity between wages frozen by government order and expanding corporate profits.

FIGHTING FOR THE FOUR FREEDOMS

Previous conflicts, including the Mexican War and World War I, had deeply divided American society. In contrast, World War II came to be remembered as the Good War, a time of national unity in pursuit of indisputably noble goals. But all wars require the mobilization of patriotic public opinion. By 1940, "To sell *goods*, we must sell *words*" had become a motto of advertisers. Foremost among the words that helped to "sell" World War II was "freedom."

Talk of freedom pervaded wartime America. To Roosevelt, the Four Freedoms expressed deeply held American values worthy of being spread worldwide. Freedom from fear meant not only a longing for peace but a more general desire for security in a world that appeared to be out of control. Freedom of speech and religion scarcely required detailed explanation. But their prominent place among the Four Freedoms accelerated the process by which First Amendment protections of free expression moved to the center of Americans' definition of liberty. In 1941, the administration celebrated with considerable fanfare the 150th anniversary of the Bill of Rights (the first ten amendments to the Constitution). FDR described their protections against tyrannical government as defining characteristics of American life, central to the rights of "free men and free women." In 1943, the Supreme Court reversed a 1940 ruling and, on First Amendment grounds, upheld the right of Jehovah's Witnesses to refuse to salute the American flag in public schools. The decision stood in sharp contrast to the coercive patriotism of World War I, and it

A patriotic fan marketed to women during World War II suggests some of the era's definitions of freedom.

affirmed the sanctity of individual conscience as a bedrock of freedom, even in times of crisis. The justices contrasted the American system of constitutional protection for unpopular minorities with Nazi tyranny.

FREEDOM FROM WANT

The "most ambiguous" of the Four Freedoms, *Fortune* magazine remarked, was freedom from want. Yet this "great inspiring phrase," as a Pennsylvania steelworker put it in a letter to the president, seemed to strike the deepest chord in a nation just emerging from the Depression. Roosevelt initially meant it to refer to the elimination of barriers to international trade. But he quickly came to link freedom from want to an economic goal more relevant to the average citizen—protecting the future "standard of living of the American worker and farmer" by guaranteeing that the Depression would not resume after the war. This, he declared, would bring "real freedom for the common man."

When Norman Rockwell's paintings of the Four Freedoms first appeared in the *Saturday Evening Post*, each was accompanied by a brief essay. Three of these essays, by the celebrated authors Stephen Vincent Benét, Booth Tarkington, and Will Durant, emphasized that the values Rockwell depicted were essentially American and the opposite of those of the Axis powers. For *Freedom from Want*, the editors chose an unknown Filipino poet, Carlos Bulosan, who had emigrated to the United States at the age of sixteen. Bulosan's essay showed how the Four Freedoms could inspire hopes for a better future as well as nostalgia for Rockwell's imagined small-town past. Bulosan wrote of those Americans still outside the social mainstream—migrant workers, cannery laborers, black victims of segregation—for whom freedom meant having enough to eat, sending their children to school, and being able to "share the promise and fruits of American life."

THE OFFICE OF WAR INFORMATION

The history of the Office of War Information (OWI), created in 1942 to mobilize public opinion, illustrates how the political divisions generated by the New Deal affected efforts to promote the Four Freedoms. The liberal Democrats who dominated the OWI's writing staff sought to make the conflict "a 'people's war' for freedom." The OWI feared that Americans had only a vague understanding of the war's purposes and that the populace seemed more fervently committed to paying back the Japanese for their attack on Pearl Harbor than ridding the world of fascism. They utilized radio, film, the press, and other media to give the conflict an ideological meaning, while seeking to avoid the nationalist hysteria of World War I.

Wartime mobilization drew on deep-seated American traditions. The portrait of the United States holding aloft the torch of liberty in a world overrun by oppression reached back at least as far as the American Revolution. The description of a world half slave and half free recalled the Great Emancipator. But critics charged that the OWI seemed most interested in promoting the definition of freedom Roosevelt had emphasized during the 1930s. One of its first pamphlets listed as elements of freedom the right to a job at fair

In this recruitment poster for the Boy Scouts, a svelte Miss Liberty prominently displays the Bill of Rights, widely celebrated during World War II as the centerpiece of American freedom.

These patriotic war posters issued by the Office of War Information invoke American history to mobilize support for the war. Left: *World War II soldiers are linked to those of the War of Independence.* Right: *The words of Abraham Lincoln are linked to the struggle against Nazi tyranny.*

pay and to adequate food, clothing, shelter, and medical care. Concerned that the OWI was devoting as much time to promoting New Deal social programs as to the war effort, Congress eliminated most of its funding.

THE FIFTH FREEDOM

After Congress curtailed the OWI, the "selling of America" became overwhelmingly a private affair. Under the watchful eye of the War Advertising Council, private companies joined in the campaign to promote wartime patriotism, while positioning themselves and their brand names for the postwar world. Alongside advertisements urging Americans to purchase war bonds, guard against revealing military secrets, and grow "victory gardens" to allow food to be sent to the army, the war witnessed a burst of messages marketing advertisers' definition of freedom. Without directly criticizing Roosevelt, they repeatedly suggested that he had overlooked a fifth freedom. The National Association of Manufacturers and individual companies bombarded Americans with press releases, radio programs, and advertisements attributing the amazing feats of wartime production to "free enterprise."

Americans on the home front enjoyed a prosperity many could scarcely remember. Despite the rationing of scarce consumer items like coffee, meat, and gasoline, consumers found more goods available in 1944 than when the war began. With the memory of the Depression still very much alive, businessmen predicted a postwar world filled with consumer goods, with "freedom of choice" among abundant possibilities assured if only private enterprise were liberated from government controls. One advertise-

THE FIFTH FREEDOM

In this advertisement by the Liberty Motors and Engineering Corporation, published in the February 1944 issue of Fortune, *Uncle Sam offers the Fifth Freedom—"free enterprise"—to war-devastated Europe. To spread its message the company offered free enlargements of its ad.*

ment for Royal typewriters, entitled "What This War Is All About," explained that victory would "hasten the day when you . . . can once more walk into any store in the land and buy anything you want." Certainly, ads suggested, the war did not imply any alteration in American institutions. "I'm fighting for freedom," said a soldier in an ad by the Nash-Kelvinator corporation. "So don't anybody tell me I'll find America changed."

WOMEN AT WAR

During the war, the nation engaged in an unprecedented mobilization of "womanpower" to fill industrial jobs vacated by men. OWI publications encouraged women to go to work, Hollywood films glorified the independent woman, and private advertising celebrated the achievements of Rosie the Riveter, the female industrial laborer depicted as muscular and self-reliant in Norman Rockwell's famous magazine cover. With 15 million men in the armed forces, women in 1944 made up over one-third of the civilian labor force, and 350,000 served in auxiliary military units.

Even though most women workers still labored in clerical and service jobs, new opportunities suddenly opened in industrial, professional, and government positions previously restricted to men. On the West Coast, one-third of the workers in aircraft manufacturing and shipbuilding were women. For the first time in history, married women in their thirties outnumbered the young and single among female workers. Women forced unions like the United Auto Workers to confront issues like equal pay for equal work, maternity leave, and childcare facilities for working mothers. Defense companies sponsored swing bands and dances to boost worker morale and arranged dates between male and female workers. Having enjoyed what one wartime worker called "a taste of freedom"—doing "men's" jobs for men's wages and, sometimes, engaging in sexual activity while unmarried—many women hoped to remain in the labor force once peace returned.

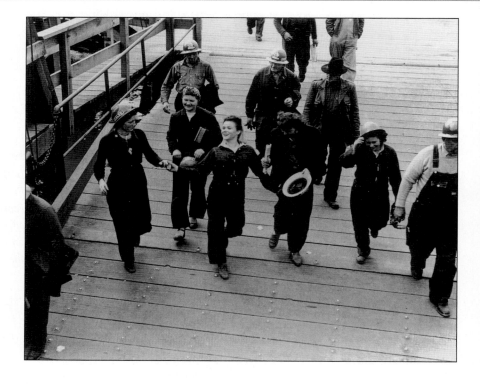

Male and female workers leaving a California shipyard at the end of their shift, in a photograph by Dorothea Lange.

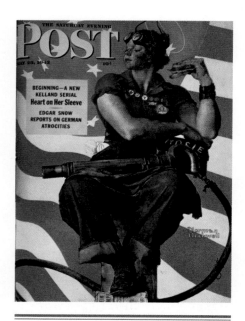

Norman Rockwell's celebrated cover for the Saturday Evening Post, May 29, 1943, shows "Rosie the Riveter" as a muscular, self-confident woman, fully capable of doing a man's job and not particularly concerned with her appearance at work.

WOMEN AT WORK

"We as a nation," proclaimed one magazine article, "must change our basic attitude toward the work of women." But change proved difficult. The government, employers, and unions depicted work as a temporary necessity, not an expansion of women's freedom. Advertisements assured women laboring in factories that they, too, were "fighting for freedom." But their language spoke of sacrifice and military victory, not rights, independence, or self-determination. One union publication even declared, "There should be a law requiring the women who have taken over men's jobs to be laid off after the war." When the war ended, most female war workers, especially those in better-paying industrial employment, did indeed lose their jobs.

Despite the upsurge in the number of working women, the advertisers' "world of tomorrow" rested on a vision of family-centered prosperity. Like Norman Rockwell's Four Freedoms paintings, these wartime discussions of freedom simultaneously looked forward to a day of material abundance and back to a time when the family stood as the bedrock of society. The "American way of life" celebrated during the war centered on the woman with "a husband to meet every night at the door," and a home stocked with household appliances and consumer goods. Advertisements portrayed working women dreaming of their boyfriends in the army and emphasized that with the proper makeup, women could labor in a factory and remain attractive to men. Men in the army seem to have assumed that they would return home to resume traditional family life. In one wartime radio program, a young man described his goal for peacetime: "Havin' a home and some kids, and breathin' fresh air out in the suburbs . . . livin' and workin' decent, like free people."

VISIONS OF POSTWAR FREEDOM

TOWARD AN AMERICAN CENTURY

The prospect of an affluent future provided a point of unity between New Dealers and conservatives, business and labor. And the promise of prosperity to some extent united two of the most celebrated blueprints for the postwar world. One was *The American Century*, publisher Henry Luce's 1941 effort to mobilize the American people both for the coming war and for an era of postwar world leadership. Americans, Luce's book insisted, must embrace the role history had thrust upon them as the "dominant power in the world." They must seize the opportunity to share with "all peoples" their "magnificent industrial products" and the "great American ideals," foremost among which stood "love of freedom." After the war, American power and American values would underpin a previously unimaginable prosperity—"the abundant life," Luce called it—produced by "free economic enterprise."

The idea of an American mission to spread democracy and freedom goes back to the Revolution. But traditionally, it had envisioned the country as an example, not an active agent imposing the American model throughout the globe. Luce's essay anticipated important aspects of the postwar world. But its bombastic rhetoric and a title easily interpreted as a call for an American imperialism aroused immediate opposition among liberals and the left. Henry Wallace offered their response in "The Price of Free World Victory," an address delivered in May 1942 to the Free World Association.

Wallace, secretary of agriculture during the 1930s and one of the more liberal New Dealers, had replaced Vice President John Nance Garner as Roosevelt's running mate in 1940. In contrast to Luce's American Century, a world of business dominance no less than of American power, Wallace predicted that the war would usher in a "century of the common man." The "march of freedom," said Wallace, would continue in the postwar world. That world, however, would be marked by international cooperation, not any single power's rule. Governments acting to "humanize" capitalism and redistribute economic resources would eliminate hunger, illiteracy, and poverty.

Luce and Wallace both spoke the language of freedom. Luce offered a confident vision of worldwide free enterprise, while Wallace anticipated a global New Deal. But they had one thing in common—a new conception of America's role in the world, tied to continued international involvement, the promise of economic abundance, and the idea that the American experience should serve as a model for all other nations. Neither took into account the ideas that other countries might have developed as to how to proceed once the war had ended.

"THE WAY OF LIFE OF FREE MEN"

Even as Congress moved to dismantle parts of the New Deal, liberal Democrats and their left-wing allies unveiled plans for a postwar economic policy that would allow all Americans to enjoy freedom from want. In 1942 and 1943, the reports of the National Resources Planning Board (NRPB) offered a blueprint for a peacetime economy based on full employment, an

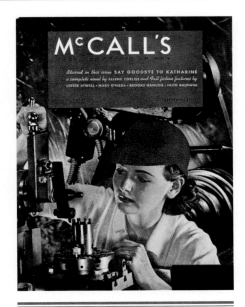

Unlike Rockwell's Rosie the Riveter, the woman operating industrial machinery on the cover of the September 1942 issue of McCall's *magazine remains glamorous, with makeup in place and hair unruffled.*

Despite the new independence enjoyed by millions of women, propaganda posters during World War II emphasized the male-dominated family as an essential element of American freedom.

expanded welfare state, and a widely shared American standard of living. Economic security and full employment were the Board's watchwords. It called for a "new bill of rights" that would include all Americans in an expanded Social Security system and guarantee access to education, health care, adequate housing, and jobs for able-bodied adults. Labor and farm organizations, church and civil rights groups, and liberal New Dealers hailed the reports as offering a "vision of freedom" for the postwar world. The NRPB's plan for a "full-employment economy" with a "fair distribution of income," said *The Nation*, embodied "the way of life of free men."

The reports continued a shift in liberals' outlook that dated from the late 1930s. Rather than seeking to reform the institutions of capitalism, liberals would henceforth rely on government spending to secure full employment, social welfare, and mass consumption, while leaving the operation of the economy in private hands. The reports appeared to reflect the views of British economist John Maynard Keynes, who, as noted in the previous chapter, had identified government spending as the best way to promote economic growth, even if it caused budget deficits. The war had, in effect, ended the Depression by implementing a military version of Keynesianism. In calling for massive spending on job creation and public works—urban redevelopment, rural electrification, an overhaul of the transportation system, and the like—the NRPB proposed the continuation of Keynesian spending in peacetime. But this went so far beyond what Congress was willing to support that it eliminated funding for the planning board.

AN ECONOMIC BILL OF RIGHTS

Roosevelt had not publicized or promoted the NRPB reports of 1942 and 1943. Yet mindful that public-opinion polls showed a large majority of Americans favoring a guarantee of employment for those who could not find work, the president in 1944 called for an "Economic Bill of Rights." The original Bill of Rights restricted the power of government in the name of liberty. FDR proposed to expand its power in order to secure full employment, an adequate income, medical care, education, and a decent home for all Americans. "True individual freedom," he declared, "cannot exist without economic security and independence."

Already ill and preoccupied with the war, Roosevelt spoke only occasionally of the Economic Bill of Rights during the 1944 presidential campaign. The replacement of Vice President Henry Wallace by Harry S. Truman, then a little-known senator from Missouri, suggested that the president did not intend to do battle with Congress over social policy. Congress did not enact the Economic Bill of Rights. But in 1944, it extended to the millions of returning veterans an array of benefits, including unemployment pay, scholarships for further education, low-cost mortgage loans, pensions, and job training. The Servicemen's Readjustment Act, or GI Bill of Rights, was one of the most far-reaching pieces of social legislation in American history. Aimed at rewarding members of the armed forces for their service and preventing the widespread unemployment and economic disruption that had followed World War I, it profoundly shaped postwar society. By 1946, over 1 million veterans were attending college under its provisions, making up half of total college enrollment. Almost 4 million would receive home mortgages, spurring the postwar suburban housing boom.

During 1945, unions, civil rights organizations, and religious groups urged Congress to enact the Full Employment Bill, which tried to do for the entire economy what the GI Bill promised veterans. The measure established a "right to employment" for all Americans and required the federal government to increase its level of spending to create enough jobs in case the economy failed to do so. The target of an intense business lobbying campaign, the bill only passed in 1946 with the word "Full" removed from its title and after its commitment to governmental job creation had been eliminated. But as the war drew to a close, most Americans embraced the idea that the government must continue to play a major role in maintaining employment and a high standard of living.

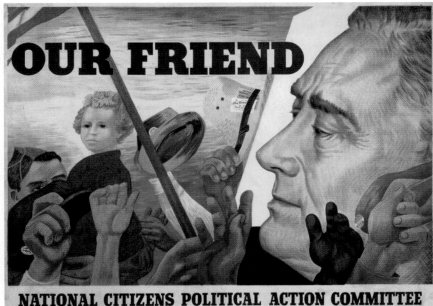

Ben Shahn's poster, Our Friend, *for the Congress of Industrial Organization's (CIO's) political action committee, urges workers to vote for FDR during his campaign for a fourth term.*

THE ROAD TO SERFDOM

The failure of the Full Employment Bill confirmed the political stalemate that had begun with the elections of 1938. It also revealed the renewed intellectual respectability of fears that economic planning represented a threat to liberty. When the *New Republic* spoke of full employment as the "road to freedom," it subtly acknowledged the impact of *The Road to Serfdom* (1944), a surprise best-seller by Friedrich A. Hayek, a previously obscure Austrian-born economist. Hayek claimed that even the best-intentioned government efforts to direct the economy posed a threat to individual liberty. He offered a simple message—"planning leads to dictatorship."

Coming at a time when the miracles of war production had reinvigorated belief in the virtues of capitalism, and with the confrontation with Nazism highlighting the danger of merging economic and political power, Hayek offered a new intellectual justification for opponents of active government. In a complex economy, he insisted, no single person or group of experts could possibly possess enough knowledge to direct economic activity intelligently. A free market, he wrote, mobilizes the fragmented and partial knowledge scattered throughout society far more effectively than a planned economy.

Unlike many of his disciples, Hayek was not a doctrinaire advocate of laissez-faire. His book endorsed measures that later conservatives would denounce as forms of socialism—minimum wage and maximum hours laws, antitrust enforcement, and a social safety net guaranteeing all citizens a basic minimum of food, shelter, and clothing. Hayek, moreover, criticized traditional conservatives for fondness for social hierarchy and authoritarian government. "I am not a conservative," he would later write. But by equating fascism, socialism, and the New Deal and by identifying economic planning with a loss of freedom, he helped lay the foundation for the rise of modern conservatism and a revival of laissez-faire economic thought. As the war drew to a close, the stage was set for a renewed battle over the government's proper role in society and the economy and the social conditions of American freedom.

THE AMERICAN DILEMMA

The unprecedented attention to freedom as the defining characteristic of American life had implications that went far beyond wartime mobilization. World War II reshaped Americans' understanding of themselves as a people. The struggle against Nazi tyranny and its theory of a master race discredited ethnic and racial inequality. Originally promoted by religious and ethnic minorities in the 1920s and the Popular Front in the 1930s, a pluralist vision of American society now became part of official rhetoric. What set the United States apart from its wartime foes, the government insisted, was not only dedication to the ideals of the Four Freedoms but also the principle that Americans of all races, religions, and national origins could enjoy those freedoms equally. Racism was the enemy's philosophy; Americanism rested on toleration of diversity and equality for all. By the end of the war, the new immigrant groups had been fully accepted as loyal ethnic Americans, rather than members of distinct and inferior "races." And the contradiction between the principle of equal freedom and the actual status of blacks had come to the forefront of national life.

PATRIOTIC ASSIMILATION

Among other things, World War II created a vast melting pot, especially for European immigrants and their children. Millions of Americans moved out of urban ethnic neighborhoods and isolated rural enclaves into the army and industrial plants where they came into contact with people of very different backgrounds. What one historian has called their "patriotic assimilation" differed sharply from the forced Americanization of World War I. While the Wilson administration had established Anglo-Saxon culture as a national norm, Roosevelt promoted pluralism as the only source of harmony in a diverse society. The American way of life, wrote the novelist Pearl Buck in an OWI pamphlet, rested on brotherhood—the principle that "persons of many lands can live together . . . and if they believe in freedom they can become a united people."

Government and private agencies eagerly promoted equality as the definition of Americanism and a counterpoint to Nazism. Officials rewrote history to establish racial and ethnic tolerance as the American way. To be an American, FDR declared, had always been a "matter of mind and heart," and "never . . . a matter of race or ancestry"—a statement more effective in mobilizing support for the war than in accurately describing the nation's past. Mindful of the intolerance spawned by World War I, the OWI highlighted nearly every group's contributions to American life and celebrated the strength of a people united in respect for diversity. One OWI pamphlet described prejudice as a foreign import rather than a homegrown product and declared bigots more dangerous than spies—they were "fighting for the enemy."

Arthur Poinier's cartoon for the Detroit Free Press, *June 19, 1941, illustrates how, during World War II, white ethnics (of British, German, Irish, French, Polish, Italian, Scandinanvian descent) were incorporated within the boundaries of American freedom.*

Horrified by the uses to which the Nazis put the idea of inborn racial difference, biological and social scientists abandoned belief in a link among race, culture, and intelligence, an idea only recently central to their disciplines. Ruth Benedict's *Races and Racism* (1942) described racism as "a travesty of scientific knowledge." In the same year, Ashley Montagu's *Man's Most Dangerous Myth: The Fallacy of Race* became a best-seller. By the war's end, racism and nativism had been stripped of intellectual respectability, at least outside the South, and were viewed as psychological disorders.

Hollywood, too, did its part, portraying fighting units whose members, representing various regional, ethnic, and religious backgrounds, put aside group loyalties and prejudices for the common cause. *Air Force* featured a bomber crew that included an Anglo-Saxon officer, a Jewish sergeant, and a Polish-American gunner. In the film *Bataan*, the ethnically balanced platoon included a black soldier, even though the real army was racially segregated. The war's most popular motion picture, *This Is the Army*, starring, among others, future president Ronald Reagan, offered a vision of postwar society that celebrated the ethnic diversity of the American people.

Intolerance, of course, hardly disappeared from American life. One correspondent complained to Norman Rockwell that he included too many "foreign-looking" faces in his *Freedom of Worship* painting. Many business and government circles still excluded Jews. Along with the fact that early reports of the Holocaust were too terrible to be believed, anti-Semitism contributed to the government's unwillingness to allow more than a handful of European Jews (21,000 during the course of the war) to find refuge in the United States. Roosevelt himself learned during the war of the extent of Hitler's "final solution" to the Jewish presence in Europe. But he failed to authorize air strikes that might have destroyed German death camps.

Nonetheless, the war made millions of ethnic Americans, especially the children of the new immigrants, feel fully American for the first time. During the war, one New York "ethnic" recalled, "the Italo-Americans stopped being Italo and started becoming Americans." But the event that inspired this comment, the Harlem race riot of 1943, suggested that patriotic assimilation stopped at the color line.

THE BRACERO PROGRAM

The war had a far more ambiguous meaning for non-white groups than for whites. On the eve of Pearl Harbor, racial barriers remained deeply entrenched in American life. Southern blacks were still trapped in a rigid system of segregation. Asians could not emigrate to the United States or become naturalized citizens. As noted in the previous chapter, over 400,000 Mexican-Americans had been "voluntarily" repatriated by local authorities in the Southwest during the Depression. Most American Indians still lived on reservations, in dismal poverty.

The war set in motion changes that would reverberate in the postwar years. Under the *bracero* program agreed to by the Mexican and American governments in 1942 (the name derives from *brazo*, the Spanish word for arm), tens of thousands of contract laborers crossed into the United States to take up jobs as domestic and agricultural workers. Initially designed as a temporary response to the wartime labor shortage, the program lasted until 1964. During the period of the *bracero* program, over 4.5 million Mexicans entered the United States under government labor contracts (while a slightly larger number was arrested for illegal entry by the Border Patrol). *Braceros* were supposed to receive decent housing and wages. But since they could not become citizens and could be deported at any time, they found it almost impossible to form unions or secure better working conditions.

Although the *bracero* program reinforced the status of immigrants from Mexico as an unskilled labor force, wartime employment opened new opportunities for second-generation Mexican-Americans. Hundreds of thousands of men and women emerged from ethnic neighborhoods, or *barrios*, to work in defense industries and serve in the army (where, unlike blacks, they fought alongside whites). A new "Chicano" culture—a fusion of Mexican heritage and American experience—was being born. Contact with other groups led many to learn English and sparked a rise in inter-ethnic marriages.

MEXICAN-AMERICAN RIGHTS

The "zoot suit" riots of 1943, in which club-wielding sailors and policemen attacked Mexican-American youths wearing flamboyant clothing on the streets of Los Angeles, illustrated the limits of wartime tolerance. "Our Latin American boys," complained one activist, "are not segregated at the front line. . . . They are dying that democracy may live." Yet when they return home, the activist continued, "they are not considered good enough to go into a café." But the contrast between the war's rhetoric of freedom and pluralism and the reality of continued discrimination inspired a heightened consciousness of civil rights. For example, Mexican-Americans brought complaints of discrimination before the Fair Employment Practices Commission (FEPC) to fight the practice in the Southwest of confining them to the lowest-paid work or paying them lower wages than white workers doing the same jobs.

Perhaps half a million Mexican-American men and women served in the armed forces. And with discrimination against Mexicans an increasing embarrassment in view of Roosevelt's Good Neighbor policy, Texas (the state with the largest population of Mexican descent) in 1943 unanimously passed the oddly named Caucasian Race—Equal Privileges resolution. It stated that since "all the nations of the North and South American continents" were united in the struggle against Nazism, "all persons of the Caucasian race" were entitled to equal treatment in places of public accommodation. Since Texas law had long defined Mexicans as white, the measure applied to them while not challenging the segregation of blacks. The resolution lacked an enforcement mechanism. Indeed, because of continued discrimination in Texas, the Mexican government for a time prohibited the state from receiving laborers under the *bracero* program.

INDIANS DURING THE WAR

The war also brought many American Indians closer to the mainstream of American life. Some 25,000 served in the army (including the famous Navajo "code-talkers," who transmitted messages in their complex native language, which the Japanese could not decipher). Insisting that the United States lacked the authority to draft Indian men into the army, the Iroquois issued their own declaration of war against the Axis powers. Tens of thousands of Indians left reservations for jobs in war industries. Exposed for the first time to urban life and industrial society, many chose not to return to the reservations after the war ended (indeed, the reservations did not share in wartime prosperity). Some Indian veterans took advantage of the GI Bill to attend college after the war, an opportunity that had been available to very few Indians previously.

ASIAN-AMERICANS IN WARTIME

Asian-Americans' war experience was paradoxical. More than 50,000—the children of immigrants from China, Japan, Korea, and the Philippines—fought in the army, mostly in all-Asian units. With China an ally in the Pacific war, Congress in 1943 ended decades of complete exclusion by establishing a nationality quota for Chinese immigrants. The annual limit of 105 hardly suggested a desire for a large-scale influx. But the image of the Chinese as gallant fighters defending their country against Japanese aggression called into question long-standing racial stereotypes. As in the case of Mexican-Americans, large numbers of Chinese-Americans moved out of ethnic ghettos to work alongside whites in jobs on the home front.

The experience of Japanese-Americans was far different. Many Americans viewed the war against Germany as an ideological struggle. But both sides saw the Pacific war as a race war. Japanese propaganda depicted Americans as a self-indulgent people contaminated by ethnic and racial diversity as opposed to the racially "pure" Japanese. In the United States, long-standing prejudices and the shocking attack on Pearl Harbor combined to produce an unprecedented hatred of Japan. "In all our history," according to one historian, "no foe has been detested as were the Japanese." Government propaganda and war films portrayed the Japanese foe as rats, dogs, gorillas, and snakes—bestial and subhuman. They blamed Japanese aggression on a violent racial or national character, not, as in the case of Germany and Italy, on tyrannical rulers.

About 70 percent of Japanese-Americans in the continental United States lived in California, where they dominated vegetable farming in the Los Angeles area. One-third were first-generation immigrants, or *issei*, but a substantial majority were *nisei*—American-born, and therefore citizens. Many of the latter spoke only English, had never been to Japan, and had tried to assimilate despite prevailing prejudice. But the Japanese-American community could not remain unaffected by the rising tide of hatred. The government bent over backward to include German-Americans and Italian-Americans in the war effort. It ordered the arrest of only a handful of the over 800,000 German and Italian nationals in the United States

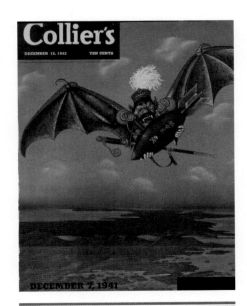

On the one-year anniversary of the Pearl Harbor attack, the cover of Collier's *magazine depicts Japanese prime minister Hideki Tojo as a vampire bat—one of many wartime images that sought to dehumanize the Pacific foe.*

when the war began. But it viewed every person of Japanese ethnicity as a potential spy.

JAPANESE-AMERICAN INTERNMENT

California, as discussed in Chapter 19, had a long history of hostility toward the Japanese. Now, inspired by exaggerated fears of a Japanese invasion of the West Coast and pressured by whites who saw an opportunity to gain possession of Japanese-American property, the military persuaded FDR to issue Executive Order 9066. Promulgated in February 1942, this ordered the expulsion of all persons of Japanese descent from the West Coast. That spring and summer, authorities removed over 110,000 men, women, and children—nearly two-thirds of them American citizens—to internment camps far from their homes. The order did not apply to persons of Japanese descent living in Hawaii, where they represented nearly 40 percent of the population. Despite Hawaii's vulnerability, its economy could not function without Japanese-American labor. But the treatment of mainland Japanese-Americans provided ammunition for Japan's claim that its aggressions in Asia were intended to defend the rights of non-white peoples against colonial rule and a racist United States.

The internees were subjected to a quasi-military discipline in the camps. Living in former horse stables, makeshift shacks, or barracks behind barbed wire fences, they were awakened for roll call at 6:45 each morning and ate their meals (which rarely included the Japanese cooking to which they were accustomed) in giant mess halls. Armed guards patrolled the camps, and searchlights shone all night. Privacy was difficult to come by, and medical facilities were often nonexistent. Nonetheless, the internees did their best to create an atmosphere of home, decorating their accommodations with pictures, flowers, and curtains, planting vegetable gardens, and setting up activities like sports clubs and art classes for themselves.

Internment revealed how easily war can undermine basic freedoms. There were no court hearings, no due process, and no writs of habeas corpus. One searches the wartime record in vain for public protests among non-Japanese against the gravest violation of civil liberties since the end of slavery. The press supported the policy almost unanimously. In Congress, only Senator Robert Taft of Ohio spoke out against it. Groups publicly committed to fighting discrimination, from the Communist Party to the NAACP and the American Jewish Committee, either defended the policy or remained silent.

The courts refused to intervene. In 1944, in *Korematsu v. United States*, the Supreme Court denied the appeal of Fred Korematsu, a Japanese-American citizen who had been arrested for refusing to present himself for internment. Speaking for a 6-3 majority, Justice Hugo Black, usually an avid defender of civil liberties, upheld the legality of the internment policy, insisting that an order applying only to persons of Japanese descent was not based on race. The Court has never overturned the *Korematsu* decision. As Justice Robert H. Jackson warned in his dissent, it "lies about like a loaded weapon ready for the hand of any authority that can bring forward a plausible claim" of national security.

A Japanese-American woman holds her sleeping child as they prepare to depart for an internment camp.

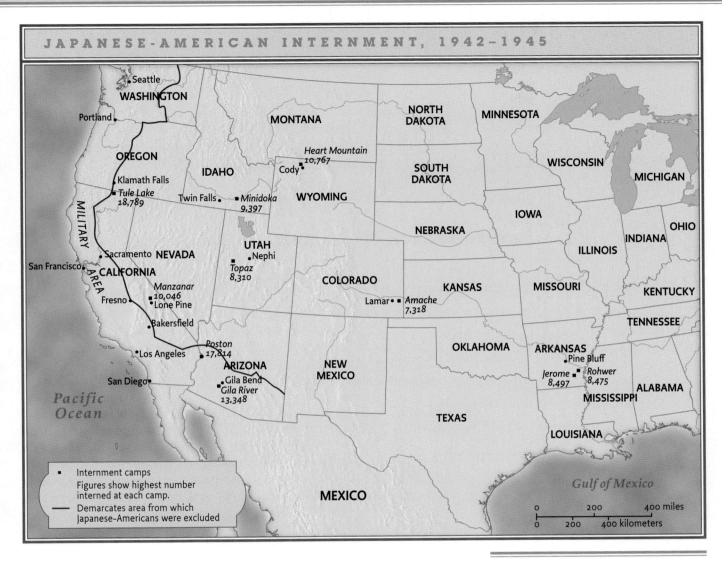

JAPANESE-AMERICAN INTERNMENT, 1942–1945

Internment camps
Figures show highest number interned at each camp.

Demarcates area from which Japanese-Americans were excluded

The government marketed war bonds to the internees. It established a loyalty oath program, expecting Japanese-Americans to swear allegiance to the government that had imprisoned them and to enlist in the army. Some young men refused, and about 200 were sent to prison for resisting the draft. "Let us out and then maybe I'll think about risking my skin for 'the land of the free,'" one of the resisters remarked. But 20,000 Japanese-Americans joined the armed forces from the camps, along with another 13,000 from Hawaii. A long campaign for acknowledgment of the injustice done to Japanese-Americans followed the end of the war. In 1988, Congress apologized for internment and provided $20,000 in compensation to each surviving victim. President Bill Clinton subsequently awarded Fred Korematsu the Presidential Medal of Freedom.

Over 100,000 Japanese-Americans, the majority American citizens, were forcibly moved from their homes to internment camps during World War II.

BLACKS AND THE WAR

Although the treatment of Japanese-Americans revealed the stubborn hold of racism in American life, the wartime message of freedom portended a major

VOICES OF FREEDOM

From Henry R. Luce, *The American Century* (1941)

Even before the United States entered World War II, some Americans were thinking of a postwar world in which the United States would exert its influence throughout the globe. One influential call for Americans to accept the burden of world leadership was a short book by Henry R. Luce, the publisher of *Life* and *Time* magazines.

In the field of national policy, the fundamental trouble with America has been, and is, that whereas their nation became in the 20th Century the most powerful and the most vital nation in the world, nevertheless Americans were unable to accommodate themselves spiritually and practically to that fact. Hence they have failed to play their part as a world power—a failure which has had disastrous consequences for themselves and for all mankind. And the cure is this: to accept wholeheartedly our duty and our opportunity as the most powerful and vital nation in the world and in consequence to exert upon the world the full impact of our influence, for such purposes as we see fit and by such means as we see fit. . . .

Our world of 2,000,000,000 human beings is for the first time in history one world, fundamentally indivisible. . . . Our world, again for the first time in human history, is capable of producing all the material needs of the entire human family. . . . The world of the 20th Century, if it is to come to life in any

nobility of health and vigor, must be to a significant degree an American Century. . . .

In postulating the indivisibility of the contemporary world, one does not necessarily imagine that anything like a world state—a parliament of men—must be brought about in this century. Nor need we assume that war can be abolished. . . . Large sections of the human family may be effectively organized into opposition to one another. Tyrannies may require a large amount of living space. But Freedom requires and will require far greater living space than Tyranny. . . . Justice will come near to losing all meaning in the minds of men unless Justice can have approximately the same fundamental meanings in many lands and among many peoples. . . .

As to the . . . promise of adequate production for all mankind, the "more abundant life," be it noted that this is characteristically an American promise. . . . What we must insist on is that the abundant life is predicated on Freedom. . . . Without Freedom, there will be no abundant life. With Freedom, there can be.

And finally there is the belief—shared let us remember by most men living—that the 20th Century must be to a significant degree an American Century. . . . As America enters dynamically upon the world scene, we need most of all to seek and to bring forth a vision of America as a world power and to bring forth a vision . . . which will guide us to the authentic creation of the 20th Century—our Century.

From Justice Robert H. Jackson,
Dissent in *Korematsu v. United States* (1944)

In the *Korematsu* case a 6-3 Supreme Court majority upheld the right of the federal government to remove Japanese-Americans to internment camps during World War II. Justice Jackson's dissent offered a sharp reminder of how easily war can undermine basic freedoms for citizens and noncitizens alike.

Korematsu was born on our soil, of parents born in Japan. The Constitution makes him a citizen of the United States by nativity and a citizen of California by residence. No claim is made that he is not loyal to this country. . . . Korematsu, however, has been convicted of an act not commonly a crime. It consists merely of being present in the state whereof he is a citizen, near the place where he was born, and where all his life he has lived. . . .

Even more unusual is the series of military orders which made this conduct a crime. . . . They were so drawn that the only way Korematsu could avoid violation was to give himself up to the military authority. This meant submission to custody, examination, and transportation out of the territory, to be followed by indefinite confinement in detention camps. . . .

If any fundamental assumption underlies our system, it is that guilt is personal and not inheritable. . . . Once a judicial opinion rationalizes such an order to show that it conforms to the Constitution, or rather rationalizes the Constitution to show that the Constitution sanctions such an order, the Court has for all time validated the principle of racial discrimination in criminal procedure and of transplanting American citizens. The principle then lies about like a loaded weapon ready for the hand of any authority that can bring forward a plausible claim of an urgent need. Every repetition imbeds the principle more deeply in our law and thinking and expands it to new purposes. All who observe the work of courts are familiar with what Judge Cardozo described as "the tendency of a principle to expand itself to the limit of its logic." A military commander may overstep the bounds of constitutionality and it is an incident. But if we review and approve, the passing incident becomes the doctrine of the Constitution. There it has a generative power of its own, and all that it created will be in its own image. Nothing better illustrates this danger than does the Court's opinion in this case.

The courts . . . must abide by the Constitution, or they cease to be civil courts and become instruments of military policy.

QUESTIONS

1. What values does Luce wish America to spread to the rest of the world?

2. Why does Justice Jackson believe that even though military authorities have the power to violate the Constitution during wartime, the Supreme Court should not approve their actions?

3. Does the experience of Japanese-Americans during the war suggest any problems with Luce's idea of an American Century?

transformation in the status of blacks. "There never has been, there isn't now, and there never will be," Roosevelt declared, "any race of people on the earth fit to serve as masters over their fellow men." Yet Nazi Germany cited American practices as proof of its own race policies. Washington remained a rigidly segregated city, and the Red Cross refused to mix blood from blacks and whites in its blood banks (thereby, critics charged, in effect accepting Nazi race theories). In 1940 and 1941, even as Roosevelt called for aid to the free peoples of Europe, thirteen lynchings took place in the United States.

The war spurred a movement of black population from the rural South to the cities of the North and West that dwarfed the Great Migration of World War I and the 1920s. About 700,000 black migrants poured out of the South on what they called "liberty trains," seeking jobs in the industrial heartland. They encountered sometimes violent hostility, nowhere more so than in Detroit, where angry white residents forced authorities to evict black tenants from a new housing project. In 1943, a fight at a Detroit city park spiraled into a race riot that left thirty-four persons dead, and a "hate strike" of 20,000 workers protested the upgrading of black employees in a plant manufacturing aircraft engines. The war failed to end lynching. Isaac Simmons, a black minister, was murdered in 1944 for refusing to sell his land to a white man who believed it might contain oil. The criminals went unpunished. This took place in Liberty, Mississippi.

BLACKS AND MILITARY SERVICE

When World War II began, the air force and marines had no black members. The army restricted the number of black enlistees and contained only five black officers, three of them chaplains. The navy accepted blacks only as waiters and cooks.

The segregated army: recruits training with their rifles at the U.S. Marine base at Parris Island, South Carolina, in 1941.

During the war, over 1 million blacks served in the armed forces. They did so in segregated units, largely confined to construction, transport, and other noncombat tasks. Many northern black draftees were sent to the South for military training, where they found themselves excluded from movie theaters and servicemen's clubs on military bases and abused when they ventured into local towns. Black soldiers sometimes had to give up their seats on railroad cars to accommodate Nazi prisoners of war. "Nothing so lowers Negro morale," wrote the NAACP's magazine, *The Crisis*, "as the frequent preferential treatment of Axis prisoners of war in contrast with Army policy toward American troops who happen to be Negro."

When southern black veterans returned home and sought benefits through the GI Bill, they encountered even more evidence of racial discrimination. On the surface, the GI Bill contained no racial differentiation in offering benefits like health care, college tuition assistance, job training, and loans to start a business or purchase a farm. But local authorities who administered its provisions allowed southern black veterans to use its education benefits only at segregated colleges, limited their job training to unskilled work and low-wage service jobs, and limited loans for farm purchase to white veterans.

BIRTH OF THE CIVIL RIGHTS MOVEMENT

In 1942, a public opinion survey sponsored by the army's Bureau of Intelligence found that the vast majority of white Americans were "unaware that there is any such thing as a 'Negro problem'" and were convinced that blacks were satisfied with their social and economic conditions. They would soon discover their mistake.

The war years witnessed the birth of the modern civil rights movement. Angered by the almost complete exclusion of African-Americans from jobs in the rapidly expanding war industries (of 100,000 aircraft workers in 1940, fewer than 300 were blacks), the black labor leader A. Philip Randolph in July 1941 called for a March on Washington. Its demands included access to defense employment, an end to segregation, and a national antilynching law. Randolph, who as founder of the Brotherhood of Sleeping Car Porters had long battled racism among both employers and unions, hurled Roosevelt's rhetoric back at the president. He declared racial discrimination "undemocratic, un-American, and pro-Hitler."

The prospect of thousands of angry blacks descending on Washington, remarked one official, "scared the government half to death." To persuade Randolph to call off the march, Roosevelt issued Executive Order 8802, which banned discrimination in defense jobs and established a Fair Employment Practices Commission (FEPC) to monitor compliance. The black press hailed the order as a new Emancipation Proclamation.

Essentially an investigative agency, the FEPC lacked enforcement powers. But its very existence marked a significant shift in public policy. Its hearings exposed patterns of racial exclusion so ingrained that firms at first freely admitted that their want ads asked for "colored" applicants for positions as porters and janitors and "white" ones for skilled jobs, and that they allowed black women to work only as laundresses and cooks. The first federal agency since Reconstruction to campaign for equal opportunity for

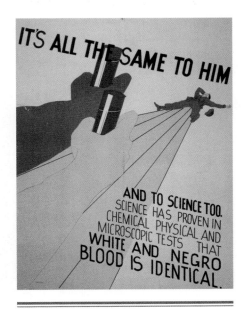

During World War II, Red Cross blood banks separated blood from black and white Americans—one illustration of the persistence of racial segregation. This 1943 poster by the NAACP points out that the concept of "Negro" and "white" blood has no scientific basis.

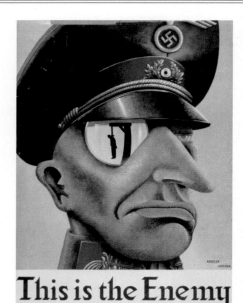

This is the Enemy

This Is the Enemy, a 1942 poster by Victor Ancona and Karl Koehler, suggests a connection between Nazism abroad and lynching at home.

black Americans, the FEPC played an important role in obtaining jobs for black workers in industrial plants and shipyards. In southern California, the aircraft manufacturer Lockheed ran special buses into black neighborhoods to bring workers to its plants. By 1944, over 1 million blacks, 300,000 of them women, held manufacturing jobs. ("My sister always said that Hitler was the one that got us out of the white folks' kitchen," recalled one black woman.)

THE DOUBLE-V

When the president "said that we should have the Four Freedoms," a black steelworker declared, he meant to include "all races." During the war, NAACP membership grew from 50,000 to nearly 500,000. The Congress of Racial Equality (CORE), founded by an interracial group of pacifists in 1942, held sit-ins in northern cities to integrate restaurants and theaters. After a Firestone tire factory in Memphis fired a black woman for trying to enter a city bus before white passengers had been seated, black workers at the plant went on strike until she was reinstated.

In February 1942, the *Pittsburgh Courier* coined the phrase that came to symbolize black attitudes during the war—the "double-V." Victory over Germany and Japan, it insisted, must be accompanied by victory over segregation at home. While the Roosevelt administration and the white press saw the war as an expression of American ideals, black newspapers pointed to the gap between those ideals and reality. Side by side with ads for war bonds, *The Crisis* insisted that a segregated army "cannot fight for a free world."

Surveying wartime public opinion, a political scientist concluded that "symbols of national solidarity" had very different meanings to white and black Americans. To blacks, freedom from fear meant, among other things, an end to lynching, and freedom from want included doing away with "discrimination in getting jobs." If, in whites' eyes, freedom was a "possession to be defended," he observed, to blacks and other racial minorities it remained a "goal to be achieved." "*Our* fight for freedom," said a returning black veteran of the Pacific war, "begins when we get to San Francisco."

WHAT THE NEGRO WANTS

During the war, a broad political coalition centered on the left but reaching well beyond it called for an end to racial inequality in America. The NAACP and American Jewish Congress cooperated closely in advocating laws to ban discrimination in employment and housing. Despite considerable resistance from rank-and-file white workers, CIO unions, especially those with strong left-liberal and communist influence, made significant efforts to organize black workers and win them access to skilled positions. AFL craft unions by and large continued their long tradition of excluding black workers. But during World War II, the CIO was probably more racially integrated than any labor organization since the Knights of Labor in the 1880s.

The new black militancy created a crisis for moderate white southerners. In 1944, the University of North Carolina Press, which had published pathbreaking works on lynching, unionism, and southern poverty, released *What the Negro Wants*, a book of essays by four-teen prominent black leaders. Virtually every contribution called for the right to vote in the South, the dismantling of seg-regation, and access to "the accepted American standard of living." Several essays also insisted that with peace must come an end to European imperialism in Africa and Asia.

When he read the manuscript, W. T. Couch, the director of the press, was stunned. "If this is what the negro wants," he told the book's editor, "noth-ing could be clearer than what he needs, and needs most urgently, is to revise his wants." Couch represented a generation of white southerners who had pressed in the 1930s for modest improvements in race relations. They now saw their mid-

Paul Robeson, the black actor, singer, and battler for civil rights, leading Oakland dockworkers in singing the national anthem in 1942. World War II gave a significant boost to the vision, shared by Robeson and others on the left, of an America based on genuine equality.

dle ground evaporating as blacks demanded an end to segregation while southern politicians took up the cry of protecting white supremacy. The latter also spoke the language of freedom. Defenders of the racial status quo interpreted freedom to mean the right to shape their region's institutions without outside interference. The "war emergency," insisted Governor Frank Dixon of Alabama, "should not be used as a pretext to bring about the abolition of the color line." Even as the war gave birth to the modern civil rights movement, it also planted the seeds for the South's "massive resis-tance" to desegregation during the 1950s.

In the rest of the country, however, the status of black Americans assumed a place at the forefront of enlightened liberalism. Far more than in the 1930s, federal officials spoke openly of the need for a dramatic change in race relations. American democracy, noted Secretary of War Stimson, had not yet addressed "the persistent legacy of the original crime of slav-ery." Progress came slowly. But the National War Labor Board banned racial wage differentials. In *Smith v. Allwright* (1944), the Supreme Court out-lawed all-white primaries, one of the mechanisms by which southern states deprived blacks of political rights. In the same year, the navy began assigning small numbers of black sailors to previously all-white ships. In the final months of the war, it ended segregation altogether, and the army established a few combat units including black and white soldiers.

After a world tour in 1942 to rally support for the Allies, Wendell Willkie, Roosevelt's opponent of 1940, published *One World*. It sold 1 mil-lion copies, faster than any nonfiction work in American history. Willkie's travels persuaded him that Asia, Africa, and Latin America would play a pivotal role in the postwar era. But the book's great surprise came in Willkie's attack on "our imperialisms at home." Unless the United States addressed the "mocking paradox" of racism, he insisted, its claim to world leadership would lack moral authority. "If we want to talk about freedom," Willkie wrote, "we must mean freedom for everyone inside our frontiers."

AN AMERICAN DILEMMA

No event reflected the new concern with the status of black Americans more than the publication in 1944 of *An American Dilemma*, a sprawling account of the country's racial past, present, and future written by the Swedish social scientist Gunnar Myrdal. The book offered an uncompromising portrait of how deeply racism was entrenched in law, politics, economics, and social behavior. But Myrdal combined this sobering analysis with admiration for what he called the American Creed—belief in equality, justice, equal opportunity, and freedom. The war, he argued, had made Americans more aware than ever of the contradiction between this Creed and the reality of racial inequality. He concluded that "there is bound to be a redefinition of the Negro's status as a result of this War."

Myrdal's notion of a conflict between American values and American racial policies was hardly new—Frederick Douglass and W. E. B. Du Bois had said much the same thing. But in the context of a worldwide struggle against Nazism and rising black demands for equality at home, his book struck a chord. It identified a serious national problem and seemed to offer an almost painless path to peaceful change, in which the federal government would take the lead in outlawing discrimination. This coupling of an appeal to American principles with federal social engineering established a liberal position on race relations that would survive for many years.

By 1945, support for racial justice had finally taken its place on the liberal-left agenda alongside full employment, civil liberties, and the expansion of the New Deal welfare state. Roosevelt himself rarely spoke out on racial issues. But many liberals insisted that racial discrimination must be confronted head-on through federal antilynching legislation, equal opportunity in the workplace, an end to segregated housing and schools, and the expansion of Social Security programs to cover agricultural and domestic workers. This wartime vision of a racially integrated full employment economy formed a bridge between the New Deal and the Great Society of the 1960s (see Chapter 25).

THE END OF THE WAR

As 1945 opened, Allied victory was assured. In December 1944, in a desperate gamble, Hitler launched a surprise counterattack in France that pushed Allied forces back fifty miles, creating a large bulge in their lines. The largest single battle ever fought by the United States Army, the Battle of the Bulge produced over 70,000 American casualties. But by early 1945 the assault had failed.

In March, American troops crossed the Rhine River and entered the industrial heartland of Germany. Hitler took his own life, and shortly afterwards Soviet forces occupied Berlin. On May 8, known as V-E Day (for victory in Europe), came the formal end to the war against Germany. In the

Pacific, American forces moved ever closer to Japan. They had reconquered Guam in August 1944 and landed in the Philippines two months later, where they destroyed most of the remainder of the enemy fleet in the naval battle of Leyte Gulf.

"THE MOST TERRIBLE WEAPON"

Franklin D. Roosevelt defeated Republican nominee Thomas E. Dewey, the governor of New York, to win an unprecedented fourth term in 1944. But FDR did not live to see the Allied victory. He succumbed to a stroke on April 12, 1945. To his successor, Harry S. Truman, fell one of the most momentous decisions ever confronted by an American president—whether to use the atomic bomb against Japan. Truman did not know about the bomb until after he became president. Then, Secretary of War Stimson informed him that the United States had secretly developed "the most terrible weapon ever known in human history."

The bomb was a practical realization of the theory of relativity, a rethinking of the laws of physics developed early in the twentieth century by the German scientist Albert Einstein. Energy and matter, Einstein showed, represented two forms of the same phenomenon. According to his famous equation $E = mc^2$, the energy contained in matter equals its mass times the speed of light squared—an enormous amount. By using certain forms of uranium, or the man-made element plutonium, an atomic reaction could be created that transformed part of the mass into energy. This energy could be harnessed to provide a form of controlled power, or it could be unleashed in a tremendous explosion.

Having fled to the United States from Hitler's Germany, Einstein in 1939 warned Roosevelt that Nazi scientists were trying to develop an atomic weapon and urged the president to do likewise. In the following year, FDR authorized what came to be known as the Manhattan Project, a top-secret program in which American scientists developed an atomic bomb during World War II. The weapon was tested successfully in New Mexico in July 1945.

THE DAWN OF THE ATOMIC AGE

On August 6, 1945, an American plane dropped an atomic bomb that detonated over Hiroshima, Japan—a target chosen because almost alone among major Japanese cities, it had not yet suffered damage. In an instant, nearly every building in the city was destroyed. Of the city's population of

Hiroshima, Japan, after the dropping of the atomic bomb on August 6, 1945.

280,000 civilians and 40,000 soldiers, approximately 70,000 died immediately. Because atomic bombs release deadly radiation, the death toll kept rising in the months that followed. By the end of the year, it reached at least 140,000. Thousands more perished over the next five years. On August 9, the United States exploded a second bomb over Nagasaki, killing 70,000 persons. On the same day, the Soviet Union declared war on Japan and invaded Manchuria. Within a week, Japan surrendered.

Because of the enormous cost in civilian lives—more than twice America's military fatalities in the entire Pacific war—the use of the bomb remains controversial. The Japanese had fought ferociously while being driven from one Pacific island after another. An American invasion of Japan, some advisers warned Truman, might cost as many as 250,000 American lives. No such invasion was planned, however, until 1946, and considerable evidence had accumulated that Japan was nearing surrender. Already some of its officials had communicated a willingness to end the war if Emperor Hirohito could remain on his throne. This fell short of the Allies' demand for "unconditional surrender," but the victors would, in the end, agree to Hirohito's survival. Japan's economy had been crippled and its fleet destroyed, and it would now have to fight the Soviet Union as well as the United States. Some of the scientists who had worked on the bomb urged Truman to demonstrate its power to international observers. But Truman did not hesitate. The bomb was a weapon, and weapons are created to be used.

THE NATURE OF THE WAR

The dropping of the atomic bombs was the logical culmination of the way World War II had been fought. All wars inflict suffering on noncombatants. But never before had civilian populations been so ruthlessly targeted. Military personnel represented 90 percent of those who died in World War I. But of the estimated 50 million persons who perished during World War II (including 400,000 American soldiers), perhaps 20 million were civilians. Germany had killed millions of members of "inferior races." It had repeatedly bombed London and other cities. The Allies carried out even more deadly air assaults on civilian populations. Early in 1945, the firebombing of Dresden killed some 100,000 people, mostly women, children, and elderly men. On March 9, nearly the same number died in an inferno caused by the bombing of Tokyo.

Four years of war propaganda had dehumanized the Japanese in American eyes, and few persons criticized Truman's decision in 1945. But public doubts began to surface, especially after John Hersey published *Hiroshima* (1946), a graphic account of the horrors suffered by the civilian population. General Dwight D. Eisenhower, who thought the use of the bomb unnecessary, later wrote, "I hated to see our country be the first to use such a weapon."

PLANNING THE POSTWAR WORLD

Even as the war raged, a series of meetings between Allied leaders formulated plans for the postwar world. Churchill, Roosevelt, and Stalin met at

Tehran, Iran, in 1943, and at Yalta, in the southern Soviet Union, early in 1945, to hammer out agreements. The final "Big Three" conference took place at Potsdam, near Berlin, in July 1945. It involved Stalin, Truman, and Churchill (replaced midway in the talks by Clement Attlee, who became prime minister when his Labour Party swept the British elections). At Potsdam, the Allied leaders established a military administration for Germany and agreed to place top Nazi leaders on trial for war crimes.

Relations among the three Allies were often uneasy, as each maneuvered to maximize its postwar power. Neither Britain nor the United States trusted Stalin. The delay in the Allied invasion of France until 1944, which left the Soviets to do the bulk of the fighting against Germany, angered the Russians. But since Stalin's troops had won the war on the eastern front, it was difficult to resist his demand that eastern Europe become a Soviet sphere of influence (a region whose governments can be counted on to do a great power's bidding).

The "Big Three"—Winston Churchill, Harry S. Truman, and Joseph Stalin—at the Potsdam conference, July 25, 1945.

YALTA AND BRETTON WOODS

At Yalta, Roosevelt and Churchill entered only a mild protest against Soviet plans to retain control of the Baltic states (Estonia, Latvia, and Lithuania) and a large part of eastern Poland. Stalin agreed to enter the war against Japan later in 1945, to include noncommunists in the pro-Soviet government of Poland, and to allow "free and unfettered elections" there. But he was intent on establishing communism in eastern Europe. He believed, as he put it to Yugoslav communist leader Josip Broz ("Tito"), that in modern war, "whoever occupies a territory also imposes his own social system." Yalta saw the highwater mark of wartime American-Soviet cooperation. But it planted seeds of conflict, since the participants soon disagreed over the fate of eastern Europe.

Tension also existed between Britain and the United States. Churchill rejected American pressure to place India and other British colonies on the road to independence. He concluded private deals with Stalin dividing southern and eastern Europe into British and Soviet spheres of influence.

Britain also resisted, unsuccessfully, American efforts to reshape and dominate the postwar economic order. A meeting of representatives of forty-five nations at Bretton Woods, New Hampshire, in July 1944 replaced the British pound with the dollar as the main currency for international transactions. During the 1930s, as noted in the previous chapter, FDR had taken the United States off the gold standard, allowing the government to issue more money in the hope of stimulating business activity. The Bretton Woods conference reestablished the link between the dollar and gold. It set the dollar's value at $35 per ounce of gold and gave other currencies a fixed relationship to the dollar. The conference also created two American-dominated financial institutions. The World Bank would provide money to developing countries and to help rebuild Europe. The

International Monetary Fund would work to prevent governments from devaluing their currencies to gain an advantage in international trade, as many had done during the Depression.

Although the details took many years to emerge, Bretton Woods created the framework for the postwar capitalist economic system, based on a freer international flow of goods and investment and a recognition of the United States as the world's financial leader. Determined to avoid a recurrence of the Great Depression, American leaders believed that the removal of barriers to free trade would encourage the growth of the world economy, an emphasis that remains central to American foreign policy to this day.

THE UNITED NATIONS

Early in the war, the Allies also agreed to establish a successor to the League of Nations. In a 1944 conference at Dumbarton Oaks, near Washington D.C., they developed the structure of the United Nations (UN). There would be a General Assembly—essentially a forum for discussion where each member enjoyed an equal voice—and a Security Council responsible for maintaining world peace. Along with six rotating members, the Council would have five permanent ones—Britain, China, France, the Soviet Union, and the United States—each with the power to veto resolutions. In June 1945, representatives of fifty-one countries met in San Francisco to adopt the UN Charter, which outlawed force or the threat of force as a means of settling international disputes. In July, the U.S. Senate endorsed the Charter. In contrast to the bitter dispute over membership in the League of Nations after World War I, only two members of the U.S. Senate voted against joining the UN. At the conclusion of the San Francisco Conference that established the United Nations, President Truman urged Americans to recognize that "no matter how great our strength, we must deny ourselves the license to do always as we please. This is the price which each nation will have to pay for world peace.... And what a reasonable price that is."

PEACE, BUT NOT HARMONY

World War II ended with the United States the world's dominant power. "What Rome was to the ancient world," wrote the journalist Walter Lippmann, "America is to be to the world of tomorrow." But peace did not usher in an era of international harmony. The Soviet occupation of eastern Europe created a division soon to be solidified in the Cold War. The dropping of the atomic bombs left a worldwide legacy of fear.

It remained to be seen how seriously the victorious Allies took their wartime rhetoric of freedom. In August 1941, four months before the United States entered the war, FDR and British prime minister Winston Churchill had met for a conference, on warships anchored off the coast of Newfoundland, and issued the Atlantic Charter. The Charter promised that "the final destruction of Nazi tyranny" would be followed by open access to markets, the right of "all peoples" to choose their form of government, and a global extension of the New Deal so that people everywhere would enjoy "improved labor standards, economic advancement and social security." It

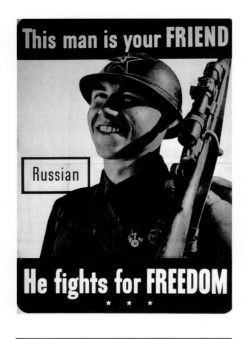

A 1942 poster celebrating the wartime alliance. Cooperation between the United States and the Soviet Union would give way to the Cold War soon after the end of World War II.

referred specifically to two of Roosevelt's Four Freedoms—freedom from want and freedom from fear. But freedom of speech and of worship had been left out because of British reluctance to apply them to its colonial possessions, especially India.

The Four Freedoms speech and the Atlantic Charter had been primarily intended to highlight the differences between Anglo-American ideals and Nazism. Nonetheless, they had unanticipated consequences. As one of Roosevelt's speechwriters remarked, "when you state a moral principle, you are stuck with it, no matter how many fingers you have kept crossed at the moment." The language with which World War II was fought helped to lay the foundation for postwar ideals of human rights that extend to all mankind.

During the war, Mahatma Gandhi, the Indian nationalist leader, wrote to Roosevelt that the idea "that the Allies are fighting to make the world safe for freedom of the individual and for democracy seems hollow, so long as India, and for that matter, Africa, are exploited by Great Britain, and America has the Negro problem in her own home." Allied victory saved mankind from a living nightmare—a worldwide system of dictatorial rule and slave labor in which peoples deemed inferior suffered the fate of European Jews and of the victims of Japanese outrages in Asia. But disputes over the freedom of colonial peoples overseas and non-whites in the United States foretold more wars and social upheavals to come.

SUGGESTED READING

Ambrose, Stephen E. *Citizen Soldiers* (1997). Discusses the experience of American soldiers fighting in Europe from D-Day to the end of the war.

Anderson, Karen. *Wartime Women: Sex Roles, Family Relations, and the Status of Women during World War II* (1981). Explores how the experience of World War II opened new opportunities for women and challenged existing gender conventions.

Blum, John M. *V Was for Victory: Politics and American Culture during World War II* (1976). A comprehensive account of the home front during World War II.

Borgwardt, Elizabeth. *A New Deal for the World: America's Vision for Human Rights* (2005). The emergence during the war of the idea of human rights as an international entitlement.

Brinkley, Alan. *The End of Reform: New Deal Liberalism in Recession and War* (1995). Describes how liberals' ideas and policies moved away, during the late New Deal and the war, from combating inequalities of economic power.

Dalfiume, Richard M. *Desegregation of the U.S. Armed Forces: Fighting in Two Fronts, 1939–1953* (1969). Presents the experience of black soldiers during and after the war.

Daniels, Rogers. *Prisoners without Trial: Japanese Americans in World War II* (1993). A brief history of the internment of Japanese-Americans during the war.

Dower, John W. *War without Mercy: Race and Power in the Pacific War* (1986). Explores how racial fears and antagonisms motivated both sides in the Pacific theater.

Isserman, Maurice. *Which Side Were You On? The American Communist Party during World War II* (1982). Traces the Communist Party's changing political positions during World War II.

Jeffries, John W. *Wartime America: The World War II Home Front* (1996). Stresses the many ways Americans were mobilized to fight the war and how this affected American society.

Kennedy, David M. *Freedom from Fear: The American People in Depression and War, 1929–1945* (1999). A detailed and lively account of American history from the Great Depression through the end of World War II.

Lichtenstein, Nelson. *Labor's War at Home: The CIO in World War II* (1982). Examines the war's impact on workers and the labor movement.

Rhodes, Richard. *The Making of the Atomic Bomb* (1986). A dramatic account of how the atomic bomb was created.

Von Eschen, Penny. *Race against Empire: Black Americans and Anticolonialism, 1937–1957* (1997). Examines how black Americans responded to the rise of movements for colonial independence overseas during and after World War II.

Wyman, David S. *The Abandonment of the Jews: America and the Holocaust, 1941–1945* (1984). A sharply critical account of the Roosevelt administration's response to Hitler's effort to exterminate European Jews.

REVIEW QUESTIONS

1. Discuss how the G.I. Bill of Rights was used by many American veterans to advance their social and economic status, while at the same time, it was manipulated by others to undermine minorities.

2. Illustrate how Franklin Roosevelt's Four Freedoms speech and the Atlantic Charter with Great Britain laid the foundation for postwar ideals of human rights.

3. How did the war affect the liberties of blacks, Indians, Japanese-Americans, and Mexican-Americans?

4. How did the war affect the lives of women on the home front?

5. Assess the controversy over the use of the atomic bomb during World War II.

REVIEW TABLE

The War and Minorities

Group	Effects of the War
Japanese-Americans	Civil liberties were stripped away while they were interned in camps for the war's duration
Chinese-Americans	Immigration restrictions in place since 1882 were reduced
African-Americans	Executive Order 8802 forbade employment discrimination in defense industries, opening up work opportunities
Mexican-Americans	The *bracero* program allowed thousands of contract workers into America and a new Chicano culture was formed
Indians	Many served in the armed forces and worked as "code talkers", and took advantage of the G.I. Bill.

KEY TERMS

Good Neighbor Policy (p. 846)

Neutrality Acts (p. 848)

Land-Lease Act (p. 849)

Pearl Harbor (p. 850)

Holocaust (p. 855)

saluting the flag (p. 858)

Korematsu v. United States (p. 870)

Executive Order 8802 (p. 875)

dropping the atomic bomb (p. 879)

Yalta (p. 881)

CHAPTER 23

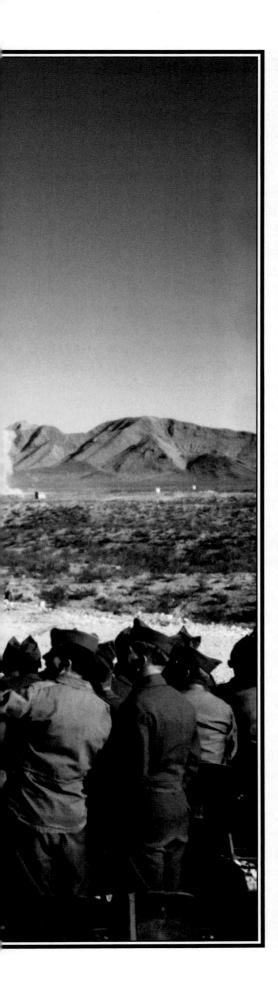

The United States and the Cold War, 1945–1953

ORIGINS OF THE COLD WAR

The Two Powers
The Roots of Containment
The Iron Curtain
The Truman Doctrine
The Marshall Plan
The Reconstruction of Japan
The Berlin Blockade and NATO
The Growing Communist
  Challenge
The Korean War
Cold War Critics
Imperialism and Decolonization

**THE COLD WAR AND
THE IDEA OF FREEDOM**

The Cultural Cold War
Freedom and Totalitarianism
The Rise of Human Rights

THE TRUMAN PRESIDENCY

The Fair Deal
The Postwar Strike Wave
The Republican Resurgence
Postwar Civil Rights
To Secure These Rights
The Dixiecrat and Wallace
  Revolts
The 1948 Campaign

**THE ANTICOMMUNIST
CRUSADE**

Loyalty and Disloyalty
The Spy Trials
McCarthy and McCarthyism
An Atmosphere of Fear
The Uses of Anticommunism
Anticommunist Politics
The Cold War and Organized
  Labor
Cold War Civil Rights

Students at the U.S. Army's Artillery School at Fort Bliss, Texas, witness a demonstration of anti-aircraft artillery, a weapon used with great effectiveness by American troops in the Korean War of 1950–1953.

FOCUS QUESTIONS

• How did the Cold War emerge in the postwar period?

• How did the Cold War reshape ideas of American freedom?

• What were the major initiatives of Truman's Fair Deal?

• What effects did the anti-communism of the Cold War have on American politics and culture?

On September 16, 1947, the 160th anniversary of the signing of the Constitution, the Freedom Train opened to the public in Philadelphia. A traveling exhibition of 133 historical documents, the train, bedecked in red, white, and blue, soon embarked on a sixteen-month tour that took it to over 300 American cities. Never before or since have so many cherished pieces of Americana—among them the Mayflower Compact, the Declaration of Independence, and the Gettysburg Address—been assembled in one place. After leaving the train, visitors were encouraged to rededicate themselves to American values by taking the Freedom Pledge and adding their names to a Freedom Scroll.

The idea for the Freedom Train, perhaps the most elaborate peacetime patriotic campaign in American history, originated in 1946 with the Department of Justice. President Harry S. Truman endorsed it as a way of contrasting American freedom with "the destruction of liberty by the Hitler tyranny." Since direct government funding raised fears of propaganda, however, the administration turned the project over to a nonprofit group, the American Heritage Foundation, headed by Winthrop W. Aldrich, chairman of Chase Manhattan Bank.

By any measure, the Freedom Train was an enormous success. It attracted over 3.5 million visitors, and millions more took part in the civic activities that accompanied its journey, including labor-management forums, educational programs, and patriotic parades. The powerful grass-roots response to the train, wrote *The New Republic*, revealed a popular hunger for "tangible evidence of American freedom." Behind the scenes, however, the Freedom Train demonstrated that the meaning of freedom remained as controversial as ever.

The liberal staff members at the National Archives who proposed the initial list of documents had included the Wagner Act of 1935, which guaranteed workers' right to form unions, as well as President Roosevelt's Four Freedoms speech of 1941, with its promise to fight "freedom from want." The more conservative American Heritage Foundation removed these documents. They also deleted from the original list the Fourteenth and Fifteenth Amendments, which had established the principle of equal civil and political rights regardless of race after the Civil War, and FDR's 1941 order establishing the Fair Employment Practices Commission, which Congress had recently allowed to expire. In the end, nothing on the train referred to organized labor or any twentieth-century social legislation. The only documents relating to blacks were the Emancipation Proclamation, the Thirteenth Amendment, and a 1776 letter by South Carolina patriot Henry Laurens criticizing slavery.

Many black Americans initially voiced doubts regarding the exhibit. On the eve of the train's unveiling, the poet Langston Hughes wondered whether there would be "Jim Crow on the Freedom Train." "When it stops in Mississippi," Hughes asked, "will it be made plain / Everybody's got a right to board the Freedom Train?" In fact, with the Truman administration about to make civil rights a major priority, the train's organizers announced that they would not permit segregated viewing. In an unprecedented move, the American Heritage Foundation canceled visits to Memphis, Tennessee, and Birmingham, Alabama, when local authorities insisted on separating visitors by race. The Freedom Train visited forty-seven other southern cities without incident and was hailed in the black press for breaching, if only temporarily, the walls of segregation.

Even as the Freedom Train reflected a new sense of national unease about expressions of racial inequality, its journey also revealed the growing impact of the Cold War. Originally intended to contrast American freedom with Nazi tyranny, the train quickly became caught up in the emerging struggle with communism. In the spring of 1947, a few months before the train was dedicated, President Truman committed the United States to the worldwide containment of Soviet power and inaugurated a program to root out "disloyal" persons from government employment. Soon, Attorney General Tom C. Clark was praising the Freedom Train as a means of preventing "foreign ideologies" from infiltrating the United States and of "aiding the country in its internal war against subversive elements." The Federal Bureau of Investigation began compiling reports on those who found the train objectionable. The Freedom Train revealed how the Cold War helped to reshape freedom's meaning, identifying it ever more closely with anticommunism, "free enterprise," and the defense of the social and economic status quo.

A page from Life *magazine, September 29, 1947, reporting on the journey of the Freedom Train. At the top, a marine stands guard over historic documents.*

ORIGINS OF THE COLD WAR

THE TWO POWERS

The United States emerged from World War II as by far the world's greatest power. Although most of the army was quickly demobilized, the country boasted the world's most powerful navy and air force. The United States accounted for half the world's manufacturing capacity. It alone possessed the atomic bomb. As discussed in the previous chapter, the Roosevelt administration was determined to avoid a retreat to isolationism like the one that followed World War I. It believed that the United States could lead the rest of the world to a future of international cooperation, expanding democracy, and ever-increasing living standards. New institutions like the United Nations and World Bank had been created to promote these goals. American leaders also believed that the nation's security depended on the security of Europe and Asia, and that American prosperity required global economic reconstruction.

The only power that in any way could rival the United States was the Soviet Union, whose armies now occupied most of eastern Europe, including the eastern part of Germany. Its crucial role in defeating Hitler and its claim that communism had wrested a vast backward nation into modernity gave the Soviet Union considerable prestige in Europe and among colonial peoples struggling for independence. Like the United States, the Soviets looked forward to a world order modeled on their own society and values. Having lost more than 20 million dead and suffered vast devastation during the war, however, Stalin's government was in no position to embark on new military adventures. "Unless they were completely out of their minds," said American undersecretary of state Dean Acheson, the Russians were hardly likely to go to war with the far more powerful United States. But having done by far the largest amount of ground fighting in the defeat of Hitler, the Soviet government remained determined to establish a sphere of influence in eastern Europe, through which Germany had twice invaded Russia in the past thirty years.

THE ROOTS OF CONTAINMENT

FDR seems to have believed that the United States could maintain friendly relations with the Soviet Union once World War II ended. In retrospect, however, it seems all but inevitable that the two major powers to emerge from the war would come into conflict. Born of a common foe rather than common long-term interests, values, or history, their wartime alliance began to unravel almost from the day that peace was declared.

The first confrontation of the Cold War took place in the Middle East. At the end of World War II, Soviet troops had occupied parts of northern Iran, hoping to pressure that country to grant it access to its rich oil fields. Under British and American pressure, however, Stalin quickly withdrew Soviet forces. At the same time, however, the Soviets installed procommunist governments in Poland, Romania, and Bulgaria, a step they claimed was no different from American domination of Latin America or Britain's determination to maintain its own empire. But many Americans became convinced that Stalin was violating the promise of free elections in Poland that had been agreed to at the Yalta conference of 1945.

Early in 1946, in his famous Long Telegram from Moscow, American diplomat George Kennan advised the Truman administration that the Soviets could not be dealt with as a normal government. Communist ideology drove them to try to expand their power throughout the world, he claimed, and only the United States had the ability to stop them. While Kennan believed that the Russians could not be dislodged from control of eastern Europe, his telegram laid the foundation for what became known as the policy of "containment," according to which the United States committed itself to preventing any further expansion of Soviet power.

THE IRON CURTAIN

Shortly afterwards, in a speech at Fulton, Missouri, Britain's former wartime prime minister Winston Churchill declared that an "iron curtain" had descended across Europe, partitioning the free West from the communist East. Churchill's speech helped to popularize the idea of an impending long-term struggle between the United States and the Soviets. But not until March 1947, in a speech announcing what came to be known as the Truman Doctrine, did the president officially embrace the Cold War as the foundation of American foreign policy and describe it as a worldwide struggle over the future of freedom.

THE TRUMAN DOCTRINE

Harry S. Truman never expected to become president. Until Democratic party leaders chose him to replace Henry Wallace as Roosevelt's running mate in 1944, he was an undistinguished senator from Missouri who had risen in politics through his connection with the boss of the Kansas City political machine, Tom Pendergast. When he assumed the presidency after Roosevelt's death in April 1945, Truman found himself forced to decide foreign policy debates in which he had previously played virtually no role.

Convinced that Stalin could not be trusted and that the United States had a responsibility to provide leadership to a world that he tended to view in stark, black-and-white terms, Truman soon determined to put the policy of containment into effect. The immediate occasion for this epochal decision came early in 1947 when Britain informed the United States that because its economy had been shattered by the war, it could no longer afford its traditional international role. Britain had no choice but to end military and financial aid to two crucial governments—Greece, a monarchy threatened by a communist-led rebellion, and Turkey, from which the Soviets were demanding joint control of the straits linking the Black Sea and the Mediterranean. Britain asked the United States to fill the vacuum.

President Harry S. Truman delivering his Truman Doctrine speech before Congress on March 12, 1947.

The Soviet Union had little to do with the internal problems of Greece and Turkey, where opposition to corrupt, undemocratic regimes was largely homegrown. Neither had held truly free elections. But they occupied strategically important sites at the gateway to southeastern Europe and the oil-rich Middle East. Truman had been told by Senate leader Arthur Vandenberg that the only way a reluctant public and Congress would support aid to these governments was for the president to "scare hell" out of the American people. To rally popular backing, Truman rolled out the heaviest weapon in his rhetorical arsenal—the defense of freedom. As the leader of the "free world," the United States must now shoulder the responsibility of supporting "freedom-loving peoples" wherever communism threatened them. Twenty-four times in the eighteen-minute speech, Truman used the words "free" or "freedom."

Building on the wartime division of the globe into free and enslaved worlds, and invoking a far older vision of an American mission to defend liberty against the forces of darkness, the Truman Doctrine created the language through which most Americans came to understand the postwar world. More than any other statement a prominent senator would write, this speech established "the guiding spirit of American foreign policy." Truman succeeded in persuading both Republicans and Democrats in Congress to support his policy, beginning a long period of bipartisan support for the containment of communism. As Truman's speech to Congress suggested, the Cold War was, in part, an ideological conflict. Both sides claimed to be promoting freedom and social justice while defending their own security, and each offered its social system as a model the rest of the world should follow.

While his request to Congress was limited to $400 million in military aid to two governments (aid that enabled both Greece and Turkey to defeat their domestic foes), Truman's rhetoric suggested that the United States had assumed a permanent global responsibility. The speech set a precedent for American assistance to anticommunist regimes throughout the world, no matter how undemocratic, and for the creation of a set of global military alliances directed against the Soviet Union. There soon followed the creation of new national security bodies immune from democratic oversight, such as the Atomic Energy Commission, National Security Council, and Central Intelligence Agency (CIA), the last established in 1947 to gather intelligence and conduct secret military operations abroad.

THE MARSHALL PLAN

The language of the Truman Doctrine and the future it sketched of open-ended worldwide responsibilities for the United States alarmed many Americans. "Are we to shoulder the mantle of nineteenth-century British imperialism?" asked the *San Francisco Chronicle*. "Are we asking for a third world war?" But the threat of American military action overseas formed only one pillar of containment. Secretary of State George C. Marshall spelled out the other in a speech at Harvard University in June 1947. Marshall pledged the United States to contribute billions of dollars to finance the economic recovery of Europe. Two years after the end of the war, much of the continent still lay in ruins. Food shortages were widespread, and inflation was rampant. The economic chaos, exacerbated by the unusually severe winter of 1946–1947, had strengthened the communist parties of France and Italy. American policymakers feared that these countries might fall into the Soviet orbit.

The Marshall Plan offered a positive vision to go along with containment. It aimed to combat the idea, widespread since the Great Depression, that capitalism was in decline and communism the wave of the future. It defined the threat to American security not so much as Soviet military power but as economic and political instability, which could be breeding grounds for communism. Avoiding Truman's language of a world divided between free and unfree blocs, Marshall insisted, "Our policy is directed not against any country or doctrine, but against hunger, poverty, desperation, and chaos." Freedom meant more than simply anticommunism—it required the emergence of the "political and social conditions in which free

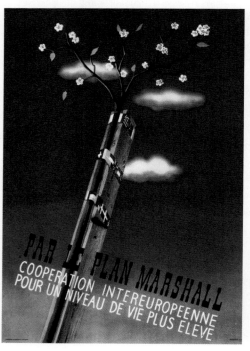

A French poster expressing European gratitude for the Marshall Plan, by which the United States aided the economic reconstruction of western Europe after the Second World War. The text reads, "Through the Marshall Plan. Inter-European Cooperation for a Higher Standard of Living."

Bales of American cotton in a warehouse at the French port of Le Havre, 1949. Part of the Marshall Plan aid program, the shipment helped to revive the French cotton industry.

institutions can exist." In effect, the Marshall Plan envisioned a New Deal for Europe, an extension to that continent of Roosevelt's wartime Four Freedoms. As a booklet explaining the idea to Europeans put it, the aim was "a higher standard of living for the entire nation; maximum employment for workers and farmers; greater production." Or, in the words of a slogan used to popularize the Marshall Plan, "Prosperity Makes You Free."

The Marshall Plan proved to be one of the most successful foreign aid programs in history. By 1950, western European production exceeded prewar levels and the region was poised to follow the United States down the road to a mass-consumption society. Since the Soviet Union refused to participate, fearing American control over the economies of eastern Europe, the Marshall Plan further solidified the division of the continent. At the same time, the United States worked out with twenty-three other western nations the General Agreement on Tariffs and Trade (GATT), which proposed to stimulate freer trade among the participants, creating an enormous market for American goods and investment.

THE RECONSTRUCTION OF JAPAN

Under the guidance of General Douglas MacArthur, the "supreme commander" in Japan until 1948, the country adopted a new, democratic constitution and eliminated absentee landlordism so that most tenant farmers became owners of land. Thanks to American insistence, and against the wishes of most Japanese leaders, the new constitution gave women the right to vote for the first time in Japan's history. (A century after the Seneca Falls convention, women's suffrage had become an intrinsic part of American understandings of freedom.) Furthermore, Article 9 of the new constitution stated that Japan would renounce forever the policy of war and armed aggression, and would maintain only a modest self-defense force.

The United States also oversaw the economic reconstruction of Japan. Initially, the United States proposed to dissolve Japan's giant industrial corporations, which had contributed so much to the nation's war effort. But this plan was abandoned in 1948 in favor of an effort to rebuild Japan's industrial base as a bastion of anticommunist strength in Asia. By the 1950s, thanks to American economic assistance, the adoption of new technologies, and low spending on the military, Japan's economic recovery was in full swing.

THE BERLIN BLOCKADE AND NATO

Meanwhile, the Cold War intensified and, despite the Marshall Plan, increasingly took a militaristic turn. At the end of World War II, each of the four victorious powers assumed control of a section of occupied Germany, and of Berlin, located deep in the Soviet zone. In June 1948, the United States, Britain, and France introduced a separate currency in their zones, a prelude to the creation of a new West German government that would be aligned with them in the Cold War. In response, the Soviets cut off road and rail traffic from the American, British, and French zones of occupied Germany to Berlin (although Stalin kept supply routes open from the east, since Soviet forces occupied part of the divided city).

An eleven-month airlift followed, with Western planes supplying fuel and food to their zones of the city. When Stalin lifted the blockade in May 1949, the Truman administration had won a major victory. Soon, two new nations emerged, East and West Germany, each allied with a side in the Cold War. Berlin itself remained divided. The city's western part survived as an isolated enclave within East Germany. Not until 1991 would Germany be reunified.

Also in 1949, the Soviet Union tested its first atomic bomb, ending the American monopoly of the weapon. In the same year, the United States, Canada, and ten western European nations established the North Atlantic Treaty Organization (NATO), pledging mutual defense against any future

Children in Berlin celebrate the arrival of a plane bringing supplies to counter the Soviet blockade of the city in 1948.

COLD WAR EUROPE, 1956

Occupation Zones
American
British
French
Soviet

Berlin Wall - 1961
West Berlin
East Berlin

ICELAND

SWEDEN
FINLAND
NORWAY

IRELAND
North Sea
DENMARK

Baltic Sea

SOVIET UNION

Atlantic Ocean

GREAT BRITAIN
London
NETHERLANDS
BELGIUM
Bonn
Berlin
POLAND
Warsaw

EAST GERMANY
Paris
WEST GERMANY
Prague
LUXEMBOURG
CZECHOSLOVAKIA

FRANCE
SWITZERLAND
AUSTRIA
Budapest
HUNGARY
ROMANIA

Bucharest

PORTUGAL
SPAIN
Corsica
ITALY
YUGOSLAVIA
Sofia
Black Sea

Lisbon
Sardinia
Tirane
BULGARIA
ALBANIA
Ankara

GREECE
TURKEY

MOROCCO
Sicily
Athens
SYRIA
IRAQ

TUNISIA
Mediterranean Sea
Crete
CYPRUS
(Great Britain)
LEBANON

ISRAEL
JORDAN

ALGERIA
(France)
SAUDI ARABIA

LIBYA
EGYPT
Red Sea

NATO countries, 1956
Warsaw Pact countries, 1956

0   250   500 miles
0   250   500 kilometers

The division of Europe between communist and noncommunist nations, solidified by the early 1950s, would last for nearly forty years.

Chinese communists carrying portraits of Mao Zedong, who took control of the country's government in 1949 after a long civil war.

Soviet attack. Soon, West Germany became a crucial part of NATO. Many Europeans feared German rearmament. But France and other victims of Nazi aggression saw NATO as a kind of "double containment," in which West Germany would serve as a bulwark against the Soviets while integration into the Western alliance tamed and "civilized" German power. The North Atlantic Treaty was the first long-term military alliance between the United States and Europe since the Treaty of Amity and Commerce with France during the American Revolution. The Soviets formalized their own eastern European alliance, the Warsaw Pact, in 1955.

THE GROWING COMMUNIST CHALLENGE

In 1949, communists led by Mao Zedong emerged victorious in the long Chinese civil war—a serious setback for the policy of containment. Assailed by Republicans for having "lost" China (which, of course, the United States never "had" in the first place), the Truman administration refused to recognize the new government and blocked it from occupying China's seat at the United Nations. Until the 1970s, the United States insisted that the ousted regime, which had been forced into exile on the island of Taiwan, remained the legitimate government of China.

In the wake of Soviet-American confrontations over southern and eastern Europe and Berlin, the communist victory in China, and Soviet success in developing an atomic bomb, the National Security Council approved a call for a permanent military build-up to enable the United States to pursue a global crusade against communism. Known as NSC-68, this 1950 manifesto described the Cold War as an epic struggle between "the idea of freedom" and the "idea of slavery under the grim oligarchy of the Kremlin." At stake in the world conflict, it insisted, was nothing less than "the survival of the free world." One of the most important policy statements of the early Cold War, NSC-68 helped to spur a dramatic increase in American military spending.

THE KOREAN WAR

Initially, American postwar policy focused on Europe. But it was in Asia that the Cold War suddenly turned hot. Occupied by Japan during World War II, Korea had been divided in 1945 into Soviet and American zones. These soon evolved into two governments: communist North Korea, and

As this map indicates, when General Douglas MacArthur launched his surprise landing at Inchon, North Korean forces controlled nearly the entire Korean peninsula.

THE KOREAN WAR, 1950-1953

North Korean offensive, June–September 1950
U.N. offensive, September–November 1950
Communist Chinese counteroffensive, November 1950–January 1951

anticommunist South Korea, undemocratic but aligned with the United States. In June 1950, the North Korean army invaded the south, hoping to reunify the country under communist control. North Korean soldiers soon occupied most of the peninsula. Viewing Korea as a clear test of the policy of containment, the Truman administration persuaded the United Nations Security Council to authorize the use of force to repel the invasion. (The Soviets, who could have vetoed the resolution, were boycotting Security Council meetings to protest the refusal to seat communist China.)

American troops did the bulk of the fighting on this first battlefield of the Cold War. In September 1950, General Douglas MacArthur launched a daring counterattack at Inchon, behind North Korean lines. The invading forces retreated northward, and MacArthur's army soon occupied most of North Korea. Truman now hoped to unite Korea under a pro-American government. But in October 1950, when UN forces neared the Chinese border, hundreds of thousands of Chinese troops intervened, driving them back in bloody fighting. MacArthur demanded the right to push north again and possibly even invade China and use nuclear weapons against it. But Truman, fearing an all-out war on the Asian mainland, refused. MacArthur did not fully accept the principle of civilian control of the military. When he went public with criticism of the president, Truman removed him from command. The war then settled into a stalemate around the thirty-eighth parallel, the original boundary between the two Koreas. Not until 1953 was an armistice agreed to, essentially restoring the prewar status quo. There has never been a formal peace treaty ending the Korean War.

Over 33,000 Americans died in Korea. The Asian death toll reached an estimated 1 million Korean soldiers and 2 million civilians (many of them victims of starvation after American bombing destroyed irrigation systems essential to rice cultivation), along with hundreds of thousands of Chinese troops. Korea made it clear that the Cold War, which began in Europe, had become a global conflict.

Taken together, the events of 1947–1953 showed that the world had moved very far from the hopes for global harmony symbolized by the founding of the United Nations in 1945. No longer did the United States speak of One World (the title of Wendell Willkie's influential wartime book). Instead, the world had been divided in two. The United States now stood as the undisputed leader of what was increasingly known as the West (although it included Japan, where permanent American military bases were established), or the Free World. NATO was soon followed by SEATO in Southeast Asia and CENTO in the Middle East, forming a web of military alliances that ringed the Soviet Union and China.

COLD WAR CRITICS

In the Soviet Union, Stalin had consolidated a brutal dictatorship that jailed or murdered millions of Soviet citizens. With its one-party rule, stringent control of the arts and intellectual life by the state, and government-controlled economy, the Soviet Union presented a stark opposite of democracy and "free enterprise." As a number of contemporary critics, few of them sympathetic to Soviet communism, pointed out, however, casting the Cold War in terms of a worldwide battle between freedom and slavery had unfortunate consequences. George Kennan, whose Long Telegram had inspired the policy of containment, observed that such language made it impossible to view international crises on a case-by-case basis, or to determine which genuinely involved either freedom or American interests.

In a penetrating critique of Truman's policies, Walter Lippmann, one of the nation's most prominent journalists, objected to turning foreign policy into an "ideological crusade." To view every challenge to the status quo as part of a contest with the Soviet Union, Lippmann correctly predicted, would require the United States to recruit and subsidize an "array of satellites, clients, dependents and puppets." It would have to intervene continuously in the affairs of nations whose political problems did not arise from Moscow and could not be easily understood in terms of the battle between freedom and slavery. World War II, he went on, had shaken the foundations of European empires. In the tide of revolutionary nationalism now sweeping the world, communists were certain to play an important role. It would be a serious mistake, Lippmann warned, for the United States to align itself against the movement for colonial independence in the name of anti-communism.

IMPERIALISM AND DECOLONIZATION

World War II had increased awareness in the United States of the problem of imperialism and had led many African-Americans to identify their own struggle for equality with the strivings of non-white colonial peoples overseas. Many movements for colonial independence borrowed the language of the American Declaration of Independence in demanding the right to self-government. Liberal Democrats and black leaders urged the Truman administration to take the lead in promoting worldwide decolonization, insisting that a Free World worthy of the name should not include colonies and empires. In 1946, the United States granted independence to the Philippines, a move hailed by nationalist movements in other colonies. But as the Cold War developed, the United States backed away from pressuring its European allies to move toward granting self-government to colonies like French Indochina, the Dutch East Indies, and British possessions like the Gold Coast and Nigeria in Africa and Malaya in Asia. Even after granting independence to India and Pakistan in 1947, Britain was determined to retain much of its empire.

In practice, geopolitical and economic interests shaped American foreign policy as powerfully as the idea of freedom. But American policymakers used the language of a crusade for freedom to justify actions around the world that had little to do with freedom by almost any definition. No matter how repressive to its own people, if a nation joined the worldwide anti-communist alliance led by the United States, it was counted as a member of the Free World. The Republic of South Africa, for example, was considered a part of the Free World even though its white minority had deprived the black population of nearly all their rights. Was there not some way, one critic asked, that the United States could accept "the aid of tyrants" on practical grounds "without corrupting our speeches by identifying tyranny with freedom"?

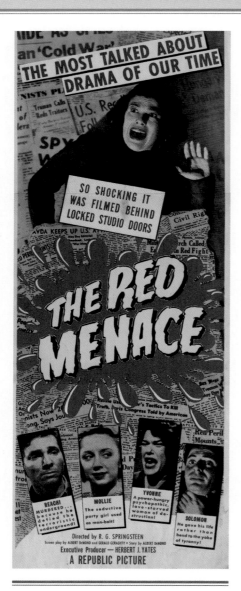

A poster for The Red Menace, *one of numerous anticommunist films produced by Hollywood during the 1950s.*

THE COLD WAR AND THE IDEA OF FREEDOM

Among other things, the Cold War was an ideological struggle, a battle, in a popular phrase of the 1950s, for the "hearts and minds" of people throughout the world. Like other wars, it required popular mobilization, in which the idea of freedom played a central role. During the 1950s, freedom became an inescapable theme of academic research, popular journalism, mass culture, and official pronouncements. Henry Luce, who had popularized the idea of an American Century, explained that freedom was the "one word out of the whole human vocabulary" through which *Time* magazine could best explain America to the rest of the world. In many ways, the Cold War established the framework for the discussion of freedom.

THE CULTURAL COLD WAR

One of the more unusual Cold War battlefields involved American history and culture. Many scholars read the American Creed of pluralism, tolerance, and equality back into the past as a timeless definition of Americanism, ignoring the powerful ethnic and racial strains with which it had always coexisted. Under the code name "Militant Liberty," national security agencies encouraged Hollywood to produce anticommunist movies, such as *The Red Menace* (1949) and *I Married a Communist* (1950), and urged that film scripts be changed to remove references to less-than-praiseworthy aspects of American history, such as Indian removal and racial discrimination.

The Central Intelligence Agency and Defense Department emerged as unlikely patrons of the arts. As noted in Chapter 21, the federal government had openly financed all sorts of artistic works during the 1930s. But Cold War funding for the arts remained top-secret—in part because Congress proved reluctant to spend money for this purpose, in part because Americans charged communist governments with imposing artistic conformity. In an effort to influence public opinion abroad, the Soviet Union sponsored tours of its world-famous ballet companies, folk dance troupes, and symphony orchestras. To counteract the widespread European view of the United States as a cultural backwater, the CIA secretly funded an array of overseas publications, conferences, publishing houses, concerts, and art exhibits. And to try to improve the international image of American race relations, the government sent jazz musicians and other black performers abroad, especially to Africa and Asia.

Works produced by artists who considered themselves thoroughly nonpolitical became weapons in the cultural Cold War. The CIA promoted the so-called New York school of painters, led by Jackson Pollock. For Pollock, the essence of art lay in the process of creation, not the final product. His "action" paintings, made by spontaneously dripping and pouring paint over large canvases, produced works of vivid color and energy but without any recognizable subject matter. Many members of Congress much preferred Norman Rockwell's readily understandable illustrations of small-town life to Pollock's "abstract expressionism." Some called Pollock's works un-American and wondered aloud if they were part of a communist plot. But the CIA funded the Museum of Modern Art in New York, which cham-

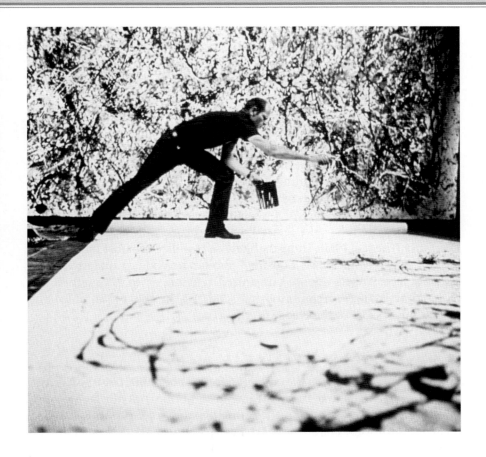

Jackson Pollack at work in his studio. Pollack's paintings exemplified the artistic school of abstract expressionism, promoted during the Cold War as a reflection of American freedom. His paintings had no recognizable subject other than reminding the viewer of how the artist had created them. "I want to express my feelings, rather than illustrate them," Pollack declared.

pioned the New York school, and helped arrange for exhibitions overseas. It hoped to persuade Europeans not only that these paintings demonstrated that the United States represented artistic leadership as well as military power, but that such art embodied the free, individual expression denied to artists in communist countries. Pollock's paintings, John Cage's musical compositions, which incorporated chance sounds rather than a fixed score, and the "graceful freedom" of George Balanchine's choreography were all described as artistic reflections of the essence of American life.

FREEDOM AND TOTALITARIANISM

Along with freedom, the Cold War's other great mobilizing concept was "totalitarianism." The term originated in Europe between the world wars to describe fascist Italy and Nazi Germany—aggressive, ideologically driven states that sought to subdue all of civil society, including churches, unions, and other voluntary associations, to their control. Such states, according to the theory of totalitarianism, left no room for individual rights or alternative values and therefore could never change from within. By 1950, the year the McCarran Internal Security Act barred "totalitarians" from entering the United States, the term had become a shorthand way of describing those on the other side in the Cold War. As the eventual collapse of communist governments in eastern Europe and the Soviet Union would demonstrate, the idea of totalitarianism greatly exaggerated the totality of government

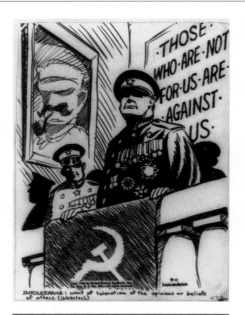

Cartoonist Bill Mauldin illustrated the essence of the idea of totalitarianism in this 1946 cartoon—a dictatorial government that refuses to accept the legitimacy of difference of opinion.

control of private life and thought in these countries. But its widespread use reinforced the view that the greatest danger to freedom lay in an overly powerful government.

Just as the conflict over slavery redefined American freedom in the nineteenth century and the confrontation with the Nazis shaped understandings of freedom during World War II, the Cold War reshaped them once again. Russia had already conquered America, the poet Archibald MacLeish complained in 1949, since politics was conducted "under a kind of upside-down Russian veto." Whatever Moscow stood for was by definition the opposite of freedom, including anything to which the word "socialized" could be attached. In the largest public relations campaign in American history, the American Medical Association raised the specter of "socialized medicine" to discredit and defeat Truman's proposal for national health insurance. The real-estate industry likewise mobilized against public housing, terming it "socialized housing," similar to policies undertaken by Moscow. The Soviets opposed organized religion, so to "strengthen our national resistance to communism," Congress in the 1950s added the words "under God" to the Pledge of Allegiance.

THE RISE OF HUMAN RIGHTS

The Cold War also affected the emerging concept of human rights. The idea that there are rights that are applicable to all of humanity originated during the eighteenth century in the Enlightenment and the American and French Revolutions. The atrocities committed during World War II, as well as the global language of the Four Freedoms and the Atlantic Charter, forcefully raised the issue of human rights in the postwar world. After the war, the victorious Allies put numerous German officials on trial before special courts at Nuremberg for crimes against humanity. For the first time, individuals were held directly accountable to the international community for violations of human rights. The trials resulted in prison terms for many Nazi officials and the execution of ten leaders.

In 1948, the United Nations General Assembly approved the Universal Declaration of Human Rights, drafted by a committee chaired by Eleanor Roosevelt. It identified a broad range of rights to be enjoyed by people everywhere, including freedom of speech, religious toleration, and protection against arbitrary government, as well as social and economic entitlements like the right to an adequate standard of living and access to housing, education, and medical care. The document had no enforcement mechanism. Some considered it an exercise in empty rhetoric. But the core principle—that a nation's treatment of its own citizens should be subject to outside evaluation—slowly became part of the language in which freedom was discussed.

After the Cold War ended, the idea of human rights would play an increasingly prominent role in world affairs. But during the 1950s, Cold War imperatives shaped the concept. Neither the United States nor the Soviet Union could resist emphasizing certain provisions of the Universal Declaration while ignoring others. The Soviets claimed to provide all citizens with social and economic rights, but violated democratic rights and civil liberties. Many Americans condemned the nonpolitical rights as a

A post–World War II cartoon shows Eleanor Roosevelt lecturing UN delegates from various countries about human rights. "Now children," she says, "all together: 'The rights of the individual are above the rights of the state.'" The Soviet ambassador to the UN, Andrei Y. Vishinsky, stands in the lower right corner.

step toward socialism. In 1950, Freedom House began yearly assessments of the status of freedom in the world's nations. It adopted purely political criteria, emphasizing citizens' rights to participate in open elections and to speak out on public issues. Considering access to employment, housing, education, medical care, and the like as part of the definition of freedom, the reports argued, would be a serious mistake.

Eleanor Roosevelt saw the Universal Declaration of Human Rights as an integrated body of principles, a combination of traditional civil and political liberties with the social conditions of freedom outlined in her husband's Economic Bill of Rights of 1944. But to make it easier for member states to ratify the document, the UN divided it into two "covenants"—Civil and Political Rights, and Economic, Social, and Cultural Rights. It took until 1992 for Congress to ratify the first. It has never approved the second.

THE TRUMAN PRESIDENCY

THE FAIR DEAL

With the end of World War II, President Truman's first domestic task was to preside over the transition from a wartime to a peacetime economy. Over 12 million men remained in uniform in August 1945. They wanted nothing more than to return home to their families. Demobilization proceeded at a rapid pace. Within a year, the armed forces had been reduced to 3 million. Some returning soldiers found the adjustment to civilian life difficult. The divorce rate in 1945 rose to double its prewar level. Others took advantage of the GI Bill of Rights (discussed in the previous chapter) to obtain home mortgages, set up small businesses, and embark on college educations. The majority of returning soldiers entered the labor force—one reason why over 2 million women workers lost their jobs. The government abolished wartime agencies that regulated industrial production and labor relations, and it dismantled wartime price controls, leading to a sharp rise in prices.

A few of the numerous World War II veterans who attended college after the war, thanks to the GI Bill.

In the immediate aftermath of World War II, President Truman, backed by party liberals and organized labor, moved to revive the stalled momentum of the New Deal. Truman's program, which he announced in September 1945 and would later call the Fair Deal, focused on improving the social safety net and raising the standard of living of ordinary Americans. He called on Congress to increase the minimum wage, enact a program of national health insurance, and expand public housing, Social Security, and aid to education. Truman, complained one Republican leader, was "out–New Dealing the New Deal."

THE POSTWAR STRIKE WAVE

In 1946, a new wave of labor militancy swept the country. The AFL and CIO launched Operation Dixie, a campaign to bring unionization to the South and, by so doing, shatter the hold of anti-labor conservatives on the region's politics. Over 200 labor organizers entered the region, seeking support especially in the southern textile industry, the steel industry in the Birmingham region, and agriculture. With war production at an end, overtime work diminished even as inflation soared following the removal of price controls. The resulting drop in workers' real income sparked the largest strike wave in American history. Nearly 5 million workers—including those in the steel, auto, coal, and other key industries—walked off their jobs, demanding wage increases. The strike of 750,000 steelworkers represented the largest single walkout in American history to that date. Even Hollywood studios shut down because of a strike of actors and other employees of the movie industry that lasted for the better part of a year. One historian calls this period "the closest thing to a national general strike in industry in the twentieth century."

President Truman feared the strikes would seriously disrupt the economy. When railroad workers stopped work and set up picket lines, the infuriated president prepared a speech in which he threatened to draft them all into the army and "hang a few traitors"—language toned down by his advisers. The walkout soon ended, as did a coal strike after the Truman administration secured a court order requiring the miners to return to work. To resolve other strikes, Truman appointed federal "fact-finding boards," which generally recommended wage increases, although not enough to restore workers' purchasing power to wartime levels.

THE REPUBLICAN RESURGENCE

In the congressional elections of 1946, large numbers of middle-class voters, alarmed by the labor turmoil, voted Republican. Many workers, disappointed by Truman's policies, stayed at home. This was a lethal combination for the Democratic Party. For the first time since the 1920s, Republicans swept to control of both houses of Congress. Meanwhile, in the face of vigorous opposition from southern employers and public officials and the reluctance of many white workers to join interracial labor unions, Operation Dixie had failed to unionize the South or dent the political control of conservative Democrats in the region. The election of 1946 ensured that a conservative coalition of Republicans and southern Democrats would continue to dominate Congress.

Congress turned aside Truman's Fair Deal program. It enacted tax cuts for wealthy Americans and, over the president's veto, in 1947 passed the Taft-Hartley Act, which sought to reverse some of the gains made by organized labor in the past decade. The measure authorized the president to suspend strikes by ordering an eighty-day "cooling-off period," and it banned sympathy strikes and secondary boycotts (labor actions directed not at an employer but at those who did business with him). It outlawed the closed shop, which required a worker to be a union member when taking up a job, and authorized states to pass "right-to-work" laws, prohibiting other forms of compulsory union membership. It also forced union officials to swear that they were not communists. While hardly a "slave-labor bill," as the AFL and CIO called it, the Taft-Hartley Act made it considerably more difficult to bring unorganized workers into unions. Over time, as population and capital investment shifted to states with "right-to-work" laws like Texas, Florida, and North Carolina, Taft-Hartley contributed to the decline of organized labor's share of the nation's workforce.

POSTWAR CIVIL RIGHTS

During his first term, Truman reached out in unprecedented ways to the nation's black community. The war, as noted in the previous chapter, had inspired a new black militancy and led many whites to reject American racial practices as reminiscent of Hitler's theory of a master race. In the years immediately following World War II, the status of black Americans enjoyed a prominence in national affairs unmatched since Reconstruction.

Between 1945 and 1951, eleven states from New York to New Mexico established fair employment practices commissions and numerous cities passed laws against discrimination in access to jobs and public accommodations. (Some of these measures addressed other racial groups besides blacks: for example, California in 1947 repealed its laws permitting local school districts to provide segregated education for children of Chinese descent and those barring aliens from owning land.) A broad civil rights

Racial segregation and exclusion were not confined to the South in the post-World War II period. Here, in 1947, picketers stand outside a Seattle grocery store that refused to serve non-whites. A campaign by black activists supported by a coalition of unions, church groups, Jewish organizations, and communists forced most of the city's stores and restaurants to treat customers on an equal basis.

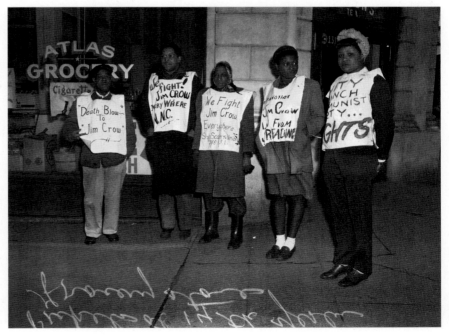

coalition involving labor, religious groups, and black organizations supported these measures. The NAACP, its ranks swollen during the war, launched a voter registration campaign in the South. By 1952, 20 percent of black southerners were registered to vote, nearly a seven-fold increase since 1940. (Most of the gains took place in the Upper South—in Alabama and Mississippi, the heartland of white supremacy, the numbers barely budged.) Law enforcement agencies finally took the crime of lynching seriously. In 1952, for the first time since record keeping began seventy years earlier, no lynchings took place in the United States.

In another indication that race relations were in flux, the Brooklyn Dodgers in 1947 challenged the long-standing exclusion of black players from major-league baseball by adding Jackie Robinson to their team. Robinson, who possessed both remarkable athletic ability and a passion for equality, had been tried and acquitted for insubordination in 1944 when he refused to move to the back of a bus at Fort Hood, Texas, while serving in the army. But he promised Dodger owner Branch Rickey that he would not retaliate when subjected to racist taunts by opposing fans and players. His dignity in the face of constant verbal abuse won Robinson nationwide respect, and his baseball prowess earned him the Rookie of the Year award. His success opened the door to the integration of baseball and led to the demise of the Negro Leagues, to which black players had previously been confined.

TO SECURE THESE RIGHTS

In October 1947, a Commission on Civil Rights appointed by the president issued *To Secure These Rights*, one of the most devastating indictments ever published of racial inequality in America. It called on the federal government to assume the responsibility for abolishing segregation and ensuring equal treatment in housing, employment, education, and the criminal justice system. Truman hailed the report as "an American charter of human freedom." The impact of America's race system on the nation's ability to conduct the Cold War was not far from his mind. Truman noted that if the United States were to offer the "peoples of the world" a "choice of freedom or enslavement," it must "correct the remaining imperfections in our practice of democracy."

In February 1948, Truman presented an ambitious civil rights program to Congress, calling for a permanent federal civil rights commission, national laws against lynching and the poll tax, and action to ensure equal access to jobs and education. Congress, as Truman anticipated, approved none of his proposals. But in July 1948, just as the presidential

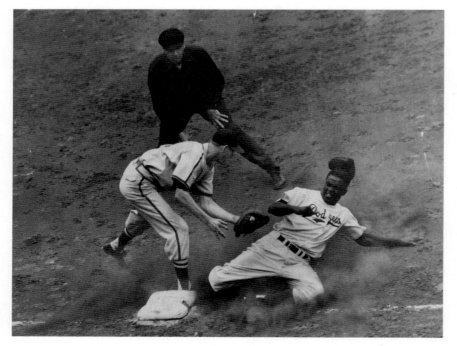

Jackie Robinson sliding into third base, 1949.

campaign was getting under way, Truman issued an executive order desegregating the armed forces. The armed services became the first large institution in American life to promote racial integration actively and to attempt to root out long-standing racist practices. The Korean War would be the first American conflict fought by an integrated army since the War of Independence.

Truman genuinely despised racial discrimination. But his focus on civil rights also formed part of a strategy to win reelection by reinvigorating and expanding the political coalition Roosevelt had created. With calls for federal health insurance, the repeal of the Taft-Hartley Act, and aid to public education, the Democratic platform of 1948 was the most progressive in the party's history. Led by Hubert Humphrey, the young mayor of Minneapolis, party liberals overcame southern resistance and added a strong civil rights plank to the platform.

THE DIXIECRAT AND WALLACE REVOLTS

"I say the time has come," Humphrey told the Democratic national convention, "to walk out of the shadow of states' rights and into the sunlight of human rights." Whereupon numerous southern delegates—dubbed Dixiecrats by the press—walked out of the gathering. They soon formed the States' Rights Democratic Party and nominated for president Governor Strom Thurmond of South Carolina. Although his platform called for the "complete segregation of the races" and his campaign drew most of its support from those alarmed by Truman's civil rights initiatives, Thurmond denied charges of racism. The real issue of the election, Thurmond insisted, was freedom—the States' Rights Democratic Party, he declared, stood for "individual liberty and freedom, the right of people to govern themselves." Truman's plans for extending federal power into the South to enforce civil rights, Thurmond charged, would "convert America into a Hitler state."

Also in 1948, a group of left-wing critics of Truman's foreign policy formed the Progressive Party and nominated former vice president Henry A. Wallace for president. Wallace advocated an expansion of social welfare programs at home and denounced racial segregation even more vigorously than Truman. When he campaigned in the South, angry white crowds attacked him. But his real difference with the president concerned the Cold War. Wallace called for international control of nuclear weapons and a renewed effort to develop a relationship with the Soviet Union based on economic cooperation rather than military confrontation. He announced his willingness to accept support from all

Blacks, led by A. Philip Randolph (left), picketing at the 1948 Democratic national convention. The delegates' adoption of a strong civil rights plank led representatives of several southern states to withdraw and nominate their own candidate for president, Strom Thurmond.

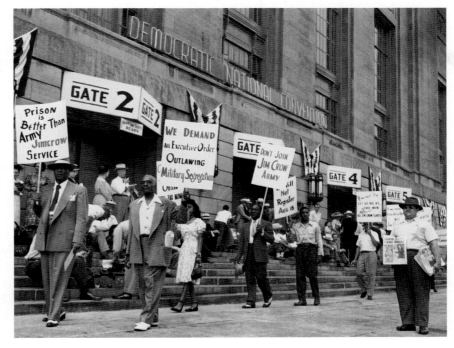

Americans who agreed with him, including socialists and communists. The influence of the now much-reduced Communist Party in Wallace's campaign led to an exodus of New Deal liberals and severe attacks on his candidacy. A vote for Wallace, Truman declared, was in effect a vote for Stalin.

THE 1948 CAMPAIGN

Wallace threatened to draw votes from Truman on the left, and Thurmond to undermine the president's support in the South, where whites had voted solidly for the Democrats throughout the twentieth century. But Truman's main opponent, fortunately for the president, was the colorless Republican Thomas A. Dewey. Certain of victory and an ineffective speaker and campaigner, Dewey seemed unwilling to commit himself on controversial issues. His speeches, wrote one hostile newspaper, amounted to nothing more than clichés: "Agriculture is important. Our rivers are full of fish. You cannot have freedom without liberty. Our future lies ahead." Truman, by contrast, ran an aggressive campaign. He crisscrossed the country by train, delivering fiery attacks on the Republican-controlled "do-nothing Congress." Truman revived New Deal rhetoric denouncing Wall Street and charged his opponent with threatening to undermine Social Security and other New Deal benefits. "Don't let them take it away," he repeated over and over.

The four-way 1948 campaign was the last before television put a premium on brief political advertisements and entertaining slogans rather than substantive debate, and the last in which a full spectrum of ideologies was presented to the American public. Virtually every public-opinion poll and newspaper report predicted a Dewey victory. Truman's success—by 303 to 189 electoral votes—represented one of the greatest upsets in American political history. Thurmond carried four Deep South states, demonstrating that the race issue, couched in terms of individual freedom, had the potential of leading traditionally Democratic white voters to desert their party. In retrospect, the States' Rights campaign offered a preview of the political transformation that by the end of the twentieth century would leave every southern state in the Republican column. As for Wallace, he suffered the humiliation of polling fewer popular votes (1.16 million) than Thurmond (1.17 million). His crushing defeat inaugurated an era in which public criticism of the foundations of American foreign policy became all but impossible.

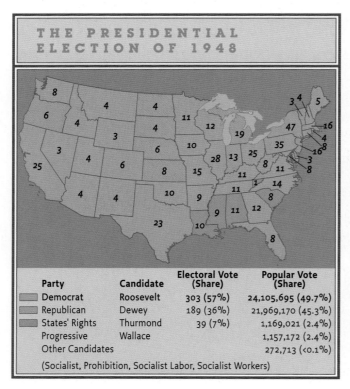

THE PRESIDENTIAL ELECTION OF 1948

Party	Candidate	Electoral Vote (Share)	Popular Vote (Share)
Democrat	Roosevelt	303 (57%)	24,105,695 (49.7%)
Republican	Dewey	189 (36%)	21,969,170 (45.3%)
States' Rights	Thurmond	39 (7%)	1,169,021 (2.4%)
Progressive	Wallace		1,157,172 (2.4%)
Other Candidates			272,713 (<0.1%)

(Socialist, Prohibition, Socialist Labor, Socialist Workers)

THE ANTICOMMUNIST CRUSADE

For nearly half a century, the Cold War profoundly affected American life. There would be no return to "normalcy" as after World War I. The military-industrial establishment created during World War II would be permanent, not temporary. The United States retained a large and active federal government and poured money into weapons development and overseas bases. National security became the stated reason for a host of government projects, including aid to higher education and the building of a new national highway system (justified by the need to speed the evacuation of major cities in the event of nuclear war). The Cold War encouraged a culture of secrecy and dishonesty. Not until decades later was it revealed that during the 1950s and 1960s both the Soviet and American governments conducted experiments in which unwitting soldiers were exposed to chemical, biological, and nuclear weapons. American nuclear tests, conducted on Pacific islands and in Nevada with no public warnings, exposed thousands of civilians to radiation that caused cancer and birth defects.

A crowd in Las Vegas, Nevada, watches a mushroom cloud rise from the test of an atomic bomb in the distance in 1951. The government publicized such tests and even broadcast one on television. It failed to issue warnings of the danger of nuclear fallout, and only years later did it admit than many onlookers had contracted diseases from radiation.

Cold War military spending helped to fuel economic growth and support scientific research that not only perfected weaponry but also led to improved aircraft, computers, medicines, and other products with a large impact on civilian life. Since much of this research took place at universities, the Cold War promoted the rapid expansion of American higher education. The Cold War reshaped immigration policy, with refugees from communism being allowed to enter the United States regardless of national-origin quotas. The international embarrassment caused by American racial policies contributed to the dismantling of segregation. And like other wars, the Cold War encouraged the drawing of a sharp line between patriotic Americans and those accused of being disloyal. Containment—not only of communism but of unorthodox opinions of all kinds—took place at home as well as abroad. At precisely the moment when the United States celebrated freedom as the foundation of American life, the right to dissent came under attack.

LOYALTY AND DISLOYALTY

Dividing the world between liberty and slavery automatically made those who could be linked to communism enemies of freedom. Although the assault on civil liberties came to be known as McCarthyism, it began before Senator Joseph R. McCarthy of Wisconsin burst onto the national scene in 1950. In 1947, less than two weeks after announcing the Truman Doctrine, the president established a loyalty review system in which government employees were required to demonstrate their patriotism without being allowed to confront accusers or, in some cases, knowing the charges against them. The loyalty program failed to uncover any cases of espionage. But the federal government dismissed several hundred persons from their

Movie stars, led by actors Humphrey Bogart and Lauren Bacall, on their way to attend the 1947 hearings of the House Un-American Activities Committee, in a demonstration of support for those called to testify about alleged communist influence in Hollywood.

jobs, and thousands resigned rather than submit to investigation.

Also in 1947, the House Un-American Activities Committee (HUAC) launched a series of hearings about communist influence in Hollywood. Calling well-known screenwriters, directors, and actors to appear before the committee ensured it a wave of national publicity, which its members relished. Celebrities like producer Walt Disney and actors Gary Cooper and Ronald Reagan testified that the movie industry harbored numerous communists. But ten "unfriendly witnesses" refused to answer the committee's questions about their political beliefs or to "name names" (identify individual communists) on the grounds that the hearings violated the First Amendment's guarantees of freedom of speech and political association. The committee charged the Hollywood Ten, who included the prominent screenwriters Ring Lardner Jr. and Dalton Trumbo, with contempt of Congress, and they served jail terms of six months to a year. Hollywood studios blacklisted them (denied them employment), along with over 200 others who were accused of communist sympathies or who refused to name names.

THE SPY TRIALS

A series of highly publicized legal cases followed, which fueled the growing anticommunist hysteria. Whittaker Chambers, an editor at *Time* magazine, testified before HUAC that during the 1930s Alger Hiss, a high-ranking State Department official, had given him secret government documents to pass to agents of the Soviet Union. Hiss vehemently denied the charge, but a jury convicted him of perjury and he served five years in prison. A young congressman from California and member of HUAC, Richard Nixon achieved national prominence because of his dogged pursuit of Hiss. In another celebrated case, the Truman administration put the leaders of the Communist Party on trial for advocating the overthrow of the government. In 1951, eleven of them were sentenced to five years in prison.

The most sensational trial involved Julius and Ethel Rosenberg, a working-class Jewish communist couple from New York City (quite different from Hiss, a member of the eastern Protestant "establishment"). In 1951, a jury convicted the Rosenbergs of conspiracy to pass secrets concerning the atomic bomb to Soviet agents during World War II (when the Soviets were American allies). Their chief accuser was David Greenglass, Ethel Rosenberg's brother, who had worked at the Los Alamos nuclear research center.

The case against Julius Rosenberg rested on highly secret documents that could not be revealed in court. (When they were released many years later, the scientific information they contained seemed too crude to justify the government's charge that Julius had passed along the "secret of the atomic bomb," although he may have helped the Soviets speed up their atomic program.) The government had almost no evidence against Ethel Rosenberg, and Greenglass later admitted that he had lied in some of his testimony about her. Indeed, prosecutors seem to have indicted her in the hope of pressuring Julius to confess and implicate others. But in the atmosphere of hysteria, their conviction was certain. Even though they had been convicted of conspiracy, a far weaker charge than spying or treason, Judge Irving Kaufman called their crime "worse than murder." They had helped, he declared, to "cause" the Korean War. Despite an international outcry, the death sentence was carried out in 1953. Controversy still surrounds the degree of guilt of both Hiss and the Rosenbergs, although almost no one today defends the Rosenbergs' execution. But these trials powerfully reinforced the idea that an army of Soviet spies was at work in the United States.

MCCARTHY AND MCCARTHYISM

In this atmosphere, a little-known senator from Wisconsin suddenly emerged as the chief national pursuer of subversives and gave a new name to the anticommunist crusade. Joseph R. McCarthy had won election to the Senate in 1946, partly on the basis of a fictional war record (he falsely claimed to have flown combat missions in the Pacific). In a speech at Wheeling, West Virginia, in February 1950, McCarthy announced that he had a list of 205 communists working for the State Department. The charge was preposterous, the numbers constantly changed, and McCarthy never identified a single person guilty of genuine disloyalty. But with a genius for self-promotion, McCarthy used the Senate subcommittee he chaired to hold hearings and level wild charges against numerous individuals as well as the Defense Department, the Voice of America, and other government agencies. Although many Republicans initially supported his rampage as a weapon against the Truman administration, McCarthy became an embarrassment to the party after the election of Republican Dwight D. Eisenhower as president in 1952. But McCarthy did not halt his campaign. He even questioned Eisenhower's anticommunism.

McCarthy's downfall came in 1954, when a Senate committee investigated his charges that the army had harbored and "coddled" communists. The nationally televised Army-McCarthy hearings revealed McCarthy as a bully who browbeat witnesses and made sweeping accusations with no basis in fact. The dramatic high point came when McCarthy attacked the loyalty of a young lawyer in the firm of Joseph Welch, the army's chief lawyer. "Let us not assassinate this lad further," Welch pleaded. "You have done enough. Have you no sense of decency, sir?" After the hearings ended, the Senate censured McCarthy for his behavior. He died three years later. But the word "McCarthyism" had entered the political vocabulary, a shorthand for character assassination, guilt by association, and abuse of power in the name of anticommunism.

AN ATMOSPHERE OF FEAR

By the early 1950s, the anticommunist crusade had created a pervasive atmosphere of fear. One commentator described Washington, D.C., as a city rife with "spying, suspicion, [and] defamation by rumor," with "democratic

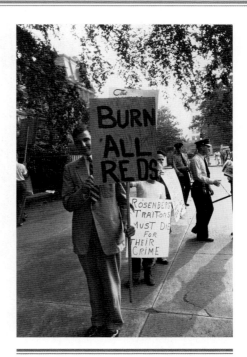

Demonstrators at a 1953 rally in Washington, D.C., demanding the execution of Julius and Ethel Rosenberg.

"Fire!" Cartoonist Herbert Block, known as "Herblock," offered this comment in 1949 on the danger to American freedom posed by the anticommunist crusade.

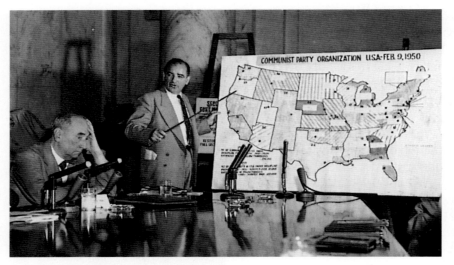

Senator Joseph R. McCarthy at the Army-McCarthy hearings of 1954. McCarthy points to a map detailing charges about the alleged extent of the communist menace, while the army's lawyer, Joseph Welch, listens in disgust.

freedoms" at risk as power slipped into the hands of those "whose values are the values of dictatorship and whose methods are the methods of the police state." But anticommunism was as much a local as a national phenomenon. States created their own committees, modeled on HUAC, that investigated suspected communists and other dissenters. States and localities required loyalty oaths of teachers, pharmacists, and members of other professions, and they banned communists from fishing, holding a driver's license, and, in Indiana, working as a professional wrestler.

Private organizations like the American Legion, National Association of Manufacturers, and Daughters of the American Revolution also persecuted individuals for their beliefs. The Better America League of southern California gathered the names of nearly 2 million alleged subversives in the region. Previous membership in organizations with communist influence or even participation in campaigns in which communists had taken part, such as the defense of the government of Spain during the Spanish Civil War of the 1930s, suddenly took on sinister implications. Throughout the country in the late 1940s and 1950s, those who failed to testify about their past and present political beliefs and to inform on possible communists frequently lost their jobs.

Local anticommunist groups forced public libraries to remove from their shelves "un-American" books like the tales of Robin Hood, who took from the rich to give to the poor. Universities refused to allow left-wing speakers to appear on campus and fired teachers who refused to sign loyalty oaths or to testify against others.

As during World War I, the courts did nothing to halt the political repression, demonstrating once again James Madison's warning that popular hysteria could override "parchment barriers" like the Bill of Rights that sought to prevent infringements on freedom. In 1951, in *Dennis v. United States*, the Supreme Court upheld the jailing of Communist Party leaders even though the charges concerned their beliefs, not any actions they had taken. Even many liberals retreated from the idea that freedom of expression was a birthright of all Americans. The American Civil Liberties Union condemned McCarthy's tactics but refused to defend the indicted Communist Party leaders.

THE USES OF ANTICOMMUNISM

There undoubtedly were Soviet spies in the United States. Yet the tiny Communist Party hardly posed a threat to American security. And the vast majority of those jailed or deprived of their livelihoods during the McCarthy era were guilty of nothing more than holding unpopular beliefs and engaging in lawful political activities.

Anticommunism had many faces and purposes. A popular mass movement, it grew especially strong among ethnic groups like Polish-Americans, with roots in eastern European countries now dominated by the Soviet Union, and among American Catholics in general, who resented and feared communists' hostility to religion. Government agencies like the Federal Bureau of Investigation (FBI) used anticommunism to expand their power. Under director J. Edgar Hoover, the FBI developed files on thousands of American citizens, including political dissenters, homosexuals, and others, most of whom had no connection to communism.

Anticommunism also served as a weapon wielded by individuals and groups in battles unrelated to defending the United States against subversion. McCarthy and his Republican followers often seemed to target not so much Stalin as the legacy of Roosevelt and the New Deal. For many Democrats, aggressive anticommunism became a form of self-defense against Republican charges of disloyalty and a weapon in a struggle for the party's future. The campaign against subversion redrew the boundaries of acceptable Democratic liberalism to exclude both communists and those willing to cooperate with them as in the days of the Popular Front. Indeed, "sympathetic association" with communists—past or present—became grounds for dismissal from one's job under the government's loyalty program.

As the historian Henry Steele Commager argued in a 1947 magazine article, the anticommunist crusade promoted a new definition of loyalty—conformity. Anything other than "uncritical and unquestioning acceptance of America as it is," wrote Commager, could now be labeled unpatriotic. For business, anticommunism became part of a campaign to identify government intervention in the economy with socialism. White supremacists employed anticommunism against black civil rights, business used it against unions, and upholders of sexual morality and traditional gender roles raised the cry of subversion against feminism and homosexuality, both supposedly responsible for eroding the country's fighting spirit. (Those barred from government service now included homosexuals and members of nudist colonies.)

ANTICOMMUNIST POLITICS

At its height, from the late 1940s to around 1960, the anticommunist crusade powerfully structured American politics and culture. Especially after their unexpected defeat in 1948, Republicans in Congress used a drumbeat of charges of subversion to block Truman's political program. The most important actions of Congress were ones the president opposed. After launching the government's loyalty program in 1947, Truman had become increasingly alarmed at the excesses of the anticommunist crusade. He vetoed the McCarran Internal Security Bill of 1950, which required "subversive" groups to register with the government, allowed the denial of passports to their members, and authorized their deportation or detention on presidential order. But Congress quickly gave the measure the two-thirds majority necessary for it to become law.

The McCarran-Walter Act of 1952, the first major piece of immigration legislation since 1924, also passed over the president's veto. Truman had appointed a Commission on Immigration, whose report, *Whom Shall We*

VOICES OF FREEDOM

FROM National Security Council, NSC-68 (1950)

A critical document of early Cold War thinking, NSC-68 called for the United States to pursue a global crusade against communism in the name of freedom. Although not made public until years later, the manifesto had a strong impact in government circles and helped to spur a sharp increase in military spending.

The Soviet Union, unlike previous aspirants to hegemony, is animated by a new fanatic faith, antithetical to our own, and seeks to impose its absolute authority over the rest of the world. . . . The Kremlin regards the United States as the only major threat to the achievement of its fundamental design. There is a basic conflict between the idea of freedom under a government of laws, and the idea of slavery under the grim oligarchy of the Kremlin, which has come to a crisis with the polarization of power . . . and the exclusive possession of atomic weapons by the two protagonists. . . . The implacable purpose of the slave state to eliminate the challenge of freedom has placed the two great powers at opposite poles. It is this fact which gives the present polarization of power the quality of crisis.

The free society values the individual as an end in himself, requiring of him only that measure of self-discipline and self-restraint which make the rights of each individual compatible with the rights of every other individual. The freedom of the individual has as its counterpart, therefore, the negative responsibility of the individual not to exercise his freedom in ways inconsistent with the freedom of other individuals and the positive responsibility to make constructive use of his freedom in the building of a just society.

From this idea of freedom with responsibility derives the marvelous diversity, the deep tolerance, the lawfulness of the free society. This is the explanation of the strength of free men. It constitutes the integrity and the vitality of a free and democratic system. The free society attempts to create and maintain an environment in which every individual has the opportunity to realize his creative powers. It also explains why the free society tolerates those within it who would use their freedom to destroy it. By the same token, in relations between nations, the prime reliance of the free society is on the strength and appeal of its idea, and it feels no compulsion sooner or later to bring all societies into conformity with it.

For the free society does not fear, it welcomes, diversity. It derives its strength from its hospitality even to antipathetic [hostile] ideas. It is a market for free trade in ideas, secure in its faith that free men will take the best wares. . . .

The idea of freedom is the most contagious idea in history, more contagious than the idea of submission to authority.

FROM HENRY STEELE COMMAGER, "Who Is Loyal to America?" *Harper's* (September 1947)

In a sharply worded essay written in 1947, the prominent historian Henry Steele Commager commented on how the anticommunist crusade was stifling the expression of dissent and promoting an idea of patriotism that equated loyalty to the nation with the uncritical acceptance of American society and institutions.

Increasingly, Congress is concerned with the eradication of disloyalty and the defense of Americanism, and scarcely a day passes . . . that the outlines of the new loyalty and the new Americanism are not etched more sharply in public policy. . . . In the making is a revival of the red hysteria of the early 1920s, one of the shabbiest chapters in the history of American democracy, and more than a revival, for the new crusade is designed not merely to frustrate Communism but to formulate a positive definition of Americanism, and a positive concept of loyalty.

What is this new loyalty? It is, above all, conformity. It is the uncritical and unquestioning acceptance of America as it is—the political institutions, the social relationships, the economic practices. It rejects inquiry into the race question or socialized medicine, or public housing, or into the wisdom or validity of our foreign policy. It regards as particularly heinous any challenge to what is called "the system of private enterprise," identifying that system with Americanism. It abandons . . . the once popular concept of progress, and regards America as a finished product, perfect and complete.

It is, it must be added, easily satisfied. For it wants not intellectual conviction nor spiritual conquest, but mere outward conformity. In matters of loyalty, it takes the word for the deed, the gesture for the principle. It is content with the flag salute. . . . It is satisfied with membership in respectable organizations and, as it assumes that every member of a liberal organization is a Communist, concludes that every member of a conservative one is a true American. It has not yet learned that everyone who saith Lord, Lord, shall enter into the kingdom of Heaven. It is designed neither to discover real disloyalty nor to foster true loyalty.

The concept of loyalty as conformity is a false one. It is narrow and restrictive, denies freedom of thought and of conscience. . . . What do men know of loyalty who make a mockery of the Declaration of Independence and the Bill of Rights?

QUESTIONS

1. What does NSC-68 see as the essential elements of the "free society"?

2. Why does Commager feel that the new patriotism makes "a mockery" of the Bill of Rights?

3. Is there any connection between the idea of a global battle over the future of freedom outlined in NSC-68 and the infringements on civil liberties at home deplored by Commager?

Welcome?, called for replacing the quotas based on national origins with a more flexible system taking into account family reunion, labor needs, and political asylum. But the McCarran-Walter Act kept the quotas in place. It also authorized the deportation of immigrants identified as communists, even if they had become citizens. But the renewed fear of aliens sparked by the anticommunist crusade went far beyond communists. In 1954, the federal government launched Operation Wetback, which employed the military to invade Mexican-American neighborhoods and round up and deport illegal aliens. Within a year, some 1 million Mexicans had been deported.

Truman did secure passage of a 1950 law that added previously excluded self-employed and domestic workers to Social Security. Otherwise, however, the idea of expanding the New Deal welfare state faded. In its place, private welfare arrangements proliferated. The labor contracts of unionized workers established health insurance plans, automatic cost of living wage increases, paid vacations, and pension plans that supplemented Social Security. Western European governments provided these benefits to all citizens. In the United States, union members in major industries enjoyed them, but not the nonunionized majority of the population, a situation that created increasing inequality among laboring Americans.

THE COLD WAR AND ORGANIZED LABOR

Every political and social organization had to cooperate with the anticommunist crusade or face destruction, a wrenching experience for movements like labor and civil rights, in which communists had been some of the most militant organizers. After the passage of the Taft-Hartley Act of 1947, which withdrew bargaining rights and legal protection from unions whose leaders failed to swear that they were not communists, the CIO expelled numerous left-wing officials and eleven communist-led unions, representing nearly 1 million workers. Organized labor emerged as a major supporter of the foreign policy of the Cold War. Internal battles over the role of communists and their allies led to the purging of some of the most militant union leaders, often the ones most committed to advancing equal rights to women and racial minorities in the workplace. This left organized labor less able to respond to the economy's shift to an emphasis on service rather than manufacturing, and to the rise of the civil rights movement.

COLD WAR CIVIL RIGHTS

The civil rights movement also underwent a transformation. At first, mainstream black organizations like the NAACP and Urban League protested the Truman administration's loyalty program. They wondered aloud why the program and congressional committees defined communism as "un-American," but not racism. Anticommunist investigators often cited attendance at interracial gatherings as evidence of disloyalty. But while a few prominent black leaders, notably the singer and actor Paul Robeson and the veteran crusader for equality W. E. B. Du Bois, became outspoken critics of the Cold War, most felt they had no choice but to go along. The NAACP purged communists from local branches. When the government deprived Robeson of his passport and indicted Du Bois for failing to register as an agent of the Soviet Union, few prominent Americans, white or black, protested. (The charge against Du Bois was so absurd that even at the height of McCarthyism, the judge dismissed it.)

The Cold War caused a shift in thinking and tactics among civil rights groups. Organizations like the Southern Conference for Human Welfare, in which communists and noncommunists had cooperated in linking racial equality with labor organizing and economic reform, had been crucial to the struggles of the 1930s and war years. Their demise left a gaping hole that the NAACP, with its narrowly legalistic strategy, could not fill. Black organizations embraced the language of the Cold War and used it for their own purposes. They insisted that by damaging the American image abroad, racial inequality played into the Russians' hands. Thus, they helped to cement Cold War ideology as the foundation of the political culture, while complicating the idea of American freedom.

President Truman, as noted above, had called for greater attention to civil rights in part to improve the American image abroad. All in all, however, the height of the Cold War was an unfavorable time to raise questions about the imperfections of American society. In 1947, two months after the Truman Doctrine speech, Undersecretary of State Dean Acheson delivered a major address defending the president's pledge to aid "free peoples" seeking to preserve their "democratic institutions." Acheson chose as his audience the Delta Council, an organization of Mississippi planters, bankers, and merchants. He seemed unaware that to make the case for the Cold War, he had ventured into what one historian has called the "American Siberia," a place of grinding poverty whose black population (70 percent of the total) enjoyed neither genuine freedom nor democracy. Most of the Delta's citizens were denied the very liberties supposedly endangered by communism.

After 1948, little came of the Truman administration's civil rights flurry. State and local laws banning discrimination in employment and housing remained largely unenforced. In 1952, the Democrats showed how quickly the issue had faded by nominating for president Adlai Stevenson of Illinois, a candidate with little interest in civil rights, with southern segregationist John Sparkman as his running mate. The following year, Hortense Gabel, director of the eminently respectable New York State Committee Against Discrimination in Housing, reported that the shadow of fear hung over the civil rights movement. Given the persecution of dissent and the widespread sentiment that equated any criticism of American society with disloyalty, "a great many people are shying away from all activity in the civil liberties and civil rights fronts."

Time would reveal that the waning of the civil rights impulse was only temporary. But it came at a crucial moment, the late 1940s and early 1950s, when the United States experienced the greatest economic boom in its history. The rise of an "affluent society" transformed American life, opening new opportunities for tens of millions of white Americans in rapidly expanding suburbs. But it left blacks trapped in the declining rural areas of the South and urban ghettos of the North. The contrast between new opportunities and widespread prosperity for whites and continued discrimination for blacks would soon inspire a civil rights revolution and, with it, yet another redefinition of American freedom.

SUGGESTED READING

Biondi, Martha. *To Stand and Fight: The Struggle for Civil Rights in Postwar New York City* (2003). A comprehensive account of the broad coalition that battled for racial justice in New York City, in areas such as jobs, education, and housing.

Donovan, Robert. *Conflict and Crisis: The Presidency of Harry S. Truman, 1945–1948* (1977). A careful account of Truman's first administration and his surprising election victory in 1948.

Dudziak, Mary L. *Cold War Civil Rights: Race and the Image of American Democracy* (2000). Analyzes how the Cold War influenced and in some ways encouraged the civil rights movement at home.

Gaddis, John. *Strategies of Containment: A Critical Analysis of Postwar American National Security* (1982). An influential analysis of the development of the containment policy central to American foreign policy during the Cold War.

Gleason, Abbott. *Totalitarianism: The Inner History of the Cold War* (1995). Traces the development and uses of a key idea in Cold War America.

Glendon, Mary Ann. *A World Made New: Eleanor Roosevelt and the Universal Declaration of Human Rights* (2001). Relates the drafting of the Universal Declaration of Human Rights and the response of governments around the world, including the United States.

Hogan, Michael. *The Marhsall Plan* (1987). A detailed look at a pillar of early Cold War policy.

Hunt, Michael. *Ideology and U.S. Foreign Policy* (1987). Discusses how ideas, including the idea of freedom, have shaped America's interactions with the rest of the world.

Leffler, Melvyn P. *A Preponderance of Power: National Security, the Truman Administration, and the Cold War* (1992). An influential account of the origins of the Cold War.

Lipsitz, George. *Rainbow at Midnight: Labor and Culture in the 1940s* (1994). Examines the labor movement and its role in American life in the decade of perhaps its greatest influence.

Saunders, Frances S. *The Cultural Cold War: The CIA and the World of Arts and Letters* (2000). Describes how the CIA and other government agencies secretly funded artists and writers as part of the larger Cold War.

Schrecker, Ellen. *Many Are the Crimes: McCarthyism in America* (1998). A full account of the anticommunist crusade at home and its impact on American intellectual and social life.

Stueck, William. *The Korean War: An International History* (1995). Studies the Korean War in its full global context.

Sugrue, Thomas. *Origins of the Urban Crisis: Race and Inequality in Postwar Detroit* (1996). Explores race relations in a key industrial city after World War II and how they set the stage for the upheavals of the 1960s.

Williams, William A. *The Tragedy of American Diplomacy* (1959). An influential critique of America's Cold War foreign policy.

CHAPTER REVIEW

 Study and Review at wwnorton.com/studyspace

REVIEW QUESTIONS

1. In their ideological war, the Cold War superpowers promoted two very different social systems. Describe them and explain why each superpower felt its social system promoted freedom and social justice.

2. What was the anticommunist crusade's impact on organized labor in the postwar period?

3. What did the 1948 presidential election say about American society's dreams and fears for postwar America?

4. What were the major factors underlying the origins of the Cold War?

5. What were the major components of Truman's Fair Deal?

KEY TERMS

Long Telegram (p. 890)

Marshall Plan (p. 892)

The Soviet bomb (p. 894)

the dismissal of Douglas MacArthur (p 898)

labor unrest (p. 904)

desegregating the armed forces (p. 907)

loyalty review system (p. 909)

Army-McCarthy hearings (p. 911)

McCarran-Walter Act (p. 913)

REVIEW TABLE

Landmark Events in the Early Cold War

Event	Date	Significance
Truman Doctrine	1947	Commited the United States to a policy of containment
Marshall Plan	1947	Provided economic aid to Europe for reconstruction
Berlin blockade and airlift	1948–1949	Demonstrated an American commitment to containment
Korean War	1950–1953	First hot war of the Cold War

Part 6

WHAT KIND OF NATION? 1953–2007

In the last half of the twentieth century, the United States experienced profound changes both at home and in its role in the larger world. The Cold War produced increasing American involvement in the affairs of other nations across the globe. Sometimes indirectly, sometimes through direct military intervention, the United States sought to prevent the further spread of communism and to ensure the existence of governments friendly to American strategic and economic interests. The sudden and unexpected collapse of communism in the Soviet Union and eastern Europe between 1989 and 1991 left the United States by far the world's foremost military power. At home, these years witnessed far-reaching changes in the nature of American society and a dramatic expansion in the rights of American citizens and their understandings of freedom.

On the surface, the decade of the 1950s seemed uneventful. It was a time of widespread affluence in the United States, the beginning of an unprecedented economic expansion that lasted until the early 1970s. Millions of Americans moved to the suburbs, where they enjoyed access to an astonishing array of consumer goods that poured out of American factories, including cars, television sets, and household appliances. The postwar "baby boom" dramatically increased the population. American understandings of freedom centered on the enjoyment of economic affluence and consumer choice within the context of traditional family life, with women finding fulfillment within their suburban homes.

Even during this time of "consensus," when sharp political divisions and economic strife seemed to have vanished from American life, seeds of discontent sprouted. A few artists and social commentators began to criticize the stifling atmosphere of conformity. The Supreme Court's decision in 1954 outlawing racial segregation in public schools, justified, in part, by the damage Jim Crow inflicted on the world standing of the United States in the Cold War, helped to inspire the revival of the struggle for racial justice. The Montgomery bus boycott of 1955 launched the southern phase of the civil rights movement, which forced the entire country to rethink whether the United States could genuinely call itself "the land of the free" if it confined millions of Americans to second-class citizenship.

These seeds of protest flowered in the 1960s, a decade of social conflict and of a dramatic expansion of the boundaries of American freedom. The civil rights revolution reached its climax with demonstrations throughout the South and the passage in 1964 and 1965 of national laws protecting blacks' civil rights and restoring to them the right to vote in the South. Although the movement splintered thereafter and the nation failed to address adequately the economic plight of non-whites trapped in decaying urban ghettos, the 1960s ended with the structure of legal segregation having been dismantled. The black movement inspired other aggrieved groups—Latinos, Indians, homosexuals, and women—to press their own grievances and claim their own "liberation." Their efforts further enlarged freedom's boundaries and helped to propel the idea of freedom into the most intimate areas of life. Under the leadership of Chief Justice Earl Warren, the Supreme Court gave constitutional recognition to the "rights revolution." By the end of the decade, both the meaning and the boundaries of freedom had expanded enormously.

At the same time, the country became more and more deeply involved in the Vietnam War. In this Cold War conflict, American policymakers viewed

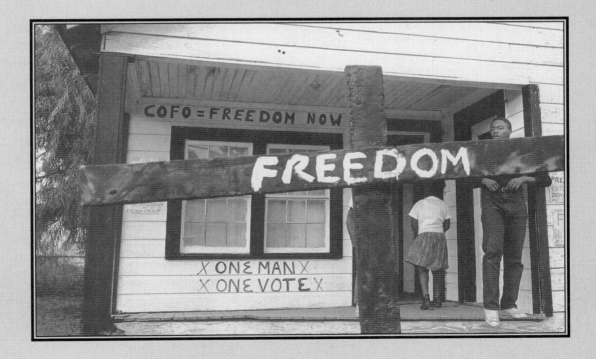

the nationalist movement in Vietnam, led by homegrown communists, as part of a worldwide conspiracy directed from Moscow. As the United States committed hundreds of thousands of soldiers to Vietnam in the mid-1960s, the foreign policy consensus disintegrated. For the first time in American history, college students took the lead in radical protest, organizing massive protests against the war. Political disaffection helped to spawn the counter-culture, a youth rebellion against prevailing middle-class mores. Having brought twentieth-century liberalism to its high point with his Great Society programs that sought to uplift the poor, encourage the arts, and provide medical care to the aged and needy, President Lyndon B. Johnson saw his party split over the war and his public support disintegrate.

Known as a time of radical protest, the 1960s also spawned a conservative backlash against the civil rights movement, the sexual revolution, public disorder, and the expansion of federal power. During the 1970s and 1980s, businessmen, antigovernment activists, a Christian Right that sought to restore what it considered to be traditional moral values, and Cold Warriors who desired a reinvigorated anticommunist crusade came together in an increasingly powerful conservative coalition. Their rise to power was hastened by the end of the postwar economic boom in 1973 and the inability of President Jimmy Carter to address the slump effectively. In 1980, conservative Ronald Reagan was elected president, ushering in the Reagan Revolution.

Reagan drastically increased military spending, cut funding for some social programs, reduced taxes, and attacked labor unions. Like Franklin D. Roosevelt, he consciously sought to redefine the meaning of freedom, associating it with anticommunism, free enterprise, and reduced government intervention in the economy. Although he put into effect conservative economic policies, Reagan failed to halt the rights revolution that had begun in the 1960s. Throughout the 1980s and 1990s, many conservatives lamented the fact that fewer and fewer women were embracing the traditional role of homemaker and that gays were gaining more and more

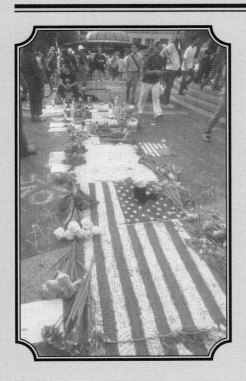

recognition of their rights. Although conservatives launched a furious campaign to overturn the Supreme Court's 1973 decision legalizing abortion, they failed to achieve success. Moreover, thanks to a 1965 law that ended the national-origins quotas for immigrants, newcomers from Asia and Latin America poured into the United States, setting off political battles over the country's increasingly visible racial and ethnic diversity.

The abrupt end of the Cold War between 1989 and 1991 left the United States as the world's lone superpower. This reinforced prevailing American understandings of freedom, emphasizing political democracy, free markets, and unrestrained individual choice in personal matters. During the 1990s, Americans became increasingly aware of the process of "globalization"—the international flow of people, investment, goods, and information across national boundaries. Some welcomed it as an expansion of economic freedom. Others worried that manufacturing jobs were leaving the United States for low-wage areas abroad and that crucial decisions affecting people's day-to-day lives were being made by institutions like the World Bank and World Trade Organization, over which no democratic control existed.

Events at the dawn of the twenty-first century revealed the extent and limitations of American power. The attacks of September 11, 2001, which killed some 3,000 persons, highlighted the nation's vulnerability at a time when terrorists, like goods and money, seemed able to cross national boundaries with ease. In response, President George W. Bush committed the United States to a "war on terrorism," a war without easily definable enemies, a predictable timetable, or a clear definition of victory. The federal government claimed the power to arrest persons suspected of involvement with terrorism, primarily individuals of Middle Eastern origin, without charge and to hold them indefinitely. The 2003 Iraq War, launched by the United States and Great Britain over the opposition of most members of the United Nations, suggested that in the post–Cold War world, America no longer needed to build alliances or concern itself with world opinion. Although the invasion successfully overthrew the Iraqi dictator Sadaam Hussein, an anti-American insurgency soon developed, along with strife between Iraq's Shiite and Sunni Muslims. By the end of 2006, the United States was bogged down in a seemingly interminable war, which was soon becoming increasingly unpopular at home.

These events raised anew vital questions already debated many times in the country's history. What is the balance between civil liberties and security in times of crisis? What are the economic conditions of freedom? Should the country consider itself a democracy or an empire? Should certain groups have their rights diminished because of their racial or ethnic origins? The answers to these questions would go a long way toward defining the meaning and boundaries of American freedom in the twenty-first century.

Chapter 24

An Affluent Society, 1953–1960

Andy Warhol's 1962 painting Green Coca-Cola Bottles *uses one of the most famous international symbols of American consumerism both to celebrate and to question the sterile uniformity of 1950s consumer culture.*

FOCUS QUESTIONS

- What were the main characteristics of the affluent society of the 1950s?

- In what ways was the 1950s a period of political consolidation?

- What were the origins of the civil rights movement?

- What was the significance of the presidential election of 1960?

In 1958, during a "thaw" in the Cold War, the United States and the Soviet Union agreed to exchange national exhibitions in order to allow citizens of each "superpower" to become acquainted with life in the other. The Soviet Exhibition, unveiled in New York City in June 1959, featured factory machinery, scientific advances, and other illustrations of how communism had modernized a backward country. The following month, the American National Exhibition opened in Moscow. A showcase of consumer goods and leisure equipment, complete with stereo sets, a movie theater, home appliances, and twenty-two different cars, the exhibit, *Newsweek* observed, hoped to demonstrate the superiority of "modern capitalism with its ideology of political and economic freedom." Yet the exhibit's real message was not freedom but consumption—or, to be more precise, the equating of the two.

When Vice President Richard Nixon prepared for his trip to Moscow to launch the exhibition, a former ambassador to Russia urged him to emphasize American values: "We are idealists; they are materialists." But the events of the opening day seemed to reverse these roles. Nixon devoted his address, entitled "What Freedom Means to Us," not to freedom of expression or differing forms of government, but to the "extraordinarily high standard of living" in the United States, with its 56 million cars and 50 million television sets. The United States, he declared, had achieved what Soviets could only dream of—"prosperity for all in a classless society."

Vice President Richard Nixon and Soviet premier Nikita Khrushchev during the "kitchen debate," a discussion, among other things, of the meaning of freedom, which took place at the 1959 American National Exposition in Moscow.

The Moscow exhibition became the site of a classic Cold War confrontation over the meaning of freedom—the "kitchen debate" between Nixon and Soviet premier Nikita Khrushchev. Twice during the first day Nixon and Khrushchev engaged in unscripted debate about the merits of capitalism and communism. The first took place in the kitchen of a model suburban ranch house, the second in a futuristic "miracle kitchen" complete with a mobile robot that swept the floors. Supposedly the home of an average steelworker, the ranch house was the exhibition's centerpiece. It represented, Nixon declared, the mass enjoyment of American freedom within a suburban setting—freedom of choice among products, colors, styles, and prices. It also implied a particular role for women. Throughout his exchanges with Khrushchev, Nixon used the words "women" and "housewives" interchangeably. Pointing to the automatic floor sweeper, the vice president remarked that in the United States "you don't need a wife."

Nixon's decision to make a stand for American values in the setting of a suburban kitchen was a brilliant stroke. Nixon recognized that "soft power"—the penetration across the globe of American goods and popular culture—was an even more potent form of influence than military might. Indeed, his stance reflected the triumph during the 1950s of a conception of freedom centered on economic abundance and consumer choice within the context of traditional family life—a vision that seemed to offer far more opportunities for the "pursuit of happiness" to men than women. In reply, Khrushchev ridiculed consumer culture and the American obsession with household gadgets. "Don't you have a machine," he quipped, "that puts food in the mouth and pushes it down?" Many of the items on display, he continued, served "no useful purpose." Yet, in a sense, the Soviet leader conceded the debate when he predicted—quite incorrectly—that within seven years his country would surpass the United States in the production of consumer goods. For if material abundance was a battleground in the Cold War, American victory was certain.

THE GOLDEN AGE

The end of World War II was followed by what one scholar has called the "golden age" of capitalism, a period of economic expansion, stable prices, low unemployment, and rising standards of living that continued until 1973. Between 1946 and 1960, the American gross national product more than doubled and much of the benefit flowed to ordinary citizens in rising wages. In every measurable way—diet, housing, income, education, recreation—most Americans lived better than their parents and grandparents had. By 1960, an estimated 60 percent of Americans enjoyed what the government defined as a middle-class standard of living. The official poverty

A portrait of affluence: In this photograph by Alex Henderson, Steve Czakalinski, an employee of DuPont, poses with his family and the food they consume in a single year.

rate, 30 percent of all families in 1950, had declined to 22 percent a decade later (still, to be sure, representing more than one in five Americans).

Numerous innovations came into widespread use in these years, transforming Americans' daily lives. They included television, home air conditioning, automatic dishwashers, inexpensive long-distance telephone calls, and jet air travel. Services like electricity, central heating, and indoor plumbing that within living memory had been enjoyed only by the rich and solidly middle class now became features of common life.

A CHANGING ECONOMY

Despite the economic recovery of western Europe and Japan after World War II, the United States remained the world's predominant industrial power. Major industries like steel, automobiles, and aircraft dominated the domestic and world markets for their products. Like other wars, the Cold War fueled industrial production and promoted a redistribution of the nation's population and economic resources. The West, especially the Seattle area, southern California, and the Rocky Mountain states, benefited enormously from government contracts for aircraft, guided missiles, and radar systems. The South became the home of numerous military bases and government-funded shipyards. Growth in the construction of aircraft engines and submarines counterbalanced the decline of New England's old textile and machinery industries, many of which relocated in the South to take advantage of low-cost nonunion labor.

In retrospect, the 1950s appear as the last decade of the industrial age in the United States. Since then, the American economy has shifted rapidly toward services, education, information, finance, and entertainment, while employment in manufacturing has declined. Even during the 1950s, the number of factory laborers fell slightly while clerical workers grew by nearly 25 percent and salaried employees in large corporate enterprises rose by 60 percent. Unions' very success in raising wages inspired employers to mechanize more and more elements of manufacturing in order to reduce labor costs. In 1956, for the first time in American history, white-collar workers outnumbered blue-collar factory and manual laborers.

The long-term trend toward fewer and larger farms continued. During the 1950s, the farm population fell from 23 million to 15 million, yet agricultural production rose by 50 percent, thanks to more efficient machinery, the application of chemical fertilizers and insecticides, increased use of irrigation to open land to cultivation in the West, and the development of new crop strains. The decade witnessed an acceleration of the transformation of southern life that had begun during World War II. New tractors and harvesting machinery and a continuing shift from cotton production to less labor-intensive soybean and poultry raising reduced the need for farm workers. More than 3 million black and white hired hands and sharecroppers migrated out of the region. The center of gravity of American farming shifted decisively to Texas, Arizona, and especially California. The large corporate farms of California, worked by Latino and Filipino migrant laborers, poured forth an endless supply of fruits and vegetables for the domestic and world markets. Items like oranges and orange juice, once luxuries, became an essential part of the American diet.

Figure 24.1 REAL GROSS DOMESTIC PRODUCT PER CAPITA, 1790–2000

A SUBURBAN NATION

The main engines of economic growth during the 1950s, however, were residential construction and spending on consumer goods. The postwar baby boom (discussed later) and the shift of population from cities to suburbs created an enormous demand for housing, television sets, home appliances, and cars. By 1960, suburban residents of single-family homes outnumbered urban dwellers and those living in rural areas. (Today, they outnumber both combined.)

Levittown, New York, perhaps the nation's most famous suburban community, photographed in 1954. Eventually, home owners would make individualized changes to their houses, so today Levittown looks far less uniform than when it was built.

This aerial view of Westchester, a community in Los Angeles, California, in 1949, illustrates how suburban "sprawl" spread over the landscape in the postwar era.

During the 1950s, the number of houses in the United States doubled, nearly all of them built in the suburbs that sprang up across the landscape. The dream of home ownership, the physical embodiment of hopes for a better life, came within reach of the majority of Americans. William and Alfred Levitt, who shortly after the war built the first Levittown on 1,200 acres of potato fields on Long Island near New York City, became the most famous suburban developers. Levittown's more than 10,000 houses were assembled quickly from prefabricated parts and priced well within the reach of most Americans. Levittown was soon home to 40,000 people. At the same time, suburbs required a new form of shopping center—the mall—to which people drove in their cars. In contrast to traditional mixed-use city centers crowded with pedestrians, malls existed solely for shopping and had virtually no public space.

THE GROWTH OF THE WEST

But it was California that became the most prominent symbol of the postwar suburban boom. Between World War II and 1975, over 30 million Americans moved west of the Mississippi River. One-fifth of the population growth of the 1950s occurred in California alone. In 1963, it surpassed New York to become the nation's most populous state.

Most western growth took place in metropolitan areas, not on farms. But "centerless" western cities like Houston, Phoenix, and Los Angeles differed greatly from traditional urban centers in the East. Rather than consisting of

Ernst Haas's 1969 photograph of Albuquerque, New Mexico, could have been taken in any one of scores of American communities. As cities spread out, "strips," consisting of motels, gas stations, and nationally franchised businesses, became common. Meanwhile, older downtown business sections stagnated.

downtown business districts linked to residential neighborhoods by public transportation, western cities were decentralized clusters of single-family homes and businesses united by a web of highways. The Los Angeles basin, the largest western suburban region, had once had an extensive system of trains, trolleys, and buses. But local governments dismantled these lines after World War II, and the state and federal governments replaced them with freeways for cars and trucks. Suburban growth spilled into farm regions like the San Fernando and San Bernardino Valleys. By one estimate, one-third of southern California's land area (presumably not including mountains and deserts) was paved over with roads and parking lots. Life centered around the car; people drove to and from work and did their shopping at malls reachable only by driving. In other sections of the country as well, shopping shifted to suburban centers, and old downtown business districts stagnated. The spread of suburban homes created millions of new lawns. Today, more land is cultivated in grass than any agricultural crop in the United States.

A family watching television, photographed by Jack Gould in 1948. Television quickly surpassed movies and live theater as the country's major form of entertainment.

A CONSUMER CULTURE

"The consumer is the key to our economy," declared Jack Straus, chairman of the board of Macy's, New York City's leading department store. "Our ability to consume is endless. The luxuries of today are the necessities of tomorrow." The roots of the consumer culture of the 1950s date back to the 1920s and even earlier. But never before had affluence, or consumerism, been so widespread. In a consumer culture, the measure of freedom became the ability to gratify market desires. Modern society, wrote Clark Kerr, president of the University of California, may well have reduced freedom "in the workplace" by subjecting workers to stringent discipline on the job, but it offered a far greater range of "goods and services," and therefore "a greater scope of freedom" in Americans' "personal lives."

In a sense, the 1950s represented the culmination of the long-term trend in which consumerism replaced economic independence and democratic participation as central definitions of American freedom. Attitudes toward debt changed as well. Low interest rates and the spread of credit cards encouraged Americans to borrow money to purchase consumer goods. Americans became comfortable living in never-ending debt, once seen as a loss of economic freedom.

Consumer culture demonstrated the superiority of the American way of life to communism and virtually redefined the nation's historic mission to extend freedom to other countries. From Coca-Cola to Levi's jeans, American consumer goods, once a status symbol for the rich in other countries,

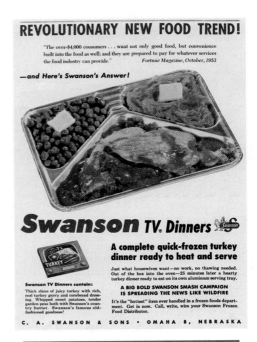

Introduced in 1954, the frozen TV dinner was marketed in a package designed to look like a TV set. Within a year, Swanson had sold 25 million dinners.

Figure 24.2 AVERAGE DAILY TELEVISION VIEWING

1950	1960	1970
4 hrs. 36 mins.	5 hrs. 6 mins.	5 hrs. 54 mins.

were now marketed to customers around the globe. The country's most powerful weapon in the Cold War, insisted a reporter for *House Beautiful* magazine, was "the freedom offered by washing machines and dishwashers, vacuum cleaners, automobiles, and refrigerators."

THE TV WORLD

Thanks to television, images of middle-class life and advertisements for consumer goods blanketed the country. By the end of the 1950s, nearly nine of ten American families owned a TV set. Television replaced newspapers as the most common source of information about public events, and TV watching became the nation's leading leisure activity. Television changed Americans' eating habits (the frozen "TV dinner," heated and eaten while watching a program, went on sale in 1954), and it provided Americans of all regions and backgrounds with a common cultural experience.

With a few exceptions like the Army-McCarthy hearings of 1954, mentioned in the previous chapter, TV avoided controversy and projected a bland image of middle-class life. Popular shows of the early 1950s, such as *The Goldbergs* (with Jewish immigrants as the central characters) and *The Honeymooners* (in which Jackie Gleason played a bus driver), featured working-class families living in urban apartments. By the end of the decade, they had been replaced as the dominant programs by quiz shows, westerns, and comedies set in suburban homes like *Leave It to Beaver* and *The Adventures of Ozzie and Harriet*. Television also became the most effective advertising medium ever invented. To polish their image, large corporations sponsored popular programs—*The General Electric Theater* (hosted for several years by Ronald Reagan), *Alcoa Presents*, and others. TV ads, aimed primarily at middle-class suburban viewers, conveyed images of the good life based on endless consumption.

A NEW FORD

"The concept of freedom," wrote one commentator in 1959, "has become as familiar to us as an old hat or a new Ford." And a new Ford—or Chrysler or Chevrolet—now seemed essential to the enjoyment of freedom's benefits. Along with a home and television set, the car became part of what sociologists called "the standard consumer package" of the 1950s. By 1960, 80 percent of American families owned at least one car, and 14 percent had two or more, nearly all manufactured in the United States. Most were designed to go out of style within a year or two, promoting further purchases.

Auto manufacturers and oil companies vaulted to the top ranks of corporate America. Detroit and its environs were home to immense auto factories. The River Rouge complex had 62,000 employees, Willow Run 42,000. Since the military increasingly needed high-technology goods rather than the trucks and tanks that had rolled off assembly lines in World War II, the region around the Great Lakes lagged in defense contracts. In the long term, the continued funneling of federal dollars from the North and Midwest to the Sunbelt would prove devastating to the old industrial heartland. But during the 1950s, the booming automobile industry, with its demand for steel, rubber, and other products, assured the region's continued prosperity.

The automobile, the pivot on which suburban life turned, transformed the nation's daily life, just as the interstate highway system (discussed later) transformed Americans' travel habits, making possible long-distance vacationing by car and commuting to work from ever-increasing distances. The result was an altered American landscape, leading to the construction of motels, drive-in movie theaters, and roadside eating establishments. The first McDonald's fast food restaurant opened in Illinois in 1954. Within ten years, having been franchised by California businessman Ray Kroc, approximately 700 McDonald's stands had been built, which had sold over 400 million hamburgers. The car symbolized the identification of freedom with individual mobility and private choice. On the road, Americans were constantly reminded in advertising, television shows, and popular songs, they truly enjoyed freedom. They could imagine themselves as modern versions of western pioneers, able to leave behind urban crowds and workplace pressures for the "open road."

Begun in 1956 and completed in 1993, the interstate highway system dramatically altered the American landscape and Americans' daily lives. It made possible more rapid travel by car and stimulated the growth of suburbs along its many routes.

THE INTERSTATE HIGHWAY SYSTEM

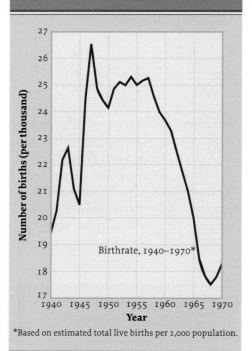

Figure 24.3 THE BABY BOOM AND ITS DECLINE

Birthrate, 1940–1970*

*Based on estimated total live births per 1,000 population.

WOMEN AT WORK AND AT HOME

The emergence of suburbia as a chief site of what was increasingly called the "American way of life" placed pressure on the family—and especially women—to live up to freedom's promise. After 1945, women lost most of the industrial jobs they had performed during the war. As during most of American history, women who worked outside the home remained concentrated in low-salary, nonunion jobs, such as clerical, sales, and service labor, rather than better-paying manufacturing positions. After a sharp postwar drop in female employment, the number of women at work soon began to rise. By 1955, it exceeded the level of World War II. But the nature and aims of women's work had changed. The modern woman, said *Look* magazine, worked part-time, to help support the family's middle-class lifestyle, not to help pull it out of poverty or to pursue personal fulfillment or an independent career. Working women in 1960 earned, on average, only 60 percent of the income of men.

Despite the increasing numbers of wage-earning women, the suburban family's breadwinner was assumed to be male, while the wife remained at home. Films, TV shows, and advertisements portrayed marriage as the most important goal of American women. And during the 1950s, men and women reaffirmed the virtues of family life. They married younger (at an average age of twenty-two for men and twenty for women), divorced less frequently than in the past, and had more children (3.2 per family). A "baby boom" that lasted into the mid-1960s followed the end of the war. At a time of low immigration, the American population rose by nearly 30 million (almost 20 percent) during the 1950s. The increase arose mostly from the large number of births, but it also reflected the fact that Americans now lived longer than in the past, thanks to the wide availability of "miracle drugs" like penicillin that had been developed during World War II to combat bacterial infections.

Jack Gould's 1946 photograph of a hospital maternity ward captures the first year of the postwar baby boom.

The family also became a weapon in the Cold War. The ability of women to remain at home, declared a government official, "separates us from the Communist world," where a high percentage of women worked. To be sure, the family life exalted during the 1950s differed from the patriarchal household of old. It was a modernized relationship, in which both partners reconciled family obligations with personal fulfillment through shared consumption, leisure activities, and sexual pleasure. Thanks to modern conveniences, the personal freedom once associated with work could now be found at home. Frozen and prepared meals, exulted one writer in 1953, offered housewives "freedom from tedium, space, work, and their own inexperience"—quite a change from the Four Freedoms of World War II.

Like other forms of dissent, feminism seemed to have disappeared from American life or was widely dismissed as evidence of mental disorder. Prominent psychologists insisted that the unhappiness of individual women or even the desire to work for wages stemmed from a failure to accept the "maternal instinct." "The independent woman," declared the book *Modern Woman: The Lost Sex* (1947) "is a contradiction in terms." The idea of domestic life as a refuge and of full-time motherhood as a woman's "sphere" had a long history in the United States. But in the postwar suburbs, where family life was physically separated from work, relatives, and the web of social organizations typical of cities, it came close to realization.

Elliott Erwitt's photograph of a young mother in New Rochelle, a suburb of New York City, suggests that life for the suburban woman could be less idyllic than many advertisements implied.

A SEGREGATED LANDSCAPE

For millions of city dwellers, the suburban utopia fulfilled the dream, postponed by depression and war, of home ownership and middle-class incomes. For beneficiaries of postwar prosperity, in the words of a Boston worker who made heroic sacrifices to move his family to the

Advertisers during the 1950s sought to convey the idea that women would find happiness in their roles as suburban homemakers, as in this ad for a Maytag washer and dryer.

suburbs, the home became "the center of freedom." The move to the suburbs also promoted Americanization, cutting residents off from urban ethnic communities and bringing them fully into the world of mass consumption. But if the suburbs offered a new site for the enjoyment of American freedom, they retained at least one familiar characteristic—rigid racial boundaries.

Suburbia has never been as uniform as either its celebrants or its critics claimed. There are upper-class suburbs, working-class suburbs, industrial suburbs, and "suburban" neighborhoods within city limits. But if the class uniformity of suburbia has been exaggerated, its racial uniformity was all too real. As late as the 1990s, nearly 90 percent of suburban whites lived in communities with non-white populations of less than 1 percent—the legacy of decisions by government, real-estate developers, banks, and residents.

During the postwar suburban boom, federal agencies continued to insure mortgages that barred resale of houses to non-whites, thereby financing housing segregation. Even after the Supreme Court in 1948 declared such provisions legally unenforceable, banks and private developers barred non-whites from the suburbs and the government refused to subsidize their mortgages except in segregated enclaves. In 1960, blacks represented less than 3 percent of the population of Chicago's suburbs. The vast new communities built by William Levitt refused to allow blacks, including army veterans, to rent or purchase homes. "If we sell one house to a Negro family," Levitt explained, "then 90 or 95 percent of our white customers will not buy into the community." After a lawsuit, Levitt finally agreed during the 1960s to sell homes to non-whites, but at a pace that can only be described as glacial. In 1990, his Long Island community, with a population of 53,000, included 127 black residents.

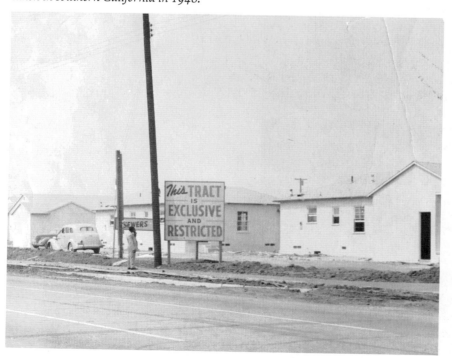

Suburban builders sometimes openly advertised the fact that their communities excluded minorities. This photograph was taken in southern California in 1948.

PUBLIC HOUSING AND URBAN RENEWAL

A Housing Act passed by Congress in 1949 authorized the construction of over 800,000 units of public housing in order to provide a "decent home for every American family." But the law set an extremely low ceiling on the income of residents—a rule demanded by private contractors seeking to avoid competition from the government in building homes for the middle class. This regulation limited housing projects to the very poor. Since white urban and suburban neighborhoods successfully opposed the construction of public housing, it was increasingly confined to segregated neighborhoods in inner cities, reinforcing the concentration of poverty in urban non-white neighborhoods. At the same time, under programs of "urban renewal," cities demolished poor neighborhoods in center cities that occupied potentially valuable real estate. In their place, developers constructed retail centers and all-white middle-income housing complexes, and states built urban public universities like Wayne State in Detroit and the University of Illinois at Chicago. Los Angeles displaced a neighborhood of mixed ethnic groups in Chavez Ravine in order to build a stadium for the Dodgers, whose move in 1958 after sixty-eight years in Brooklyn seemed to symbolize the growing importance of California on the national scene. White residents displaced by urban renewal often moved to the suburbs. Non-whites, unable to do so, found housing in run-down city neighborhoods.

An aerial photograph of Boulevard Houses, a low-income housing project in Brooklyn, illustrates how public housing concentrated poor Americans in structures separated from surrounding neighborhoods.

THE DIVIDED SOCIETY

Suburbanization hardened the racial lines of division in American life. Between 1950 and 1970, about 7 million white Americans left central cities for the suburbs. Meanwhile, nearly 3 million blacks moved from South to North, greatly increasing the size of existing urban ghettos and creating entirely new ones. And half a million Puerto Ricans, mostly small coffee and tobacco farmers and agricultural laborers forced off the land when American sugar companies expanded their landholdings on the island, moved to the mainland. Most ended up in New York City's East Harlem, until then an Italian-American community. Although set in a different part of New York, the popular Broadway musical *West Side Story* dramatized the tensions between Puerto Rican newcomers and longtime urban residents. By the late 1960s, more Puerto Ricans lived in New York City than San Juan, the island's capital.

The process of racial exclusion became self-reinforcing. Non-whites remained concentrated in manual and unskilled jobs, the result of employment discrimination and their virtual exclusion from educational opportunities at public and private universities, including those outside the South. In 1950, only 12 percent of employed blacks held white-collar positions, compared with 45 percent of whites. As the white population and industrial jobs fled the old central cities for suburbs, poorer blacks and Latinos remained trapped in urban ghettos, seen by many whites as places of crime, poverty, and welfare.

Suburbanites, for whom the home represented not only an emblem of freedom but the family's major investment, became increasingly fearful that any non-white presence would lower the quality of life and destroy property values. *Life* magazine quoted a white suburbanite discussing a prospective black neighbor: "he's probably a nice guy, but every time I see him, I see

Students at an East Harlem elementary school in 1947. Most have recently migrated from Puerto Rico to the mainland with their families, although some are probably children of the area's older Italian-American community.

$2,000 drop off the value of my house." Residential segregation was reinforced by "blockbusting"—a tactic of real-estate brokers who circulated exaggerated warnings of an impending influx of non-whites, to persuade alarmed white residents to sell their homes hastily. Because of this practice, some all-white neighborhoods quickly became all-minority enclaves rather than places where members of different races lived side by side.

"Freedom is equal housing too" became a slogan in the campaign for residential integration. But suburban home ownership long remained a white entitlement, with the freedom of non-whites to rent or purchase a home where they desired overridden by the claims of private property and "freedom of association." Even as the old divisions between white ethnic Americans faded in the suburban melting pot, racial barriers in housing, and therefore in public education and jobs, were reinforced.

THE END OF IDEOLOGY

Cold War affluence coexisted with urban decay and racism, the seeds from which protest would soon flower. Yet to many observers in the 1950s it seemed that the ills of American society had been solved. In contrast to the turmoil of the 1930s and the immediate postwar years, the 1950s was a placid time, because of both widespread affluence and the narrowing of the boundaries of permissible political debate. The boom and bust cycles, mass unemployment, and economic insecurity of the past seemed largely to have disappeared. Scholars celebrated the "end of ideology" and the triumph of a democratic, capitalist "consensus" in which all Americans except the maladjusted and fanatics shared the same liberal values of individualism, respect for private property, and belief in equal opportunity. If problems remained, their solutions required technical adjustments, not structural change or aggressive political intervention.

As for religious differences, the source of persistent tension in American history, these were absorbed within a common "Judeo-Christian" heritage, a notion that became central to the cultural and political dialogue of the 1950s. This newly invented tradition sought to demonstrate that Catholics, Protestants, and Jews shared the same history and values and had all contributed to the evolution of American society. In the era of McCarthyism, ideological differences may have been un-American, but group pluralism reigned supreme, with the free exercise of religion yet another way of differentiating the American way of life from life under communism.

The idea of a unified Judeo-Christian tradition overlooked the long history of hostility among religious denominations. But it reflected the decline of anti-Semitism and anti-Catholicism in the wake of World War II, as well as the ongoing secularization of American life. During the 1950s, a majority of Americans—the highest proportion in the nation's history—were affiliated with a church or synagogue. Evangelists like Billy Graham used radio and television to spread the message of Christianity and anti-communism to millions. But as Will Herberg argued in his influential book *Protestant-Catholic-Jew* (1955), religion now had less to do with spiritual activities or sacred values than with personal identity and group assimilation. In an affluent suburban society, Herberg argued, the "common religion" was the American way of life, a marriage of democratic values and economic prosperity—in a phrase, "free enterprise."

SELLING FREE ENTERPRISE

The economic content of Cold War freedom increasingly came to focus on consumer capitalism, or, as it was now universally known, "free enterprise." More than political democracy or freedom of speech, which many allies of the United States outside western Europe lacked, an economic system resting on private ownership united the nations of the Free World. A week before his Truman Doctrine speech, in a major address on economic policy, the president reduced Roosevelt's Four Freedoms to three. Freedom of speech and worship remained, but freedom from want and fear had been replaced by freedom of enterprise, "part and parcel," said Truman, of the American way of life.

Even more than during World War II, what one historian calls the "selling of free enterprise" became a major industry, involving corporate advertising, school programs, newspaper editorials, and civic activities. Convinced that ads represented "a new weapon in the world-wide fight for freedom," the Advertising Council invoked cherished symbols like the Statue of Liberty and the Liberty Bell in the service of "competitive free enterprise." To be sure, the free enterprise campaigners did not agree on every issue. Some businessmen believed that defending free enterprise required rolling back much of the power labor unions had gained in the past decade, dismantling New Deal regulations, and restricting the economic role of government. Representing what might be called business's more liberal wing, the Advertising Council, in its "American Economic System" ad campaign of 1949, reaffirmed labor's right to collective bargaining and the importance of government-business cooperation. Indeed, despite talk of the glories of the free market, government policies played a crucial role in the postwar boom. The rapid expansion of the suburban middle class owed much to federal tax subsidies, mortgage guarantees for home purchases, dam and highway construction, military contracts, and benefits under the GI Bill.

PEOPLE'S CAPITALISM

Free enterprise seemed an odd way of describing an economy in which a few large corporations dominated key sectors. Until well into the twentieth century, most ordinary Americans had been deeply suspicious of big business, associating it with images of robber barons who manipulated politics, suppressed economic competition, and treated their workers unfairly. Americans, wrote David Lilienthal, chairman of the Atomic Energy Commission, must abandon their traditional fear that concentrated economic power endangered "our very liberties." Large-scale production was not only necessary to fighting the Cold War, but it enhanced freedom by multiplying consumer goods. "By freedom," wrote Lilienthal, "I mean essentially *freedom to choose.* . . . It means a maximum range of choice for the consumer when he spends his dollar." By the end of the 1950s, public-opinion surveys revealed that over 80 percent of Americans believed that "our freedom depends on the free enterprise system."

The United States, declared *Fortune* magazine, anticipating Vice President Nixon's remark in the 1959 kitchen debate, had achieved the Marxist goal of a classless society. A sharp jump in the number of individuals investing in Wall Street inspired talk of a new "people's capitalism." In 1953, 4.5 million

TV became the most effective advertising medium in history. Here, an advertisement for Ford, one of the largest American corporations, is being filmed. The background evokes the idea of driving on the open road as a form of individual freedom.

Americans—only slightly more than in 1928—owned shares of stock. By the mid-1960s, the number had grown to 25 million. In the face of widespread abundance, who could deny that the capitalist marketplace embodied individual freedom or that poverty would soon be a thing of the past? "It was American Freedom," proclaimed *Life* magazine, "by which and through which this amazing achievement of wealth and power was fashioned."

THE LIBERTARIAN CONSERVATIVES

During the 1950s, a group of thinkers began the task of reviving conservatism and reclaiming the idea of freedom from liberals. Although largely ignored outside their own immediate circle, they developed ideas that would define conservative thought for the next half-century. One was opposition to a strong national government, an outlook that had been given new political life in conservatives' bitter reaction against the New Deal. To these "libertarian" conservatives, freedom meant individual autonomy, limited government, and unregulated capitalism.

These ideas had great appeal to conservative entrepreneurs, especially in the rapidly growing South and West. Many businessmen who desired to pursue their economic fortunes free of government regulation, high taxes, and labor unions found intellectual reinforcement in the writings of the young economist Milton Friedman. In 1962, Friedman published *Capitalism and Freedom*, which identified the free market as the necessary foundation for individual liberty. This was not an uncommon idea during the Cold War, but Friedman pushed it to extreme conclusions. He called for turning over to the private sector virtually all government functions and the repeal of minimum wage laws, the graduated income tax, and the Social Security system. Friedman extended the idea of unrestricted free choice into virtually every realm of life. Government, he insisted, should seek to regulate neither the economy nor individual conduct.

THE NEW CONSERVATISM

Friedman was indirectly criticizing not only liberalism but also the "new conservatism," a second strand of thought that became increasingly prominent in the 1950s. Convinced that the Free World needed to arm itself morally and intellectually, not just militarily, for the battle against communism, "new conservatives" like writers Russell Kirk and Richard Weaver insisted that toleration of difference—a central belief of modern liberalism—offered no substitute for the search for absolute truth. Weaver's book, *Ideas Have Consequences* (1948), a rambling philosophical treatise that surprisingly became the most influential statement of this new traditionalism, warned that the West was suffering from moral decay and called for a return to a civilization based on values grounded in the Christian tradition and in timeless notions of good and evil.

The "new conservatives" understood freedom as first and foremost a moral condition. It required a decision by independent men and women to lead virtuous lives, or governmental action to force them to do so. Although they wanted government expelled from the economy, new conservatives trusted it to regulate personal behavior, to restore a Christian morality they saw as growing weaker and weaker in American society.

Here lay the origins of a division in conservative ranks that would persist into the twenty-first century. Unrestrained individual choice and moral virtue are radically different starting points from which to discuss freedom. Was the purpose of conservatism, one writer wondered, to create the "free man" or the "good man"? Libertarian conservatives spoke the language of progress and personal autonomy; the "new conservatives" emphasized tradition, community, and moral commitment. The former believed that too many barriers existed to the pursuit of individual liberty. The latter condemned an excess of individualism and a breakdown of common values.

Fortunately for conservatives, political unity often depends less on intellectual coherence than on the existence of a common foe. And two powerful enemies became focal points for the conservative revival—the Soviet Union abroad and the federal government at home. Anti-communism, however, did not clearly distinguish conservatives from liberals, who also supported the Cold War. What made conservatism distinct was its antagonism to "big government" in America, at least so long as it was controlled by liberals who, conservatives believed, tolerated or encouraged immorality. Republican control of the presidency did not lessen conservatives' hostility to the federal government, partly because they did not consider President Eisenhower one of their own.

THE EISENHOWER ERA

IKE AND NIXON

Dwight D. Eisenhower, or "Ike," as he was affectionately called, emerged from World War II as the military leader with the greatest political appeal, partly because his public image of fatherly warmth set him apart from other successful generals like the arrogant Douglas MacArthur. Eisenhower's party affiliation was unknown. In 1948, he voted for Truman, and

Dwight D. Eisenhower's popularity was evident at this appearance in Baltimore during the 1952 presidential campaign.

he accepted Truman's invitation to return to Europe as Supreme Commander of NATO forces. Both parties wanted him as their candidate in 1952. But Eisenhower became convinced that Senator Robert A. Taft of Ohio, a leading contender for the Republican nomination, would lead the United States back toward isolationism. Eisenhower entered the contest and won the Republican nomination.

As his running mate, Eisenhower chose Richard Nixon of California, a World War II veteran who had made a name for himself by vigorous anticommunism. In his first campaign for Congress, in 1946, Nixon attacked his opponent as an advocate of "state socialism." He gained greater fame by his pursuit of Alger Hiss while a member of the House Un-American Activities Committee. Nixon won election to the U.S. Senate in 1950 in a campaign in which he suggested that the Democratic candidate, Congresswoman Helen Gahagan Douglas, had communist sympathies.

These tactics gave Nixon a lifelong reputation for opportunism and dishonesty. But Nixon was also a shrewd politician, who pioneered efforts to transform the Republican Party's image from defender of business to champion of the "forgotten man"—the hardworking citizen burdened by heavy taxation and unresponsive government bureaucracies. "Freedom for the individual, for private enterprise," he insisted, had made America great. In using populist language to promote free market economics, Nixon helped to lay the foundation for the triumph of conservatism a generation later.

THE 1952 CAMPAIGN

Almost as soon as he won the vice-presidential nomination, Nixon ran into trouble over press reports that wealthy Californians had created a private fund for his family. Eisenhower considered dropping him from the ticket. But in an emotional nationally televised thirty-minute address in which he drew attention to his ordinary upbringing, war service, and close-knit family, Nixon denied the accusations. The "Checkers speech," named after the family dog—the one gift Nixon acknowledged receiving, but insisted he would not return—rescued his political career. It illustrated how television was beginning to transform politics by allowing candidates to bring a carefully crafted image directly into Americans' living rooms. The 1952 campaign became the first to make extensive use of TV ads. Parties, one observer complained, were "selling the president like toothpaste."

More important to the election's outcome, however, was Eisenhower's popularity (invoked in the Republican campaign slogan "I Like Ike") and public weariness with the Korean War. Ike's pledge to "go to Korea" in search of peace signaled his intention to bring the conflict to an end. He won a resounding victory over the Democratic candidate, Adlai Stevenson. Four years later, Eisenhower again defeated Stevenson, by an even wider margin. His popularity, however, did not extend to his party. Republicans won a razor-thin majority in Congress in 1952, but Democrats regained control in 1954 and retained it for the rest of the decade. In 1956, Eisenhower became the first president to be elected without his party controlling either house of Congress.

During the 1950s, voters at home and abroad seemed to find reassurance in selecting familiar, elderly leaders to govern them. At age sixty-two, Eisenhower was one of the oldest men ever elected president. But he seemed positively youthful compared with Winston Churchill, who returned to office as prime minister of Great Britain at age seventy-seven, Charles DeGaulle, who assumed the presidency of France at sixty-eight, and Konrad Adenauer, who served as chancellor of West Germany from age seventy-three until well into his eighties. In retrospect, Eisenhower's presidency seems almost uneventful, at least in domestic affairs—an interlude between the bitter party battles of the Truman administration and the social upheavals of the 1960s.

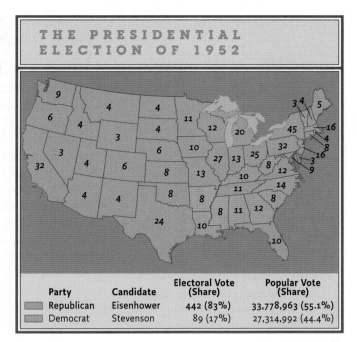

THE PRESIDENTIAL ELECTION OF 1952

Party	Candidate	Electoral Vote (Share)	Popular Vote (Share)
Republican	Eisenhower	442 (83%)	33,778,963 (55.1%)
Democrat	Stevenson	89 (17%)	27,314,992 (44.4%)

MODERN REPUBLICANISM

With a Republican serving as president for the first time in twenty years, the tone in Washington changed. Wealthy businessmen dominated Eisenhower's cabinet. Defense Secretary Charles Wilson, the former president of General Motors, made the widely publicized statement: "What is good for the country is good for General Motors, and vice versa." A champion of the business community and a fiscal conservative, Ike worked to scale back government spending, including the military budget. But while right-wing Republicans saw his victory as an invitation to roll back the New Deal, Eisenhower realized that such a course would be disastrous. "Should any political party attempt to abolish Social Security, unemployment insurance, and eliminate labor laws and farm programs," he declared, "you would not hear of that party again in our political history."

Eisenhower called his domestic agenda Modern Republicanism. It aimed to sever his party's identification in the minds of many Americans with Herbert Hoover, the Great Depression, and indifference to the economic conditions of ordinary citizens. The core New Deal programs not only remained in place, but expanded. In 1955, millions of agricultural workers became eligible for the first time for Social Security. Nor did Ike reduce the size and scope of government. Despite the use of "free enterprise" as a weapon in the Cold War, the idea of a "mixed economy" in which the government played a major role in planning economic activity was widely accepted throughout the Western world. America's European allies like Britain and France expanded their welfare states and nationalized

"Do you call C-minus catching up with Russia?" Alan Dunn's cartoon for the New Yorker *magazine comments on how Soviet success in launching an artificial earth satellite spurred a focus on improving scientific education in the United States.*

key industries like steel, shipbuilding, and transportation (that is, the government bought them from private owners and operated and subsidized them).

The United States had a more limited welfare state than western Europe and left the main pillars of the economy in private hands. But it too used government spending to promote productivity and boost employment. Eisenhower presided over the largest public-works enterprise in American history, the building of the 41,000-mile interstate highway system. As noted in the previous chapter, Cold War arguments—especially the need to provide rapid exit routes from cities in the event of nuclear war—justified this multibillion-dollar project. But automobile manufacturers, oil companies, suburban builders, and construction unions had very practical reasons for supporting highway construction regardless of any Soviet threat. When the Soviets launched *Sputnik*, the first artificial earth satellite, in 1957, the administration responded with the National Defense Education Act, which for the first time offered direct federal funding to higher education.

All in all, rather than dismantling the New Deal, Eisenhower's modern Republicanism consolidated and legitimized it. By accepting its basic premises, he ensured that its continuation no longer depended on Democratic control of the presidency.

THE SOCIAL CONTRACT

The 1950s also witnessed an easing of the labor conflict of the two previous decades. The passage of the Taft-Hartley Act in 1947 (discussed in the previous chapter) had reduced labor militancy. In 1955, the AFL and CIO merged to form a single organization representing 35 percent of all nonagricultural workers. In leading industries, labor and management hammered out what has been called a new "social contract." Unions signed long-term agreements that left decisions regarding capital investment, plant location, and output in management's hands, and they agreed to try to prevent unauthorized "wildcat" strikes. Employers stopped trying to eliminate existing unions and granted wage increases and fringe benefits such as private pension plans, health insurance, and automatic adjustments to pay to reflect rises in the cost of living.

Unionized workers shared fully in 1950s prosperity. Although the social contract did not apply to the majority of workers, who did not belong to unions, it did bring benefits to those who labored in nonunion jobs. For example, trade unions in the 1950s and 1960s were able to use their political power to win a steady increase in the minimum wage, which was earned mostly by nonunion workers at the bottom of the employment pyramid. But these "spillover effects" were limited. The majority of workers did not enjoy anything close to the wages, benefits, and job security of unionized workers in such industries as automobiles and steel.

Indeed, nonunion employers continued to fight vehemently against labor organization, and groups like the National Association of Manufacturers still viewed unions as an unacceptable infringement on the power of employers. Some firms continued to shift jobs to the less-unionized suburbs and South. By the end of the 1950s, the social contract was weakening. In 1959, the steel industry sought to tighten work rules and limit wage increases in an attempt to boost profits battered by a recession that hit two years earlier. The plan sparked a strike of 500,000 steelworkers, which successfully beat back the proposed changes.

MASSIVE RETALIATION

Soon after he entered office, Eisenhower approved an armistice that ended fighting in Korea. But this failed to ease international tensions. Ike took office at a time when the Cold War had entered an extremely dangerous phase. In 1952, the United States exploded the first hydrogen bomb—a weapon far more powerful than those that had devastated Hiroshima and Nagasaki. The following year, the Soviets matched this achievement. Both sides feverishly developed long-range bombers capable of delivering weapons of mass destruction around the world.

A professional soldier, Ike hated war, which he viewed as a tragic waste. "Every gun that is made," he said in 1953, "every warship launched . . . signifies a theft from those who hunger and are not fed." But his secretary of state, John Foster Dulles, was a grim Cold Warrior. In 1954, Dulles announced an updated version of the doctrine of containment. "Massive retaliation," as it was called, declared that any Soviet attack on an American ally would be countered by a nuclear assault on the Soviet Union itself. In some ways, this reliance on the nuclear threat was a way to enable the budget-conscious Eisenhower to reduce spending on conventional military forces. During his presidency, the size of the armed services fell by nearly half. But the number of American nuclear warheads rose from 1,000 in 1953 to 18,000 in 1960.

Massive retaliation ran the risk that any small conflict, or even a miscalculation, could escalate into a war that would destroy both the United States and the Soviet Union. Critics called the doctrine "brinksmanship," warning of the danger of Dulles's apparent willingness to bring the world to the brink of nuclear war. The reality that all-out war would result in "mutual assured destruction" (or MAD, in military short-hand) did succeed in making both great powers cautious in their direct dealings with one another. But it also inspired widespread fear of impending nuclear war. Government programs encouraging Americans to build bomb shelters in their backyards, and school drills that trained children to hide under their desks in the event of an atomic attack, aimed to convince Americans that nuclear war was survivable. But these measures only increased the atmosphere of fear.

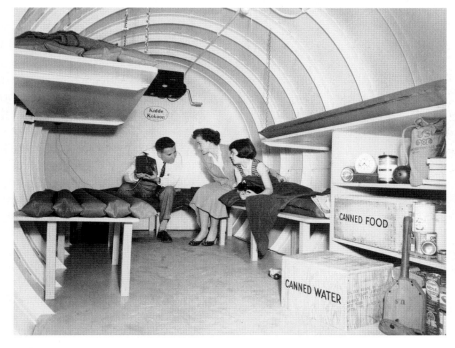

H-Bomb Hideaway, *a photograph taken in 1955, shows a family in their underground bomb shelter, where, the manufacturer claimed, the occupants could survive for five days after a nuclear war.*

IKE AND THE RUSSIANS

In his inaugural address, Eisenhower repeated the familiar Cold War formula: "Freedom is pitted against slavery; lightness against dark." But the end of the Korean War and the death of Stalin, both of which occurred in 1953, convinced him that rather than being blind zealots, the Soviets were reasonable and could be dealt with in conventional diplomatic terms. In 1955, Ike met in Geneva, Switzerland, with Nikita Khrushchev, the new Soviet leader, at the first "summit" conference since Potsdam a decade earlier. The following year, Khrushchev delivered a speech to the Communist Party Congress in Moscow that detailed Stalin's crimes, including purges of political opponents numbering in the millions. The revelations created a crisis of belief among communists throughout the world. In the United States, three-quarters of the remaining Communist Party members abandoned the organization, realizing that they had been blind to the nature of Stalin's rule.

Khrushchev's call in the same 1956 speech for "peaceful coexistence" with the United States raised the possibility of an easing of the Cold War. The "thaw" was abruptly shaken that fall, however, when Soviet troops put down an anticommunist uprising in Hungary. Many conservative Republicans had urged eastern Europeans to resist communist rule, and Secretary of State Dulles himself had declared "liberation," rather than containment, to be the goal of American policy. But Eisenhower refused to extend aid to the Hungarian rebels, an indication that he believed it impossible to "roll back" Soviet domination of eastern Europe.

In 1958, the two superpowers agreed to a voluntary halt to the testing of nuclear weapons. The pause lasted until 1961. It had been demanded by the National Committee for a Sane Nuclear Policy, which publicized the danger to public health posed by radioactive fallout from nuclear tests. In 1959, Khrushchev toured the United States and had a friendly meeting with Eisenhower at Camp David. But the spirit of cooperation ended abruptly in 1960, when the Soviets shot down an American U-2 spy plane over their territory. Eisenhower first denied that the plane had been involved in espionage and refused to apologize even after the Russians produced the captured pilot. The incident torpedoed another planned summit meeting.

THE EMERGENCE OF THE THIRD WORLD

Even as Europe, where the Cold War began, settled into what appeared to be a permanent division between a communist East and a capitalist West, an intense rivalry, which sometimes took a military form, persisted in what came to be called the Third World. The term was invented to describe developing countries aligned with neither of the two Cold War powers and desirous of finding their own model of development between Soviet centralized economic planning and free market capitalism. The Bandung Conference, which brought leaders of twenty-nine Asian and African nations together in Indonesia in 1955, seemed to announce the emergence of a new force in global affairs, representing a majority of the world's population. But none of these countries could avoid being strongly affected by the political, military, and economic contest of the Cold War.

The post–World War II era witnessed the crumbling of European empires. The "winds of change," said British prime minister Harold Macmillan, were sweeping Africa and Asia. Decolonization began when India and Pakistan (the latter carved out of India to give Muslims their own nation) achieved independence in 1947. Ten years later, Britain's Gold

Coast colony in West Africa emerged as the independent nation of Ghana. Other new nations—including Indonesia, Malaysia, Nigeria, Kenya, Tanzania—soon followed. In 1975, Portugal, which five centuries earlier had created the first modern overseas empire, granted independence to its African colonies of Mozambique and Angola.

Decolonization presented the United States with a complex set of choices. It created power vacuums in the former colonies into which, Americans feared, communists would move. The Soviet Union strongly supported the dissolution of Europe's overseas empires, and communists participated in movements for colonial independence. Many noncommunist leaders, like Jawaharlal Nehru of India and Kwame Nkrumah of Ghana, saw socialism of one sort or another as the best route to achieving economic independence and narrowing the social inequalities fostered by imperialism. Most of the new Third World nations resisted alignment with either major power bloc, hoping to remain neutral in the Cold War. On the other hand, many nationalists sincerely admired the United States and, indeed, saw the American struggle for independence as a model for their own struggles. Ho Chi Minh, the communist leader of the Vietnamese movement against rule by France, modeled his 1945 proclamation of nationhood on the American Declaration of Independence. He even requested that President Truman establish a protectorate over Vietnam to guarantee its independence.

THE COLD WAR IN THE THIRD WORLD

By the end of the 1950s, the division of Europe appeared to be set in stone. Much of the focus of the Cold War shifted to the Third World. The policy of containment easily slid over into opposition to any government, whether communist or not, that seemed to threaten American strategic or economic interests. Jacobo Arbenz Guzmán in Guatemala and Mohammed Mossadegh in Iran were elected, homegrown nationalists, not agents of Moscow. But they were determined to reduce foreign corporations' control over their countries' economies. Arbenz embarked on a sweeping land-reform policy that threatened the domination of Guatemala's economy by the American-owned United Fruit Company. Mossadegh nationalized the Anglo-Iranian Oil Company, whose refinery in Iran was Britain's largest remaining overseas asset. Their foes quickly branded both as communists. In 1953 and 1954, the Central Intelligence Agency organized the ouster of both governments—a clear violation of the UN Charter, which barred a member state from taking military action against another except in self-defense.

In 1956, Israel, France, and Britain—without prior consultation with the United States—invaded Egypt after the

The military junta installed in Guatemala by the CIA in 1954, entering Guatemala City in a Jeep driven by CIA agent Carlos Castillo Armas. Although hailed by the Eisenhower administration as a triumph for freedom, the new government suppressed democracy in Guatemala and embarked on a murderous campaign to stamp out opposition.

"Save the Holy Places": Herbert Block's 1948 cartoon suggests that American diplomacy in the Middle East was primarily concerned with access to oil.

country's nationalist leader, Gamal Abdel Nasser, nationalized the Suez Canal, jointly owned by Britain and France. A furious Eisenhower forced them to abandon the invasion. After the Suez fiasco, the United States moved to replace Britain as the dominant Western power in the Middle East, and American companies increasingly dominated the region's oil fields. In 1957, Eisenhower extended the principle of containment to the region, issuing the Eisenhower Doctrine, which pledged the United States to defend Middle Eastern governments threatened by communism or Arab nationalism. A year later, Ike dispatched 5,000 American troops to Lebanon to protect a government dominated by pro-Western Christians against Nasser's effort to bring all Arab states into a single regime under his rule.

ORIGINS OF THE VIETNAM WAR

In Vietnam, the expulsion of the Japanese in 1945 led not to independence but to a French military effort to preserve their Asian empire, which dated to the late nineteenth century, against Ho Chi Minh's nationalist forces. Anticommunism led the United States into deeper and deeper involvement. Following a policy initiated by Truman, the Eisenhower administration funneled billions of dollars in aid to bolster French efforts. By the early 1950s, the United States was paying four-fifths of the cost of the war. Wary of becoming bogged down in another land war in Asia immediately after Korea, however, Ike declined to send in American troops when France requested them to avert defeat in 1954. He also rejected the National Security Council's advice to use nuclear weapons, leaving France no alternative but to agree to Vietnamese independence.

A peace conference in Geneva divided Vietnam temporarily into northern and southern districts, with elections scheduled for 1956 to unify the country. But the staunchly anticommunist southern leader Ngo Dinh Diem, urged on by the United States, refused to hold elections, which would almost certainly have resulted in a victory for Ho Chi Minh's communists. Diem's close ties to wealthy Catholic families—in predominantly Buddhist South Vietnam—and to landlords in a society dominated by small farmers who had been promised land by Ho alienated an increasing number of his subjects. American aid poured into South Vietnam in order to bolster the Diem regime. By the time Eisenhower left office, Diem nevertheless faced a full-scale guerrilla revolt by the communist-led National Liberation Front.

Events in Guatemala, Iran, and Vietnam, considered great successes at the time by American policymakers, cast a long shadow over American foreign relations. Little by little, the United States was becoming accustomed to intervention, both open and secret, in far-flung corners of the world. Despite the Cold War rhetoric of freedom, American leaders seemed more comfortable dealing with reliable military regimes than democratic governments. A series of military governments succeeded Arbenz. They reversed his social reforms and inaugurated three decades of repression in which some 200,000 Guatemalans perished. The shah of Iran replaced Mossadegh and agreed to give British and American oil companies 40 percent of his nation's oil revenues. He remained in office until 1979 as one of the world's most tyrannical rulers, until his overthrow in a revolution led by the fiercely anti-American radical Islamist Ayatollah Khomeini. In Vietnam, the American decision to prop up Diem's regime laid the groundwork for what would soon become the most disastrous military involvement in American history.

MASS SOCIETY AND ITS CRITICS

The fatherly Eisenhower seemed the perfect leader for the placid society of the 1950s. Consensus was the dominant ideal in an era in which McCarthyism had defined criticism of the social and economic order as disloyalty and most Americans located the enjoyment of freedom in private pleasures rather than the public sphere. With the mainstreams of both parties embracing the Cold War, political debate took place within extremely narrow limits. Even *Life* magazine commented that American freedom might be in greater danger from "disuse" than from communist subversion.

Dissenting voices could be heard. Some intellectuals wondered whether the celebration of affluence and the either-or mentality of the Cold War obscured the extent to which the United States itself fell short of the ideal of freedom. In 1957, political scientist Hans J. Morgenthau noted that free enterprise had created "new accumulations" of power, "as dangerous to the freedom of the individual as the power of the government had ever been." More radical in pointing to the problem of unequal power in American society, the sociologist C. Wright Mills challenged the self-satisfied vision of democratic pluralism that dominated mainstream social science in the 1950s. Mills wrote of a "power elite"—an interlocking directorate of corporate leaders, politicians, and military men whose domination of government and society had made political democracy obsolete. Freedom, Mills insisted, meant more than "the chance to do as one pleases." It rested on the ability "to formulate the available choices," and this most Americans were effectively denied.

Even as the government and media portrayed the United States as a beacon of liberty locked in a titanic struggle with its opposite, one strand of social analysis in the 1950s contended that Americans did not enjoy genuine freedom. These critics identified as the culprit not the unequal structure of power criticized by Mills, but the modern age itself, with its psychological and cultural discontents. Modern mass society, some writers worried, inevitably produced loneliness and anxiety, causing mankind to yearn for stability and authority, not freedom. In *The Lonely Crowd* (1950), the decade's most influential work of social analysis, the sociologist David Riesman described Americans as "other-directed" conformists who lacked the inner resources to lead truly independent lives. Other social critics charged that corporate bureaucracies had transformed employees into "organization men" incapable of independent thought.

Some commentators feared that the Russians had demonstrated a greater ability to sacrifice for common public goals than Americans. What kind of nation, the economist John Kenneth Galbraith asked in *The Affluent Society* (1958), neglected investment in schools, parks, and public services, while producing ever more goods to fulfill desires created by advertising? Was the spectacle of millions of educated middle-class women seeking happiness in suburban dream houses a reason for cele-

Commuters returning from work in downtown Chicago, leaving the railroad station at suburban Park Forest, Illinois, in 1953. Social critics of the 1950s claimed that Americans had become "organization men," too conformist to lead independent lives.

bration or a waste of precious "woman power" at a time when the Soviets trumpeted the accomplishments of their female scientists, physicians, and engineers? Books like Galbraith's, along with William Whyte's *The Organization Man* (1956) and Vance Packard's *The Hidden Persuaders* (1957), which criticized the monotony of modern work, the emptiness of suburban life, and the pervasive influence of advertising, created the vocabulary for an assault on the nation's social values that lay just over the horizon. In the 1950s, however, while criticism of mass society became a minor industry among intellectuals, it failed to dent widespread complacency about the American way.

REBELS WITHOUT A CAUSE

The social critics did not offer a political alternative or have any real impact on the parties or government. Nor did other stirrings of dissent. With teenagers a growing part of the population thanks to the baby boom, the emergence of a popular culture geared to the emerging youth market suggested that significant generational tensions lay beneath the bland surface of 1950s life. J. D. Salinger's 1951 novel *Catcher in the Rye* and the 1955 films *Blackboard Jungle* and *Rebel without a Cause* (the latter starring James Dean as an aimlessly rebellious youth) highlighted the alienation of at least some young people from the world of adult respectability. These works helped to spur a mid-1950s panic about "juvenile delinquency." *Time* magazine devoted a cover story to "Teenagers on the Rampage," and a Senate committee held hearings in 1954 on whether violent comic books caused criminal behavior among young people. (One witness even criticized Superman comics for arousing violent emotions among its readers.) To head off federal regulation, publishers—like movie producers in the 1920s—adopted a code of conduct for their industry that strictly limited the portrayal of crime and violence in comic books.

Cultural life during the 1950s seemed far more daring than politics. Indeed, many adults found the emergence of a mass-marketed teenage culture that rejected middle-class norms more alarming than the actual increase in juvenile arrests. Teenagers wore leather jackets and danced to rock-and-roll music that brought the hard-driving rhythms and sexually provocative movements of black musicians and dancers to enthusiastic young white audiences. They made Elvis Presley, a rock-and-roll singer with an openly sexual performance style, an immensely popular entertainment celebrity.

Challenges of various kinds also arose to the family-centered image of personal fulfillment. *Playboy* magazine, which began publication in 1953, reached a circulation of over 1 million copies per

Rebels without a cause. Teenage members of a youth gang, photographed at Coney Island, Brooklyn, in the late 1950s.

month by 1960. It extended the consumer culture into the most intimate realms of life, offering men a fantasy world of sexual gratification outside the family's confines. Although considered sick or deviant by the larger society and subject to constant police harassment, gay men and lesbians created their own subcultures in major cities.

THE BEATS

In New York City and San Francisco, as well as college towns like Madison, Wisconsin, and Ann Arbor, Michigan, the Beats, a small group of poets and writers, railed against mainstream culture. The novelist Jack Kerouac coined the term "beat"—a play on "beaten down" and "beatified" (or saint-like). His *On the Road*, written in the early 1950s but not published until 1957, recounted in a seemingly spontaneous rush of sights, sounds, and images its main character's aimless wanderings across the American land-scape. The book became a bible for a generation of young people who rejected the era's middle-class culture but had little to put in its place.

"I saw the best minds of my generation destroyed by madness, starving hysterical naked," wrote the Beat poet Allen Ginsberg in *Howl* (1955), a brilliant protest against materialism and conformism written while the author was under the influence of hallucinogenic drugs. Ginsberg became nationally known when San Francisco police in 1956 confiscated his book and arrested bookstore owners for selling an obscene work. (A judge later overturned the ban on the grounds that *Howl* possessed redeeming social value.) Rejecting the work ethic, the "desperate materialism" of the suburban middle class, and the militarization of American life by the Cold War, the Beats celebrated impulsive action, immediate pleasure (often enhanced by drugs), and sexual experimentation. Despite Cold War slogans, they insisted, personal and political repression, not freedom, were the hallmarks of American society.

Elvis Presley's gyrating hips appealed to teenagers but alarmed many adults during the 1950s.

A Beat coffeehouse in San Francisco, photographed in 1958, where poets, artists, and others who rejected 1950s mainstream culture gathered.

VOICES OF FREEDOM

FROM DAVID E. LILIENTHAL,
Big Business: A New Era (1952)

While some Americans worried that the domination of important sectors of the economy by a few large corporations threatened economic freedom, others saw "bigness" as an inevitable characteristic of the modern economy. One of the latter was David Lilienthal, chairman of the Atomic Energy Commission.

I conceive the purpose of American economic society not as the production and consumption of so many billions of units of steel, copper, automobiles, refrigerators. The purpose of our economic society and system is to promote freedom for the individual, as one prime essential of happiness and human fulfillment. By freedom, I mean essentially *freedom to choose* to the maximum degree possible. . . .

Freedom of choice in economic matters means freedom to choose between competing ideas or services or goods. It means the maximum freedom to choose one job or one profession or one line of business as against some other. It means a maximum range of choice for the consumer when he spends his dollar. It means a maximum possible area of choice for the man who has saved up capital to invest.

These are economic choices. They are, however, more than economic or business acts. They are the mark of men who are free. . . . It is the vital role of Big Business in furthering this freedom of choice. . . . And yet we still carry around our inherited conviction that Bigness means monopoly, which implies the absence of free choice. . . . I was brought up, like most men and women of my generation, to be suspicious and distrustful of things that are big. My father and his friends, who were small businessmen, spoke with deep apprehension of the trusts and cheered Teddy Roosevelt in his Bull Moose campaign. . . .

[This] economic and political philosophy and emotion . . . badly needs re-examination. It is by the new facts of the fifties in contrast to the essential facts about our country as it was a generation or two ago, that we need to judge whether Bigness should today be penalized or encouraged, feared or promoted.

Such a fundamental re-examination is appropriate, is indeed essential and vital, at a time like the present. In such a period of crisis and strain, of heart-searching and anxiety about basic things, we need to examine such an all-pervasive issue as this. If, by that inexplicable process of general public consensus by which Americans decide fundamental issues, we decide that Bigness is our ally, that its risk and dangers are now manageable and with wisdom can be surmounted, if we conclude to end this contradiction between our enjoyment of the fruits of Bigness and the suspicions we visit upon it, then we can accelerate our progress toward the goals of America in a way that takes one's breath away to contemplate.

FROM MARTIN LUTHER KING JR.,
Speech at Montgomery, Alabama (December 5, 1955)

On the evening of Rosa Parks's arrest for refusing to give up her seat on a Montgomery bus to a white passenger, a mass rally of local African-Americans decided to boycott city buses in protest. In his speech to the gathering, the young Baptist minister Martin Luther King Jr. invoked Christian and American ideals of justice and democracy—themes he would strike again and again during his career as the leading national symbol of the civil rights struggle.

We are here this evening . . . because first and foremost we are American citizens, and we are determined to apply our citizenship to the fullness of its means. We are here also because of our love for democracy. . . . Just the other day . . . one of the finest citizens in Montgomery—not one of the finest Negro citizens but one of the finest citizens in Montgomery—was taken from a bus and carried to jail and arrested because she refused to give her seat to a white person. . . .

Mrs. Rosa Parks is a fine person. And since it had to happen I'm happy that it happened to a person like Mrs. Parks, for nobody can doubt the boundless outreach of her integrity! Nobody can doubt the height of her character, nobody can doubt that depth of her Christian commitment and devotion to the teachings of Jesus. And I'm happy since it had to happen, it happened to a person that nobody can call a disturbing factor in the community. Mrs. Parks is a fine Christian person, unassuming, and yet there is integrity and character there. And just because she refused to get up, she was arrested.

I want to say, that we are not here advocating violence. We have never done that. . . . We believe in the teachings of Jesus. The only weapon that we have in our hands this evening is the weapon of protest. . . . There will be no white persons pulled out of their homes and taken out to some distant road and lynched. . . .

We are not wrong in what we are doing. If we are wrong, then the Supreme Court of this nation is wrong. If we are wrong, the Constitution of the United States is wrong. If we are wrong, God Almighty is wrong. . . . If we are wrong, justice is a lie. . . .

We, the disinherited of this land, we who have been oppressed so long, are tired of going through the long night of captivity. And now we are reaching out for the daybreak of freedom and justice and equality. . . . Right here in Montgomery when the history books are written in the future, somebody will have to say, "There lived a race of people, a *black* people, . . . a people who had the moral courage to stand up for their rights. And thereby they injected a new meaning into the veins of history and of civilization."

===

QUESTIONS

1. How does Lilienthal's definition of freedom reflect the concerns of a consumer society?

2. How do religious convictions shape King's definition of freedom?

3. How do these documents illustrate the contradictions in American society of the 1950s?

THE FREEDOM MOVEMENT

Not until the 1960s would young white rebels find their cause, as the seeds of dissent planted by the social critics and Beats flowered in an outpouring of political activism, new attitudes toward sexuality, and a full-fledged generational rebellion. A more immediate challenge to the complacency of the 1950s arose from the twentieth century's greatest citizens' movement—the black struggle for equality.

ORIGINS OF THE MOVEMENT

Today, with the birthday of Martin Luther King Jr. a national holiday and the struggles of Montgomery, Little Rock, Birmingham, and Selma celebrated as heroic episodes in the history of freedom, it is easy to forget that at the time, the civil rights revolution came as a great surprise. Looking back, its causes seem clear: the destabilization of the racial system during World War II; the mass migration out of the segregated South that made black voters an increasingly important part of the Democratic Party coalition; and the Cold War and rise of independent states in the Third World, both of which made the gap between America's rhetoric and its racial reality an international embarrassment. Yet few predicted the emergence of the southern mass movement for civil rights.

In *An American Dilemma* (1944), Gunnar Myrdal had suggested that the challenge to racial inequality would arise in the North, where blacks had far greater opportunities for political organization than in the South. With blacks' traditional allies on the left decimated by McCarthyism, most union leaders unwilling to challenge racial inequalities within their own ranks, and the NAACP concentrating on court battles, new constituencies and new tactics were sorely needed. The movement found in the southern black church the organizing power for a militant, nonviolent assault on segregation.

The United States in the 1950s was still a segregated, unequal society. Half of the nation's black families lived in poverty. Because of labor contracts that linked promotions and firings to seniority, non-white workers, who had joined the industrial labor force later than whites, lost their jobs first in times of economic downturn. In the South, evidence of Jim Crow abounded—in separate public institutions and the signs "white" and "colored" at entrances to buildings, train carriages, drinking fountains, restrooms, and the like. In the North and West, the law did not require segregation, but custom barred blacks from many colleges, hotels, and restaurants, and from most suburban housing. Las Vegas, Nevada, for example, was as strictly segregated as any southern city. Hotels and casinos did not admit blacks except in the most menial jobs. Lena Horne, Sammy Davis Jr., Louis Armstrong, and other black entertainers played the hotel-casinos on the "strip" but could not stay as guests where they performed.

In 1950, seventeen southern and border states and Washington, D.C., had laws requiring the racial segregation of public schools, and several others permitted local districts to impose it. Around 40 percent of the nation's 28 million schoolchildren studied in legally segregated schools, and millions more attended classes in northern communities where housing patterns and school district lines created de facto segregation—separation in fact if not in law. Few white Americans felt any urgency about confronting racial inequality. "Segregation," the white writer John Egerton later recalled, "didn't restrict me in any way, so it was easy to accept things the way they were, to take my freedom for granted and not worry about anyone else's."

THE LEGAL ASSAULT ON SEGREGATION

With Truman's civil rights initiative having faded and the Eisenhower administration being reluctant to address the issue, it fell to the courts to confront the problem of racial segregation. In the Southwest, the League of United Latin American Citizens (LULAC), the equivalent of the NAACP, challenged restrictive housing, employment discrimination, and the segregation of Latino students. They won an important victory in 1946 in the case of *Mendez v. Westminster*, when the California Supreme Court ordered the schools of Orange County desegregated. In response, the state legislature repealed all school laws requiring racial segregation. The governor who signed the measure, Earl Warren, had presided over the internment of Japanese-Americans during World War II as the state's attorney general. After the war, he became convinced that racial inequality had no place in American life. When Chief Justice Fred Vinson died in 1953, Eisenhower appointed Earl Warren to replace him. Warren would play the key role in deciding *Brown v. Board of Education*, the momentous case that outlawed school segregation.

For years, the NAACP, under the leadership of attorney Thurgood Marshall, had pressed legal challenges to the "separate but equal" doctrine laid down by the Court in 1896 in *Plessy v. Ferguson* (see Chapter 17). At first, the NAACP sought to gain admission to white institutions of higher learning

A segregated school in West Memphis, Arkansas, photographed for Life *magazine in 1949. Education in the South was separate but hardly equal.*

for which no black equivalent existed. In 1938, the Supreme Court ordered the University of Missouri Law School to admit Lloyd Gaines, a black student, because the state had no such school for blacks. Missouri responded by setting up a segregated law school, satisfying the courts. But in 1950, the Supreme Court unanimously ordered Heman Sweatt admitted to the University of Texas Law School even though the state had established a "school" for him in a basement containing three classrooms and no library. There was no way, the Court declared, that this hastily constructed law school could be "equal" to the prestigious all-white institution.

THE *BROWN* CASE

Marshall now launched a frontal assault on segregation itself. He brought the NAACP's support to local cases that had arisen when black parents challenged unfair school policies. To do so required remarkable courage. In Clarendon County, South Carolina, Levi Pearson, a black farmer who brought a lawsuit on behalf of his children, saw his house burned to the ground. The Clarendon case attacked not segregation itself but the unequal funding of schools. The local school board spent $179 per white child and $43 per black, and unlike white pupils, black children attended class in buildings with no running water or indoor toilets and were not provided with buses to transport them to classes. Five such cases from four states and the District of Columbia were combined in a single appeal that reached the Supreme Court late in 1952.

When cases are united, they are listed alphabetically and the first case gives the entire decision its name. In this instance, the first case arose from a state outside the old Confederacy. Oliver Brown went to court because his daughter, a third grader, was forced to walk across dangerous railroad tracks each morning rather than being allowed to attend a nearby school restricted to whites. His lawsuit became *Brown v. Board of Education of Topeka, Kansas.*

Thurgood Marshall decided that the time had come to attack not the unfair applications of the "separate but equal" principle but the doctrine itself. Even with the same funding and facilities, he insisted, segregation was inherently unequal since it stigmatized one group of citizens as unfit to associate with others. Drawing on studies by New York psychologists Kenneth and Mamie Clark, Marshall argued that segregation did lifelong damage to black children, undermining their self-esteem. In its legal brief, the Eisenhower administration did not directly support Marshall's position, but it urged the justices to consider "the problem of racial discrimination . . . in the context of the present world struggle between freedom and tyranny." Other peoples, it noted, "cannot understand how such a practice can exist in a country which professes to be a staunch supporter of freedom, justice, and democracy."

The new chief justice, Earl Warren, managed to create unanimity on a divided Court, some of whose members disliked segregation but feared that a decision to outlaw it would spark widespread violence. On May 17, 1954, Warren himself read aloud the decision, only eleven pages long. Segregation in public education, he concluded, violated the equal protection of the laws guaranteed by the Fourteenth Amendment. "In the field of education, the doctrine of 'separate but equal' has no place. Separate educational facilities are inherently unequal."

The black press hailed the *Brown* decision as a "second Emancipation Proclamation." And like its predecessor it was in many ways a limited document. The decision did not address segregation in institutions other than public schools or ban all racial classifications in the law, such as statutes prohibiting interracial marriage. It did not address the de facto school segregation of the North, which rested on housing patterns rather than state law. It did not order immediate implementation but instead called for hearings as to how segregated schooling should be dismantled. But *Brown* marked the emergence of the "Warren Court" as an active agent of social change. And it inspired a wave of optimism that discrimination would soon disappear. "What a wonderful world of possibilities are unfolded for the children," wrote the black novelist Ralph Ellison.

THE MONTGOMERY BUS BOYCOTT

Brown did not cause the modern civil rights movement, which, as noted in the previous two chapters, began during World War II and continued in cities like New York after the war. But the decision did ensure that when the movement resumed after waning in the early 1950s, it would have the backing of the federal courts. Mass action against Jim Crow soon reappeared. On December 1, 1955, Rosa Parks, a black tailor's assistant who had just completed her day's work in a Montgomery, Alabama, department store, refused to surrender her seat on a city bus to a white rider, as required by local law. Parks's arrest sparked a year-long bus boycott, the beginning of the mass phase of the civil rights movement in the South. Within a decade, the civil rights revolution had overturned the structure of legal segregation and regained the right to vote for black southerners. In 2000, *Time* magazine named Rosa Parks one of the 100 most significant persons of the twentieth century.

Parks is widely remembered today as a "seamstress with tired feet," a symbol of ordinary blacks' determination to resist the daily injustices and indignities of the Jim Crow South. In fact, her life makes clear that the civil rights revolution built on earlier struggles. Parks was a veteran of black politics. During the 1930s, she took part in meetings protesting the conviction of the Scottsboro Boys. She served for many years as secretary to E. D. Nixon, the local leader of the NAACP. In 1943, she tried to register to vote, only to be turned away because she supposedly failed a literacy test. After two more attempts, Parks succeeded in becoming one of the few blacks in Montgomery able to cast a ballot. In 1954, she attended a training session for political activists at the Highlander School in Tennessee, a meeting ground for labor and civil rights radicals.

No one knows exactly why Parks decided not to give up her seat that day. Perhaps it was because an all-white jury in Mississippi had just acquitted the murderers of Emmett Till, a black teenager who had allegedly whistled at a white woman. Jo Ann Robinson, a professor at the all-black Alabama State University, had been calling for a boycott of public transportation since 1954. When news of Parks's arrest spread, hundreds of blacks gathered in a local church and vowed to refuse to ride the buses until accorded equal treatment. For 381 days, despite legal harassment and occasional

The mug shot of Rosa Parks, taken in December 1955 at a Montgomery, Alabama police station after she was arrested for refusing to give up her seat on a city bus to a white passenger.

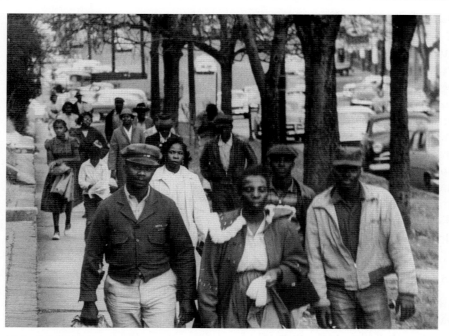

Black residents of Montgomery, Alabama, walking to work during the bus boycott of 1955–1956.

violence, black maids, janitors, teachers, and students walked to their destinations or rode an informal network of taxis. Finally, in November 1956, the Supreme Court ruled segregation in public transportation unconstitutional. The boycott ended in triumph.

THE DAYBREAK OF FREEDOM

The Montgomery bus boycott marked a turning point in postwar American history. It launched the movement for racial justice as a nonviolent crusade based in the black churches of the South. It gained the support of northern liberals and focused unprecedented and unwelcome international attention on the country's racial policies. And it marked the emergence of twenty-six-year-old Martin Luther King Jr., who had recently arrived in Montgomery to become pastor of a Baptist church, as the movement's national symbol. On the night of the first protest meeting, King's call to action electrified the audience: "We, the disinherited of this land, we who have been oppressed so long, are tired of going through the long night of captivity. And now we are reaching out for the daybreak of freedom and justice and equality."

From the beginning, the language of freedom pervaded the black movement. It resonated in the speeches of civil rights leaders and in the hand-lettered placards of the struggle's foot soldiers. On the day of Rosa Parks's court appearance in December 1955, even before the bus boycott had officially been announced, a torn piece of cardboard appeared on a bus shelter in Montgomery's Court Square, advising passengers: "Don't ride the buses today. Don't ride it for freedom." During the summer of 1964, when civil rights activists established "freedom schools" for black children across Mississippi, lessons began with students being asked to define the word. Some gave specific answers ("going to public libraries"), some more abstract ("standing up for your rights"). Some insisted that freedom meant legal equality, others saw it as liberation from years of deference to and fear of whites. "Freedom of the mind," wrote one, was the greatest freedom of all.

For adults as well, freedom had many meanings. It meant enjoying the political rights and economic opportunities taken for granted by whites. It required eradicating historic wrongs such as segregation, disenfranchisement, confinement to low-wage jobs, and the ever-present threat of violence. It meant the right to be served at lunch counters and downtown department stores, central locations in the consumer culture, and to be addressed as "Mr.," "Miss," and "Mrs.," rather than "boy" and "auntie."

THE LEADERSHIP OF KING

In King's soaring oratory, the protesters' understandings of freedom fused into a coherent whole. For the title of his first book, relating the boycott's history, King chose the title *Stride Toward Freedom*. His most celebrated oration, the "I Have a Dream" speech of 1963, began by invoking the unfulfilled promise of emancipation ("one hundred years later, the Negro still is not free") and closed with a cry borrowed from a black spiritual: "Free at last! Free at last! Thank God Almighty, we are free at last!"

A master at appealing to the deep sense of injustice among blacks and to the conscience of white America, King presented the case for black rights in a vocabulary that merged the black experience with that of the nation. Having studied the writings on peaceful civil disobedience of Henry David Thoreau and Mohandas (Mahatma) Gandhi, as well as the nonviolent protests the Congress of Racial Equality had organized in the 1940s, King outlined a philosophy of struggle in which evil must be met with good, hate with Christian love, and violence with peaceful demands for change. "There will be no white persons pulled out of their homes and taken out to some distant road and lynched," he declared in his speech at the launching of the Montgomery bus boycott.

Echoing Christian themes derived from his training in the black church, King's speeches resonated deeply in both black communities and the broader culture. He repeatedly invoked the Bible to preach justice and forgiveness, even toward those "who desire to deprive you of freedom." Like Frederick Douglass before him, King appealed to white America by stressing the protesters' love of country and devotion to national values. The "daybreak of freedom," King made clear, meant a new dawn for the whole of American society. And like W. E. B. Du Bois, he linked the American "color line" with the degradation of non-white peoples overseas. "The great struggle of the Twentieth Century," he declared in a 1956 sermon, "has been between the exploited masses questing for freedom and the colonial powers seeking to maintain their domination." If Africa was gaining its freedom, he asked, why must black America lag behind?

MASSIVE RESISTANCE

Buoyed by success in Montgomery, King in 1956 took the lead in forming the Southern Christian Leadership Conference, a coalition of black ministers and civil rights activists, to press for desegregation. But despite the movement's success in popular mobilization, the fact that Montgomery's city fathers agreed to the boycott's demands only after a Supreme Court ruling indicated that without national backing, local action might not be enough to overturn Jim Crow. The white South's refusal to accept the *Brown* decision reinforced the conviction that black citizens could not gain their constitutional rights without Washington's intervention. This was not immediately forthcoming. When the Supreme Court finally issued its implementation ruling in 1955, the justices declared that desegregation should proceed "with all deliberate speed." This vague formulation unintentionally encouraged a campaign of "massive resistance" that paralyzed civil rights progress in much of the South.

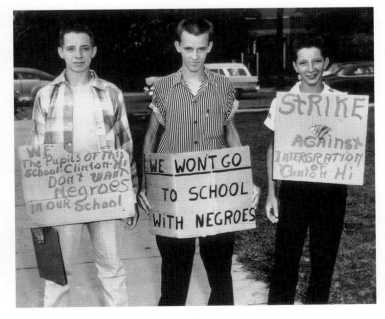

Students at Clinton High School, in Tennessee, opposing racial integration in 1956.

In 1956, 82 of 106 southern congressmen—and every southern senator except Lyndon B. Johnson of Texas and Albert Gore and Estes Kefauver of Tennessee—signed a Southern Manifesto, denouncing the *Brown* decision as a "clear abuse of judicial power," and calling for resistance to "forced integration" by "any lawful means." State after state passed laws to block desegregation. Some made it illegal for the NAACP to operate within their borders. Virginia pioneered the strategy of closing any public schools ordered to desegregate and offering funds to enable white pupils, but not black, to attend private institutions. Prince Edward County, Virginia, shut its schools entirely in 1959; not until 1964 did the Supreme Court order them reopened. Many states adopted "freedom of choice" plans that allowed white students to opt out of integrated schools. As a symbol of defiance, Georgia's legislature incorporated the Confederate battle flag into its state flag in 1956, and Alabama and South Carolina soon began flying the battle flag over their state capitol buildings.

EISENHOWER AND CIVIL RIGHTS

The federal government tried to remain aloof from the black struggle. Thanks to the efforts of Senate majority leader Lyndon B. Johnson, who hoped to win liberal support for a run for president in 1960, Congress in 1957 passed the first national civil rights law since Reconstruction. It targeted the denial of black voting rights in the South, but with weak enforcement provisions it added few voters to the rolls. President Eisenhower failed to provide moral leadership. He called for Americans to abide by the law, but he made it clear that he found the whole civil rights issue distasteful. He privately told aides that he disagreed with the Supreme Court's reasoning. Ike failed to act in 1956 when a federal court ordered that Autherine Lucy be admitted to the University of Alabama; a mob prevented her from registering and the board of trustees expelled her. The university remained all-white into the 1960s.

In 1957, however, after Governor Orval Faubus of Arkansas used the National Guard to prevent the court-ordered integration of Little Rock's Central High School, Eisenhower dispatched federal troops to the city. In the face of a howling mob, soldiers of the 101st Airborne Division escorted nine black children into the school. Events in Little Rock showed that in the last instance, the federal government would not allow the flagrant violation of court orders. But because of massive resistance, the pace of the movement slowed in the final years of the 1950s. When Eisenhower

Federal troops at Little Rock's Central High School, enforcing a court order for integration in 1957.

left office, fewer than 2 percent of black students attended desegregated schools in the states of the old Confederacy.

THE ELECTION OF 1960

KENNEDY AND NIXON

The presidential campaign of 1960 turned out to be one of the closest in American history. Republicans chose Vice President Richard Nixon as their candidate to succeed Eisenhower. Democrats nominated John F. Kennedy, a senator from Massachusetts and a Roman Catholic, whose father, a millionaire Irish-American businessman, had served as ambassador to Great Britain during the 1930s. Kennedy's chief rivals for the nomination were Hubert Humphrey, leader of the party's liberal wing, and Lyndon B. Johnson of Texas, the Senate majority leader, who accepted Kennedy's offer to run for vice president.

The atmosphere of tolerance promoted by World War II had weakened traditional anti-Catholicism. But as recently as 1949, Paul Blanshard's *American Freedom and Catholic Power*, which accused the Church of being antidemocratic, morally repressive, and essentially un-American, had become a national best-seller. Many Protestants remained reluctant to vote for a Catholic, fearing that Kennedy would be required to support church doctrine on controversial public issues or, in a more extreme version, take orders from the pope. Kennedy addressed the question directly. "I do not speak for my church on public matters," he insisted, and "the church does not speak for me." His defeat of Humphrey in the Democratic primary in overwhelmingly Protestant West Virginia put the issue of his religion to rest. At age forty-three, Kennedy became the youngest major-party nominee for president in the nation's history.

Both Kennedy and Nixon were ardent Cold Warriors. But Kennedy pointed to Soviet success in putting *Sputnik*, the first earth satellite, into orbit and subsequently testing the first intercontinental ballistic missile (ICBM) as evidence that the United States had lost the sense of national purpose necessary to fight the Cold War. He warned that Republicans had allowed a "missile gap" to develop in which the Soviets had achieved technological and military superiority over the United States. In fact, as both Kennedy and Nixon well knew, American economic and military capacity far exceeded that of the Soviets. But the charge persuaded many Americans that the time had come for new leadership. The stylishness of Kennedy's wife, Jacqueline, which stood in sharp contrast to the more dowdy public appearance of Mamie Eisenhower and Pat Nixon, reinforced the impression that Kennedy would conduct a more youthful, vigorous presidency.

In the first televised debate between presidential candidates, judging by viewer response, the handsome Kennedy bested Nixon, who was suffering from a cold and appeared tired and nervous. Those who heard the encounter on the

John F. Kennedy and Richard M. Nixon, the presidential candidates of 1960, shaking hands at their televised debate.

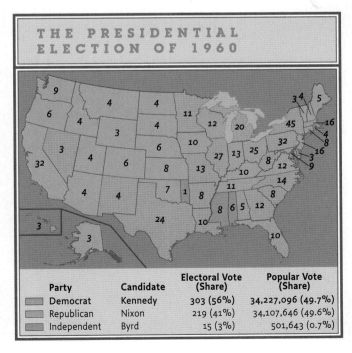

THE PRESIDENTIAL ELECTION OF 1960

Party	Candidate	Electoral Vote (Share)	Popular Vote (Share)
Democrat	Kennedy	303 (56%)	34,227,096 (49.7%)
Republican	Nixon	219 (41%)	34,107,646 (49.6%)
Independent	Byrd	15 (3%)	501,643 (0.7%)

A photograph of John F. Kennedy and his wife, Jacqueline, strolling along the pier at Hyannisport, Massachusetts, illustrates their youthful appeal.

Residents of Los Angeles don gas masks at a 1954 luncheon to protest the government's failure to combat the air pollution, or "smog," that hung over the city.

radio thought Nixon had won, but, on TV, image counted for more than substance. In November, Kennedy eked out a narrow victory, winning the popular vote by only 120,000 out of 69 million votes cast (and, Republicans charged, benefiting from a fraudulent vote count by the notoriously corrupt Chicago Democratic machine).

THE END OF THE 1950S

In January 1961, shortly before leaving office, Eisenhower delivered a televised Farewell Address, modeled to some extent on George Washington's address of 1796. Knowing that the missile gap was a myth, Ike warned against the drumbeat of calls for a new military buildup. He urged Americans to think about the dangerous power of what he called the "military-industrial complex"—the conjunction of "an immense military establishment" with a "permanent arms industry"—with an influence felt in "every office" in the land. "We must never let the weight of this combination," he advised his countrymen, "endanger our liberties or democratic processes." Few Americans shared Ike's concern—far more saw the alliance of the Defense Department and private industry as a source of jobs and national security rather than a threat to democracy. A few years later, however, with the United States locked in an increasingly unpopular war, Eisenhower's warning would come to seem prophetic.

By then, other underpinnings of 1950s life were also in disarray. The tens of millions of cars that made suburban life possible were spewing toxic lead, an additive to make gasoline more efficient, into the atmo-sphere. Penned in to the east by mountains that kept automobile emissions from being dispersed by the wind, Los Angeles had become synonymous with smog, a type of air pollution produced by cars. Chlorofluorocarbons, used in air conditioners, deodorants, and aerosol hair sprays, were releasing chemicals into the atmosphere that damaged the ozone layer, producing global warming and an increase in skin cancer. (Both leaded gasoline and chlorofluorocarbons had been invented by General Motors research scientist Thomas Midgley. He "had more impact on the atmosphere," writes one historian, "than any other single organism" in the history of the world.) The chemical insecticides that enabled agricultural conglomerates to produce the country's remarkable abundance of food were poisoning farm workers, consumers, and the water supply. Housewives were rebelling against a life centered in suburban dream houses. Blacks were increasingly impatient with the slow progress of racial change. The United States, in other words, had entered that most turbulent of decades, the 1960s.

Andy Warhol (1928–1987), Green Coca-Cola Bottles, *1962, synthetic polymer, silkscreen ink, and graphite on canvas.*

SUGGESTED READING

Belgrad, Daniel. *The Culture of Spontaneity: Improvisation and the Arts in Postwar America* (1998). Explores how developments in the arts reflected and encouraged the idea of the free individual.

Branch, Taylor. *Parting the Waters: America in the King Years, 1954–1963* (1988). A comprehensive account of the civil rights movement from the *Brown* decision to the early 1960s.

Cohen, Lizabeth. *A Consumer's Republic: The Politics of Mass Consumption in Postwar America* (2003). Considers how the glorification of consumer freedom shaped American public policy and the physical landscape.

De Grazia, Victoria. *Irresistible Empire: America's Advance through Twentieth-Century Europe* (2005). An examination of American "soft power" and its triumphant penetration of twentieth-century Europe.

Fones-Wolf, Elizabeth A. *Selling Free Enterprise: The Business Assault on Labor and Liberalism, 1945–1960* (1994). Examines the carefully developed campaign whereby business leaders associated capitalism and a union-free work place with freedom.

Freeman, Joshua B. *Working-Class New York: Life and Labor since World War II* (2000). An account of the lives of laborers in the nation's largest city, tracing the rise and decline of the labor movement.

Hirsch, Arnold R. *Making the Second Ghetto: Race and Housing in Chicago, 1940–1960* (1983). Describes how the migration of African-Americans from the South to Chicago during the 1940s and 1950s reshaped the city.

Jackson, Kenneth T. *Crabgrass Frontier: The Suburbanization of America* (1985). The standard account of the development of American suburbia.

Jacobs, Meg. *Pocketbook Politics: Economic Citizenship in Twentieth-Century America* (2005). Discusses how consumer freedom became central to Americans' national identity after World War II.

Klarman, Michael J. *From Jim Crow to Civil Rights: The Supreme Court and the Struggle for Racial Equality* (2004). A full study of Supreme Court cases dealing with civil rights, and how they both reflected and helped to stimulate social change.

May, Elaine T. *Homeward Bound: American Families in the Cold War Era* (1988). Studies the nuclear family as a bastion of American freedom during the Cold War, at least according to official propaganda.

Nicolaides, Becky M. *My Blue Heaven: Life and Politics in the Working-Class Suburbs of Los Angeles, 1920–1965* (2002). Traces the transformation of Southgate, an industrial neighborhood of Los Angeles, into an all-white suburb, and the political results.

Patterson, James T. *Grand Expectations: The United States, 1945–1974* (1996). A comprehensive account of American history over the three decades following World War II.

Pells, Richard. *The Liberal Mind in a Conservative Age: American Intellectuals in the 1940s and 1950s* (1984). Examines how American writers and artists responded to the Cold War.

Westad, Odd Arne. *The Global Cold War* (2005). A wide-ranging analysis of how the Cold War played out in the Third World.

REVIEW QUESTIONS

1. Illustrate how the automobile transformed American society and culture in the 1950s.

2. Explain why the conservatives in American politics did not view President Eisenhower as one of their own.

3. What new meanings did Americans give to freedom in the 1950s?

4. In what ways did the cultural critics of the 1950s voice their dissent with the "golden age"?

5. Describe what President Eisenhower meant by "Modern Republicanism" and discuss his motivations for pursuing such a policy.

6. What were the most significant factors that contributed to the growing momentum of the civil rights movement in the 1950s?

KEY TERMS

television (p. 932)

women at work (p. 934)

housing discrimination (p. 936)

Sputnik (p. 944)

The U-2 incident (p. 946)

The Iranian coup (p. 947)

rock-and-roll music (p. 950)

League of United Latin American Citizens (LULAC) (p. 955)

Sweatt v. Painter (p. 956)

REVIEW TABLE

Landmark Events in the Civil Rights Movement in the 1950s

Event	Date	Significance
Brown v. Board of Education	1954	Ended segregation in public education, reversing the 1896 *Plessy v. Ferguson* decision
Montgomery bus boycott	1955–1956	Mobilized a community to successfully fight Jim Crow, ending segregation on public buses and launching the leadership career of Martin Luther King, Jr.
Integration of Little Rock's Central High School	1957	Forced the federal government to uphold the law of the nation and enforce the *Brown* decision
Greensboro, N.C. Woolworth sit-in	1960	Launched a decade of political activism and social change, especially by students

CHAPTER 25

The Sixties, 1960–1968

James Karales's dramatic photograph for Look *magazine depicts the March 1965 civil rights march from Selma to Montgomery, Alabama, demanding voting rights.*

☞ FOCUS QUESTIONS

• What were the major events in the civil rights movement of the early 1960s?

• What were the major initiatives of the Kennedy presidency?

• What was the significance of LBJ's Great Society programs?

• How did the civil rights movement change in the mid-1960s?

• How did the Vietnam War transform American politics and culture?

• What were the sources and significance of the rights revolution of the late 1960s?

• In what ways was 1968 a climactic year for the Sixties?

On the afternoon of February 1, 1960, four students from North Carolina Agricultural and Technical State University, a black college in Greensboro, North Carolina, entered the local Woolworth's department store. After making a few purchases, they sat down at the lunch counter, an area reserved for whites. Told that they could not be served, they remained in their seats until the store closed. They returned the next morning and the next. As the protest continued, other students, including a few local whites, joined in. Demonstrations spread across the country. After resisting for five months, Woolworth's in July agreed to serve black customers at its lunch counters.

The sit-in reflected mounting frustration at the slow pace of racial change. White Greensboro prided itself on being free of prejudice. In 1954, the city had been the first in the South to declare its intention of complying with the *Brown* decision. But by 1960 only a handful of black students had been admitted to all-white schools, the economic gap between blacks and whites had not narrowed, and Greensboro was still segregated.

More than any other event, the Greensboro sit-in launched the 1960s: a decade of political activism and social change. Sit-ins had occurred before, but never had they sparked so massive a response. Similar demonstrations soon took place throughout the South, demanding the integration not only of lunch counters but of parks, pools, restaurants, bowling alleys, libraries, and other facilities as well. By the end of 1960, some 70,000 demonstrators had taken part in sit-ins. Angry whites often assaulted them. But having been trained in nonviolent resistance, the protesters did not strike back.

Even more than elevating blacks to full citizenship, declared the writer James Baldwin, the civil rights movement challenged the United States to rethink "what it really means by freedom"—including whether freedom applied to all Americans or only to part of the population. With their freedom rides, freedom schools, freedom marches, and the insistent cry "freedom now," black Americans and their white allies made freedom once again the rallying cry of the dispossessed. Thousands of ordinary men and women—maids and laborers alongside students, teachers, businessmen, and ministers—risked physical and economic retribution to lay claim to freedom. Their courage inspired a host of other challenges to the status quo, including a student movement known as the New Left, the "second wave" of feminism, and activism among other minorities.

By the time the decade ended, these movements had challenged the 1950s' understanding of freedom linked to the Cold War abroad and consumer choice at home. They exposed the limitations of traditional New Deal liberalism. They forced a reconsideration of the nation's foreign policy and extended claims to freedom into the most intimate areas of life. They

Participants in a sit-in in Raleigh, North Carolina in 1960. The protesters, probably students from a local college, brought books and newspapers to emphasize the seriousness of their intentions and their commitment to nonviolence.

made American society confront the fact that certain groups, including students, women, members of racial minorities, and homosexuals, felt themselves excluded from full enjoyment of American freedom.

Reflecting back years later on the struggles of the 1960s, one black organizer in Memphis remarked, "All I wanted to do was to live in a free country." Of the movement's accomplishments, he added, "You had to fight for every inch of it. Nobody gave you anything. Nothing."

THE FREEDOM MOVEMENT

THE RISING TIDE OF PROTEST

With the sit-ins, college students for the first time stepped onto the stage of American history as the leading force for social change. In April 1960, Ella Baker, a longtime civil rights organizer, called a meeting of young activists in Raleigh, North Carolina. About 200 black students and a few whites attended. Out of the gathering came the Student Non-Violent Coordinating Committee (SNCC), dedicated to replacing the culture of segregation with a "beloved community" of racial justice and to empowering ordinary blacks to take control of the decisions that affected their lives. "We can't count on adults," declared SNCC organizer Robert Moses. "Very few . . . are not afraid of the tremendous pressure they will face. This leaves the young people to be the organizers, the agents of social and political change."

Other forms of direct action soon followed the sit-ins. Blacks in Biloxi and Gulfport, Mississippi, engaged in "wade-ins," demanding access to segregated public beaches. Scores were arrested and two black teenagers were killed. In 1961, the Congress of Racial Equality (CORE) launched the Freedom Rides. Integrated groups traveled by bus into the Deep South to test

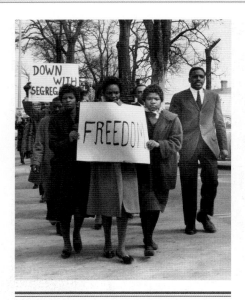

Civil rights demonstrators in Orangeburg, South Carolina, in 1960.

Demonstrators in downtown Birmingham, Alabama, during the civil rights campaign of 1963.

compliance with court orders banning segregation on interstate buses and trains and in terminal facilities. Violent mobs assaulted them. Near Anniston, Alabama, a firebomb was thrown into the vehicle and the passengers beaten as they escaped. In Birmingham, Klansmen attacked riders with bats and chains, while police refused to intervene. Many of the Freedom Riders were arrested. But their actions led the Interstate Commerce Commission to order buses and terminals desegregated.

As protests escalated, so did the resistance of local authorities. Late in 1961, SNCC and other groups launched a campaign of nonviolent protests against racial discrimination in Albany, Georgia. The protests lasted a year, but despite filling the jails with demonstrators—a tactic adopted by the movement to gain national sympathy—they failed to achieve their goals. In September 1962, a court ordered the University of Mississippi to admit James Meredith, a black student. The state police stood aside as a mob, encouraged by Governor Ross Barnett, rampaged through the streets of Oxford, where the university is located. Two bystanders lost their lives in the riot. President Kennedy was forced to dispatch the army to restore order.

BIRMINGHAM

The high point of protest came in the spring of 1963, when demonstrations took place in towns and cities across the South, dramatizing black discontent over inequality in education, employment, and housing. In one week in June, there were over 15,000 arrests in 186 cities. The dramatic culmination came in Birmingham, Alabama, a citadel of segregation. Even for the Deep South, Birmingham was a violent city—there had been over fifty bombings of black homes and institutions since World War II. Local blacks had been demonstrating, with no result, for greater economic opportunities and an end to segregation by local businesses.

With the movement flagging, some of its leaders invited Martin Luther King Jr. to come to Birmingham. While serving a nine-day prison term in April 1963 for violating a ban on demonstrations, King composed one of his most eloquent pleas for racial justice, the "Letter from Birmingham Jail." Responding to local clergymen who counseled patience, King related the litany of abuses faced by black southerners, from police brutality to the daily humiliation of having to explain to their children why they could not enter amusement parks or public swimming pools. The "white moderate," King declared, must put aside fear of disorder and commit himself to racial justice.

In May, King made the bold decision to send black schoolchildren into the streets of Birmingham. Police chief Eugene "Bull" Connor unleashed his forces against the thousands of young marchers. The images, broadcast on television, of children being assaulted with nightsticks, high-pressure fire hoses, and attack dogs produced a wave of revulsion throughout the world and turned the Birmingham campaign into a triumph for the civil rights movement. It led President Kennedy, as will be related later, to endorse the movement's goals. Leading businessmen, fearing that the city was becoming an international symbol of brutality, brokered an end to the demonstrations that desegregated downtown stores and restaurants and promised that black salespeople would be hired.

But more than these modest gains, the events in Birmingham forced white Americans to decide whether they had more in common with fellow citizens demanding their basic rights or with violent segregationists. The question became more insistent in the following weeks. In June 1963, a sniper killed Medgar Evers, field secretary of the NAACP in Mississippi. In September, a bomb exploded at a black Baptist church in Birmingham, killing four young girls. (Not until the year 2002 was the last of those who committed this act of domestic terrorism tried and convicted.)

A fireman assaulting young African-American demonstrators with a high-pressure hose during the climactic demonstrations in Birmingham. Broadcast on television, such pictures proved a serious problem for the United States in its battle for the "hearts and minds" of people around the world and forced the Kennedy administration to confront the contradiction between the rhetoric of freedom and the reality of racism.

THE MARCH ON WASHINGTON

On August 28, 1963, two weeks before the Birmingham church bombing, 250,000 black and white Americans converged on the nation's capital for the March on Washington, often considered the high point of the nonviolent civil rights movement. Organized by a coalition of civil rights, labor, and church organizations led by A. Philip Randolph, the black unionist who had threatened a similar march in 1941, it was the largest public demonstration in the nation's history to that time. Calls for the passage of a civil rights bill pending before Congress took center stage. But the march's goals also included a public-works program to reduce unemployment, an increase in the minimum wage, and a law barring discrimination in employment. These demands, and the marchers' slogan, "Jobs and Freedom," revealed how the black movement had, for the moment, forged an alliance with white liberal groups. On the steps of the Lincoln Memorial, King delivered his most famous speech, including the words, "I have a dream that one day this nation will rise up and live out the true meaning of its creed: 'We hold these truths to be self-evident, that all men are created equal.'" (See the Appendix for the full text.)

The March on Washington reflected an unprecedented degree of black-white cooperation in support of racial and economic justice. But it also revealed some of the movement's limitations, and the tensions within it. Even though female activists like Jo Ann Robinson and Ella Baker had played crucial roles in civil rights organizing, every speaker at the Lincoln Memorial was male. The organizers ordered SNCC leader John Lewis (later a congressman from Georgia) to tone down his speech, the original text of which called on blacks to "free ourselves of the chains of political and economic slavery" and march "through the heart of Dixie the way Sherman did . . . and burn Jim Crow to the ground." Lewis's rhetoric forecast the more militant turn many in the movement would soon be taking.

"Seek the freedom in 1963 promised in 1863," read one banner at the March on Washington. And civil rights activists resurrected the Civil War–era vision of national authority as the custodian of American freedom. Despite the fact that the federal government had for many decades promoted segregation, blacks' historical experience suggested that they had more hope for justice from national power than from local governments or civic institutions—home owners' associations, businesses, private clubs—still riddled with racism. It remained unclear whether the federal government would take up this responsibility.

Part of the crowd that gathered at the Lincoln Memorial for the 1963 March on Washington to demand "Jobs and Freedom."

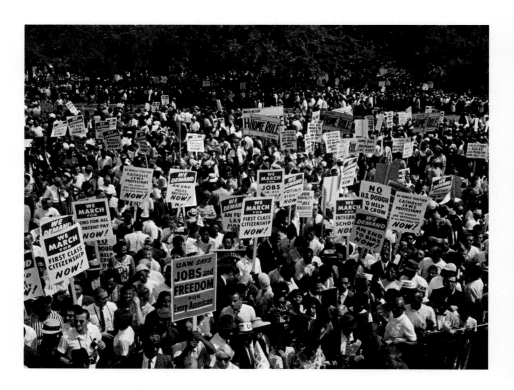

THE KENNEDY YEARS

John F. Kennedy served as president for less than three years and, in domestic affairs, had few tangible accomplishments. But his administration is widely viewed today as a moment of youthful glamour, soaring hopes, and dynamic leadership at home and abroad. Later revelations of the sexual liaisons Kennedy obsessively pursued while in the White House have not significantly damaged his reputation among the general public.

Kennedy's inaugural address of January 1961 announced a watershed in American politics: "The torch has been passed," he declared, "to a new generation of Americans" who would "pay any price, bear any burden," to "assure the survival and success of liberty." The speech seemed to urge Americans to move beyond the self-centered consumer culture of the 1950s: "Ask not what your country can do for you; ask what you can do for your country." But while the sit-ins were by now a year old, the speech said nothing about segregation or race. At the outset of his presidency, Kennedy regarded civil rights as a distraction from his main concern—vigorous conduct of the Cold War.

KENNEDY AND THE WORLD

Kennedy's agenda envisioned new initiatives aimed at countering communist influence in the world. One of his administration's first acts was to establish the Peace Corps, which sent young Americans abroad to aid in the economic and educational progress of developing countries and to improve the image of the United States there. By 1966, over 15,000 young men and women were serving as Peace Corps volunteers. When the Soviets in April 1961 launched a satellite carrying the first man into orbit around the earth, Kennedy announced that the United States would mobilize its resources to land a man on the moon by the end of the decade. The goal seemed almost impossible when announced, but it was stunningly accomplished in 1969.

Kennedy also formulated a new policy toward Latin America, the Alliance for Progress. A kind of Marshall Plan for the Western Hemisphere, although involving far smaller sums of money, it aimed, Kennedy said, to promote both "political" and "material freedom." Begun with much fanfare about alleviating poverty and counteracting the appeal of communism, the Alliance for Progress failed. Unlike the Marshall Plan, military regimes and local elites controlled Alliance for Progress aid. They enriched themselves while the poor saw little benefit.

Like his predecessors, Kennedy viewed the entire world through the lens of the Cold War. This outlook shaped his dealings with Fidel Castro, who had led a revolution that in 1959 ousted Cuban dictator Fulgencio Batista. Until Castro took power, Cuba was an economic dependency of the United States. When his government began nationalizing American landholdings and other investments and signed an agreement to sell sugar to the Soviet Union, the Eisenhower administration suspended trade with the island. The CIA began training anti-Castro exiles for an invasion of Cuba.

In April 1961, Kennedy allowed the CIA to launch its invasion, at a site known as the Bay of Pigs. Military advisers predicted a popular uprising that would quickly topple the Castro government. But the assault proved to be a total failure. Of 1,400 invaders, over 100 were killed and 1,100 captured. Cuba became ever more closely tied to the Soviet Union. The Kennedy administration tried other methods, including assassination attempts, to get rid of Castro's government.

THE MISSILE CRISIS

Meanwhile, relations between the two "superpowers" deteriorated. In August 1961, in order to stem a growing tide of emigrants fleeing from East to West Berlin, the Soviets constructed a wall separating the two parts of the city. Until its demolition in 1989, the Berlin Wall would stand as a tangible symbol of the Cold War and the division of Europe.

The most dangerous crisis of the Kennedy administration, and in many ways of the entire Cold War, came in October 1962, when American spy planes discovered that the Soviet Union was installing missiles in Cuba capable of reaching the United States with nuclear weapons. The Russians' motive—whether they hoped to alter the world balance of power or simply stave off another American invasion of Cuba—may never be known. But the Kennedy administration considered the missiles' presence intolerable. Rejecting advice from military leaders that he authorize an attack on Cuba, which would almost certainly have triggered a Soviet response in Berlin and perhaps a nuclear war, Kennedy imposed a blockade or "quarantine" of the island and demanded the missiles' removal. After tense behind-the-scenes negotiations, Soviet premier Nikita Khrushchev agreed to withdraw the missiles; Kennedy pledged that the United States would not invade Cuba and secretly agreed to remove American Jupiter missiles from Turkey, from which they could reach the Soviet Union.

For thirteen days, the world teetered on the brink of all-out nuclear war. The crisis seems to have lessened Kennedy's passion for the Cold War. Indeed, he appears to have been shocked by the casual way military leaders spoke of "winning" a nuclear exchange in which tens of millions of Americans and Russians were certain to die. In 1963, Kennedy moved to reduce Cold War tensions. In a speech at American University, he called for greater cooperation with the Soviets. He warned against viewing the Cold War simply as a battle between the forces of light and those of darkness: "No government or social system is so evil that its people must be considered as lacking in virtue." That summer, the two countries agreed to a treaty banning the testing of nuclear weapons in the atmosphere and in space. In announcing the agreement, Kennedy paid tribute to the small movement against nuclear weapons that had been urging such a ban for several years. He even sent word to Castro through a journalist that he desired a more constructive relationship with Cuba.

KENNEDY AND CIVIL RIGHTS

In his first two years in office, Kennedy was preoccupied with foreign policy. But in 1963, the crisis over civil rights eclipsed other concerns. Until then, Kennedy had been reluctant to take a forceful stand on black

demands. He seemed to share FBI director J. Edgar Hoover's fear that the movement was inspired by communism.
Attorney General Robert F. Kennedy, the
president's brother, approved FBI wire-
taps on King. Despite promising during
the 1960 campaign to ban discrimination in federally assisted housing,
Kennedy waited until the end of 1962 to
issue the order. He used federal force
when obstruction of the law became
acute, as at the University of Mississippi.
But he failed to protect civil rights workers from violence, insisting that law
enforcement was a local matter.

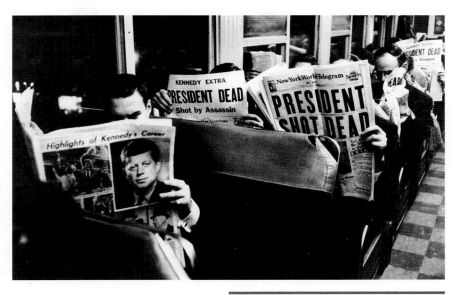

New York City train passengers reading the news of President Kennedy's assassination, November 22, 1963.

Events in Birmingham in May 1963
forced Kennedy's hand. Kennedy real-
ized that the United States simply could not declare itself the champion of
freedom throughout the world while maintaining a system of racial
inequality at home. In June, he went on national television to call for the
passage of a law banning discrimination in all places of public accommodation, a major goal of the civil rights movement. The nation, he asserted,
faced a moral crisis: "We preach freedom around the world . . . , but are we
to say to the world, and much more importantly, to each other, that this is
a land of the free except for Negroes?"

Kennedy did not live to see his civil rights bill enacted. On November 22,
1963, while riding in a motorcade through Dallas, Texas, he was shot and
killed. Most likely, the assassin was Lee Harvey Oswald, a troubled former
marine. Partly because Oswald was murdered two days later by a local
nightclub owner while in police custody, speculation about a possible conspiracy continues to this day. In any event, Kennedy's death brought an
abrupt and utterly unexpected end to his presidency. As with Pearl Harbor
or September 11, 2001, an entire generation would always recall the
moment when they first heard the news of Kennedy's death. It fell to his
successor, Lyndon B. Johnson, to secure passage of the civil rights bill and to
launch a program of domestic liberalism far more ambitious than anything
Kennedy had envisioned.

LYNDON JOHNSON'S PRESIDENCY

Unlike John F. Kennedy, raised in a wealthy and powerful family, Lyndon
Johnson grew up in one of the poorest parts of the United States, the central Texas hill country. Kennedy seemed to view success as his birthright;
Johnson had to struggle ferociously to achieve wealth and power. By the
1950s, he had risen to become majority leader of the U.S. Senate. But Johnson never forgot the poor Mexican and white children he had taught in a
Texas school in the early 1930s. Far more interested than Kennedy in
domestic reform, he continued to hold the New Deal view that government
had an obligation to assist less-fortunate members of society.

Lyndon B. Johnson being sworn in as president on the plane taking him to Washington from Dallas. On the left is Lady Bird Johnson, and on the right, Jacqueline Kennedy.

THE CIVIL RIGHTS ACT OF 1964

When he became president, nobody expected that Johnson would make the passage of civil rights legislation his first order of business or that he would come to identify himself with the black movement more passionately than any previous president. Just five days after Kennedy's assassination, however, Johnson called on Congress to enact the civil rights bill as the most fitting memorial to his slain predecessor. "We have talked long enough about equal rights in this country," he declared. "It is now time to write the next chapter and write it in the books of law."

In 1964, Congress passed the Civil Rights Act, which prohibited racial discrimination in employment, institutions like hospitals and schools, and privately owned public accommodations such as restaurants, hotels, and theaters. It also banned discrimination on the grounds of sex—a provision added by opponents of civil rights in an effort to derail the entire bill and embraced by liberal and female members of Congress as a way to broaden its scope. Johnson knew that many whites opposed the new law. After signing it, he turned to an aide and remarked, "I think we delivered the South to the Republican Party."

FREEDOM SUMMER

The 1964 law did not address a major concern of the civil rights movement—the right to vote in the South. That summer, a coalition of civil rights groups including SNCC, CORE, and the NAACP launched a voter registration drive in Mississippi. Hundreds of white college students from the North traveled to the state to take part in Freedom Summer. An outpouring of violence greeted the campaign, including thirty-five bombings and numerous beatings of civil rights workers. In June, three young activists—Michael Schwerner and Andrew Goodman, white students from the North, and James Chaney, a local black youth, were kidnapped by a group headed by a deputy sheriff and murdered near Philadelphia, Mississippi. Between 1961 and 1965, an estimated twenty-five black civil rights workers paid with their lives. But the deaths of the two white students focused unprecedented attention on Mississippi and on the apparent inability of the federal government to protect citizens seeking to enjoy their constitutional rights. (In June 2005, forty-one years after Freedom Summer, a Mississippi jury convicted a member of the Ku Klux Klan of manslaughter in the deaths of the three civil rights workers.)

Freedom Summer led directly to one of the most dramatic confrontations of the civil rights era—the campaign by the Mississippi Freedom Democratic Party (MFDP) to take the seats of the state's all-white official party at the 1964

Fannie Lou Hamer testifying at the Democratic National Convention of 1964 on behalf of the Mississippi Freedom Democratic Party.

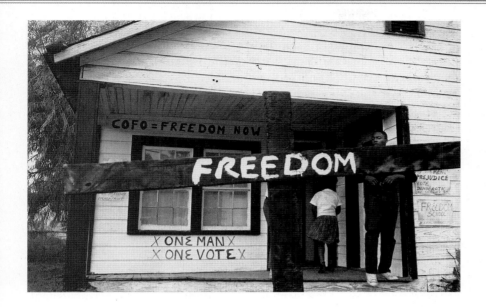

A burned cross in front of a Freedom House during the Mississippi Freedom Summer of 1964 was left in place by civil rights workers, who painted the movement's byword on it.

Democratic national convention in Atlantic City, New Jersey. With blacks unable to participate in the activities of the Democratic Party or register to vote, the civil rights movement in Mississippi had created the MFDP, open to all residents of the state. At televised hearings before the credentials committee, Fannie Lou Hamer of the MFDP held a national audience spellbound with her account of growing up in poverty in the Yazoo-Mississippi Delta and of the savage beatings she had endured at the hands of police. Like many other black activists, Hamer was a deeply religious person who believed that Christianity rested on the idea of freedom and that the movement had been divinely inspired. "Is this America," she asked, "the land of the free and home of the brave, where . . . we [are] threatened daily because we want to live as decent human beings?" Johnson feared a southern walkout, as had happened at the 1948 party convention, if the MFDP were seated. Party liberals, including Johnson's running mate, Hubert Humphrey, pressed for a compromise in which two black delegates would be granted seats. But the MFDP rejected the proposal.

THE 1964 ELECTION

The events at Atlantic City severely weakened black activists' faith in the responsiveness of the political system and forecast the impending breakup of the coalition between the civil rights movement and the liberal wing of the Democratic Party. For the moment, however, the movement rallied behind Johnson's campaign for reelection. Johnson's opponent, Senator Barry Goldwater of Arizona, had published *The Conscience of a Conservative* (1960), which sold over 3 million copies. The book demanded a more aggressive conduct of the Cold War (he even suggested that nuclear war might be "the price of freedom"). But Goldwater directed most of his critique against

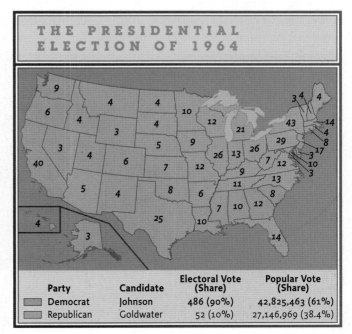

THE PRESIDENTIAL ELECTION OF 1964

Party	Candidate	Electoral Vote (Share)	Popular Vote (Share)
Democrat	Johnson	486 (90%)	42,825,463 (61%)
Republican	Goldwater	52 (10%)	27,146,969 (38.4%)

"internal" dangers to freedom, especially the New Deal welfare state, which he believed stifled individual initiative and independence. He called for the substitution of private charity for public welfare programs and Social Security, and the abolition of the graduated income tax. Goldwater had voted against the Civil Rights Act of 1964. His acceptance speech at the Republican national convention contained the explosive statement, "Extremism in the defense of liberty is no vice."

Stigmatized by the Democrats as an extremist who would repeal Social Security and risk nuclear war, Goldwater went down to a disastrous defeat. Johnson received almost 43 million votes to Goldwater's 27 million. Democrats swept to two-to-one majorities in both houses of Congress. Although few realized it, the 1964 campaign marked a milestone in the resurgence of American conservatism. Goldwater's success in the Deep South, where he carried five states, coupled with the surprisingly strong showing of segregationist governor George Wallace of Alabama in Democratic primaries in Wisconsin, Indiana, and Maryland, suggested that politicians could strike electoral gold by appealing to white opposition to the civil rights movement.

One indication of problems for the Democrats came in California, with the passage by popular referendum of Proposition 14, which repealed a 1963 law banning racial discrimination in the sale of real estate. Backed by the state's realtors and developers, California conservatives made the "freedom" of home owners to control their property the rallying cry of the campaign against the fair housing law. Although Johnson carried California by over 1 million votes, Proposition 14 received a considerable majority, winning three-fourths of the votes cast by whites.

THE CONSERVATIVE SIXTIES

The 1960s, today recalled as a decade of radicalism, clearly had a conservative side as well. With the founding in 1960 of Young Americans for Freedom (YAF), conservative students emerged as a force in politics. There were striking parallels between the Sharon Statement, issued by ninety young people who gathered at the estate of conservative intellectual William F. Buckley in Sharon, Connecticut, to establish YAF, and the Port Huron Statement of SDS of 1962 (discussed below). Both manifestos portrayed youth as the cutting edge of a new radicalism, and both claimed to offer a route to greater freedom. The Sharon Statement summarized beliefs that had circulated among conservatives during the past decade—the free market underpinned "personal freedom," government must be strictly limited, and "international communism," the gravest threat to liberty, must be destroyed.

YAF aimed initially to take control of the Republican Party from leaders who

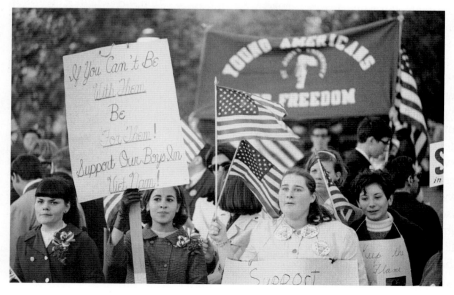

A 1967 rally by members of Young Americans for Freedom, a conservative group that flourished in the 1960s.

had made their peace with the New Deal and seemed willing to coexist with communism. YAF members became Barry Goldwater's shock troops in 1964. Despite his landslide defeat in the general election, Goldwater's nomination was a remarkable triumph for a movement widely viewed as composed of fanatics out to "repeal the twentieth century."

Goldwater also brought new constituencies to the conservative cause. His campaign aroused enthusiasm in the rapidly expanding suburbs of southern California and the Southwest. Orange County, California, many of whose residents had recently arrived from the East and Midwest and worked in defense-related industries, became a nationally known center of grassroots conservative activism. The funds that poured into the Goldwater campaign from the Sunbelt's oilmen and aerospace entrepreneurs established a new financial base for conservatism. And by carrying five states of the Deep South, Goldwater showed that the civil rights revolution had redrawn the nation's political map, opening the door to a "southern strategy" that would eventually lead the entire region into the Republican Party.

Well before the rise of Black Power, a reaction against civil rights gains offered conservatives new opportunities and threatened the stability of the Democratic coalition. During the 1950s, many conservatives had responded favorably to southern whites' condemnation of the *Brown v. Board of Education* desegregation decision as an invasion of states' rights. The *National Review*, an influential conservative magazine, referred to whites as "the advanced race" and defended black disenfranchisement on the grounds that "the claims of civilization supersede those of universal suffrage." In 1962, YAF bestowed its Freedom Award on Senator Strom Thurmond of South Carolina, one of the country's most prominent segregationists. During the 1960s, most conservatives abandoned talk of racial superiority and inferiority. But conservative appeals to law and order, "freedom of association," and the evils of welfare often had strong racial overtones. Racial divisions would prove to be a political gold mine for conservatives.

THE VOTING RIGHTS ACT

One last legislative triumph, however, lay ahead for the civil rights movement. In January 1965, King launched a voting rights campaign in Selma, Alabama, a city where only 355 of 15,000 black residents had been allowed to register to vote. In March, defying a ban by Governor Wallace, King attempted to lead a march from Selma to the state capital, Montgomery. When the marchers reached the bridge leading out of the city, state police assaulted them with cattle prods, whips, and tear gas.

Once again, violence against nonviolent demonstrators flashed across television screens throughout the world, compelling the federal government to take action. Calling Selma a milestone in "man's unending search for freedom," Johnson asked Congress to enact a law securing the right to vote. He closed his speech by quoting the demonstrators' song, "We Shall Overcome." Never before had the movement received so powerful an endorsement from the federal government. Congress quickly passed the Voting Rights Act of 1965, which allowed federal officials to register voters. Black southerners finally regained the suffrage that had been stripped from them at the turn of the twentieth century. In addition, the Twenty-Fourth

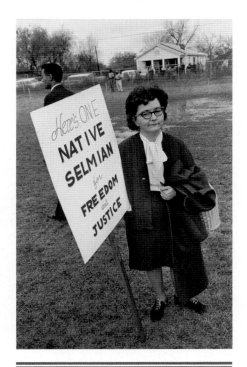

A white resident of Selma offers her support to civil rights demonstrators.

Amendment to the Constitution outlawed the poll tax, which had long prevented poor blacks (and some whites) from voting in the South.

IMMIGRATION REFORM

By 1965, with court orders and new federal laws prohibiting discrimination in public accommodations, employment, and voting, the civil rights movement had succeeded in eradicating the legal bases of second-class citizenship. The belief that racism should no longer serve as a basis of public policy spilled over into other realms. In 1965, the Hart-Celler Act abandoned the national-origins quota system of immigration, which had excluded Asians and severely restricted southern and eastern Europeans. The law established new, racially neutral criteria for immigration, notably family reunification and possession of skills in demand in the United States. On the other hand, because of growing hostility in the Southwest to Mexican immigration, the law established the first limit, 120,000, on newcomers from the Western Hemisphere. This created, for the first time, the category of "illegal aliens" from the Americas. The Act set the quota for the rest of the world at 170,000. The total annual number of available immigrants, 290,000, represented a lower percentage of the American population than had the nationality quotas established in 1924. However, because of special provisions for refugees from communist countries, immigration soon exceeded these caps.

The new law had many unexpected results. At the time, immigrants represented only 5 percent of the American population—the lowest proportion since the 1830s. No one anticipated that the new quotas not only would lead to an explosive rise in immigration but also would spark a dramatic shift in which newcomers from Latin America, the Caribbean, and Asia came to outnumber those from Europe. Taken together, the civil rights revolution and immigration reform marked the triumph of a pluralist conception of Americanism. By 1976, 85 percent of respondents to a public-opinion survey agreed with the statement, "The United States was meant to be . . . a country made up of many races, religions, and nationalities."

THE GREAT SOCIETY

After his landslide victory of 1964, Johnson outlined the most sweeping proposal for governmental action to promote the general welfare since the New Deal. Johnson's initiatives of 1965–1967, known collectively as the Great Society, provided health services to the poor and elderly in the new Medicaid and Medicare programs and poured federal funds into education and urban development. New cabinet offices—the Departments of Transportation and of Housing and Urban Development—and new agencies, such as the Equal Employment Opportunity Commission, the National Endowments for the Humanities and for the Arts, and a national public broadcasting network, were created. These measures greatly expanded the powers of the federal government, and they completed and extended the social agenda (with the exception of national health insurance) that had been stalled in Congress since 1938.

Unlike the New Deal, however, the Great Society was a response to prosperity, not depression. The mid-1960s were a time of rapid economic expansion, fueled by increased government spending and a tax cut on individuals and businesses initially proposed by Kennedy and enacted in 1964. Johnson and Democratic liberals believed that economic growth made it possible to fund ambitious new government programs and to improve the quality of life.

THE WAR ON POVERTY

The centerpiece of the Great Society, however, was the crusade to eradicate poverty, launched by Johnson early in 1964. After the talk of universal affluence during the 1950s, economic deprivation had been rediscovered by political leaders, thanks in part to Michael Harrington's 1962 book *The Other America*. Harrington revealed that 40 to 50 million Americans lived in poverty, often in isolated rural areas or urban slums "invisible" to the middle class. He showed that technological improvements like the mechanization of agriculture and the automation of industry, which produced a higher standard of living overall, eliminated the jobs of farm laborers and unskilled workers, locking them in poverty. The civil rights movement heightened the urgency of the issue, even though, as Harrington made clear, whites made up a majority of the nation's poor.

During the 1930s, Democrats had attributed poverty to an imbalance of economic power and flawed economic institutions. In the 1960s, the administration attributed it to an absence of skills and a lack of proper attitudes and work habits. Thus, the War on Poverty did not consider the most direct ways of eliminating poverty—guaranteeing an annual income for all Americans, creating jobs for the unemployed, promoting the spread of unionization, or making it more difficult for businesses to shift production to the low-wage South or overseas. Nor did it address the economic changes that were reducing the number of well-paid manufacturing jobs and leaving poor families in rural areas like Appalachia and decaying urban ghettos with little hope of economic advancement.

One of the Great Society's most popular and successful components, food stamps, offered direct aid to the poor. But, in general, the War on Poverty concentrated not on direct economic aid but on equipping the poor with skills and rebuilding their spirit and motivation. The new Office of Economic Opportunity oversaw a series of initiatives designed to lift the poor into the social and economic mainstream. It provided Head Start (an early childhood education program), job training, legal services, and scholarships for poor college students. It also created VISTA, a domestic version of the Peace Corps for the inner cities. In an echo of SNCC's philosophy of empowering ordinary individuals to take control of their lives, the War on Poverty required that poor people play a leading part in the design and implementation of local policies, a recipe for continuing conflict with local political leaders accustomed to controlling the flow of federal dollars.

FREEDOM AND EQUALITY

Johnson defended the Great Society in a vocabulary of freedom derived from the New Deal, when his own political career began, and reinforced by the civil rights movement. Soon after assuming office in 1963, he resurrected the phrase "freedom from want," all but forgotten during the 1950s. Echoing FDR, Johnson told the 1964 Democratic convention, "The man

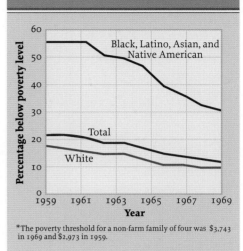

Figure 25.1 PERCENTAGE OF POPULATION BELOW POVERTY LEVEL, BY RACE, 1959–1969*

*The poverty threshold for a non-farm family of four was $3,743 in 1969 and $2,973 in 1959.

During the 1960s, an expanding economy and government programs assisting the poor produced a steady decrease in the percentage of Americans living in poverty.

who is hungry, who cannot find work or educate his children, who is bowed by want, that man is not fully free." Recognizing that black poverty was fundamentally different from white, since its roots lay in "past injustice and present prejudice," Johnson sought to redefine the relationship between freedom and equality. Economic liberty, he insisted, meant more than equal opportunity: "You do not wipe away the scars of centuries by saying: Now you are free to go where you want, do as you desire, and choose the leaders you please.... We seek ... not just equality as a right and a theory, but equality as a fact and as a result."

Johnson's Great Society may not have achieved equality "as a fact," but it represented a remarkable reaffirmation of the idea of social citizenship. It was the most expansive effort in the nation's history to mobilize the powers of the national government to address the needs of the least-advantaged Americans, especially those, like blacks, largely excluded from the original New Deal entitlements such as Social Security.

Coupled with the decade's high rate of economic growth, the War on Poverty succeeded in reducing the incidence of poverty from 22 percent to 13 percent of American families during the 1960s. It has fluctuated around the latter figure ever since. The sum spent, however, was too low to end poverty altogether or to transform conditions of life in poor urban neighborhoods. By the 1990s, thanks to the civil rights movement and the Great Society, the historic gap between whites and blacks in education, income, and access to skilled employment narrowed considerably. But with deindustrialization and urban decay affecting numerous families and most suburbs still being off-limits to non-whites, the median wealth of white households remained ten times greater than that of blacks, and nearly a quarter of all black children still lived in poverty.

THE CHANGING BLACK MOVEMENT

Even at its moment of triumph, the civil rights movement confronted a crisis as it sought to move from access to schools, public accommodations, and the voting booth to the economic divide separating blacks from other Americans. In the mid-1960s, economic issues rose to the forefront of the civil rights agenda. Violent outbreaks in black ghettos outside the South drew attention to the national scope of racial injustice and to inequalities in jobs, education, and housing that the dismantling of legal segregation left intact. Much of the animosity that came to characterize race relations arose from the belief of many whites that the legislation of 1964 and 1965 had fulfilled the nation's obligation to assure blacks equality before the law, while blacks, aware of the discrimination they still faced in jobs, education, housing, and the criminal justice system, pushed for more government action, sparking fears of "reverse discrimination."

THE GHETTO UPRISINGS

The first riots—really, battles between angry blacks and the predominantly white police (widely seen by many ghetto residents as an occupying army)—erupted in Harlem in 1964. Far larger was the Watts uprising of

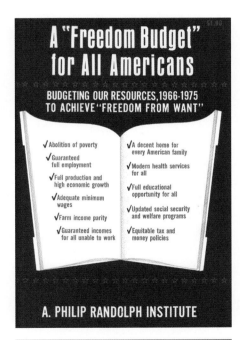

A burned store mannequin lies on the street and smoke rises in the background as a policeman patrols Los Angeles during the Watts riot of 1965.

1965, which took place in the black ghetto of Los Angeles only days after Johnson signed the Voting Rights Act. An estimated 50,000 persons took part in this "rebellion," attacking police and firemen, looting white-owned businesses, and burning buildings. It required 15,000 police and National Guardsmen to restore order, by which time thirty-five people lay dead, 900 were injured, and $30 million worth of property had been destroyed.

By the summer of 1967, violence had become so widespread that some feared racial civil war. Urban uprisings in that year left twenty-three dead in Newark and forty-three in Detroit, where entire blocks went up in flames and property damage ran into the hundreds of millions of dollars. The violence led Johnson to appoint a commission headed by Illinois governor Otto Kerner to study the causes of urban rioting. Released in 1968, the Kerner Report blamed the violence on "segregation and poverty" and offered a powerful indictment of "white racism." It depicted a country in danger of being torn apart by racial antagonism: "Our nation is moving toward two societies, one black, one white—separate and unequal." But the report failed to offer any clear proposals for change.

With black unemployment twice that of whites and the average black family income little more than half the white norm, the movement looked for ways to "make freedom real" for black Americans. In 1964, King called for a "Bill of Rights for the Disadvantaged" to mobilize the nation's resources to abolish economic deprivation. His proposal was directed against poverty in general, but King also insisted that after "doing something special *against* the Negro for hundreds of years," the United States had an obligation to "do something special *for* him now"—an early call for what would come to be known as "affirmative action." A. Philip Randolph and civil rights veteran Bayard Rustin proposed a Freedom Budget, which envisioned spending $100 billion over ten years on a federal program of job creation and urban redevelopment.

In 1965, Martin Luther King Jr., and the black labor leader A. Philip Randolph called for a Freedom Budget, which they claimed would eliminate poverty by 1975. The proposal illustrated how the focus of the civil rights movement was shifting from desegregation to economic inequality.

Martin Luther King Jr. (on the left) and Malcolm X at their only meeting, on March 26, 1964, during the congressional debate on the Civil Rights Act.

In 1966, King launched the Chicago Freedom Movement, with demands quite different from its predecessors in the South—an end to discrimination by employers and unions, equal access to mortgages, the integration of public housing, and the construction of low-income housing scattered throughout the region. Confronting the entrenched power of Mayor Richard J. Daley's political machine and the ferocious opposition of white home owners, the movement failed. King's tactics—marches, sit-ins, mass arrests—proved ineffective in the face of the North's less pervasive but still powerful system of racial inequality. As he came to realize the difficulty of combating the economic plight of black America, King's language became more and more radical. He called for nothing less than a "revolution in values" that would create a "better distribution of wealth" for "all God's children."

MALCOLM X

The civil rights movement's first phase had produced a clear set of objectives, far-reaching accomplishments, and a series of coherent if sometimes competitive organizations. The second witnessed political fragmentation and few significant victories. Even during the heyday of the integration struggle, the fiery orator Malcolm X had insisted that blacks must control the political and economic resources of their communities and rely on their own efforts rather than working with whites. Having committed a string of crimes as a youth, Malcolm Little was converted in jail to the teachings of the Nation of Islam, or Black Muslims, who preached a message of white evil and black self-discipline. Malcolm dropped his "slave surname" in favor of "X," symbolizing blacks' separation from their African ancestry. On his release from prison he became a spokesman for the Muslims and a sharp critic of the ideas of integration and nonviolence, and of King's practice of appealing to American values. "I don't see any American dream," he proclaimed. "I see an American nightmare."

On a 1964 trip to Mecca, Saudi Arabia, Islam's spiritual home, Malcolm X witnessed harmony among Muslims of all races. He now began to speak of the possibility of interracial cooperation for radical change in the United States. But when members of the Nation of Islam assassinated him in February 1965 after he had formed his own Organization of Afro-American Unity, Malcolm X left neither a consistent ideology nor a coherent movement. Most whites considered him an apostle of racial violence. However, his call for blacks to rely on their own resources struck a chord among the urban poor and younger civil rights activists. His *Autobiography*, published in 1966, became a great best-seller. Today, streets, parks, and schools are named after him.

THE RISE OF BLACK POWER

Malcolm X was the intellectual father of "Black Power," a slogan that came to national attention in 1966 when SNCC leader Stokely Carmichael used it during a civil rights march in Mississippi. Black Power immediately became a rallying cry for those bitter over the federal government's failure to stop violence against civil rights workers, white attempts to determine movement strategy (as at the Democratic convention of 1964), and the civil rights movement's failure to have any impact on the economic problems of black ghettos.

One who embraced the idea proclaimed, "Black Power means Black Freedom"—freedom, especially, from whites who tried to dictate the movement's goals. A highly imprecise idea, Black Power suggested everything from the election of more black officials (hardly a radical notion) to the belief that black Americans were a colonized people whose freedom could only be won through a revolutionary struggle for self-determination. But however employed, the idea reflected the radicalization of young civil rights activists and sparked an explosion of racial self-assertion, reflected in the slogan "black is beautiful." The abandonment of the word "Negro" in favor of "Afro-American," as well as the popularity of black beauty pageants, African styles of dress, and the "natural," or "Afro," hairdo among both men and women, signified much more than a change in language and fashion. They reflected a new sense of racial pride and a rejection of white norms.

Inspired by the idea of black self-determination, SNCC and CORE repudiated their previous interracialism and new militant groups sprang into existence. Many of these groups proved short-lived. But both traditional civil rights organizations and black politicians adopted some of their ideas. Most prominent of the new groups, in terms of publicity, if not numbers, was the Black Panther Party. Founded in Oakland, California, in 1966, it became notorious for advocating armed self-defense in response to police brutality. It demanded the release of black prisoners because of racism in the criminal justice system. The party's youthful members alarmed whites by wearing military garb, although they also ran health clinics, schools, and children's breakfast programs. But internal disputes and a campaign against the Black Panthers by police and the FBI, which left several leaders dead in shootouts, destroyed the organization.

Black unemployment declined throughout the second half of the 1960s. But by 1967, with the escalation of U.S. military involvement in Vietnam, the War on Poverty had ground to a halt. By then, with ghetto uprisings punctuating the urban landscape, the antiwar movement assuming massive proportions, and millions of young people ostentatiously rejecting mainstream values, American society faced its greatest crisis since the Depression.

VIETNAM AND THE NEW LEFT

OLD AND NEW LEFTS

To most Americans, the rise of a protest movement among white youth came as a complete surprise. For most of the century, colleges had been conservative institutions that drew their students from a privileged segment of the population. During the 1950s, young people had been called a "silent generation." If blacks' grievances appeared self-evident, those of white college students were difficult to understand. What persuaded large numbers of children of affluence to reject the values and institutions of their society? In part, the answer lay in a redefinition of the meaning of freedom by what came to be called the New Left.

Betye Saar's 1972 installation, The Liberation of Aunt Jemima, *illustrates modes of thought associated with Black Power. Quaker Oats Company has long used an image of a black woman reminiscent of the stereotypical slave "mammy" as a symbol for its brand of pancake mix. Saar gives Aunt Jemima a rifle to go along with her broom. In front of her is another Aunt Jemima, holding a light-skinned baby, a symbol, according to the artist, of the sexual exploitation of black women by white men. Images in the background reveal how Quaker Oats had already modified its advertising image, giving her a smaller kerchief and an Afro hairdo. By the end of the twentieth century, the kerchief had disappeared entirely, and Aunt Jemima had become slimmer and younger and was not smiling quite so broadly.*

What made the New Left new was its rejection of the intellectual and political categories that had shaped radicalism and liberalism for most of the twentieth century. It challenged not only mainstream America but also what it dismissively called the Old Left. Unlike the Communist Party, it did not take the Soviet Union as a model or see the working class as the main agent of social change. Instead of economic equality and social citizenship, the language of New Deal liberals, the New Left spoke of loneliness, isolation, and alienation, of powerlessness in the face of bureaucratic institutions and a hunger for authenticity that affluence could not provide. These discontents galvanized a mass movement among what was rapidly becoming a major sector of the American population. By 1968, thanks to the coming of age of the baby-boom generation and the growing number of jobs that required post–high school skills, over 7 million students attended college, more than the number of farmers or steelworkers.

The New Left was not as new as it claimed. Its call for a democracy of citizen participation harked back to the American Revolution, its critique of the contrast between American values and American reality, to the abolitionists. Its emphasis on authenticity in the face of conformity recalled the bohemians of the years before World War I, and its critique of consumer culture drew inspiration from 1950s writers on mass society. But the New Left's greatest inspiration was the black freedom movement. More than any other event, the sit-ins catalyzed white student activism.

Here was the unlikely combination that created the upheaval known as The Sixties—the convergence of society's most excluded members demanding full access to all its benefits, with the children of the middle class rejecting the social mainstream. The black movement and white New Left shared basic assumptions—that the evils to be corrected were deeply embedded in social institutions and that only direct confrontation could persuade Americans of the urgency of far-reaching change.

THE FADING CONSENSUS

The years 1962 and 1963 witnessed the appearance of several path-breaking books that challenged one or another aspect of the 1950s consensus. James Baldwin's *The Fire Next Time* gave angry voice to the black revolution. Rachel Carson's *Silent Spring* exposed the environmental costs of economic growth. Michael Harrington's *The Other America* revealed the persistence of poverty amid plenty. *The Death and Life of Great American Cities*, by Jane Jacobs, criticized urban renewal, the removal of the poor from central cities, and the destruction of neighborhoods to build highways, accommodating cities to the needs of drivers rather than pedestrians. What made cities alive, she insisted, was density and diversity, the social interaction of people of different backgrounds encountering each other on urban streets.

Yet in some ways the most influential critique of all arose in 1962 from the Students for a Democratic Society (SDS), an offshoot of the socialist League for Industrial Democracy. Meeting at Port Huron, Michigan, some sixty college students adopted a document that captured the mood and summarized the beliefs of this generation of student protesters.

The Port Huron Statement devoted four-fifths of its text to criticism of institutions ranging from political parties to corporations, unions, and the military-industrial complex. But what made the document the guiding spirit of a new radicalism was the remainder, which offered a new vision of social change. "We seek the establishment," it proclaimed, of "a democracy of individual participation, [in which] the individual shares in those social decisions determining the quality and direction of his life." Freedom, for the New Left, meant "participatory democracy." Although rarely defined with precision, this became a standard by which students judged existing social arrangements—workplaces, schools, government—and found them wanting. The idea suggested a rejection of the elitist strain that had marked liberal thinkers from the Progressives to postwar advocates of economic planning, in which government experts would establish national priorities in the name of the people.

THE RISE OF SDS

By the end of 1962, SDS had grown to 8,000 members. Then, in 1964, events at the University of California at Berkeley revealed the possibility for a far broader mobilization of students in the name of participatory democracy. A Cold War "multiversity," Berkeley was an immense, impersonal institution where enrollments in many classes approached 1,000 students. The spark that set student protests alight was a new rule prohibiting political groups from using a central area of the campus to spread their ideas. Students—including conservatives outraged by being barred from distributing their own literature—responded by creating the Free Speech movement. Freedom of expression, declared Mario Savio, a student leader, "represents the very dignity of what a human being is. . . . That's what marks us off from the stones and the stars. You can speak freely." Likening the university to a factory, Savio called on students to "throw our body against the machines."

Thousands of Berkeley students became involved in the protests in the months that followed. Their program moved from demanding a repeal of the new rule to a critique of the entire structure of the university and of an education geared toward preparing graduates for corporate jobs. When the university gave in on the speech ban early in 1965, one activist exulted that the students had succeeded in reversing "the world-wide drift from freedom."

Police arresting Mario Savio, a leader of the Free Speech Movement, as he addresses a crowd on the campus of the University of California, Berkeley in 1966.

AMERICA AND VIETNAM

By 1965 the black movement and the emergence of the New Left had shattered the climate of consensus of the 1950s. But what transformed protest into a full-fledged generational rebellion was the war in Vietnam. What one historian has called "the greatest miscalculation in the history of American foreign relations"

VOICES OF FREEDOM

FROM YOUNG AMERICANS FOR FREEDOM, The *Sharon Statement* (September 1960)

Although the 1960s is usually thought of as a decade of youthful radicalism, it also witnessed the growth of conservative movements. The Sharon Statement marked the emergence of Young Americans for Freedom as a force for conservatism in American politics.

In this time of moral and political crisis, it is the responsibility of the youth of America to affirm certain eternal truths. We, as young conservatives, believe:

That foremost among the transcendent values is the individual's use of his God-given free will, whence derives his right to be free from the restrictions of arbitrary force;

That liberty is indivisible, and that political freedom cannot long exist without economic freedom;

That the purposes of government are to protect those freedoms through the preservation of internal order, the provision of national defense, and the administration of justice;

That when government ventures beyond these lawful functions, it accumulates power which tends to diminish order and liberty; . . .

That the market economy, allocating resources by the free play of supply and demand, is the single economic system compatible with the requirements of personal freedom and constitutional government, and that it is at the same time the most productive supplier of human needs; . . .

That the forces of international Communism are, at present, the greatest single threat to these liberties;

That the United States should stress victory over, rather than coexistence with, this menace.

FROM TOM HAYDEN AND OTHERS,
The *Port Huron Statement* (June 1962)

One of the most influential documents of the 1960s emerged in 1962 from a meeting sponsored by the Students for a Democratic Society in Port Huron, Michigan. Its call for a "democracy of individual participation" inspired many of the social movements of the decade and offered a critique of institutions ranging from the government to universities that failed to live up to this standard.

———————

We are the people of this generation, bred in at least modest comfort, housed now in universities, looking uncomfortably to the world we inherit. . . . Freedom and equality for each individual, government of, by, and for the people—these American values we found good principles by which we could live as men.

As we grew, however, our comfort was penetrated by events too troubling to dismiss. First, the . . . Southern struggle against racial bigotry compelled most of us from silence to activism. Second, . . . the proclaimed peaceful intentions of the United States contradicted its economic and military investments in the Cold War. . . . The conventional moral terms of the age, the politician moralities—"free world," "people's democracies"—reflect realities poorly if at all, and seem to function more as ruling myths than as descriptive principles. But neither has our experience in the universities brought us moral enlightenment. Our professors and administrators sacrifice controversy to public relations; . . . their skills and silence are purchased by investors in the arms race. . . .

We regard *men* as infinitely precious and possessed of unfulfilled capacities for reason, freedom, and love.

In affirming these principles we are aware of countering perhaps the dominant conceptions of man in the twentieth century: that he is a thing to be manipulated, and that he is inherently incapable of directing his own affairs. We oppose the depersonalization that reduces human beings to the status of things—if anything, the brutalities of the twentieth century teach that means and ends are intimately related, that vague appeals to "posterity" cannot justify the mutilations of the present. . . . We see little reason why men cannot meet with increasing skill the complexities and responsibilities of their situation, if society is organized not for minority, but for majority, participation in decision-making.

We would replace power rooted in possession, privilege, or circumstance by power and uniqueness rooted in love, reflectiveness, reason, and creativity. As a social system we seek the establishment of a democracy of individual participation [so] that the individual [can] share in those social decisions determining the quality and direction of his life. . . . A new left must consist of younger people. . . . [It] must start controversy throughout the land, if national policies and national apathy are to be reversed.

———————

QUESTIONS

1. How do the young conservatives who wrote the Sharon Statement understand freedom?

2. What do the authors of the Port Huron Statement appear to mean by participatory democracy?

3. What are the main differences, and are there any similarities, between the outlooks of the young conservatives and the young radicals?

was a logical extension of Cold War policies and assumptions. The war tragically revealed the danger that Walter Lippmann had warned of at the outset of the Cold War—viewing the entire world and every local situation within it through the either-or lens of an anticommunist crusade. A Vietnam specialist in the State Department who attended a policy meeting in August 1963 later recalled "the abysmal ignorance around the table of the particular facts of Vietnam. . . . They made absolutely no distinctions between countries with completely different historical experiences. . . . They [believed] that we could manipulate other states and build nations; that we knew all the answers."

Few Americans had any knowledge of Vietnam's history and culture. Successive administrations reduced a complex struggle for national independence, led by homegrown communists who enjoyed widespread support throughout their country in addition to Soviet backing, to a test of "containment." As noted in the previous chapter, the Truman and Eisenhower administrations had cast their lot with French colonialism in the region. After the French defeat, they financed the creation of a pro-American South Vietnamese government, in violation of the Geneva Accords of 1954 that had promised elections to unify Vietnam. By the 1960s, the United States was committed to the survival of this corrupt regime.

Fear that the public would not forgive them for "losing" Vietnam made it impossible for Presidents Kennedy and Johnson to remove the United States from an increasingly untenable situation. Kennedy's foreign policy advisers saw Vietnam as a test of whether the United States could, through "counterinsurgency"—intervention to counter internal uprisings in noncommunist countries—halt the spread of Third World revolutions. Despite the dispatch of increased American aid and numerous military advisers, South Vietnamese leader Ngo Dinh Diem lost control of the countryside to the communist-led Viet Cong. Diem resisted American advice to broaden his government's base of support. In October 1963, after large Buddhist demonstrations against his regime, the United States approved a military coup that led to Diem's death. When Kennedy was assassinated the following month, there were 17,000 American military advisers in South Vietnam. Shortly before his death, according to the notes of a White House meeting, Kennedy questioned "the wisdom of involvement in Vietnam." But he took no action to end the American presence.

LYNDON JOHNSON'S WAR

Lyndon B. Johnson came to the presidency with little experience in foreign relations. Johnson had misgivings about sending American troops to Vietnam. "I don't see that we can ever hope to get out of there once we are committed," he remarked to one senator in 1964. But he knew that Republicans had used the "loss" of China as a weapon against

Secretary of Defense Robert McNamara, on the left, and his deputy, Cyrus Vance, at a May 1965 meeting at the White House where the war in Vietnam was discussed. A bust of President Kennedy stands in the background. McNamara later wrote in his memoirs that his misgivings only grew as the war progressed.

Truman. "I am not going to be the president," he vowed, "who saw Southeast Asia go the way China went."

In August 1964, North Vietnamese vessels encountered an American ship on a spy mission off its coast. Claiming that the North Vietnamese had fired on the American vessel, Johnson proclaimed that the United States was a victim of "aggression." In response, Congress passed the Gulf of Tonkin resolution, authorizing the president to take "all necessary

A war of aerial bombing and small guerilla skirmishes rather than fixed land battles, Vietnam was the longest war in American history and the only one the United States has lost.

THE VIETNAM WAR, 1964–1975

CHINA

NORTH VIETNAM

BURMA (MYANMAR)

Dien Bien Phu•

U.S. air raids 1966–1968, 1972

Hanoi ⊗

Haiphong•

Gulf of Tonkin

LAOS

Thanh Hoa•

⊗ Gulf of Tonkin incident August 1964

Hainan

•Vinh

Vientiane•

Mekong R.

•Dong Hoi — Demilitarized zone

17th Parallel demarcation line Geneva accords, July 1954

Invasion of Laos February–March 1971

Hue ⊗ — Tet offensive January–February 1968

•Da Nang

THAILAND

Ho Chi Minh Trail

⊗ My Lai massacre March 1968

•Pleiku

•Qui Nhon

CAMBODIA

Invasion of Cambodia April–June 1970

SOUTH VIETNAM

South China Sea

Phnom Penh•

•Na Trang

Saigon ⊗

Tet offensive January–February 1968 Surrender of South Vietnam April 30, 1975

Gulf of Thailand

Mekong Delta

0   100   200 miles
0   100   200 kilometers

⊗ Major battles or actions
— U.S. and South Vietnamese offensives
━ North Vietnamese offensives
--- North Vietnamese supply routes

American soldiers in South Vietnam carrying wounded men to safety after a 1966 battle.

measures to repel armed attack" in Vietnam. Only two members—Senators Ernest Gruening of Alaska and Wayne Morse of Oregon—voted against giving Johnson this blank check. The nearest the United States ever came to a formal declaration of war, the resolution passed without any discussion of American goals and strategy in Vietnam. (Over forty years later, in December 2005, the National Security Agency finally released hundreds of pages of secret documents that made it clear that no North Vietnamese attack had actually taken place.)

During the 1964 campaign, Johnson insisted that he had no intention of sending American troops to Vietnam. But immediately after Johnson's reelection, the National Security Council recommended that the United States begin air strikes against North Vietnam and introduce American ground troops in the south. When the Viet Cong in February 1965 attacked an American air base in South Vietnam, Johnson put the plan into effect. At almost the same time, he intervened in the Dominican Republic. Here, military leaders in 1963 had overthrown the left-wing but noncommunist Juan Bosch, the country's first elected president since 1924. In April 1965, another group of military men attempted to restore Bosch to power but were defeated by the ruling junta. Fearing the unrest would lead to "another Cuba," Johnson dispatched 22,000 American troops. The intervention outraged many Latin Americans. But the operation's success seemed to bolster Johnson's determination in Vietnam.

By 1968, the number of American troops in Vietnam exceeded half a million, and the conduct of the war had become more and more brutal. American planes dropped more tons of bombs on the small countries of North and South Vietnam than both sides used in all of World War II. They spread chemicals that destroyed forests to deprive the Viet Cong of hiding places and dropped bombs filled with napalm, a gelatinous form of gasoline that burns the skin of anyone exposed to it. The army pursued Viet Cong and North Vietnamese forces in "search and destroy" missions that often did not distinguish between combatants and civilians. Weekly reports of enemy losses or "body counts" became a fixation of the administration. But the United States could not break its opponents' ability to fight or make the South Vietnamese government any more able to survive on its own.

THE ANTIWAR MOVEMENT

As casualties mounted and American bombs poured down on North and South Vietnam, the Cold War foreign policy consensus began to unravel. By 1968, the war had sidetracked much of the Great Society and had torn families, universities, and the Democratic Party apart. With the entire political leadership, liberal no less than conservative, committed to the war for most of the 1960s, young activists lost all confidence in "the system."

A massive 1969 antiwar demonstration on the Mall in Washington.

Opposition to the war became the organizing theme that united people with all kinds of doubts and discontents. "We recoil with horror," said a SNCC position paper, "at the inconsistency of a supposedly 'free' society where responsibility to freedom is equated with the responsibility to lend oneself to military aggression." With college students exempted from the draft, the burden of fighting fell on the working class and the poor. In 1967, Martin Luther King Jr. condemned the administration's Vietnam policy as an unconscionable use of violence and for draining resources from needs at home. At this point, King was the most prominent American to speak out against the war.

As for SDS, the war seemed the opposite of participatory democracy, since American involvement had come through secret commitments and decisions made by political elites, with no real public debate. In April 1965,

An antiwar demonstrator places flowers in the rifles of U.S. soldiers outside the Pentagon in 1967.

SDS invited opponents of American policy in Vietnam to assemble in Washington, D.C. The turnout of 25,000 amazed the organizers, offering the first hint that the antiwar movement would soon enjoy a mass constituency. At the next antiwar rally, in November 1965, SDS leader Carl Ogelsby openly challenged the foundations of Cold War thinking. He linked Vietnam to a critique of American interventions in Guatemala and Iran, support for South African apartheid, and Johnson's dispatch of troops to the Dominican Republic, all rooted in obsessive anticommunism. Some might feel, Ogelsby concluded, "that I sound mighty anti-American. To these, I say: 'Don't blame *me* for *that!* Blame those who mouthed my liberal

Two young members of the counterculture at their wedding in New Mexico.

Timothy Leary, promoter of the hallucinogenic drug LSD, listening to the band Quicksilver Messenger Service at the Human Be-In in San Francisco in 1967.

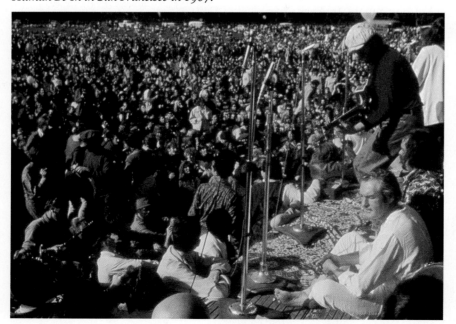

values and broke my American heart.'" The speech, observed one reporter, marked a "declaration of independence" for the New Left.

By 1967, young men were burning their draft cards or fleeing to Canada to avoid fighting in what they considered an unjust war. In October of that year, 100,000 antiwar protestors assembled at the Lincoln Memorial in Washington, D.C. Many marched across the Potomac River to the Pentagon, where photographers captured them placing flowers in the rifle barrels of soldiers guarding the nerve center of the American military.

THE COUNTERCULTURE

The New Left's definition of freedom initially centered on participatory democracy, a political concept. But as the 1960s progressed, young Americans' understanding of freedom increasingly expanded to include cultural freedom as well. Although many streams flowed into the generational rebellion known as the "counterculture," the youth revolt was inconceivable without the war's destruction of young Americans' belief in authority. By the late 1960s, millions of young people openly rejected the values and behavior of their elders. Their ranks included not only college students but also numerous young workers, even though most unions strongly opposed antiwar demonstrations and countercultural displays (a reaction that further separated young radicals from former allies on the traditional left). For the first time in American history, the flamboyant rejection of respectable norms in clothing, language, sexual behavior, and drug use, previously confined to artists and bohemians, became the basis of a mass movement. Its rallying cry was "liberation."

Here was John Winthrop's nightmare of three centuries earlier come to pass—a massive redefinition of freedom as a rejection of all authority. "Your sons and your daughters are beyond your command," Bob Dylan's song "The Times They Are A-Changin'" bluntly informed mainstream America. To be sure, the counterculture in some ways represented not rebellion but the fulfillment of the consumer marketplace. It extended into every realm of life the definition of freedom as the right to individual choice. Given the purchasing power of students and young adults, countercultural emblems—colorful clothing, rock music, images of sexual freedom, even symbols of black revolution and Native American resistance—were soon being mass-marketed as fashions of the day. Self-indulgence and self-destructive behavior were built into the counterculture. To followers of Timothy Leary, the Harvard scientist turned prophet of mind-expansion, the psychedelic drug LSD embodied a new freedom—"the freedom to expand your own consciousness." In 1967, Leary organized a Human Be-In in San Francisco, where he urged a crowd of 20,000 to "turn on, tune in, drop out."

PERSONAL LIBERATION AND THE FREE INDIVIDUAL

But there was far more to the counterculture than new consumer styles or the famed trio of sex, drugs, and rock and roll. To young dissenters, personal liberation represented a spirit of creative experimentation, a search for a way of life in which friendship and pleasure eclipsed the single-minded pursuit of wealth. It meant a release from bureaucratized education and work, repressive rules of personal behavior, and, above all, a militarized state that, in the name of freedom, rained destruction on a faraway people. It also encouraged new forms of radical action. "Underground" newspapers pioneered a personal and politically committed style of journalism. The Youth International Party, or "yippies," introduced humor and theatricality as elements of protest. From the visitor's gallery of the New York Stock Exchange, yippie founder Abbie Hoffman showered dollar bills onto the floor, bringing trading to a halt as brokers scrambled to retrieve the money.

The counterculture emphasized the ideal of community, establishing quasi-independent neighborhoods in New York City's East Village and San Francisco's Haight-Ashbury district and, in an echo of nineteenth-century utopian communities like New Harmony, some 2,000 communes nationwide. Rock festivals, like Woodstock in upstate New York in 1969, brought together hundreds of thousands of young people to celebrate their alternative lifestyle and independence from adult authority. The opening song at Woodstock, performed by Richie Havens, began with eight repetitions of the single word "freedom."

The counterculture's notion of liberation centered on the free individual. Nowhere was this more evident than in the place occupied by sexual freedom in the generational rebellion. Starting in 1960, the mass marketing of birth-control pills made possible what "free lovers" had long demanded—the separation of sex from procreation. By the late 1960s, sexual freedom had become as much an element of the youth rebellion as long hair and drugs. Rock music celebrated the free expression of sexuality. The musical *Hair*, which gave voice to the youth rebellion, flaunted nudity on Broadway. The sexual revolution was central to another mass movement that emerged in the 1960s—the "second wave" of feminism.

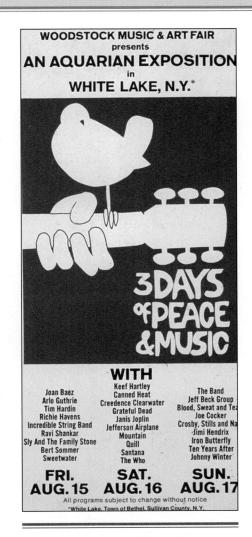

A poster listing some of the performers who took part in the Woodstock Festival in 1969. A dove of peace sits on the guitar, symbolizing the overlap between the antiwar movement and counterculture.

THE NEW MOVEMENTS AND THE RIGHTS REVOLUTION

The civil rights revolution, soon followed by the rise of the New Left, inspired other Americans to voice their grievances and claim their rights. Many borrowed the confrontational tactics of the black movement and activist students, adopting their language of "power" and "liberation" and their rejection of traditional organizations and approaches. By the late 1960s, new social movements dotted the political landscape.

THE FEMININE MYSTIQUE

The achievement of the vote had not seemed to affect women's lack of power and opportunity. When the 1960s began, only a handful of women held political office, newspapers divided job ads into "male" and "female" sections, with the latter limited to low-wage clerical positions, and major universities limited the number of female students they accepted. In many states, husbands still controlled their wives' earnings. As late as 1970, the Ohio Supreme Court held that a wife was "at most a superior servant to her husband," without "legally recognized feelings or rights."

During the 1950s, some commentators had worried that the country was wasting its "woman power," a potential weapon in the Cold War. But the public reawakening of feminist consciousness did not get its start until the publication in 1963 of Betty Friedan's *The Feminine Mystique*. Friedan had written pioneering articles during the 1940s on pay discrimination against women workers and racism in the workplace for the newspaper of the United Electrical Workers' union. But, like other social critics of the 1950s, she now took as her themes the emptiness of consumer culture and the discontents of the middle class. Her opening chapter, "The Problem That Has No Name," painted a devastating picture of talented, educated women trapped in a world that viewed marriage and motherhood as their primary goals. Somehow, after more than a century of agitation for access to the public sphere, women's lives still centered on the home. In Moscow in 1959, Richard Nixon had made the suburban home an emblem of American freedom. For Friedan, invoking the era's most powerful symbol of evil, it was a "comfortable concentration camp."

Few books have had the impact of *The Feminine Mystique*. Friedan was deluged by desperate letters from female readers relating how the suburban dream had become a nightmare. "Freedom," wrote an Atlanta woman, "was a word I had always taken for granted. [I now realized that] I had voluntarily enslaved myself." To be sure, a few of Friedan's correspondents insisted that for a woman to create "a comfortable, happy home for her family" was "what God intended." But the immediate result of *The Feminine Mystique* was to focus attention on yet another gap between American rhetoric and American reality.

The law slowly began to address feminist concerns. In 1963, Congress passed the Equal Pay Act, barring sex discrimination among holders of the same jobs. The Civil Rights Act of 1964, as noted earlier, prohibited inequalities based on sex as well as race. Deluged with complaints of discrimination by working women, the Equal Employment Opportunity Commission established by the law became a major force in breaking down barriers to female employment. The year 1966 saw the formation of the National Organization for Women (NOW), with Friedan as president. Modeled on civil rights organizations, it demanded equal opportunity in jobs, education, and political participation and attacked the "false image of women" spread by the mass media.

WOMEN'S LIBERATION

If NOW grew out of a resurgence of middle-class feminism, a different female revolt was brewing within the civil rights and student movements. As in the days of abolitionism, young women who had embraced an ideology of social equality and personal freedom and learned methods of political organizing encountered inequality and sexual exploitation. Women like Ella Baker and Fannie Lou Hamer had played major roles in grassroots civil rights organizing. But many women in the movement found themselves relegated to typing, cooking, and cleaning for male coworkers. Some were pressured to engage in sexual liaisons. Echoing the words of Abby

Kelley a century earlier, a group of female SNCC activists concluded in a 1965 memorandum that "there seem to be many parallels that can be drawn between the treatment of Negroes and the treatment of women in our society as a whole." What bothered them most was the status of women within the movement, where assumptions of male supremacy seemed as deeply rooted as in society at large.

The same complaints arose in SDS. "The Movement is supposed to be for human liberation," wrote one student leader. "How come the condition of women inside it is no better than outside?" The rapidly growing number of women in college provided a ready-made constituency for the new feminism. By 1967, women throughout the country were establishing "consciousness-raising" groups to discuss the sources of their discontent. The time, many concluded, had come to establish a movement of their own, more radical than NOW. The new feminism burst onto the national scene at the Miss America beauty pageant of 1968, when protesters filled a "freedom trash can" with objects of "oppression"—girdles, brassieres, high-heeled shoes, and copies of *Playboy* and *Cosmopolitan*. (Contrary to legend, they did not set the contents on fire, which would have been highly dangerous on the wooden boardwalk. But the media quickly invented a new label for radical women—"bra burners.") Inside the hall, demonstrators unfurled banners carrying the slogans "Freedom for Women" and "Women's Liberation."

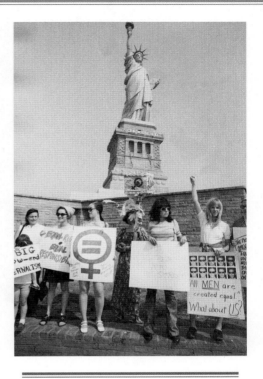

A 1970 women's liberation demonstration at the Statue of Liberty.

PERSONAL FREEDOM

The women's liberation movement inspired a major expansion of the idea of freedom by insisting that it should be applied to the most intimate realms of life. Introducing the terms "sexism" and "sexual politics" and the phrase "the personal is political" into public debate, they insisted that sexual relations, conditions of marriage, and standards of beauty were as much "political" questions as the war, civil rights, and the class tensions that had traditionally inspired the Left to action. The idea that family life is not off-limits to considerations of power and justice repudiated the family-oriented public culture of the 1950s, and it permanently changed Americans' definition of freedom.

Radical feminists' first public campaign demanded the repeal of state laws that underscored women's lack of self-determination by banning abortions or leaving it up to physicians to decide whether a pregnancy could be terminated. Without the right to control her own reproduction, wrote one activist, "woman's other 'freedoms' are tantalizing mockeries that cannot be exercised." In 1969, a group of feminists disrupted legislative hearings on New York's law banning abortions, where the experts scheduled to testify consisted of fourteen men and a Roman Catholic nun.

The call for legalized abortions merged the nineteenth-century demand that a woman control her own body with the Sixties emphasis on sexual freedom. But the concerns of women's liberation went far beyond sexuality. *Sisterhood Is Powerful*, an influential collection of essays, manifestos, and personal accounts published in 1970, touched on a remarkable array of issues, from violence against women to inequalities in the law, churches, workplaces, and family life. By this time, feminist ideas had entered the mainstream. In 1962, a poll showed that two-thirds of American women did not feel themselves to be victims of discrimination. By 1974, two-thirds did.

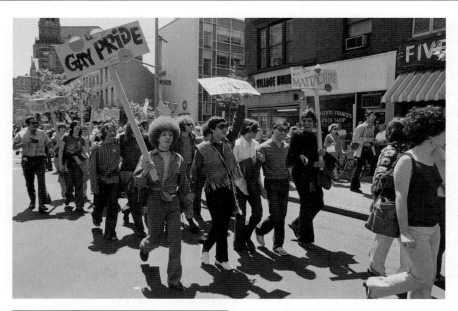

Part of the Gay Liberation Day demonstration in New York City in June 1970.

GAY LIBERATION

In a decade full of surprises, perhaps the greatest of all was the emergence of the movement for gay liberation. Efforts of one kind or another for greater rights for racial minorities and women had a long history. Homosexuals, wrote Harry Hay, who in 1951 founded the Mattachine Society, the first gay rights organization, were "the one group of disadvantaged people who didn't even think of themselves as a group." Gay men and lesbians had long been stigmatized as sinful or mentally disordered. Most states made homosexual acts illegal, and police regularly harassed the gay subcultures that existed in major cities like San Francisco and New York. McCarthyism, which viewed homosexuality as a source of national weakness, made the discrimination to which gays were subjected even worse. Although homosexuals had achieved considerable success in the arts and fashion, most kept their sexual orientation secret, or "in the closet."

The Mattachine Society had worked to persuade the public that apart from their sexual preferences, gays were average Americans who ought not to be persecuted. But as with other groups, the Sixties transformed the gay movement. If one moment marked the advent of "gay liberation," it was a 1969 police raid on the Stonewall Bar in New York's Greenwich Village, a gathering place for homosexuals. Rather than bowing to police harassment, as in the past, gays fought back. Five days of rioting followed, and a militant movement was born. Gay men and lesbians stepped out of the "closet" to insist that sexual orientation is a matter of rights, power, and identity. Prejudice against homosexuals persisted. But within a few years, "gay pride" marches were being held in numerous cities.

LATINO ACTIVISM

As in the case of blacks, a movement for legal rights had long flourished among Mexican-Americans. But the mid-1960s saw the flowering of a new militancy challenging the group's second-class economic status. Like Black Power advocates, the movement emphasized pride in both the Mexican past and the new Chicano culture that had arisen in the United States. Unlike the Black Power movement and SDS, it was closely linked to labor struggles. Beginning in 1965, César Chavez, the son of migrant farm workers and a disciple of King, led a series of nonviolent protests, including marches, fasts, and a national boycott of California grapes, to pressure growers to agree to labor contracts with the United Farm Workers union (UFW). The UFW was as much a mass movement for civil rights as a campaign for economic betterment. The boycott mobilized Latino communities throughout the Southwest and drew national attention to the pitifully low wages and oppressive working conditions of migrant laborers. In 1970, the major growers agreed to contracts with the UFW.

César Chavez leading a march of striking Chicano farm workers in 1968. Huelga *means "strike" in Spanish.*

In New York City, the Young Lords Organization, modeled on the Black Panthers, staged street demonstrations to protest the high unemployment rate among the city's Puerto Ricans and the lack of city services in Latino neighborhoods. (In one protest, they dumped garbage on city streets to draw attention to the city's failure to collect refuse in poor areas.) Like SNCC and SDS, the Latino movement gave rise to feminist dissent. Many Chicano and Puerto Rican men regarded feminist demands as incompatible with the Latino heritage of *machismo* (an exaggerated sense of manliness, including the right to dominate women). Young female activists, however, viewed the sexual double standard and the inequality of women as incompatible with freedom for all members of *la raza* (the race, or people).

The occupation of Alcatraz Island in San Francisco Bay in 1969 by "Indians of All Tribes" symbolized the emergence of a new militancy among Native Americans.

RED POWER

The 1960s also witnessed an upsurge of Indian militancy. The Truman and Eisenhower administrations had sought to dismantle the reservation system and integrate Indians into the American mainstream—a policy known as "termination," since it meant ending recognition of the remaining elements of Indian sovereignty. Many Indian leaders protested vigorously against this policy, and it was abandoned by President Kennedy. Johnson's War on Poverty channeled increased federal funds to reservations. But like other minority groups, Indian activists compared their own status to that of underdeveloped countries overseas. They demanded not simply economic aid but self-determination, like the emerging nations of the Third World. Using language typical of the late 1960s, Clyde Warrior, president of the National Indian Youth Council, declared, "We are not free in the most basic sense of the word. We are not allowed to make those basic human choices about our personal life and the destiny of our communities."

Founded in 1968, the American Indian Movement staged protests demanding greater tribal self-government and the

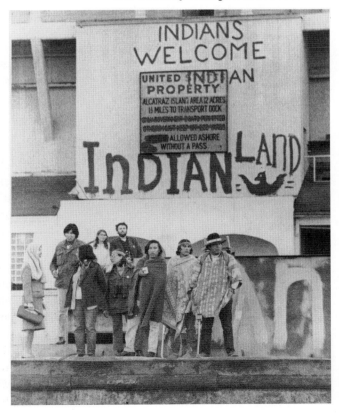

restoration of economic resources guaranteed in treaties. In 1969, a group calling itself "Indians of All Nations" occupied (or from their point of view, re-occupied) Alcatraz Island in San Francisco Bay, claiming that it had been illegally seized from its original inhabitants. The protest, which lasted into 1971, launched the Red Power movement. In the years that followed, many Indian tribes would win greater control over education and economic development on the reservations. Indian activists would bring land claims suits, demanding and receiving monetary settlements for past dispossession. As a result of a rising sense of self-respect, the number of Americans identifying themselves as Indians doubled between 1970 and 1990.

SILENT SPRING

Liberation movements among racial minorities, women, and gays challenged long-standing social inequalities. Another movement, environmentalism, called into question different pillars of American life—the equation of progress with endless increases in consumption and the faith that science, technology, and economic growth would advance the social welfare. Concern for preserving the natural environment dated back to the creation of national parks and other conservation efforts during the Progressive era. But in keeping with the spirit of the Sixties, the new environmentalism was more activist and youth-oriented, and it spoke the language of empowering citizens to participate in decisions that affected their lives. Its emergence reflected the very affluence celebrated by proponents of the American Way. As the "quality of life"—including physical fitness, health, and opportunities to enjoy leisure activities—occupied a greater role in the lives of middle-class Americans, the environmental consequences of economic growth received increased attention. When the 1960s began, complaints were already being heard about the bulldozing of forests for suburban development and the contamination produced by laundry detergents and chemical lawn fertilizers seeping into drinking supplies.

The publication in 1962 of *Silent Spring* by the marine biologist Rachel Carson brought home to millions of readers the effects of DDT, an insecticide widely used by home owners and farmers against mosquitoes, gypsy moths, and other insects. In chilling detail, Carson related how DDT killed birds and animals and caused sickness among humans. Chemical and pesticide companies launched a campaign to discredit her—some critics called the book part of a communist plot. *Time* magazine even condemned Carson as "hysterical" and "emotional"—words typically used by men to discredit women.

THE NEW ENVIRONMENTALISM

Carson's work launched the modern environmental movement. The Sierra Club, founded in the 1890s to preserve forests, saw its membership more than triple, and other groups sprang into existence to alert the country to the dangers of water contamination, air pollution, lead in paint, and the extinction of animal species. Nearly every state quickly banned the use of DDT. In 1969, television brought home to a national audience the death of birds and fish and the despoiling of beaches caused by a major oil spill off the coast of California, exposing the environmental dangers of oil transportation and ocean drilling for oil.

Despite vigorous opposition from business groups that considered its proposals a violation of property rights, environmentalism attracted the broadest bipartisan support of any of the new social movements. Under Republican president Richard Nixon, Congress during the late 1960s and early 1970s passed a series of measures to protect the environment, including the Clean Air and Clean Water Acts and the Endangered Species Act. On April 22, 1970, the first Earth Day, some 20 million people, most of them under the age of thirty, participated in rallies, concerts, and teach-ins.

Closely related to environmentalism was the consumer movement, spearheaded by the lawyer Ralph Nader. His book *Unsafe at Any Speed* (1965) exposed how auto manufacturers produced highly dangerous vehicles. General Motors, whose Chevrolet Corvair Nader singled out for its tendency to roll over in certain driving situations, hired private investigators to discredit him. When their campaign was exposed, General Motors paid Nader a handsome settlement, which he used to fund investigations of other dangerous products and of misleading advertising.

Nader's campaigns laid the groundwork for the numerous new consumer protection laws and regulations of the 1970s. Unlike 1960s movements that emphasized personal liberation, environmentalism and the consumer movement called for limiting some kinds of freedom—especially the right to use private property in any way the owner desired—in the name of a greater common good.

THE RIGHTS REVOLUTION

It is one of the more striking ironies of the 1960s that although the "rights revolution" began in the streets, it achieved constitutional legitimacy through the Supreme Court, historically the most conservative branch of government. Under the guidance of Chief Justice Earl Warren, the Court vastly expanded the rights enjoyed by all Americans and placed them beyond the reach of legislative and local majorities.

As noted in Chapter 21, the Court's emergence as a vigorous guardian of civil liberties had been foreshadowed in 1937, when it abandoned its commitment to freedom of contract while declaring that the right of free expression deserved added protection. The McCarthy era halted progress toward a broader conception of civil liberties. It resumed on June 17, 1957, known as "Red Monday" by conservatives, when the Court moved to rein in the anticommunist crusade. The justices overturned convictions of individuals for advocating the overthrow of the government, failing to answer questions before the House Un-American Activities Committee, and refusing to disclose their political beliefs to state officials. The government, Warren declared, could prosecute illegal actions, but not "unorthodoxy or dissent." By the time Warren retired in 1969, the Court had reaffirmed the right of even the most unpopular viewpoints to First Amendment protection and had dismantled the Cold War loyalty security system.

Civil liberties had gained strength in the 1930s because of association with the rights of labor; in the 1950s and 1960s, they became intertwined with civil rights. Beginning with *NAACP v. Alabama* in 1958, the Court struck down southern laws that sought to destroy civil rights organizations by forcing them to make public their membership lists. In addition, in the landmark ruling in *New York Times v. Sullivan* (1964), it overturned a libel judgment by an Alabama

Karl Hubenthal's December 8, 1976, cartoon for the Los Angeles Herald-Examiner *celebrates the rights revolution as an expansion of American liberty.*

jury against the nation's leading newspaper for carrying an advertisement critical of how local officials treated civil rights demonstrators. The "central meaning of the First Amendment," the justices declared, lay in the right of citizens to criticize their government. For good measure, they declared the Sedition Act of 1798 unconstitutional over a century and a half after it had expired. Before the 1960s, few Supreme Court cases had dealt with newspaper publishing. *Sullivan* created the modern constitutional law of freedom of the press.

The Court in the 1960s continued the push toward racial equality, overturning numerous local Jim Crow laws. In *Loving v. Virginia* (1967), it declared unconstitutional the laws still on the books in sixteen states that prohibited interracial marriage. In the following year, in *Jones v. Alfred H. Mayer Co.*, it forbade discrimination in the rental or sale of housing. Eliminating "badges of slavery," such as unequal access to housing, the ruling suggested, was essential to fulfilling at long last the promise of emancipation.

POLICING THE STATES

The Court simultaneously pushed forward the process of imposing upon the states the obligation to respect the liberties outlined in the Bill of Rights. It required states to abide by protections against illegal search and seizure, the right of a defendant to a speedy trial, the prohibition against cruel and unusual punishment, and the right of poor persons accused of a crime to receive counsel from publicly supplied attorneys. Among the most important of these decisions was the 5-4 ruling in *Miranda v. Arizona* (1966). This held that an individual in police custody must be informed of the rights to remain silent and to confer with a lawyer before answering questions and must be told that any statements might be used in court. The decision made "Miranda warnings" standard police practice.

The Court also assumed the power to oversee the fairness of democratic procedures at the state and local levels. *Baker v. Carr* (1962) established the principle that districts electing members of state legislatures must be equal in population. This "one-man, one-vote" principle overturned apportionment systems in numerous states that had allowed individuals in sparsely inhabited rural areas to enjoy the same representation as residents of populous city districts.

The justices also moved to reinforce the "wall of separation" between church and state. In 1961, they unanimously declared unconstitutional a clause in Maryland's constitution requiring that public officials declare their belief "in the existence of God." In the following two years, they decreed that prayers and Bible readings in public schools also violated the First Amendment. President Kennedy pointed out that Americans remained perfectly free to pray at home or in church, but these rulings proved to be the most unpopular of all the Warren Court's decisions. Polls showed that 80 percent of Americans favored allowing prayer in public schools.

THE RIGHT TO PRIVACY

The Warren Court not only expanded existing liberties but also outlined entirely new rights in response to the rapidly changing contours of American society. Most dramatic was its assertion of a constitutional right to privacy in *Griswold v. Connecticut* (1965), which overturned a state law prohibiting the use of contraceptives. Justice William O. Douglas, who wrote the decision, had once declared, "The right to be let alone is the beginning of all freedom." Apart from decisions of the 1920s that affirmed the right to marry and raise children without government interference, however, few legal precedents existed regarding privacy. The Constitution does not mention the word. Nonetheless, Douglas argued that a constitutionally protected "zone of privacy" within marriage could be inferred from the "penumbras" (shadows) of the Bill of Rights.

Griswold linked privacy to the sanctity of marriage. But the Court soon transformed it into a right of individuals. It extended access to birth control to unmarried adults and ultimately to minors—an admission by the Court that law could not reverse the sexual revolution. These decisions led directly to the most controversial decision that built on the rulings of the Warren Court (even though it occurred in 1973, four years after Warren's retirement). This was *Roe v. Wade*, which created a constitutional right to terminate a pregnancy. The Court declared access to abortion a fundamental freedom protected by the Constitution, a fulfillment of radical feminists' earliest demand. *Roe* provoked vigorous opposition, which has continued to this day. Only two states banned contraception when *Griswold* was decided; *Roe* invalidated the laws of no fewer than forty-six.

Griswold and *Roe* unleashed a flood of rulings and laws that seemed to accept the feminist view of the family as a collection of sovereign individuals rather than a unit with a single head. The legal rights of women within the domestic sphere expanded dramatically. Law enforcement authorities for the first time began to prosecute crimes like rape and assault by husbands against their wives. Today, some notion of privacy is central to most Americans' conception of freedom.

The rights revolution completed the transformation of American freedom from a set of entitlements enjoyed mainly by white men into an open-ended claim to equality, recognition, and self-determination. For the rest of the century, the government and legal system would be inundated by demands by aggrieved groups of all kinds, and the Supreme Court would devote much of its time to defining the rights of Americans.

1968

A YEAR OF TURMOIL

The Sixties reached their climax in 1968, a year when momentous events succeeded each other so rapidly that the foundations of society seemed to be dissolving. Late January 1968 saw the Tet offensive, in which Viet Cong and North Vietnamese troops launched well-organized uprisings in cities throughout South Vietnam, completely surprising American military leaders. The United States drove back the offensive and inflicted heavy losses. But the intensity of the fighting, brought into America's homes on television, shattered public confidence in the Johnson administration, which had repeatedly proclaimed victory to be "just around the corner." Leading members of the press and political establishment joined the chorus criticizing American involvement. Eugene McCarthy, an antiwar senator from Minnesota, announced that he would seek the Democratic nomination. In

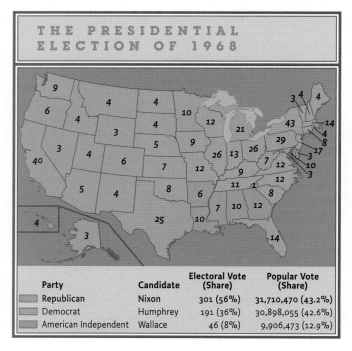

Striking sanitation workers in Memphis, Tennessee. As their signs suggest, they demanded respect as well as higher wages. Having traveled to Memphis to support the strikers, Martin Luther King Jr. was assassinated on April 4, 1968.

THE PRESIDENTIAL ELECTION OF 1968

Party	Candidate	Electoral Vote (Share)	Popular Vote (Share)
Republican	Nixon	301 (56%)	31,710,470 (43.2%)
Democrat	Humphrey	191 (36%)	30,898,055 (42.6%)
American Independent	Wallace	46 (8%)	9,906,473 (12.9%)

March, aided by a small army of student volunteers, McCarthy received over 40 percent of the vote in the New Hampshire primary. With public support dissolving, Johnson rejected the military's request to send 200,000 more troops to Vietnam. In March, he stunned the nation by announcing that he had decided not to seek reelection. Peace talks soon opened in Paris.

Meanwhile, Martin Luther King Jr. was organizing a Poor People's March, hoping to bring thousands of demonstrators to Washington to demand increased antipoverty efforts. On April 4, having traveled to Memphis to support a strike of the city's grossly underpaid black garbage collectors, King was killed by a white assassin. The greatest outbreak of urban violence in the nation's history followed in ghettos across the country. Washington, D.C., had to be occupied by soldiers before order was restored. As a gesture to King's memory, Congress passed its last major civil rights law, the Open Housing Act, which prohibited discrimination in the sale and rental of homes and apartments, although with weak enforcement mechanisms.

At the end of April, students protesting Columbia University's involvement in defense research and its plan to build a gymnasium in a public park occupied seven campus buildings. New York police removed them in an assault that left hundreds of protesters and bystanders injured and led to a strike that closed the campus. In June, a young Palestinian nationalist assassinated Robert F. Kennedy, who was seeking the Democratic nomination as an opponent of the war. In August, tens of thousands of antiwar activists descended on Chicago for protests at the Democratic national convention, where the delegates nominated Vice President Hubert Humphrey as their presidential candidate. The city's police, never known for restraint, assaulted the marchers with nightsticks, producing hundreds of injuries outside the convention hall and pandemonium inside it.

A later investigation called the event a "police riot." Nonetheless, the government indicted eight political radicals for conspiring to incite the violence. They included Tom Hayden of SDS, yippie leader Abbie Hoffman, and Bobby Seale of the Black Panthers. Five were found guilty after a tumultuous trial. But an appeals court overturned the convictions because Judge Julius Hoffman (no relation to Abbie Hoffman) had been flagrantly biased against the defendants.

NIXON'S COMEBACK

Like 1848 and 1919, 1968 was a year of worldwide upheaval, and a "turning point at which history failed to turn." In Paris, a nationwide student uprising began in May 1968 that echoed American demands for educational reform and personal liberation. French workers soon joined it, producing a general strike that paralyzed the country before it ended. Leaders bent on reform came to power in communist Czechoslovakia, only to be ousted by a Soviet invasion. Soldiers fired on students demonstrating for greater democracy on the eve of the opening of the Olympic Games in Mexico City, leading to over 500 deaths.

In the United States, instead of radical change, the year's events opened the door for a conservative reaction. Turmoil in the streets produced a demand for public order. Black militancy produced white "backlash," which played an increasing role in politics. The fact that the unelected Supreme Court was inventing and protecting "rights" fed the argument that faraway bureaucrats rode roughshod over local traditions.

In August, Richard Nixon capped a remarkable political comeback by winning the Republican nomination. He campaigned as the champion of the "silent majority"—ordinary Americans who believed that change had gone too far—and called for a renewed commitment to "law and order." Humphrey could not overcome the deep divide in his party. With 43 percent of the vote, Nixon had only a razor-thin margin over his Democratic rival. But George Wallace, running as an independent and appealing to resentments against blacks' gains, Great Society programs, and the Warren Court, received an additional 13 percent. Taken together, the Nixon and Wallace totals, which included a considerable number of former Democratic voters, indicated that four years after Johnson's landslide election ushered in the Great Society, liberalism was on the defensive.

The year 1968 did not mark the end of the 1960s. The Great Society would achieve an unlikely culmination during the Nixon administration. The second wave of feminism achieved its largest following during the 1970s. Nixon's election did, however, inaugurate a period of growing conservatism in American politics. The conservative ascendancy would usher in yet another chapter in the story of American freedom.

THE LEGACY OF THE SIXTIES

The 1960s transformed American life in ways unimaginable when the decade began. It produced new rights and new understandings of freedom. It made possible the entrance of numerous members of racial minorities into the mainstream of American life, while leaving unsolved the problem of urban poverty. It set in motion a transformation of the status of women. It changed what Americans expected from government, from clean air and water to medical coverage in old age. At the same time, it undermined public confidence in national leaders. Relations between young and old, men and women, and white and non-white, along with every institution in society, changed as a result.

Just as the Civil War and New Deal established the framework for future political debates, so, it seemed, Americans were condemned to refight the battles of the 1960s long after the decade had ended. Race relations, feminism, social policy, the nation's proper role in world affairs—these issues hardly originated in the 1960s. But the events of those years made them

Signs, *a 1970 painting by Robert Rauschenberg, presents a collage of images from the turbulent 1960s, including troops putting down urban rioting, Robert F. Kennedy, singer Janis Joplin, peace demonstrators, John F. Kennedy, Martin Luther King Jr. after his assassination, and an astronaut on the moon.*

more pressing and more divisive. As the country became more conservative, the Sixties would be blamed for every imaginable social ill, from crime and drug abuse to a decline of respect for authority. Yet during the 1960s, the United States had become a more open, more tolerant—in a word, a freer country.

SUGGESTED READING

Anderson, John A., III. *The Other Side of the Sixties: Young Americans for Freedom and the Rise of Conservative Politics* (1997). Considers conservative students of the 1960s and how they laid the groundwork for the later growth of their movement.

Anderson, Terry H. *The Movement and the Sixties: Protest in America from Greensboro to Wounded Knee* (1995). Offers an account of the numerous social protests that took place in the 1960s.

Brick, Howard. *Age of Contradiction: American Thought and Culture in the 1960s* (1998). A careful examination of the complex currents of thought that circulated during the decade.

Carson, Clayborne. *In Struggle: SNCC and the Black Awakening of the 1960s* (1981). A study of the Student Non-Violent Coordinating Committee and its impact on the 1960s.

D'Emilio, John. *Sexual Politics, Sexual Communities: The Making of a Homosexual Minority in the United States, 1940–1970* (1983). Explores the status of gay men and lesbians in mid-twentieth-century America and the rise of the gay movement.

Dittmer, John. *Local People: The Struggle for Civil Rights in Mississippi* (1994). Traces the civil rights movement in one state, looked at from the experience of grass-roots activists.

Herring, George C. *America's Longest War: The United States and Vietnam, 1950–1975* (2002 ed.). The fullest study of how the United States became involved in the war in Vietnam, and the course of the conflict.

Horwitz, Morton J. *The Warren Court and the Pursuit of Justice* (1998). Analyzes how the Supreme Court redefined the rights of Americans under Chief Justice Earl Warren.

Isserman, Maurice, and Michael Kazin. *America Divided: The Civil War of the 1960s* (2000). A comprehensive account of the social movements and political debates of the 1960s.

Matusow, Allen J. *The Unraveling of America: A History of Liberalism in the 1960s* (1984). Examines how liberalism triumphed and then dissolved during the 1960s.

Porter, Gareth. *Perils of Dominance: Imbalance of Power and the Road to Vietnam* (2005). Discusses the assumptions of policymakers and their effect on foreign policy, especially the idea that American power could not be resisted.

Rosen, Ruth. *The World Split Open: How the Modern Women's Movement Changed America* (2000). Considers how the "second wave" of feminism transformed the lives of American women and men.

Rossinow, Douglas C. *The Politics of Authenticity: Liberalism, Christianity, and the New Left in America* (1998). A careful look at some of the intellectual roots of New Left radicalism.

Sale, Kirkpatrick. *The Green Revolution: The American Environmental Movement, 1962–1992* (1993). A brief history of one of the most significant movements to emerge from the 1960s.

Skretny, John. *The Minority Rights Revolution* (2002). An account of the rights revolution and how it affected American society and its understanding of the rights of citizens.

REVIEW QUESTIONS

1. Explain why many blacks, especially in the North, did not believe that the civil rights legislation passed in 1964 and 1965 went far enough.

2. Although some monies from the War on Poverty helped Indians on reservations, many desired self-determination. Analyze why Indians desired self-determination, its benefits to them, and any possible disadvantages.

3. Illustrate how Lyndon Johnson's War on Poverty redefined the relationship between freedom and equality.

4. What were the main reasons for the increased American involvement in Vietnam?

5. How did the civil rights movement influence the rights revolution of the 1960s?

KEY TERMS

Freedom Rides (p. 969)

Bay of Pigs (p. 973)

Voting Rights Act of 1965 (p. 979)

Hart-Celler Act (p. 980)

War on Poverty (p. 981)

Chicago Freedom Movement (p. 984)

Red Power (p. 1000)

Baker v. Carr (p. 1002)

Chicago Seven (p. 1004)

George Wallace presidential candidacy (p. 1005)

REVIEW TABLE

The Rights Revolution

Group	Leading Figure	Major Organization	Platform
Feminists	Betty Friedan	National Organization for Women	To increase opportunities for women in the workplace and in education
Environmentalists	Rachel Carson	Sierra Club	To reduce harmful chemicals in the environment and bring awareness through the celebration of Earth Day
Latinos	César Chavez	United Farm Workers Union	To improve work conditions and obtain civil rights for migrant farm workers
Gays	Harry Hay	Mattachine Society	To persuade the public that sexual preferences ought not to be persecuted
Indians	Clyde Warrior	American Indian Movement	To demand greater tribal self-government and the restoration of economic resources

CHAPTER 26

The Triumph of Conservatism, 1969–1988

A delegate to the Republican national convention of 1980 wears a hat festooned with the flags of the United States and Texas and a button with a picture of her hero, Ronald Reagan, who brought conservatism to the White House and launched the Reagan Revolution.

FOCUS QUESTIONS

• What were the major policies of the Nixon administration on social and economic issues?

• What was the significance of the Watergate scandal?

• In what ways did Americans experience the 1970s as a period of limits?

• How did the rising conservatism of the 1970s affect social and economic issues?

• What was the significance of the Reagan presidency?

eginning with the dramatic 1960 contest between John F. Kennedy and Richard M. Nixon, the journalist Theodore White published best-selling accounts of four successive races for the presidency. Covering the 1964 election, White attended civil rights demonstrations and rallies for Barry Goldwater, the Republican nominee. White noticed something that struck him as odd: "The dominant word of these two groups, which loathe each other, is 'freedom.' Both demand either Freedom Now or Freedom for All. The word has such emotive power behind it that . . . a reporter is instantly denounced for questioning what they mean by the word 'freedom.'" The United States, White concluded, sorely needed "a commonly agreed-on concept of freedom."

White had observed firsthand the struggle over the meaning of freedom set in motion by the 1960s, as well as the revival of conservatism in the midst of an era known for radicalism. Goldwater's campaign helped to crystalize and popularize ideas that would remain the bedrock of conservatism for years to come. To intense anticommunism, Goldwater added a critique of the welfare state for destroying "the dignity of the individual." He demanded a reduction in taxes and governmental regulations. Goldwater showed that with liberals in control in Washington, conservatives could claim for themselves the tradition of antigovernment populism, thus broadening their electoral base and countering their image as upper-crust elitists.

The second half of the 1960s and the 1970s would witness pivotal developments that reshaped American politics—the breakup of the political coalition forged by Franklin D. Roosevelt; an economic crisis that traditional liberal remedies seemed unable to solve; a shift of population and economic resources to conservative strongholds in the "Sunbelt" of the South and West; the growth of an activist, conservative Christianity increasingly aligned with the Republican Party; and a series of setbacks for the United States overseas. Together, they led to growing popularity for conservatives' ideas, including their understanding of freedom.

PRESIDENT NIXON

From the vantage point of the early twenty-first century, it is difficult to recall how marginal conservatism seemed at the end of World War II. Associated in many minds with conspiracy theories, anti-Semitism, and preference for social hierarchy over democracy and equality, conservatism seemed a relic of a discredited past. "In the United States at this time," wrote the social critic Lionel Trilling in 1949, "liberalism is not only the dominant but even the sole intellectual tradition. For it is the plain fact that nowadays there are no conservative or reactionary ideas in general cir-

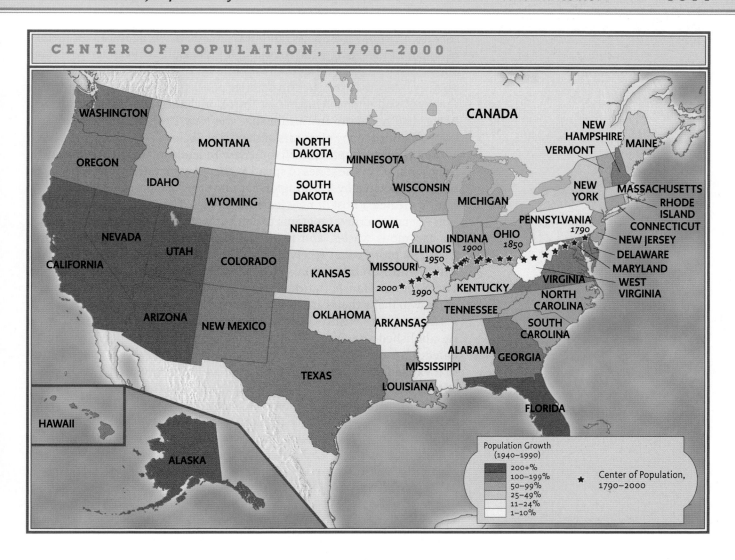

CENTER OF POPULATION, 1790–2000

Population Growth
(1940–1990)

- 200+%
- 100–199%
- 50–99%
- 25–49%
- 11–24%
- 1–10%

★ Center of Population, 1790–2000

culation." When conservative ideas did begin to spread, liberals like Trilling explained them as a rejection of the modern world by the alienated or psychologically disturbed.

Nonetheless, as noted in the previous two chapters, the 1950s and 1960s witnessed a conservative rebirth. And in 1968, a "backlash" among formerly Democratic voters against both black assertiveness and antiwar demonstrations helped to propel Richard Nixon into the White House. But conservatives found Nixon no more to their liking than his predecessors. Nixon echoed conservative language, especially in his condemnation of student protesters and his calls for law and order, but in office he expanded the welfare state and moved to improve American relations with the Soviet Union and China. During his presidency, the social changes set in motion by the 1960s—seen by conservatives as forces of moral decay—continued apace.

NIXON'S DOMESTIC POLICIES

Having won the presidency by a very narrow margin, Nixon moved toward the political center on many issues. A shrewd politician, he worked to solidify his support among Republicans while reaching out to disaffected elements of the Democratic coalition. It is difficult to characterize Nixon's domestic agenda according to the traditional categories of liberal and conservative. Mostly interested in foreign policy, he had no desire to battle Congress, still under Democratic control, on domestic issues. Just as Eisenhower had helped to institutionalize the New Deal, Nixon accepted and even expanded many elements of the Great Society.

Conservatives applauded Nixon's New Federalism, which offered federal "block grants" to the states to spend as they saw fit, rather than for specific purposes dictated by Washington. On the other hand, the Nixon administration created a host of new federal agencies. The Environmental Protection Agency oversaw programs to combat water and air pollution, cleaned up hazardous wastes, and required "environmental impact" statements from any project that received federal funding. The Occupational Safety and Health Administration sent inspectors into the nation's workplaces. The National Transportation Safety Board instructed automobile makers on how to make their cars safer.

Nixon spent lavishly on social services and environmental initiatives. He abolished the Office of Economic Opportunity, which had coordinated Johnson's War on Poverty. But he signed congressional measures that expanded the food stamp program and indexed Social Security benefits to inflation—meaning that they would rise automatically as the cost of living increased. The Endangered Species Act prohibited spending federal funds on any project that might extinguish an animal species. The Clean Air Act set air quality standards for carbon monoxide and other chemicals released by cars and factories and led to a dramatic decline in air pollution.

NIXON AND WELFARE

Perhaps Nixon's most startling initiative was his proposal for a Family Assistance Plan, or "negative income tax," that would replace Aid to Families with Dependent Children (AFDC) by having the federal government guarantee a minimum income for all Americans. Universally known as "welfare," AFDC provided assistance, often quite limited, to poor families who met local eligibility requirements. Originally a New Deal program that mainly served the white poor, welfare had come to be associated with blacks, who by 1970 accounted for nearly half the recipients. The AFDC rolls expanded rapidly during the 1960s. This arose from an increase in births to unmarried women, which produced a sharp rise in the number of poor female-headed households, and from an aggressive campaign by welfare rights groups to encourage people to apply for benefits. Conservative politicians now attacked recipients of welfare as people who preferred to live at the expense of honest taxpayers rather than by working.

A striking example of Nixon's willingness to break the political mold, his plan to replace welfare with a guaranteed annual income failed to win approval by Congress. It proved too radical for conservatives, who saw it as a reward for laziness, while liberals denounced the proposed level of $1,600 per year for a needy family of four as inadequate.

NIXON AND RACE

Nixon's racial policies offer a similarly mixed picture. To consolidate support in the white South, he nominated to the Supreme Court Clement Haynsworth and G. Harold Carswell, conservative southern jurists with records of support for segregation. Both were rejected by the Senate. On the other hand, because the courts finally lost patience with southern delaying tactics, extensive racial integration at last came to public schools in the South. In Nixon's first three years in office, the proportion of southern black students attending integrated schools rose from 32 percent to 77 percent.

For a time, the Nixon administration also pursued "affirmative action" programs to upgrade minority employment. Under Johnson, the Department of Labor had required contractors receiving federal money to establish "specific goals and timetables"—that is, to establish what number of minorities should be hired, and by when—to implement equal employment opportunity. Soon after taking office, the Nixon administration expanded this initiative with the Philadelphia Plan, which required that construction contractors on federal projects hire specific numbers of minority workers. Secretary of Labor George Shultz, who initiated the idea, sincerely hoped to open more jobs for black workers. Nixon seems to have viewed the plan mainly as a way of fighting inflation by weakening the power of the building trades unions. Their control over the labor market, he believed, pushed wages to unreasonably high levels, raising the cost of construction. And, he calculated, if the plan caused dissension between blacks and labor unions—two pillars of the Democratic coalition—Republicans could only benefit.

Trade unions of skilled workers like plumbers and electrical workers, which had virtually no black members, strongly opposed the Philadelphia Plan. After a widely publicized incident in May 1970, when a group of construction workers assaulted antiwar demonstrators in New York City, Nixon suddenly decided that he might be able to woo blue-collar workers in preparation for his 1972 reelection campaign. He soon attacked the very affirmative action goals his administration had initiated. He abandoned the Philadelphia Plan in favor of an ineffective one that stressed voluntary local efforts toward minority hiring instead of federal requirements.

Richard Nixon (on the right) and former Alabama governor George Wallace at an "Honor America" celebration in February 1974. Nixon's "southern strategy" sought to woo Wallace's supporters into the Republican party.

THE BURGER COURT

When Earl Warren retired as chief justice in 1969, Nixon appointed Warren Burger, a federal court-of-appeals judge, to succeed him. An outspoken critic of the "judicial activism" of the Warren Court—its willingness to expand old rights and create new ones by overturning acts of Congress and the states—Burger was expected to lead the justices in a conservative direction. But like Nixon, he surprised many of his supporters. While the pace of change slowed, the Burger Court, at least initially, consolidated and expanded many of the judicial innovations of the 1960s.

In 1971, in *Swann v. Charlotte-Mecklenburg Board of Education*, which arose from North Carolina, the justices unanimously approved a lower court's plan that required the extensive transportation of students to achieve

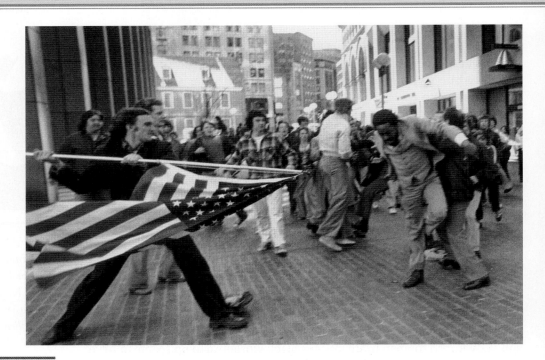

The battle over busing students to achieve racial integration in Boston produced a series of violent incidents, this one in April 1976. The photographer, Stanley Forman, won a Pulitzer Prize for this image, to which he gave the title The Soiling of Old Glory.

school integration. The decision led to hundreds of cases in which judges throughout the country ordered the use of busing as a tool to achieve integration. With many white parents determined to keep their children in neighborhood schools and others willing to move to the suburbs or enroll them in private academies to avoid integration, busing became a lightning rod for protests. One of the most bitter fights took place in Boston in the mid-1970s. Residents of the tightly knit Irish-American community of South Boston demonstrated vociferously and sometimes violently against a busing plan decreed by a local judge.

The Supreme Court soon abandoned the idea of overturning local control of schools, or moving students great distances to achieve integration. In 1973, it rebuffed a group of Texas Latinos who sued to overturn the use of property taxes to finance public education. Because of the great disparity in wealth between districts, spending on predominantly Mexican-American schools stood far below that for white ones. But in *San Antonio Independent School District v. Rodriguez*, a 5-4 Court majority ruled that the Constitution did not require equality of school funding. In the following year, in *Milliken v. Bradley* (1974), the justices overturned a lower court order that required Detroit's predominantly white suburbs to enter into a regional desegregation plan with the city's heavily minority school system. By absolving suburban districts of responsibility for assisting in integrating urban schools, the decision guaranteed that housing segregation would be mirrored in public education. Indeed, by the 1990s, public schools in the North were considerably more segregated than those in the South.

THE COURT AND AFFIRMATIVE ACTION

Efforts to promote greater employment opportunities for minorities also spawned politically divisive legal issues. Many whites came to view affirmative action programs as a form of "reverse discrimination," claiming that, in violation of the Fourteenth Amendment's equal protection clause, they granted minorities special advantages over whites. Even as affirmative action programs quickly spread from blacks to encompass women, Latinos, Asian-Americans, and Native Americans, conservatives demanded that the Supreme Court invalidate all such policies. The justices refused, but they found it difficult to devise a consistent approach to this politically charged issue.

In *Griggs v. Duke Power Company* (1971), the Court ruled that even racially neutral job requirements such as a written examination were illegal if they operated to exclude a disproportionate number of non-white applicants and were not directly related to job performance. Later in the decade, in *United Steelworkers of America v. Weber* (1979), it upheld a program devised by the Kaiser Aluminum & Chemical Corporation and its union that set quotas for training and hiring non-white workers in skilled jobs. Since this private, voluntary agreement did not involve government action, the Court ruled, it did not violate the Fourteenth Amendment's ban on state policies that discriminated among citizens.

The justices, however, proved increasingly hostile to governmental affirmative action policies. In *Regents of the University of California v. Bakke* (1978), the Court overturned an admissions program of the University of California at Davis, a public university, which set aside 16 of 100 places in the entering medical school class for minority students. Justice Lewis F. Powell, a Nixon appointee who cast the deciding vote in the 5-4 decision, rejected the idea of fixed affirmative action quotas. He added, however, that race could be used as one factor among many in admissions decisions, so affirmative action continued at most colleges and universities. During the 1990s, as courts in different parts of the country interpreted *Bakke* in different ways, the legal status of affirmative action would remain ambiguous. In 2003, a 5-4 majority reaffirmed the *Bakke* principle that institutions of higher learning may use race as a consideration in admissions decisions.

THE CONTINUING SEXUAL REVOLUTION

To the alarm of conservatives, during the 1970s the sexual revolution passed from the counterculture into the social mainstream. The number of Americans who told public-opinion polls that premarital sex was wrong plummeted. The number of divorces soared, reaching over 1 million in 1975, double the number ten years earlier. The age at which both men and women married rose dramatically. The figure for divorces in 1975 exceeded the number of first-time marriages. A popular 1978 film, *An Unmarried Woman*, portrayed the dissolution of a marriage as a triumph for the wife, who discovered her potential for individual growth only after being abandoned by her husband. As a result of women's changing aspirations and the availability of birth control and legal abortions, the American birthrate declined dramatically. By 1976, the average woman was bearing 1.7 children during her lifetime, less than half the figure of 1957 and below the level at which a population reproduces itself. A 1971 survey of the last five graduating classes at Bryn Mawr, an elite women's college, reported the birth of over seventy children. A similar survey covering the classes of 1971 through 1975 found that only three had been born.

Table 26.1 RATE OF DIVORCE: DIVORCES OF EXISTING MARRIAGES PER 1,000 NEW MARRIAGES, 1950–1980	
Year	**Divorces**
1950	385
1955	377
1960	393
1965	479
1970	708
1975	1,036
1980	1,189

One result of the "sexual revolution" was a sharp rise in the age at which Americans chose to marry, and an increase in the number of divorces.

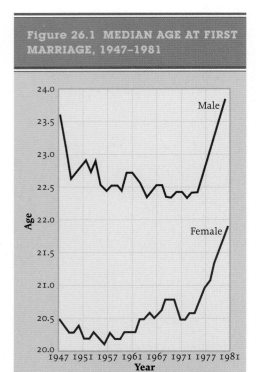

Figure 26.1 MEDIAN AGE AT FIRST MARRIAGE, 1947–1981

During the Nixon years, women made inroads into areas from which they had long been excluded. In 1972, Congress approved Title IX, which banned gender discrimination in higher education, and the Equal Credit Opportunity Act, which required that married women be given access to credit in their own name. The giant corporation American Telephone and Telegraph (AT&T) entered into a landmark agreement in which it agreed to pay millions of dollars to workers who had suffered gender discrimination and to upgrade employment opportunities for women. The number of women at work continued its upward climb. In 1960, only 20 percent of women with young children had been in the workforce. The figure reached 40 percent in 1980, and 55 percent in 1990. Working women were motivated by varied aims. Some sought careers in professions and skilled jobs previously open only to men. Others, spurred by the need to bolster family income as the economy faltered, flooded into the traditional, low-wage, "pink-collar" sector, working as cashiers, secretaries, and telephone operators.

In addition, the gay and lesbian movement, born at the end of the 1960s, expanded greatly during the 1970s and became a major concern of the right. In 1969, there had been about fifty local gay rights groups in the United States; ten years later, their numbers reached into the thousands. They began to elect local officials, persuaded many states to decriminalize homosexual relations, and succeeded in convincing cities with large gay populations to pass antidiscrimination laws. They actively encouraged gay men and lesbians to "come out of the closet"—that is, to reveal their sexual orientation. During the 1970s, the American Psychiatric Association removed homosexuality from its list of mental diseases.

As pre–World War I bohemians saw many of their ideas absorbed into the mass culture of the 1920s, values and styles of the 1960s became part of 1970s America, dubbed by the writer Tom Wolfe the "Me Decade." When asked in a Gallup poll to rate a series of ideas, respondents gave the highest

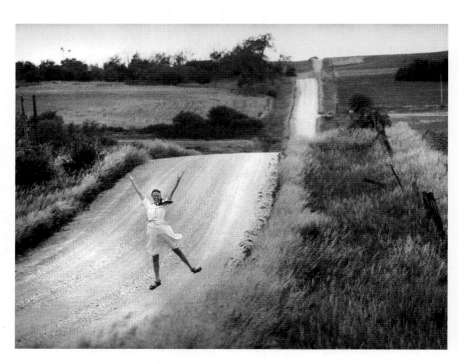

Daryl Koehn, of Kansas, celebrates in 1977 on learning that she has been chosen as one of the first group of women allowed to study at Oxford University as a Rhodes Scholar. Since their establishment in 1903, the scholarships had been limited to men.

ranking not to "following God's will," "high income," or "a sense of accomplishment," but to "freedom to choose." The demand of student protesters that individuals be empowered to determine their own "lifestyle" emerged in depoliticized form in Americans' obsession with self-improvement through fitness programs, health food diets, and new forms of psychological therapy.

NIXON AND DÉTENTE

Just as domestic policies and social trends under Nixon disappointed conservatives, they viewed his foreign policy as dangerously "soft" on communism. To be sure, in the Third World, Nixon and Henry Kissinger, his national security adviser and secretary of state, continued their predecessors' policy of attempting to undermine governments deemed dangerous to American strategic or economic interests. Nixon funneled arms to dictatorial pro-American regimes in Iran, the Philippines, and South Africa. After Chile in 1970 elected socialist Salvador Allende as president, the CIA worked with his domestic opponents to destabilize the regime. On September 11, 1973, Allende was overthrown and killed in a military coup, which installed a bloody dictatorship under General Augusto Pinochet. Thousands of Allende backers, including a few Americans then in Chile, were tortured and murdered, and many others fled the country. The Nixon administration knew of the coup plans in advance but failed to warn Allende, and it continued to back Pinochet despite his brutal policies. Democracy did not return to Chile until the end of the 1980s.

In his relations with the major communist powers, however, Nixon fundamentally altered Cold War policies. Nixon had launched his political career as a fierce and, critics charged, unscrupulous anticommunist. But in the language of foreign relations, he and Kissinger were "realists." They had more interest in power than ideology and preferred international stability to relentless conflict. Nixon also hoped that if relations with the Soviet Union improved, the Russians would influence North Vietnam to agree to an end to the Vietnam War on terms acceptable to the United States.

Richard Nixon at a banquet celebrating his visit to China in February 1972. To his right is Premier Chou En-lai.

Nixon realized that far from being part of a unified communist bloc, China had its own interests, different from those of the Soviet Union, and was destined to play a major role on the world stage. The policy of refusing to recognize China's communist government had reached a dead end. In 1971, Kissinger flew secretly to China, paving the way for Nixon's own astonishing public visit of February 1972. The trip led to the Beijing government's taking up China's seat at the United Nations, previously occupied by the exiled regime on Taiwan. Full diplomatic relations between the United States and the People's Republic of China were not established until 1979. But Nixon's visit sparked a dramatic increase in trade between the two countries.

Three months after his trip to Beijing, Nixon became the first American president to visit the Soviet Union, where he engaged in intense negotiations with his Soviet counterpart, Leonid Brezhnev. Out of this "summit" meeting came agreements for increased trade and two landmark arms-control treaties. SALT (named for the Strategic Arms Limitation Talks under way since 1969) froze each country's arsenal of intercontinental missiles capable of carrying nuclear warheads. The Anti–Ballistic Missile Treaty banned the development of systems designed to intercept incoming missiles, so that neither side would be tempted to attack the other without fearing devastating retaliation. Nixon and Brezhnev proclaimed a new era of "peaceful coexistence," in which "détente" (cooperation) would replace the hostility of the Cold War.

VIETNAM AND WATERGATE

NIXON AND VIETNAM

Despite Nixon's foreign policy triumphs, one issue would not go away—Vietnam. Nixon ran for president in 1968 declaring that he had a "secret plan" to end the war. On taking office, he announced a new policy, Vietnamization. Under this plan, American troops would gradually be withdrawn while South Vietnamese soldiers, backed by continued American bombing, did more and more of the fighting. But Vietnamization neither limited the war nor ended the antiwar movement. Hoping to cut North Vietnamese supply lines, Nixon in 1970 ordered American troops into neutral Cambodia. The invasion did not achieve its military goals, but it destabilized the Cambodian government and set in motion a chain of events that eventually brought to power the Khmer Rouge. Before being ousted by a Vietnamese invasion in 1979, this local communist movement attempted to force virtually all Cambodians into rural communes and committed widespread massacres in that unfortunate country.

As the war escalated, protests again spread on college campuses. In the wake of the killing of four antiwar protesters at Kent State University by the Ohio National Guard and two by police at Jackson State University in Mississippi, the student movement reached its high-water mark. In the spring of 1970, more than 350 colleges and universities experienced strikes, and troops occupied 21 campuses. The protests at Kent State, a public university with a largely working-class student body, and Jackson State, a

A distraught young woman kneels beside one of the four Kent State University students killed by members of the Ohio National Guard at an antiwar demonstration in 1970.

black institution, demonstrated how antiwar sentiment had spread far beyond elite campuses like Berkeley and Columbia.

At the same time, troop morale in Vietnam plummeted. Although all young men were subject to the draft, for most of the war college students received exemptions. As a result, the army was predominantly composed of working-class whites and members of racial minorities. Unlike in previous wars, blacks complained not about exclusion from the army but about the high number of black soldiers among the casualties.

In 1965 and 1966, blacks accounted for over 20 percent of American casualties, double their proportion in the army as a whole. After protests from black leaders, President Johnson ordered the number of black soldiers in combat units reduced. For the war as a whole, blacks made up 14 percent of deaths among enlisted men.

In 1971, in one of the most dramatic demonstrations of the entire era, hundreds of veterans deposited on the steps of the Capitol medals they had received while fighting in Vietnam.

The same social changes sweeping the home front were evident among troops in Vietnam. Soldiers experimented with drugs, openly wore peace and black power symbols, refused orders, and even assaulted unpopular officers. In 1971, thousands deserted the army, while at home Vietnam veterans held antiwar demonstrations. The decline of discipline within the army convinced increasing numbers of high-ranking officers that the United States must extricate itself from Vietnam.

Public support for the war was rapidly waning. In 1969, the *New York Times* published details of the My Lai massacre of 1968, in which a company of American troops had killed some 350 South Vietnamese civilians. After a military investigation, one soldier, Lieutenant William Calley, was found guilty of directing the atrocity. (Nixon released him from prison in 1974.) In 1971, the *Times* began publishing the Pentagon Papers, a classified report prepared by the Defense Department that traced American involvement in Vietnam back to World War II and revealed how successive presidents had misled the American people about it. In a landmark freedom-of-the-press decision, the Supreme Court rejected Nixon's request for an injunction to halt publication. In 1973, Congress passed the War Powers Act. The most vigorous assertion of congressional control over foreign policy in the nation's history, it required the president to seek congressional approval for the commitment of American troops overseas.

THE END OF THE VIETNAM WAR

Early in 1973, Nixon achieved what had eluded his predecessors—a negotiated settlement in Vietnam. The Paris peace agreement, the result of five years of talks, made possible the final withdrawal of American troops. The compromise left in place the government of South Vietnam, but it also left

North Vietnamese and Viet Cong soldiers in control of parts of the South. American bombing ceased, and the military draft came to an end. Henceforth, volunteers would make up the armed forces. But the agreement did not solve the basic issue of the war—whether Vietnam would be one country or two. That question was answered in the spring of 1975, when the North Vietnamese launched a final military offensive. The government of South Vietnam collapsed; the United States did not intervene except to evacuate the American Embassy, and Vietnam was reunified under communist rule.

The only war the United States has ever lost, Vietnam was a military, political, and social disaster. By the time it ended, 58,000 Americans had been killed, along with 3 million to 4 million Vietnamese. The war cost the United States an estimated $100 billion. But the nonmonetary price was far higher. Vietnam undermined Americans' confidence in their own institutions and challenged long-standing beliefs about the country and its purposes.

Two decades after the war ended, former secretary of defense Robert McNamara published a memoir in which he admitted that the policy he had helped to shape had been "terribly wrong." Ignorance of the history and culture of Vietnam and a misguided belief that every communist movement in the world was a puppet of Moscow, he wrote, had led the country into a war that he now profoundly regretted. The *New York Times* rejected McNamara's apology. The "ghosts of those unlived lives," the young men sent to their death "for no purpose," it declared, could not so easily be wished away. But the *Times* itself, like the rest of the political establishment, had supported the war for most of its duration. For far too long, they had accepted its basic premise—that the United States had the right to decide the fate of a faraway people about whom it knew almost nothing.

WATERGATE

By the time the war ended, Richard Nixon was no longer president. His domestic policies and foreign policy successes had contributed greatly to his reelection in 1972. He won a landslide victory over liberal Democrat George McGovern, receiving 60 percent of the popular vote. Nixon made deep inroads into former Democratic strongholds in the South and among working-class white northerners. He carried every state but Massachusetts. But his triumph soon turned into disaster.

Nixon was obsessed with secrecy and could not accept honest difference of opinion. He viewed every critic as a threat to national security and developed an "enemies list" that included reporters, politicians, and celebrities unfriendly to the administration. When the Pentagon Papers were published, Nixon created a special investigative unit known as the "plumbers" to gather information about Daniel Ellsberg, the former government official who had leaked them to the press. The plumbers raided the office of Ellsberg's psychiatrist in search of incriminating records. In June 1972, five former employees of Nixon's reelection committee took part in a break-in at Democratic Party headquarters in the Watergate apartment complex in Washington, D.C. A security guard called police, who arrested the intruders.

No one knows precisely what the Watergate burglars were looking for (perhaps they intended to install listening devices), and the botched robbery played little role in the 1972 presidential campaign. But in 1973, Judge John J. Sirica, before whom the burglars were tried, determined to find out who had sponsored the break-in. A pair of *Washington Post* journalists began publishing investigative stories that made it clear that persons close to the president had ordered the burglary and then tried to "cover up" White House involvement. Congressional hearings followed that revealed a wider pattern of wiretapping, break-ins, and attempts to sabotage political opposition. When it became known that Nixon had made tape recordings of conversations in his office, a special prosecutor the president had reluctantly appointed to investigate the Watergate affair demanded copies. The Supreme Court unanimously ordered Nixon to provide them—a decision that reaffirmed the principle that the president is not above the law.

NIXON'S FALL

Week after week, revelations about the scandal unfolded. By mid-1974, it had become clear that although Nixon did not know in advance of the Watergate break-in, he had become involved immediately afterwards in authorizing payments to the burglars to remain silent or commit perjury, and he had ordered the FBI to halt its investigation of the crime. In August 1974, the House Judiciary Committee voted to recommend that Nixon be impeached for conspiracy to obstruct justice. His political support having evaporated, Nixon became the only president in history to resign.

Nixon's presidency remains a classic example of the abuse of political power. In 1973, his vice president, Spiro T. Agnew, resigned after revelations that he had accepted bribes from construction firms while serving as governor of Maryland. Nixon's attorney general, John Mitchell, and White House aides H. R. Haldeman and John Ehrlichman were convicted of obstruction of justice in the Watergate affair and went to jail. As for the president, he insisted that he had done nothing wrong—or at any rate, that previous presidents had also been guilty of lying and illegality.

Although it hardly excused his behavior, Nixon had a point. His departure from office was followed by Senate hearings headed by Frank Church of Idaho that laid bare a history of abusive actions that involved every administration since the beginning of the Cold War. In violation of the law, the FBI had spied on millions of Americans and had tried to disrupt the civil rights movement. The CIA had conducted secret operations to overthrow foreign governments and had tried to assassinate foreign leaders. It had even recruited a secret army to fight in Laos, a neighbor of Vietnam. Abuses of power, in other words, went far beyond the misdeeds of a single president.

Along with Watergate, the Pentagon Papers, and the Vietnam War itself, the Church Committee revelations seriously undermined Americans' confidence in their own government. They led Congress to enact new restrictions on the power of the FBI and CIA to spy on American citizens or conduct operations abroad without the knowledge of lawmakers. Congress also strengthened the Freedom of Information Act (FOIA), initially enacted in 1966. Since 1974, the FOIA has allowed scholars, journalists, and ordinary citizens to gain access to millions of pages of records of federal agencies.

Liberals, who had despised Nixon throughout his career, celebrated his downfall. They did not realize that the revulsion against Watergate under-

Herbert Block's 1973 cartoon depicts Americans' disbelief as revelations related to the Watergate scandal unfolded in Washington.

mined the foundations of liberalism itself, already weakened by the divisions of the 1960s. For liberalism rests, in part, on belief in the ability of government, especially the federal government, to solve social problems and promote both the public good and individual freedom. Nixon's fall and the revelations of years of governmental misconduct helped to convince many Americans that conservatives were correct when they argued that to protect liberty it was necessary to limit Washington's power over Americans' lives. The Watergate crisis also distracted attention from the economic crisis that began in the fall of 1973. Its inability to fashion a response to this crisis, which gripped the United States for much of the 1970s, dealt liberalism yet another blow.

THE END OF THE GOLDEN AGE

THE DECLINE OF MANUFACTURING

During the 1970s, the long period of postwar economic expansion and consumer prosperity came to an end, succeeded by slow growth and high inflation. There were many reasons for the end of capitalism's "golden age." With American prosperity seemingly unassailable and the military-industrial complex thriving, successive administrations had devoted little attention to the less positive economic consequences of the Cold War. To strengthen its anticommunist allies, the United States promoted the industrial reconstruction of Japan and Germany and the emergence of new centers of manufacturing in places like South Korea and Taiwan. It encouraged American companies to invest in overseas plants and did not complain when allies protected their own industries while seeking unrestricted access to the American market. Imports of foreign steel, for example, led to growing problems for this key industry at home. The strong dollar, linked to gold by the Bretton Woods agreement of 1944, made it harder to sell American goods overseas (discussed in Chapter 22).

In 1971, for the first time in the twentieth century, the United States experienced a merchandise trade deficit—that is, it imported more goods than it exported. By 1980, nearly three-quarters of goods produced in the United States were competing with foreign-made products and the number of manufacturing workers, 38 percent of the American workforce in 1960, had fallen to 28 percent. Moreover, the war in Vietnam produced ever-higher federal deficits and rising inflation.

In 1971, Nixon announced the most radical change in economic policy since the Great Depression. He took the United States off the gold standard, ending the Bretton Woods agreement that fixed the value of the dollar and other currencies in terms of gold. Henceforth, the world's currencies would "float" in relation to one another, their worth determined not by treaty but by international currency markets. Nixon hoped that lowering the dollar's value in terms of the German mark and Japanese yen would promote exports by making American goods cheaper overseas and reduce imports since foreign products would be more expensive in the United States. But the end of fixed currency rates injected a new element of instability into the world economy. Nixon also ordered wages and prices frozen for ninety days.

STAGFLATION

These policies temporarily curtailed inflation and reduced imports. But in 1973, a brief war broke out between Israel and its neighbors Egypt and Syria. Middle Eastern Arab states retaliated for Western support of Israel by quadrupling the price of oil and suspending the export of oil to the United States for several months. Long lines of cars appeared at American gas stations, which either ran out of fuel or limited how much a customer could buy. A second "oil shock" occurred in 1979 as a result of the revolution that overthrew the shah of Iran, discussed later.

Because the rapidly growing demand for fuel by cars and factories outstripped domestic supplies, by 1973 the United States imported one-third of its oil. Europe and Japan depended even more heavily on oil imports. To promote energy conservation, Congress lowered the speed limit on interstate highways to fifty-five miles per hour, and many public buildings reduced heat and lighting.

The energy crisis of the 1970s drew increased attention to domestic energy resources like oil, coal, and natural gas. While the rest of the economy stagnated, western energy production grew apace. Oil was discovered in Alaska in 1968, and in 1977 a pipeline opened to facilitate its shipment to the rest of the country. Coal production in Wyoming boomed. Western energy companies benefited from the high oil prices set by OPEC—the Organization of Petroleum Exporting Countries.

But rising oil prices rippled through the world economy, contributing to the combination of stagnant economic growth and high inflation known as "stagflation." Between 1973 and 1981, the rate of inflation in developed countries was 10 percent per year, and the rate of economic growth only 2.4 percent, a sharp deterioration from the economic conditions of the 1960s. The so-called misery index—the sum of the unemployment and inflation rates—stood at 10.8 when the decade began. By 1980, it had almost doubled. As oil prices rose, many Americans shifted from large domestically produced cars, known for high gasoline consumption, to smaller, more fuel-efficient imports. By the end of the decade, Japan had become the world's leading automobile producer, and imports accounted for nearly 25 percent of car sales in the United States.

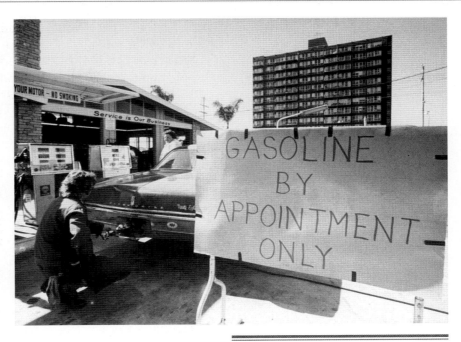

During the oil crisis of 1973, Americans confronted rising gasoline prices and widespread shortages. This photograph shows a gas station in San Diego, California, in 1974.

THE BELEAGUERED SOCIAL COMPACT

The economic crisis contributed to a breakdown of the postwar social compact. Faced with declining profits and rising overseas competition, corporations stepped up the trend, already under way before 1970, toward eliminating well-paid manufacturing jobs through automation and shifting

	Table 26.2 THE MISERY INDEX, 1970–1980		
Year	Rate of Inflation (%)	Rate of Unemployment (%)	Misery Index (%)
1970	5.9	4.9	10.8
1971	4.3	5.9	10.2
1972	3.3	5.6	8.9
1973	6.2	4.9	11.1
1974	11.0	5.6	16.6
1975	9.1	8.5	17.6
1976	5.8	7.7	13.5
1977	6.5	7.1	13.6
1978	7.7	6.1	13.8
1979	11.3	5.8	17.1
1980	13.5	7.1	20.6

production to low-wage areas of the United States and overseas. The effects on older industrial cities were devastating. By 1980, Detroit and Chicago had lost over half the manufacturing jobs that had existed three decades earlier.

Smaller industrial cities suffered even sharper declines. As their tax bases shriveled, many found themselves unable to maintain public services. In Paterson, New Jersey, where great silk factories had arisen in the early twentieth century, deindustrialization left a landscape of abandoned manufacturing plants. The poverty rate reached 20 percent, the city sold off public library buildings to raise cash, and the schools became so run down and overcrowded that the state government took control. The accelerating flow of jobs, investment, and population to the nonunion, low-wage states of the Sunbelt increased the political influence of this conservative region. Of population growth in metropolitan areas, during the 1970s, 96 percent occurred in the South and West. San Jose and Phoenix, with populations around 100,000 in 1950, neared 1 million by 1990.

In some manufacturing centers, political and economic leaders welcomed the opportunity to remake their cities as finance, information, and entertainment hubs. In New York, the construction of the World Trade Center, completed in 1977, symbolized this shift in the economy. Until destroyed by terrorists twenty-four years later, the 110-story "twin towers" stood as a symbol of New York's grandeur. But to make way for the World Trade Center, the city displaced hundreds of small electronics, printing, and other firms, causing the loss of thousands of manufacturing jobs.

LABOR ON THE DEFENSIVE

Always a junior partner in the Democratic coalition, the labor movement found itself forced onto the defensive. It has remained there ever since. One example of the weakening of unions' power came in 1975 with the New York City fiscal crisis. Deeply in debt and unable to market its bonds, the city faced the prospect of bankruptcy. The solution to the crisis required a reduction of the city's workforce, severe cuts in the budgets of schools, parks, and the subway system, and an end to the century-old policy of free tuition at the City University. Even in this center of unionism, working-class New Yorkers had no choice but to absorb job losses and a drastic decline in public services.

The weakening of unions and the continuation of the economy's long-term shift from manufacturing to service employment had an adverse impact on ordinary Americans. Between 1953 and 1973, median family income had doubled. But beginning in 1973, real wages essentially did not rise for twenty years. The 1970s was one of only two decades in the twentieth century (the other being the 1930s) that ended with Americans on average poorer than when it began. The popular song "The River," by Bruce Springsteen, captured the woes of blue-collar workers: "Is a dream a lie if it don't come true / Or is it something worse?"

FORD AS PRESIDENT

Economic problems dogged the presidencies of Nixon's successors. Gerald Ford, who had been appointed to replace Vice President Agnew, succeeded to the White House when Nixon resigned. Ford named Nelson Rockefeller of New York as his own vice president. Thus, for the only time in American history, both offices were occupied by persons for whom no one had actually voted. Among his first acts as president, Ford pardoned Nixon, shielding him from prosecution for obstruction of justice. Ford claimed that he wanted the country to put the Watergate scandal behind it. But the pardon proved to be widely unpopular.

In domestic policy, Ford's presidency lacked significant accomplishment. Ford and his chief economic adviser, Alan Greenspan, believed that Americans spent too much on consumption and saved too little, leaving business with insufficient money for investment. They called for cutting taxes on business and lessening government regulation of the economy. But the Democratic majority in Congress was in no mood to accept these traditional Republican policies. To combat inflation, Ford urged Americans to shop wisely, reduce expenditures, and wear WIN buttons (for "Whip Inflation Now"). Although inflation fell, joblessness continued to rise. During the steep recession of 1974–1975 unemployment exceeded 9 percent, the highest level since the Depression.

In the international arena, 1975 witnessed the major achievement of Ford's presidency. In a continuation of Nixon's policy of détente, the United States and Soviet Union signed an agreement at Helsinki, Finland, that recognized the permanence of Europe's post–World War II boundaries (including the division of Germany). In addition, both superpowers agreed to respect the basic liberties of their citizens. Secretary of State Kissinger and his Soviet counterpart, Andrey Gromyko, assumed that this latter pledge would have little practical effect. But over time, the Helsinki Accords inspired movements for greater freedom within the communist countries of eastern Europe.

The World Trade Center under construction in New York City during the 1970s.

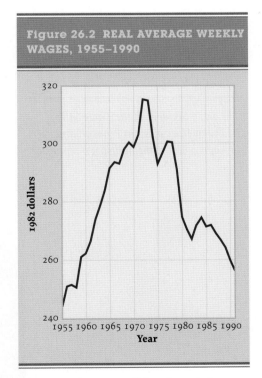

Figure 26.2 REAL AVERAGE WEEKLY WAGES, 1955–1990

Because of economic dislocations and deindustrialization, Americans' real wages (wages adjusted to take account of inflation) peaked in the early 1970s and then began a sharp, prolonged decline.

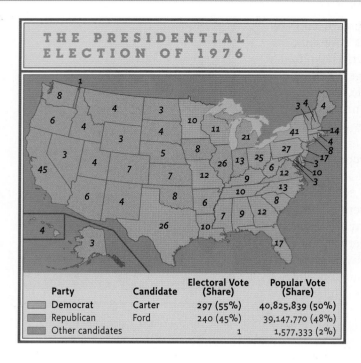

THE PRESIDENTIAL ELECTION OF 1976

Party	Candidate	Electoral Vote (Share)	Popular Vote (Share)
Democrat	Carter	297 (55%)	40,825,839 (50%)
Republican	Ford	240 (45%)	39,147,770 (48%)
Other candidates		1	1,577,333 (2%)

THE CARTER ADMINISTRATION

In the presidential election of 1976, Jimmy Carter, a former governor of Georgia, narrowly defeated Ford. A graduate of the U.S. Naval Academy who later became a peanut farmer, Carter was virtually unknown outside his state when he launched his campaign for the Democratic nomination. But realizing that Watergate and Vietnam had produced a crisis in confidence in the federal government, he turned his obscurity into an advantage. Carter ran for president as an "outsider," making a virtue of the fact that he had never held federal office. A devout "born-again" Baptist, he spoke openly of his religious convictions. His promise, "I'll never lie to you," resonated with an electorate tired of official dishonesty.

Carter had much in common with Progressives of the early twentieth century. His passions were making government more efficient, protecting the environment, and raising the moral tone of politics. Unlike the Progressives, however, he embraced the aspirations of black Americans. His inaugural address as governor of Georgia in 1971 had apologized for past mistreatment of the state's black population. As president, Carter appointed an unprecedented number of blacks to important positions, including Andrew Young, a former lieutenant of Martin Luther King Jr., as ambassador to the United Nations.

CARTER AND THE ECONOMIC CRISIS

The 1979 accident at the Three Mile Island nuclear plant in Pennsylvania brought a halt to the industry's expansion.

Although his party controlled both houses, Carter often found himself at odds with Congress. He viewed inflation, not unemployment, as the country's main economic problem, and to combat it he promoted cuts in spending on domestic programs. In the hope that increased competition would reduce prices, his administration deregulated the trucking and airline industries. Carter supported the Federal Reserve Bank's decision to raise interest rates to curtail economic activity until both wages and prices fell, traditionally a Republican policy. But oil prices kept rising, thanks to the overthrow of the shah of Iran, discussed later, and inflation did not decline.

Carter also believed that expanded use of nuclear energy could help reduce dependence on imported oil. For years, proponents of nuclear power had hailed it as an inexpensive way of meeting the country's energy needs. By the time Carter took office, over 200 nuclear plants were operating or on order. But in 1979 the industry suffered a near-fatal blow when an accident at the Three Mile Island plant in Pennsylvania released a large amount of radioactive steam into the atmosphere. The rise of the environmental movement had promoted public skepticism about scientific experts who touted the miraculous promise of technological innovations without concern for their social consequences. The Three Mile Island mishap reinforced fears about the environmental hazards associated with nuclear energy and put a halt to the industry's expansion.

Since the New Deal, Democrats had presented themselves as the party of affluence and economic growth. But Carter seemed to be presiding over a period of national decline. It did not help his popularity when, in a speech in 1979, he spoke of a national "crisis of confidence" and seemed to blame it on the American people themselves and their "mistaken idea of freedom" as "self-indulgence and consumption."

CARTER AND HUMAN RIGHTS

Carter believed that in the post-Vietnam era, American foreign policy should de-emphasize Cold War thinking. Combating poverty in the Third World, preventing the spread of nuclear weapons, and promoting human rights should take priority over what he called "the inordinate fear of communism that once led us to embrace any dictator who joined us in that fear." In one of his first acts as president, he offered an unconditional pardon to Vietnam-era draft resisters. In a 1977 address, he insisted that foreign policy could not be separated from "questions of justice, equity, and human rights."

Carter's emphasis on pursuing peaceful solutions to international problems and his willingness to think outside the Cold War framework yielded important results. In 1979, he brought the leaders of Egypt and Israel to the presidential retreat at Camp David and brokered a historic peace agreement between the two countries. He improved American relations with Latin America by agreeing to a treaty, ratified by the Senate in 1978, that provided for the transfer of

President Jimmy Carter (center), *Egyptian president Anwar Sadat* (left), *and Israeli prime minister Menachem Begin* (right) *celebrating the signing of the 1979 peace treaty between Israel and Egypt.*

the Panama Canal to local control by the year 2000. In 1979, he resisted calls for intervention when a popular revolution led by the left-wing Sandinista movement overthrew Nicaraguan dictator Anastasio Somoza, a longtime ally of the United States. Carter attempted to curb the murderous violence of death squads allied to the right-wing government of El Salvador, and in 1980 he suspended military aid after the murder of four American nuns by members of the country's army. He signed the SALT II agreement with the Soviets, which reduced the number of missiles, bombers, and nuclear warheads.

Both conservative Cold Warriors and foreign policy "realists" severely criticized Carter's emphasis on human rights. He himself found it impossible to translate rhetoric into action. He criticized American arms sales to the rest of the world. But with thousands of jobs and billions of dollars in corporate profits at stake, he did nothing to curtail them. The United States continued its support of allies with records of serious human rights violations such as the governments of Guatemala, the Philippines, South Korea, and Iran. Indeed, the American connection with the shah of Iran, whose secret police regularly jailed and tortured political opponents, proved to be Carter's undoing.

THE IRAN CRISIS AND AFGHANISTAN

Occupying a strategic location on the southern border of the Soviet Union, Iran was a major supplier of oil and an importer of American military equipment. At the end of 1977, Carter traveled there to help celebrate the shah's rule, causing the internal opposition to become more and more anti-American. Early in 1979, a popular revolution inspired by the exiled Muslim cleric Ayatollah Khomeini overthrew the shah and declared Iran an Islamic republic.

The Iranian revolution marked an ideological shift in opposition movements in the Middle East from socialism and Arab nationalism to religious fundamentalism. This would have important long-term consequences for the United States. More immediately, when Carter in November 1979 allowed the deposed shah to seek medical treatment in the United States, Khomeini's followers invaded the American embassy in Tehran and seized fifty-three hostages. They did not regain their freedom until January 1981, on the day Carter's term as president ended. Events in Iran made Carter seem helpless and inept and led to a rapid fall in his popularity.

Another crisis that began in 1979 undermined American relations with Moscow. At the end of that year, the Soviet Union sent thousands of troops into Afghanistan to support a friendly government threatened by an Islamic rebellion. In the long run, Afghanistan became the Soviet Vietnam, an unwinnable conflict whose mounting casualties seriously weakened the government at home. Initially, however, it seemed another example of declining American power.

Declaring the invasion the greatest crisis since World War II (a considerable exaggeration), the president announced the Carter Doctrine, declaring that the United States would use military force, if necessary, to protect its interests in the Persian Gulf. He placed an embargo on grain exports to the Soviet Union and organized a Western boycott of the 1980 Olympics,

Television gave extensive coverage to the plight of American hostages in Iran in 1979–1980, leading many Americans to view the Carter administration as weak and inept.

which took place in Moscow. He withdrew the SALT II treaty from consideration by the Senate and dramatically increased American military spending. In a reversion to the Cold War principle that any opponent of the Soviet Union deserved American support, the United States funneled aid to fundamentalist Muslims in Afghanistan who fought a decade-long guerrilla war against the Soviets. The alliance had unforeseen consequences. A faction of Islamic fundamentalists known as the Taliban eventually came to power in Afghanistan. Tragically, they would prove as hostile to the United States as to Moscow.

In an unsuccessful attempt to bring down inflation, Carter had abandoned the Keynesian economic policy of increased government spending to combat recession in favor of high interest rates. He had cut back on social spending and the federal government's economic regulations, while projecting a major increase in the military budget. By 1980, détente had been eclipsed and the Cold War reinvigorated. Thus, many of the conservative policies associated with his successor, Ronald Reagan, were already in place when Carter's presidency ended.

THE RISING TIDE OF CONSERVATISM

The combination of domestic and international dislocations during the 1970s created a widespread sense of anxiety among Americans and offered conservatives new political opportunities. Economic problems heightened the appeal of lower taxes, reduced government regulation, and cuts in social spending to spur business investment. Fears about a decline of American power in the world led to calls for a renewal of the Cold War. The civil rights and sexual revolutions produced resentments that undermined the Democratic coalition. Rising urban crime rates reinforced demands for law and order and attacks on courts considered too lenient toward criminals. These issues brought new converts to the conservative cause.

One set of recruits was the "neoconservatives," a group of intellectuals who charged that the 1960s had produced a decline in moral standards and respect for authority. Once supporters of liberalism, they had come to believe that even well-intentioned government social programs did more harm than good. Welfare, for example, not only failed to alleviate poverty but also encouraged single motherhood and undermined the work ethic. High taxes and expensive government regulations drained resources from productive enterprises, stifling economic growth. Neoconservatives repudiated the attempt by Nixon, Ford, and Carter to reorient foreign policy away from the Cold War. Carter's focus on human rights and alleged blindness to the Soviet threat, they argued, endangered the "survival of freedom." Conservative "think tanks" created during the 1970s, like the Heritage Foundation and the American Enterprise Institute, refined and spread these ideas.

THE RELIGIOUS RIGHT

The rise of religious fundamentalism during the 1970s expanded conservatism's popular base. Challenged by the secular and material concerns of

The Reverend Jerry Falwell, leader of the Moral Majority, with some of his followers.

American society, some denominations tried to bring religion into harmony with these interests; others reasserted more traditional religious values. The latter approach seemed to appeal to growing numbers of Americans. Even as membership in mainstream denominations like Episcopalianism and Presbyterianism declined, evangelical Protestantism flourished. Some observers spoke of a Third Great Awakening (like those of the 1740s and early nineteenth century). The election of Carter, the first "born-again" Christian to become president, highlighted the growing influence of evangelical religion. But unlike Carter, most fundamentalists who entered politics did so as conservatives.

Evangelical Christians had become more and more alienated from a culture that seemed to them to trivialize religion and promote immorality. They demanded the reversal of Supreme Court decisions banning prayer in public schools, protecting pornography as free speech, and legalizing abortion. Although it spoke of restoring traditional values, the Religious Right proved remarkably adept at using modern technology, including mass mailings and televised religious programing, to raise funds for their crusade and spread their message. In 1979, Jerry Falwell, a Virginia minister, created the self-styled Moral Majority, devoted to waging a "war against sin" and electing "pro-life, pro-family, pro-America" candidates to office. Falwell identified supporters of abortion rights, easy divorce, and "military unpreparedness" as the forces of Satan, who sought to undermine God's "special plans for this great, free country of ours."

Christian conservatives seemed most agitated by the ongoing sexual revolution, which they saw as undermining the traditional family and promoting immorality. As a result of the 1960s, they believed, American freedom was out of control. The growing assertiveness of the new gay movement spurred an especially fierce reaction. In 1977, after a campaign led by the popular singer Anita Bryant, a familiar fixture in televised orange juice commercials, Dade County, Florida, passed an anti-gay ordinance under the banner "Save Our Children."

THE BATTLE OVER THE EQUAL RIGHTS AMENDMENT

During the 1970s, "family values" moved to the center of conservative politics, nowhere more so than in the battle over the Equal Rights Amendment (ERA). Originally proposed during the 1920s by Alice Paul and the Women's Party, the ERA had been revived by second-wave feminists. In the wake of the rights revolution, the amendment's affirmation that "equality of rights under the law" could not be abridged "on account of sex" hardly seemed controversial. In 1972, with little opposition, Congress approved the ERA and sent it to the states for ratification. Designed to eliminate

Doug Marlette's cartoon comments on the continuing gap in pay between men and women, the kind of inequality that inspired support for the proposed Equal Rights Amendment.

obstacles to the full participation of women in public life, it aroused un-expected protest from those who claimed it would discredit the role of wife and homemaker.

The ERA debate reflected a division among women as much as a battle of the sexes. To its supporters, the amendment offered a guarantee of women's freedom in the public sphere. To its foes, freedom for women still resided in the divinely appointed roles of wife and mother. Phyllis Schlafly, who helped to organize opposition to the ERA, insisted that the "free enterprise system" was the "real liberator of women," since labor-saving home appli-ances offered more genuine freedom than "whining about past injustices" or seeking fulfillment outside the home. Opponents claimed that the ERA would let men "off the hook" by denying their responsibility to provide for their wives and children. Polls consistently showed that a majority of Americans, male and female, favored the ERA. But thanks to the mobiliza-tion of conservative women, the amendment failed to achieve ratification by the required thirty-eight states.

THE ABORTION CONTROVERSY

An even more bitter battle emerged in the 1970s over abortion rights, another example, to conservatives, of how liberals in office promoted sexual immorality at the expense of moral values. The movement to reverse the 1973 *Roe v. Wade* decision began among Roman Catholics, whose church condemned abortion under any circumstances. But it soon enlisted evan-gelical Protestants and social conservatives more generally. Life, the move-ment insisted, begins at conception, and abortion is nothing less than murder. Between this position and the feminist insistence that a woman's right to control her body includes the right to a safe, legal abortion, com-promise was impossible. Ironically, both sides showed how the rights revo-lution had reshaped the language of politics. Defenders of abortion exalted "the right to choose" as the essence of freedom. Opponents called them-selves the "right to life" movement and claimed to represent the rights of the "unborn child."

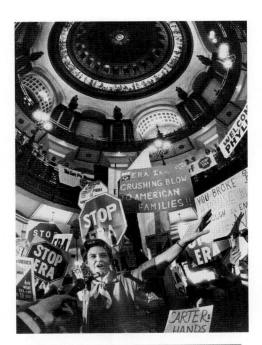

Conservative Phyllis Schlafly campaigning against the Equal Rights Amendment at the Illinois State Capitol in 1978.

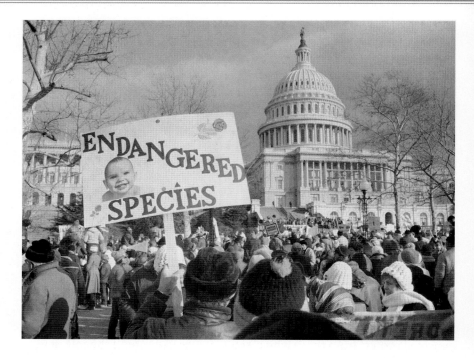

A 1979 anti-abortion rally in Washington, D.C., on the sixth anniversary of the Supreme Court's decision in Roe v. Wade, *which barred states from limiting a woman's right to terminate a pregnancy.*

The abortion issue drew a bitter, sometimes violent line through American politics. It affected battles over nominees to judicial positions and led to demonstrations at family-planning and abortion clinics. The anti-abortion movement won its first victory in 1976 when Congress, over President Ford's veto, ended federal funding for abortions for poor women through the Medicaid program. By the 1990s, a few fringe anti-abortion activists were placing bombs at medical clinics and murdering doctors who terminated pregnancies. To the end of the century, most women would continue to have the legal right of access to abortion. But in many areas the procedure became more and more difficult to obtain as hospitals and doctors stopped providing it.

THE TAX REVOLT

With liberals unable to devise an effective policy to counteract deindustrialization and declining real wages, economic anxieties also created a growing constituency for conservative economics. Unlike during the Great Depression, economic distress inspired a critique of government rather than of business. New environmental regulations led to calls for less government intervention in the economy. These were most strident in the West, where measures to protect the environment threatened irrigation projects and private access to public lands. But everywhere, the economy's descent from affluence to "stagflation" increased the appeal of the conservative argument that government regulation raised business costs and eliminated jobs.

Economic decline also broadened the constituency receptive to demands for lower taxes. To conservatives, tax reductions served the dual purpose of enhancing business profits and reducing the resources available to government, thus making new social programs financially impossible. Many Americans found taxes increasingly burdensome. On paper, their incomes were rising, although the gains were nullified by inflation. Rising wages

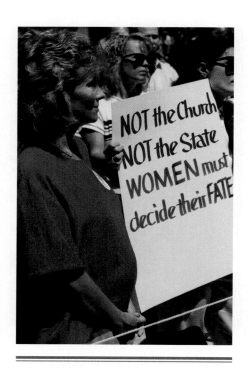

Demonstrators at a rally supporting abortion rights.

pushed families into higher tax brackets, increasing the percentage of their income they had to pay the government.

In 1978, conservatives sponsored and California voters approved Proposition 13, a ban on further increases in property taxes. The vote demonstrated that the level of taxation could be a powerful political issue. Proposition 13 proved to be a windfall for businesses and home owners, while reducing funds available for schools, libraries, and other public services. Many voters, however, proved willing to accept this result of lower taxes. As anti-tax sentiment flourished throughout the country, many states followed California's lead.

A parallel upsurge of grassroots conservatism was reflected in the Sagebrush Rebellion (the name given to a bill passed by the Nevada legislature in 1979). Using the language of freedom from government tyranny, leaders in western states denounced control of large areas of land by the Bureau of Land Management in Washington, D.C., and insisted that the states themselves be given decision-making power over issues like grazing rights, mining development, and whether public lands should be closed to fishing and hunting. With the federal government reluctant to give up control over public lands in the West, the Sagebrush Rebellion had few concrete accomplishments, but it underscored the rising tide of antigovernment sentiment.

THE ELECTION OF 1980

By 1980, Carter's approval rating had fallen to 21 percent—lower than Nixon's at the time of his resignation. A conservative tide seemed to be rising throughout the western world. In 1979, Margaret Thatcher became prime minister of Great Britain. She promised to restore economic competitiveness by curtailing the power of unions, reducing taxes, selling state-owned industries to private owners, and cutting back the welfare state. In the United States, Ronald Reagan's 1980 campaign for the presidency brought together the many strands of 1970s conservatism. He pledged to end stagflation and restore the country's dominant role in the world and its confidence in itself. "Let's make America great again," he proclaimed. "The era of self-doubt is over."

Reagan also appealed skillfully to "white backlash." He kicked off his campaign in Philadelphia, Mississippi, where three civil rights workers had been murdered in 1964, with a speech emphasizing his belief in states' rights. Many white southerners understood this doctrine as including opposition to federal intervention on behalf of civil rights. During the campaign, Reagan repeatedly condemned welfare "cheats," school busing, and affirmative action. The Republican platform reversed the party's long-standing support for the Equal Rights Amendment and condemned moral permissiveness. Although not personally religious and the first divorced man to run for president, Reagan won the support of the Religious Right and conservative upholders of "family values."

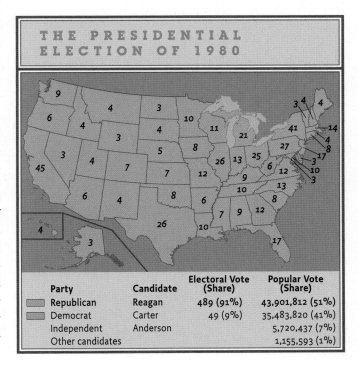

THE PRESIDENTIAL ELECTION OF 1980

Party	Candidate	Electoral Vote (Share)	Popular Vote (Share)
Republican	Reagan	489 (91%)	43,901,812 (51%)
Democrat	Carter	49 (9%)	35,483,820 (41%)
Independent	Anderson		5,720,437 (7%)
Other candidates			1,155,593 (1%)

VOICES OF FREEDOM

FROM Redstockings Manifesto (1969)

Redstockings was one of the radical feminist movements that arose in the late 1960s. Based in New York, it issued this manifesto, which, in language typical of the era, illustrates how at its most radical edge, feminism had evolved from demands for equal treatment for women to a total critique of male power and a call for women's "liberation."

After centuries of individual and preliminary political struggle, women are uniting to achieve their final liberation from male supremacy. Redstockings is dedicated to building this unity and winning our freedom.

Women are an oppressed class. Our oppression is total, affecting every facet of our lives. We are exploited as sex objects, breeders, domestic servants, and cheap labor. We are considered inferior beings, whose only purpose is to enhance men's lives. Our humanity is denied. Our prescribed behavior is enforced by the threat of physical violence.

Because we have lived so intimately with our oppressors, in isolation from each other, we have been kept from seeing our personal suffering as a political condition....

We identify the agents of our oppression as men. Male supremacy is the oldest, most basic form of domination.... Men have controlled all political, economic, and cultural institutions and backed up this control with physical force....

Our chief task at present is to develop female class consciousness through sharing experience and publicly exposing the sexist foundation of all our institutions. Consciousness-raising is not "therapy," which implies the existence of individual solutions and falsely assumes that the male-female relationship is purely personal, but the only method by which we can ensure that our program for liberation is based on the concrete realities of our lives.... The first requirement for raising class consciousness is honesty, in private and in public, with ourselves and other women.

We identify with all women. We define our best interest as that of the poorest, most brutally exploited women....

We call on all our sisters to unite with us in struggle.

We call on all men to give up their male privileges and support women's liberation in the interest of our humanity and their own.

FROM PHYLLIS SCHLAFLY,
"The Fraud of the Equal Rights Amendment" (1972)

Phyllis Schlafly, a conservative political writer from Illinois, led the campaign against the proposed Equal Rights Amendment to the Constitution. This document is excerpted from an article in her newsletter, *The Phyllis Schlafly Report.* The defeat of the ERA was a major conservative victory of the 1970s.

In the last couple of years, a noisy movement has sprung up agitating for "women's rights." Suddenly, everywhere we are afflicted with aggressive females on television talk shows yapping about how mistreated American women are, suggestions that marriage has put us in some kind of "slavery," that housework is menial and degrading, and—perish the thought—that women are discriminated against. . . . It's time to set the record straight. The claim that American women are downtrodden and unfairly treated is the fraud of the century. Why should we lower ourselves to "equal rights" when we already have the status of special privilege? . . .

The proposed Equal Rights Amendment . . . will absolutely and positively make women subject to the draft. . . . Another bad effect of the Equal Rights Amendment is that it will abolish a woman's right to child support and alimony, and substitute what the women's libbers think is a more "equal" policy. . . . Under present American laws, the man is *always* required to support his wife and each child he caused to be brought into the world. Why should women abandon these good laws? . . .

The law now requires a husband to support his wife as best as his financial situation permits, but a wife is not required to support her husband (unless he is about to become a public charge). A husband cannot demand that his wife go to work to help pay for family expenses. He has the duty of financial support under our laws and customs. Why should we abandon these mandatory wife-support and child-support laws so that a wife would have an "equal" obligation to take a job?

By law and custom in America, in case of divorce, the mother always is given custody of her children unless there is overwhelming evidence of mistreatment, neglect or bad character. This is our special privilege because of the high rank that is placed on motherhood in our society. Do women really want to give up this special privilege and lower themselves to "equal rights"? . . .

The women's libbers are radicals who are waging a total assault on the family, on marriage, and on children.

QUESTIONS

1. How do the authors of the Redstockings Manifesto seem to define women's freedom?

2. Why does Schlafly believe that the Equal Rights Amendment will actually harm women?

3. How do the two documents differ in their portrayal of the status of women in American society?

Riding a wave of dissatisfaction with the country's condition, Reagan swept into the White House. He carried such Democratic strongholds as Illinois, Texas, and New York. Because moderate Republican John Anderson, running for president as an independent, received about 7 percent of the popular vote, Reagan won only a bare majority, although he commanded a substantial margin in the electoral college. Carter received 41 percent, a humiliating defeat for a sitting president.

Jimmy Carter's reputation improved after he left the White House. He went to work for Habitat for Humanity, an organization that constructs homes for poor families. In the 1990s, he negotiated a cease-fire between warring Muslim and Serb forces in Bosnia and arranged a peaceful transfer of power from the military to an elected government in Haiti. In 2002, Carter was awarded the Nobel Peace Prize. His presidency, however, is almost universally considered a failure. And his defeat in 1980 launched the Reagan Revolution, which completed the transformation of freedom from the rallying cry of the left to a possession of the right.

THE REAGAN REVOLUTION

Ronald Reagan followed a most unusual path to the presidency. Originally a New Deal Democrat and head of the Screen Actors Guild (the only union leader ever to reach the White House), he emerged in the 1950s as a spokesman for the General Electric Corporation, preaching the virtues of unregulated capitalism. His nominating speech for Barry Goldwater at the 1964 Republican convention brought Reagan to national attention. Two years later, California voters elected Reagan as governor, establishing him as conservatives' best hope of capturing the presidency. In 1976, he challenged President Ford for the Republican nomination and came close to winning it. His victory in 1980 brought to power a diverse coalition of old and new conservatives: Sunbelt suburbanites and urban working-class ethnics; antigovernment crusaders and advocates of a more aggressive foreign policy; libertarians who believed in freeing the individual from restraint and the Christian Right, which sought to restore what they considered traditional moral values to American life.

REAGAN AND AMERICAN FREEDOM

Reagan's opponents often underestimated him. By the time he left office at the age of seventy-seven, he had become the oldest man ever to serve as president. He "rose at the crack of noon," as one reporter put it, and relied on his wife to arrange his official schedule. Unlike most modern presidents, he was content to outline broad policy themes and leave their implementation to others.

Reagan, however, was hardly a political novice, having governed California during the turbulent 1960s. An excellent public speaker, his optimism and affability appealed to large numbers of Americans. Reagan made conservatism seem progressive, rather than an attempt to turn back the tide of progress. He frequently quoted Thomas Paine: "We have it in our power to begin the world over again." Reagan repeatedly invoked the idea that Amer-

Ronald Reagan delivering a speech during his presidency. His aides often positioned him so he could be photographed with patriotic symbols like the American flag in the background.

ica has a divinely appointed mission as a "beacon of liberty and freedom." Freedom, indeed, became the watchword of the Reagan Revolution. In his public appearances and state papers, Reagan used the word more often than any president before him.

Reagan reshaped the nation's agenda and political language more effectively than any president since Franklin D. Roosevelt. Like FDR, he seized on the vocabulary of his opponents and gave it new meaning. Reagan promised to free government from control by "special interests," but these were racial minorities, unionists, and others hoping to use Washington's power to attack social inequalities, not businessmen seeking political favors, the traditional target of liberals. His Justice Department made the principle that the Constitution must be "color-blind"—a remark hurled at the Supreme Court majority by Justice John Marshall Harlan in 1896 to challenge a system of legal segregation—a justification for gutting civil-rights enforcement.

REAGANOMICS

Like Roosevelt and Johnson before him, Reagan spoke of "economic freedom" and proposed an "economic Bill of Rights." But in contrast to his predecessors, who used these phrases to support combating poverty and strengthening economic security, economic freedom for Reagan meant curtailing the power of unions, dismantling regulations, and radically reducing taxes. Taxation, he declared, violated the principle that "the right to earn your own keep and keep what you earn" was "what it means to be free."

In 1981, Reagan persuaded Congress to reduce the top tax rate from 70 percent to 50 percent and to index tax brackets to take inflation into account. Five years later, the Tax Reform Act reduced the rate on the wealthiest Americans to 28 percent. These measures marked a sharp retreat from the principle of progressivity (the idea that the wealthy should pay a higher percentage of their income in taxes than other citizens), one of the ways twentieth-century societies tried to address the unequal distribution of wealth. Reagan also appointed conservative heads of regulatory agencies, who cut back on environmental protection and workplace safety rules about which business had complained for years.

Since the New Deal, liberals had tried to promote economic growth by using the power of the government to bolster ordinary Americans' purchasing power. Reagan's economic program, known as "supply-side economics" by proponents and "trickle-down economics" by critics, relied on high interest rates to curb inflation and lower tax rates, especially for businesses and high-income Americans, to stimulate private investment. The policy assumed that cutting taxes would inspire Americans at all income levels to work harder, since they would keep more of the money they earned. Everyone would benefit from increased business profits, and because of a growing economy, government receipts would rise despite lower tax rates.

REAGAN AND LABOR

Reagan inaugurated an era of hostility between the federal government and organized labor. In August 1981, when 13,000 members of PATCO, the

This photograph of the remains of the Sprague Electric Company in North Adams, Massachusetts, which closed in 1985, depicts the aftermath of deindustrialization. Today, the building is the site of the Massachusetts Museum of Contemporary Art.

union of air traffic controllers, began a strike in violation of federal law, Reagan fired them all. He used the military to oversee the nation's air traffic system until new controllers could be trained. Reagan's action inspired many private employers to launch anti-union offensives. The hiring of workers to replace permanently those who had gone on strike, a rare occurrence before 1980, became widespread. Manufacturing employment, where union membership was concentrated, meanwhile continued its long-term decline. By the mid-1990s, the steel industry employed only 170,000 persons—down from 600,000 in 1973. When Reagan left office, both the service and retail sectors employed more Americans than manufacturing, and only 11 percent of workers with non-government jobs were union members.

"Reaganomics," as critics dubbed the administration's policies, initially produced the most severe recession since the 1930s. A long period of economic expansion, however, followed the downturn of 1981–1982. As companies "downsized" their workforces, shifted production overseas, and took advantage of new technologies such as satellite communications, they became more profitable. At the same time, the rate of inflation, 13.5 percent at the beginning of 1981, declined to 3.5 percent in 1988, partly because a period of expanded oil production that drove down prices succeeded the shortages of the 1970s. The stock market rose substantially. In October 1987, the market suffered its sharpest drop since 1929, but stocks soon resumed their upward climb.

THE PROBLEM OF INEQUALITY

Together, Reagan's policies, rising stock prices, and deindustrialization resulted in a considerable rise in economic inequality. By the mid-1990s, the richest 1 percent of Americans owned 40 percent of the nation's wealth, twice their share twenty years earlier. They spent their income not on productive investments, as supply-side economists had promised, but on luxury goods, real-estate speculation, and corporate buyouts that often led to plant closings as operations were consolidated. The income of middle-class Americans stagnated while that of the poorest one-fifth of the population declined. Because of falling investment in public housing, the release of mental patients from state hospitals, and cuts in welfare, homeless persons became a visible fixture on the streets of cities from New York to Los Angeles.

Deindustrialization and the decline of the labor movement had a particularly devastating impact on minority workers, who had only recently gained a foothold in better-paying manufacturing jobs. Thanks to the opening of colleges and professional schools to minority students as a result of the civil rights movement and affirmative action programs, the black middle class expanded considerably. But black workers, traditionally the last hired and first fired, were hard hit by economic changes.

During the 1970s, Jim Crow had finally ended in many workplaces and unions. But just as decades of painful efforts to obtain better jobs bore fruit, hundreds of thousands of black workers lost their jobs when factories closed their doors. In South Gate, a working-class suburb of Los Angeles, for example, the giant Firestone tire factory shut down in 1980, only a few years after black and Latino workers had made their first breakthroughs in employment. When the national unemployment rate reached 8.9 percent at the end of 1981, the figure for blacks exceeded 20 percent. Nor did black workers share fully in the recovery that followed. Few had the education to take advantage of job openings in growing "knowledge-based" industries like technology and information services. Overall, during the 1980s black males fell further than any other group in the population in terms of wages and jobs.

THE SECOND GILDED AGE

In retrospect, the 1980s, like the 1890s, would be widely remembered as a decade of misplaced values. Buying out companies generated more profits than running them; making deals, not making products, became the way to get rich. The merger of Nabisco and R.J. Reynolds Tobacco Company in 1988 produced close to 1 billion dollars in fees for lawyers, economic advisers, and stockbrokers. "Greed is healthy," declared Wall Street financier Ivan Boesky (who ended up in prison for insider stock trading). "Yuppie"—the young urban professional who earned a high income working in a bank or stock brokerage firm and spent lavishly on designer clothing and other

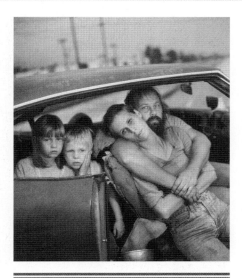

A homeless Los Angeles family, forced to live in their car, photographed in 1983.

A family of affluent "yuppies"—young urban professionals—posing in their New York City apartment with their child-care worker and baby.

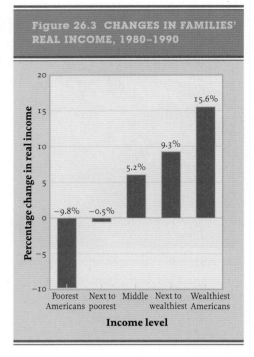

Figure 26.3 CHANGES IN FAMILIES' REAL INCOME, 1980–1990

The wealthiest American families benefited the most from economic expansion during the 1980s, while the poorest 40 percent of the population saw their real incomes decline. (Real income indicates income adjusted to take account of inflation.)

trappings of the good life—became a household word. Television shows like *Dallas* and *Dynasty* chronicled the activities of the very rich for a mass audience.

Taxpayers footed the bill for some of the consequences. The deregulation of Savings and Loans Associations—banks that had generally confined themselves to financing home mortgages—allowed these institutions to invest in unsound real-estate ventures and corporate mergers. Losses piled up, and the Federal Savings and Loan Insurance Corporation, which insured depositors' accounts, faced bankruptcy. After Reagan left office, the federal government bailed out the savings and loan institutions, at a cost to taxpayers estimated at $250 billion.

Supply-side advocates insisted that lowering taxes would enlarge government revenue by stimulating economic activity. But spurred by large increases in funds for the military, federal spending far outstripped income, producing the largest budget deficits in American history. During Reagan's presidency, the national debt tripled to $2.7 trillion. Nonetheless, Reagan remained immensely popular. He took credit for economic expansion while blaming congressional leaders for the ballooning federal deficit. He won a triumphant reelection in 1984. His opponent, Walter Mondale (best remembered for choosing Congresswoman Geraldine Ferraro of New York as his running mate, the first woman candidate on a major-party presidential ticket), carried only his home state of Minnesota and the District of Columbia.

CONSERVATIVES AND REAGAN

While he implemented their economic policies, Reagan in some ways disappointed ardent conservatives. The administration sharply reduced funding for Great Society antipoverty programs such as food stamps, school lunches, and federal financing of low-income housing. But it left intact core elements of the welfare state, such as Social Security, Medicare, and Medicaid, which many conservatives wished to curtail significantly or repeal. The Reagan era did little to advance the social agenda of the Christian Right. Abortion remained legal, women continued to enter the labor force in unprecedented numbers, and Reagan even appointed the first female member of the Supreme Court, Sandra Day O'Connor. In 1986, in *Bowers v. Hardwick*, in a rare victory for cultural conservatives, the Supreme Court did uphold the constitutionality of state laws outlawing homosexual acts. (In 2003, the justices would reverse the *Bowers* decision, declaring laws that criminalized homosexuality unconstitutional.)

Reagan gave verbal support to a proposed constitutional amendment restoring prayer in public schools but did little to promote its passage. The administration launched a "Just Say No" campaign against illegal drug use. But this failed to halt the spread in urban areas of crack, a potent, inexpensive form of cocaine that produced an upsurge of street crime and family breakdown. Reagan's Justice Department cut back on civil rights enforcement and worked to curtail affirmative action programs. But to the end of Reagan's presidency, the Supreme Court continued to approve plans by private employers and city and state governments to upgrade minority employment.

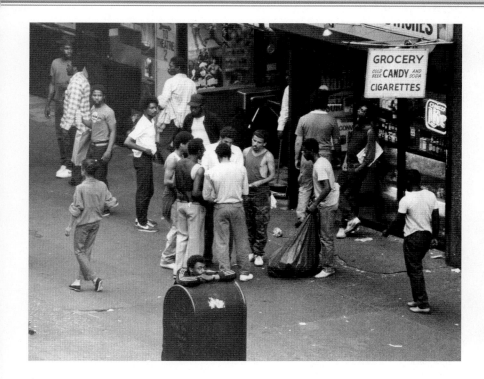

The drug crack being openly sold on the streets of New York City in 1986.

REAGAN AND THE COLD WAR

In foreign policy, Reagan breathed new life into the rhetorical division of the world into a free West and unfree East. He resumed vigorous denunciation of the Soviet Union—calling it an "evil empire"—and sponsored the largest military buildup in American history, including new long-range bombers and missiles. He proposed an entirely new strategy, the Strategic Defense Initiative, based on developing a space-based system to intercept and destroy enemy missiles. The idea was not remotely feasible technologically, and, if deployed, it would violate the Anti-Ballistic Missile Treaty of 1972. But it appealed to Reagan's desire to reassert America's worldwide power. He persuaded NATO, over much opposition, to introduce short-range nuclear weapons into Europe to counter Soviet forces. But the renewed arms race and Reagan's casual talk of winning a nuclear war caused widespread alarm at home and abroad. In the early 1980s, a movement for a nuclear freeze—a halt to the development of nuclear weapons—attracted millions of supporters in the United States and Europe. In 1983, half of the American population watched *The Day After*, a television program that unflinchingly depicted the devastation that would be caused by a nuclear war.

Reagan came into office determined to overturn the "Vietnam syndrome"—as widespread public reluctance to commit American forces overseas was called. He sent American troops to the Caribbean island of Grenada to oust a pro-Cuban government, and he ordered the bombing of Libya in retaliation for the country's alleged involvement in a terrorist attack on a West Berlin nightclub in which an American died. In 1982, Reagan dispatched marines as a peacekeeping force to Lebanon, where a civil war raged between the Christian government, supported by Israeli forces,

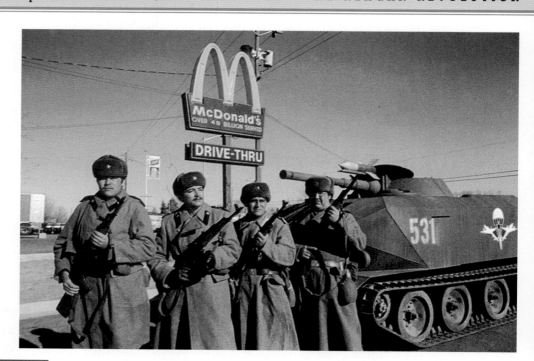

Hollywood joined enthusiastically in the revived Cold War. The 1984 film Red Dawn *depicted a Soviet invasion of the United States.*

and Muslim insurgents. But he quickly withdrew them after a bomb exploded at their barracks, killing 241 Americans. The public, Reagan realized, would support minor operations like Grenada but remained unwilling to sustain heavy casualties abroad.

Reagan generally relied on military aid rather than American troops to pursue his foreign policy objectives. Abandoning the Carter administration's emphasis on human rights, Reagan embraced the idea, advanced in 1979 by neoconservative writer Jeane Kirkpatrick, that the United States should oppose "totalitarian" communists but assist "authoritarian" noncommunist regimes. Kirkpatrick became the American ambassador to the United Nations, and the United States stepped up its alliances with Third World anticommunist dictatorships like the governments of Chile and South Africa. The administration poured in funds to combat insurgencies against the governments of El Salvador and Guatemala, whose armies and associated death squads committed flagrant abuses against their own citizens. When El Salvador's army massacred hundreds of civilians in the town of El Mozote in 1981, the State Department denied that the event, widely reported in the press, had taken place.

THE IRAN-CONTRA AFFAIR

American involvement in Central America produced the greatest scandal of Reagan's presidency, the Iran-Contra affair. In 1984, Congress banned military aid to the Contras (derived from the Spanish word for "against") fighting the Sandinista government of Nicaragua, which, as noted earlier, had ousted the American-backed dictator Anastasio Somoza in 1979. In 1985, Reagan secretly authorized the sale of arms to Iran—now involved in a war with its neighbor, Iraq—in order to secure the release of a number of American hostages held by Islamic groups in the Middle East. CIA director William Casey and Lieutenant Colonel Oliver North of the National Security Council set up a system that diverted some of the proceeds to buy military supplies for the Contras in defiance of the congressional ban. The scheme continued for nearly two years.

In 1987, after a Middle Eastern newspaper leaked the story, Congress held televised hearings that revealed a pattern of official duplicity and violation of the law reminiscent of the Nixon era. Eleven members of the administration eventually were convicted of perjury or destroying documents, or pleaded guilty before being tried. Reagan denied knowledge of the illegal proceedings, but the Iran-Contra affair undermined confidence that he controlled his own administration.

As in the first part of the twentieth century, the United States intervened frequently in Caribbean and Central American countries during and immediately after the Cold War.

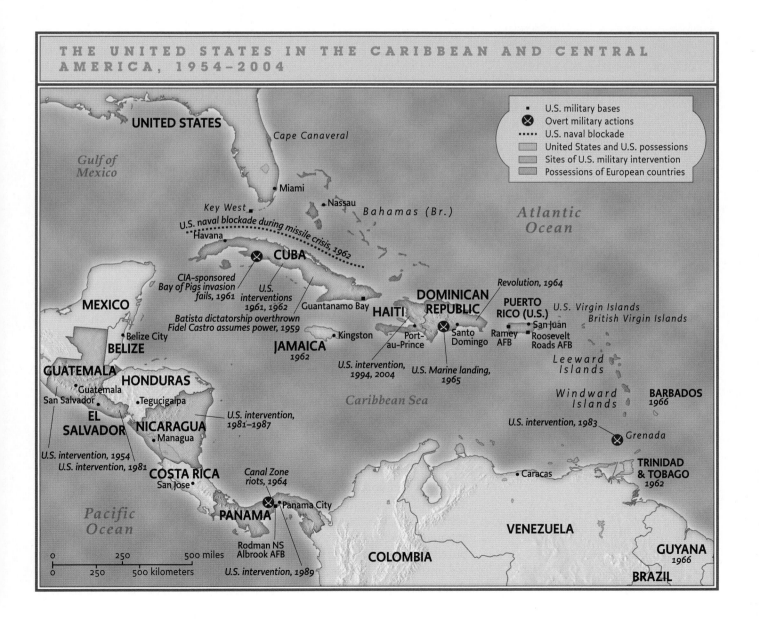

THE UNITED STATES IN THE CARIBBEAN AND CENTRAL AMERICA, 1954–2004

Legend:
- U.S. military bases
- ⊗ Overt military actions
- ••••• U.S. naval blockade
- United States and U.S. possessions
- Sites of U.S. military intervention
- Possessions of European countries

President Reagan visited Moscow in 1988, cementing his close relationship with Soviet leader Mikhail Gorbachev. They were photographed in Red Square.

REAGAN AND GORBACHEV

In his second term, to the surprise of both his foes and supporters, Reagan softened his anticommunist rhetoric and established good relations with Soviet premier Mikhail Gorbachev. Gorbachev had come to power in 1985, bent on reforming the Soviet Union's repressive political system and re-invigorating its economy. The country had fallen further and further behind the United States in the production and distribution of consumer goods, and it relied increasingly on agricultural imports to feed itself. Gorbachev inaugurated policies known as *glasnost* (political openness) and *perestroika* (economic reform).

Gorbachev realized that significant change would be impossible without reducing his country's military budget. Reagan was ready to negotiate. A series of talks between 1985 and 1987 yielded more progress on arms control than in the entire postwar period to that point, including an agreement to eliminate intermediate and short-range nuclear missiles in Europe. In 1988, Gorbachev began pulling Soviet troops out of Afghanistan. Having entered office as an ardent Cold Warrior, Reagan left with hostilities between the superpowers much diminished. He even repudiated his earlier comment that the Soviet Union was an "evil empire," saying that it referred to "another era."

REAGAN'S LEGACY

Reagan's presidency revealed the contradictions at the heart of modern conservatism. Rhetorically, he sought to address the concerns of the Religious Right, advocating a "return to spiritual values" as a way to strengthen traditional families and local communities. But in some ways, the Reagan Revolution undermined the very values and institutions conservatives held dear. Intended to discourage reliance on government handouts by rewarding honest work and business initiative, Reagan's policies inspired a speculative frenzy that enriched architects of corporate takeovers and investors in the stock market while leaving in their wake plant closings, job losses, and devastated communities. Nothing proved more threatening to local traditions or family stability than deindustrialization, insecurity about employment, and the relentless downward pressure on wages. Nothing did more to undermine a sense of common national purpose than the widening gap between rich and poor.

Because of the Iran-Contra scandal and the enormous deficits the government had accumulated, Reagan left the presidency with his reputation somewhat tarnished. Nonetheless, few figures have so successfully changed the landscape and language of politics. Reagan's vice president, George H. W. Bush, defeated Michael Dukakis, the governor of Massachusetts, in the 1988 election partly because Dukakis could not respond effectively to the charge that he was a "liberal"—now a term of political abuse. Conservative assumptions about the virtues of the free market and the evils of "big government" dominated the mass media and political debates. Those receiving public assistance had come to be seen not as citizens entitled to help in coping with economic misfortune, but as a drain on taxes. During the 1990s, these and other conservative ideas would be embraced almost as fully by President Bill Clinton, a Democrat, as by Reagan and the Republicans.

Conservatives celebrate the inauguration of George H. W. Bush, January 1989.

THE ELECTION OF 1988

The 1988 election seemed to show politics sinking to new lows. Television advertisements and media exposés now dominated political campaigns. The race for the Democratic nomination had hardly begun before the front-runner, Senator Gary Hart of Colorado, withdrew after a newspaper reported that he had spent the night at his Washington town house with a woman other than his wife. Both parties ran negative campaigns. Democrats ridiculed the Republican vice-presidential nominee, Senator Dan Quayle of Indiana, for factual and linguistic mistakes. Republicans spread unfounded rumors that Michael Dukakis's wife had burned an American flag during the 1960s. The low point of the campaign came in a Republican television ad depicting the threatening image of Willie Horton, a black murderer and rapist who had been furloughed from prison during Dukakis's term as governor of Massachusetts. Rarely in the modern era had a major party appealed so blatantly to racial fears. Before his death in 1991, Lee Atwater, who masterminded Bush's campaign, apologized for the Horton ad.

Although he did not match Reagan's landslide victory of 1984, Bush achieved a substantial majority, winning 54 percent of the popular vote. Democratic success in retaining control of Congress suggested that an electoral base existed for a comeback. But this would only occur if the party fashioned a new appeal to replace traditional liberalism, which had been eclipsed by the triumph of conservatism.

SUGGESTED READING

Adler, William M. *Mollie's Job: A Story of Life and Work on the Global Assembly Line* (2000). Tracks how a manufacturing job moved from the North to the South and eventually out of the country, and what happened to the workers who held it.

Allitt, Patrick. *Religion in America since 1945* (2003). A survey of the main trends of religious development since World War II.

Anderson, Terry H. *The Pursuit of Fairness: A History of Affirmative Action* (2004). A careful study of the origins and development of affirmative action policies.

Busch, Andrew E. *Ronald Reagan and the Politics of Freedom* (2001). Discusses how Ronald Reagan interpreted the idea of freedom and how it influenced his presidency.

Dallek, Matthew. *The Right Moment: Ronald Reagan's First Victory and the Decisive Turning Point in American Politics* (2000). An examination of the causes of Reagan's election in 1980 and its impact on American politics.

Fitzgerald, Frances. *Way Out There in the Blue: Reagan, Star Wars and the End of the Cold War* (2000). A critical appraisal of one of the key military initiatives of Reagan's presidency.

Greenberg, David. *Nixon's Shadow: The History of an Image* (2003). Explores how Nixon's supporters and enemies thought about him during his long political career.

Himmelstein, Jerome L. *To the Right: The Transformation of American Conservatism* (1990). Studies the development of conservative ideas since World War II.

Kutler, Stanley I. *The Wars of Watergate: The Last Crisis of Richard Nixon* (1990). The most thorough analysis of the Watergate scandal that brought down President Nixon.

Luker, Kristin. *Abortion and the Politics of Motherhood* (1984). Describes how the abortion issue affected American politics and the ideas about gender relations that lay behind the debate.

Martin, William. *With God on Our Side: The Rise of the Religious Right in America* (1996). Traces the development of religious conservatism and its impact on American society.

Mathews, Donald G., and Jane S. De Hart. *Sex, Gender, and the Politics of ERA* (1990). An in-depth examination of the debate over the Equal Rights Amendment and why its opponents were successful.

McGirr, Lisa. *Suburban Warriors: The Origins of the New American Right* (2001). An influential study of the rise of conservatism in Orange County, California, once one its more powerful centers.

Schulman, Bruce J. *The Seventies: The Great Shift in American Culture, Society, and Politics* (2001). A survey of the numerous political, social, and economic changes that took place during the 1970s.

Stein, Judith. *Running Steel, Running America: Race, Economic Policy, and the Decline of Liberalism* (1998). Examines the decline of the American steel industry and how the Cold War and presidential policies from Eisenhower to Carter contributed to it.

REVIEW QUESTIONS

1. Like Dwight Eisenhower before him, President Richard Nixon was not often seen as conservative enough for the political right. Examine Nixon's presidency and explain what policies the conservative agreed or disagreed with and why.

2. Explain how Ronald Reagan's 1980 presidential campaign brought together the many strands of 1970s conservatism.

3. Illustrate how the changing morale in the Army during the last years of the Vietnam conflict mirrored the social changes sweeping America at home.

4. What were the reasons for the economic recessions of the 1970s?

5. How did Ronald Reagan shift the meanings of freedom during his presidency?

KEY TERMS

Family Assistance Plan (p. 1012)

San Antonio Independent School District v. Rodriguez (p. 1014)

Title IX (p. 1016)

Nixon and China (p. 1017)

oil crisis (p. 1023)

The Nixon pardon (p. 1025)

Iranian hostage crisis (p. 1028)

Iran-Contra affair (p. 1042)

REVIEW TABLE

Triumph of Conservatism

Event	Dates	Background	Significance
Sharon Statement	1960	Platform of the Young Americans for Freedom	Conservative students emerged as a force in politics
Goldwater campaign	1964	Barry Goldwater (R) lost presidential election to Lyndon Johnson (D)	His victory in five southern states identified a growing conservative electorate frustrated with civil rights and big government
Equal Rights Amendment battle	1972–1982	Ten-year battle over ratification of the ERA by the states	Conservatives who saw the ERA as anti-family succeeded in its defeat
Moral Majority	1979	Organized by Jerry Falwell to wage a war against sin	It was used as a vehicle for political influence, helping elect Ronald Reagan
Sagebrush Rebellion	1979	Bill passed by Nevada legislature denouncing federal control over land	Grassroots initiative that argued the states, not D.C., ought to determine grazing rights, mining development, and land use
Reagan election	1980	Ronald Reagan (R) defeated Jimmy Carter (D)	His overwhelming victory marked the high tide of conservatism
Air Traffic Controllers' Strike	1981	ATC strikers' demands go unmet and all are fired who did not return to work	Ronald Reagan's actions inspired other employers to take anti-union offensives
Bowers v. Hardwick	1986	Held that state laws outlawing homosexual acts were constitutional	Victory for cultural conservatives

CHAPTER 27

Globalization and Its Discontents, 1989–2000

Workers trying to deal with crowds of customers at the opening of the first McDonald's restaurant in Beijing, 1992. By the end of the century, there were 200 McDonald's in China, one small example of the globalization of the world economy during the 1990s.

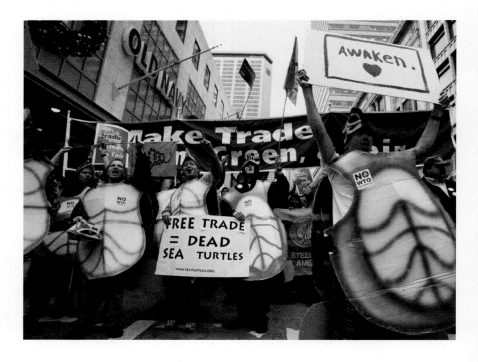

FOCUS QUESTIONS

- What were the domestic and international strategies of the Clinton administration in the aftermath of the Cold War?

- What drove the economic resurgence of the 1990s?

- How did the social fabric of America change in the 1990s?

- What did the election of 2000 reveal about American politics?

- What were the prevailing ideas of American freedom at the end of the century?

In December 1999, delegates from around the world gathered in Seattle for a meeting of the World Trade Organization (WTO), a 135-nation group created five years earlier to reduce barriers to international commerce and settle trade disputes. To the astonishment of residents of the city, over 30,000 persons gathered to protest the meeting. Their marches and rallies brought together factory workers who claimed that global free trade encouraged corporations to shift production to low-wage centers overseas and "tree-huggers," as some reporters called environmentalists, who complained about the impact on the earth's ecology of unregulated economic development.

Some of the latter dressed in costumes representing endangered species—monarch butterflies whose habitats were disappearing because of the widespread destruction of forests by lumber companies, and sea turtles threatened by unrestricted ocean fishing. Protesters drew attention to the depletion of ozone in the atmosphere, which shields the earth from harmful solar radiation. The heightened use of aerosol sprays and refrigerants containing damaging chemicals had caused a large hole in the ozone layer. A handful of self-proclaimed anarchists embarked on a window-breaking spree at local stores. The police sealed off the downtown and made hundreds of arrests, and the WTO gathering disbanded.

Once a center of labor radicalism, the Seattle area in 1999 was best known as the home of Microsoft, developer of the operating system for most of the world's computers. The company's worldwide reach symbolized "globalization," the process by which people, investment, goods, information, and culture increasingly flowed across national boundaries.

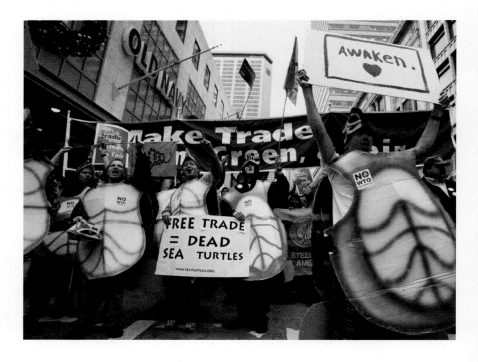

Protesters dressed as sea turtles, an endangered species, at the demonstrations against the World Trade Organization in Seattle, December 1999.

Globalization has been called "*the* concept of the 1990s." During that decade, the media resounded with announcements that a new era in human history had opened, with a borderless economy and a "global civilization" that would soon replace traditional cultures. Some commentators claimed that the nation-state itself had become obsolete in the globalized world.

Globalization, of course, was hardly a new phenomenon. The internationalization of commerce and culture and the reshuffling of the world's peoples had been going on since the explorations of the fifteenth century. But the scale and scope of late-twentieth-century globalization was unprecedented. Thanks to satellites and the Internet, information and popular culture flowed instantaneously to every corner of the world. Manufacturers and financial institutions scoured the world for profitable investment opportunities.

Perhaps most important, the collapse of communism between 1989 and 1991 opened the entire world to the spread of market capitalism and to the idea that government should interfere as little as possible with economic activity. The Free World triumphed over its communist rival, the free market over the idea of a planned economy, and the free individual over ideas of shared community and social citizenship. American politicians and social commentators increasingly criticized the regulation of wages and working conditions, assistance to the less fortunate, and environmental protections as burdens on international competitiveness. During the 1990s, presidents George H. W. Bush, a Republican, and Bill Clinton, a Democrat, both spoke of an American mission to create a single global free market as the path to rising living standards, the spread of democracy, and greater worldwide freedom.

Similar demonstrations at economic summits overseas followed the Seattle protests. The media called the loose coalition of groups who organized the protests the "antiglobalization" movement. In fact, they challenged not globalization itself but its social consequences. Globalization, the demonstrators claimed, accelerated the worldwide creation of wealth but widened gaps between rich and poor countries and between haves and have-nots within societies. Decisions affecting the day-to-day lives of millions of people were made by institutions—the World Trade Organization, International Monetary Fund, World Bank, and multinational corporations—that operated without any democratic input. These international organizations required developing countries seeking financial aid to open their economies to penetration from abroad while reducing spending on domestic social concerns. Demonstrators demanded not an end to global trade and capital flows, but the establishment of international standards for wages, labor conditions, and the environment, and greater investment in health and education in poor countries.

Douglas Harp's 1993 lithograph drew attention to the development of a hole in the atmosphere's ozone layer that exposed human beings to increased solar radiation.

Even President Clinton, a staunch advocate of free trade, told the Seattle delegates that the protesters were "telling us in the streets" that "we've been silent" about the effects of globalization. The Battle of Seattle placed on the national and international agendas a question that promises to be among the most pressing concerns of the twenty-first century—the relationship between globalization, economic justice, and freedom.

THE POST-COLD WAR WORLD

THE CRISIS OF COMMUNISM

The year 1989 was one of the most momentous of the twentieth century. In April, tens of thousands of student demonstrators occupied Tiananmen Square in the heart of Beijing, demanding greater democracy in China. Workers, teachers, and even some government officials joined them, until their numbers swelled to nearly 1 million. Both the reforms Mikhail Gorbachev had introduced in the Soviet Union and the example of American institutions inspired the protesters. The students erected a figure reminiscent of the Statue of Liberty, calling it "The Goddess of Democracy and Freedom." In June, Chinese troops crushed the protest, killing an unknown number of people, possibly thousands.

In the fall of 1989, pro-democracy demonstrations spread across eastern Europe. Gorbachev made it clear that unlike in the past, the Soviet Union would not intervene. The climactic event took place on November 9 when crowds breached the Berlin Wall, which since 1961 had stood as the Cold War's most prominent symbol. One by one, the region's communist gov-

Demonstrators dancing atop the Berlin Wall on November 10, 1989. The next day, crowds began dismantling it, in the most dramatic moment of the collapse of communist rule in eastern Europe.

ernments agreed to give up power. In 1990, a reunified German nation absorbed East Germany. The remarkably swift and almost entirely peaceful collapse of communism in eastern Europe became known as the "velvet revolution."

Meanwhile, the Soviet Union itself slipped deeper and deeper into crisis. Gorbachev's attempts at economic reform produced only chaos, and his policy of political openness allowed long-suppressed national and ethnic tensions to rise to the surface. In 1990, the Baltic republics of Estonia, Latvia, and Lithuania, which had been absorbed into the Soviet Union in 1940, declared their independence. In August 1991, a group of military leaders attempted to seize power to overturn the government's plan to give greater autonomy to the various parts of the Soviet Union. Russian president Boris Yeltsin mobilized crowds in Moscow that restored Gorbachev to office. Gorbachev then resigned from the Communist Party, ending its eighty-four-year rule. One after another, the republics of the Soviet Union declared themselves sovereign states. At the end of 1991, the Soviet Union ceased to exist; in its place were fifteen new independent nations.

Pro-democracy advocates displayed the Goddess of Democracy and Freedom, a statue reminiscent of the Statue of Liberty, during the 1989 demonstrations in Beijing's Tiananmen Square.

The sudden and unexpected collapse of communism marked the end of the Cold War and a stunning victory for the United States and its allies. For the first time since 1917, there existed a truly worldwide capitalist system. Even China, while remaining under Communist Party rule, had already embarked on market reforms and rushed to attract foreign investment. Other events suggested that the 1990s would also be a "decade of democracy." In 1990, South Africa released Nelson Mandela, head of the African National Congress, from prison. Four years later, as a result of the first democratic elections in the country's history, Mandela became president, ending the system of state-sponsored racial inequality, known as "apartheid," and white minority government. Peace came to Central America, with negotiated ends to the civil war in El Salvador and an election in Nicaragua won by opponents of the Sandinistas in 1990. Throughout Latin America and Africa, civilian governments replaced military rule.

A NEW WORLD ORDER?

The sudden shift from a bipolar world to one of unquestioned American predominance promised to redefine the country's global role. President George H. W. Bush spoke of the coming of a "new world order." But no one knew what its characteristics would be.

Bush's first major foreign policy action was a throwback to the days of American interventionism in the Western Hemisphere. At the end of 1989, he dispatched troops to Panama to overthrow the government of General

EASTERN EUROPE AFTER THE COLD WAR

The end of the Cold War and breakup of the Soviet Union, Czechoslovakia, and Yugoslavia redrew the map of eastern Europe (compare this map with the map of Cold War Europe in Chapter 23). Two additional nations that emerged from the Soviet Union lie to the east and are not indicated here: Kyrgyzstan and Tajikistan.

Manuel Antonio Noriega, a former ally of the United States who had become involved in the international drug trade. Although the invasion cost the lives of over 3,000 Panamanians and was condemned by the United Nations General Assembly as a violation of international law, the administration deemed it a great success. The United States installed a new government and flew Noriega to Florida, where he was tried and convicted on drug charges.

THE GULF WAR

A far more serious crisis arose in 1990 when Iraq invaded and annexed Kuwait, an oil-rich sheikdom on the Persian Gulf. Fearing that Iraqi dictator Saddam Hussein might next attack Saudi Arabia, a longtime ally that supplied more oil to the United States than any other country, Bush rushed troops to defend the kingdom and warned Iraq to withdraw from Kuwait or face war. His policy aroused intense debate in the United States. Critics insisted that diplomacy be given a chance to resolve the crisis. Bush spoke of defending the freedom of Saudi Arabia and restoring that of Kuwait. Antiwar activists pointed out that neither qualified as a free country—both, for example, denied women the right to vote. But the Iraqi invasion so flagrantly violated international law that Bush succeeded in building a forty-nation coalition committed to restoring Kuwait's independence, secured the support of the United Nations, and sent half a million American troops along with a naval armada to the region.

In February 1991, the United States launched Operation Desert Storm, which quickly drove the Iraqi army from Kuwait. Tens of thousands of Iraqis and 184 Americans died in the conflict. The United Nations ordered Iraq to disarm and imposed economic sanctions that produced widespread civilian suffering for the rest of the decade. But Hussein remained in place. So did a large American military establishment in Saudi Arabia, to the outrage of Islamic fundamentalists who deemed their presence an affront to their faith.

The Gulf War was the first post–Cold War international crisis. Despite assembling a broad coalition, the United States did nearly all of the fighting itself. Relying on high-tech weaponry like cruise missiles that reached Iraq from bases and aircraft carriers hundreds of miles away, the United States was able to prevail quickly and avoid the prolonged involvement and high casualties of Vietnam. The Soviet Union, in the process of disintegration, remained on the sidelines. In the war's immediate aftermath, Bush's public approval rating rose to an unprecedented 89 percent.

President Bush, with Defense Secretary Dick Cheney (left) *and General Colin Powell* (right), *chair of the Joint Chiefs of Staff, at a meeting in January 1991, shortly before the beginning of the Gulf War. Cheney and Powell would play major roles in the administration of Bush's son, President George W. Bush.*

VISIONS OF AMERICA'S ROLE

In a speech to Congress, the president identified the Gulf War as the first step in the struggle to create a world rooted in democracy and global free trade. But it remained unclear how this broad vision would be translated into policy. Soon after the end of the war, General Colin Powell, chairman of the Joint Chiefs of Staff, and Dick Cheney, the secretary of defense, outlined different visions of the future. Powell predicted that the post–Cold War world would be a dangerous environment with conflicts popping up in unexpected places. To avoid being drawn into an unending role as global policeman, he insisted, the United States should not commit its troops abroad without clear objectives and a timetable for withdrawal. Cheney argued that with the demise of the Soviet Union, the United States possessed the power to reshape the world and prevent hostile states from achieving regional power. It must be willing to use force, independently if necessary, to maintain its strategic dominance. For the rest of the 1990s, it was not certain which definition of the American role in the post–Cold War world would predominate.

THE ELECTION OF CLINTON

Had a presidential election been held in 1991, Bush would undoubtedly have been victorious. But in that year the economy slipped into recession. In a kind of hangover from the speculative excesses of the Reagan years, unem-

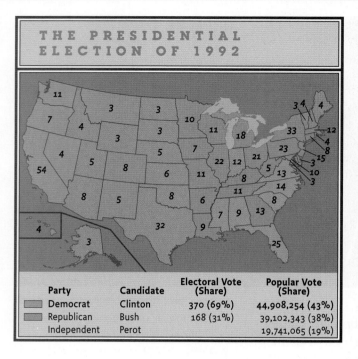

THE PRESIDENTIAL ELECTION OF 1992

Party		Candidate	Electoral Vote (Share)	Popular Vote (Share)
	Democrat	Clinton	370 (69%)	44,908,254 (43%)
	Republican	Bush	168 (31%)	39,102,343 (38%)
	Independent	Perot		19,741,065 (19%)

ployment rose and family income stagnated. Despite victory in the Cold War and the Gulf, public-opinion polls showed that more and more Americans believed that the country was on the wrong track. No one seized more effectively on the widespread sense of unease than Bill Clinton, a former governor of Arkansas. In 1992, Clinton won the Democratic nomination by combining social liberalism (he supported abortion rights, gay rights, and affirmative action for racial minorities) with elements of conservatism (he pledged to reduce government bureaucracy and, borrowing a page from Republicans, promised to "end welfare as we know it").

A charismatic campaigner, Clinton conveyed sincere concern for voters' economic anxieties. To counter Republican rhetoric urging voters to blame their woes on "welfare queens" and others who cheated honest taxpayers, Clinton argued that deindustrialization caused rising inequality and the loss of good jobs. In his speech accepting the nomination, he spoke of people "working harder than ever, spending less time with their children, working nights and weekends," while "those who cut corners and cut deals have been rewarded."

Bush, by contrast, seemed out of touch with the day-to-day lives of ordinary Americans. On the wall of Democratic headquarters, Clinton's campaign director posted the slogan, "It's the Economy, Stupid"—a reminder that the economic downturn was the Democrats' strongest card. Bush was further weakened when conservative leader Pat Buchanan delivered a fiery televised speech at the Republican national convention that declared cultural war against gays, feminists, and supporters of abortion rights. This seemed to confirm the Democratic portrait of Republicans as intolerant and divisive. From a peak of 89 percent in 1991, Bush's popularity slumped to 29 percent during the 1992 campaign.

A third candidate, the eccentric Texas billionaire Ross Perot, also entered the fray. He attacked Bush and Clinton as lacking the economic know-how to deal with the recession and the ever-increasing national debt. That millions of Americans considered Perot a credible candidate—at one point, polls showed him leading both Clinton and Bush—testified to widespread dissatisfaction with the major parties. Perot's support faded as election day approached, but he still received 19 percent of the popular vote, the best result for a third-party candidate since Theodore Roosevelt in 1912. Clinton won by a substantial margin, a humiliating outcome for Bush, given his earlier popularity.

CLINTON IN OFFICE

In his first two years in office, Clinton turned away from some of the social and economic policies of the Reagan and Bush years. He appointed several blacks and women to his cabinet, including Janet Reno, the first female attorney general, and named two supporters of abortion rights, Ruth Bader Ginsburg and Stephen Breyer, to the Supreme Court. He modified the military's strict ban on gay soldiers, instituting a "don't ask, don't tell" policy by which officers would not seek out gays for dismissal from the armed forces. His first budget raised taxes on the wealthy and significantly expanded the Earned Income Tax Credit (EITC)—a cash payment for low-income workers begun during the Ford administration. The most effective antipoverty policy since the Great Society, the EITC raised over 4 million Americans, half of them children, above the poverty line during Clinton's presidency.

Clinton shared his predecessor's passion for free trade. Despite strong opposition from unions and environmentalists, he obtained congressional approval of the North American Free Trade Agreement (NAFTA), a treaty negotiated by Bush that created a free-trade zone consisting of Canada, Mexico, and the United States.

The major policy initiative of Clinton's first term was a plan devised by a panel headed by his wife, Hillary, a lawyer who had pursued an independent career after their marriage, to address the rising cost of health care and the increasing number of Americans who lacked health insurance. In Canada and western Europe, governments provided universal medical coverage. The United States had the world's most advanced medical technology and a woefully incomplete system of health insurance. The Great Society had provided coverage for the elderly and poor through the Medicare and Medicaid programs. Many employers offered health insurance to their workers. But tens of millions of Americans lacked any coverage at all. Beginning in the 1980s, moreover, businesses shifted their employees from individual doctors to Health Maintenance Organizations (HMOs), which reduced costs by limiting physicians' fees and, critics charged, denying patients needed medical procedures.

Announced with great fanfare by Hillary Rodham Clinton at congressional hearings in 1993, Clinton's plan would have provided universal coverage through large groupings of organizations like the HMOs. Doctors and health insurance and drug companies attacked it vehemently, fearing government regulations that would limit reimbursement for medical procedures, insurance rates, and the price of drugs. Too complex to be easily understood by most voters and vulnerable to criticism for further expanding the unpopular federal bureaucracy, the plan died in 1994. Nothing took its place. By 2000, some 40 million Americans, most of them persons who held full-time jobs, still lacked health insurance, meaning that illness could quickly become a financial disaster.

Edward Sorel's illustration for the cover of the New Yorker *depicts Bill Clinton at his 1993 inauguration, flanked by some of his predecessors as president.*

THE "FREEDOM REVOLUTION"

With the economy recovering slowly from the recession and Clinton's first two years in office seemingly lacking in significant accomplishments, voters in 1994 turned against the administration. The health care fiasco enabled his opponents to portray Clinton as the embodiment of big government. For the first time since the 1950s, Republicans won control of both houses of Congress. They proclaimed their triumph the "Freedom Revolution." Newt Gingrich, a conservative congressman from Georgia who became the new Speaker of the House, masterminded their campaign. Gingrich had devised a platform called the "Contract with America," which promised to curtail the scope of government, cut back on taxes and economic and environmental regulations, overhaul the welfare system, and end affirmative action.

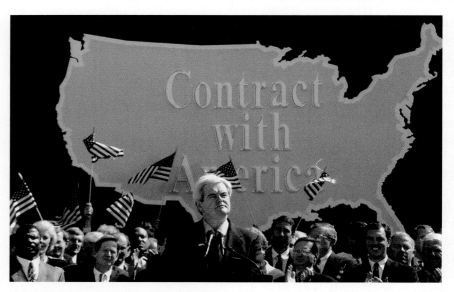

Congressman Newt Gingrich of Georgia at a rally in September 1994 announcing the "Contract with America," the Republican program for the congressional elections that fall. The Republican sweep resulted in Gingrich's election as Speaker of the House.

Viewing their electoral triumph as an endorsement of the Contract, Republicans moved swiftly to implement its provisions. The House approved deep cuts in social, educational, and environmental programs, including the popular Medicare system. With the president and Congress unable to reach agreement on a budget, the government in December 1995 shut down all nonessential operations, including Washington, D.C., museums and national parks.

Gingrich had assumed that the public shared his intense ideological convictions. He discovered that in 1994 they had voted against Clinton, not for the full implementation of the Contract with America. Most Americans blamed Congress for the impasse, and Gingrich's popularity plummeted.

CLINTON'S POLITICAL STRATEGY

Like Truman after the Republican sweep of 1946, Clinton rebuilt his popularity by campaigning against a radical Congress. He opposed the most extreme parts of his opponents' program, while adopting others. In his state of the union address of January 1996, he announced that "the era of big government is over," in effect turning his back on the tradition of Democratic Party liberalism and embracing the antigovernment outlook associated with Republicans since the days of Barry Goldwater. He also approved the Telecommunications Act of 1996, which deregulated broadcasting and telephone companies and gave billions of dollars worth of digital frequencies to existing broadcasters without charge.

Also in 1996, ignoring the protests of most Democrats, Clinton signed into law a Republican bill that abolished the program of Aid to Families with Dependent Children (AFDC), commonly known as "welfare." Grants of money to the states, with strict limits on how long recipients could receive payments, replaced it. At the time of its abolition, AFDC assisted 14 million individuals, 9 million of them children. Thanks to stringent new eligibility requirements imposed by the states and the economic boom of the late 1990s, welfare rolls plummeted. But the number of children living in poverty remained essentially unchanged. Nonetheless, Clinton had succeeded in one of his primary goals: by the late 1990s, welfare, a hotly contested issue for twenty years or more, had disappeared from political debate.

Commentators called Clinton's political strategy "triangulation." This meant embracing the most popular Republican policies, like welfare reform, while leaving his opponents with extreme positions unpopular among suburban middle-class voters, such as hostility to abortion rights and environmental protection. Clinton's strategy enabled him to neutralize Republican claims that Democrats were the party of high taxes and lavish spending on persons who preferred dependency to honest labor. Clinton's passion for free trade alienated many working-class Democrats but convinced middle-class voters that the party was not beholden to the unions.

Clinton easily defeated Republican Bob Dole in the presidential contest of 1996, becoming the first Democrat elected to two terms since FDR. Clinton had accomplished for Reaganism what Eisenhower had done for the New Deal, and Nixon for the Great Society—consolidating a basic shift in American politics by accepting many of the premises of his opponents.

CLINTON AND WORLD AFFAIRS

Like Jimmy Carter before him, Clinton's primary political interests concerned domestic, not international, affairs. But with the United States now indisputably the world's dominant power, Clinton, like Carter, took steps to encourage the settlement of long-standing international conflicts and tried to elevate support for human rights to a central place in international relations. He met only mixed success.

Clinton strongly supported a 1993 agreement, negotiated at Oslo, Norway, in which Israel for the first time recognized the legitimacy of the Palestine Liberation Organization. The Oslo accords seemed to outline a road to Mideast peace. But neither side proved willing to implement them fully. Israeli governments continued to build Jewish settlements on Palestinian land in the West Bank—a part of Jordan that Israel had occupied during the 1967 Six-Day War. The new Palestinian Authority, which shared in governing parts of the West Bank as a stepping stone to full statehood, proved to be corrupt, powerless, and unable to curb the growth of groups bent on violence against Israel. At the end of his presidency, Clinton brought Israeli and Palestinian leaders to Camp David to try to work out a final peace treaty. But the meeting failed, and violence soon resumed.

Like Carter, Clinton found it difficult to balance concern for human rights with strategic and economic interests and to formulate clear guidelines for humanitarian interventions overseas. For example, the United States did nothing in 1994 when tribal massacres racked Rwanda, in central Africa. Over 800,000 people were slaughtered, and 2 million refugees fled the country. On the other hand, with Carter taking the lead in negotiations, the Clinton administration in 1994 arranged the peaceful return to power of Haiti's elected president, Jean-Bertrand Aristide, who had been ousted in a military coup. American troops landed on the island not, as earlier in the century, to occupy it but to assist an elected government and to keep the peace.

THE BALKAN CRISIS

The most complex foreign policy crisis of the Clinton years arose from the disintegration of Yugoslavia, a multi-ethnic state in southeastern Europe that had been carved from the old Austro-Hungarian empire after World War I. As in the rest of eastern Europe, the communist government that had ruled Yugoslavia since the 1940s collapsed in 1989. Within a few years, the country's six provinces dissolved into five new states. Ethnic conflict plagued several of these new nations. In 1992, Serbs in Bosnia, which straddled the historic boundary between Christianity and Islam in southeastern Europe, launched a war aimed at driving out Muslims and Croats. They conducted

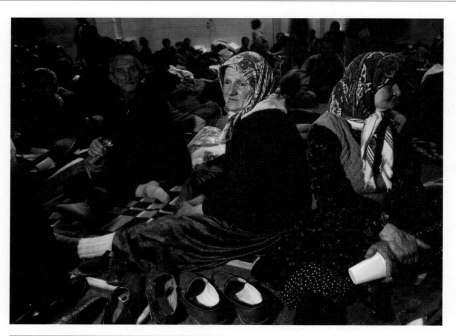

A 1992 photograph of refugees in war-torn Bosnia illustrates the humanitarian crisis in the Balkans during the 1990s.

the war with unprecedented ferocity, using mass murder and rape as military strategies. "Ethnic cleansing"—a terrible new term meaning the forcible expulsion from an area of a particular ethnic group—now entered the international vocabulary. By the end of 1993, over 100,000 Bosnians, nearly all of them civilians, had perished.

With the Cold War over, protection of human rights in the Balkans gave NATO a new purpose. After considerable indecision, NATO launched air strikes against Bosnian Serb forces, with American planes contributing. UN troops, including 20,000 Americans, arrived as peacekeepers. In 1998, ethnic cleansing again surfaced, this time by Yugoslavian troops and local Serbs against the Albanian population of Kosovo, a province of Serbia. Over 800,000 Albanians fled the region. To halt the bloodshed, NATO launched a two-month war against Yugoslavia that led to the deployment of American and UN forces in Kosovo.

HUMAN RIGHTS

During Clinton's presidency, human rights played an increasingly important role in international affairs. At the time, hundreds of nongovernmental agencies throughout the world defined themselves as protectors of human rights. During the 1990s, the agenda of international human rights organizations expanded to include access to health care, women's rights, and the rights of indigenous peoples like the Aborigines of Australia and the descendants of the original inhabitants of the Americas. Reports by Amnesty International and Human Rights Watch—international organizations that monitored how governments treated their citizens—strongly influenced world public opinion. Human rights emerged as a justification for interventions in matters once considered to be the internal affairs of sovereign nations. The United States dispatched the military to distant parts of the world to assist in international missions to protect civilians.

New institutions emerged that sought to punish violations of human rights. The Rwandan genocide produced a UN-sponsored war crimes court that sentenced the country's former prime minister to life in prison. An international tribunal put Yugoslav president Slobodan Milošević on trial for sponsoring the massacre of civilians. The European Court of Human Rights overruled legal decisions by national courts that violated individual rights. Spanish and British courts considered charging former Chilean dictator Augusto Pinochet with murder, although he proved to be too ill to stand trial. It remained to be seen whether these initiatives would grow into an effective international system of protecting human rights across national boundaries, partly because despite adopting human rights as a slogan, many governments continued to violate them in practice.

A NEW ECONOMY?

Clinton's popularity rested in part on the American economy's remarkable performance in the mid- and late 1990s. After recovery from the recession of 1990–1991, economic expansion continued for the rest of the decade. By 2000, unemployment stood below 4 percent, a figure not seen since the 1960s. Many economists had insisted that if unemployment fell that low, inflation would inevitably increase. Yet prices barely rose during the boom, because rising worldwide oil production kept the cost of energy low and weak unions and increased global competition made it difficult for workers to achieve significant wage increases and for corporations to raise prices. The boom became the longest uninterrupted period of economic expansion in the nation's history. Because Reagan and Bush had left behind massive budget deficits, Clinton worked hard to balance the federal budget—a goal traditionally associated with fiscal conservatives. Since economic growth produced rising tax revenues, Clinton during his second term not only balanced the budget but actually produced budget surpluses.

The first Starbucks store, which opened in Seattle in 1971. By the early twenty-first century, Starbucks had over 7,000 such establishments in countries around the globe.

THE COMPUTER REVOLUTION

Many commentators spoke of the 1990s as the dawn of a "new economy," in which computers and the Internet would produce vast new efficiencies and the production and sale of information would occupy the central place once held by the manufacture of goods. Computers had first been developed during and after World War II to solve scientific problems and do calculations involving enormous amounts of data. The early ones were extremely large, expensive, and, by modern standards, slow. Research for the space program of the 1960s spurred the development of improved computer technology, notably the miniaturization of parts thanks to the development of the microchip on which circuits could be imprinted.

Microchips made possible the development of entirely new consumer products. Video cassette recorders, handheld video games, cellular phones, and digital cameras were mass-produced at affordable prices during the 1990s, mostly in Asia and Latin America rather than the United States. But it was the computer that transformed American life. Beginning in the 1980s, companies like Apple and IBM marketed computers for business and home use. As computers became smaller, faster, and less expensive, they found a place in businesses of every kind. In occupations as diverse as clerical work, banking, architectural design, medical diagnosis, and even factory production, they transformed the American workplace. They also changed private life. By the year 2000, nearly half of all American households owned a personal computer, used for entertainment, shopping, and

Two architects of the computer revolution, Steve Jobs (standing), *the head of Apple Computers, and Bill Gates, founder of Microsoft, via the Internet, at a 1997 convention.*

Young people seemed to adapt to the computer revolution more readily than their elders. Here, nine-year-old Anna Walter teaches several adults how to use the Internet in Wichita, Kansas.

sending and receiving electronic mail. Centers of computer technology, such as Silicon Valley south of San Francisco, the Seattle and Austin metropolitan areas, and lower Manhattan, boomed during the 1990s.

At the same time, the Internet, first developed as a high-speed military communications network, was simplified and opened to commercial and individual use through personal computers. The Internet expanded the flow of information and communications more radically than any invention since the printing press. Since English quickly emerged as the dominant language on the Internet, it also accelerated the global spread of American culture. At a time when the ownership of newspapers, television stations, and publishing houses was becoming concentrated in the hands of a few giant media conglomerates, the fact that anyone with a computer could post his or her ideas for worldwide circulation led "netizens" ("citizens" of the Internet) to hail the advent of a new, democratic public sphere in cyberspace.

GLOBAL ECONOMIC PROBLEMS

American economic expansion in the 1990s seemed all the more remarkable since other advanced countries found themselves bogged down in difficulty. In western Europe, unemployment remained far higher than in the United States. Japan, which some commentators of the 1980s had expected to surpass the United States as the world's leading economic power, was locked in a long-term recession. Despite an influx of Western loans and investment, Russia moved from one economic crisis to another. Relying strongly on advice from American free-market economists and the Clinton administration, Russian president Boris Yeltsin presided over a policy of "shock therapy" that privatized state-owned enterprises and imposed severe cuts in wages and in the guaranteed jobs, health care, and housing Russians had become used to under communism. Foreign investors and a new Russian business class (many of them Yeltsin's relatives and cronies, and former party officials) reaped a windfall, while most of the population plunged into poverty.

Many Third World countries faced large trade deficits and problems repaying loans from foreign banks and other institutions. A sharp decline in the value of the Thai currency in 1997 sparked a fiscal crisis throughout Asia, only resolved by massive loans from the International Monetary Fund. These bailouts inspired criticisms, echoed at the Seattle protests of 1999, that globalization increased social inequality. Foreign investors had their loans repaid, but receiving nations were required to balance their budgets by stringent cutbacks in public spending, so that the burden fell disproportionately on the poor.

THE STOCK MARKET BOOM AND BUST

In the United States, economic growth and talk of a new economy sparked a frenzied boom in the stock market that was reminiscent of the 1920s. Investors, large and small, poured funds into stocks, spurred by the rise of discount and online firms that advertised aggressively and charged lower fees than traditional brokers. By 2000, a majority of American households owned stocks directly or through investment in mutual funds and pension and retirement accounts.

Investors were especially attracted to the new "dot coms"—companies that conducted business via the Internet and seemed to symbolize the

Technicians at the offices of FHP Wireless in Belmont, California, one of numerous technology companies launched with great fanfare in the late 1990s. Unlike many, FHP survived. In 2002, Fortune magazine listed it as one of the country's "cool companies." It is now called Tropos Networks.

promise of the new economy. Standard and Poor's index of 500 stocks (S&P 500) increased 20 percent or more each year from 1996 to 1999, a remarkable performance. But the NASDAQ, a stock exchange dominated by new technology companies, rose over 500 percent from 1998 to 1999. Many of these "high-tech" companies never turned a profit. But economic journalists and stock brokers explained that the new economy had so revolutionized business that traditional methods of assessing a company's value no longer applied

Inevitably, the bubble burst. On April 14, 2000, stocks suffered their largest one-day drop in history. They did not soon recover. For the first time since the Depression, stock prices declined for three successive years (2000–2002), wiping out billions of dollars in Americans' net worth and pension funds. The value of NASDAQ stocks fell by nearly 80 percent between 2000 and 2002. Not until 2006 would the general stock index again reach the level of early 2000, and the NASDAQ remained far below its record high. Stock brokerage firms "downsized" their staffs, state and federal tax revenues plummeted, and technology companies that had expended hundreds of billions of dollars of investors' funds disappeared. By 2001, the American economy had fallen into a recession. Talk of a new economy, it appeared, had been premature.

THE ENRON SYNDROME

Only after the market dropped did it become apparent that the stock boom of the 1990s had been fueled in part by fraud. For a time in 2001 and 2002, Americans were treated to daily revelations of almost incredible greed and corruption on the part of respected brokerage firms, accountants, and company executives. During the late 1990s, accounting firms like Arthur Andersen, giant banks like J.P. Morgan Chase and Citigroup, and corporate lawyers pocketed extravagant fees for devising complex schemes to help

Cartoonist Harley Schwadron's comment on the Enron scandal.

push up companies' stock prices by hiding their true financial condition. Enron, a Houston-based energy company that epitomized the new economy—it bought and sold electricity rather than actually producing it—reported as profits billions of dollars in operating losses. Brokers at respected Wall Street firms advised favored clients to sell risky stocks while foisting them on ordinary customers. When stock prices began to fall, insiders jumped ship while brokers urged hapless individual investors to hold on to their shares, many of which ended up being worthless.

In many companies, corporate boards of directors, charged with looking out for the interests of shareholders, secretly approved lavish payments to present and former company leaders. Only because of court papers filed in his divorce case, for example, did it become known that the board of General Electric (GE) had agreed that after his retirement, the company would provide its former head, Jack Welch Jr., with access to a private jet, a Manhattan apartment, and payment of his restaurant bills. Welch could have afforded the cost of his meals—in 2000, his last year running GE, he was paid $123 million.

In the early twenty-first century, the bill came due for many corporate criminals. The founder of Adelphia Communications was convicted of misuse of company funds. A jury found the chairman of Tyco International guilty of looting the company of millions of dollars. A number of former chief executives faced long prison terms. Kenneth Lay and Jeffrey Skilling, chief officers of Enron, were convicted by a Texas jury of multiple counts of fraud. (Lay died before sentencing.) Even reputable firms like J. P. Morgan, Chase, and Citigroup agreed to pay billions of dollars to compensate investors on whom they had pushed worthless stocks.

FRUITS OF DEREGULATION

At the height of the 1990s boom, with globalization in full swing, stocks rising, and the economy expanding, the economic model of free trade and deregulation appeared unassailable. But the retreat from government economic regulation, a policy embraced by both the Republican Congress and President Clinton, left no one to represent the public interest.

The sectors of the economy most affected by the scandals—energy, telecommunications, and stock trading—had all been subjects of deregulation. Enron could manipulate energy prices because Congress had granted it an exemption from laws regulating the price of natural gas and electricity. WorldCom, a communications giant that, like Enron, issued fraudulent earnings statements, had benefited from the Telecommunications Act of 1996, mentioned earlier, that privatized the airwaves. Many stock frauds stemmed directly from the repeal in 1999 of the Glass-Steagall Act, a New Deal measure that had separated commercial banking from Wall Street investing. The repeal made conflicts of interest all but inevitable. Banks financed risky new stock offerings by fledgling Internet companies while their investment arms peddled the shares to an unsuspecting public.

Like the scandals of the 1920s, those of the 1990s severely damaged confidence in the stock market and in the ethics of corporate leaders. Indeed, striking parallels existed between the two decades—the stock market frenzy, get-rich-quick ethos, close connection between business and government, passion for deregulation, and widespread corruption. Henry M. Paulson, Jr., chairman of the major investment company Goldman Sachs, said that never in his lifetime had the reputation of business leaders been lower than at the dawn of the twenty-first century. Unlike during the New Deal, however, public outrage at business practices did not translate into a legislative agenda.

RISING INEQUALITY

The boom that began in 1995 benefited nearly all Americans. For the first time since the early 1970s, average real wages and family incomes began to grow significantly. Economic expansion at a time of low unemployment brought rapid increases in wages for families at all income levels. It aided low-skilled workers, especially non-whites, who had been left out of previous periods of growth. By 2000, the number of long-term unemployed, 2 million in 1993, had declined to around 700,000. Yet, despite these gains, average wages for nonsupervisory workers, adjusted for inflation, remained below the level of the 1970s. Overall, in the last two decades of the twentieth century, the poor and the middle class became worse off while the rich became significantly richer.

Between 1977 and 1999, the average after-tax income of the poorest one-fifth of Americans fell 12 percent, and that of the middle one-fifth decreased by 3 percent. In contrast, thanks to the soaring stock market and increasingly generous pay for top executives, the income of the top one-fifth rose 38 percent. The wealth of the richest Americans exploded during the 1990s. Sales of luxury goods like yachts and mansions boomed. Bill Gates, head of Microsoft and the country's richest person, owned as much wealth as the bottom 40 percent of the American population put together. In 1965, the salary of the typical corporate chief executive officer (CEO) had been 26 times the annual income of the typical worker. In 2000, the ratio had increased to 310 to 1.

Dot-com millionaires and well-paid computer designers and programmers received much publicity. But companies continued to shift manufacturing jobs overseas. Thanks to NAFTA, which eliminated barriers to imports from Mexico, a thriving industrial zone emerged just across the southern border of the United States, where American manufacturers built plants to take advantage of cheap labor and weak environmental and safety regulations. Despite low unemployment, companies' threats to shut down and move exerted downward pressure on American wages. In 2000, the United States no longer led the world in the hourly wages of manufacturing workers, lagging behind several countries in Europe. In terms of the distribution of income and wealth, the United States was the most unequal society in the developed world.

High-tech firms did not create enough high-paying jobs to compensate. Microsoft, symbol of the new economy, employed only 30,000 people. In 1970, General Motors had been the country's largest corporate employer. In the early twenty-first century, it had been replaced by Wal-Mart, a giant discount retail chain that paid most of its 1.6 million workers slightly more than the minimum wage. Wal-Mart aggressively opposed efforts at collective bargaining. In 2000, not a single one of its employees belonged to a union.

Figure 27.1 U.S. INCOME INEQUALITY, 1913–2003

Index of economic inequality

Higher = more unequal

Year

The "Gini index" measures economic inequality; the higher the number, the more unequally income is distributed. As the graph shows, inequality peaked just before the Great Depression, fell dramatically during the New Deal, World War II, and the postwar economic boom, and then began a steady upward climb in the early 1970s.

In 2000, well over half the labor force worked for less than fourteen dollars per hour, a wage on which families found it very difficult to make ends meet. Because of the decline in union membership and the spread of part-time employment, fewer and fewer workers enjoyed fringe benefits common in union contracts, such as employer-provided health insurance. In "dual cities" like Los Angeles and New York, high-tech computer companies and firms engaging in international finance coexisted with sweatshops reminiscent of the Progressive era, where workers toiled in overcrowded conditions for the minimum wage or less. Poverty was not limited to urban areas. The highest rates of poverty could be found in isolated rural regions that experienced the continuation of the long-term decline in family farming. Of the twenty-five poorest counties in the United States in 2000, nine were located in Nebraska and South Dakota.

At the end of the twentieth century, the United States, more than ever before, was a suburban nation. Two-thirds of new jobs were created in the suburbs. Suburbs were no longer places from which people commuted to jobs in central cities—their office parks, industrial plants, and huge shopping malls employed many local residents. Nor were suburbs as racially segregated as in the past. In 2000, one-quarter of the suburban population was black, and Hispanics represented a majority of the population in the suburbs of Los Angeles and Miami. But suburbs remained divided by income—there were rich suburbs, middle-class suburbs, and poor suburbs, with little connection between them.

Barbie's Liberty, *a satirical work by the artist Hans Haacke, recasts the Barbie doll, one of America's most successful toys, in the image of the Statue of Liberty to comment on the loss of manufacturing jobs to low-wage areas overseas.*

CULTURE WARS

The end of the Cold War ushered in hopes for a new era of global harmony. Instead, what one observer called a "rebellion of particularisms"—renewed emphasis on group identity and insistent demands for group recognition and power—racked the international arena during the 1990s. In the nineteenth and twentieth centuries, socialism and nationalism had united people of different backgrounds in pursuit of common goals. Now, in Africa, Asia, the Middle East, and parts of Europe, the waning of movements based on socialism and the declining power of nation-states arising from globalization seemed to unleash long-simmering ethnic and religious antagonisms. Partly in reaction to the global spread of a secular culture based on consumption and mass entertainment, intense religious movements attracted increasing numbers of followers—Hindu nationalism in India, orthodox Judaism in Israel, Islamic fundamentalism in much of the Muslim world, and evangelical Christianity in the United States. Like other nations, although in a far less extreme way and with little accompanying violence, the United States experienced divisions arising from the intensification of ethnic and racial identities and religious fundamentalism.

THE NEWEST IMMIGRANTS

Because of shifts in immigration, cultural and racial diversity became increasingly visible in the United States. Until the immigration law of 1965, the vast majority of twentieth-century newcomers had hailed from

VOICES OF FREEDOM

FROM PUWAT CHARUKAMNOETKANOK, "Triple Identity: My Experience as an Immigrant in America" (1990)

Like all immigrants, those of the late twentieth century faced painful adjustments in America. In this essay, a student at the State University of New York who had entered the country from Thailand four years earlier reflects on his experiences. His grandfather had moved from China to Thailand in 1937 and later married a Chinese woman.

"America is the land of opportunity." Is this a myth or reality? I came to America four years ago with a faith that I would find opportunity here. However, I realize a reality: racism exists and most people will not easily accept immigrants. In the spring of 1990, I took a course, "Immigration and Ethnicity in the United States," in which I learned that I am not alone. Many immigrants encountered similar barriers. My grandparents are also immigrants, and I have learned about their experiences....

My grandparents ignored the prejudice they faced [in Thailand]. They worked hard, hoping that when they became established economically people would accept them for who they really were—kind, generous, and peaceful persons. I believe they have succeeded.... The ultimate act of assimilation came when [my grandparents] changed their nationality to Thai. They changed their last name from Wong ... to Charukamnoetkanok. ... Because of my grandparents' willingness to assimilate and the generous attitude of the majority of Thai people, I never experienced an identity crisis in Thailand ... not until I came to America.

In April 1986 I was told that we would go to America. I only knew about America from movies and television shows. ... When we went to New York City, I saw tall buildings just like in the movies. But I experienced many things that have never been shown accurately by Hollywood.

The major difference between my immigration and my grandparents' is the motivation. [My grandfather] migrated from China [to Thailand] mainly for economic reasons. My parents' main objective for migrating was the education of their children. This point can be proven by the fact that my parents left their established business behind and have started from scratch in America....

However, both migration experiences are similar in many ways. For the first time in my life, I have learned about prejudice and discrimination. ... In America, many values are different. I, like many children from Asia, have been taught to respect elders, including parents, relatives, and teachers. Needless to say, it is quite different here in America....

Living in America, I learn about racism and cultural differences, and experience language difficulties. For the first time, I experience an identity crisis. ... Am I Chinese, Thai, or American? ... If I am willing to work hard at it, hopefully someday people will accept me for who I am. America really is a land of opportunity, but as with all good land, hard work and patience are needed to harvest the crops.

FROM GLOBAL EXCHANGE, SEATTLE, Declaration for Global Democracy (December 1999)

The demonstrations that disrupted the December 1999 meeting of the World Trade Organization in Seattle brought to public attention a widespread dissatisfaction with the effects of economic "globalization." In this declaration, organizers of the protest offered their critique.

———————————

As citizens of global society, recognizing that the World Trade Organization is unjustly dominated by corporate interests and run for the enrichment of the few at the expense of all others, we demand:

Representatives from all sectors of society must be included in all levels of trade policy formulations. All global citizens must be democratically represented in the formulation, implementation, and evaluation of all global social and economic policies.

Global trade and investment must not be ends in themselves, but rather the instruments for achieving equitable and sustainable development including protection for workers and the environment.

Global trade agreements must not undermine the ability of each nation-state or local community to meet its citizens' social, environmental, cultural or economic needs.

The World Trade Organization must be replaced by a democratic and transparent body accountable to citizens—not to corporations.

No globalization without representation!

———————————

QUESTIONS

1. What are the most unfamiliar features of American life to the immigrant from Thailand?

2. Why do the Seattle protesters feel that the World Trade Organization is a threat to democracy?

3. How do these documents reflect the contradictory impact of globalization in the United States?

Table 27.1 IMMIGRATION TO THE UNITED STATES, 1960–2000						
Decade	Total	Europe	Asia	Western Hemisphere	Africa	Oceania
1961–1970	3,321,584	1,123,492	427,642	1,716,374	28,954	25,122
1971–1980	4,493,302	800,368	1,588,178	1,982,735	80,779	41,242
1981–1990	7,337,030	761,550	2,738,157	3,615,225	176,893	45,205
1991–2000	9,052,999	1,359,737	2,795,672	4,486,806	354,939	55,845

Europe. That measure, as noted in Chapter 25, sparked a wholesale shift in immigrants' origins. Between 1965 and 2000, nearly 24 million immigrants entered the United States, a number only slightly lower than the 27 million during the peak period of immigration between 1880 and 1924. About 50 percent came from Latin America and the Caribbean, 35 percent from Asia, and smaller numbers from the Middle East and Africa. Only 10 percent arrived from Europe, mostly from the war-torn Balkans and the former Soviet Union.

In 2000, the number of foreign-born persons living in the United States stood at over 31 million, or 11 percent of the population. Although less than the peak proportion of 14 percent in 1910, in absolute numbers this represented the largest immigrant total in the nation's history. The immigrant influx changed the country's religious and racial map. By 2000, over 3 million Muslims resided in the United States, and the combined population of Buddhists and Hindus exceeded 1 million.

As in the past, most immigrants became urban residents, with New York City, Los Angeles, Chicago, and Miami the most common destinations. New ethnic communities emerged, homes to shops, restaurants, foreign-language newspapers and radio and television stations, and ethnic professionals like businessmen and lawyers. Unlike in the past, rather than being concentrated in one or two parts of central cities, immigrants quickly moved into outlying neighborhoods and older suburbs. The immigrant influx revitalized neighborhoods like New York City's Washington Heights (a Dominican enclave) and Flushing (a center for Asian newcomers). By the turn of the century, more than half of all Latinos lived in suburbs. Orange County, California, which had been a stronghold of suburban conservatism between 1960 and 1990, elected a Latina Democrat to Congress in the late 1990s. While most immigrants settled on the East and West Coasts, some moved to other parts of the country. They brought cultural and racial diversity to once-homogeneous communities in the American heartland.

Post-1965 immigration formed part of the worldwide uprooting of labor arising from globalization. In 2000, the global immigrant population was estimated at 100 million. Those who migrated to the United States came from a wide variety of backgrounds. They included poor, illiterate refugees from places of economic and political crisis—Central Americans escaping the region's civil wars and poverty, Haitians and Cambodians fleeing

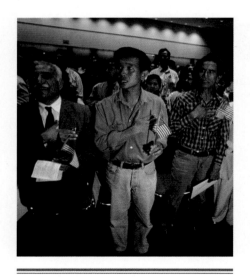

Recent immigrants reciting the Pledge of Allegiance during a naturalization ceremony.

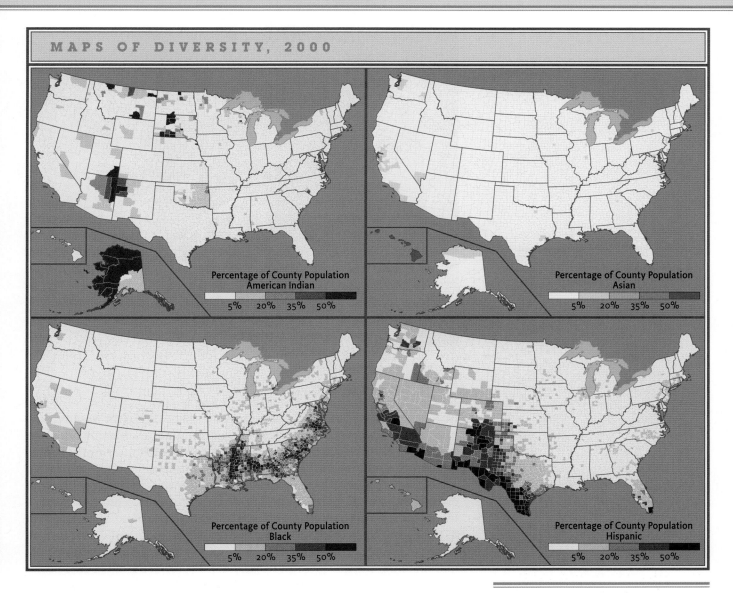

MAPS OF DIVERSITY, 2000

Percentage of County Population
American Indian

5%　20%　35%　50%

Percentage of County Population
Asian

5%　20%　35%　50%

Percentage of County Population
Black

5%　20%　35%　50%

Percentage of County Population
Hispanic

5%　20%　35%　50%

repressive governments. But many immigrants were well-educated professionals from countries like India and South Korea, where the availability of skilled jobs had not kept pace with the spread of higher education.

For the first time in American history, women made up the majority of newcomers, reflecting the decline of manufacturing jobs that had previously absorbed immigrant men, as well as the spread of employment opportunities in traditionally female fields like care of children and the elderly and retail sales. (Many were paid by their employers "off the books," without withholding taxes. This practice became a focus of public discussion in 1993 when President Clinton was forced to withdraw two female cabinet nominees when it came to light that they had hired undocumented immigrants as housekeepers and paid them in this manner.) Thanks to cheap global communications and jet travel, the immigrants of the 1990s retained strong ties with their countries of origin, frequently phoning and visiting home.

Based on the 2000 Census, these maps show that nearly every state has a significant non-white population.

Latina nannies pushing baby carriages in Beverly Hills, California. In the 1990s, for the first time in American history, female immigrants outnumbered male immigrants.

THE NEW DIVERSITY

Latinos formed the largest single immigrant group. This term was invented in the United States and included people from quite different origins—Mexicans, Central and South Americans, and migrants from Spanish-speaking Caribbean islands like Cuba, the Dominican Republic, and Puerto Rico (although the last group, of course, were American citizens, not immigrants). With 95 million people, Mexico in 2000 had become the world's largest Spanish-speaking nation. Its poverty, high birthrate, and proximity to the United States made it a source of massive legal and illegal immigration. In 2000, Mexican-Americans made up a majority of the Hispanic population of the United States and nearly half the residents of Los Angeles.

Numbering over 41 million in 2006, Latinos had become the largest minority group in the United States. Latinos were highly visible in entertainment, sports, and politics. Indeed, the Hispanic presence transformed American life. José was now the most common name for baby boys in Texas and the third most popular in California. Smith remained the most common American surname, but Garcia, Rodriguez, Gonzales, and other Hispanic names were all in the top fifty.

Latino communities remained far poorer than the rest of the country. A flourishing middle class developed in Los Angeles, Miami, and other cities with large Spanish-speaking populations. But most immigrants from Mexico and Central America competed at the lowest levels of the job market. The influx of legal and illegal immigrants swelled the ranks of low-wage urban workers and agricultural laborers. Latinos lagged far behind other Americans in education. In 2000, their poverty rate stood at double the national figure of 11.3 percent. Living and working conditions among predominantly Latino farm workers in the West fell back to levels as dire as when César Chavez established the United Farm Workers union in the 1960s.

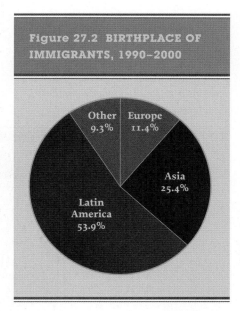

The U.S. Border Patrol apprehending Mexicans who had entered the country in violation of immigration laws, near San Diego, California. In 1990, over 1 million immigrants were arrested and deported after crossing the border illegally.

Asian-Americans also became increasingly visible in the 1990s. There had long been a small population of Asian ancestry in California and New York City, but only after 1965 did immigration from Asia assume large proportions. By 2000, the number of Asian-Americans stood at 11.9 million, eight times the figure of 1970. Like Latinos, Asian-Americans were a highly diverse population, including well-educated Koreans, Indians, and Japanese, as well as poor refugees from Cambodia, Vietnam, and China. Growing up in tight-knit communities that placed great emphasis on education, young Asian-Americans poured into American colleges and universities. Once subjected to harsh discrimination, Asian-Americans now achieved remarkable success. White Americans hailed them as a "model minority." By 2000, the average family income of Asian-Americans, $53,000, surpassed that of whites. But more than any other group, Asian-Americans clustered at opposite ends of the income spectrum. Large numbers earned either more than $75,000 per year (doctors, engineers, and entrepreneurs) or under $5,000 (unskilled laborers in sweatshops and restaurants).

The United States, of course, had long been a multiracial society. But for centuries race relations had been shaped by the black-white divide and the experience of slavery and segregation. The growing visibility of Latinos and Asians suggested that a two-race system no longer adequately described American life. Multiracial imagery filled television, films, and advertising. Interracial marriage, at one time banned in forty-two states, became more common and acceptable. Among Asian-Americans at the turn of the century, half of all marriages involved a non-Asian partner. The figure for Latinos was 30 percent. Some commentators spoke of the "end of racism" and the emergence of a truly color-blind society. Others argued that while Asians and some Latinos were being absorbed into an expanded category of "white" Americans, the black-white divide remained almost as impenetrable as ever.

One thing, however, seemed clear at the dawn of the twenty-first century: diversity was here to stay. In 2000, whites made up around 70 percent

During the 1990s, immigration from Latin America and Asia eclipsed immigration from Europe, traditionally the main source of newcomers to the United States.

Korean youngsters rehearsing a dance at the Veterans' Administration Medical Center in Columbia, South Carolina, an illustration of the growing diversity of American society.

of the population, blacks and Hispanics around 13 percent each, and Asians 6 percent. Because the birthrate of racial minorities is higher than that of whites, the Census Bureau projected that by 2050, only 50 percent of the American population would be white, a little less than 25 percent would be Hispanic, and blacks and Asians would account for around 13 percent each.

AFRICAN-AMERICANS IN THE 1990S

Compared with the situation in 1900 or 1950, the most dramatic change in American life at the turn of the century was the absence of legal segregation and the presence of blacks in areas of American life from which they had once been almost entirely excluded. Thanks to the decline in overt discrimination and the effectiveness of many affirmative action programs, blacks now worked in unprecedented numbers alongside whites in corporate board rooms, offices, and factories. The number of black policemen, for example, rose from 24,000 to 65,000 between 1970 and 2000, and in the latter year, 37 percent of the black population reported having attended college. The economic boom of the late 1990s aided black Americans enormously; the average income of black families rose more rapidly than that of whites.

One major change in black life was the growing visibility of Africans among the nation's immigrants. Between 1970 and 2000, twice as many Africans immigrated to the United States as had entered during the entire period of the Atlantic slave trade. For the first time, all the elements of the African diaspora—natives of Africa, Caribbeans, Central and South Americans of African descent, Europeans with African roots—could be found in the United States alongside the descendants of American slaves.

Despite the ups and downs of unemployment, the rate for non-whites remains persistently higher than that for whites.

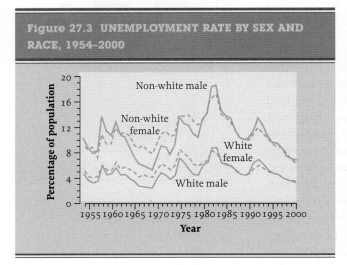

Figure 27.3 UNEMPLOYMENT RATE BY SEX AND RACE, 1954–2000

Table 27.2 HOME OWNERSHIP RATES BY GROUP, 1970–2000				
	1970	*1980*	*1990*	*2000*
Whites	65.0%	67.8%	68.2%	73.8%
Blacks	41.6	44.4	43.4	47.2
Latinos	43.7	43.4	42.4	46.3
All Families	62.9	64.4	64.2	67.4

Nigeria, Ghana, and Ethiopia provided the largest number of African immigrants, and they settled overwhelmingly in urban areas, primarily in New York, California, Texas, and the District of Columbia. Some were impoverished refugees fleeing civil wars in Somalia, Sudan, and Ethiopia, but many more were professionals—over half the African newcomers had college educations, the highest percentage for any immigrant group. Indeed, some African countries complained of a "brain drain" as physicians, teachers, and other highly skilled persons sought opportunities in the United States that did not exist in their own underdeveloped countries. While some prospered, others found it difficult to transfer their credentials to the United States and found jobs driving taxis and selling African crafts at street fairs.

Most African-Americans, nonetheless, remained in a more precarious situation than whites or many recent immigrants. The black unemployment rate remained double that of whites, and their median family income of $29,000 and poverty rate of 26 percent put them behind whites, Asians, and Latinos. Half of all black children lived in poverty, two-thirds were born out of wedlock, and in every index of social well-being from health to quality of housing, blacks continued to lag. Despite the continued expansion of the black middle class, a far lower percentage of blacks than whites owned their homes or held professional and managerial jobs. Housing segregation remained pervasive. In 2000, over one-third of the black population lived in suburbs, but mostly in predominantly black communities.

THE ROLE OF THE COURTS

As in the late nineteenth century, the Supreme Court in the last years of the twentieth century little by little retreated from the civil rights revolution. The justices made it increasingly difficult for victims of discrimination to win lawsuits and proved increasingly sympathetic to the pleas of whites that affirmative action plans discriminated against them. In *Patterson v. McLean Credit Union* (1989), the Court barred a black employee who suffered racial harassment while working from suing for damages under the Civil Rights Act of 1866. That law, the justices maintained, only prohibited discrimination at the moment of signing a contract, not on the job.

In the same year, the Court overturned a Richmond law reserving 30 percent of city construction contracts for minority businesses. Less than 1 percent of such contracts had gone to black-owned companies in the five years before the city council enacted the new law. But Justice Sandra Day O'Connor, who wrote the opinion, insisted that in the absence of clear statements of racism by government officials (hardly a likely occurrence), one could not prove the existence of discrimination. Blacks, she speculated, may have been "attracted to other industries than construction," as if their distribution among the occupations had historically been a matter of free choice.

Despite the nation's growing racial diversity, school segregation—now resulting from housing patterns and the divide between urban and suburban school districts rather than laws requiring racial separation—was on the rise. Most city public school systems consisted overwhelmingly of minority students, large numbers of whom failed to receive an adequate education. The courts released more and more districts from desegregation orders. By 2000, the nation's black and Latino students were more isolated from white pupils than in 1970. Nearly 80 percent of white students attended schools where they encountered few if any pupils of another race. Since school funding rested on property taxes, poor communities continued to have less to spend on education than wealthy ones.

THE SPREAD OF IMPRISONMENT

During the 1960s, the nation's prison population had declined. But in the 1970s, with urban crime rates rising, politicians of both parties sought to convey the image of being "tough on crime." They insisted that the judicial system should focus on locking up criminals for long periods rather than rehabilitating them. They treated drug addiction as a violation of the law rather than as a disease. State governments greatly increased the penalties for crime and reduced the possibility of parole. Successive presidents launched "wars" on the use of illegal drugs. As a result, the number of Americans in prison rose dramatically, most of them incarcerated for non-violent drug offenses.

During the 1990s, thanks to the waning of the "crack" epidemic and more effective urban police tactics, crime rates dropped dramatically across the country. But because of the sentencing laws of the previous two decades, this did nothing to stem the increase of the prison population. In 2006, it reached 2.2 million, ten times the figure of 1970. Several million more individuals were on parole, probation, or under some other kind of criminal supervision. These figures dwarfed those of every other Western society.

As the prison population grew, a "prison-industrial complex" emerged. Struggling communities battered by deindustrialization saw prisons as a source of jobs and income. Between 1990 and 1995, the federal government and the states constructed over 200 new prisons. California spent more money on its prison system than on its state universities. Convict labor, a practice the labor movement had managed to curtail in the late nineteenth century, revived in the late twentieth. Private companies in Oregon "leased" prisoners for three dollars per day. A call to Trans World Airlines for a flight reservation was likely to be answered by a California inmate.

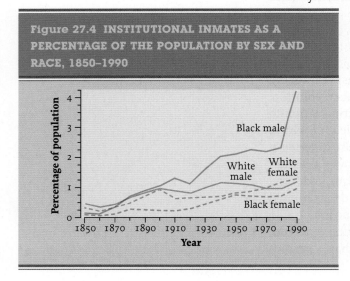

Figure 27.4 INSTITUTIONAL INMATES AS A PERCENTAGE OF THE POPULATION BY SEX AND RACE, 1850–1990

THE BURDEN OF IMPRISONMENT

Members of racial minorities experienced most strongly the paradox of growing islands of unfreedom in a nation that prided itself on liberty. In 1950, whites accounted for 70 percent of the nation's prison population and non-whites 30 percent. By 2000, these figures had been reversed. One reason was that severe penalties faced those convicted of using or selling crack, a particularly potent form of cocaine concentrated among the urban poor, while the use of powder cocaine, the drug of choice in suburban America, led to far lighter sentences.

The percentage of the black population in prison stood eight times higher than the proportion for white Americans. Over one-quarter of all black men could expect to serve time in prison at some time during their lives. A criminal record made it very difficult for ex-prisoners to find jobs. Partly because so many young men were in prison, blacks had a significantly lower rate of marriage than other Americans. Their children became "prison orphans," forced to live with relatives or in foster homes. With twenty-nine states denying the vote to those on probation and seven barring ex-felons from voting for their entire lives, an estimated 4 million black men (13 percent of the black male population) could not cast a ballot at the end of the twentieth century. In the seven states that denied the vote to ex-offenders (Alabama, Florida, Iowa, Kentucky, Mississippi, Nevada, and Virginia), one black man in four was permanently disenfranchised.

Blacks convicted of crimes were also more likely than whites to receive the death penalty. In 1972, the Supreme Court had temporarily suspended states' use of this punishment. But the Court soon allowed it to resume, despite evidence of racial disparities in its application. Even as western Europe and other countries abolished the death penalty, the United States executed 598 persons between 1977 and 1999. In the 1830s, Alexis de Tocqueville had described executions as common in Europe but rare in America. At the close of the twentieth century, with over 3,000 prisoners on death row, the United States ranked with China, Iran, and Saudi Arabia as the nations that most often executed their citizens.

A private, for-profit, maximum-security prison under construction in 1999 in California City, in the Mohave Desert, illustrates the expansion of the "prison-industrial complex."

The continuing frustration of urban blacks exploded in 1992 when an all-white suburban jury found four Los Angeles police officers not guilty of beating black motorist Rodney King, even though an onlooker had captured their assault on videotape. The deadliest urban uprising since the New York draft riots of 1863 followed. Some fifty-two people died, and property damage approached $1 billion. Many Latino youths, who shared blacks' resentment over mistreatment by the police, joined in the violence. The uprising suggested that despite the civil rights revolution, the nation had failed to address the plight of the urban poor. Racial minorities benefited enormously from the dramatic decline in unemployment that accompanied the economic boom of the mid- and late 1990s. But when the boom ended in 2000, these gains once again began to disappear.

THE CONTINUING RIGHTS REVOLUTION

Reflecting the continued power of the rights revolution, the 1990s also witnessed the emergence of new movements for public recognition. In 1990, newly organized disabled Americans won passage of the Americans with Disabilities Act. This far-reaching measure prohibited discrimination in hiring and promotion against persons with disabilities and required that entrances to public buildings be redesigned so as to ensure access for the disabled.

Some movements that were descended from the late 1960s achieved their greatest visibility in the 1990s. Prominent among these was the campaign for gay rights, which in the last two decades of the century increasingly turned its attention to combating acquired immunodeficiency syndrome (AIDS), a fatal disease spread by sexual contact, drug use, and transfusions of contaminated blood. AIDS first emerged in the early 1980s. It quickly became epidemic among homosexual men. The gay movement mobilized to promote "safe sex," prevent discrimination against people suffering from AIDS, and press the federal government to devote greater resources to fighting the disease. By 2000, even though over 400,000 Americans had died of AIDS, its spread among gays had been sharply curtailed. But in other parts of the world, such as Africa, the AIDS epidemic remained out of control.

Gay groups also played an increasing role in politics. In cities with large gay populations, such as New York and San Francisco, politicians vied to attract their votes. Overall, the growth of public tolerance of homosexuality was among the most striking changes in American social attitudes in the last two decades of the century.

NATIVE AMERICANS IN 2000

Another social movement spawned by the 1960s that continued to flourish was the American Indian Movement. The Indian population reached 4 million in the 2000 Census—a sign not only of population growth but also of a renewed sense of pride that led many Indians for the first time to identify themselves as such to census enumerators. Meanwhile, with the assistance of the Native American Rights Fund, established in 1971, some tribes embarked on a campaign for restitution for past injustices. In 2001, for example, a New York court awarded the Cayuga Nation $248 million for illegal land seizures two centuries earlier.

The AIDS quilt, each square of which represents a person who had died of AIDS, on display in Washington, D.C. The quilt was exhibited throughout the country, heightening public awareness of the AIDS epidemic.

The legal position of Indians as American citizens who enjoy a kind of quasi-sovereignty still survives in some cases. Notable examples are the lucrative Indian casinos now operating in states that otherwise prohibit gambling. Indian casinos take in around $15 billion each year, making some tribes very rich. One such group is the Pequot tribe of Connecticut. In 1637, as the result of a brief, bloody war, Puritan New Englanders exterminated or sold into slavery most of the tribe's members. The treaty that restored peace decreed that the tribe's name should be wiped from the historical record. Today, the 280 members of the Pequot tribe operate Foxwoods, reputedly the world's largest casino.

The Census of 2000 listed a Native American population of around 2.5 million, 80 percent of them of mixed Indian and non-Indian ancestry. Half of today's Indians live in five western states (California, Oklahoma, Arizona, New Mexico, and Washington). Although some tribes have reinvested casino profits in improved housing and health care and college scholarships for Native American students, most Indian casinos are marginal operations whose low-wage jobs as cashiers, waitresses, and the like have done little to relieve Indian poverty. Native Americans continue to occupy the lowest rung on the economic ladder. At least half of those living on reservations have incomes below the poverty line.

This "public sculpture" by the Native American artist Lewis deSoto links his own surname with over four centuries of American history. The wall label invokes the depredations of the sixteenth-century Spanish conquistador Hernán DeSoto. The car reminds the viewer that the Chrysler Corporation chose the name DeSoto for a now-defunct automobile. On the rear of the car is an insignia based on traditional Indian basket designs, encircled by the Latin word for smallpox, which the conquistadores transmitted to the Indian population.

MULTICULTURALISM

The new face of American society went hand in hand with one of the most striking developments of the 1990s—the celebration of group difference and demands for group recognition. "Multiculturalism" became the term for a new awareness of the diversity of American society, past and present, and for vocal demands that jobs, education, and politics reflect that diversity. As the numbers of minority and female students at the nation's colleges and universities rose, these institutions moved aggressively to diversify their faculties and revise the traditional curriculum.

One sign of multiculturalism could be seen in the spread of academic programs dealing with the experience of specific groups—Black Studies, Latino Studies, Women's Studies, and the like. Literature departments added the writings of female and minority authors to those of white men. Numerous scholars now taught and wrote history in ways that stressed the experiences of diverse groups of Americans, rather than a common national narrative.

At the same time, public opinion polls revealed a remarkable growth of toleration. The number of respondents who accepted interracial dating without objection rose from 45 percent in 1987 to 78 percent in 2003.

Those who believed gays should automatically be fired from teaching jobs fell from 50 to 35 percent over the same period. In addition, popular television shows portrayed gay characters in a sympathetic light.

THE IDENTITY DEBATE

Among some Americans, the heightened visibility of immigrants, racial minorities, and inheritors of the sexual revolution inspired not celebration of pluralism but alarm over perceived cultural fragmentation. Conservatives, and some traditional liberals as well, decried "identity politics" and multiculturalism for undermining a common sense of nationhood. As in the debates over the Alien Act of the 1790s, Irish immigration in the 1850s, and the "new immigrants" of the early twentieth century, the definition of American nationality again became a contentious political question. Bill Clinton's 1992 slogan, "It's the Economy, Stupid," was directed, in part, at members of the Democratic Party who preferred to focus on racial and gender issues rather than traditional economic concerns. Republicans appealed most directly to those alarmed by the influx of non-white immigrants and the decline of traditional "family values." But differences over diversity did not follow party lines.

Increased cultural diversity and changes in educational policy inspired harsh debates over whether immigrant children should be required to learn English and whether further immigration should be discouraged. These issues entered politics most dramatically in California, whose voters in 1994 approved Proposition 187, which denied illegal immigrants and their children access to welfare, education, and most health services. A federal judge soon barred implementation of the measure on the grounds that control over immigration policy rests with the federal government. But during the 1990s, California voters also approved measures banning bilingual education in public schools, and affirmative action in admission to public colleges and universities. By 2000, twenty-three states had passed laws establishing English as their official language (similar to measures enacted in the aftermath of World War I). The 1996 law that abolished welfare also barred most immigrants who had not become citizens from receiving food stamps.

For a time, nativism gained renewed respectability. *The Bell Curve* (1994), a best-seller by Charles Murray and Richard Herrnstein, claimed to demonstrate scientifically the innate intellectual inferiority of non-whites. Peter Brimelow, a naturalized citizen born in England, argued in *Alien Nation* (1995) that non-white immigration posed a threat to the country's historical cultural identity and should be curtailed. Both works echoed turn-of-the-twentieth-century theorists who warned that "lesser" races might overwhelm real

Demonstrators for and against Proposition 187, with police separating them, at a rally in Los Angeles in August 1996. Approved by California voters two years earlier, the measure severely restricted the services available to undocumented immigrants.

Americans—that is, whites. But since 1900, the United States had become a far more tolerant society. Efforts to appeal to prejudice for political gain often backfired. In California, Republicans' anti-immigrant campaigns inspired minorities to mobilize politically and offended many white Americans. In 2000, Republican presidential candidate George W. Bush emphasized that his brand of conservatism was multicultural, not exclusionary.

CULTURAL CONSERVATISM

Immigration occupied only one front in what came to be called the Culture Wars—battles over moral values that raged throughout the 1990s. The Christian Coalition, founded by evangelical minister Pat Robertson, became a major force in Republican politics. It launched crusades against gay rights, abortion, secularism in public schools, and government aid to the arts. Pat Buchanan's Republican convention speech of 1992 calling for a "religious war for the soul of America," mentioned earlier, alarmed many voters. But cultural conservatives hailed it as their new rallying cry.

It sometimes appeared during the 1990s that the country was refighting old battles between traditional religion and modern secular culture. In an echo of the 1920s, a number of localities required the teaching of creationism, a religious alternative to Darwin's theory of evolution. The battles of the 1960s seemed to be forever unresolved. Many conservatives railed against the erosion of the nuclear family, the changing racial landscape produced by immigration, and what they considered a general decline of traditional values. Cultural conservatives were not satisfied with a few victories over what they considered immorality, such as rules banning the National Endowment for the Arts from making grants to artists who produced sexually explicit material, or the Defense of Marriage Act of 1996, which barred gay couples from spousal benefits provided by federal law.

"FAMILY VALUES" IN RETREAT

The census of 2000 showed "family values" increasingly in disarray. Half of all marriages ended in divorce (70 percent on the West Coast), and over one-third of all births were to unmarried women, including not only sexually active teenagers but growing numbers of professional women in their thirties and forties, as well. Two-thirds of married women worked outside the home, and less than one-fourth of all households consisted of a "traditional" family—a wife, husband, and their children. Although dominated by conservatives, the Supreme Court, in *Casey v. Planned Parenthood of Pennsylvania* (1992), reaffirmed a woman's right to obtain an abortion. The decision allowed states to enact mandatory waiting periods and anti-abortion counseling, but it overturned a requirement that the husband be given notification before the procedure was undertaken. "At the heart of liberty," said the Court, "is the right to . . . make the most intimate and personal choices" without outside interference. In effect, *Casey* repudiated the centuries-old doctrine that a husband has a legal claim to control the body of his wife.

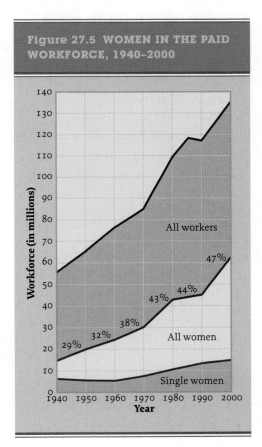

Figure 27.5 WOMEN IN THE PAID WORKFORCE, 1940–2000

By 2000, women represented nearly half of the American workforce, and unlike in the nineteenth century, a majority of women working outside the home were married.

Figure 27.6 CHANGES IN FAMILY STRUCTURE, 1970–2000*

*Not shown are single people living alone and nonrelated people living together. "Children" are a family's own children under age eighteen living at home.

1970	1980	1990	2000
40.3%	30.9%	26.3%	23.5%
30.3%	29.9%	29.8%	28.2%
5.0%	7.5%	8.3%	9.3%
5.6%	5.4%	6.5%	7.1%

- Married couples with children
- Married couples without children
- Other families with children
- Other families without children

At the beginning of the twenty-first century, less than one-quarter of American households consisted of a "traditional" family—a married couple living with their children.

The narrowness of the 5-4 vote in *Casey* and the vehemence of the dissenters, including Chief Justice William Rehnquist, in insisting that *Roe v. Wade* must be reversed, left the legal status of abortion rights dependent on future changes in the Court's membership. As of 2000, however, although conservatives had controlled the presidency under Reagan and Bush, Congress after 1994, and the Supreme Court, they had not eliminated abortion rights, restored prayer to public schools, or persuaded women to abandon public aspirations and "go about the business of marrying and raising children," as Republican congressional leader Richard Armey indelicately demanded. Women did not listen to Armey. At the dawn of the twentieth-century, women received over 60 percent of all college degrees (as opposed to 35 percent in 1960) and over 40 percent of advanced law, medical, and business degrees (up from around 5 percent forty years earlier). The abortion rate declined throughout the 1990s, but this was mostly because teenagers had increasing access to contraception. The sexual revolution and feminism, it seemed, were here to stay.

THE ANTIGOVERNMENT EXTREME

At the radical fringe of conservatism, the belief that the federal government posed a threat to American freedom led to the creation of private militias who armed themselves to fend off oppressive authority. Groups like Aryan Nation, Posse Comitatus, and other self-proclaimed "Christian patriots" spread a mixture of racist, anti-Semitic, and antigovernment ideas. Private armies, like the Militia of Montana, vowed to resist enforcement of federal gun control laws. For millions of Americans, owning a gun became a prime symbol of liberty. "We're here because we love freedom," declared a participant in a 1995 Washington rally against proposed legislation banning semiautomatic assault weapons.

Items on sale at Michigan's "Gun Stock '95," an antigovernment convention.

Many militia groups employed the symbolism and language of the American Revolution, sprinkling their appeals with warnings about the dangers of government tyranny drawn from the writings of Thomas Jefferson, Patrick Henry, and Thomas Paine. They warned that leaders of both major parties formed part of a conspiracy to surrender American sovereignty to the United Nations, or to some shadowy international conspiracy. Although such organizations had been growing for years, they burst into the national spotlight in 1995 when Timothy McVeigh, a member of the militant antigovernment movement, exploded a bomb at a federal office building in Oklahoma City. The blast killed 168 persons, including numerous children at a day-care center. McVeigh was captured, convicted, and executed. The worst act of terrorism in American history until the twenty-first century, the bombing alerted the nation to the danger of violent antigovernment right-wing groups.

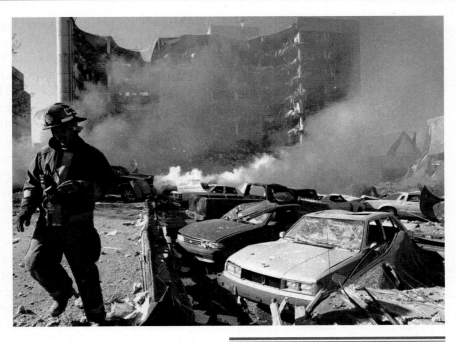

The aftermath of the bombing of a federal office building in Oklahoma City in 1995, the worst act of terrorism in the United States during the twentieth century.

IMPEACHMENT AND THE ELECTION OF 2000

The unusually intense partisanship of the 1990s seemed ironic, given Clinton's move toward the political center. Republicans' intense dislike of Clinton could only be explained by the fact that he seemed to symbolize everything conservatives hated about the 1960s. As a college student, the president had smoked marijuana and participated in antiwar demonstrations. He had married a feminist, made a point of leading a multicultural administration, and supported gay rights. Clinton's popularity puzzled and frustrated conservatives, reinforcing their conviction that something was deeply amiss in American life. From the very outset of his administration, Clinton's political opponents and a scandal-hungry media stood ready to pounce. Clinton himself provided the ammunition.

THE IMPEACHMENT OF CLINTON

Charges of sexual misconduct by public officials had a long history. Federalists had accused Thomas Jefferson of having sexual relations with his slave Sally Hemings, a charge apparently confirmed by DNA tests during the 1990s. But in the 1980s and 1990s, scrutiny of politicians' private lives became far more intense than in the past. Gary Hart, as noted in the previous chapter, had been driven from the 1988 campaign because of an extramarital liaison. In 1991, Senate hearings on the nomination to the Supreme Court of Clarence Thomas, a black conservative, became embroiled in sensational charges of sexual harassment leveled against Thomas by law

BALANCE

BUDGET

Herbert Block's 1998 cartoon comments humorously on Clinton's talent for political survival.

professor Anita Hill. To the outrage of feminists, the Senate narrowly confirmed him.

From the day Clinton took office, charges of misconduct bedeviled him. In 1993, an investigation began of an Arkansas real-estate deal known as Whitewater, from which he and his wife had profited. The following year, an Arkansas woman, Paula Jones, filed a civil suit charging that Clinton had sexually harassed her while he served as governor of that state. In 1998, it became known that Clinton had carried on an affair with Monica Lewinsky, a White House intern. Kenneth Starr, the special counsel who had been appointed to investigate Whitewater, shifted his focus to Lewinsky. He issued a lengthy report containing almost pornographic details of Clinton's sexual acts with the young woman and accused the president of lying when he denied the affair in a deposition for the Jones lawsuit. In December 1998, the Republican-controlled House of Representatives voted to impeach Clinton for perjury and obstruction of justice. He became the second president to be tried before the Senate. Early in 1999, the vote took place. Neither charge mustered a simple majority, much less than the two-thirds required to remove Clinton from office.

Karl Marx once wrote that historical events occur twice—first as tragedy, the second time as farce. The impeachment of Andrew Johnson in 1868 had revolved around some of the most momentous questions in American history—the Reconstruction of the South, the rights of the former slaves, relations between the federal government and the states. Clinton's impeachment had to do with what many considered to be a juvenile escapade. Polls suggested that the obsession of Kenneth Starr and members of Congress with Clinton's sexual acts appalled Americans far more than the president's irresponsible behavior. Clinton's continuing popularity throughout the impeachment controversy demonstrated how profoundly traditional attitudes toward sexual morality had changed.

THE DISPUTED ELECTION

Had Clinton been eligible to run for reelection in 2000, he would probably have won. But after the death of FDR, the Constitution had been amended to limit presidents to two terms in office. Democrats nominated Vice President Al Gore to succeed Clinton (pairing him with Senator Joseph Lieberman of Connecticut, the first Jewish vice-presidential nominee). Republicans chose George W. Bush, the governor of Texas and son of Clinton's predecessor, as their candidate, with former secretary of defense Dick Cheney as his running mate.

The election proved to be one of the closest in the nation's history. The outcome remained uncertain until a month after the ballots had been cast. Gore won the popular vote by a tiny margin—540,000 of 100 million cast, or one-half of 1 percent. Victory in the electoral college hinged on which candidate had carried Florida. There, amid widespread confusion at the polls and claims of irregularities in counting the ballots, Bush claimed a margin of a few hundred votes. In the days after the election, Democrats demanded a hand recount of the Florida ballots for which machines could not determine a voter's intent. The Florida Supreme Court ordered the recount to proceed.

Just as Clinton's impeachment recalled the trial of Andrew Johnson, the battle for the presidency in 2000 seemed to repeat the disputed election that ended Reconstruction (a contest in which Florida had also played a crucial role). As in 1877, it fell to Supreme Court justices to decide the outcome. On December 12, 2000, by a 5-4 vote, the Court ordered a halt to the recounting of Florida ballots, allowing the state's governor Jeb Bush (George W. Bush's brother) to certify that the Republican candidate had carried the state and had therefore won the presidency.

The decision in *Bush v. Gore* was one of the oddest in Supreme Court history. In the late 1990s, the Court had reasserted the powers of the states within the federal system, reinforcing their immunity from lawsuits by individuals who claimed to be victims of discrimination and denying the power of Congress to force states to carry out federal policies. Now, however, it overturned a decision of the Florida Supreme Court interpreting the state's election laws. Many observers did not expect the justices to consider the matter at all, since it did not seem to raise a federal constitutional question. They justified their decision by insisting that the "equal protection" clause of the Fourteenth Amendment required that all ballots within a state be counted in accordance with a single standard, something impossible given the wide variety of machines and paper ballots used in Florida. Perhaps recognizing that this new constitutional principle threatened to throw into question results throughout the country—since many states had voting systems as complex as Florida's—the Court added that it applied only in this single case.

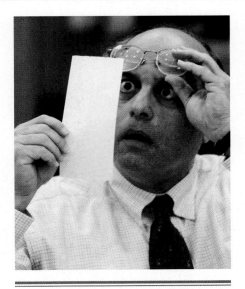

A member of a Florida election board trying to determine a voter's intent during the recount of presidential ballots in November 2000. The U.S. Supreme Court eventually ordered the recount halted.

THE 2000 RESULT

The most remarkable thing about the election of 2000 was not so much its controversial ending as the even division of the country it revealed. Bush and Gore each received essentially half of the popular vote. The final count in the electoral college stood at 271-266, the narrowest margin since 1876. The Senate ended up divided 50-50 between the two parties. But these figures concealed deep political and social fissures. Bush carried the entire South and nearly all the states of the trans-Mississippi farm belt and Rockies. Gore won almost all the states of the Northeast, Old Northwest, and West Coast. Residents of urban areas voted overwhelmingly for Gore. Rural areas went just as solidly for Bush. Members of racial minorities gave Gore large majorities, while white voters preferred Bush. The results also revealed a significant "gender gap." Until the 1960s, women had tended to vote disproportionately Republican. In 2000, women favored Gore by 11 percent, while men preferred Bush by the same margin.

Democrats blamed the Supreme Court, Ralph Nader, and sheer bad luck for Bush's narrow victory. Running as the candidate of the environmentalist Green Party, Nader had won tens of thousands of votes in Florida that otherwise may have gone to Gore. In one county, a faulty ballot

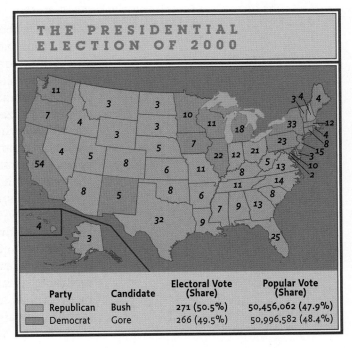

THE PRESIDENTIAL ELECTION OF 2000

Party	Candidate	Electoral Vote (Share)	Popular Vote (Share)
Republican	Bush	271 (50.5%)	50,456,062 (47.9%)
Democrat	Gore	266 (49.5%)	50,996,582 (48.4%)

"IT'S STILL A REPRESENTATIVE FORM OF GOVERNMENT—THEY REPRESENT US"

Another cartoon by Herbert Block, from 2000, suggests that democracy has been corrupted by the influence of "big money interests" on government.

design led several thousand Gore voters accidentally to cast their votes for independent conservative candidate Pat Buchanan. Had their votes been counted for Gore, he would have been elected president. But the largest reason for Gore's loss of Florida was that 600,000 persons—overwhelmingly black and Latino men—had lost the right to vote for their entire lives after being convicted of a felony. (For the nation as a whole, over 5 million persons were denied the right to vote because of criminal records.) For fear of being labeled soft on crime, Democrats had gone along with the policy of lifetime felony disenfranchisement, even though it primarily affected members of racial minorities who would likely have voted Democratic. In this sense, they themselves helped to place Bush in the White House. In 2007, Florida's clemency board voted to allow a large majority of the states's ex-felons, by then estimated at 950,000, to regain the right to vote.

A CHALLENGED DEMOCRACY

Coming at the end of the "decade of democracy," the 2000 election revealed troubling features of the American political system at the close of the twentieth century. The electoral college, devised by the founders to enable the country's prominent men rather than ordinary voters to choose the president, gave the White House to a candidate opposed by a majority of voters, an odd result in a political democracy. A country that prided itself on modern technology had a voting system in which citizens' choices could not be reliably determined. Counting both congressional and presidential races, the campaign cost over $1.5 billion, mostly raised from wealthy individuals and corporate donors. This reinforced the widespread belief that money dominated the political system. It remained for future generations to ponder the implications for democracy of the ever-closer connection between power in the economic marketplace and power in the marketplace of politics and ideas.

Evidence abounded in 2000 of a broad disengagement from public life. As governments at all levels competed to turn their activities over to private contractors, and millions of Americans walled themselves off from their fellow citizens by taking up residence in socially homogeneous gated communities, the very idea of a shared public sphere seemed to dissolve. Organizations like parent-teacher associations, the Boy Scouts, and the Red Cross all suffered declining membership and volunteering. With politicians and political parties still in disrepute and neither candidate able to generate much enthusiasm, voter turnout remained far below that of other democracies. Nearly half the eligible voters did not bother to go to the polls, and in state and local elections, turnouts typically ranged between only 20 and 30 percent. More people watched the televised Nixon-Kennedy debates of 1960 than the Bush-Gore debates of 2000, even though the population had risen by 100 million. Both candidates sought to occupy the political center and relied on public-opinion polls and media consultants to shape their messages. Major issues like health care, race relations, and economic inequality went virtually unmentioned during the campaign.

FREEDOM AND THE NEW CENTURY

The century that ended with the 2000 election witnessed vast human progress and unimaginable human tragedy. It saw the decolonization of Asia and Africa, the emergence of women into full citizenship in most parts of the world, and amazing advances in science, medicine, and technology. Thanks to the spread of new products, available at ever-cheaper prices, it brought more improvement in the daily conditions of life to more human beings than any other century in history. Worldwide life expectancy in the twentieth century rose from forty to sixty-seven years, and the literacy rate increased from 25 percent to 80 percent. This was the first century in which the primary economic activity for most of mankind moved beyond the acquisition of basic food, clothing, and shelter. But the twentieth century also witnessed the death of uncounted millions in wars and genocides and the widespread degradation of the natural environment, the underside of progress.

EXCEPTIONAL AMERICA

In the United States, people lived longer and healthier lives in 2000 compared to previous generations, and they enjoyed a level of material comfort unimagined a century before. In 1900, the average annual income was $3,000 in today's dollars. The typical American had no indoor plumbing, no telephone or car, and had not graduated from high school. As late as 1940, one-third of American households did not have running water. In 2000, health conditions had improved so much that the average life expectancy for men had risen to seventy-four and for women to seventy-nine (from

At the beginning of the twenty-first century, more than 7 million American families lived in gated communities, where the wealthy, and some members of the middle class as well, walled themselves off from the rest of society. This one is in the Brentwood section of Los Angeles.

forty-six and forty-eight in 1900). Over 14 million Americans attended college in 2000, more than three times the figure for 1960.

In 2000, nearly one American in seven was older than sixty-five. Certain to continue rising in the twenty-first century, this figure sparked worries about the future cost of health care and the economic stability of the Social Security system. But it also suggested that people would enjoy far longer and more productive periods of retirement than in the past. On the other hand, poverty, income inequality, and infant mortality in the United States considerably exceeded that of other economically advanced countries, and fewer than 10 percent of workers in private firms belonged to unions, a figure not seen since the nineteenth century.

Many of the changes affecting American life, such as the transformed role of women, the better health and longer lifespan of the population, the spread of suburbanization, and the decline of industrial employment, have taken place in all economically advanced societies. In other ways, however, the United States at the dawn of the twenty-first century differed sharply from other developed countries. Prevailing ideas of freedom in the United States seemed more attuned to individual advancement than to broad social welfare. In 2003, when asked whether it was more important for the government to guarantee freedom from want or freedom to pursue individual goals, only 35 percent of Americans selected freedom from want, as opposed to 58 percent in Germany, 62 percent in France and Great Britain, and 65 percent in Italy. The United States was a far more religious country. Sixty percent of Americans agreed with the statement, "religion plays a very important part in my life," while the comparable figure was 32 percent in Britain, 26 percent in Italy, and only 11 percent in France. One in three Americans said he or she believed in the literal truth of the Bible, and half that the United States enjoys "special protection from God." Religion and nationalism reinforced one another far more powerfully in the United States than in the more secular nations of western Europe.

Other forms of American exceptionalism had a darker side. Among advanced countries, the United States has by far the highest rate of murder using guns. In 1998, the last year for which comparative statistics are available, there were 11,789 murders with guns in the United States, as opposed to 373 in Germany, 151 in Canada, 54 in Great Britain, and 19 in Japan.

VARIETIES OF FREEDOM

In a speech at midnight on January 1, 2000 (strictly speaking, a year before the twenty-first century actually began), President Clinton proclaimed, "the great story of the twentieth century is the triumph of freedom and free people." Freedom remained a crucial point of self-definition for individuals and society at large. When asked in a public-opinion survey what they were proudest of about America, 69 percent of respondents answered, "freedom." Americans were increasingly tolerant of divergent personal lifestyles, cultural backgrounds, and religious persuasions. They enjoyed a degree of freedom of expression unmatched in virtually any country in the world. But their definition of freedom had changed markedly during the course of the twentieth century. Thanks to the rights revolution and the political ascendancy of antigovernment conservatives, the dominant definition of freedom stressed the capacity of individuals to realize their desires and fulfill their potential unrestricted by authority. Other American traditions—freedom as economic security, freedom as active participation in democratic government, freedom as social justice for those long disadvantaged—seemed to be in eclipse. Americans sought freedom within themselves, not through social institutions or public engagement.

It was an irony of late-twentieth-century life that Americans enjoyed more personal freedom than ever before but less of what earlier generations called "industrial freedom." The sustained recovery from the recession of the early 1990s did not entirely relieve a widespread sense of economic insecurity. Globalization—which treated workers at home and abroad as interchangeable factors of production, capable of being uprooted or dismissed without warning—seemed to render individual and even national sovereignty all but meaningless. Since economic liberty has long been associated with economic security, and rights have historically been linked to democratic participation and membership in a nation-state, these processes had ominous implications for traditional understandings of freedom. It remained to be seen whether a conception of freedom grounded in access to the consumer marketplace and the glorification of individual self-fulfillment unrestrained by government, social citizenship, or a common public culture could provide an adequate way of comprehending the world of the twenty-first century.

SUGGESTED READING

Brands, H. W. *The Strange Death of American Liberalism* (2001). Explores how liberals' discrediting of the federal government through their criticisms of the Vietnam War and Watergate paved the way for the triumph of antigovernment conservatism.

Cassidy, John. *Dot.con* (2002). Describes the rise and fall of the "new economy."

Christianson, Scott. *With Liberty for Some: 500 Years of Imprisonment in America* (1998). A full-scale study of the history of imprisonment in the United States and its recent dramatic expansion.

Foner, Nancy. *From Ellis Island to JFK: New York's Two Great Waves of Immigration* (2000). Studies the new immigration of the 1980s and 1990s, and considers how it does and does not differ from earlier waves of newcomers.

Friedman, Thomas L. *The Lexus and the Olive Tree* (1999). An influential account of globalization and its economic promise.

Hodgson, Godfrey. *More Equal Than Others: America from Nixon to the New Century* (2004). A survey of recent American history that identifies growing inequality as a major trend of these years.

Johnson, Haynes. *The Best of Times: America in the Clinton Years* (2001). A sympathetic account of Clinton's presidency.

Judis, John B. *The Paradox of American Democracy* (2000). Discusses how the democratic tradition has been weakened by the growing influence of money and declining voter participation.

Katz, Michael B. *The Price of Citizenship: Redefining the American Welfare State* (2001). Presents the history of welfare policy, with attention to the origins and impact of Clinton's welfare reform.

Levitas, Daniel. *The Terrorist Next Door: The Militia Movement and the Radical Right* (2003). A careful study of right-wing extremism of the 1990s.

Phillips, Kevin. *Wealth and Democracy* (2002). A critique of the influence of money on American politics.

Power, Samantha. *A Problem from Hell: America and the Age of Genocide* (2002). Discusses genocides of the 1990s and the problem of the appropriate American response.

Roberts, Sam. *Who We Are Now: The Changing Face of America in the Twenty-First Century* (2004). A social portrait of the American people, based on the 2000 Census.

Smelser, Neil J., and Jeffrey C. Alexander. *Diversity and Its Discontents: Cultural Conflict and Common Ground in Contemporary American Society* (1999). Describes the new social diversity of the 1990s and the cultural and political tensions arising from it.

Stiglitz, Joseph. *Globalization and Its Discontents* (2002). A leading economist's criticism of some of the consequences of economic globalization.

REVIEW QUESTIONS

1. Assess the significance of globalization in the 1990s?

2. Recent public opinion polls in America have reflected a growing toleration for gays and interracial relationships, but a lessening concern about the responsibility of the federal government to relieve poverty. Analyze why Americans are becoming more tolerant of diversity, yet less concerned with alleviating poverty.

3. What brought about the crisis in communism that led to the eventual break-up of the Soviet Union?

4. What were the major characteristics of Clinton's foreign policy?

5. How was the language of freedom used by various sides in the culture wars?

KEY TERMS

The Gulf War (p. 1054)

The Perot candidacy (p. 1056)

North American Free Trade Agreement (p. 1057)

welfare reform (p. 1058)

The Balkan crisis (p. 1059)

Patterson v. McLean Credit Union (p. 1075)

race and imprisonment (p. 1077)

Defense of Marriage Act of 1996 (p. 1081)

The Clinton impeachment (p. 1083)

REVIEW TABLE

The New Diversity of America

Group	Origins	Population in 2000	Demographics
Latinos	Mexico, Caribbean, Central and South America	35 million	Largest minority group in the United States as of 2001
Asian-Americans	Korea, China, Southeast Asia, Japan	11.9 million	Fastest-growing immigrant group in America
African-Americans	Africa, Caribbean	36.4 million	Majority still live in South and three-fifths of all blacks live in only ten states
Indians	North America	4 million	Growth from natural births as well as a renewed sense of pride identifying oneself as Indian

CHAPTER 28

September 11 and the Next American Century

In this photo taken in February 2006, Iraqi civilians warily pass two American soldiers on patrol.

<table>
<tr><td>

FOCUS QUESTIONS

• What were the major thrusts of the war on terrorism in the wake of September 11, 2001?

• How did the war in Iraq unfold in the wake of 9/11?

• What were the domestic repercussions of the September 11 attacks?

• How did post-9/11 politics change during Bush's second term?

</td></tr>
</table>

No member of the present generation will ever forget when he or she first learned of the events of September 11, 2001. That beautiful late-summer morning began with the sun rising over the East Coast of the United States in a crystal-clear sky. But September 11 soon became one of the most tragic dates in American history.

Around 8 A.M., hijackers seized control of four jet airliners filled with passengers. They crashed two into the World Trade Center in New York City, igniting infernos that soon caused these buildings, which dominated the lower Manhattan skyline, to collapse. A third plane hit a wing of the Pentagon, the country's military headquarters, in Washington, D.C. On the fourth aircraft, passengers who had learned of these events via their cell phones overpowered the hijackers. The plane crashed in a field near Pittsburgh, killing all aboard. Counting the nineteen hijackers, over 200 passengers, pilots, and flight attendants, and victims on the ground, around 3,000 people died on September 11. The victims included nearly 400 police and firefighters who had rushed to the World Trade Center in a rescue effort and perished when the "twin towers" collapsed. Most of the dead were Americans, but citizens of over eighty other countries also lost their lives. Relatives and friends desperately seeking information about the fate of those lost in the attacks printed thousands of "missing" posters. These remained in public places in New York and Washington for weeks, grim reminders of the lives extinguished on September 11.

The attack dealt New York City and the country as a whole a severe blow. Immediate damage and recovery costs ran into the billions of dollars. An estimated 80,000 persons lost their jobs in the New York area. They included employees of financial firms housed in the World Trade Center, as well as waiters, retail sales clerks, and cleaning workers dismissed when business in lower Manhattan ground to a halt and tourism to the city plummeted. The loss of tax revenue plunged the city into a deep fiscal crisis. Major airlines also faced bankruptcy as Americans became afraid to fly.

The Bush administration quickly blamed Al Qaeda, a shadowy terrorist organization headed by Osama bin Laden, for the attacks. A wealthy Islamic fundamentalist from Saudi Arabia, bin Laden had joined the fight against the Soviet occupation of Afghanistan in the 1980s. He had developed a relationship with the Central Intelligence Agency and received American funds to help build his mountain bases. But after the Gulf War of 1991, his anger increasingly

Firemen amid the ruins of the World Trade Center after its collapse as a result of the terrorist attacks of September 11, 2001.

A bystander gazes at some of the missing posters with photographs of those who died on September 11.

turned against the United States. Bin Laden was especially outraged by the presence of American military bases in Saudi Arabia and by American support for Israel in its ongoing conflict with the Palestinians. More generally, bin Laden and his followers saw the United States, with its religious pluralism, consumer culture, and open sexual mores, as the antithesis of the rigid values in which they believed. He feared that American influence was corrupting Saudi Arabia, Islam's spiritual home, and helping to keep the Saudi royal family, which failed to oppose this development, in power. But if Al Qaeda believed in traditional Islamic values, it also acted much like a modern transnational organization, taking full advantage of globalization. The terrorists moved freely across national borders, financed themselves through international capital flows, and communicated via e-mail and the Internet.

Terrorism—the targeting of civilian populations by violent organizations who hope to spread fear for a political purpose—has a long history, including in the United States. During the Reconstruction era after the Civil War, the Ku Klux Klan and similar groups launched a reign of terror that led to the deaths of thousands of American citizens, most of them newly emancipated slaves. Between the assassination of President William McKinley in 1901 and the Wall Street bombing of 1920, anarchists committed numerous acts of violence. Antigovernment extremist Timothy McVeigh killed 168 persons when he exploded a bomb at a federal office building in Oklahoma City in 1995.

In the last three decades of the twentieth century, terrorist groups who held the United States and other Western countries responsible for the plight of the Palestinians had engaged in hijackings and murders. In October 1985, a group of Palestinians seized control of the *Achille Lauro*, an Italian cruise ship, and killed an American Jewish passenger. In 1988, a bomb planted by operatives based in Libya destroyed a Pan American

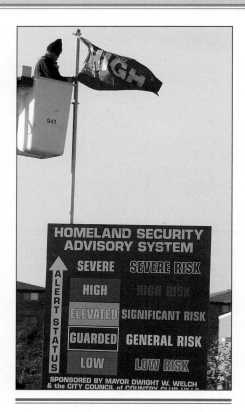

In the years following September 11, 2001, fear remained a prominent feature of American life. The federal government adopted a color-coded system to indicate the likelihood of further terrorist attacks, raising or lowering the danger level in accordance with intelligence reports, rumors, and, critics charged, political advantage. Here, in December 2003, a government employee in Country Club Hills, Illinois, changes the alert level from "elevated" to "high" in response to an announcement from the Department of Homeland Security in Washington.

flight over Scotland, killing all 259 persons on board. After the Gulf War, Osama bin Laden declared "war" on the United States. Terrorists associated with Al Qaeda exploded a truck-bomb at the World Trade Center in 1993, killing six persons, and set off blasts in 1998 at American embassies in Kenya and Tanzania, in which over 200 persons, mostly African embassy workers, died. Thus, a rising terrorist threat was visible before September 11. Nonetheless, the attack came as a complete surprise. With the end of the Cold War in 1991, most Americans felt more secure, especially within their own borders, than they had for decades.

September 11 enveloped the country in a cloud of fear. The sense of being under assault was heightened in the following weeks, when unknown persons sent letters to prominent politicians and television journalists, containing spores that cause the deadly disease anthrax. Five individuals—postal workers and others who handled the letters—died. In the months that followed, as the government periodically issued "alerts" concerning possible new attacks, national security remained at the forefront of Americans' consciousness, and fear of terrorism powerfully affected their daily lives.

In the immediate aftermath of September 11, the Bush administration announced a "war on terrorism." Over the next two years, the United States embarked on wars in Afghanistan and Iraq, the second with very limited international support. It created a new Department of Homeland Security to coordinate efforts to improve security at home, and it imposed severe limits on the civil liberties of those suspected of a connection with terrorism and, more generally, on immigrants from the Middle East.

The attacks of September 11, 2001, gave new prominence to ideas deeply embedded in the American past—that freedom was the central quality of American life, and that the United States had a mission to spread freedom throughout the world and to fight those it saw as freedom's enemies. The attacks and events that followed also lent new urgency to questions that had recurred many times in American history: Should the United States act in the world as a republic or an empire? What is the proper balance between liberty and security? Who deserves the full enjoyment of American freedom? None had an easy answer.

THE WAR ON TERRORISM

BUSH BEFORE SEPTEMBER 11

Before becoming president, George W. Bush had been an executive in the oil industry and had served as governor of Texas. He had worked to dissociate the Republican Party from the harsh anti-immigrant rhetoric of the mid-1990s and had proven himself an effective proponent of what he called "compassionate conservatism." Because of his narrow margin of victory in the election of 2000, he came into office without a broad popular mandate. He had received fewer votes than his opponent, Al Gore, and his party commanded only tiny majorities in the House of Representatives and Senate. Nonetheless, from the outset Bush pursued a strongly conservative agenda. In 2001, he persuaded Congress to enact the largest tax cut in American history. With the economy slowing, he promoted the plan as a way of stimulating renewed growth. In keeping with the "supply-side" economic outlook embraced twenty years earlier by Ronald Reagan, most of the tax cuts were directed toward the wealthiest Americans, on the assumption that they would invest the money they saved in taxes in economically productive activities.

Bush also proposed changes in environmental policies, including opening Alaska's Arctic National Wildlife Refuge to drilling for oil and allowing timber companies to operate in national forests, claiming that this would reduce forest fires. But soon after the passage of the tax bill, Senator Jim Jeffords of Vermont, a moderate Republican, abandoned the party and declared himself an independent. His action gave Democrats a one-vote margin in the Senate and made it difficult for Bush to achieve further legislative victories.

BUSH AND THE WORLD

In foreign policy, Bush emphasized American freedom of action, unrestrained by international treaties and institutions. During the 2000 campaign, he had criticized the Clinton administration's penchant for "nation-building"—American assistance in creating stable governments in chaotic parts of the world. Once in office, Bush announced plans to push ahead with a national missile defense system (another inheritance from the Reagan era) even though this required American withdrawal from the Anti–Ballistic Missile Treaty of 1972, which barred the deployment of such systems. He repudiated a treaty establishing an International Criminal Court to try violators of human rights, fearing that it would assert its jurisdiction over Americans. Critics charged that Bush was resuming the tradition of American isolationism, which had been abandoned after World War II.

To great controversy, the Bush administration announced that it would not abide by the Kyoto Protocol of 1997, which sought to combat global warming—a slow rise in the earth's temperature that scientists warned could have disastrous effects on the world's climate. Global warming is caused when gases released by burning fossil fuels such as coal and oil remain in the upper atmosphere, trapping heat reflected from the earth. Evidence of this development first surfaced in the 1990s, when scientists studying layers of ice in Greenland concluded that the earth's temperature had risen significantly during the past century. Further investigations revealed that areas of the Antarctic once under ice had become covered by grass, and that glaciers across the globe are retreating.

Today, most scientists consider global warming a serious situation. Climate change threatens to disrupt long-established patterns of agriculture, and the melting of glaciers and the polar ice caps because of rising temperatures may raise ocean levels and flood coastal cities.

By the time Bush took office, some 180 nations, including the United States, had agreed to accept the goals set in the Kyoto Protocol for reducing the output of gases from fossil fuels. Since the United States burns far more fossil fuels than any other nation, Bush's repudiation of the treaty, on the grounds that it would weaken the American economy, infuriated much of the world, as well as environmentalists at home.

"THEY HATE FREEDOM"

September 11 transformed the international situation, the domestic political environment, and the Bush presidency. An outpouring of popular patriotism followed the attacks, all the more impressive because it was spontaneous, not orchestrated by the government or private organizations. Throughout the country, people demonstrated their sense of resolve and their sympathy for the victims by displaying the American flag. Public trust in government rose dramatically, and public servants like firemen and policemen became national heroes. After two decades in which the dominant language of American politics centered on deregulation and individualism, the country experienced a renewed feeling of common social purposes. Americans of all backgrounds shared the sense of having lived through a traumatic experience.

The Bush administration benefited from this patriotism and identification with government. The president's popularity soared. As in other crises, Americans looked to the federal government, and especially the president, for reassurance, leadership, and decisive action. Bush seized the opportunity to give his administration a new direction and purpose. Like presidents before him, he made freedom the rallying cry for a nation at war.

On September 20, 2001, Bush addressed a joint session of Congress and a national television audience. His speech echoed the words of FDR, Truman, and Reagan: "Freedom and fear are at war. The advance of human freedom . . .

This photograph of three emergency-response workers at the World Trade Center site suggests that the composition of the construction industry labor force had become more diverse as a result of the civil rights movement.

A homemade float in a July 4, 2002, parade in Amherst, Massachusetts, illustrates how the "twin towers" had become a symbol of American patriotism.

now depends on us." The country's antagonists, Bush went on, "hate our freedoms, our freedom of religion, our freedom of speech, our freedom to assemble and disagree with each other." In later speeches, he repeated this theme. Why did terrorists attack the United States, the president repeatedly asked. His answer: "Because we love freedom, that's why. And they hate freedom."

THE BUSH DOCTRINE

Bush's speech announced a new foreign policy principle, which quickly became known as the Bush Doctrine. The United States would launch a war on terrorism. Unlike previous wars, this one had a vaguely defined enemy—terrorist groups around the world that might threaten the United States or its allies—and no predictable timetable for victory. The American administration would make no distinction between terrorists and the governments that harbored them, and it would recognize no middle ground in the new war: "Either you are with us, or you are with the terrorists." Bush demanded that Afghanistan, ruled by a group of Islamic fundamentalists called the Taliban, surrender Osama bin Laden, who had established a base in the country. When the Taliban refused, the United States on October 7, 2001, launched air strikes against its strongholds.

Bush gave the war in Afghanistan the name "Enduring Freedom." By the end of the year, the combination of American bombing and ground combat by the Northern Alliance (Afghans who had been fighting the Taliban for years) had driven the regime from power. A new government, friendly to and dependent on the United States, took its place. It repealed Taliban laws denying women the right to attend school and banning movies, music, and other expressions of Western culture but found it difficult to establish full control over the country. Fewer than 100 Americans died in the war, while Afghan military and civilian casualties numbered in the thousands. But bin Laden had not been found, and many Taliban supporters continued to pose a threat to the new government's stability. Indeed, by early 2007, the

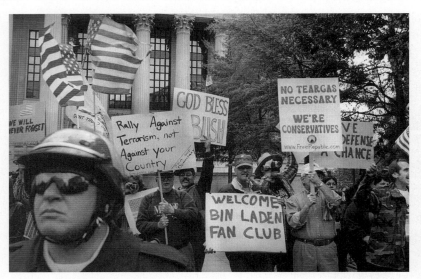

Supporters of the Bush administration who turned out in Washington, D.C., late in 2001, to confront demonstrators opposed to the war in Afghanistan.

Taliban had reasserted their power in some parts of Afghanistan, and no end was in sight to the deployment of American troops there.

THE "AXIS OF EVIL"

Like the surprise attack on Pearl Harbor in 1941, September 11 not only plunged the United States into war but also transformed American foreign policy, inspiring a determination to reshape the world in terms of American ideals and interests. Remarkable changes quickly followed the assault on Afghanistan. To facilitate further military action in the Middle East, the United States established military bases in Central Asia, including former republics of the Soviet Union like Kyrgyzstan, Uzbekistan, and Tajikistan. Such an action would have been inconceivable before the end of the Cold War. The administration sent troops to the Philippines to assist that government in combating an Islamic insurgency, and it announced plans to establish a greater military presence in Africa. It solidified its ties with the governments of Pakistan and Indonesia, which confronted opposition from Islamic fundamentalists.

The toppling of the Taliban, Bush repeatedly insisted, marked only the beginning of the war on terrorism. In his State of the Union address of January 2002, the president accused Iraq, Iran, and North Korea of harboring terrorists and developing "weapons of mass destruction"—nuclear, chemical, and biological—that posed a potential threat to the United States. He called the three countries an "axis of evil," even though no evidence connected them with the attacks of September 11 and they had never cooperated with one another (Iraq and Iran, in fact, had fought a long and bloody war in the 1980s).

THE NATIONAL SECURITY STRATEGY

In September 2002, one year after the September 11 attacks, the Bush administration released a document called the National Security Strategy. Like NSC-68 of 1950 (discussed in Chapter 23), the National Security Strategy outlined a fundamental shift in American foreign policy. And like NSC-68, it began with a discussion not of weaponry or military strategy, but of freedom.

The document defined freedom as consisting of political democracy, freedom of expression, religious toleration, free trade, and free markets. These, it proclaimed, were universal ideals, "right and true for every person, in every society." It went on to promise that the United States would "extend the benefits of freedom" by fighting not only "terrorists" but also "tyrants" around the world. Since nothing less than freedom was at stake, the document insisted that the United States must maintain an overwhelming preponderance of military power, not allowing any other country to challenge either its overall strength or its dominance in any region of the world. And to replace the Cold War doctrine of deterrence, which assumed that the certainty of retaliation would prevent attacks on the United States and its allies, the National Security Strategy announced a new foreign policy principle—"preemptive" war. If the United States believed that a nation posed a possible future threat to its security, it had the right to attack before such a threat materialized.

AN AMERICAN EMPIRE?

The "axis of evil" speech and National Security Strategy sent shock waves around the world. In the immediate aftermath of September 11, a wave of sympathy for the United States had swept across the globe. Most of the world supported the war in Afghanistan as a legitimate response to the terrorist attacks. By late 2002, however, many persons overseas feared that the United States was claiming the right to act as a world policeman in violation of international law.

Relations between the United States and Europe, warned Ivo Daalder, a Dutch-born former official of the Clinton administration, were on a "collision course," because Washington had become "dismissive of the perspectives of others." Critics, including leaders of close American allies, wondered whether dividing the world into friends and enemies of freedom ran the danger of repeating some of the mistakes of the Cold War. Anti-Americanism in the Middle East, they argued, reached far beyond bin Laden's organization and stemmed not simply from dislike of American freedom but, rightly or wrongly, from opposition to specific American policies—toward Israel, the Palestinians, and the region's corrupt and undemocratic regimes. And like the battle against communism, the war on terrorism seemed to be leading the United States to forge closer and closer ties with repressive governments like Pakistan and the republics of Central Asia that consistently violated human rights.

Charges quickly arose that the United States was bent on establishing itself as a new global empire. Indeed, September 11 and its aftermath highlighted not only the vulnerability of the United States but also its overwhelming strength. In every index of power—military, economic, cultural—the United States far outpaced the rest of the world. It accounted for just under one-third of global economic output and more than one-third of global military spending. Its defense budget exceeded that of the next twenty powers combined. The United States maintained military bases throughout the world and deployed its navy on every ocean. It was not surprising that in such circumstances many American policymakers felt that the country had a responsibility to impose order in a dangerous world, even if this meant establishing its own rules of international conduct.

In public discussion in the United States after September 11, the word "empire," once a term of abuse, came back into widespread use. The need to "shoulder the burdens of empire" emerged as a common theme in discussions among foreign policy analysts and political commentators who embraced the new foreign policy. As we have seen, the idea of the United States as an empire has a long history, dating back to Jefferson's "empire of liberty" (see Chapter 7) and McKinley's "benevolent imperialism" (see Chapter 17). But talk of a new American empire alarmed people at home

VOICES OF FREEDOM

FROM

The National Security Strategy of the United States (September 2002)

The National Security Strategy, issued in 2002 by the Bush administration, outlined a new foreign and military policy for the United States in response to the terrorist attacks of September 11, 2001. It announced the doctrine of preemptive war—that the United States retained the right to use its military power against countries that might pose a threat in the future. But the document began with a statement of the administration's definition of freedom and its commitment to spreading freedom to the entire world.

The great struggles of the twentieth century between liberty and totalitarianism ended with a decisive victory for the forces of freedom—and a single sustainable model for national success: freedom, democracy, and free enterprise. . . . These values of freedom are right and true for every person, in every society. . . .

Today, the international community has the best chance since the rise of the nation-state in the seventeenth century to build a world where great powers compete in peace instead of continually prepare for war. . . . The United States will use this moment of opportunity to extend the benefits of freedom across the globe. We will actively work to bring the hope of democracy, development, free markets, and free trade to every corner of the world. . . .

In building a balance of power that favors freedom, the United States is guided by the conviction that all nations have important responsibilities. Nations that enjoy freedom must actively fight terror. Nations that depend on international stability must help prevent the spread of weapons of mass destruction. . . . Throughout history, freedom has been threatened by war and terror; it has been challenged by the clashing wills of powerful states and the evil designs of tyrants; and it has been tested by widespread poverty and disease. Today, humanity holds in its hands the opportunity to further freedom's triumph over all these foes. The United States welcomes our opportunity to lead in this great mission.

FROM Speech of Senator Robert Byrd of West Virginia in the Senate (February 2003)

As the United States moved toward war with Iraq, few voices in Congress were raised in opposition. One senator who did criticize the administration's policies was Robert Byrd. His warnings about the lack of postwar planning and the possible consequences of an invasion proved remarkably prescient.

To contemplate war is to think about the most horrible of human experiences. On this February day, as this nation stands at the brink of battle, every American on some level must be contemplating the horrors of war.

Yet, this Chamber [the Senate] is, for the most part, silent. . . . There is no debate, no discussion, no attempt to lay out for the nation the pros and cons of this particular war. . . . Yet . . . this coming battle, if it materializes, represents a turning point in U.S. foreign policy and possibly a turning point in the recent history of the world.

This nation is about to embark upon the first test of a revolutionary doctrine applied in an extraordinary way at an unfortunate time. The doctrine of preemption—the idea that the United States or any other nation can legitimately attack a nation that is not imminently threatening but may be threatening in the future—is a radical new twist on the traditional idea of self defense. It appears to be in contravention of international law and the UN Charter. And it is being tested at a time of world-wide terrorism, making many countries around the globe wonder if they will soon be on our—or some other nation's—hit list. . . . There are huge cracks emerging in our time-honored alliances, and U.S. intentions are suddenly subject to damaging worldwide speculation. . . . Here at home, people are warned of imminent terrorist attacks with little guidance as to when or where such attacks might occur. Family members are being called to active duty, with no idea of the duration of the stay or what horrors they may face. . . . The mood of the nation is grim. . . .

We may have massive military might, but we cannot fight a global war on terrorism alone. . . . This administration has not finished the first war against terrorism and yet it is eager to embark on another conflict with perils much greater than those in Afghanistan. Is our attention span that short? Have we not learned that after winning the war one must always secure the peace? And yet we hear little about the aftermath of war in Iraq. . . . To whom do we propose to hand the reins of power after Saddam Hussein? . . . Has our senselessly bellicose language and our callous disregard of the interests and opinions of other nations increased the global race to join the nuclear club? . . . This war is not necessary at this time.

QUESTIONS

1. How does the National Security Strategy define the global mission of the United States?

2. What are Senator Byrd's main arguments against going to war with Iraq?

3. In what ways is Byrd's speech a repudiation of the assumptions of the National Security Strategy?

A cartoon from the French newspaper Le Monde *illustrates worldwide skepticism about American claims to be promoting liberty in Iraq.*

and abroad who did not desire to have the United States reconstruct the world in its own image.

CONFRONTING IRAQ

These tensions became starkly evident in the Bush administration's next initiative. The Iraqi dictatorship of Saddam Hussein had survived its defeat in the Gulf War of 1991. Hussein's opponents charged that he had flouted United Nations resolutions barring the regime from developing new weapons. During the Clinton administration, the United States had occasionally bombed Iraqi military sites in retaliation for Hussein's lack of cooperation with UN weapons inspectors.

From the outset of the Bush administration, a group of conservative policymakers including Vice President Dick Cheney, Secretary of Defense Donald Rumsfeld, and Deputy Defense Secretary Paul D. Wolfowitz were determined to oust Hussein from power. They developed a military strategy to accomplish this—massive initial air strikes followed by invasion by a relatively small number of troops. They insisted that the oppressed Iraqi people would welcome an American army as liberators and quickly establish a democratic government, allowing for the early departure of American soldiers. This group seized on the opportunity presented by the attacks of September 11 to press their case, and President Bush adopted their outlook. Secretary of State Colin Powell, who believed the conquest and stabilization of Iraq would require hundreds of thousands of American soldiers and should not be undertaken without the support of America's allies, found himself marginalized in the administration.

Even though Hussein was not an Islamic fundamentalist, and no known evidence linked him to the terrorist attacks of September 11, the Bush administration in 2002 announced a goal of "regime change" in Iraq. Hussein, administration spokesmen insisted, must be ousted from power because he had developed an arsenal of chemical and bacterial "weapons of mass destruction" and was seeking to acquire nuclear arms. American newspaper and television journalists repeated these claims with almost no independent investigation. The UN Security Council agreed to step up weapons inspections, but the Bush administration soon declared that inspectors could never uncover Hussein's military capabilities. Early in 2003, despite his original misgivings, Secretary of State Powell delivered a speech before the UN outlining the administration's case. He claimed that Hussein possessed a mobile chemical weapons laboratory, had hidden weapons of mass destruction in his many palaces, and was seeking to acquire uranium in Africa to build nuclear weapons. (Every one of these assertions later turned out to be false.) Shortly after Powell's address, the president announced his intention to go to war with or without the approval of the United Nations. Congress passed a resolution authorizing the president to use force if he deemed it necessary.

THE IRAQ WAR

The decision to go to war split the Western alliance and inspired a massive antiwar movement throughout the world. In February 2003, between

10 million and 15 million people across the globe demonstrated against the impending war. There were large-scale protests in the United States, which brought together veterans of the antiwar movement during the Vietnam era and a diverse group of young activists united in the belief that launching a war against a nation because it might pose a security threat in the future violated international law and the UN Charter.

Foreign policy "realists," including members of previous Republican administrations like Brent Scowcroft, the national security adviser under the first President Bush, warned that the administration's preoccupation with Iraq deflected attention from its real foe, Al Qaeda, which remained capable of launching terrorist attacks. They insisted that the United States could not unilaterally transform the Middle East into a bastion of democracy, as the administration claimed was its long-term aim.

Both traditional foes of the United States like Russia and China, and traditional allies like Germany and France, refused to support a "preemptive" strike against Iraq. Many Americans resented international criticism. Some restaurants stopped selling French wines, and the Senate dining room renamed french fries as "freedom fries," recalling the rechristening of items with German names during World War I.

Unable to obtain approval from the United Nations for attacking Iraq, the United States went to war anyway in March 2003, with Great Britain as its sole significant ally. President Bush called the war "Operation Iraqi Freedom." Its purpose, he declared, was to "defend our freedom" and "bring freedom to others." The Hussein regime proved no match for the American armed forces, with their precision bombing, satellite-guided missiles, and well-trained soldiers. Within a month, American troops occupied Baghdad. After hiding out for several months, Hussein was captured by American forces and subsequently put on trial before an Iraqi court. Late in 2006, he was found guilty of ordering the killing of many Iraqis during his reign, was sentenced to death and executed.

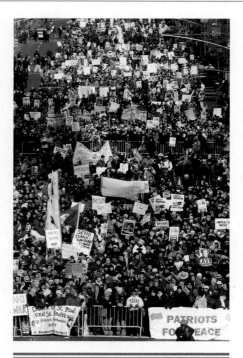

Part of the massive crowd that gathered in New York City on February 15, 2003, a day of worldwide demonstrations against the impending war against Iraq.

ANOTHER VIETNAM?

Soon after the fall of Baghdad, a triumphant President Bush appeared in an air force flight suit on the deck of an aircraft carrier beneath a banner reading "Mission Accomplished." But after the fall of Hussein, everything seemed to go wrong. Rather than parades welcoming American liberators, looting and chaos followed the fall of the Iraqi regime. With too few American troops to establish order, mobs promptly sacked libraries, museums, government offices, and businesses, and seized caches of weapons. An insurgency quickly developed that targeted American soldiers and Iraqis cooperating with them. Sectarian violence soon swept throughout Iraq, with militias of Shiite and Sunni Muslims fighting each other. (Under Hussein, Sunnis, a minority of Iraq's population, had dominated the government and army; now, the Shiite majority sought to exercise power and exact revenge.) Despite holding a number of elections in Iraq, the United States found it impossible to create an Iraqi government strong enough to impose order on the country. By 2006, American intelligence agencies concluded, Iraq had become what it had not been before—a haven for terrorists bent on attacking Americans.

U.S. PRESENCE IN THE MIDDLE EAST, 1947-2006

EGYPT
-Suez crisis, 1956
-Kissinger's shuttle diplomacy, 1974-1975
-Camp David accords, 1978

-Recognition, 1948
-Camp David accords, 1978
-Wye Memorandum, concerning peace with the Palestinians, 1998

IRAQ
-Gulf War, 1990
-Iraq War, 2003

IRAN
-American embassy occupied, 1979-1981

AFGHANISTAN
-War against Taliban and Terrorists, 2001

Oil fields
Air bases
Naval bases

Since World War II, the United States has become more and more deeply involved in the affairs of the Middle East, whose countries are together the world's largest exporter of oil.

Fewer than 200 American soldiers died in the initial phase of the Iraq War. But by the end of 2006, Iraq stood at the brink of civil war. American deaths had reached nearly 3,000, with 20,000 or more wounded. According to the estimates of U.S. and Iraqi scientists, hundreds of thousands of Iraqis, most of them civilians, had also died, and tens of thousands more had fled to neighboring countries seeking safety. Initially, the Bush administration had estimated that the war would cost $60 billion, to be paid for largely by Iraq's own oil revenues. By early 2006, expenditures had reached $200 billion and were climbing fast, and the insurgency prevented Iraq from resuming significant oil production. Some economists estimated that the Iraq War would end up costing the United States nearly $2 trillion, an almost unimaginable sum.

With no end in sight to the conflict, comparisons with the American experience in Vietnam became commonplace. Iraq and Vietnam, of course, have very different histories, cultures, and geographies. But in both wars, American policy was made by officials who had little or no knowledge of the countries to which they were sending troops and distrusted State Department experts on these regions, who tended be skeptical about the possibility of achieving quick military and long-term political success. The war's architects preferred to get their knowledge of Iraq from Saddam Hussein's exiled opponents, who exaggerated their own popularity and the degree of popular support for an American invasion. Administration officials gave little thought to postwar planning.

THE WORLD AND THE WAR

The war marked a new departure in American foreign policy. The United States had frequently intervened unilaterally in the affairs of Latin American countries. But outside the Western Hemisphere it had previously been reluctant to use force except as part of an international coalition. And while the United States had exerted enormous influence in the Middle East since World War II, never before had it occupied a nation in the center of the world's most volatile region.

Rarely in its history had the United States found itself so isolated from world public opinion. Initially, the war in Iraq proved to be popular in the United States. After all, unlike earlier wars, this one brought no calls for public sacrifice from the administration. There were no tax increases, and no reintroduction of the draft to augment the hard-pressed all-volunteer army. Many Americans believed the administration's claims that Saddam Hussein had something to do with September 11 and had stockpiled weapons of mass destruction. The realization that in fact Hussein had no such weapons discredited the administration's rationale for the war. Subsequent investigations revealed that intelligence reports at variance with administration claims had been sidetracked or ignored. With the weapons argument discredited, the Bush administration increasingly defended the war as an effort to bring freedom to the people of Iraq. This argument resonated with deeply rooted American values. But by early 2007, polls showed that a large majority of Americans considered the invasion of Iraq a mistake, and the war a lost cause.

Much of the outside world now viewed the United States as a superpower unwilling to abide by the rules of international law. They believed that a nation whose Declaration of Independence had proclaimed its signers' "decent respect to the opinions of mankind" had become indifferent or

ISRAEL, THE WEST BANK, AND GAZA STRIP

1967 Cease-Fire line

Mediterranean Sea

Jordan River

Nablus

West Bank

1949 Armistice line

Ramallah

Jerusalem

ISRAEL

Bethlehem

Gaza Strip

Hebron

Dead Sea

1950 Armistice line

▨ Territory under full Palestinian Authority control

▢ Palestinian Authority responsible for social and civil services only

▢ Gaza Strip and West Bank territory under full Israeli control

▨ Jewish settlements

▨ Israeli military bases

Soldiers with the 321st Psychological Operations Company cover Anti-American graffiti with posters in Falluja, Iraq, 2003. The posters display coalition efforts for Iraqi improvement and are intended not only to cover the Anti-American sentiments, but to help dispel them altogether.

hostile to the views of others. As early as 2003, a survey of global opinion had found that even in western Europe, large numbers of people viewed the United States as a threat to world peace. The fact that Iraq possessed the world's second-largest reserves of oil reinforced suspicions that American motives had less to do with freedom than self-interest.

The Iraq War severely strained the United Nations and the Western alliance created in the aftermath of World War II. But whatever the outcome, for the third time in less than a century, the United States had embarked on a crusade to create a new world order.

THE AFTERMATH OF SEPTEMBER 11 AT HOME

SECURITY AND LIBERTY

Like earlier wars, the war on terrorism raised anew the problem of balancing security and liberty. In the immediate aftermath of the attacks, Congress rushed to passage the USA Patriot Act, a mammoth bill (it ran to over 300 pages) that few members of the House or Senate had actually read. It conferred unprecedented powers on law-enforcement agencies charged with preventing the new, vaguely defined crime of "domestic terrorism," including the power to wiretap, spy on citizens, open letters, read e-mail, and obtain personal records from third parties like universities and libraries without the knowledge of a suspect. Unlike during World Wars I and II, with their campaigns of hatred against German-Americans and Japanese-Americans, the Bush administration made a point of discouraging anti-Arab and anti-Muslim sentiment. Nonetheless, at least 5,000 foreigners with Middle Eastern connections were rounded up, and more than 1,200 arrested. Many with no link to terrorism were held for months, without either a formal charge or a public notice of their fate. The administration also set up a detention camp at the U.S. naval base at Guantànamo Bay, Cuba, for persons captured in Afghanistan or otherwise accused of terrorism. Over 700 persons, the nationals of many foreign countries, were detained there.

In November 2001, the Bush administration issued an executive order authorizing the holding of secret military tribunals for noncitizens deemed to have assisted terrorism. In such trials, traditional constitutional protections, such as the right of the accused to choose a lawyer and see all the evidence, would not apply. A few months later, the Justice Department declared that American citizens could be held indefinitely without charge and not allowed to see a lawyer, if the government declared them to be "enemy combatants." The president's press secretary, Ari Fleischer, warned Americans to "watch what they say," and Attorney General John Ashcroft declared that criticism of administration policies aided the country's terrorist enemies.

THE POWER OF THE PRESIDENT

In the new atmosphere of heightened security, numerous court orders and regulations of the 1970s, inspired by abuses of the CIA, FBI, and local police forces, were rescinded, allowing these agencies to resume surveillance of Americans without evidence that a crime had been committed. Some of these measures were authorized by Congress, but the president implemented many of them unilaterally, claiming the authority to ignore laws that restricted his power as commander-in-chief in wartime. Thus, soon after September 11, President Bush authorized the National Security Agency (NSA) to eavesdrop on Americans' telephone conversations without a court warrant, a clear violation of a law limiting the NSA to foreign intelligence gathering.

"War," Randolph Bourne had written during World War I, "is the health of the state." Especially, one might add, of the presidency. Previous presidents had initiated "wars of choice" like Iraq—for example, the Mexican and Spanish-American Wars—and leaders from Abraham Lincoln to Richard Nixon had claimed the right to act as commander-in-chief in ways that violated specific legal prohibitions. But no other president had ever made so sweeping an assertion of the power to violate both long-standing constitutional principles, such as the right to trial by jury, and any law he chooses during wartime.

The majority of Americans seemed willing to accept the administration's contention that restraints on time-honored liberties were necessary to fight terrorism, especially since these restraints applied primarily to Muslims and immigrants from the Middle East. Others recalled previous times when wars produced limitations on civil liberties and public officials equated political dissent with lack of patriotism: the Alien and Sedition Acts during the "quasi-war" with France in 1798, the suspension of the writ of habeas corpus during the Civil War, the severe repression of free speech and persecution of German-Americans during World War I, Japanese-American internment in World War II, and McCarthyism during the Cold War. These episodes underscored the fragility of principles most Americans have learned to take for granted—civil liberties and the ideal of equality before the law, regardless of race and ethnicity. The debate over liberty and security seemed certain to last as long as the war on terrorism itself.

THE TORTURE CONTROVERSY

Officials of the Bush administration also insisted in the aftermath of September 11 that the United States need not be bound by international law in pursuing the war on terrorism. They were especially eager to sidestep the Geneva Conventions and the International Convention Against Torture, which regulate the treatment of prisoners of war and prohibit torture and other forms of physical and mental coercion. In January 2002, the Justice Department produced a memorandum stating that these rules did not apply to captured members of Al Qaeda as they were "unlawful combatants," not members of regularly constituted armies. White House counsel Alberto Gonzales, who later became attorney general, advised the president that the Geneva accords were "quaint" and "obsolete" in this "new

Based on an infamous photograph, circulated around the world, of an Iraqi prisoner abused while in American custody, this 2004 cartoon suggests how such mistreatment damaged the image of the United States.

kind of war." In February 2003, President Bush issued a directive that denied Al Qaeda and Taliban prisoners the Geneva protections.

Amid strong protests from Secretary of State Powell and senior military officers who feared that the new policy would encourage the retaliatory mistreatment of American prisoners of war, in April 2003 the president prohibited the use of torture except where special permission had been granted. Nonetheless, the Defense Department approved methods of interrogation that most observers considered torture. In addition, the CIA set up a series of jails in foreign countries outside the traditional chain of military command and took part in the "rendition" of suspects—that is, kidnapping them and spiriting them to prisons in Egypt, Yemen, Syria, and former communist states of eastern Europe, where torture is practiced.

In this atmosphere and lacking clear rules of behavior, some military personnel—in Afghanistan, at Abu Ghraib prison in Iraq, and at Guantànamo—beat prisoners who were being held for interrogation, subjected them to electric shocks, let them be attacked by dogs, and forced them to strip naked and lie atop other prisoners. Some prisoners in U.S. custody died from their maltreatment. As it turned out, the military guards and interrogators who committed these acts had not been adequately trained for their missions. Indeed, some took photographs of the maltreatment of prisoners and circulated them by e-mail. Inevitably, the photos became public. Their exposure around the world in newspapers, on television, and on the Internet undermined the reputation of the United States as a country that adheres to standards of civilized behavior and the rule of law.

The military investigated prisoner abuse but punished only a few low-level soldiers, not the commanders who were supposed to be in charge of these prisons and had tolerated or failed to halt the abuse. After much debate, Congress in 2005 inserted in the Defense Appropriations Act a measure sponsored by Senator John McCain of Arizona (a former prisoner of war in Vietnam) banning the use of torture. President Bush signed the bill but issued a "signing statement" reaffirming his right as commander-in-chief to set rules for the military by himself.

THE ECONOMY UNDER BUSH

In the congressional elections of 2002, Bush took full advantage of his post–September 11 popularity, campaigning actively for Republican candidates. His intervention was credited with helping his party increase its small majorities in the House and Senate, in defiance of the traditional pattern in which the president's party loses seats in midterm elections. Continuing chaos in Iraq began to undermine support for Bush's foreign policy.

But the main threat to the president's reelection appeared to be the condition of the American economy. During 2001, the economy slipped into a recession—that is, it contracted rather than grew. Growth resumed at the end of the year, but, with businesses reluctant to make new investments after the overexpansion of the 1990s, it failed to generate new jobs.

THE "JOBLESS" RECOVERY

Talk of "economic pain" reappeared in public discussions. The sectors that had expanded the most in the previous decade contracted rapidly. The computer industry slashed over 40 percent of its jobs during the first two years of the Bush presidency. Thanks to the Internet, jobs as computer programmers and other highly skilled technology positions could be shifted to India, which had a large number of well-educated persons willing to work for far less than their American counterparts. Employment in the media, advertising, and telecommunications industries also fell.

The difficulties of these sectors received much publicity. But in fact, 90 percent of the jobs lost during the recession of 2001–2002 were in manufacturing. Despite the renewed spirit of patriotism, deindustrialization continued. Textile firms closed southern plants and shifted production to cheap-labor factories in China and India. Maytag, a manufacturer of washing machines, refrigerators, and other home appliances, announced plans to close its factory in Galesburg, Illinois, where wages averaged fifteen dollars per hour, to open a new one in Mexico, where workers earned less than one-seventh that amount.

Even after economic recovery began, the problems of traditional industries continued. Employment in steel—520,000 in 1970—had dropped to 120,000 by 2004. Late in 2005, facing declining profits and sales, General Motors, which once had 600,000 employees, announced plans to reduce its American workforce to 86,000. Major companies also moved to eliminate the remnants of the post–World War II "social contract," in which industries provided manufacturing workers with both high-paying jobs and the promise that they would be provided for in old age. Many eliminated or sharply reduced pensions and health benefits for retired workers. Between 1988 and 2004, the number of private businesses with pension plans fell by two-thirds.

Rapid job creation during the 1990s had benefited those at the bottom of the economic scale, and especially racial minorities. Now, they suffered the most from the economy's continued shedding of jobs in the early 2000s. For example, the black and Latino unemployment rates stood at double that for whites. Indeed, Bush became the first president since Herbert Hoover to see the economy lose jobs over the course of a four-year term.

The Bush administration responded to economic difficulties by supporting the Federal Reserve Board's policy of reducing interest rates and by proposing another round of tax cuts. In 2003, the president signed into law a $320-billion tax reduction, one of the largest in American history. In accordance with supply-side theory, the cuts were again geared to reducing the tax burden on wealthy individuals and corporations. Left to future generations were the questions of how to deal with a rapidly mounting federal deficit (which exceeded $400 billion, a record, in 2004) and how to pay for the obligations of the federal government and the needs of American society.

The economy grew at the healthy rate of 4.2 percent in 2004. But job creation proceeded more slowly than during previous recoveries. Because of the continuing decline in union membership (which fell to 8 percent of private sector employees in 2006), the failure of Congress to raise the minimum wage (which between 1997 and 2006 remained at $5.15 per hour, thereby steadily falling in real value), the continuing shift of higher-paying manufacturing jobs overseas, and the skewing of the tax cuts toward the most wealthy Americans, economic inequality continued to increase. The real income of average American families fell slightly despite the economic recovery. The number of Americans without health insurance continued its upward climb, reaching 16 percent of the population by 2005. Nearly all the benefits of growth went to the top 5 percent of the population.

THE WINDS OF CHANGE

THE 2004 ELECTION

With Bush's popularity sliding because of the war in Iraq and a widespread sense that many Americans were not benefiting from economic growth, Democrats in 2004 sensed a golden opportunity to retake the White House. They nominated as their candidate John Kerry, a senator from Massachusetts and the first Catholic to run for president since John F. Kennedy in 1960. A decorated combat veteran in Vietnam, Kerry had joined the antiwar movement after leaving the army. The party hoped that Kerry's military experience would insulate him from Republican charges that Democrats were too weak-willed to be trusted to protect the United States from further terrorist attacks, while his antiwar credentials in Vietnam would appeal to voters opposed to the invasion of Iraq.

Kerry proved a surprisingly ineffective candidate. An aloof man who lacked the common touch, he failed to generate the same degree of enthusiasm among his supporters as Bush did among his. Kerry's inability to explain why he voted in favor of the Iraq War in the Senate only to denounce it later as a major mistake enabled Republicans to portray him as lacking the kind of resolution necessary in dangerous times. Meanwhile, Karl Rove, Bush's chief political adviser, worked assiduously to mobilize the Republican Party's conservative base by having Republicans stress the president's stance on cultural issues—opposition to the extension of the right to marry to homosexuals (which the Supreme Court of Massachusetts had ruled must receive legal recognition in that state), opposition to abortion rights, and so on.

Throughout the campaign, polls predicted a very close election. Bush won a narrow victory, with a margin of 2 percent of the popular vote and thirty-four electoral votes. The results revealed a remarkable electoral stability. Both sides had spent tens of millions of dollars in advertising and had mobilized new voters—nearly 20 million since 2000. But in the end, only three states voted differently

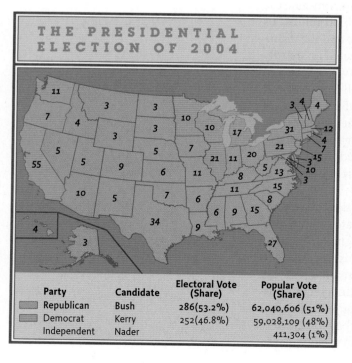

THE PRESIDENTIAL
ELECTION OF 2004

Party	Candidate	Electoral Vote (Share)	Popular Vote (Share)
Republican	Bush	286 (53.2%)	62,040,606 (51%)
Democrat	Kerry	252 (46.8%)	59,028,109 (48%)
Independent	Nader		411,304 (1%)

than four years earlier—New Hampshire, which Kerry carried, and Iowa and New Mexico, which swung to Bush.

Post-election polls initially suggested that "moral values" held the key to the election outcome, leading some commentators to urge Democrats to make peace with the Religious Right. Most evangelical Christians, indeed, voted for Bush. But the "moral values" category was a grab-bag indicating everything from hostility to abortion rights to the desire for a leader who says what he means and apparently means what he says. More important to the outcome were the attacks of September 11 and the sense of being engaged in a worldwide war on terror. No American president who has sought reelection during wartime has ever been defeated (although Harry S. Truman and Lyndon Johnson declined to run again during unpopular wars). The Bush campaign consistently and successfully appealed to fear, with continuous reminders of September 11 and warnings of future attacks.

Republicans also slightly increased their majorities in the House of Representatives and the Senate. But the most striking feature of congressional races was that by the careful drawing of district lines in state legislatures, both parties had managed to make a majority of the seats "safe" ones. Only three incumbents were defeated for reelection, and nearly all the House seats were won by a margin of 10 percent or more. In the old days, one commentator quipped, voters chose their political leaders. Today, politicians choose their voters.

BUSH'S SECOND TERM

In his second inaugural address, in January 2005, Bush outlined a new American goal—"ending tyranny in the world." Striking a more conciliatory tone than during his first administration, he promised that the United States would not try to impose "our style of government" on others and that it would in the future seek the advice of allies. He said nothing specific about Iraq but tried to shore up falling support for the war by invoking the ideal of freedom: "the survival of liberty in our land increasingly depends on the success of liberty in other lands." In his first inaugural, in January 2001, Bush had used the words "freedom," "free," or "liberty" seven times. In his second, they appeared forty-nine times. Again and again, Bush insisted that the United States stands for the worldwide triumph of freedom.

Republicans were overjoyed by Bush's electoral triumph. "Now comes the revolution," declared one conservative leader. But the ongoing chaos in Iraq, coupled with a spate of corruption scandals surrounding Republicans in Congress and the White House, eroded Bush's standing. Vice President Cheney's chief of staff was convicted of perjury in connection with an investigation of the illegal "leak" to the press of the name of a CIA operative whose husband had criticized the manipulation of intelligence before the invasion of Iraq. He was the first White House official to be indicted while holding office since Orville Babcock, Grant's chief of staff, in 1875. A Texas grand jury indicted Tom DeLay, the House majority leader, for violating campaign finance laws, and Jack Abramoff, a Republican activist and lobbyist, pleaded guilty to defrauding his clients and bribing public officials. A "culture of corruption," Demo-crats charged, had overtaken the nation's capital.

Bush's popularity continued to decline. At one point in 2006, his approval rating fell to 31 percent. Bush did get Congress in 2005 to extend the life of the Patriot Act, with a few additional safeguards for civil liberties. But otherwise, the first two years of his second term were devoid of significant legislative achievement. Bush launched a highly publicized campaign to "reform" the Social Security system, the most enduring and popular legacy of the New Deal, by allowing workers to set up private retirement accounts—a step toward eliminating the entire system, Democrats charged—but it got nowhere. Congress rejected the president's proposal to open the Arctic National Wildlife Preserve to oil drilling, and it refused to eliminate the estate tax, a tax on property owned at a person's death, which affected only the richest 1 percent of Americans.

HURRICANE KATRINA

A further blow to the Bush administration's standing came in August 2005, when Hurricane Katrina slammed ashore near New Orleans. Situated below sea level between the Mississippi River and Lake Pontchartrain, New Orleans has always been vulnerable to flooding. For years, scientists had predicted a catastrophe if a hurricane hit the city. But requests to strengthen its levee system had been ignored by the federal government. When the storm hit on August 29 the levees broke, and nearly the entire city, with a population of half a million, was inundated. Nearby areas of the Louisiana and Mississippi Gulf Coast were also hard hit.

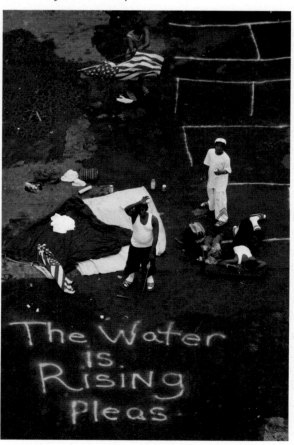

Residents of New Orleans, stranded on a rooftop days after flood waters engulfed the city, frantically attempt to attract the attention of rescue helicopters.

The natural disaster quickly became a man-made one, with ineptitude evident from local government to the White House. The mayor of New Orleans had been slow to order an evacuation, fearing this would damage the city's tourist trade. When he finally instructed residents to leave, a day before the storm's arrival, he neglected to provide for the thousands who did not own automobiles and were too poor to find other means of transportation. In November 2002, a new Department of Homeland Security had been created, absorbing many existing intelligence agencies, including the Federal Emergency Management Agency (FEMA), which is responsible for disaster planning and relief within the United States. FEMA was headed by Michael Brown, who lacked experience in disaster management and had apparently been appointed because he was a college friend of his predecessor in the office. Although warned of impending disaster by the National Weather Service, FEMA had done almost no preparation. Vacationing in Texas, the president announced that New Orleans had "dodged the bullet" when the storm veered away from a direct hit. When he finally visited the city, he seemed unaware of the scope of devastation. If the Bush administration had prided itself on anything, it was competence in dealing with disaster. Katrina shattered that image.

THE NEW ORLEANS DISASTER

For days, vast numbers of people, most of them poor African-Americans, remained abandoned amid the floodwaters. The government was not even aware that thousands had gathered at the New Orleans Convention Center, without food, water, or shelter, until television reporters asked federal officials about their status. For days, bodies floated in the streets and people died in city hospitals and nursing homes. By the time aid began to arrive, damage stood at $80 billion, the death toll was around 1,500, and two-thirds of the city's population had been displaced. The televised images of misery in the streets of New Orleans shocked the world and shamed the country. To leave the poorest behind and unhelped, one editorial writer commented, was like abandoning wounded soldiers on a battlefield.

Hurricane Katrina shone a bright light on both the heroic and the less praiseworthy sides of American life. Where government failed, individual citizens stepped into the breach. People with boats rescued countless survivors from rooftops and attics, private donations flowed in to aid the victims, and neighboring states like Texas opened their doors to thousands of refugees. Like the publication of Jacob Riis's *How the Other Half Lives* (1890) and Michael Harrington's *The Other America* (1962), the hurricane's aftermath alerted Americans to the extent of poverty in the world's richest country. Generations of state and local policies pursuing economic growth via low-wage, nonunion employment and low investment in education, health, and social welfare had produced a large impoverished population in the South. Once a racially mixed city, New Orleans was now essentially segregated, with a population two-thirds black, surrounded by mostly white suburbs. Nearly 30 percent of New Orleans's population lived in poverty, and of these, seven-eighths were black.

For a moment, people previously invisible to upper- and middle-class America appeared on television screens and magazine covers. Stung by criticism of his response to the hurricane, President Bush spoke of the need to take aggressive action against "deep, persistent poverty" whose roots lay in "a history of racial discrimination." But unwilling to raise taxes, the Republican Congress instead cut billions of dollars from Medicaid, food stamps, and other social programs to help pay for rebuilding efforts along the Gulf Coast. A year after the hurricane hit, the population of New Orleans stood at half the pre-storm total, and reconstruction had barely begun in many neighborhoods.

Hurricane Katrina had another result as well. The shutting down of oil refining capacity on the Gulf Coast led to an immediate rise in the price of oil, and thus of gasoline for American drivers. With the rapidly growing economies of China and India needing more and more oil, and with instability in the Middle East threatening to affect oil production, prices remained at historic highs throughout 2006. Despite decades of talk about the need to develop alternative energy supplies, the United States remained as dependent as ever on imported oil and extremely vulnerable to potential disruptions of oil imports. Rising prices threatened to derail the economic recovery by dampening consumer spending on other goods. They also dealt yet another blow to American automobile manufacturers, who had staked their futures on sales of light trucks and suburban utility vehicles (SUVs). These vehicles generated high profits for the car companies but achieved very low gas mileage. When gas prices rose, consumers shifted their purchasing to smaller cars with better fuel efficiency, most of which were produced by Japanese and other foreign automakers.

President George W. Bush speaking in Jackson Square, New Orleans on September 15, 2005, two and a half weeks after Hurricane Katrina flooded the city. In the background is St. Louis Cathedral.

THE IMMIGRATION DEBATE

In the spring of 2006, an issue as old as the American nation suddenly burst again onto the center stage of politics—immigration. As we have seen, the Hart-Celler Act of 1965 led to a radical shift in the origins of those entering the United States, and especially the rapid growth of the Hispanic population. The influx of immigrants proceeded apace during the first five years of the twenty-first century. By 2005, immigrants represented 12.4 percent of the nation's population, up from 11.2 percent in 2000. Many of these newcomers were bypassing traditional immigrant destinations and heading for areas in the Midwest, small-town New England, and the Upper South. The city with the highest rate of growth of its immigrant population from 1990 to 2005 was Nashville, Tennessee. Racial and ethnic diversity was now a fact of life in the American heartland.

Alongside legal immigrants, undocumented newcomers made their way to the United States, mostly from Mexico. At the end of 2005, it was estimated, there were 11 million illegal aliens in the United States, 7 million of them members of the workforce. Economists disagree about their impact. It seems clear that the presence of large numbers of uneducated, low-skilled workers pushes down wages at the bottom of the economic ladder, especially affecting African-Americans. On the other hand, immigrants both legal and illegal receive regular paychecks, spend money, and pay taxes. They fill jobs for which American workers seem to be unavailable because the wages are so low. It is estimated that over one-fifth of construction workers, domestic workers and agricultural workers are in the United States illegally.

As noted in previous chapters, Mexican immigration has long been a controversial subject, especially in the Southwest. Before 1924, there were no limits on immigration from the Western Hemisphere. During the 1930s, hundreds of thousands of Mexican-Americans were repatriated. The *bracero* program of the 1940s and 1950s brought thousands of Mexicans into the United States under labor contracts as migrant agricultural workers. Operation Wetback in 1954 sent 1 million Mexicans home. Since the rise of the Chicano movement of the late 1960s and 1970s, the Mexican-American community has generally defended the rights of undocumented workers, although some advocates have feared that the presence of illegal aliens lowers the standing—in the eyes of other Americans—of everyone of Mexican descent. Unions generally fear that such workers lower wages for all low-skilled workers and make labor organizing more difficult.

In 1986, the Reagan administration had granted amnesty—that is, the right to remain in the United States and become citizens—to 3 million illegal immigrants. During the 1990s, conservatives in states with significant populations of illegal immigrants, especially California, had called for a tough crackdown on their entry and rights within the United States. As governor of Texas, by contrast, George W. Bush had strived to win Hispanic support and downplayed the immigration issue. But in 2006, with many Americans convinced that the United States had lost control of its borders and that immigration was in part responsible for the stagnation of real wages, the House of Representatives approved a bill making it a felony to be in the country illegally and a crime to offer aid to illegal immigrants.

THE IMMIGRANT RIGHTS MOVEMENT

The response was utterly unexpected: a series of massive demonstrations in the spring of 2006 by immigrants—legal and illegal—and their supporters, demanding the right to remain in the country as citizens. In cities from New York to Chicago, Los Angeles, Phoenix, and Dallas, hundreds of thousands of protesters took to the streets. Nashville experienced the largest public demonstration in its history, a march of more than 10,000 mostly Hispanic immigrants. People living at the margins of American society suddenly found their voice. "All that we want is to have a shot at the American dream," said one. Another, an Iraq War veteran who marched with his parents, who had come to the country illegally, said, "I've fought for freedom overseas. Now I'm fighting for freedom here."

At the same time, church groups used to sheltering and feeding the destitute denounced the proposed bill as akin to the Fugitive Slave Law of 1850 for making it a crime to help a suffering human being and vowed to resist it. On the other hand, many conservatives condemned the marches as "ominous" and their display of the flags of the marchers' homelands as "repellant." When the Senate passed a different immigrant bill, tightening patrols of the border but offering a route to citizenship for illegal aliens, the House refused to approve it. All Congress could agree on was a measure to build a 700-mile wall along part of the U.S.-Mexico border. In early 2007, the immigration issue was at a stalemate and its ultimate resolution impossible to predict.

THE CONSTITUTION AND LIBERTY

As in the 1980s and 1990s, conservatives proved far more successful in implementing their views in economic and foreign policy than in the ongoing culture wars. Two significant Supreme Court decisions in June

In April 2006, millions of people demonstrated for immigrant rights. This photograph shows part of the immense crowd in Chicago, bearing the flags of many nations.

2003 revealed how the largely conservative justices had come to accept that the social revolution that began during the 1960s could not be undone.

In two cases arising from challenges to the admissions policies of the University of Michigan, the Supreme Court issued its most important rulings on affirmative action since the *Bakke* case twenty-five years earlier. A 5-4 majority upheld the right of colleges and universities to take race into account in admissions decisions. Writing for the majority, Justice Sandra Day O'Connor argued that such institutions have a legitimate interest in creating a "diverse" student body to enhance education. The Bush administration had urged the Court to reject affirmative action. But O'Connor was strongly influenced by briefs on its behalf filed by corporate executives and retired military officers. In today's world, they argued, the United States cannot compete in the global economy or maintain effective armed services without drawing its college-trained business and military leaders from a wide variety of racial and ethnic backgrounds.

In the second decision, in *Lawrence v. Texas*, a 6-3 majority declared unconstitutional a Texas law making homosexual acts a crime. Written by Justice Anthony Kennedy, the majority opinion overturned the Court's 1986 ruling in *Bowers v. Hardwick*, which had upheld a similar Georgia law. Today, Kennedy insisted, the idea of liberty includes not only "freedom of thought, belief, [and] expression" but "intimate conduct" as well. The decision was a triumph for the feminist and gay movements, which had long campaigned to extend the idea of freedom into the most personal realms of life. And it repudiated the conservative view that constitutional interpretation must rest either on the "original intent" of the founding fathers or on a narrow reading of the document's text. Instead, Kennedy reaffirmed the liberal view of the Constitution as a living document whose protections expand as society changes. "Times can blind us to certain truths," he wrote, "and later generations can see that laws once thought necessary and proper in fact serve only to oppress. As the Constitution endures, persons in every generation can invoke its principles in their own search for greater freedom."

THE COURT AND THE PRESIDENT

Nor did the Supreme Court prove receptive to President Bush's claim of authority to disregard laws and treaties and to suspend constitutional protections of individual liberties. In a series of decisions, the Court reaffirmed the rule of law both for American citizens and for foreigners held prisoner by the United States.

The first cases were decided in 2004. In *Rasul v. Bush*, the Court allowed a British citizen held at Guantánamo Bay, Cuba, to challenge his incarceration in federal court. In *Hamdi v. Rumsfeld*, it considered the lawsuit of Yasir Hamdi, an American citizen who had moved to Saudi Arabia and been captured in Afghanistan. Hamdi was imprisoned in a military jail in South Carolina without charge or the right to see a lawyer. The Court ruled that he had a right to a judicial hearing. "A state of war," wrote Sandra Day O'Connor for the 8-1 majority, "is not a blank check for the president when it comes to the rights of the nation's citizens." Even Justice Antonin Scalia, the Court's most prominent conservative, rejected the president's claim of authority to imprison a citizen at will as antithetical to "the very core of liberty." After claiming in court that Hamdi was so dangerous that he could not even be allowed a hearing, the administration allowed him to return to Saudi Arabia on condition that he relinquish his American citizenship.

By the time the next significant case, *Hamdan v. Rumsfeld*, came before the Court in 2006, President Bush had appointed two new justices—Chief Justice John Roberts, to replace William Rehnquist, who died in 2005, and Samuel Alito Jr., who succeeded the retiring Sandra Day O'Connor. The Court was clearly becoming more conservative. But in June 2006, by a 5-3 margin (with Roberts not participating because he had ruled on the case while serving on an appeals court), the justices offered a stinging rebuke to the key presumptions of the Bush administration—that the Geneva Conventions do not apply to prisoners captured in the war on terrorism, that the president can unilaterally set up secret military tribunals in which defendants have very few if any rights, and that the Constitution does not apply at Guantànamo. Congress, the majority noted, had never authorized such tribunals, and they clearly violated the protections afforded to prisoners of war by the Geneva Conventions, which, the Court declared, was the law of the land.

Like the Nixon tapes case of 1974, the decision was a striking illustration of the separation of powers envisioned by the Constitution's framers, an affirmation that the courts have the right and responsibility to oversee actions by the president. However, it was unusual that the decision came in wartime. The Court had upheld jailings under the Sedition Act in World War I, and Japanese internment in World War II. Previously, the Court had only exerted its oversight authority once peace arrived. But Bush's claims of presidential authority had been so sweeping that a judicial reaction was all but inevitable.

As the "war on terror" entered its sixth year later in 2006, the scope of the president's power to detain and punish suspects outside of normal legal procedures remained unresolved. In September 2006, in response to the *Hamdan* decision, Congress enacted a bill authorizing the establishment of special military tribunals to try accused terrorists and giving the president the authority to jail without charge anyone he declared to be an "illegal enemy combatant." The measure authorized certain kinds of harsh treatment of prisoners, with evidence obtained during coercive interrogations usable in these new courts, and stripped detainees in military prisons of the right to challenge their detention in federal courts. Many military lawyers objected strongly to these provisions, as did other army officials, fearing that captured U.S. soldiers might be subjected to the same treatment. It remained to be seen whether the Supreme Court would allow Congress to override the Geneva Conventions and eliminate judicial oversight of the treatment of prisoners.

THE MIDTERM ELECTIONS OF 2006

With President Bush's popularity having plummeted because of the war in Iraq and the Hurricane Katrina disaster, Congress beset by scandal after scandal, and public opinion polls revealing that a majority of Americans believed the country to be "on the wrong track," Democrats expected to reap major gains in the congressional elections of 2006. They were not disappointed. Interest in the election ran high. Voter turnout in 2006 exceeded 40 percent of those eligible, the highest figure for a midterm election since 1990. In a sweeping repudiation of the administration, voters gave Democrats control of both houses of Congress for the first time since the Republican sweep of 1994. In January 2007, Democrat Nancy Pelosi of California became the first female Speaker of the House in American history. No sooner had the votes been counted than political observers began to speculate about the presidential election of 2008—the first time since 1952 that the major party candidates for the highest office in the land would not include a sitting president or vice president.

LEARNING FROM HISTORY

"The owl of Minerva takes flight at dusk." Minerva was the Roman goddess of wisdom, and this saying suggests that the meaning of events only becomes clear once they are over. It is still far too soon to assess the full impact of September 11 on American life and the long-term consequences of the changes at home and abroad it inspired.

As of 2006, the world seemed far more unstable than anyone could have predicted when the Cold War ended fifteen years before. An end to the war on terror seemed as remote as ever. Chaos continued in Iraq. War raged during the summer between Israel and radical Muslims in Lebanon. Iran, its power in the region enhanced by the American removal of its chief rival, Saddam Hussein's regime in Iraq, seemed bent on acquiring nuclear weapons. Other regions of the world also presented daunting problems for American policymakers. North Korea had acquired nuclear weapons and refused international pressure to give them up. China's rapidly growing economic power posed a challenge to American predominance. A series of Latin American countries elected presidents who rejected the doctrines of globalization and global free trade pressed so insistently by the United States. No one could predict how any of these crises, or others yet unimagined, would be resolved.

What *is* clear is that September 11 and its aftermath drew new attention to essential elements of the history of American freedom. As in the past, freedom is central to Americans' sense of themselves as individuals and as a nation. Americans continue to debate contemporary issues in a political landscape shaped by ideas of freedom. Indeed, freedom remains, as it has always been, an evolving

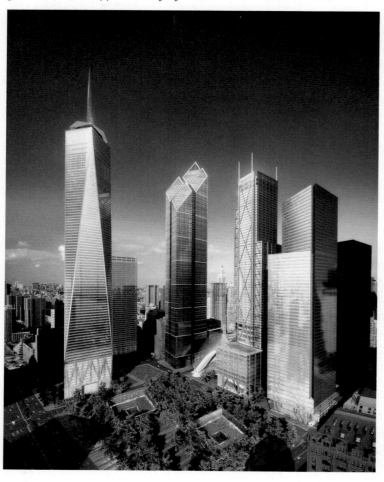

The design for a series of office buildings that will replace the World Trade Center illustrate the juxtaposition of optimism and fear in the aftermath of September 11, 2001. The soaring towers underscore Americans' capacity for recovery and regeneration. But at the insistence of the New York City police, the base of the Freedom Tower, at the left, consists of reinforced concrete, giving the building, at ground level, the appearance of a fortress.

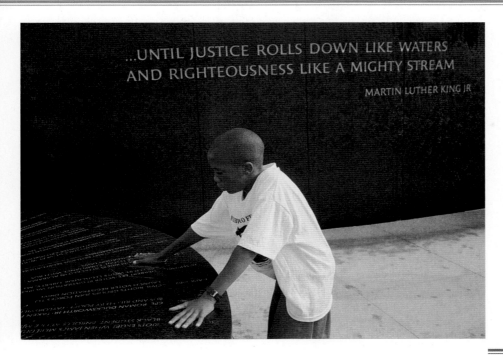

Seeking the lessons of history: a young visitor at the Civil Rights Memorial in Montgomery, Alabama.

concept, its definition open to disagreement, its boundaries never fixed or final. Freedom is neither self-enforcing nor self-correcting. It cannot be taken for granted, and its preservation requires eternal vigilance, especially in times of crisis.

Over half a century ago, the African-American poet Langston Hughes urged Americans both to celebrate the freedoms they enjoy and to remember that freedom has always been incomplete:

> There are words like *Freedom*
> Sweet and wonderful to say.
> On my heartstrings freedom sings
> All day everyday.
>
> There are words like *Liberty*
> That almost make me cry.
> If you had known what I know
> You would know why.

SUGGESTED READING

Bacevich, Andrew. *American Empire: The Realities and Consequences of U.S. Diplomacy* (2003). Examines how the idea of an American empire reemerged after September 11, and some of the results.

Brinkley, Douglas. *The Great Deluge: Hurricane Katrina, New Orleans, and the Mississippi Gulf Coast* (2006). A scathing account of how government at all levels failed the people of New Orleans.

Cole, David. *Terrorism and the Constitution* (rev. ed., 2006). Explores the constitutional issues raised by the war on terrorism.

Lakoff, George. *Whose Freedom? The Battle over America's Most Important Idea* (2006). Describes how conservatives and liberals continue to interpret freedom in very different ways.

Levitas, Mitchell, ed. *A Nation Challenged: A Visual History of 9/11 and Its Aftermath* (2002). Presents striking photographs of the terrorist attacks and the days that followed.

Little, Douglas. *American Orientalism: The United States and the Middle East since 1945* (2003). A careful study of American relations with a volatile region since World War II.

Nye, Joseph S., Jr. *The Paradox of American Power* (2002). An argument that despite its overwhelming power, the United States cannot do as it pleases in international affairs.

Packer, George. *The Assassin's Gate: America in Iraq* (2005). An early supporter of the war in Iraq explains what went wrong.

Zakaria, Fareed. *The Future of Freedom: Illiberal Democracy at Home and Abroad* (2003). A foreign policy analyst discusses how the United States should respond to threats to freedom in the world.

REVIEW QUESTIONS

1. In what ways did the war in Iraq significantly alter American foreign policy?

2. What actions demonstrated that the Bush administration practiced a conservative agenda?

3. How did the Bush administration use the language of freedom in the aftermath of September 11?

4. How did the Supreme Court decisions of 2003 indicate that the rights revolution was here to stay?

5. Discuss the major changes in American freedom since 1865.

REVIEW TABLE

Significant Changes in American Policy Since September 11

Policy	Explanation
Bush Doctrine	America commits itself to a war against terrorism
U.S.A. Patriot Act	Confers unprecedented powers on law-enforcement agencies
National Security Strategy	Advocates preemptive war for the first time in American history

KEY TERMS

tax cuts (p. 1097)

Kyoto Protocol (p. 1097)

War in Afghanistan (p. 1099)

signing statements (p. 1110)

Election of 2004 (p. 1112)

Hurricane Katrina (p. 1114)

immigration and globalization (p. 1116)

Lawrence v. Texas (p. 1118)

Appendix

The Declaration of Independence (1776)

When in the course of human events, it becomes necessary for one people to dissolve the political bands which have connected them with another, and to assume among the Powers of the earth, the separate and equal station to which the Laws of Nature and of Nature's God entitle them, a decent respect to the opinions of mankind requires that they should declare the causes which impel them to the separation.

We hold these truths to be self-evident, that all men are created equal, that they are endowed by their Creator with certain unalienable rights, that among these are Life, Liberty, and the pursuit of Happiness. That to secure these rights, Governments are instituted among Men, deriving their just powers from the consent of the governed. That whenever any Form of Government becomes destructive of these ends, it is the Right of the People to alter or to abolish it, and to institute new Government, laying its foundation on such principles and organizing its powers in such form, as to them shall seem most likely to effect their Safety and Happiness. Prudence, indeed, will dictate that Governments long established should not be changed for light and transient causes; and accordingly all experience hath shown, that mankind are more disposed to suffer, while evils are sufferable, than to right themselves by abolishing the forms to which they are accustomed. But when a long train of abuses and usurpations, pursuing invariably the same Object evinces a design to reduce them under absolute Despotism, it is their right, it is their duty, to throw off such Government, and to provide new Guards for their future security.—Such has been the patient sufferance of these Colonies; and such is now the necessity which constrains them to alter their former Systems of Government. The history of the present King of Great Britain is a history of repeated injuries and usurpations, all having in direct object the establishment of an absolute Tyranny over these States. To prove this, let Facts be submitted to a candid world.

He has refused his Assent to Laws, the most wholesome and necessary for the public good.

He has forbidden his Governors to pass Laws of immediate and pressing importance, unless suspended in their operation till his Assent should be obtained; and when so suspended, he has utterly neglected to attend to them.

He has refused to pass other Laws for the accommodation of large districts of people, unless those people would relinquish the right of Representation in the Legislature, a right inestimable to them and formidable to tyrants only.

He has called together legislative bodies at places unusual, uncomfortable, and distant from the depository of their public Records, for the sole purpose of fatiguing them into compliance with his measures.

He has dissolved Representative Houses repeatedly, for opposing with manly firmness his invasions on the rights of the people.

He has refused for a long time, after such dissolutions, to cause others to be elected; whereby the Legislative powers, incapable of Annihilation, have returned to the People at large for their exercise; the State remaining in the mean time exposed to all dangers of invasion from without, and convulsions within.

He has endeavoured to prevent the population of these States; for that purpose obstructing the Laws of Naturalization of Foreigners; refusing to pass others to encourage their migrations hither, and raising the conditions of new Appropriations of Lands.

He has obstructed the Administration of Justice, by refusing his Assent to Laws for establishing Judiciary powers.

He has made Judges dependent on his Will alone, for the tenure of their offices, and the amount and payment of their salaries.

He has erected a multitude of New Offices, and sent hither swarms of Officers to harass our People, and eat out their substance.

He has kept among us, in times of peace, Standing Armies without the Consent of our legislatures.

He has affected to render the Military independent of and superior to the Civil Power.

He has combined with others to subject us to a jurisdiction foreign to our constitution, and unacknowledged by our laws; giving his Assent to their Acts of pretended Legislation:

For quartering large bodies of armed troops among us:

For protecting them, by a mock Trial, from Punishment for any Murders which they should commit on the Inhabitants of these States:

For cutting off our Trade with all parts of the world:

For imposing taxes on us without our Consent:

For depriving us of many cases, of the benefits of Trial by jury:

For transporting us beyond Seas to be tried for pretended offences:

For abolishing the free System of English Laws in a neighbouring Province, establishing therein an Arbitrary government, and enlarging its Boundaries so as to render it at once an example and fit instrument for introducing the same absolute rule into these Colonies:

For taking away our Charters, abolishing our most valuable Laws, and altering fundamentally the Forms of our Governments:

For suspending our own Legislatures, and declaring themselves invested with Power to legislate for us in all cases whatsoever.

He has abdicated Government here, by declaring us out of his Protection and waging War against us.

He has plundered our seas, ravaged our Coasts, burnt our towns, and destroyed the lives of our people.

He is at this time transporting large armies of foreign mercenaries to compleat the works of death, desolation, and tyranny, already begun with circumstances of Cruelty & perfidy scarcely paralleled in the most barbarous ages, and totally unworthy the Head of a civilized nation.

He has constrained our fellow Citizens taken Captive on the high Seas to bear Arms against their Country, to become the executioners of their friends and Brethren, or to fall themselves by their Hands.

He has excited domestic insurrections amongst us, and has endeavoured to bring on the inhabitants of our frontiers, the merciless Indian Savages, whose known rule of warfare, is an undistinguished destruction of all ages, sexes, and conditions.

In every stage of these Oppressions We have Petitioned for Redress in the most humble terms: Our repeated Petitions have been answered only by repeated injury. A Prince, whose character is thus marked by every act which may define a Tyrant, is unfit to be the ruler of a free people.

Nor have We been wanting in attention to our British brethren. We have warned them from time to time of attempts by their legislature to extend an unwarrantable jurisdiction over us. We have reminded them of the circumstances of our emigration and settlement here. We have appealed to their native justice and magnanimity, and we have conjured them by the ties of our common kindred to disavow these usurpations, which, would inevitably interrupt our connections and correspondence. They too must have been deaf to the voice of justice and of consanguinity. We must, therefore, acquiesce in the necessity, which denounces our Separation, and hold them, as we hold the rest of mankind, Enemies in War, in Peace Friends.

WE, THEREFORE, the Representatives of the UNITED STATES OF AMERICA, in General Congress, Assembled, appealing to the Supreme Judge of the world for the rectitude of our intentions, do, in the Name, and by Authority of the good People of these Colonies, solemnly publish and declare, That these United Colonies are, and of Right ought to be FREE AND INDEPENDENT STATES; that they are Absolved from all Allegiance to the British Crown, and that all political connection between them and the State of Great Britain, is and ought to be totally dissolved; and that as Free and Independent States, they have full Power to levy War, conclude Peace, contract Alliances, establish Commerce, and to do all other Acts and Things which Independent States may of right do. And for the support of this Declaration, with a firm reliance on the Protection of Divine Providence, we mutually pledge to each other our Lives, our Fortunes, and our sacred Honor.

The foregoing Declaration was, by order of Congress, engrossed, and signed by the following members:

John Hancock

NEW HAMPSHIRE	NEW JERSEY	VIRGINIA
Josiah Bartlett	*Richard Stockton*	*George Wythe*
William Whipple	*John Witherspoon*	*Richard Henry Lee*
Matthew Thornton	*Francis Hopkinson*	*Thomas Jefferson*
	John Hart	*Benjamin Harrison*
	Abraham Clark	*Thomas Nelson, Jr.*
MASSACHUSETTS BAY		*Francis Lightfoot Lee*
Samuel Adams		*Carter Braxton*
John Adams	PENNSYLVANIA	
Robert Treat Paine	*Robert Morris*	
Elbridge Gerry	*Benjamin Rush*	NORTH CAROLINA
	Benjamin Franklin	*William Hooper*
	John Morton	*Joseph Hewes*
RHODE ISLAND	*George Clymer*	*John Penn*
Stephen Hopkins	*James Smith*	
William Ellery	*George Taylor*	
	James Wilson	SOUTH CAROLINA
	George Ross	*Edward Rutledge*
CONNECTICUT		*Thomas Heyward, Jr.*
Roger Sherman		*Thomas Lynch, Jr.*
Samuel Huntington		*Arthur Middleton*
William Williams	DELAWARE	
Oliver Wolcott	*Caesar Rodney*	
	George Read	GEORGIA
	Thomas M'Kean	*Button Gwinnett*
NEW YORK		*Lyman Hall*
William Floyd		*George Walton*
Philip Livingston	MARYLAND	
Francis Lewis	*Samuel Chase*	
Lewis Morris	*William Paca*	
	Thomas Stone	
	Charles Carroll, of	
	Carrollton	

Resolved, That copies of the Declaration be sent to the several assemblies, conventions, and committees, or councils of safety, and to the several commanding officers of the continental troops; that it be proclaimed in each of the United States, at the head of the army.

THE CONSTITUTION OF THE UNITED STATES (1787)

We the People of the United States, in order to form a more perfect Union, establish Justice, insure domestic Tranquility, provide for the common defence, promote the general Welfare, and secure the Blessings of Liberty to ourselves and our Posterity, do ordain and establish this Constitution for the United States of America.

ARTICLE. I.

Section. 1. All legislative Powers herein granted shall be vested in a Congress of the United States, which shall consist of a Senate and House of Representatives.

Section. 2. The House of Representatives shall be composed of Members chosen every second Year by the People of the several States, and the Electors in each State shall have the Qualifications requisite for Electors of the most numerous Branch of the State Legislature.

No Person shall be a Representative who shall not have attained to the Age of twenty five Years, and been seven Years a Citizen of the United States, and who shall not, when elected, be an Inhabitant of that State in which he shall be chosen.

Representatives and direct Taxes shall be apportioned among the several States which may be included within this Union, according to their respective Numbers, which shall be determined by adding to the whole Number of free Persons, including those bound to Service for a Term of Years, and excluding Indians not taxed, three fifths of all other Persons. The actual Enumeration shall be made within three Years after the first Meeting of the Congress of the United States, and within every subsequent Term of ten Years, in such Manner as they shall by Law direct. The Number of Representatives shall not exceed one for every thirty Thousand, but each State shall have at Least one Representative; and until such enumeration shall be made, the State of New Hampshire shall be entitled to chuse three, Massachusetts eight, Rhode-Island and Providence Plantations one, Connecticut five, New York six, New Jersey four, Pennsylvania eight, Delaware one, Maryland six, Virginia ten, North Carolina five, South Carolina five, and Georgia three.

When vacancies happen in the Representation from any state, the Executive Authority thereof shall issue Writs of Election to fill such Vacancies.

The House of Representatives shall chuse their Speaker and other Officers; and shall have the sole Power of Impeachment.

Section. 3. The Senate of the United States shall be composed of two Senators from each State, chosen by the legislature thereof, for six Years; and each Senator shall have one Vote.

Immediately after they shall be assembled in Consequence of the first Election, they shall be divided as equally as may be into three Classes. The Seats of the Senators of the first Class shall be vacated at the Expiration of the second Year, of the second Class at the Expiration of the fourth Year, and of the third Class at the Expiration of the sixth Year, so that one third may be chosen every second Year; and if Vacancies happen by Resignation, or otherwise, during the Recess of the Legislature of any State, the Executive thereof may make temporary Appointments until the next Meeting of the Legislature, which shall then fill such Vacancies.

No Person shall be a Senator who shall not have attained to the Age of thirty Years, and been nine Years a Citizen of the United States, and who shall not, when elected, be an Inhabitant of that State for which he shall be chosen.

The Vice President of the United States shall be President of the Senate, but shall have no Vote, unless they be equally divided.

The Senate shall chuse their other Officers, and also a President pro tempore, in the Absence of the Vice President, or when he shall exercise the Office of President of the United States.

The Senate shall have the sole Power to try all Impeachments. When sitting for that Purpose, they shall be on Oath or Affirmation. When the President of the United States is tried, the Chief Justice shall preside: And no Person shall be convicted without the Concurrence of two thirds of the Members present.

Judgment in Cases of Impeachment shall not extend further than to removal from Office, and disqualification to hold and enjoy any Office of honor, Trust or Profit under the United States: but the Party convicted shall nevertheless be liable and subject to Indictment, Trial, Judgment and Punishment, according to Law.

Section. 4. The Times, Places and Manner of holding Elections for Senators and Representatives, shall be prescribed in each State by the Legislature thereof; but the Congress may at any time by Law make or alter such Regulations, except as to the Places of chusing Senators.

The Congress shall assemble at least once in every Year, and such Meeting shall be on the first Monday in December, unless they shall by Law appoint a different Day.

Section. 5. Each House shall be the Judge of the Elections, Returns and Qualifications of its own Members, and a Majority of each shall constitute a Quorum to do Business; but a smaller Number may adjourn from day to day, and may be authorized to compel the Attendance of absent Members, in such Manner, and under such Penalties as each House may provide.

Each House may determine the Rules of its Proceedings, punish its Members for disorderly Behaviour, and, with the Concurrence of two thirds, expel a Member.

Each House shall keep a Journal of its Proceedings, and from time to time publish the same, excepting such Parts as may in their Judgment require Secrecy; and the Yeas and Nays of the Members of either House on any question shall, at the Desire of one fifth of those Present, be entered on the Journal.

Neither House, during the Session of Congress, shall, without the Consent of the other, adjourn for more than three days, not to any other Place than that in which the two Houses shall be sitting.

Section. 6. The Senators and Representatives shall receive a Compensation for their Services, to be ascertained by Law, and paid out of the Treasury of the United States. They shall in all Cases, except Treason, Felony and Breach of the Peace, be privileged from Arrest during their Attendance at the Session of their respective Houses, and in going to and returning from the same; and for any Speech or Debate in either House, they shall not be questioned in any other Place.

No Senator or Representative shall, during the Time for which he was elected, be appointed to any civil Office under the Authority of the United States, which shall have been created, or the Emoluments whereof shall have been encreased during such time; and no Person holding any Office under the United States, shall be a Member of either House during his Continuance in Office.

Section. 7. All Bills for raising Revenue shall originate in the House of Representatives; but the Senate may propose or concur with Amendments as on other Bills.

Every Bill which shall have passed the House of Representatives and the Senate shall, before it become a Law, be presented to the President of the United States; If he approve he shall sign it, but if not he shall return it, with his Objections to that House in which it shall have originated, who shall enter the Objections at large on their Journal, and proceed to reconsider it. If after such Reconsideration two thirds of that House shall agree to pass the Bill, it shall be sent, together with the Objections, to the other House, by which it shall likewise be reconsidered, and if approved by two thirds of that House, it shall become a Law. But in all such Cases the Votes of both Houses shall be determined by Yeas and Nays, and the Names of the Persons voting for and against the Bill shall be entered on the Journal of each House respectively. If any Bill shall not be returned by the President within ten Days (Sundays excepted) after it shall have been presented to him, the Same shall be a Law, in like Manner as if he had signed it, unless the Congress by their Adjournment prevent its Return, in which Case it shall not be a Law.

Every Order, Resolution, or Vote to which the Concurrence of the Senate and House of Representatives may be necessary (except on a question of Adjournment) shall be presented to the President of the United States; and before the Same shall take Effect, shall be approved by him, or being disapproved by him, shall be repassed by two thirds of the Senate and House of Representatives, according to the Rules and Limitations prescribed in the Case of a Bill.

Section. 8. The Congress shall have Power To lay and collect Taxes, Duties, Imposts and Excises, to pay the Debts and provide for the common Defence and general Welfare of the United States; but all Duties, Imposts and Excises shall be uniform throughout the United States;

To borrow Money on the credit of the United States;

To regulate Commerce with foreign Nations, and among the several States, and with the Indian Tribes;

To establish an uniform Rule of Naturalization, and uniform Laws on the subject of Bankruptcies throughout the United States;

To coin Money, regulate the Value thereof, and of foreign Coin, and fix the Standard of Weights and Measures;

To provide for the Punishment of counterfeiting the Securities and current Coin of the United States;

To establish Post Offices and Post Roads;

To promote the Progress of Science and useful Arts, by securing for limited Times to Authors and Inventors the exclusive Right to their respective Writings and Discoveries;

To constitute Tribunals inferior to the supreme Court;

To define and punish Piracies and Felonies committed on the high Seas, and Offences against the Law of Nations;

To declare War, grant Letters of Marque and Reprisal, and make Rules concerning Captures on Land and Water;

To raise and support Armies, but no Appropriation of Money to that Use shall be for a longer Term than two Years;

To provide and maintain a Navy;

To make Rules for the Government and Regulation of the land and naval Forces;

To provide for calling forth the Militia to execute the Laws of the Union, suppress Insurrections and repel Invasions;

To provide for organizing, arming, and disciplining, the Militia, and for governing such Part of them as may be employed in the Service of the United States, reserving to the States respectively, the Appointment of the Officers, and the Authority of training the Militia according to the discipline prescribed by Congress;

To exercise exclusive Legislation in all Cases whatsoever, over such District (not exceeding ten Miles square) as may, by Cession of Particular States, and the Acceptance of Congress, become the Seat of the Government of the United States, and to exercise like Authority over all Places purchased by the Consent of the Legislature of the State in which the Same shall be, for the Erection of Forts, Magazines, Arsenals, dock-Yards, and other needful Buildings;—And

To make all Laws which shall be necessary and proper for carrying into Execution the foregoing Powers, and all other Powers vested by this Constitution in the Government of the United States, or in any Department or Officer thereof.

Section. 9. The Migration or Importation of such Persons as any of the States now existing shall think proper to admit, shall not be prohibited by the Congress prior to the Year one thousand eight hundred and eight, but a Tax or duty may be imposed on such Importation, not exceeding ten dollars for each Person.

The Privilege of the Writ of Habeas Corpus shall not be suspended, unless when in Cases of Rebellion or Invasion the public Safety may require it.

No Bill of Attainder or ex post facto Law shall be passed.

No Capitation, or other direct, Tax shall be laid, unless in Proportion to the Census or Enumeration herein before directed to be taken.

No Tax or Duty shall be laid on Articles exported from any State.

No Preference shall be given by any Regulation of Commerce or Revenue to the Ports of one State over those of another: nor shall Vessels bound to, or from, one State, be obliged to enter, clear, or pay Duties in another.

No Money shall be drawn from the Treasury, but in Consequence of Appropriations made by Law; and a regular Statement and Account of the Receipts and Expenditures of all public Money shall be published from time to time.

No Title of Nobility shall be granted by the United States: And no Person holding any Office of Profit or Trust under them, shall, without the Consent of the Congress, accept of any present, Emolument, Office, or Title, of any kind whatever, from any King, Prince, or foreign State.

Section. 10. No State shall enter into any Treaty, Alliance, or Confederation; grant Letters of Marque and Reprisal; coin Money; emit Bills of Credit; make any Thing but gold and silver Coin a Tender in Payment of Debts; pass any Bill of Attainder, ex post facto Law, or Law impairing the Obligation of Contracts, or grant any Title of Nobility.

No State shall, without the Consent of the Congress, lay any Imposts or Duties on Imports or Exports, except what may be absolutely necessary for executing its inspection Laws: and the net Produce of all Duties and Imposts, laid by any State on Imports or Exports, shall be for the Use of the Treasury of the United States; and all such Laws shall be subject to the Revision and Controul of the Congress.

No State shall, without the Consent of Congress, lay any Duty of Tonnage, keep Troops, or Ships of War in time of Peace, enter into any Agreement or Compact with another State, or with a foreign Power, or engage in War, unless actually invaded, or in such imminent Danger as will not admit of delay.

ARTICLE. II.

Section. 1. The executive Power shall be vested in a President of the United States of America. He shall hold his Office during the term of four Years, and, together with the Vice President, chosen for the same Term, be elected, as follows:

Each State shall appoint, in such Manner as the Legislature thereof may direct, a Number of Electors, equal to the whole Number of Senators and Representatives to which the State may be entitled in the Congress: but no Senator or Representa-

tive, or Person holding an Office of Trust or Profit under the United States, shall be appointed an Elector.

The Electors shall meet in their respective States, and vote by Ballot for two Persons, of whom one at least shall not be an Inhabitant of the same State with themselves. And they shall make a List of all the Persons voted for, and of the Number of Votes for each; which List they shall sign and certify, and transmit sealed to the Seat of the Government of the United States, directed to the President of the Senate. The President of the Senate shall, in the Presence of the Senate and House of Representatives, open all the Certificates, and the Votes shall then be counted. The Person having the greatest Number of Votes shall be the President, if such Number be a Majority of the whole Number of Electors appointed; and if there be more than one who have such Majority, and have an equal Number of Votes, then the House of Representatives shall immediately chuse by Ballot one of them for President; and if no Person have a Majority, then from the five highest on the List the said House shall in like Manner chuse the President. But in chusing the President, the Votes shall be taken by States, the Representation from each State having one Vote; A quorum for this Purpose shall consist of a Member or Members from two thirds of the States, and a Majority of all the States shall be necessary to a Choice. In every Case, after the Choice of the President, the Person having the greatest Number of Votes of the Electors shall be the Vice President. But if there should remain two or more who have equal Votes, the Senate shall chuse from them by Ballot the Vice President.

The Congress may determine the Time of chusing the Electors, and the Day on which they shall give their Votes; which Day shall be the same throughout the United States.

No Person except a natural born Citizen, or a Citizen of the United States, at the time of the Adoption of this Constitution, shall be eligible to the Office of President; neither shall any Person be eligible to that Office who shall not have attained to the Age of thirty five Years, and been fourteen Years a Resident within the United States.

In Case of the Removal of the President from Office, or of his Death, Resignation, or Inability to discharge the Powers and Duties of the said Office, the Same shall devolve on the Vice President, and the Congress may by Law provide for the Case of Removal, Death, Resignation or Inability, both of the President and Vice President, declaring what Officer shall then act as President, and such Officer shall act accordingly, until the Disability be removed, or a President shall be elected.

The President shall, at stated Times, receive for his Services, a Compensation, which shall neither be encreased or diminished during the Period for which he shall have been elected, and he shall not receive within that Period any other Emolument from the United States, or any of them.

Before he enters on the Execution of his Office, he shall take the following Oath or Affirmation:—"I do solemnly swear (or affirm) that I will faithfully execute the Office of President of the United States, and will to the best of my Ability, preserve, protect and defend the Constitution of the United States."

Section. 2. The President shall be Commander in Chief of the Army and Navy of the United States, and of the Militia of the several States, when called into the actual Service of the United States; he may require the Opinion, in writing, of the principal Officer in each of the executive Departments, upon any Subject relating to the Duties of their respective Offices, and he shall have Power to grant Reprieves and Pardons for Offences against the United States, except in Cases of Impeachment.

He shall have Power, by and with the Advice and Consent of the Senate, to make Treaties, provided two thirds of the Senators present concur; and he shall nominate, and by and with the Advice and Consent of the Senate, shall appoint Ambassadors, other public Ministers and Consuls, Judges of the supreme Court, and all other Officers of the United States, whose Appointments are not herein otherwise provided for, and which shall be established by Law; but the Congress may by Law vest the Appointment of such inferior Officers, as they think proper, in the President alone, in the Courts of Law, or in the Heads of Departments.

The President shall have Power to fill up all Vacancies that may happen during the Recess of the Senate, by granting Commissions which shall expire at the End of their next Session.

Section. 3. He shall from time to time give to the Congress Information of the State of the Union, and recommend to their Consideration such Measures as he shall judge necessary and expedient; he may, on extraordinary Occasions, convene both Houses, or either of them, and in Case of Disagreement between them, with Respect to the Time of Adjournment, he may adjourn them to such Time as he shall think proper; he shall receive Ambassadors and other public Ministers; he shall take Care that the Laws be faithfully executed, and shall Commission all the Officers of the United States.

Section. 4. The President, Vice President and all civil Officers of the United States, shall be removed from Office on Impeachment for, and Conviction of, Treason, Bribery, or other high Crimes and Misdemeanors.

ARTICLE. III.

Section. 1. The judicial Power of the United States, shall be vested in one supreme Court, and in such inferior Courts as the Congress may from time to time ordain and establish. The Judges, both of the supreme and inferior Courts, shall hold their Offices during good Behavior, and shall, at stated Times, receive for their Services, a Compensation, which shall not be diminished during their Continuance in Office.

Section. 2. The judicial Power shall extend to all Cases, in Law and Equity, arising under this Constitution, the Laws of the United States, and Treaties made, or which shall be made, under their Authority;—to all Cases affecting Ambassadors, other public Ministers and Consuls;—to all Cases of admiralty and maritime Jurisdiction;—the Controversies to which the United States shall be a Party;—to Controversies between two or more States;—between a State and Citizens of another State;—between Citizens of different States;—between Citizens of the same State claiming Lands under Grants of different States, and between a State, or the Citizens thereof, and foreign States, Citizens or Subjects.

In all cases affecting Ambassadors, other public Ministers and Consuls, and those in which a State shall be Party, the supreme Court shall have original Jurisdiction. In all the other Cases before mentioned, the supreme Court shall have appellate Jurisdiction, both as to Law and Fact, with such Exceptions, and under such Regulations as the Congress shall make.

The Trial of all Crimes, except in Cases of Impeachment, shall be by Jury; and such Trial shall be held in the State where the said Crimes shall have been committed; but when not committed within any State, the Trial shall be at such Place or Places as the Congress may by Law have directed.

Section. 3. Treason against the United States, shall consist only in levying War against them, or in adhering to their Enemies, giving them Aid and Comfort. No Person shall be convicted of Treason unless on the Testimony of two Witnesses to the same overt Act, or on Confession in open Court.

The Congress shall have Power to declare the Punishment of Treason, but no Attainder of Treason shall work Corruption of Blood, or Forfeiture except during the Life of the Person attainted.

ARTICLE. IV.

Section. 1. Full Faith and Credit shall be given in each State to the public Acts, Records, and judicial Proceedings of every other State. And the Congress may by general Laws prescribe the Manner in which such Acts, Records and Proceedings shall be proved, and the Effect thereof.

Section. 2. The Citizens of each State shall be entitled to all Privileges and Immunities of Citizens in the several States.

A Person charged in any State with Treason, Felony, or other Crime, who shall flee from Justice, and be found in another State, shall on Demand of the executive Authority of the State from which he fled, be delivered up, to be removed to the State having Jurisdiction of the Crime.

No Person held to Service or Labour in one State, under the Laws thereof, escaping into another, shall, in Consequence of any Law or Regulation therein, be discharged from such Service or Labour, but shall be delivered up on Claim of the Party to whom such Service or Labour may be due.

Section. 3. New States may be admitted by the Congress into this Union; but no new State shall be formed or erected within the Jurisdiction of any other State; nor any State be formed by the Junction of two or more States, or Parts of States, without the consent of the Legislatures of the States concerned as well as of the Congress.

The Congress shall have Power to dispose of and make all needful Rules and Regulations respecting the Territory or other Property belonging to the United States; and nothing in this Constitution shall be so construed as to Prejudice any Claims of the United States, or of any particular States.

Section. 4. The United States shall guarantee to every State in this Union a Republican Form of Government, and shall protect each of them against Invasion; and on Application of the Legislature, or of the Executive (when the Legislature cannot be convened) against domestic Violence.

ARTICLE. V.

The Congress, whenever two thirds of both Houses shall deem it necessary, shall propose Amendments to this Constitution, or, on the Application of the Legislatures of two thirds of the several States, shall call a Convention for proposing Amendments, which, in either Case, shall be valid to all Intents and Purposes, as Part of this Constitution, when ratified by the Legislatures of three fourths of the several States, or by Conventions in three fourths thereof, as the one or the other Mode of Ratification may be proposed by the Congress; Provided that no Amendment which may be made prior to the Year One thousand eight hundred and eight shall in any Manner affect the first and fourth Clauses in the Ninth Section of the first Article; and that no State, without its Consent, shall be deprived of its equal Suffrage in the Senate.

ARTICLE. VI.

All Debts contracted and Engagements entered into, before the Adoption of this Constitution, shall be as valid against the United States under this Constitution, as under the Confederation.

This Constitution, and the Laws of the United States which shall be made in Pursuance thereof; and all Treaties made, or which shall be made, under the Authority of the United States, shall be the supreme Law of the Land; and the Judges in every State shall be bound thereby, any Thing in the Constitution or Laws of any State to the Contrary notwithstanding.

The Senators and Representatives before mentioned, and the Members of the several State Legislatures, and all executive and judicial Officers, both of the United States and of the several States, shall be bound by Oath or Affirmation, to support this Constitution; but no religious Test shall ever be required as a Qualification to any Office or public Trust under the United States.

ARTICLE. VII.

The Ratification of the Conventions of nine States, shall be sufficient for the Establishment of this Constitution between the States so ratifying the Same.

Done in Convention by the Unanimous Consent of the States present the Seventeenth Day of September in the Year of our Lord one thousand seven hundred and Eighty seven and of the Independence of the United States of America the Twelfth. In witness thereof We have hereunto subscribed our Names,

G°. WASHINGTON—Presd[t].
and deputy from Virginia

NEW HAMPSHIRE
John Langdon
Nicholas Gilman

MASSACHUSETTS
Nathaniel Gorham
Rufus King

CONNECTICUT
W[m] Sam[l] Johnson
Roger Sherman

NEW YORK
Alexander Hamilton

NEW JERSEY
Wil: Livingston
David A. Brearley
W[m] Paterson
Jona: Dayton

PENNSYLVANIA
B Franklin
Thomas Mifflin
Rob[t] Morris
Geo. Clymer
Tho[s] FitzSimons
Jared Ingersoll
James Wilson
Gouv Morris

DELAWARE
Geo: Read
Gunning Bedford jun
John Dickinson
Richard Bassett
Jaco: Broom

MARYLAND
James M[c]Henry
Dan of S[t] Tho[s] Jenifer
Dan[l] Carroll

VIRGINIA
John Blair—
James Madison Jr.

NORTH CAROLINA
W[m] Blount
Rich[d] Dobbs Spaight
Hu Williamson

SOUTH CAROLINA
J. Rutledge
Charles Cotesworth Pinckney
Charles Pinckney
Pierce Butler

GEORGIA
William Few
Abr Baldwin

AMENDMENTS TO THE CONSTITUTION

Articles in addition to, and Amendment of the Constitution of the United States of America, proposed by Congress, and ratified by the Legislatures of the several States, pursuant to the fifth Article of the original Constitution.

AMENDMENT I.*

Congress shall make no law respecting an establishment of religion, or prohibiting the free exercise thereof; or abridging the freedom of speech, or of the press; or the right of the people peaceably to assemble, and to petition the Government for a redress of grievances.

AMENDMENT II.

A well regulated Militia, being necessary to the security of a free State, the right of the people to keep and bear Arms, shall not be infringed.

AMENDMENT III.

No Soldier shall, in time of peace be quartered in any house, without the consent of the Owner, nor in time of war, but in a manner to be prescribed by law.

AMENDMENT IV.

The right of the people to be secure in their persons, houses, papers, and effects, against unreasonable searches and seizures, shall not be violated, and no Warrants shall issue, but upon probable cause, supported by Oath or affirmation, and particularly describing the place to be searched, and the persons or things to be seized.

AMENDMENT V.

No person shall be held to answer for a capital, or otherwise infamous crime, unless on a presentment or indictment of a Grand Jury, except in cases arising in the land or naval forces, or in the Militia, when in actual service in time of War or public danger; nor shall any person be subject for the same offence to be twice put in jeopardy of life or limb; nor shall be compelled in any criminal case to be a witness against himself, nor be deprived of life, liberty, or property, without due process of law; nor shall private property be taken for public use, without just compensation.

AMENDMENT VI.

In all criminal prosecutions, the accused shall enjoy the right to a speedy and public trial, by an impartial jury of the State

and district wherein the crime shall have been committed, which district shall have been previously ascertained by law, and to be informed of the nature and cause of the accusation; to be confronted with the witnesses against him; to have compulsory process for obtaining witnesses in his favor, and to have the Assistance of Counsel for his defence.

AMENDMENT VII.

In Suits at common law, where the value in controversy shall exceed twenty dollars, the right of trial by jury shall be preserved, and no fact tried by a jury, shall be otherwise re-examined in any Court of the United States, than according to the rules of the common law.

AMENDMENT VIII.

Excessive bail shall not be required, nor excessive fines imposed, nor cruel and unusual punishments inflicted.

AMENDMENT IX.

The enumeration in the Constitution, of certain rights, shall not be construed to deny or disparage others retained by the people.

AMENDMENT X.

The powers not delegated to the United States by the Constitution, nor prohibited by it to the States, are reserved to the States respectively, or to the people.

AMENDMENT XI.

The Judicial power of the United States shall not be construed to extend to any suit in law or equity, commenced or prosecuted against one of the United States by Citizens of another State, or by Citizens or Subjects of any Foreign State. [January 8, 1798]

AMENDMENT XII.

The Electors shall meet in their respective states, and vote by ballot for President and Vice-President, one of whom, at least, shall not be an inhabitant of the same state with themselves; they shall name in their ballots the person voted for as President, and in distinct ballots the person voted for as Vice-President, and they shall make distinct lists of all persons voted for as President, and of all persons voted for as Vice President, and of the number of votes for each, which lists they shall sign and certify, and transmit sealed to the seat of the government of the United States, directed to the President of the Senate;—The President of the Senate shall, in the presence of the Senate and

*The first ten Amendments (the Bill of Rights) were ratified in 1791.

House of Representatives, open all the certificates and the votes shall then be counted;—The person having the greatest number of votes for President, shall be the President, if such number be a majority of the whole number of Electors appointed; and if no person have such majority, then from the persons having the highest numbers not exceeding three on the list of those voted for as President, the House of Representatives shall choose immediately, by ballot, the President. But in choosing the President, the votes shall be taken by states, the representation from each state having one vote; a quorum for this purpose shall consist of a member or members from two-thirds of the states, and a majority of all the states shall be necessary to a choice. And if the House of Representatives shall not choose a President whenever the right of choice shall devolve upon them, before the fourth day of March next following, then the Vice-President shall act as President, as in the case of the death or other constitutional disability of the President.—The person having the greatest number of votes as Vice-President, shall be the Vice-President, if such number be a majority of the whole number of Electors appointed, and if no person have a majority, then from the two highest numbers on the list, the Senate shall choose the Vice-President; a quorum for the purpose shall consist of two-thirds of the whole number of Senators, and a majority of the whole number shall be necessary to a choice. But no person constitutionally ineligible to the office of President shall be eligible to that of Vice-President of the United States. [September 25, 1804]

Amendment XIII.

Section 1. Neither slavery nor involuntary servitude, except as a punishment for crime whereof the party shall have been duly convicted, shall exist within the United States, or any place subject to their jurisdiction.

Section 2. Congress shall have power to enforce this article by appropriate legislation. [December 18, 1865]

Amendment XIV.

Section 1. All persons born or naturalized in the United States, and subject to the jurisdiction thereof, are citizens of the United States and of the State wherein they reside. No State shall make or enforce any law which shall abridge the privileges or immunities of citizens of the United States; nor shall any State deprive any person of life, liberty, or property, without due process of law; nor deny to any person within its jurisdiction the equal protection of the laws.

Section 2. Representatives shall be apportioned among the several States according to their respective numbers, counting the whole number of persons in each State, excluding Indians not taxed. But when the right to vote at any election for the choice of electors for President and Vice President of the United States, Representatives in Congress, the Executive and Judicial officers of a State, or the members of the Legislature thereof, is denied to any of the male inhabitants of such State, being twenty-one years of age, and citizens of the United States, or in any way abridged, except for participation in rebellion, or other crime, the basis of representation therein shall be reduced in the proportion which the number of such male citizens shall bear to the whole number of male citizens twenty-one years of age in such State.

Section 3. No person shall be a Senator or Representative in Congress, or elector of President and Vice President, or hold any office, civil or military, under the United States, or under any State, who, having previously taken an oath, as a member of Congress, or as an officer of the United States, or as a member of any State legislature, or as an executive or judicial officer of any State, to support the Constitution of the United States, shall have engaged in insurrection or rebellion against the same, or given aid or comfort to the enemies thereof. But Congress may by a vote of two-thirds of each House, remove such disability.

Section 4. The validity of the public debt of the United States, authorized by law, including debts incurred for payment of pensions and bounties for services in suppressing insurrection or rebellion, shall not be questioned. But neither the United States nor any State shall assume or pay any debt or obligation incurred in aid of insurrection or rebellion against the United States, or any claim for the loss or emancipation of any slave; but all such debts, obligations and claims shall be held illegal and void.

Section 5. The Congress shall have power to enforce, by appropriate legislation, the provisions of this article. [July 28, 1868]

Amendment XV.

Section 1. The right of citizens of the United States to vote shall not be denied or abridged by the United States or by any State on account of race, color, or previous condition of servitude—

Section 2. The Congress shall have power to enforce this article by appropriate legislation. [March 30, 1870]

Amendment XVI.

The Congress shall have power to lay and collect taxes on incomes, from whatever source derived, without apportionment among the several States, and without regard to any census or enumeration. [February 25, 1913]

Amendment XVII.

The Senate of the United States shall be composed of two senators from each State, elected by the people thereof, for six years; and each Senator shall have one vote. The electors in each State shall have the qualifications requisite for electors of the most numerous branch of the State legislatures.

When vacancies happen in the representation of any State in the Senate, the executive authority of such State shall issue writs of election to fill such vacancies: *Provided,* That the legislature of any State may empower the executive thereof to make temporary appointments until the people fill the vacancies by election as the legislature may direct.

This amendment shall not be so construed as to affect the election or term of any senator chosen before it becomes valid as part of the Constitution. [May 31, 1913]

AMENDMENT XVIII.

After one year from the ratification of this article, the manufacture, sale, or transportation of intoxicating liquors within, the importation thereof into, or the exportation thereof from the United States and all territory subject to the jurisdiction thereof for beverage purposes is hereby prohibited.

The Congress and the several States shall have concurrent power to enforce this article by appropriate legislation.

This article shall be inoperative unless it shall have been ratified as an amendment to the Constitution by the legislatures of the several States, as provided in the Constitution, within seven years from the date of the submission thereof to States by Congress. [January 29, 1919]

AMENDMENT XIX.

The right of citizens of the United States to vote shall not be denied or abridged by the United States or by any State on account of sex.

The Congress shall have power by appropriate legislation to enforce the provisions of this article. [August 26, 1920]

AMENDMENT XX.

Section 1. The terms of the President and Vice-President shall end at noon on the twentieth day of January, and the terms of Senators and Representatives at noon on the third day of January, of the years in which such terms would have ended if this article had not been ratified; and the terms of their successors shall then begin.

Section 2. The Congress shall assemble at least once in every year, and such meeting shall begin at noon on the third day of January, unless they shall by law appoint a different day.

Section 3. If, at the time fixed for the beginning of the term of the President, the President-elect shall have died, the Vice-President-elect shall become President. If a President shall not have been chosen before the time fixed for the beginning of his term, or if the President-elect shall have failed to qualify,

then the Vice-President-elect shall act as President until a President shall have qualified; and the Congress may by law provide for the case wherein neither a President-elect nor a Vice-President-elect shall have qualified, declaring who shall then act as President, or the manner in which one who is to act shall be selected, and such person shall act accordingly until a President or Vice-President shall have qualified.

Section 4. The Congress may by law provide for the case of the death of any of the persons from whom the House of Representatives may choose a President whenever the right of choice shall have devolved upon them, and for the case of the death of any of the persons from whom the Senate may choose a Vice-President whenever the right of choice shall have devolved upon them.

Section 5. Sections 1 and 2 shall take effect on the 15th day of October following the ratification of this article.

Section 6. This article shall be inoperative unless it shall have been ratified as an amendment to the Constitution by the legislatures of three-fourths of the several States within seven years from the date of its submission. [February 6, 1933]

AMENDMENT XXI.

Section 1. The eighteenth article of amendment to the Constitution of the United States is hereby repealed.

Section 2. The transportation or importation into any State, Territory or possession of the United States for delivery or use therein of intoxicating liquors, in violation of the laws thereof, is hereby prohibited.

Section 3. This article shall be inoperative unless it shall have been ratified as an amendment to the Constitution by convention in the several States, as provided in the Constitution, within seven years from the date of the submission thereof to the States by the Congress. [December 5, 1933]

AMENDMENT XXII.

Section 1. No person shall be elected to the office of the President more than twice, and no person who has held the office of President, or acted as President, for more than two years of a term to which some other person was elected President shall be elected to the office of the President more than once. But this Article shall not apply to any person holding the office of President when this Article was proposed by the Congress, and shall not prevent any person who may be holding the office of President, or acting as President, during the term within which this Article becomes operative from holding the office of President or acting as President during the remainder of such term.

Section 2. This article shall be inoperative unless it shall have been ratified as an amendment to the Constitution by the legislatures of three-fourths of the several States within seven years from the date of its submission to the States by the Congress. [February 27, 1951]

AMENDMENT XXIII.

Section 1. The District constituting the seat of government of the United States shall appoint in such manner as the Congress may direct:

A number of electors of President and Vice-President equal to the whole number of Senators and Representatives in Congress to which the District would be entitled if it were a State, but in no event more than the least populous State; they shall be in addition to those appointed by the States, but they shall be considered, for the purposes of the election of President and Vice-President, to be electors appointed by a State; and they shall meet in the District and perform such duties as provided by the twelfth article of amendment.

Section 2. The Congress shall have the power to enforce this article by appropriate legislation. [March 29, 1961]

AMENDMENT XXIV.

Section 1. The right of citizens of the United States to vote in any primary or other election for President or Vice President, for electors for President or Vice President, or for Senator or Representative in Congress, shall not be denied or abridged by the United States or any State by reason of failure to pay any poll tax or other tax.

Section 2. The Congress shall have power to enforce this article by appropriate legislation. [January 23, 1964]

AMENDMENT XXV.

Section 1. In case of the removal of the President from office or of his death or resignation, the Vice President shall become President.

Section 2. Whenever there is a vacancy in the office of Vice President, the President shall nominate a Vice President who shall take office upon confirmation by a majority vote of both Houses of Congress.

Section 3. Whenever the President transmits to the President pro tempore of the Senate and the Speaker of the House of Representatives his written declaration that he is unable to discharge the powers and duties of his office, and until he transmits to them a written declaration to the contrary, such powers and duties shall be discharged by the Vice President as Acting President.

Section 4. Whenever the Vice President and a majority of either the principal officers of the executive departments or of such other body as Congress may by law provide, transmit to the President pro tempore of the Senate and the Speaker of the House of Representatives their written declaration that the President is unable to discharge the powers and duties of his office, the Vice President shall immediately assume the powers and duties of the office as Acting President.

Thereafter, when the President transmits to the President pro tempore of the Senate and the Speaker of the House of Representatives his written declaration that no inability exists, he shall resume the powers and duties of his office unless the Vice President and a majority of either the principal officers of the executive departments or of such other body as Congress may by law provide, transmit within four days to the President pro tempore of the Senate and the Speaker of the House of Representatives their written declaration that the President is unable to discharge the powers and duties of his office. Thereupon Congress shall decide the issue, assembling within forty-eight hours for that purpose if not in session. If the Congress, within twenty-one days after receipt of the latter written declaration, or, if Congress is not in session, within twenty-one days after Congress is required to assemble, determines by two-thirds vote of both Houses that the President is unable to discharge the powers and duties of his office, the Vice President shall continue to discharge the same as Acting President; otherwise, the President shall resume the powers and duties of his office. [February 10, 1967]

AMENDMENT XXVI.

Section 1. The right of citizens of the United States, who are eighteen years of age or older, to vote shall not be denied or abridged by the United States or by any State on account of age.

Section 2. The Congress shall have power to enforce this article by appropriate legislation. [June 30, 1971]

AMENDMENT XXVII.

No law, varying the compensation for the services of the Senators and Representatives shall take effect, until an election of Representatives shall have intervened. [May 8, 1992]

FROM George Washington's Farewell Address (1796)

Friends and Citizens:

The period for a new election of a citizen to administer the executive government of the United States being not far distant, and the time actually arrived when your thoughts must be employed in designating the person who is to be clothed with that important trust, it appears to me proper, especially as it may conduce to a more distinct expression of the public voice, that I should now apprise you of the resolution I have formed, to decline being considered among the number of those out of whom a choice is to be made.

* * *

In looking forward to the moment which is intended to terminate the career of my public life, my feelings do not permit me to suspend the deep acknowledgment of that debt of gratitude which I owe to my beloved country for the many honors it has conferred upon me; still more for the steadfast confidence with which it has supported me; and for the opportunities I have thence enjoyed of manifesting my inviolable attachment, by services faithful and persevering, though in usefulness unequal to my zeal. If benefits have resulted to our country from these services, let it always be remembered to your praise, and as an instructive example in our annals, that under circumstances in which the passions, agitated in every direction, were liable to mislead, amidst appearances sometimes dubious, vicissitudes of fortune often discouraging, in situations in which not unfrequently want of success has countenanced the spirit of criticism, the constancy of your support was the essential prop of the efforts, and a guarantee of the plans by which they were effected. Profoundly penetrated with this idea, I shall carry it with me to my grave, as a strong incitement to unceasing vows that heaven may continue to you the choicest tokens of its beneficence; that your union and brotherly affection may be perpetual; that the free Constitution, which is the work of your hands, may be sacredly maintained; that its administration in every department may be stamped with wisdom and virtue; that, in fine, the happiness of the people of these States, under the auspices of liberty, may be made complete by so careful a preservation and so prudent a use of this blessing as will acquire to them the glory of recommending it to the applause, the affection, and adoption of every nation which is yet a stranger to it.

Here, perhaps, I ought to stop. But a solicitude for your welfare, which cannot end but with my life, and the apprehension of danger, natural to that solicitude, urge me, on an occasion like the present, to offer to your solemn contemplation, and to recommend to your frequent review, some sentiments which are the result of much reflection, of no inconsiderable observation, and which appear to me all-important to the permanency of your felicity as a people. These will be offered to you with the more freedom, as you can only see in them the disinterested warnings of a parting friend, who can possibly have no personal motive to bias his counsel. Nor can I forget, as an encouragement to it, your indulgent reception of my sentiments on a former and not dissimilar occasion.

Interwoven as is the love of liberty with every ligament of your hearts, no recommendation of mine is necessary to fortify or confirm the attachment.

The unity of government which constitutes you one people is also now dear to you. It is justly so, for it is a main pillar in the edifice of your real independence, the support of your tranquility at home, your peace abroad; of your safety; of your prosperity; of that very liberty which you so highly prize. But as it is easy to foresee that, from different causes and from different quarters, much pains will be taken, many artifices employed to weaken in your minds the conviction of this truth; as this is the point in your political fortress against which the batteries of internal and external enemies will be most constantly and actively (though often covertly and insidiously) directed, it is of infinite moment that you should properly estimate the immense value of your national union to your collective and individual happiness; that you should cherish a cordial, habitual, and immovable attachment to it; accustoming yourselves to think and speak of it as of the palladium of your political safety and prosperity; watching for its preservation with jealous anxiety; discountenancing whatever may suggest even a suspicion that it can in any event be abandoned; and indignantly frowning upon the first dawning of every attempt to alienate any portion of our country from the rest, or to enfeeble the sacred ties which now link together the various parts.

For this you have every inducement of sympathy and interest. Citizens, by birth or choice, of a common country, that country has a right to concentrate your affections. The name of American, which belongs to you in your national capacity, must always exalt the just pride of patriotism more than any appellation derived from local discriminations. With slight shades of difference, you have the same religion, manners, habits, and political principles. You have in a common cause fought and triumphed together; the independence and liberty you possess are the work of joint counsels, and joint efforts of common dangers, sufferings, and successes.

But these considerations, however powerfully they address themselves to your sensibility, are greatly outweighed by those which apply more immediately to your interest. Here every portion of our country finds the most commanding motives for carefully guarding and preserving the union of the whole.

The North, in an unrestrained intercourse with the South, protected by the equal laws of a common government, finds in the productions of the latter great additional resources of maritime and commercial enterprise and precious materials of manufacturing industry. The South, in the same intercourse, benefiting by the agency of the North, sees its agriculture grow and its commerce expand. Turning partly into its own channels the seamen of the North, it finds its particular navigation invigorated; and, while it contributes, in different ways, to nourish and increase the general mass of the national navigation, it looks forward to the protection of a maritime strength, to which itself is unequally adapted. The East, in a like intercourse with the West, already finds, and in the progressive improvement of interior communications by land and water, will more and more find a valuable vent for the commodities which it brings from abroad, or manufactures at home. The West derives from the East supplies requisite to its growth and comfort, and, what is perhaps of still greater consequence, it must of necessity owe the secure enjoyment of indispensable outlets for its own productions to the weight, influence, and the future maritime strength of the Atlantic side of the Union, directed by an indissoluble community of interest as one nation. Any other tenure by which the West can hold this essential advantage, whether derived from its own separate strength, or from an apostate and unnatural connection with any foreign power, must be intrinsically precarious.

While, then, every part of our country thus feels an immediate and particular interest in union, all the parts combined cannot fail to find in the united mass of means and efforts greater strength, greater resource, proportionably greater security from external danger, a less frequent interruption of their peace by foreign nations; and, what is of inestimable value, they must derive from union an exemption from those broils and wars between themselves, which so frequently afflict neighboring countries not tied together by the same governments, which their own rival ships alone would be sufficient to produce, but which opposite foreign alliances, attachments, and intrigues would stimulate and embitter. Hence, likewise, they will avoid the necessity of those overgrown military establishments which, under any form of government, are inauspicious to liberty, and which are to be regarded as particularly hostile to republican liberty. In this sense it is that your union ought to be considered as a main prop of your liberty, and that the love of the one ought to endear to you the preservation of the other.

These considerations speak a persuasive language to every reflecting and virtuous mind, and exhibit the continuance of the Union as a primary object of patriotic desire. Is there a doubt whether a common government can embrace so large a sphere? Let experience solve it. To listen to mere speculation in such a case were criminal. We are authorized to hope that a proper organization of the whole with the auxiliary agency of governments for the respective subdivisions, will afford a happy issue to the experiment. It is well worth a fair and full experiment. With such powerful and obvious motives to union, affecting all parts of our country, while experience

shall not have demonstrated its impracticability, there will always be reason to distrust the patriotism of those who in any quarter may endeavor to weaken its bands.

* * *

To the efficacy and permanency of your Union, a government for the whole is indispensable. No alliance, however strict, between the parts can be an adequate substitute; they must inevitably experience the infractions and interruptions which all alliances in all times have experienced. Sensible of this momentous truth, you have improved upon your first essay, by the adoption of a constitution of government better calculated than your former for an intimate union, and for the efficacious management of your common concerns. This government, the offspring of our own choice, uninfluenced and unawed, adopted upon full investigation and mature deliberation, completely free in its principles, in the distribution of its powers, uniting security with energy, and containing within itself a provision for its own amendment, has a just claim to your confidence and your support. Respect for its authority, compliance with its laws, acquiescence in its measures, are duties enjoined by the fundamental maxims of true liberty. The basis of our political systems is the right of the people to make and to alter their constitutions of government. But the Constitution which at any time exists, till changed by an explicit and authentic act of the whole people, is sacredly obligatory upon all. The very idea of the power and the right of the people to establish government presupposes the duty of every individual to obey the established government.

* * *

I have already intimated to you the danger of parties in the State, with particular reference to the founding of them on geographical discriminations. Let me now take a more comprehensive view, and warn you in the most solemn manner against the baneful effects of the spirit of party generally.

This spirit, unfortunately, is inseparable from our nature, having its root in the strongest passions of the human mind. It exists under different shapes in all governments, more or less stifled, controlled, or repressed; but, in those of the popular form, it is seen in its greatest rankness, and is truly their worst enemy.

The alternate domination of one faction over another, sharpened by the spirit of revenge, natural to party dissension, which in different ages and countries has perpetrated the most horrid enormities, is itself a frightful despotism. But this leads at length to a more formal and permanent despotism. The disorders and miseries which result gradually incline the minds of men to seek security and repose in the absolute power of an individual; and sooner or later the chief of some prevailing faction, more able or more fortunate than his competitors, turns this disposition to the purposes of his own elevation, on the ruins of public liberty.

Without looking forward to an extremity of this kind (which nevertheless ought not to be entirely out of sight), the common and continual mischiefs of the spirit of party are sufficient to make it the interest and duty of a wise people to discourage and restrain it.

It serves always to distract the public councils and enfeeble the public administration. It agitates the community with ill-founded jealousies and false alarms, kindles the animosity of one part against another, foments occasionally riot and insurrection. It opens the door to foreign influence and corruption, which finds a facilitated access to the government itself through the channels of party passions. Thus the policy and the will of one country are subjected to the policy and will of another.

There is an opinion that parties in free countries are useful checks upon the administration of the government and serve to keep alive the spirit of liberty. This within certain limits is probably true; and in governments of a monarchical cast, patriotism may look with indulgence, if not with favor, upon the spirit of party. But in those of the popular character, in governments purely elective, it is a spirit not to be encouraged. From their natural tendency, it is certain there will always be enough of that spirit for every salutary purpose. And there being constant danger of excess, the effort ought to be by force of public opinion, to mitigate and assuage it. A fire not to be quenched, it demands a uniform vigilance to prevent its bursting into a flame, lest, instead of warming, it should consume.

It is important, likewise, that the habits of thinking in a free country should inspire caution in those entrusted with its administration, to confine themselves within their respective constitutional spheres, avoiding in the exercise of the powers of one department to encroach upon another. The spirit of encroachment tends to consolidate the powers of all the departments in one, and thus to create, whatever the form of government, a real despotism. A just estimate of that love of power, and proneness to abuse it, which predominates in the human heart, is sufficient to satisfy us of the truth of this position. The necessity of reciprocal checks in the exercise of political power, by dividing and distributing it into different depositaries, and constituting each the guardian of the public weal against invasions by the others, has been evinced by experiments ancient and modern; some of them in our country and under our own eyes. To preserve them must be as necessary as to institute them. If, in the opinion of the people, the distribution or modification of the constitutional powers be in any particular wrong, let it be corrected by an amendment in the way which the Constitution designates. But let there be no change by usurpation; for though this, in one instance, may be the instrument of good, it is the customary weapon by which free governments are destroyed. The precedent must always greatly overbalance in permanent evil any partial or transient benefit, which the use can at any time yield.

* * *

Observe good faith and justice towards all nations; cultivate peace and harmony with all. Religion and morality enjoin this conduct; and can it be, that good policy does not equally enjoin it? It will be worthy of a free, enlightened, and at no distant period, a great nation, to give to mankind the magnanimous and too novel example of a people always guided by an exalted justice and benevolence. Who can doubt that, in the course of time and things, the fruits of such a plan would richly repay any temporary advantages which might be lost by a steady adherence to it? Can it be that Providence has not connected the permanent felicity of a nation with its virtue? The experiment, at least, is recommended by every sentiment which ennobles human nature. Alas! is it rendered impossible by its vices?

In the execution of such a plan, nothing is more essential than that permanent, inveterate antipathies against particular nations, and passionate attachments for others, should be excluded; and that, in place of them, just and amicable feelings towards all should be cultivated. The nation which indulges towards another a habitual hatred or a habitual fondness is in some degree a slave. It is a slave to its animosity or to its affection, either of which is sufficient to lead it astray from its duty and its interest. Antipathy in one nation against another disposes each more readily to offer insult and injury, to lay hold of slight causes of umbrage, and to be haughty and intractable, when accidental or trifling occasions of dispute occur. Hence, frequent collisions, obstinate, envenomed, and bloody contests. The nation, prompted by ill-will and resentment, sometimes impels to war the government, contrary to the best calculations of policy. The government sometimes participates in the national propensity, and adopts through passion what reason would reject; at other times it makes the animosity of the nation subservient to projects of hostility instigated by pride, ambition, and other sinister and pernicious motives. The peace often, sometimes perhaps the liberty, of nations, has been the victim.

* * *

The great rule of conduct for us in regard to foreign nations is in extending our commercial relations, to have with them as little political connection as possible. So far as we have already formed engagements, let them be fulfilled with perfect good faith. Here let us stop. Europe has a set of primary interests which to us have none; or a very remote relation. Hence she must be engaged in frequent controversies, the causes of which are essentially foreign to our concerns. Hence, therefore, it must be unwise in us to implicate ourselves by artificial ties in the ordinary vicissitudes of her politics, or the ordinary combinations and collisions of her friendships or enmities.

Our detached and distant situation invites and enables us to pursue a different course. If we remain one people under an efficient government, the period is not far off when we may defy material injury from external annoyance; when we may take such an attitude as will cause the neutrality we may at any time resolve upon to be scrupulously respected; when belligerent nations, under the impossibility of making acquisitions upon us, will not lightly hazard the giving us provocation; when we may choose peace or war, as our interest, guided by justice, shall counsel.

Why forego the advantages of so peculiar a situation? Why quit our own to stand upon foreign ground? Why, by interweaving our destiny with that of any part of Europe, entangle our peace and prosperity in the toils of European ambition, rivalship, interest, humor or caprice?

It is our true policy to steer clear of permanent alliances with any portion of the foreign world; so far, I mean, as we are now at liberty to do it; for let me not be understood as capable of patronizing infidelity to existing engagements. I hold the maxim no less applicable to public than to private affairs, that honesty is always the best policy. I repeat it, therefore, let those engagements be observed in their genuine sense. But, in my opinion, it is unnecessary and would be unwise to extend them.

Taking care always to keep ourselves by suitable establishments on a respectable defensive posture, we may safely trust to temporary alliances for extraordinary emergencies.

Harmony, liberal intercourse with all nations, are recommended by policy, humanity, and interest. But even our commercial policy should hold an equal and impartial hand; neither seeking nor granting exclusive favors or preferences; consulting the natural course of things; diffusing and diversifying by gentle means the streams of commerce, but forcing nothing; establishing (with powers so disposed, in order to give trade a stable course, to define the rights of our merchants, and to enable the government to support them) conventional rules of intercourse, the best that present circumstances and mutual opinion will permit, but temporary, and liable to be from time to time abandoned or varied, as experience and circumstances shall dictate; constantly keeping in view that it is folly in one nation to look for disinterested favors from another; that it must pay with a portion of its independence for whatever it may accept under that character; that, by such acceptance, it may place itself in the condition of having given equivalents for nominal favors, and yet of being reproached with ingratitude for not giving more.

* * *

Relying on its kindness in this as in other things, and actuated by that fervent love towards it, which is so natural to a man who views in it the native soil of himself and his progenitors for several generations, I anticipate with pleasing expectation that retreat in which I promise myself to realize, without alloy, the sweet enjoyment of partaking, in the midst of my fellow-citizens, the benign influence of good laws under a free government, the ever-favorite object of my heart, and the happy reward, as I trust, of our mutual cares, labors, and dangers.

Geo. Washington

The Seneca Falls Declaration of Sentiments and Resolutions (1848)

1. Declaration of Sentiments

When, in the course of human events, it becomes necessary for one portion of the family of man to assume among the people of the earth a position different from that which they have hitherto occupied, but one to which the laws of nature and of nature's God entitle them, a decent respect to the opinions of mankind requires that they should declare the causes that impel them to such a course.

We hold these truths to be self-evident: that all men and women are created equal; that they are endowed by their Creator with certain inalienable rights; that among these are life, liberty, and the pursuit of happiness; that to secure these rights governments are instituted, deriving their just powers from the consent of the governed. Whenever any form of government becomes destructive of these ends, it is the right of those who suffer from it to refuse allegiance to it, and to insist upon the institution of a new government, laying its foundation on such principles, and organizing its powers in such form, as to them shall seem most likely to effect their safety and happiness. Prudence, indeed, will dictate that governments long established should not be changed for light and transient causes; and accordingly all experience hath shown that mankind are more disposed to suffer, while evils are sufferable, than to right themselves by abolishing the forms to which they are accustomed. But when a long train of abuses and usurpations, pursuing invariably the same object, evinces a design to reduce them under absolute despotism, it is their duty to throw off such government, and to provide new guards for their future security. Such has been the patient sufferance of the women under this government, and such is now the necessity which constrains them to demand the equal station to which they are entitled. The history of mankind is a history of repeated injuries and usurpations on the part of man toward woman, having in direct object the establishment of an absolute tyranny over her. To prove this, let facts be submitted to a candid world.

He has never permitted her to exercise her inalienable right to the elective franchise.

He has compelled her to submit to laws, in the formation of which she had no voice.

He has withheld from her rights which are given to the most ignorant and degraded men—both natives and foreigners.

Having deprived her of this first right of a citizen, the elective franchise, thereby leaving her without representation in the halls of legislation, he has oppressed her on all sides.

He has made her, if married, in the eye of the law, civilly dead. He has taken from her all right in property, even to the wages she earns.

He has made her, morally, an irresponsible being, as she can commit many crimes with impunity, provided they be done in the presence of her husband.

In the covenant of marriage, she is compelled to promise obedience to her husband, he becoming, to all intents and purposes, her master—the law giving him power to deprive her of her liberty, and to administer chastisement.

He has so framed the laws of divorce, as to what shall be the proper causes, and in case of separation, to whom the guardianship of the children shall be given, as to be wholly regardless of the happiness of women—the law, in all cases, going upon a false supposition of the supremacy of man, and giving all power into his hands.

After depriving her of all rights as a married woman, if single, and the owner of property, he has taxed her to support a government which recognizes her only when her property can be made profitable to it.

He has monopolized nearly all the profitable employments, and from those she is permitted to follow, she receives but a scanty remuneration. He closes against her all the avenues to wealth and distinction which he considers most honorable to himself. As a teacher of theology, medicine, or law, she is not known.

He has denied her the facilities for obtaining a thorough education, all colleges being closed against her.

He allows her in Church, as well as State, but a subordinate position, claiming Apostolic authority for her exclusion from the ministry, and, with some exceptions, from any public participation in the affairs of the Church.

He has created a false public sentiment by giving to the world a different code of morals for men and women, by which moral delinquencies which exclude women from society, are not only tolerated, but deemed of little account in man.

He has usurped the prerogative of Jehovah himself, claiming it as his right to assign for her a sphere of action, when that belongs to her conscience and to her God.

He has endeavored, in every way that he could, to destroy her confidence in her own powers, to lessen her self-respect and to make her willing to lead a dependent and abject life.

Now, in view of this entire disfranchisement of one-half the people of this country, their social and religious degradation—in view of the unjust laws above mentioned, and because women do feel themselves aggrieved, oppressed, and fraudulently deprived of their most sacred rights, we insist that they have immediate admission to all the rights and privileges which belong to them as citizens of the United States.

In entering upon the great work before us, we anticipate no small amount of misconception, misrepresentation, and ridicule; but we shall use every instrumentality within our power to effect our object. We shall employ agents, circulate tracts, petition the State and National legislatures, and endeavor to enlist the pulpit and the press in our behalf. We hope this Convention will be followed by a series of Conventions embracing every part of the country.

2. RESOLUTIONS

WHEREAS, The great precept of nature is conceded to be, that "man shall pursue his own true and substantial happiness." Blackstone in his Commentaries remarks, that this law of Nature being coeval with mankind, and dictated by God himself, is of course superior in obligation to any other. It is binding over all the globe, in all countries and at all times; no human laws are of any validity if contrary to this, and such of them as are valid, derive all their force, and all their validity, and all their authority, mediately and immediately, from this original; therefore,

Resolved, That such laws as conflict, in any way, with the true and substantial happiness of woman, are contrary to the great precept of nature and of no validity, for this is "superior in obligation to any other."

Resolved, That all laws which prevent woman from occupying such a station in society as her conscience shall dictate, or which place her in a position inferior to that of man, are contrary to the great precept of nature, and therefore of no force or authority.

Resolved, That woman is man's equal—was intended to be so by the Creator, and the highest good of the race demands that she should be recognized as such.

Resolved, That the women of this country ought to be enlightened in regard to the laws under which they live, that they may no longer publish their degradation by declaring themselves satisfied with their present position, nor their ignorance, by asserting that they have all the rights they want.

Resolved, That inasmuch as man, while claiming for himself intellectual superiority, does accord to woman moral superiority, it is pre-eminently his duty to encourage her to speak and teach, as she has an opportunity, in all religious assemblies.

Resolved, That the same amount of virtue, delicacy, and refinement of behavior that is required of woman in the social state, should also be required of man, and the same transgressions should be visited with equal severity on both man and woman.

Resolved, That the objection of indelicacy and impropriety, which is so often brought against woman when she addresses a public audience, comes with a very ill-grace from those who encourage, by their attendance, her appearance on the stage, in the concert. Or in feats of the circus.

Resolved, That woman has too long rested satisfied in the circumscribed limits which corrupt customs and a perverted application of the Scriptures have marked out for her, and that it is time she should move in the enlarged sphere which her great Creator has assigned her.

Resolved, That it is the duty of the women of this country to secure to themselves their sacred right to the elective franchise.

Resolved, That the equality of human rights results necessarily from the fact of the identity of the race in capabilities and responsibilities.

Resolved, therefore, That, being invested by the Creator with the same capabilities, and the same consciousness of responsibility for their exercise, it is demonstrably the right and duty of woman, equally with man, to promote every righteous cause by every righteous means; and especially in regard to the great subjects of morals and religion, it is self-evidently her right to participate with her brother in teaching them, both in private and in public, by writing and by speaking, by any instrumentalities proper to be used, and in any assemblies proper to be held; and this being a self-evident truth growing out of the divinely implanted principles of human nature, any custom or authority adverse to it, whether modern or wearing the hoary sanction of antiquity, is to be regarded as a self-evident falsehood, and at war with mankind.

Resolved, That the speedy success of our cause depends upon the zealous and untiring efforts of both men and women, for the overthrow of the monopoly of the pulpit, and for the securing to women an equal participation with men in the various trades, professions, and commerce.

FROM FREDERICK DOUGLASS'S "WHAT, TO THE SLAVE, IS THE FOURTH OF JULY?" SPEECH (1852)

* * *

This, for the purpose of this celebration, is the Fourth of July. It is the birthday of your National Independence, and of your political freedom. This, to you, is what the Passover was to the emancipated people of God. It carries your minds back to the day, and to the act of your great deliverance; and to the signs and to the wonders associated with that act and that day. This celebration also marks the beginning of another year of your national life; and reminds you that the Republic of America is now seventy-six years old. I am glad, fellow citizens, that your nation is so young. Seventy-six years, though a good old age for a man, is but a mere speck in the life of a nation. Three score years and ten is the allotted time for individual men; but nations number their years by thousands. According to this fact, you are, even now, only in the beginning of your national career, still lingering in the period of childhood. I repeat, I am glad this is so. There is hope in the thought, and hope is much needed, under the dark clouds which lower above the horizon. The eye of the reformer is met with angry flashes, portending disastrous times; but his heart may well beat lighter at the thought that America is young, and that she is still in the impressible stage of her existence. May he not hope that high lessons of wisdom, of justice and of truth, will yet give direction to her destiny? Were the nation older, the patriot's heart might be sadder and the reformer's brow heavier. Its future might be shrouded in gloom and the hope of its prophets go out in sorrow. There is consolation in the thought that America is young. Great streams are not easily turned from channels worn deep in the course of ages. They may sometimes rise in quiet and stately majesty, and inundate the land, refreshing and fertilizing the earth with their mysterious properties. They may also rise in wrath and fury, and bear away on their angry waves the accumulated wealth of years of toil and hardship. They, however, gradually flow back to the same old channel and flow on as serenely as ever. But, while the river may not be turned aside, it may dry up and leave nothing behind but the withered branch and the unsightly rock, to howl in the abyss-sweeping wind, the sad tale of departed glory. As with rivers, so with nations.

Fellow citizens, I shall not presume to dwell at length on the associations that cluster about this day. The simple story of it is, that seventy-six years ago the people of this country were British subjects. The style and title of your "sovereign people" (in which you now glory) was not then born. You were under the British Crown. Your fathers esteemed the English government as the home government, and England as the fatherland. This home government, you know, although a considerable distance from your home, did, in the exercise of its parental prerogatives, impose upon its colonial children such restraints, burdens and limitations as, in its mature judgment, it deemed wise, right and proper.

* * *

Feeling themselves harshly and unjustly treated by the home government, your fathers, like men of honesty and men of spirit, earnestly sought redress. They petitioned and remonstrated, they did so in a decorous, respectful and loyal manner. Their conduct was wholly unexceptionable. This, however, did not answer the purpose. They saw themselves treated with sovereign indifference, coldness and scorn. Yet they persevered. They were not the men to look back.

* * *

Citizens, your fathers . . . succeeded; and today you reap the fruits of their success. The freedom gained is yours; and you, therefore, may properly celebrate this anniversary. The Fourth of July is the first great fact in your nation's history—the very ringbolt in the chain of your yet undeveloped destiny.

Pride and patriotism, not less than gratitude, prompt you to celebrate and to hold it in perpetual remembrance. I have said that the Declaration of Independence is the ringbolt to the chain of your nation's destiny; so, indeed, I regard it. The principles contained in that instrument are saving principles. Stand by those principles, be true to them on all occasions, in all places, against all foes, and at whatever cost.

* * *

[The fathers of this republic] were peace men, but they preferred revolution to peaceful submission to bondage. They were quiet men; but they did not shrink from agitating against oppression. They showed forbearance, but that they knew its limits. They believed in order, but not in the order of tyranny. With them, nothing was "settled" that was not right. With them, justice, liberty and humanity were "final," not slavery and oppression. You may well cherish the memory of such men. They were great in their day and generation. Their solid manhood stands out the more as we contrast it with these degenerate times.

* * *

Fellow citizens, pardon me, allow me to ask, why am I called upon to speak here today? What have I, or those I represent, to do with your national independence? Are the great principles of political freedom and of natural justice, embodied in that Declaration of Independence, extended to us? and am I, therefore, called upon to bring our humble offering to the national altar and to confess the benefits and express devout gratitude for the blessings resulting from your independence to us?

* * *

But such is not the state of the case. I say it with a sad sense of the disparity between us. I am not included within the pale of this glorious anniversary! Your high independence only reveals the immeasurable distance between us. The blessings in which you, this day, rejoice, are not enjoyed in common. The rich inheritance of justice, liberty, prosperity and independence, bequeathed by your fathers, is shared by you, not by me. The sunlight that brought light and healing to you, has brought stripes and death to me. This Fourth of July is *yours*, not *mine*. *You* may rejoice, *I* must mourn.

* * *

Fellow citizens, above your national, tumultuous joy I hear the mournful wail of millions! whose chains, heavy and grievous yesterday, are today rendered more intolerable by the jubilee shouts that reach them. If I do forget, if I do not faithfully remember those bleeding children of sorrow this day, "may my right hand forget her cunning, and may my tongue cleave to the roof of my mouth!" To forget them, to pass lightly over their wrongs and to chime in with the popular theme would be treason most scandalous and shocking and would make me a reproach before God and the world. My subject, then, fellow citizens, is American slavery. I shall see this day and its popular characteristics from the slave's point of view. Standing there identified with the American bondman, making his wrongs mine, I do not hesitate to declare, with all my soul, that the character and conduct of this nation never looked blacker to me than on this Fourth of July. Whether we turn to the declarations of the past or to the professions of the present, the conduct of the nation seems equally hideous and revolting. America is false to the past, false to the present, and solemnly binds herself to be false to the future.

* * *

For the present, it is enough to affirm the equal manhood of the Negro race. It is not astonishing that, while we are plowing, planting and reaping, using all kinds of mechanical tools, erecting houses, constructing bridges, building ships, working in metals of brass, iron, copper, silver and gold; that, while we are reading, writing and ciphering, acting as clerks, merchants and secretaries, having among us lawyers, doctors, ministers, poets, authors, editors, orators and teachers; that, while we are engaged in all manner of enterprises common to other men, digging gold in California, capturing the whale in the Pacific, feeding sheep and cattle on the hillside, living, moving, acting, thinking, planning, living in families as husbands, wives and children, and, above all, confessing and worshiping the Christian's God and looking hopefully for life and immortality beyond the grave, we are called upon to prove that we are men!

Would you have me argue that man is entitled to liberty? that he is the rightful owner of his own body? You have already declared it. Must I argue the wrongfulness of slavery?

Is that a question for republicans? Is it to be settled by the rules of logic and argumentation, as a matter beset with great difficulty, involving a doubtful application of the principle of justice, hard to be understood? How should I look today, in the presence of Americans, dividing and subdividing a discourse, to show that men have a natural right to freedom, speaking of it relatively and positively, negatively and affirmatively? To do so would be to make myself ridiculous and to offer an insult to your understanding. There is not a man beneath the canopy of heaven that does not know that slavery is wrong *for him*.

* * *

What, to the American slave, is your Fourth of July? I answer: a day that reveals to him, more than all other days in the year, the gross injustice and cruelty to which he is the constant victim. To him, your celebration is a sham; your boasted liberty an unholy license; your national greatness swelling vanity; your sounds of rejoicing are empty and heartless; your denunciation of tyrants brass-fronted impudence; your shouts of liberty and equality hollow mockery; your prayers and hymns, your sermons and thanksgivings, with all your religious parade and solemnity, are to Him mere bombast, fraud, deception, impiety and hypocrisy—a thin veil to cover up crimes which would disgrace a nation of savages. There is not a nation on the earth guilty of practices more shocking and bloody than are the people of the United States at this very hour.

Go where you may, search where you will, roam through all the monarchies and despotisms of the Old World, travel through South America, search out every abuse, and when you have found the last, lay your facts by the side of the everyday practices of this nation, and you will say with me, that, for revolting barbarity and shameless hypocrisy, America reigns without a rival.

* * *

Americans! your republican politics, not less than your republican religion, are flagrantly inconsistent. You boast of your love of liberty, your superior civilization and your pure Christianity, while the whole political power of the nation (as embodied in the two great political parties) is solemnly pledged to support and perpetuate the enslavement of three millions of your countrymen. You hurl your anathemas at the crowned-headed tyrants of Russia and Austria and pride yourselves on your democratic institutions, while you yourselves consent to be the mere *tools* and *bodyguards* of the tyrants of Virginia and Carolina. You invite to your shores fugitives of oppression from abroad, honor them with banquets, greet them with ovations, cheer them, toast them, salute them, protect them, and pour out your money to them like water; but the fugitives from your own land you advertise, hunt, arrest, shoot and kill. You glory in your refinement and your universal education; yet you maintain a system as barbarous and dreadful as ever stained the character of a nation—a system begun in avarice, supported in pride, and perpetuated in cruelty. You shed tears over fallen Hungary, and make the sad story of her wrongs the theme of your poets, statesmen and orators, till your gallant sons are ready to fly to arms to vindicate her cause against the oppressor;* but, in regard to the ten thousand wrongs of the American slave, you would enforce the strictest silence and would hail him as an enemy of the nation who dares to make those wrongs the subject of public discourse! You are all on fire at the mention of liberty for France or for Ireland, but are as cold as an iceberg at the thought of liberty for the enslaved of America. You discourse eloquently on the dignity of labor; yet, you sustain a system which, in its very essence, casts a stigma upon labor. You can bare your bosom to the storm of British artillery to throw off a three-penny tax on tea, and yet wring the last hard-earned farthing from the grasp of the black laborers of your country. You profess to believe "that of one blood God made all nations of men to dwell on the face of all the earth"† and hath commanded all men, everywhere, to love one another; yet you notoriously hate (and glory in your hatred) all men whose skins are not colored like your own. You declare before the world, and are understood by the world to declare, that you *"hold these truths to be self-evident, that all men are created equal; and are endowed by their Creator with certain unalienable rights; and that among these are, life, liberty and the pursuit of happiness"*; and yet, you hold securely, in a bondage which, according to your own Thomas Jefferson, *"is worse than ages of that which your fathers rose in rebellion to oppose,"* a seventh part of the inhabitants of your country.

Fellow citizens, I will not enlarge further on your national inconsistencies. The existence of slavery in this country brands your republicanism as a sham, your humanity as a base pretense, and your Christianity as a lie. It destroys your moral power abroad; it corrupts your politicians at home. It saps the foundation of religion; it makes your name a hissing and a byword to a mocking earth. It is the antagonistic force in your government, the only thing that seriously disturbs and endangers your union. It fetters your progress; it is the enemy of improvement; the deadly foe of education; it fosters pride; it breeds insolence; it promotes vice; it shelters crime; it is a curse to the earth that supports it; and yet you cling to it as if it were the sheet anchor of all your hopes.

* * *

Allow me to say, in conclusion, notwithstanding the dark picture I have this day presented, of the state of the nation, I do not despair of this country. There are forces in operation which must inevitably work the downfall of slavery.

* * *

---

*The fledgling Hungarian republic was invaded by Austria and Russia in 1849.

†Acts 17:26.

The Gettysburg Address (1863)

Four score and seven years ago our fathers brought forth on this continent, a new nation, conceived in Liberty, and dedicated to the proposition that all men are created equal.

Now we are engaged in a great civil war, testing whether that nation, or any nation so conceived and so dedicated, can long endure. We are met on a great battle field of that war. We have come to dedicate a portion of that field, as a final resting place for those who here gave their lives that that nation might live. It is altogether fitting and proper that we should do this.

But, in a larger sense, we can not dedicate—we can not consecrate—we can not hallow—this ground. The brave men, living and dead, who struggled here, have consecrated it, far above our poor power to add or detract. The world will little note, nor long remember what we say here, but it can never forget what they did here. It is for us the living, rather, to be dedicated here to the unfinished work which they who fought here have thus far so nobly advanced. It is rather for us to be here dedicated to the great task remaining before us—that from these honored dead we take increased devotion to that cause for which they gave the last full measure of devotion—that we here highly resolve that these dead shall not have died in vain—that this nation, under God, shall have a new birth of freedom—and that government of the people, by the people, for the people, shall not perish from the earth.

Abraham Lincoln
November 19, 1863

Abraham Lincoln's Second Inaugural Address (1865)

Fellow Countrymen:

At this second appearing to take the oath of the presidential office, there is less occasion for an extended address than there was at the first. Then a statement, somewhat in detail, of a course to be pursued, seemed fitting and proper. Now, at the expiration of four years, during which public declarations have been constantly called forth on every point and phase of the great contest which still absorbs the attention, and engrosses the energies of the nation, little that is new could be presented. The progress of our arms, upon which all else chiefly depends, is as well known to the public as to myself; and it is, I trust, reasonably satisfactory and encouraging to all. With high hope for the future, no prediction in regard to it is ventured.

On the occasion corresponding to this four years ago, all thoughts were anxiously directed to an impending civil war. All dreaded it—all sought to avert it. While the inaugural address was being delivered from this place, devoted altogether to *saving* the Union without war, insurgent agents were in the city seeking to *destroy* it without war—seeking to dissolve the Union, and divide effects, by negotiation. Both parties deprecated war; but one of them would *make* war rather than let the nation survive; and the other would *accept* war rather than let it perish. And the war came.

One eighth of the whole population were colored slaves, not distributed generally over the Union, but localized in the southern part of it. These slaves constituted a peculiar and powerful interest. All knew that this interest was, somehow, the cause of the war. To strengthen, perpetuate, and extend this interest was the object for which the insurgents would rend the Union, even by war; while the government claimed no right to do more than to restrict the territorial enlargement of it. Neither party expected for the war, the magnitude, or the duration, which it has already attained. Neither anticipated that the *cause* of the conflict might cease with, or even before, the conflict itself should cease. Each looked for an easier triumph, and a result less fundamental and astounding. Both read the same Bible, and pray to the same God; and each invokes His aid against the other. It may seem strange that any men should dare to ask a just God's assistance in wringing their bread from the sweat of other men's faces; but let us judge not that we be not judged. The prayers of both could not be answered; that of neither has been answered fully. The Almighty has His own purposes. "Woe unto the world because of offences! for it must needs be that offences come; but woe to that man by whom the offence cometh." If we shall suppose that American slavery is one of those offences which, in the providence of God, must needs come, but which, having continued through His appointed time, He now wills to remove, and that He gives to both North and South, this terrible war, as the woe due to those by whom the offence came, shall we discern therein any departure from those divine attributes which the believers in a living God always ascribe to Him? Fondly do we hope, fervently do we pray—that this mighty scourge of war may speedily pass away. Yet, if God wills that it continue until all the wealth piled by the bondsman's two hundred and fifty years of unrequited toil shall be sunk, and until every drop of blood drawn with the lash shall be paid by another drawn with the sword, as was said three thousand years ago, so still it must be said "the judgments of the Lord are true and righteous altogether."

With malice toward none; with charity for all; with firmness in the right as God gives us to see the right, let us strive on to finish the work we are in; to bind up the nation's wounds; to care for him who shall have borne the battle and for his widow and his orphan, to do all which may achieve and cherish a just and a lasting peace, among ourselves and with all nations.

The Populist Platform of 1892

Assembled upon the 116th anniversary of the Declaration of Independence, the People's Party of America, in their first national convention, invoking upon their action the blessing of Almighty God, puts forth in the name and on behalf of the people of this country, the following preamble and declaration of principles:

PREAMBLE

The conditions which surround us best justify our co-operation; we meet in the midst of a nation brought to the verge of moral, political, and material ruin. Corruption dominates the ballot-box, the Legislatures, the Congress, and touches even the ermine of the bench. The people are demoralized; most of the States have been compelled to isolate the voters at the polling places to prevent universal intimidation and bribery. The newspapers are largely subsidized or muzzled, public opinion silenced, business prostrated, homes covered with mortgages, labor impoverished, and the land concentrating in the hands of the capitalists. The urban workmen are denied the right to organize for self-protection, imported pauperized labor beats down their wages, a hireling standing army, unrecognized by our laws, is established to shoot them down, and they are rapidly degenerating into European conditions. The fruits of the toil of millions are boldly stolen to build up the fortunes for a few, unprecedented in the history of mankind; and the possessors of these, in turn, despise the Republic and endanger liberty. From the same prolific womb of governmental injustice we breed the two great classes—tramps and millionaires.

The national power to create money is appropriated to enrich bondholders; a vast public debt, payable in legal tender currency, has been funded into gold-bearing bonds, thereby adding millions to the burdens of the people. Silver, which has been accepted as coin since the dawn of history, has been demonetized to add to the purchasing power of gold by decreasing the value of all forms of property as well as human labor, and the supply of currency is purposely abridged to fatten usurers, bankrupt enterprise, and enslave industry. A vast conspiracy against mankind has been organized on two continents, and it is rapidly taking possession of the world. If not met and overthrown at once it forebodes terrible social convulsions, the destruction of civilization, or the establishment of an absolute despotism.

We have witnessed for more than a quarter of a century the struggles of the two great political parties for power and plunder, while grievous wrongs have been inflicted upon the suffering people. We charge that the controlling influences dominating both these parties have permitted the existing dreadful conditions to develop without serious effort to prevent or restrain them. Neither do they now promise us any substantial reform. They have agreed together to ignore in the coming campaign every issue but one. They propose to drown the outcries of a plundered people with the uproar of a sham battle over the tariff, so that capitalists, corporations, national banks, rings, trusts, watered stock, the demonetization of silver, and the oppressions of the usurers may all be lost sight of. They propose to sacrifice our homes, lives, and children on the altar of mammon; to destroy the multitude in order to secure corruption funds from the millionaires.

Assembled on the anniversary of the birthday of the nation, and filled with the spirit of the grand general and chief who established our independence, we seek to restore the government of the Republic to the hands of "the plain people," with which class it originated. We assert our purpose to be identical with the purposes of the National Constitution, "to form a more perfect union and establish justice, insure domestic tranquility, provide for the common defense, promote the general welfare, and secure the blessings of liberty for ourselves and our posterity." We declare that this Republic can only endure as a free government while built upon the love of the whole people for each other and for the nation; that it cannot be pinned together by bayonets; that the civil war is over, and that every passion and resentment which grew out of it must die with it; and that we must be in fact, as we are in name, one united brotherhood of free men.

Our country finds itself confronted by conditions for which there is no precedent in the history of the world; our annual agricultural productions amount to billions of dollars in value, which must, within a few weeks or months, be exchanged for billions of dollars of commodities consumed in their production; the existing currency supply is wholly inadequate to make this exchange; the results are falling prices, the formation of combines and rings, the impoverishment of the producing class. We pledge ourselves, if given power, we will labor to correct these evils by wise and reasonable legislation, in accordance with the terms of our platform. We believe that the power of government—in other words, of the people—should be expanded (as in the case of the postal service) as rapidly and as far as the good sense of an intelligent people and the teaching of experience shall justify, to the end that oppression, injustice, and poverty shall eventually cease in the land.

While our sympathies as a party of reform are naturally upon the side of every proposition which will tend to make men intelligent, virtuous, and temperate, we nevertheless regard these questions—important as they are—as secondary to the great issues now pressing for solution, and upon which not only our individual prosperity but the very existence of free institutions depend; and we ask all men to first help us to determine whether we are to have a republic to administer before we differ as to the conditions upon which it is to be administered, believing that the forces of reform this day organized will never cease to move forward until every wrong is remedied, and equal rights and equal privileges securely established for all the men and women of this country.

PLATFORM

We declare, therefore—

First.—That the union of the labor forces of the United States this day consummated shall be permanent and perpetual; may its spirit enter into all hearts for the salvation of the Republic and the uplifting of mankind!

Second.—Wealth belongs to him who creates it, and every dollar taken from industry without an equivalent is robbery. "If any will not work, neither shall he eat." The interests of rural and civic labor are the same; their enemies are identical.

Third.—We believe that the time has come when the railroad corporations will either own the people or the people must own the railroads; and, should the government enter upon the work of owning and managing all railroads, we should favor an amendment to the Constitution by which all persons engaged in the government service shall be placed under a civil-service regulation of the most rigid character, so as to prevent the increase of the power of the national administration by the use of such additional government employees.

FINANCE.—We demand a national currency, safe, sound, and flexible, issued by the general government only, a full legal tender for all debts, public and private, and that without the use of banking corporations, a just, equitable, and efficient means of distribution direct to the people, at a tax not to exceed two per cent per annum, to be provided as set forth in the sub-treasury plan of the Farmers' Alliance, or a better system; also by payments in discharge of its obligations for public improvements.

1. We demand free and unlimited coinage of silver and gold at the present legal ratio of 16 to 1.

2. We demand that the amount of circulating medium be speedily increased to not less than $50 per capita.

3. We demand a graduated income tax.

4. We believe that the money of the country should be kept as much as possible in the hands of the people, and hence we demand that all State and national revenues shall be limited to the necessary expenses of the government, economically and honestly administered.

5. We demand that postal savings banks be established by the government for the safe deposit of the earnings of the people and to facilitate exchange.

TRANSPORTATION.—Transportation being a means of exchange and a public necessity, the government should own and operate the railroads in the interest of the people. The telegraph and telephone, like the post-office system, being a necessity for the transmission of news, should be owned and operated by the government in the interest of the people.

LAND.—The land, including all the natural sources of wealth, is the heritage of the people, and should not be monopolized for speculative purposes, and alien ownership of land should be prohibited. All land now held by railroads and other corporations in excess of their actual needs, and all lands now owned by aliens should be reclaimed by the government and held for actual settlers only.

EXPRESSION OF SENTIMENTS

Your committee on Platform and Resolutions beg leave unanimously to report the following:

Whereas, Other questions have been presented for our consideration, we hereby submit the following, not as a part of the Platform of the People's Party, but as resolutions expressive of the sentiment of this Convention:

1. *Resolved*, That we demand a free ballot and a fair count in all elections, and pledge ourselves to secure it to every legal voter without federal intervention, through the adoption by the States of the unperverted Australian or secret ballot system.

2. *Resolved*, That the revenue derived from a graduated income tax should be applied to the reduction of the burden of taxation now levied upon the domestic industries of this country.

3. *Resolved*, That we pledge our support to fair and liberal pensions to ex-Union soldiers and sailors.

4. *Resolved*, That we condemn the fallacy of protecting American labor under the present system, which opens our ports to the pauper and criminal classes of the world, and crowds out our wage-earners; and we denounce the present ineffective laws against contract labor, and demand the further restriction of undesirable emigration.

5. *Resolved*, that we cordially sympathize with the efforts of organized workingmen to shorten the hours of labor, and demand a rigid enforcement of the existing eight-hour law on Government work, and ask that a penalty clause be added to the said law.

6. *Resolved*, That we regard the maintenance of a large standing army of mercenaries, known as the Pinkerton system, as a menace to our liberties, and we demand its abolition; and we condemn the recent invasion of the Territory of Wyoming by the hired assassins of plutocracy, assisted by federal officers.

7. *Resolved*, That we commend to the favorable consideration of the people and the reform press the legislative system known as the initiative and referendum.

8. *Resolved*, That we favor a constitutional provision limiting the office of President and Vice-President to one term, and providing for the election of Senators of the United States by a direct vote of the people.

9. *Resolved*, That we oppose any subsidy or national aid to any private corporation for any purpose.

10. *Resolved*, That this convention sympathizes with the Knights of Labor and their righteous contest with the tyrannical combine of clothing manufacturers of Rochester, and declare it to be the duty of all who hate tyranny and oppression to refuse to purchase the goods made by the said manufacturers, or to patronize any merchants who sell such goods.

FRANKLIN D. ROOSEVELT'S FIRST INAUGURAL ADDRESS (1933)

I am certain that my fellow Americans expect that on my induction into the Presidency I will address them with a candor and a decision which the present situation of our Nation impels. This is preeminently the time to speak the truth, the whole truth, frankly and boldly. Nor need we shrink from honestly facing conditions in our country today. This great Nation will endure as it has endured, will revive and will prosper. So, first of all, let me assert my firm belief that the only thing we have to fear is fear itself—nameless, unreasoning, unjustified terror which paralyzes needed efforts to convert retreat into advance. In every dark hour of our national life a leadership of frankness and vigor has met with that understanding and support of the people themselves which is essential to victory. I am convinced that you will again give that support to leadership in these critical days.

In such a spirit on my part and on yours we face our common difficulties. They concern, thank God, only material things. Values have shrunken to fantastic levels; taxes have risen; our ability to pay has fallen; government of all kinds is faced by serious curtailment of income; the means of exchange are frozen in the currents of trade; the withered leaves of industrial enterprise lie on every side; farmers find no markets for their produce; the savings of many years in thousands of families are gone.

More important, a host of unemployed citizens face the grim problem of existence, and an equally great number toil with little return. Only a foolish optimist can deny the dark realities of the moment.

Yet our distress comes from no failure of substance. We are stricken by no plague of locusts. Compared with the perils which our forefathers conquered because they believed and were not afraid, we have still much to be thankful for. Nature still offers her bounty and human efforts have multiplied it. Plenty is at our doorstep, but a generous use of it languishes in the very sight of the supply. Primarily this is because the rulers of the exchange of mankind's goods have failed, through their own stubbornness and their own incompetence, have admitted their failure, and abdicated. Practices of the unscrupulous money changers stand indicted in the court of public opinion, rejected by the hearts and minds of men.

True they have tried, but their efforts have been cast in the pattern of an outworn tradition. Faced by failure of credit they have proposed only the lending of more money. Stripped of the lure of profit by which to induce our people to follow their false leadership, they have resorted to exhortations, pleading tearfully for restored confidence. They know only the rules of a generation of self-seekers. They have no vision, and when there is no vision the people perish.

The money changers have fled from their high seats in the temple of our civilization. We may now restore that temple to the ancient truths. The measure of the restoration lies in the extent to which we apply social values more noble than mere monetary profit.

Happiness lies not in the mere possession of money; it lies in the joy of achievement, in the thrill of creative effort. The joy and moral stimulation of work no longer must be forgotten in the mad chase of evanescent profits. These dark days will be worth all they cost us if they teach us that our true destiny is not to be ministered unto but to minister to ourselves and to our fellow men.

Recognition of the falsity of material wealth as the standard of success goes hand in hand with the abandonment of the false belief that public office and high political position are to be valued only by the standards of pride of place and personal profit; and there must be an end to a conduct in banking and in business which too often has given to a sacred trust the likeness of callous and selfish wrongdoing. Small wonder that confidence languishes, for it thrives only on honesty, on honor, on the sacredness of obligations, on faithful protection, on unselfish performance; without them it cannot live.

Restoration calls, however, not for changes in ethics alone. This Nation asks for action, and action now.

Our greatest primary task is to put people to work. This is no unsolvable problem if we face it wisely and courageously. It can be accomplished in part by direct recruiting by the Government itself, treating the task as we would treat the emergency of a war, but at the same time, through this employment, accomplishing greatly needed projects to stimulate and reorganize the use of our natural resources.

Hand in hand with this we must frankly recognize the overbalance of population in our industrial centers and, by engaging on a national scale in a redistribution, endeavor to provide a better use of the land for those best fitted for the land. The task can be helped by definite efforts to raise the values of agricultural products and with this the power to purchase the output of our cities. It can be helped by preventing realistically the tragedy of the growing loss through foreclosure of our small homes and our farms. It can be helped by insistence that the Federal, State, and local governments act forthwith on the demand that their cost be drastically reduced. It can be helped by the unifying of relief activities which today are often scattered, uneconomical, and unequal. It can be helped by national planning for and supervision of all forms of transportation and of communications and other utilities which have a definitely public character. There are many ways in which it can be helped, but it can never be helped merely by talking about it. We must act and act quickly.

Finally, in our progress toward a resumption of work we require two safeguards against a return of the evils of the old order; there must be a strict supervision of all banking and credits and investments; there must be an end to speculation with other people's money, and there must be provision for an adequate but sound currency.

There are the lines of attack. I shall presently urge upon a new Congress, in special session, detailed measures for their fulfillment, and I shall seek the immediate assistance of the several States.

Through this program of action we address ourselves to putting our own national house in order and making income balance outgo. Our international trade relations, though vastly important, are in point of time and necessity secondary to the establishment of a sound national economy. I favor as a practical policy the putting of first things first. I shall spare no effort to restore world trade by international economic readjustment, but the emergency at home cannot wait on that accomplishment.

The basic thought that guides these specific means of national recovery is not narrowly nationalistic. It is the insistence, as a first consideration, upon the interdependence of the various elements in all parts of the United States—a recognition of the old and permanently important manifestation of the American spirit of the pioneer. It is the way to recovery. It is the immediate way. It is the strongest assurance that the recovery will endure.

In the field of world policy I would dedicate this Nation to the policy of the good neighbor—the neighbor who resolutely respects himself and, because he does so, respects the rights of others—the neighbor who respects his obligations and respects the sanctity of his agreements in and with a world of neighbors.

If I read the temper of our people correctly, we now realize as we have never realized before our interdependence on each other; that we cannot merely take but we must give as well; that if we are to go forward, we must move as a trained and loyal army willing to sacrifice for the good of a common discipline, because without such discipline no progress is made, no leadership becomes effective. We are, I know, ready and willing to submit our lives and property to such discipline, because it makes possible a leadership which aims at a larger good. This I propose to offer, pledging that the larger purposes will bind upon us all as a sacred obligation with a unity of duty hitherto evoked only in time of armed strife.

With this pledge taken, I assume unhesitatingly the leadership of this great army of our people dedicated to a disciplined attack upon our common problems.

Action in this image and to this end is feasible under the form of government which we have inherited from our ancestors. Our Constitution is so simple and practical that it is possible always to meet extraordinary needs by changes in emphasis and arrangement without loss of essential form. That is why our constitutional system has proved itself the most superbly enduring political mechanism the modern world has produced. It has met every stress of vast expansion of territory, of foreign wars, of bitter internal strife, of world relations.

It is to be hoped that the normal balance of executive and legislative authority may be wholly adequate to meet the unprecedented task before us. But it may be that an unprecedented demand and need for undelayed action may call for temporary departure from that normal balance of public procedure.

I am prepared under my constitutional duty to recommend the measures that a stricken nation in the midst of a stricken world may require. These measures, or such other measures as the Congress may build out of its experience and wisdom, I shall seek, within my constitutional authority, to bring to speedy adoption.

But in the event that the Congress shall fail to take one of these two courses, and in the event that the national emergency is still critical, I shall not evade the clear course of duty that will then confront me. I shall ask the Congress for the one remaining instrument to meet the crisis—broad Executive power to wage a war against the emergency, as great as the power that would be given to me if we were in fact invaded by a foreign foe.

For the trust reposed in me I will return the courage and the devotion that befit the time. I can do no less.

We face the arduous days that lie before us in the warm courage of national unity; with the clear consciousness of seeking old and precious moral values; with the clean satisfaction that comes from the stern performance of duty by old and young alike. We aim at the assurance of a rounded and permanent national life.

We do not distrust the future of essential democracy. The people of the United States have not failed. In their need they have registered a mandate that they want direct, vigorous action. They have asked for discipline and direction under leadership. They have made me the present instrument of their wishes. In the spirit of the gift I take it.

In this dedication of a Nation we humbly ask the blessing of God. May He protect each and every one of us. May He guide me in the days to come.

Martin Luther King Jr.'s, "I Have a Dream" Speech (1963)

I am happy to join with you today in what will go down in history as the greatest demonstration for freedom in the history of our nation.

Five score years ago, a great American, in whose symbolic shadow we stand today, signed the Emancipation Proclamation. This momentous decree came as a great beacon light of hope to millions of Negro slaves who had been seared in the flames of withering injustice. It came as a joyous daybreak to end the long night of captivity.

But one hundred years later, the Negro still is not free. One hundred years later, the life of the Negro is still sadly crippled by the manacles of segregation and the chains of discrimination. One hundred years later, the Negro is still languishing in the corners of American society and finds himself an exile in his own land. And so we've come here today to dramatize a shameful condition.

In a sense we have come to our nation's capital to cash a check. When the architects of our republic wrote the magnificent words of the Constitution and the Declaration of Independence, they were signing a promissory note to which every American was to fall heir. This note was a promise that all men, yes black men as well as white men, would be guaranteed the "unalienable Rights of Life, Liberty, and the pursuit of Happiness." It is obvious today that America has defaulted on this promissory note insofar as her citizens of color are concerned. Instead of honoring this sacred obligation, America has given the Negro people a bad check,—a check which has come back marked "insufficient funds."

But we refuse to believe that the bank of justice is bankrupt. We refuse to believe that there are insufficient funds in the great vaults of opportunity of this nation. And so we've come to cash this check,—a check that will give us upon demand the riches of freedom and the security of justice.

We have also come to this hallowed spot to remind America of the fierce urgency of now. This is no time to engage in the luxury of cooling off or to take the tranquilizing drug of gradualism. Now is the time to make real the promises of democracy. Now is the time to rise from the dark and desolate valley of segregation to the sunlit path of racial justice. Now is the time to lift our nation from the quicksands of racial injustice to the solid rock of brotherhood. Now is the time to make justice a reality for all of God's children.

It would be fatal for the nation to overlook the urgency of the moment. This sweltering summer of the Negro's legitimate discontent will not pass until there is an invigorating autumn of freedom and equality. Nineteen sixty-three is not an end, but a beginning. And those who hope that the Negro needed to blow off steam and will now be content will have a rude awakening if the nation returns to business as usual. There will be neither rest nor tranquility in America until the Negro is granted his citizenship rights. The whirlwinds of revolt will continue to shake the foundation of our nation until the bright day of justice emerges.

But there is something that I must say to my people, who stand on the warm threshold which leads into the palace of justice: In the process of gaining our rightful place, we must not be guilty of wrongful deeds. Let us not seek to satisfy our thirst for freedom by drinking from the cup of bitterness and hatred. We must forever conduct our struggle on the high plane of dignity and discipline. We must not allow our creative protest to degenerate into physical violence. Again and again, we must rise to the majestic heights of meeting physical force with soul force. The marvelous new militancy which has engulfed the Negro community must not lead us to a distrust of all white people, for many of our white brothers, as evidenced by their presence here today, have come to realize that their destiny is tied up with our destiny. And they have come to realize that their freedom is inextricably bound to our freedom. We cannot walk alone.

And as we walk, we must make the pledge that we shall march ahead. We cannot turn back. There are those who are asking the devotees of civil rights, "When will you be satisfied?"

We can never be satisfied as long as the Negro is the victim of unspeakable horrors of police brutality. We can never be satisfied as long as our bodies, heavy with the fatigue of travel, cannot gain lodging in the motels of the highways and the hotels of the cities. We cannot be satisfied as long as the Negro's basic mobility is from a smaller ghetto to a larger one. We can never be satisfied as long as our children are stripped of their selfhood and robbed of their dignity by signs stating "for whites only." We cannot be satisfied as long as a Negro in Mississippi cannot vote and a Negro in New York believes he has nothing for which to vote. No, no, we are not satisfied, and we will not be satisfied until, "justice rolls down like waters and righteousness like a mighty stream."

I am not unmindful that some of you have come here out of great trials and tribulations. Some of you have come fresh from narrow jail cells. Some of you have come from areas where your quest for freedom left you battered by the storms of persecution and staggered by the winds of police brutality. You have been the veterans of creative suffering. Continue to work with the faith that unearned suffering is redemptive.

Go back to Mississippi, go back to Alabama, go back to South Carolina, go back to Georgia, go back to Louisiana, go back to the slums and ghettos of our northern cities, knowing that somehow this situation can and will be changed. Let us not wallow in the valley of despair.

I say to you today, my friends, so even though we face the difficulties of today and tomorrow, I still have a dream. It is a dream deeply rooted in the American dream.

I have a dream that one day this nation will rise up and live out the true meaning of its creed: "We hold these truths to be self-evident, that all men are created equal."

I have a dream that one day on the red hills of Georgia, the sons of former slaves and the sons of former slave owners will be able to sit down together at the table of brotherhood.

I have a dream that one day even the state of Mississippi, a state sweltering with the heat of injustice, sweltering with the heat of oppression, will be transformed into an oasis of freedom and justice.

I have a dream that my four little children will one day live in a nation where they will not be judged by the color of their skin but by the content of their character. I have a dream today.

I have a dream that one day down in Alabama, with its vicious racists, with its governor having his lips dripping with the words of "interposition" and "nullification," one day right there in Alabama little black boys and black girls will be able to join hands with little white boys and white girls as sisters and brothers. I have a dream today.

I have a dream that one day "every valley shall be exalted, and every hill and mountain shall be made low; the rough places will be made plain, and the crooked places will be made straight; and the glory of the Lord shall be revealed, and all flesh shall see it together."

This is our hope. This is the faith that I go back to the South with. With this faith we will be able to hew out of the mountain of despair a stone of hope. With this faith will be able to transform the jangling discords of our nation into a beautiful symphony of brotherhood. With this faith we will be able to work together, to pray together, to struggle together, to go to jail together, to stand up for freedom together, knowing that we will be free one day. This will be the day, this will be the day when all of God's children will be able to sing with a new meaning:

My country, 'tis of thee, sweet land of liberty, of thee I sing.
Land where my fathers died, land of the pilgrim's pride,
From every mountainside, let freedom ring.

And if America is to be a great nation this must become true.

And so let freedom ring from the prodigious hilltops of New Hampshire.

Let freedom ring from the mighty mountains of New York.

Let freedom ring from the heightening Alleghenies of Pennsylvania.

Let freedom ring from the snowcapped Rockies of Colorado.

Let freedom ring from the curvaceous peaks of California.

But not only that: let freedom ring from Stone Mountain of Georgia.

Let freedom ring from Lookout Mountain of Tennessee.

Let freedom ring from every hill and molehill of Mississippi.

From every mountainside, let freedom ring.

And when this happens, when we allow freedom to ring, when we let it ring from every village and every hamlet, from every state and every city, we will be able to speed up that day when all of God's children, black men and white men, Jews and Gentiles, Protestants and Catholics, will be able to join hands and sing in the words of the old Negro spiritual:

Free at last! Free at last!
Thank God Almighty, we are free at last!

Ronald Reagan's First Inaugural Address (1981)

WEST FRONT OF THE U.S. CAPITOL
JANUARY 20, 1981

Senator Hatfield, Mr. Chief Justice, Mr. President, Vice President Bush, Vice President Mondale, Senator Baker, Speaker O'Neill, Reverend Moomaw, and my fellow citizens.

To a few of us here today this is a solemn and most momentous occasion, and yet in the history of our nation it is a commonplace occurrence. The orderly transfer of authority as called for in the Constitution routinely takes place, as it has for almost two centuries, and few of us stop to think how unique we really are. In the eyes of many in the world, this every-four-year ceremony we accept as normal is nothing less than a miracle.

Mr. President, I want our fellow citizens to know how much you did to carry on this tradition. By your gracious cooperation in the transition process, you have shown a watching world that we are a united people pledged to maintaining a political system which guarantees individual liberty to a greater degree than any other, and I thank you and your people for all your help in maintaining the continuity which is the bulwark of our republic. The business of our nation goes forward. These United States are confronted with an economic affliction of great proportions. We suffer from the longest and one of the worst sustained inflations in our national history. It distorts our economic decisions, penalizes thrift, and crushes the struggling young and the fixed-income elderly alike. It threatens to shatter the lives of millions of our people.

Idle industries have cast workers into unemployment, human misery, and personal indignity. Those who do work are denied a fair return for their labor by a tax system which penalizes successful achievement and keeps us from maintaining full productivity. But great as our tax burden is, it has not kept pace with public spending. For decades we have piled deficit upon deficit, mortgaging our future and our children's future for the temporary convenience of the present. To continue this long trend is to guarantee tremendous social, cultural, political, and economic upheavals.

You and I, as individuals, can, by borrowing, live beyond our means, but for only a limited period of time. Why, then, should we think that collectively, as a nation, we're not bound by that same limitation? We must act today in order to preserve tomorrow. And let there be no misunderstanding: We are going to begin to act, beginning today. The economic ills we suffer have come upon us over several decades. They will not go away in days, weeks, or months, but they will go away. They will go away because we as Americans have the capacity now, as we've had in the past, to do whatever needs to be done to preserve this last and greatest bastion of freedom.

In this present crisis, government is not the solution to our problem; government is the problem. From time to time we've been tempted to believe that society has become too complex to be managed by self-rule, that government by an elite group is superior to government for, by, and of the people. Well, if no one among us is capable of governing himself, then who among us has the capacity to govern someone else? All of us together, in and out of government, must bear the burden. The solutions we seek must be equitable, with no one group singled out to pay a higher price.

We hear much of special interest groups. Well, our concern must be for a special interest group that has been too long neglected. It knows no sectional boundaries or ethnic and racial divisions, and it crosses political party lines. It is made up of men and women who raise our food, patrol our streets, man our mines and factories, teach our children, keep our homes, and heal us when we're sick—professionals, industrialists, shopkeepers, clerks, cabbies, and truck drivers. They are, in short, "we the people," this breed called Americans.

Well, this administration's objective will be a healthy, vigorous, growing economy that provides equal opportunities for all Americans, with no barriers born of bigotry or discrimination. Putting America back to work means putting all Americans back to work. Ending inflation means freeing all Americans from the terror of runaway living costs. All must share in the productive work of this "new beginning," and all must share in the bounty of a revived economy. With the idealism and fair play which are the core of our system and our strength, we can have a strong and prosperous America, at peace with itself and the world.

So, as we begin, let us take inventory. We are a nation that has a government—not the other way around. And this makes us special among the nations of the Earth. Our government has no power except that granted it by the people. It is time to check and reverse the growth of government, which shows signs of having grown beyond the consent of the governed.

It is my intention to curb the size and influence of the federal establishment and to demand recognition of the distinction between the powers granted to the federal government and those reserved to the states or to the people. All of us need to be reminded that the federal government did not create the states; the states created the federal government.

Now, so there will be no misunderstanding, it's not my intention to do away with government. It is rather to make it work—work with us, not over us; to stand by our side, not ride on our back. Government can and must provide opportunity, not smother it; foster productivity, not stifle it.

If we look to the answer as to why for so many years we achieved so much, prospered as no other people on earth, it was because here in this land we unleashed the energy and individual genius of man to a greater extent than has ever been done before. Freedom and the dignity of the individual have been more available and assured here than in any other place on earth. The price for this freedom at times has been high, but we have never been unwilling to pay the price.

It is no coincidence that our present troubles parallel and are proportionate to the intervention and intrusion in our lives that result from unnecessary and excessive growth of government. It is time for us to realize that we're too great a nation to limit ourselves to small dreams. We're not, as some would have us believe, doomed to an inevitable decline. I do not believe in a fate that will fall on us no matter what we do. I do believe in a fate that will fall on us if we do nothing. So, with all the creative energy at our command, let us begin an era of national renewal. Let us renew our determination, our courage, and our strength. And let us renew our faith and our hope.

We have every right to dream heroic dreams. Those who say that we're in a time when there are no heroes, they just don't know where to look. You can see heroes every day going in and out of factory gates. Others, a handful in number, produce enough food to feed all of us and then the world beyond. You meet heroes across a counter, and they're on both sides of that counter. There are entrepreneurs with faith in themselves and faith in an idea who create new jobs, new wealth and opportunity. They're individuals and families whose taxes support the government and whose voluntary gifts support church, charity, culture, art, and education. Their patri-

otism is quiet, but deep. Their values sustain our national life.

Now, I have used the words "they" and "their" in speaking of these heroes. I could say "you" and "your," because I'm addressing the heroes of whom I speak—you, the citizens of this blessed land. Your dreams, your hopes, your goals are going to be the dreams, the hopes, and the goals of this administration, so help me God.

We shall reflect the compassion that is so much a part of your makeup. How can we love our country and not love our countrymen; and loving them, reach out a hand when they fall, heal them when they're sick, and provide opportunity to make them self-sufficient so they will be equal in fact and not just in theory?

Can we solve the problems confronting us? Well, the answer is an unequivocal and emphatic "yes." To paraphrase Winston Churchill, I did not take the oath I've just taken with the intention of presiding over the dissolution of the world's strongest economy.

In the days ahead I will propose removing the roadblocks that have slowed our economy and reduced productivity. Steps will be taken aimed at restoring the balance between the various levels of government. Progress may be slow, measured in inches and feet, not miles, but we will progress. It is time to reawaken this industrial giant, to get government back within its means, and to lighten our punitive tax burden. And these will be our first priorities, and on these principles there will be no compromise.

On the eve of our struggle for independence a man who might have been one of the greatest among the Founding Fathers, Dr. Joseph Warren, president of the Massachusetts Congress, said to his fellow Americans, "Our country is in danger, but not to be despaired of . . . On you depend the fortunes of America. You are to decide the important questions upon which rests the happiness and the liberty of millions yet unborn. Act worthy of yourselves." Well, I believe we, the Americans of today, are ready to act worthy of ourselves, ready to do what must be done to ensure happiness and liberty for ourselves, our children, and our children's children. And as we renew ourselves here in our own land, we will be seen as having greater strength throughout the world. We will again be the exemplar of freedom and a beacon of hope for those who do not now have freedom.

To those neighbors and allies who share our freedom, we will strengthen our historic ties and assure them of our support and firm commitment. We will match loyalty with loyalty. We will strive for mutually beneficial relations. We will not use our friendship to impose on their sovereignty, for our own sovereignty is not for sale. As for the enemies of freedom, those who are potential adversaries, they will be reminded that peace is the highest aspiration of the American people. We will negotiate for it, sacrifice for it; we will not surrender for it, now or ever.

Our forbearance should never be misunderstood. Our reluctance for conflict should not be misjudged as a failure of will. When action is required to preserve our national security, we will act. We will maintain sufficient strength to prevail if need be, knowing that if we do so we have the best chance of never having to use that strength. Above all, we must realize that no arsenal or no weapon in the arsenals of the world is so formidable as the will and moral courage of free men and women. It is a weapon our adversaries in today's world do not have. It is a weapon that we as Americans do have. Let that be understood by those who practice terrorism and prey upon their neighbors. I'm told that tens of thousands of prayer meetings are being held on this day, and for that I'm deeply grateful. We are a nation under God, and I believe God intended for us to be free. It would be fitting and good, I think, if on each Inaugural Day in future years it should be declared a day of prayer.

This is the first time in our history that this ceremony has been held, as you've been told, on the West Front of the Capitol. Standing here, one faces a magnificent vista, opening up on the city's special beauty and history. At the end of this open mall are those shrines to the giants on whose shoulders we stand.

Directly in front of me, the monument to a monumental man, George Washington, father of our country. A man of humility who came to greatness reluctantly. He led Americans out of revolutionary victory into infant nationhood. Off to one side, the stately memorial to Thomas Jefferson. The Declaration of Independence flames with his eloquence. And then, beyond the Reflecting Pool, the dignified columns of the Lincoln Memorial. Whoever would understand in his heart the meaning of America will find it in the life of Abraham Lincoln.

Beyond those monuments to heroism is the Potomac River, and on the far shore the sloping hills of Arlington National Cemetery, with its row upon row of simple white markers bearing crosses of Stars of David. They add up to only a tiny fraction of the price that has been paid for our freedom. Each one of those markers is a monument to the kind of hero I spoke of earlier. Their lives ended in places called Belleau Wood, the Argonne, Omaha Beach, Salerno, and halfway around the world on Guadalcanal, Tarawa, Pork Chop Hill, the Chosin Reservoir, and in a hundred rice paddies and jungles of a place called Vietnam.

Under one such marker lies a young man, Martin Treptow, who left his job in a small town barbershop in 1917 to go to France with the famed Rainbow Division. There, on the western front, he was killed trying to carry a message between battalions under heavy artillery fire.

We're told that on his body was found a diary. On the flyleaf under the heading "My Pledge," he had written these words: "America must win this war. Therefore I will work, I will save, I will sacrifice, I will endure, I will fight cheerfully and do my utmost, as if the issue of the whole struggle depended on me alone."

The crisis we are facing today does not require of us the kind of sacrifice that Martin Treptow and so many thousands of others were called upon to make. It does require, however, our best effort and our willingness to believe in ourselves and to believe in our capacity to perform great deeds, to believe that together with God's help we can and will resolve the problems which now confront us.

And after all, why shouldn't we believe that? We are Americans.

God bless you, and thank you.

PRESIDENTIAL ELECTIONS

Year	Number of States	Candidates	Parties	Popular Vote	% of Popular Vote	Electoral Vote	% Voter Participation
1789	11	**GEORGE WASHINGTON**	NO PARTY			69	
		John Adams	DESIGNATIONS			34	
		Other candidates				35	
1792	15	**GEORGE WASHINGTON**	NO PARTY			132	
		John Adams	DESIGNATIONS			77	
		George Clinton				50	
		Other candidates				5	
1796	16	**JOHN ADAMS**	FEDERALIST			71	
		Thomas Jefferson	Republican			68	
		Thomas Pinckney	Federalist			59	
		Aaron Burr	Republican			30	
		Other candidates				48	
1800	16	**THOMAS JEFFERSON**	REPUBLICAN			73	
		Aaron Burr	Republican			73	
		John Adams	Federalist			65	
		Charles C. Pinckney	Federalist			64	
		John Jay	Federalist			1	
1804	17	**THOMAS JEFFERSON**	REPUBLICAN			162	
		Charles C. Pinckney	Federalist			14	
1808	17	**JAMES MADISON**	REPUBLICAN			122	
		Charles C. Pinckney	Federalist			47	
		George Clinton	Republican			6	
1812	18	**JAMES MADISON**	REPUBLICAN			128	
		DeWitt Clinton	Federalist			89	

Year	Number of States	Candidates	Parties	Popular Vote	% of Popular Vote	Electoral Vote	% Voter Participation
1816	19	**JAMES MONROE**	REPUBLICAN			183	
		Rufus King	Federalist			34	
1820	24	**JAMES MONROE**	REPUBLICAN			231	
		John Quincy Adams	Independent			1	
1824	24	**JOHN QUINCY ADAMS**	NO PARTY	108,740	31.0	84	26.9
		Andrew Jackson	DESIGNATIONS	153,544	43.0	99	
		William H. Crawford		46,618	13.0	41	
		Henry Clay		47,136	13.0	37	
1828	24	**ANDREW JACKSON**	DEMOCRAT	647,286	56.0	178	57.6
		John Quincy Adams	National Republican	508,064	44.0	83	
1832	24	**ANDREW JACKSON**	DEMOCRAT	687,502	54.5	219	55.4
		Henry Clay	National Republican	530,189	37.5	49	
		William Wirt	Anti-Masonic	101,051	8.0	7	
		John Floyd	Democrat			11	
1836	26	**MARTIN VAN BUREN**	DEMOCRAT	765,483	51.0	170	57.8
		William H. Harrison	Whig			73	
		Hugh L. White	Whig	739,795	49.0	26	
		Daniel Webster	Whig			14	
		William P. Mangum	Whig			11	
1840	26	**WILLIAM H. HARRISON**	WHIG	1,274,624	53.0	234	80.2
		Martin Van Buren	Democrat	1,127,781	47.0	60	

Year	Number of States	Candidates	Parties	Popular Vote	% of Popular Vote	Electoral Vote	% Voter Participation
1844	26	**JAMES K. POLK**	DEMOCRAT	1,338,464	50.0	170	78.9
		Henry Clay	Whig	1,300,097	48.0	105	
		James G. Birney	Liberty	62,300	2.0		
1848	30	**ZACHARY TAYLOR**	WHIG	1,360,967	47.5	163	72.7
		Lewis Cass	Democrat	1,222,342	42.5	127	
		Martin Van Buren	Free Soil	291,263	10.0		
1852	31	**FRANKLIN PIERCE**	DEMOCRAT	1,601,117	51.0	254	69.6
		Winfield Scott	Whig	1,385,453	44.0	42	
		John P. Hale	Free Soil	155,825	5.0		
1856	31	**JAMES BUCHANAN**	DEMOCRAT	1,832,955	45.0	174	78.9
		John C. Frémont	Republican	1,339,932	33.0	114	
		Millard Fillmore	American	871,731	22.0	8	
1860	33	**ABRAHAM LINCOLN**	REPUBLICAN	1,865,593	40.0	180	81.2
		Stephen A. Douglas	Northern Democrat	1,382,713	29.0	12	
		John C. Breckinridge	Southern Democrat	848,356	18.0	72	
		John Bell	Constitutional Union	592,906	13.0	39	
1864	36	**ABRAHAM LINCOLN**	REPUBLICAN	2,206,938	55.0	212	73.8
		George B. McClellan	Democrat	1,803,787	45.0	21	
1868	37	**ULYSSES S. GRANT**	REPUBLICAN	3,013,421	53.0	214	78.1
		Horatio Seymour	Democrat	2,706,829	47.0	80	

Year	Number of States	Candidates	Parties	Popular Vote	% of Popular Vote	Electoral Vote	% Voter Participation
1872	37	ULYSSES S. GRANT	REPUBLICAN	3,596,745	55.6	286	71.3
		Horace Greeley	Democrat	2,843,446	43.9	66	
1876	38	RUTHERFORD B. HAYES	REPUBLICAN	4,036,572	48.0	185	81.8
		Samuel J. Tilden	Democrat	4,284,020	51.0	184	
1880	38	JAMES A. GARFIELD	REPUBLICAN	4,453,295	48.4	214	79.4
		Winfield S. Hancock	Democrat	4,414,082	48.3	155	
		James B. Weaver	Greenback-Labor	308,578	3.5		
1884	38	GROVER CLEVELAND	DEMOCRAT	4,879,507	48.5	219	77.5
		James G. Blaine	Republican	4,850,293	48.2	182	
		Benjamin F. Butler	Greenback-Labor	175,370	1.8		
		John P. St. John	Prohibition	150,369	1.5		
1888	38	BENJAMIN HARRISON	REPUBLICAN	5,447,129	47.9	233	79.3
		Grover Cleveland	Democrat	5,537,857	48.6	168	
		Clinton B. Fisk	Prohibition	249,506	2.2		
		Anson J. Streeter	Union Labor	146,935	1.3		
1892	44	GROVER CLEVELAND	DEMOCRAT	5,555,426	46.1	277	74.7
		Benjamin Harrison	Republican	5,182,690	43.0	145	
		James B. Weaver	People's	1,029,846	8.5	22	
		John Bidwell	Prohibition	264,133	2.2		
1896	45	WILLIAM McKINLEY	REPUBLICAN	7,102,246	51.0	271	79.3
		William J. Bryan	Democrat	6,492,559	47.0	176	

Year	Number of States	Candidates	Parties	Popular Vote	% of Popular Vote	Electoral Vote	% Voter Participation
1900	45	**WILLIAM McKINLEY**	REPUBLICAN	7,218,491	52.0	292	73.2
		William J. Bryan	Democrat; Populist	6,356,734	46.0	155	
		John C. Wooley	Prohibition	208,914	1.5		
1904	45	**THEODORE ROOSEVELT**	REPUBLICAN	7,628,461	56.4	336	65.2
		Alton B. Parker	Democrat	5,084,223	37.6	140	
		Eugene V. Debs	Socialist	402,283	3.0		
		Silas C. Swallow	Prohibition	258,536	1.9		
1908	46	**WILLIAM H. TAFT**	REPUBLICAN	7,675,320	52.0	321	65.4
		William J. Bryan	Democrat	6,412,294	43.4	162	
		Eugene V. Debs	Socialist	420,793	2.8		
		Eugene W. Chafin	Prohibition	253,840	1.7		
1912	48	**WOODROW WILSON**	DEMOCRAT	6,296,547	41.9	435	58.8
		Theodore Roosevelt	Progressive	4,118,571	27.4	88	
		William H. Taft	Republican	3,486,720	23.2	8	
		Eugene V. Debs	Socialist	900,672	6.0		
		Eugene W. Chafin	Prohibition	206,275	1.4		
1916	48	**WOODROW WILSON**	DEMOCRAT	9,127,695	49.4	277	61.6
		Charles E. Hughes	Republican	8,533,507	46.2	254	
		A. L. Benson	Socialist	585,113	3.2		
		J. Frank Hanly	Prohibition	220,506	1.2		
1920	48	**WARREN G. HARDING**	REPUBLICAN	16,153,115	60.6	404	49.2
		James M. Cox	Democrat	9,133,092	34.3	127	
		Eugene V. Debs	Socialist	915,490	3.4		
		P. P. Christensen	Farmer-Labor	265,229	1.0		
1924	48	**CALVIN COOLIDGE**	REPUBLICAN	15,719,921	54.0	382	48.9
		John W. Davis	Democrat	8,386,704	29.0	136	
		Robert M. La Follette	Progressive	4,832,532	16.5	13	

Year	Number of States	Candidates	Parties	Popular Vote	% of Popular Vote	Electoral Vote	% Voter Participation
1928	48	**HERBERT C. HOOVER**	REPUBLICAN	21,437,277	58.2	444	56.9
		Alfred E. Smith	Democrat	15,007,698	40.9	87	
1932	48	**FRANKLIN D. ROOSEVELT**	DEMOCRAT	22,829,501	57.7	472	56.9
		Herbert C. Hoover	Republican	15,760,684	39.8	59	
		Norman Thomas	Socialist	884,649	2.2		
1936	48	**FRANKLIN D. ROOSEVELT**	DEMOCRAT	27,757,333	60.8	523	61.0
		Alfred M. Landon	Republican	16,684,231	36.6	8	
		William Lemke	Union	892,267	2.0		
1940	48	**FRANKLIN D. ROOSEVELT**	DEMOCRAT	27,313,041	54.9	449	62.5
		Wendell L. Willkie	Republican	22,348,480	44.9	82	
1944	48	**FRANKLIN D. ROOSEVELT**	DEMOCRAT	25,612,610	53.5	432	55.9
		Thomas E. Dewey	Republican	22,017,617	46.0	99	
1948	48	**HARRY S. TRUMAN**	DEMOCRAT	24,179,345	49.7	303	53.0
		Thomas E. Dewey	Republican	21,991,291	45.3	189	
		J. Strom Thurmond	States' Rights	1,176,125	2.4	39	
		Henry A. Wallace	Progressive	1,157,326	2.4		
1952	48	**DWIGHT D. EISENHOWER**	REPUBLICAN	33,936,234	55.1	442	63.3
		Adlai E. Stevenson	Democrat	27,314,992	44.4	89	

Year	Number of States	Candidates	Parties	Popular Vote	% of Popular Vote	Electoral Vote	% Voter Participation
1956	48	**DWIGHT D. EISENHOWER**	REPUBLICAN	35,590,472	57.6	457	60.6
		Adlai E. Stevenson	Democrat	26,022,752	42.1	73	
1960	50	**JOHN F. KENNEDY**	DEMOCRAT	34,226,731	49.7	303	62.8
		Richard M. Nixon	Republican	34,108,157	49.6	219	
1964	50	**LYNDON B. JOHNSON**	DEMOCRAT	43,129,566	61.0	486	61.9
		Barry M. Goldwater	Republican	27,178,188	38.4	52	
1968	50	**RICHARD M. NIXON**	REPUBLICAN	31,785,480	43.2	301	60.9
		Hubert H. Humphrey	Democrat	31,275,166	42.6	191	
		George C. Wallace	American Independent	9,906,473	12.9	46	
1972	50	**RICHARD M. NIXON**	REPUBLICAN	47,169,911	60.7	520	55.2
		George S. McGovern	Democrat	29,170,383	37.5	17	
		John G. Schmitz	American	1,099,482	1.4		
1976	50	**JIMMY CARTER**	DEMOCRAT	40,830,763	50.0	297	53.5
		Gerald R. Ford	Republican	39,147,793	48.0	240	
1980	50	**RONALD REAGAN**	REPUBLICAN	43,904,153	50.9	489	52.6
		Jimmy Carter	Democrat	35,483,883	41.1	49	
		John B. Anderson	Independent	5,720,060	6.6		
		Ed Clark	Libertarian	921,299	1.1		

Year	Number of States	Candidates	Parties	Popular Vote	% of Popular Vote	Electoral Vote	% Voter Participation
1984	50	**RONALD REAGAN**	REPUBLICAN	54,455,075	58.8	525	53.1
		Walter F. Mondale	Democrat	37,577,185	40.5	13	
1988	50	**GEORGE H. BUSH**	REPUBLICAN	48,886,097	53.4	426	50.1
		Michael Dukakis	Democrat	41,809,074	45.6	111	
1992	50	**BILL CLINTON**	DEMOCRAT	44,909,326	42.9	370	55.0
		George H. Bush	Republican	39,103,882	37.4	168	
		H. Ross Perot	Independent	19,741,657	18.9		
1996	50	**BILL CLINTON**	DEMOCRAT	47,402,357	49.2	379	49.0
		Bob Dole	Republican	39,198,755	40.7	159	
		H. Ross Perot	Reform Party	8,085,402	8.4		
2000	50	**GEORGE W. BUSH**	REPUBLICAN	50,455,156	47.9	271	50.4
		Albert Gore	Democrat	50,992,335	48.4	266	
		Ralph Nader	Green Party	2,882,738	2.7		
2004	50	**GEORGE W. BUSH**	REPUBLICAN	62,040,610	50.7	286	56.2
		John F. Kerry	Democrat	59,028,111	48.3	251	

Candidates receiving less than 1 percent of the popular vote have been omitted. Thus, the percentage of popular vote given for any election year may not total 100 percent. Before the passage of the Twelfth Amendment in 1804, the electoral college voted for two presidential candidates; the runner-up became vice president.

ADMISSION OF STATES

Order of Admission	State	Date of Admission	Order of Admission	State	Date of Admission
1	Delaware	December 7, 1787	26	Michigan	January 26, 1837
2	Pennsylvania	December 12, 1787	27	Florida	March 3, 1845
3	New Jersey	December 18, 1787	28	Texas	December 29, 1845
4	Georgia	January 2, 1788	29	Iowa	December 28, 1846
5	Connecticut	January 9, 1788	30	Wisconsin	May 29, 1848
6	Massachusetts	February 7, 1788	31	California	September 9, 1850
7	Maryland	April 28, 1788	32	Minnesota	May 11, 1858
8	South Carolina	May 23, 1788	33	Oregon	February 14, 1859
9	New Hampshire	June 21, 1788	34	Kansas	January 29, 1861
10	Virginia	June 25, 1788	35	West Virginia	June 30, 1863
11	New York	July 26, 1788	36	Nevada	October 31, 1864
12	North Carolina	November 21, 1789	37	Nebraska	March 1, 1867
13	Rhode Island	May 29, 1790	38	Colorado	August 1, 1876
14	Vermont	March 4, 1791	39	North Dakota	November 2, 1889
15	Kentucky	June 1, 1792	40	South Dakota	November 2, 1889
16	Tennessee	June 1, 1796	41	Montana	November 8, 1889
17	Ohio	March 1, 1803	42	Washington	November 11, 1889
18	Louisiana	April 30, 1812	43	Idaho	July 3, 1890
19	Indiana	December 11, 1816	44	Wyoming	July 10, 1890
20	Mississippi	December 10, 1817	45	Utah	January 4, 1896
21	Illinois	December 3, 1818	46	Oklahoma	November 16, 1907
22	Alabama	December 14, 1819	47	New Mexico	January 6, 1912
23	Maine	March 15, 1820	48	Arizona	February 14, 1912
24	Missouri	August 10, 1821	49	Alaska	January 3, 1959
25	Arkansas	June 15, 1836	50	Hawaii	August 21, 1959

POPULATION OF THE UNITED STATES

Year	Number of States	Population	% Increase	Population per Square Mile
1790	13	3,929,214		4.5
1800	16	5,308,483	35.1	6.1
1810	17	7,239,881	36.4	4.3
1820	23	9,638,453	33.1	5.5
1830	24	12,866,020	33.5	7.4
1840	26	17,069,453	32.7	9.8
1850	31	23,191,876	35.9	7.9
1860	33	31,443,321	35.6	10.6
1870	37	39,818,449	26.6	13.4
1880	38	50,155,783	26.0	16.9
1890	44	62,947,714	25.5	21.1
1900	45	75,994,575	20.7	25.6
1910	46	91,972,266	21.0	31.0
1920	48	105,710,620	14.9	35.6
1930	48	122,775,046	16.1	41.2
1940	48	131,669,275	7.2	44.2
1950	48	150,697,361	14.5	50.7
1960	50	179,323,175	19.0	50.6
1970	50	203,235,298	13.3	57.5
1980	50	226,504,825	11.4	64.0
1985	50	237,839,000	5.0	67.2
1990	50	250,122,000	5.2	70.6
1995	50	263,411,707	5.3	74.4
2000	50	281,421,906	6.8	77.0

Historical Statistics of the United States

LABOR FORCE—SELECTED CHARACTERISTICS EXPRESSED AS A PERCENTAGE OF THE LABOR FORCE: 1800–2000

Year	Agriculture	Manufacturing	Domestic service	Clerical, sales, and service	Professions	Slave	Nonwhite	Foreign-born	Female
1800	74.4	—	2.4	—	—	30.2	32.6	—	21.4
1860	55.8	13.8	5.4	4.8[1]	3.0[1]	21.7	23.6	24.5[1]	19.6
1910	30.7	20.8	5.5	14.1	4.7	—	13.4	22.0	20.8
1950	12.0	26.4	2.5	27.3	8.9	—	10.0	8.7	27.9
2000	2.4	14.7	0.6	38.0[2]	15.6	—	16.5	10.3[2]	46.6

[1]Values for 1870 are presented here because the available data for 1860 exclude slaves.
[2]1990.
Note: "Clerical, sales, and service" excludes domestic service.

IMMIGRATION, BY ORIGIN (in thousands)

Period	Europe	Americas	Asia
1820–30	106	12	—
1831–40	496	33	—
1841–50	1,597	62	—
1851–60	2,453	75	42
1861–70	2,065	167	65
1871–80	2,272	404	70
1881–90	4,735	427	70
1891–1900	3,555	39	75
1901–10	8,065	362	324
1911–20	4,322	1,144	247
1921–30	2,463	1,517	112
1931–40	348	160	16
1941–50	621	355	32
1951–60	1,326	997	150
1961–70	1,123	1,716	590
1971–80	800	1,983	1,588
1981–90	762	3,616	2,738
1991–2000	1,100	3,800	2,200

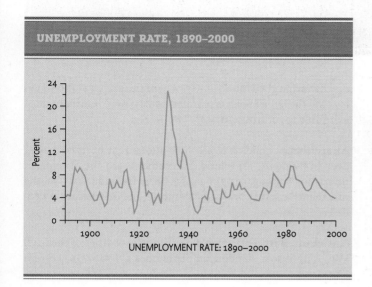

UNEMPLOYMENT RATE, 1890–2000

UNEMPLOYMENT RATE: 1890–2000

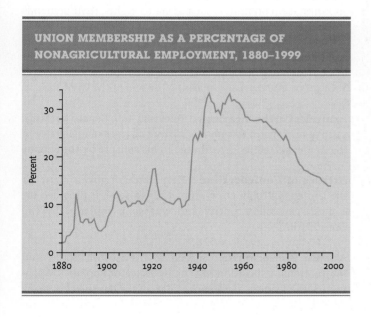

UNION MEMBERSHIP AS A PERCENTAGE OF
NONAGRICULTURAL EMPLOYMENT, 1880–1999

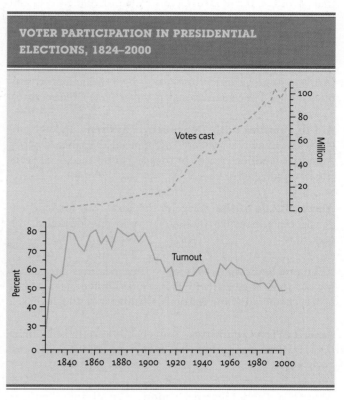

VOTER PARTICIPATION IN PRESIDENTIAL
ELECTIONS, 1824–2000

Abolitionism Social movement of the pre–Civil War era that advocated the immediate emancipation of the slaves and their incorporation into American society as equal citizens.

Agricultural Adjustment Act (1933) New Deal legislation that established the Agricultural Adjustment Administration (AAA) to improve agricultural prices by limiting market supplies; declared unconstitutional in *United States v. Butler* (1936).

Aid to Families with Dependent Children Federal program, also known as "welfare," of financial assistance to needy American families; created in 1935 as part of the Social Security Act; abolished in 1996.

Alamo, Battle of the Siege in the Texas War for Independence, 1836, in which the San Antonio mission fell to the Mexicans.

Alien and Sedition Acts (1798) Four measures passed during the undeclared war with France that limited the freedoms of speech and press and restricted the liberty of noncitizens.

America First Committee Largely midwestern isolationist organization supported by many prominent citizens, 1940–1941.

American Civil Liberties Union Organization founded during World War I to protest the suppression of freedom of expression in wartime; played a major role in court cases that achieved judicial recognition of Americans' civil liberties.

American Colonization Society Organized in 1816 to encourage colonization of free blacks to Africa; West African nation of Liberia founded in 1822 to serve as a homeland for them.

American Federation of Labor Founded in 1881 as a federation of trade unions composed mostly of skilled, white, native-born workers; its long-term president was Samuel Gompers.

American System Program of internal improvements and protective tariffs promoted by Speaker of the House Henry Clay in his presidential campaign of 1824; his proposals formed the core of Whig ideology in the 1830s and 1840s.

Amistad Ship that transported slaves from one port in Cuba to another, seized by the slaves in 1839. They made their way northward to the United States, where the status of the slaves became the subject of a celebrated court case; eventually most were able to return to Africa.

Anarchism Belief that all institutions that exercise power over individuals, especially government, are illegitimate; it flourished among certain native-born individualists in the nineteenth century and radical immigrants in the early twentieth century.

Antietam, Battle of One of the bloodiest battles of the Civil War, fought to a standoff on September 17, 1862, in western Maryland.

Antifederalists Opponents of the Constitution who saw it as a limitation on individual and states' rights; their demands led to the addition of a Bill of Rights to the document.

Appomattox Court House, Virginia Site of the surrender of Confederate general Robert E. Lee to Union general Ulysses S. Grant on April 9, 1865, marking the end of the Civil War.

Army-McCarthy hearings Televised U.S. Senate hearings in 1954 on Senator Joseph McCarthy's charges of disloyalty in the Army; his tactics contributed to his censure by the Senate.

Articles of Confederation First frame of government for the United States; in effect from 1781 to 1788, it provided for a weak central authority and was soon replaced by the Constitution.

Atlanta Compromise Speech to the Cotton States and International Exposition in 1895 by educator Booker T. Washington, the leading black spokesman of the day; black scholar W. E. B. Du Bois gave the speech its derisive name and criticized Washington for encouraging blacks to accommodate segregation and disenfranchisement.

Atlantic Charter Issued August 12, 1941, following meetings in Newfoundland between President Franklin D. Roosevelt and British prime minister Winston Churchill, the charter signaled the allies' cooperation and stated their war aims.

Atomic Energy Commission Created in 1946 to supervise peacetime uses of atomic energy.

Axis powers In World War II, the nations of Germany, Italy, and Japan.

Aztec Mesoamerican people who were conquered by the Spanish under Hernán Cortés, 1519–1528.

Baby boom Markedly higher birthrate in the years following World War II; led to the biggest demographic "bubble" in American history.

Bacon's Rebellion Unsuccessful 1676 revolt led by planter Nathaniel Bacon against Virginia governor William Berkeley's administration because of governmental corruption and because Berkeley had failed to protect settlers from Indian raids and did not allow them to occupy Indian lands.

***Baker v. Carr* (1962)** U.S. Supreme Court decision that established the principle of "one man, one vote," that is, that legislative districts must be equal in population.

***Bakke v. Regents of the University of California* (1978)** Case in which the U.S. Supreme Court ruled against the California university system's use of racial quotas in admissions but allowed the use of race as one factor in admissions decisions.

Balance of trade Ratio of imports to exports.

Bank of the United States Proposed by the first secretary of the treasury, Alexander Hamilton, the bank opened in 1791 and operated until 1811 to issue a uniform currency, make business loans, and collect tax monies. The Second Bank of the United States was chartered in 1816 but President Andrew Jackson vetoed the recharter bill in 1832.

Barbary pirates Plundering pirates off the Mediterranean coast of Africa; President Thomas Jefferson's refusal to pay them tribute to protect American ships sparked an undeclared naval war with North African nations, 1801–1805.

Barbed wire First practical fencing material for the Great Plains was invented in 1873 and rapidly spelled the end of the open range.

Bay of Pigs Invasion Hoping to inspire a revolt against Fidel Castro, the CIA sent 1,500 Cuban exiles to invade their homeland on April 17, 1961, but the mission was a spectacular failure.

Bill of Rights First ten amendments to the U.S. Constitution, adopted in 1791 to guarantee individual rights against infringement by the federal government.

Black Codes (1865–1866) Laws passed in southern states to restrict the rights of former slaves; to nullify the codes, Congress passed the Civil Rights Act of 1866 and the Fourteenth Amendment.

Black Legend Idea that the Spanish New World empire was more oppressive toward the Indians than other European empires; was used as a justification for English imperial expansion.

Black Power Post-1966 rallying cry of a more militant civil rights movement.

Bland-Allison Act (1878) Passed over President Rutherford B. Hayes's veto, the inflationary measure authorized the purchase each month of 2 to 4 million dollars' worth of silver for coinage.

"Bleeding Kansas" Violence between pro- and antislavery settlers in the Kansas Territory, 1856.

Boston Massacre Clash between British soldiers and a Boston mob, March 5, 1770, in which five colonists were killed.

Boston Tea Party On December 16, 1773, the Sons of Liberty, dressed as Indians, dumped hundreds of chests of tea into Boston harbor to protest the Tea Act of 1773, under which the British exported to the colonies millions of pounds of cheap— but still taxed—tea, thereby undercutting the price of smuggled tea and forcing payment of the tea duty.

Boxer Rebellion Chinese nationalist protest against Western commercial domination and cultural influence, 1900; a coalition of American, European, and Japanese forces put down the rebellion and reclaimed captured embassies in Peking (Beijing) within the year.

***Bracero* program** System agreed to by Mexican and American governments in 1942 under which tens of thousands of Mexicans entered the United States to work temporarily in agricultural jobs in the Southwest; lasted until 1964 and inhibited labor organization among farm workers since *braceros* could be deported at any time.

Brains trust Group of advisers—many of them academics—assembled by Franklin D. Roosevelt to recommend New Deal policies during the early months of his presidency.

Bretton Woods Town in New Hampshire and site of international agreement in 1944 by which the American dollar replaced the British pound as the most important international currency, and the World Bank and World Trade Organization were created to promote rebuilding after World War II and to insure that countries did not devalue their currencies.

Brook Farm Transcendentalist commune in West Roxbury, Massachusetts, populated from 1841 to 1847 principally by writers (Nathaniel Hawthorne, for one) and other intellectuals.

Brown v. Board of Education of Topeka (1954) U.S. Supreme Court decision that struck down racial segregation in public education and declared "separate but equal" unconstitutional.

Bull Run, Battles of (First and Second Manassas) First land engagement of the Civil War took place on July 21, 1861, at Manassas Junction, Virginia, at which Union troops quickly retreated; one year later, on August 29–30, Confederates captured the federal supply depot and forced Union troops back to Washington.

Bunker Hill, Battle of First major battle of the Revolutionary War; it actually took place at nearby Breed's Hill, Massachusetts, on June 17, 1775.

"Burned-over district" Area of western New York strongly influenced by the revivalist fervor of the Second Great Awakening; Disciples of Christ and Mormons are among the many sects that trace their roots to the phenomenon.

Bush v. Gore (2000) U.S. Supreme Court case that determined the winner of the disputed 2000 presidential election.

Calvinism Doctrine of predestination expounded by Swiss theologian John Calvin in 1536; influenced the Puritan, Presbyterian, German and Dutch Reformed, and Huguenot churches in the colonies.

Camp David accords Peace agreement between the leaders of Israel and Egypt, brokered by President Jimmy Carter in 1978.

Carpetbaggers Derisive term for northern emigrants who participated in the Republican governments of the Reconstruction South.

Chancellorsville, Battle of Confederate general Robert E. Lee won his last major victory and General "Stonewall" Jackson died in this Civil War battle in northern Virginia on May 1–4, 1863.

Chinese Exclusion Act (1882) Halted Chinese immigration to the United States.

Civil Rights Act of 1866 Along with the Fourteenth Amendment, guaranteed the rights of citizenship to former slaves.

Civil Rights Act of 1957 First federal civil rights law since Reconstruction; established the Civil Rights Commission and the Civil Rights Division of the Department of Justice.

Civil Rights Act of 1964 Outlawed discrimination in public accommodations and employment.

Closed shop Hiring requirement that all workers in a business must be union members.

Coercive Acts/Intolerable Acts (1774) Four parliamentary measures in reaction to the Boston Tea Party that forced payment for the tea, disallowed colonial trials of British soldiers, forced their quartering in private homes, and reduced the number of elected officials in Massachusetts.

Cold War Term for tensions, 1945–1989, between the Soviet Union and the United States, the two major world powers after World War II.

Commonwealth v. Hunt (1842) Landmark ruling of the Massachusetts Supreme Court establishing the legality of labor unions.

Communitarianism Social reform movement of the nineteenth century driven by the belief that by establishing small communities based on common ownership of property, a less competitive and individualistic society could be developed.

Compromise of 1850 Complex compromise devised by Senator Henry Clay that admitted California as a free state, included a stronger fugitive slave law, and delayed determination of the slave status of the New Mexico and Utah territories.

Compromise of 1877 Deal made by a Republican and Demo-cratic special congressional commission to resolve the disputed presidential election of 1876; Republican Rutherford B. Hayes, who had lost the popular vote, was declared the winner in exchange for the withdrawal of federal troops from involvement in politics in the South, marking the end of Reconstruction.

Congress of Industrial Organizations (CIO) Umbrella organization of semiskilled industrial unions, formed in 1935 as the Committee for Industrial Organization and renamed in 1938.

Congress of Racial Equality (CORE) Civil rights organization started in 1942 and best known for its Freedom Rides, bus journeys challenging racial segregation in the South in 1961.

Conspicuous consumption Phrase referring to extravagant spending to raise social standing, coined by Thorstein Veblen in *The Theory of the Leisure Class* (1899).

Constitutional Convention Meeting in Philadelphia, May 25–September 17, 1787, of representatives from twelve colonies—excepting Rhode Island—to revise the existing Articles of Confederation; convention soon resolved to produce an entirely new constitution.

Containment   General U.S. strategy in the Cold War that called for containing Soviet expansion; originally devised by U.S. diplomat George F. Kennan.

Continental army   Army authorized by the Continental Congress in 1775 to fight the British; commanded by General George Washington.

Continental Congress   Representatives of the colonies met first in Philadelphia in 1774 to formulate actions against British policies; the Second Continental Congress (1775–1789) conducted the war and adopted the Declaration of Independence and the Articles of Confederation.

Convict leasing   System developed in the post–Civil War South that generated income for the states and satisfied planters' need for cheap labor by renting prisoners out; the convicts were often treated poorly.

Copperheads   Republican term for northerners opposed to the Civil War; it derived from the name of a poisonous snake.

Coral Sea, Battle of the   Fought on May 7–8, 1942, near the eastern coast of Australia, it was the first U.S. naval victory over Japan in World War II.

Cotton gin   Invented by Eli Whitney in 1793, the machine separated cotton seed from cotton fiber, speeding cotton processing and making profitable the cultivation of the more hardy, but difficult to clean, short-staple cotton; led directly to the dramatic nineteenth-century expansion of slavery in the South.

Counterculture   "Hippie" youth culture of the 1960s, which rejected the values of the dominant culture in favor of illicit drugs, communes, free sex, and rock music.

Court-packing plan   President Franklin D. Roosevelt's failed 1937 attempt to increase the number of U.S. Supreme Court justices from nine to fifteen in order to save his Second New Deal programs from constitutional challenges.

Coverture   Principle in English and American law that a married woman lost her legal identity, which became "covered" by that of her husband, who therefore controlled her person and the family's economic resources.

Credit Mobilier scandal   Millions of dollars in overcharges for building the Union Pacific Railroad were exposed; high officials of the Ulysses S. Grant administration were implicated but never charged.

Creoles (*Criollos* in Spanish)   Persons born in the New World of European ancestry.

Cuban missile crisis   Caused when the United States discovered Soviet offensive missile sites in Cuba in October 1962; the U.S.-Soviet confrontation was the Cold War's closest brush with nuclear war.

Crop-lien system   Merchants extended credit to tenants based on their future crops, but high interest rates and the uncertainties of farming often led to inescapable debts.

D-Day   June 6, 1944, when an Allied amphibious assault landed on the Normandy coast and established a foothold in Europe, leading to the liberation of France from German occupation.

***Dartmouth College v. Woodward* (1819)**   U.S. Supreme Court upheld the original charter of the college against New Hampshire's attempt to alter the board of trustees; set precedent of support of contracts against state interference.

Dawes Act   Law passed in 1887 meant to encourage adoption of white norms among Indians; broke up tribal holdings into small farms for Indian families, with the remainder sold to white purchasers.

Declaration of Independence   Document adopted on July 4, 1776, that made the break with Britain official; drafted by a committee of the Second Continental Congress, including principal writer Thomas Jefferson.

Deindustrialization   Term describing decline of manufacturing in old industrial areas in the late twentieth century as companies shifted production to low-wage centers in the South and West or in other countries.

Deism   Enlightenment thought applied to religion; emphasized reason, morality, and natural law.

Democratic-Republican Societies   Organizations created in the mid-1790s by opponents of the policies of the Washington administration and supporters of the French Revolution.

Department of Homeland Security   Created to coordinate federal antiterrorist activity following the 2001 terrorist attacks on the World Trade Center and Pentagon.

Depression   Period in which economic output declines sharply and unemployment rises; it applied especially to the Great Depression of the 1930s.

Depression of 1893   Worst depression of the nineteenth century, set off by a railroad failure, too much speculation on Wall Street, and low agricultural prices.

Disenfranchise   To deprive of the right to vote; in the United States, exclusionary policies were used to deny groups, especially African-Americans and women, their voting rights.

Division of Powers The division of political power between the state and federal governments under the U.S. Constitution (also known as federalism).

Dixiecrats Deep South delegates who walked out of the 1948 Democratic National Convention in protest of the party's support for civil rights legislation and later formed the States' Rights Democratic (Dixiecrat) Party, which nominated Strom Thurmond of South Carolina for president.

Dominion of New England Consolidation into a single colony of the New England colonies—and later New York and New Jersey—by royal governor Edmund Andros in 1686; dominion reverted to individual colonial governments three years later.

Dred Scott v. Sandford (1857) U.S. Supreme Court decision in which Chief Justice Roger B. Taney ruled that Congress could not prohibit slavery in the territories, on the grounds that such a prohibition would violate the Fifth Amendment rights of slaveholders, and that no black person could be a citizen of the United States.

Due-process clause Clause in the Fifth and the Fourteenth Amendments to the U.S. Constitution guaranteeing that states could not "deprive any person of life, liberty, or property, without due process of law."

Dust Bowl Great Plains counties where millions of tons of topsoil were blown away from parched farmland in the 1930s; massive migration of farm families followed.

Eighteenth Amendment (1919) Prohibition amendment that made illegal the manufacture, sale, or transportation of alcoholic beverages; repealed in 1933.

Ellis Island Reception center in New York Harbor through which most European immigrants to America were processed from 1892 to 1954.

Emancipation Proclamation (1863) President Abraham Lincoln issued a preliminary proclamation on September 22, 1862, freeing the slaves in areas under Confederate control as of January 1, 1863, the date of the final proclamation, which also authorized the enrollment of black soldiers into the Union army.

Embargo Act of 1807 Attempt to exert economic pressure by prohibiting all exports from the United States, instead of waging war in reaction to continued British impressment of American sailors; smugglers easily circumvented the embargo, and it was repealed two years later.

Emergency Banking Relief Act (1933) First New Deal measure that provided for reopening the banks under strict conditions and took the United States off the gold standard.

Emergency Immigration Act of 1921 Limited U.S. immigration to 3 percent of each foreign-born nationality in the 1910 census; three years later, Congress restricted immigration even further.

Encomienda System under which officers of the Spanish conquistadores gained ownership of Indian land.

Enlightenment Revolution in thought in the eighteenth century that emphasized reason and science over the authority of traditional religion.

Environmental Protection Agency (EPA) Created in 1970 during the first administration of President Richard M. Nixon to oversee federal pollution control efforts.

Equal Rights Amendment Amendment to guarantee equal rights for women, introduced in 1923 but not passed by Congress until 1972; it failed to be ratified by the states.

Era of Good Feelings Contemporary characterization of the administration of popular Republican president James Monroe, 1817–1825.

Erie Canal Most important and profitable of the canals of the 1820s and 1830s; stretched from Buffalo to Albany, New York, connecting the Great Lakes to the East Coast and making New York City the nation's largest port.

Espionage and Sedition Acts (1917–1918) Limited criticism of government leaders and policies by imposing fines and prison terms on those who opposed American participation in the First World War.

Eugenics "Science" of improving the human race by regulating who can bear children; flourished in early twentieth century and led to laws for involuntary sterilization of the "feeble-minded."

Fair Deal Domestic reform proposals of the Truman administration; included civil rights legislation, national health insurance, and repeal of the Taft-Hartley Act, but only extensions of some New Deal programs were enacted.

Fair Employment Practices Commission Created in 1941 by executive order, the FEPC sought to eliminate racial discrimination in jobs; it possessed little power but represented a step toward civil rights for African-Americans.

Family Wage Idea that male workers should earn a wage sufficient to enable them to support their entire family without their wives having to work outside the home.

Federal Trade Commission Act (1914) Established the Federal Trade Commission to enforce existing antitrust laws that prohibited business combinations in restraint of trade.

The Federalist Collection of eighty-five essays that appeared in the New York press in 1787–1788 in support of the Constitution; written by Alexander Hamilton, James Madison, and John Jay and published under the pseudonym "Publius."

Federalist Party One of the two first national political parties; led by George Washington, John Adams, and Alexander Hamilton, it favored a strong central government.

Feminism Term that entered the lexicon in the early twentieth century to describe the movement for full equality for women, in political, social, and personal life.

Fifteenth Amendment Constitutional Amendment ratified in 1870, which prohibited states from discriminating in voting privileges on the basis of race.

"Fifty-four forty or fight" Democratic campaign slogan in the presidential election of 1844, urging that the northern border of Oregon be fixed at 54°40′ north latitude.

Filibuster In the nineteenth century, invasions of Central American countries launched privately by groups of Americans seeking to establish personal rule and spread slavery; in the twentieth century, term for the practice of members of the U.S. Senate delivering interminable speeches in order to prevent voting on legislation.

Fletcher v. Peck (1810) U.S. Supreme Court decision in which Chief Justice John Marshall upheld the initial fraudulent sale contracts in the Yazoo Fraud cases; it upheld the principle of sanctity of a contract.

Fordism Early twentieth-century term describing the economic system pioneered by Ford Motor Company based on high wages and mass consumption.

Fort McHenry Fort in Baltimore Harbor unsuccessfully bombarded by the British in September 1814; Francis Scott Key, a witness to the battle, was moved to write the words to "The Star-Spangled Banner."

Fort Sumter First battle of the Civil War, in which the federal fort in Charleston (South Carolina) Harbor was captured by the Confederates on April 14, 1861, after two days of shelling.

Fourteen Points President Woodrow Wilson's 1918 plan for peace after World War I; at the Versailles peace conference, however, he failed to incorporate all of the points into the treaty.

Fourteenth Amendment (1868) Guaranteed rights of citizenship to former slaves, in words similar to those of the Civil Rights Act of 1866.

Franchise The right to vote.

"Free person of color" Negro or mulatto person not held in slavery; immediately before the Civil War, there were nearly a half million in the United States, split almost evenly between North and South.

Free Soil Party Formed in 1848 to oppose slavery in the territory acquired in the Mexican War; nominated Martin Van Buren for president in 1848. By 1854 most of the party's members had joined the Republican Party.

Free Speech Movement Founded in 1964 at the University of California at Berkeley by student radicals protesting restrictions on their right to distribute political publications.

Freedmen's Bureau Reconstruction agency established in 1865 to protect the legal rights of former slaves and to assist with their education, jobs, health care, and landowning.

French and Indian War Known in Europe as the Seven Years' War, the last (1755–1763) of four colonial wars fought between England and France for control of North America east of the Mississippi River.

Fugitive Slave Act of 1850 Gave federal government authority in cases involving runaway slaves; aroused considerable opposition in the North.

Fundamentalism Anti-modernist Protestant movement started in the early twentieth century that proclaimed the literal truth of the Bible; the name came from *The Fundamentals*, published by conservative leaders.

Gadsden Purchase (1853) Thirty thousand square miles in present-day Arizona and New Mexico bought by Congress from Mexico primarily for the Southern Pacific Railroad's transcontinental route.

Gag Rule Rule adopted by House of Representatives in 1836 prohibiting consideration of abolitionist petitions; opposition, led by former president John Quincy Adams, succeeded in having it repealed in 1844.

Gentlemen's Agreement (1907) The United States would not exclude Japanese immigrants if Japan would voluntarily limit the number of immigrants coming to the United States.

Gettysburg, Battle of Fought in southern Pennsylvania, July 1–3, 1863; the Confederate defeat and the simultaneous loss at Vicksburg marked the military turning point of the Civil War.

Gibbons v. Ogden (1824) U.S. Supreme Court decision reinforcing the "commerce clause" (the federal government's right to regulate interstate commerce) of the Constitution; Chief Justice John Marshall ruled against the State of New York's granting of steamboat monopolies.

Gideon v. Wainwright **(1963)**   U.S. Supreme Court decision guaranteeing legal counsel for indigent felony defendants.

The Gilded Age   Mark Twain and Charles Dudley Warner's 1873 novel, the title of which became the popular name for the period from the end of the Civil War to the turn of the century.

Glass-Steagall Act (Banking Act of 1933)   Established the Federal Deposit Insurance Corporation and included banking reforms, some designed to control speculation. Repealed in 1999, opening the door to scandals involving banks and stock investment companies.

Globalization   Term that became prominent in the 1990s to describe the rapid acceleration of international flows of commerce, financial resources, labor, and cultural products.

Gold Standard   Policy at various points in American history by which the value of a dollar is set at a fixed price in terms of gold (in the post–World War II era, for example, $35 per ounce of gold).

Good Neighbor Policy   Proclaimed by President Franklin D. Roosevelt in his first inaugural address in 1933, it sought improved diplomatic relations between the United States and its Latin American neighbors.

Grandfather clause   Loophole created by southern disfranchising legislatures of the 1890s for illiterate white males whose grandfathers had been eligible to vote in 1867.

Granger movement   Political movement that grew out of the Patrons of Husbandry, an educational and social organization for farmers founded in 1867; the Grange had its greatest success in the Midwest of the 1870s, lobbying for government control of railroad and grain elevator rates and establishing farmers' cooperatives.

Great Awakening   Fervent religious revival movement in the 1720s through the 1740s that was spread throughout the colonies by ministers like New England Congregationalist Jonathan Edwards and English revivalist George Whitefield.

Great Compromise (Connecticut Compromise)   Settled the differences between the New Jersey and Virginia delegations to the Constitutional Convention by providing for a bicameral legislature, the upper house of which would have equal representation for each state and the lower house of which would be apportioned by population.

Great Depression   Worst economic depression in American history; it was spurred by the stock market crash of 1929 and lasted until World War II.

Great Migration   Large-scale migration of southern blacks during and after World War I to the North, where jobs had become available during the labor shortage of the war years.

Great Society   Term coined by President Lyndon B. Johnson in his 1965 State of the Union address, in which he proposed legislation to address problems of voting rights, poverty, diseases, education, immigration, and the environment.

Greenback-Labor Party   Formed in 1876 in reaction to economic depression, the party favored issuance of unsecured paper money to help farmers repay debts; the movement for free coinage of silver took the place of the greenback movement by the 1880s.

Griswold v. Connecticut **(1965)**   Supreme Court decision that, in overturning Connecticut law prohibiting the use of contraceptives, established a constitutional right to privacy.

Gulf War   Military action in 1991 in which an international coalition led by the United States drove Iraq from Kuwait, which it had occupied the previous year.

Habeas corpus, Writ of   An essential component of English common law and of the U.S. Constitution that guarantees that citizens may not be imprisoned without due process of law; literally means, "you may have the body"; suspended by President Lincoln during the Civil War and limited by President Bush after the attacks of September 11, 2001.

Hacienda   Large-scale farm in the Spanish New World empire worked by Indian laborers.

Harlem Renaissance   African-American literary and artistic movement of the 1920s centered in New York City's Harlem district; writers Langston Hughes, Jean Toomer, Zora Neale Hurston, and Countee Cullen were among those active in the movement.

Harpers Ferry, Virginia   Site of abolitionist John Brown's failed raid on the federal arsenal, October 16–17, 1859; Brown became a martyr to his cause after his capture and execution.

Hart-Celler Act (1965)   Eliminated the national origins quota system for immigration established by laws in 1921 and 1924; led to radical change in the origins of immigrants to the United States, with Asians and Latin Americans outnumbering Europeans.

Hartford Convention Meeting of New England Federalists on December 15, 1814, to protest the War of 1812; proposed seven constitutional amendments (limiting embargoes and changing requirements for officeholding, declaration of war, and admission of new states), but the war ended before Congress could respond.

Hawley-Smoot Tariff Act (1930) Raised tariffs to an unprecedented level and worsened the Great Depression by raising prices and discouraging foreign trade.

Haymarket affair Violence during an anarchist protest at Haymarket Square in Chicago on May 4, 1886; the deaths of eight, including seven policemen, led to the trial of eight anarchist leaders for conspiracy to commit murder.

Hessians German soldiers, most from Hesse-Cassel principality (hence the name), paid to fight for the British in the Revolutionary War.

Holding company Investment company that holds controlling interest in the securities of other companies.

Homestead Act (1862) Authorized Congress to grant 160 acres of public land to a western settler, who had to live on the land for five years to establish title.

Homestead Strike Violent strike at the Carnegie Steel Company near Pittsburgh in 1892 that culminated in the defeat of the Amalgamated Association of Iron and Steel Workers, the first steelworkers' union.

House Un-American Activities Committee (HUAC) Formed in 1938 to investigate subversives in the government and holders of radical ideas more generally; best-known investigations were of Hollywood notables and of former State Department official Alger Hiss, who was accused in 1948 of espionage and Communist Party membership. Abolished in 1975.

Hundred Days Extraordinarily productive first three months of President Franklin D. Roosevelt's administration in which a special session of Congress enacted fifteen of his New Deal proposals.

Impeachment Bringing charges against a public official; for example, the House of Representatives can impeach a president for "treason, bribery, or other high crimes and misdemeanors" by majority vote, and after the trial the Senate can remove the president by a vote of two-thirds. Two presidents, Andrew Johnson and Bill Clinton, have been impeached and tried before the Senate; neither was convicted.

Implied powers Federal powers beyond those specifically enumerated in the U.S. Constitution; based on the "elastic clause" of Article I, Section 8, of the Constitution that allows Congress to enact laws that promote the "general welfare."

"In God We Trust" Phrase placed on all new U.S. currency as of 1954.

Indentured servant Settler who signed on for a temporary period of servitude to a master in exchange for passage to the New World; Virginia and Pennsylvania were largely peopled in the seventeenth and eighteenth centuries by English and German indentured servants.

Indian Removal Act (1830) Signed by President Andrew Jackson, the law permitted the negotiation of treaties to obtain the Indians' lands in exchange for their relocation to what would become Oklahoma.

Individualism Term that entered the language in the 1820s to describe the increasing emphasis on the pursuit of personal advancement and private fulfillment free of outside interference.

Industrial Workers of the World Radical union organized in Chicago in 1905 and nicknamed the Wobblies; its opposition to World War I led to its destruction by the federal government under the Espionage Act.

Inflation An economic condition in which prices rise continuously.

Insular Cases Series of cases between 1901 and 1904 in which the Supreme Court ruled that constitutional protection of individual rights did not fully apply to residents of "insular" territories acquired by the United States in the Spanish-American War, such as Puerto Rico and the Philippines.

Interstate Commerce Commission Reacting to the U.S. Supreme Court's ruling in *Wabash Railroad v. Illinois* (1886), Congress established the ICC to curb abuses in the railroad industry by regulating rates.

Iran-Contra affair Scandal of the second Reagan administration involving sales of arms to Iran in partial exchange for release of hostages in Lebanon and use of the arms money to aid the Contras in Nicaragua, which had been expressly forbidden by Congress.

Iraq War Military campaign in 2003 in which the United States, unable to gain approval by the United Nations, unilaterally occupied Iraq and removed dictator Saddam Hussein from power.

Iron Curtain Term coined by Winston Churchill to describe the Cold War divide between western Europe and the Soviet Union's eastern European satellites.

Jamestown, Virginia Site in 1607 of the first permanent English settlement in the New World.

Japanese-American Internment Policy adopted by the Roosevelt administration in 1942 under which 110,000 persons of Japanese descent, most of them American citizens, were removed from the West Coast and forced to spend most of World War II in internment camps; it was the largest violation of American civil liberties in the twentieth century.

Jay's Treaty Treaty with Britain negotiated in 1794 by Chief Justice John Jay; Britain agreed to vacate forts in the Northwest Territories, and festering disagreements (border with Canada, prewar debts, shipping claims) would be settled by commission.

Jim Crow Minstrel show character whose name became synonymous with racial segregation.

Kansas-Nebraska Act (1854) Law sponsored by Illinois senator Stephen A. Douglas to allow settlers in newly organized territories north of the Missouri border to decide the slavery issue for themselves; fury over the resulting repeal of the Missouri Compromise of 1820 led to violence in Kansas and to the formation of the Republican Party.

Kellogg-Briand Pact Representatives of sixty-two nations in 1928 signed the pact (also called the Pact of Paris) to outlaw war.

Keynesianism Economic theory derived from the writings of British economist John Maynard Keynes, which rejected the laissez-faire approach in favor of public spending to stimulate economic growth, even at the cost of federal deficits; dominated economic policies of administrations from the 1940s to the mid-1970s.

Knights of Labor Founded in 1869, the first national union lasted, under the leadership of Terence V. Powderly, only into the 1890s; supplanted by the American Federation of Labor.

Know-Nothing (American) Party Nativist, anti-Catholic third party organized in 1854 in reaction to large-scale German and Irish immigration; the party's only presidential candidate was Millard Fillmore in 1856.

Korean War Conflict touched off in 1950 when Communist North Korea invaded South Korea; fighting, largely by U.S. forces, continued until 1953.

Ku Klux Klan Organized in Pulaski, Tennessee, in 1866 to terrorize former slaves who voted and held political offices during Reconstruction; a revived organization in the 1910s and 1920s stressed white, Anglo-Saxon, fundamentalist Protestant supremacy; the Klan revived a third time to fight the civil rights movement of the 1950s and 1960s in the South.

Laissez-faire Term adopted from French, meaning "let people do as they choose," describing opposition to government action to regulate economic or personal behavior.

Land Ordinance of 1785 Directed surveying of the Northwest Territory into townships of thirty-six sections (square miles) each, the sale of the sixteenth section of which was to be used to finance public education.

League of Nations Organization of nations to mediate disputes and avoid war established after World War I as part of the Treaty of Versailles; President Woodrow Wilson's "Fourteen Points" speech to Congress in 1918 proposed the formation of the league, which the United States never joined.

Lend-Lease Act (1941) Permitted the United States to lend or lease arms and other supplies to the Allies, signifying increasing likelihood of American involvement in World War II.

Levittown Low-cost, mass-produced developments of suburban tract housing built by William Levitt after World War II on Long Island and elsewhere.

Lexington and Concord, Battle of The first shots fired in the Revolutionary War, on April 19, 1775, near Boston; approximately 100 minutemen and 250 British soldiers were killed.

Leyte Gulf, Battle of Largest sea battle in history, fought on October 25, 1944, and won by the United States off the Philippine island of Leyte; Japanese losses were so great that they could not rebound.

Liberalism Originally, political philosophy that emphasized the protection of liberty by limiting the power of government to interfere with the natural rights of citizens; in the twentieth century, belief in an activist government promoting greater social and economic equality.

Liberty Party Abolitionist political party that nominated James G. Birney for president in 1840 and 1844; merged with the Free Soil Party in 1848.

Lincoln-Douglas debates Series of senatorial campaign debates in 1858 focusing on the issue of slavery in the territories; held in Illinois between Republican Abraham Lincoln, who made a national reputation for himself, and incumbent Democratic senator Stephen A. Douglas, who managed to hold onto his seat.

Little Bighorn, Battle of Most famous battle of the Great Sioux War took place in 1876 in the Montana Territory; combined Sioux and Cheyenne warriors massacred a vastly outnumbered U.S. Cavalry commanded by Lieutenant Colonel George Armstrong Custer.

Lochner v. New York **(1905)** Decision by Supreme Court overturning a New York law establishing a limit on the number of hours per week bakers could be compelled to work; "Lochnerism" became a way of describing the liberty of contract jurisprudence, which opposed all governmental intervention in the economy.

Louisiana Purchase President Thomas Jefferson's 1803 purchase from France of the important port of New Orleans and 828,000 square miles west of the Mississippi River to the Rocky Mountains; it more than doubled the territory of the United States at a cost of only $15 million.

Loyalists Colonists who remained loyal to Great Britain during the War of Independence.

Lusitania British passenger liner sunk by a German U-boat, May 7, 1915, creating a diplomatic crisis and public outrage at the loss of 128 Americans (roughly 10 percent of the total aboard); Germany agreed to pay reparations, and the United States waited two more years to enter World War I.

Lyceum movement Founded in 1826, the movement promoted adult public education through lectures and performances.

Lynching Practice, particularly widespread in the South between 1890 and 1940, in which persons (usually black) accused of a crime were murdered by mobs before standing trial. Lynchings often took place before large crowds, with law enforcement authorities not intervening.

Manhattan Project Secret American program during World War II to develop an atomic bomb; J. Robert Oppenheimer led the team of physicists at Los Alamos, New Mexico.

Manifest Destiny Phrase first used in 1845 to urge annexation of Texas; used thereafter to encourage American settlement of European colonial and Indian lands in the Great Plains and the West and, more generally, as a justification for American empire.

Marbury v. Madison **(1803)** First U.S. Supreme Court decision to declare a federal law—the Judiciary Act of 1801—unconstitutional.

March on Washington Civil rights demonstration on August 28, 1963, where the Reverend Martin Luther King Jr., gave his "I Have a Dream" speech on the steps of the Lincoln Memorial.

Marshall Plan U.S. program for the reconstruction of post–World War II Europe through massive aid to former enemy nations as well as allies; proposed by General George C. Marshall in 1947.

Massive resistance In reaction to the *Brown* decision of 1954, effort by southern states to defy federally mandated school integration.

Maya Pre-Columbian society in Mesoamerica before about A.D. 900.

Mayflower Compact Signed in 1620 aboard the *Mayflower* before the Pilgrims landed at Plymouth, the document committed the group to majority-rule government.

McCarran Internal Security Act (1950) Passed over President Harry S. Truman's veto, the law required registration of American Communist Party members, denied them passports, and allowed them to be detained as suspected subversives.

McCarthyism Post–World War II Red Scare focused on the fear of Communists in U.S. government positions; peaked during the Korean War; most closely associated with Joseph McCarthy, a major instigator of the hysteria.

McCulloch v. Maryland **(1819)** U.S. Supreme Court decision in which Chief Justice John Marshall, holding that Maryland could not tax the Second Bank of the United States, supported the authority of the federal government versus the states.

McNary-Haugen Bill Vetoed by President Calvin Coolidge in 1927 and 1928, the bill to aid farmers would have artificially raised agricultural prices by selling surpluses overseas for low prices and selling the reduced supply in the United States for higher prices.

Meat Inspection Act (1906) Passed largely in reaction to Upton Sinclair's *The Jungle,* the law set strict standards of cleanliness in the meatpacking industry.

Medicaid Great Society program established in 1965 that provided free medical care to the poor.

Medicare Key component of Great Society of Lyndon B. Johnson; government program created in 1965 to pay medical costs of elderly and disabled Americans.

Mercantilism Policy of Great Britain and other imperial powers of regulating the economies of colonies to benefit the mother country.

Mestizo Spanish word for person of mixed Native American and European ancestry.

Mexican War Controversial war with Mexico for control of California and New Mexico, 1846–1848; the Treaty of Guadalupe Hidalgo fixed the border at the Rio Grande and extended the United States to the Pacific coast, annexing more than a half-million square miles of Mexican territory.

Midway, Battle of Decisive American victory near Midway Island in the South Pacific on June 4, 1942; the Japanese navy never recovered its superiority over the U.S. navy.

Minstrel show Blackface vaudeville entertainment popular in the decades surrounding the Civil War.

***Miranda v. Arizona* (1966)** U.S. Supreme Court decision required police to advise persons in custody of their rights to legal counsel and against self-incrimination.

Missouri Compromise Deal proposed by Kentucky senator Henry Clay in 1820 to resolve the slave/free imbalance in Congress that would result from Missouri's admission as a slave state; Maine's admission as a free state offset Missouri, and slavery was prohibited in the remainder of the Louisiana Territory north of the southern border of Missouri.

Molly Maguires Secret organization of Irish coal miners that used violence to intimidate mine officials in the 1870s.

***Monitor* and *Merrimac*, Battle of the** First engagement between ironclad ships; fought at Hampton Roads, Virginia, on March 9, 1862.

Monroe Doctrine President James Monroe's declaration to Congress on December 2, 1823, that the American continents would be thenceforth closed to European colonization, and that the United States would not interfere in European affairs.

Moral Majority Televangelist Jerry Falwell's political lobbying organization, the name of which became synonymous with the Religious Right—conservative evangelical Protestants who helped ensure President Ronald Reagan's 1980 victory.

Mormons Founded in 1830 by Joseph Smith, the sect (officially, the Church of Jesus Christ of Latter-day Saints) was a product of the intense revivalism of the "burned-over district" of New York; Smith's successor Brigham Young led 15,000 followers to Utah in 1847 to escape persecution.

Montgomery bus boycott Sparked by Rosa Parks's arrest on December 1, 1955, for refusing to surrender her seat to a white passenger, a successful year-long boycott protesting segregation on city buses; led by the Reverend Martin Luther King Jr.

Muckrakers Writers who exposed corruption and abuses in politics, business, meatpacking, child labor, and more, primarily in the first decade of the twentieth century; their popular books and magazine articles spurred public interest in reform.

Mugwumps Reform wing of the Republican Party that supported Democrat Grover Cleveland for president in 1884 over Republican James G. Blaine, whose influence peddling had been revealed in the Mulligan letters of 1876.

Multiculturalism Term that became prominent in the 1990s to describe a growing emphasis on group racial and ethnic identity and demands that jobs, education, and politics reflect the increasingly diverse nature of American society.

***Munn v. Illinois* (1877)** U.S. Supreme Court ruling that upheld a Granger law allowing the state to regulate grain elevators.

NAFTA Approved in 1993, the North American Free Trade Agreement with Canada and Mexico allowed goods to travel across their borders free of tariffs; critics argued that American workers would lose their jobs to cheaper Mexican labor.

Nat Turner Rebellion Most important slave uprising in nineteenth-century America, led by a slave preacher who, with his followers, killed about sixty white persons in Southampton County, Virginia, in 1831.

National Association for the Advancement of Colored People (NAACP) Founded in 1910, this civil rights organization brought lawsuits against discriminatory practices and published *The Crisis*, a journal edited by African-American scholar W. E. B. Du Bois.

National Defense Education Act (1958) Passed in reaction to America's perceived inferiority in the space race; encouraged education in science and modern languages through student loans, university research grants, and aid to public schools.

National Industrial Recovery Act (1933) Passed on the last of the Hundred Days, it created public-works jobs through the Federal Emergency Relief Administration and established a system of self-regulation for industry through the National Recovery Administration, which was ruled unconstitutional in 1935.

National Organization for Women Founded in 1966 by writer Betty Friedan and other feminists, NOW pushed for abortion rights, nondiscrimination in the workplace, and other forms of equality for women.

National Road First federal interstate road, built between 1811 and 1838 and stretching from Cumberland, Maryland, to Vandalia, Illinois.

National Security Act (1947) Authorized the reorganization of government to coordinate military branches and security agencies; created the National Security Council, the Central Intelligence Agency, and the National Military Establishment (later renamed the Department of Defense).

National Youth Administration Created in 1935 as part of the Works Progress Administration, it employed millions of youths who had left school.

Nativism Anti-immigrant and anti-Catholic feeling especially prominent in the 1830s through the 1850s; the largest group was New York's Order of the Star-Spangled Banner, which expanded into the American (Know-Nothing) Party in 1854.

Naval stores Tar, pitch, and turpentine made from pine resin and used in shipbuilding; an important industry in the southern colonies, especially North Carolina.

Navigation Acts Passed by the English Parliament to control colonial trade and bolster the mercantile system, 1650–1775; enforcement of the acts led to growing resentment by colonists.

Neutrality Acts Series of laws passed between 1935 and 1939 to keep the United States from becoming involved in war by prohibiting American trade and travel to warring nations.

New Deal Franklin D. Roosevelt's campaign promise, in his speech to the Democratic National Convention of 1932, to combat the Great Depression with a "new deal for the American people"; the phrase became a catchword for his ambitious plan of economic programs.

New Freedom Democrat Woodrow Wilson's political slogan in the presidential campaign of 1912; Wilson wanted to improve the banking system, lower tariffs, and, by breaking up monopolies, give small businesses freedom to compete.

New Frontier John F. Kennedy's program, stymied by a Republican Congress and his abbreviated term; his successor Lyndon B. Johnson had greater success with many of the same concepts.

New Harmony Founded in Indiana by British industrialist Robert Owen in 1825, the short-lived New Harmony Community of Equality was one of the few nineteenth-century communal experiments not based on religious ideology.

New Left Radical youth protest movement of the 1960s, named by leader Tom Hayden to distinguish it from the Old (Marxist-Leninist) Left of the 1930s.

New Nationalism Platform of the Progressive Party and slogan of former president Theodore Roosevelt in the presidential campaign of 1912; stressed government activism, including regulation of trusts, conservation, and recall of state court decisions that had nullified progressive programs.

New Orleans, Battle of Last battle of the War of 1812, fought on January 8, 1815, weeks after the peace treaty was signed but prior to the news reaching America; General Andrew Jackson led the victorious American troops.

New South *Atlanta Constitution* editor Henry W. Grady's 1886 term for the prosperous post–Civil War South he envisioned: democratic, industrial, urban, and free of nostalgia for the defeated plantation South.

Nineteenth Amendment (1920) Granted women the right to vote.

Nisei Japanese-Americans; literally, "second generation."

Normalcy Word coined by future president Warren G. Harding as part of a 1920 campaign speech—"not nostrums, but normalcy"—signifying public weariness with Woodrow Wilson's internationalism and domestic reforms.

North Atlantic Treaty Organization (NATO) Alliance founded in 1949 by ten western European nations, the United States, and Canada to deter Soviet expansion in Europe.

Northwest Ordinance of 1787 Created the Northwest Territory (area north of the Ohio River and west of Pennsylvania), established conditions for self-government and statehood, included a Bill of Rights, and permanently prohibited slavery.

Nullification Concept of invalidation of a federal law within the borders of a state; first expounded in Thomas Jefferson's draft of Kentucky resolution against Alien and Sedition Acts (1798); cited by South Carolina in its Ordinance of Nullification (1832) of the Tariff of Abominations, used by southern states to explain their secession from the Union (1861), and cited again by southern states to oppose the *Brown v. Board of Education* decision (1954).

Office of Price Administration Created in 1941 to control wartime inflation and price fixing resulting from shortages of many consumer goods, the OPA imposed wage and price freezes and administered a rationing system.

Okies Displaced farm families from the Oklahoma dust bowl who migrated to California during the 1930s in search of jobs.

Oneida Community Utopian community founded in 1848; the Perfectionist religious group practiced "complex marriage" under leader John Humphrey Noyes.

OPEC Organization of Petroleum Exporting Countries.

Open Door Policy In hopes of protecting the Chinese market for U.S. exports, Secretary of State John Hay demanded in 1899 that Chinese trade be open to all nations.

Open Shop Situation in which union membership is not a condition of employment in a factory or other business.

Operation Dixie CIO's largely ineffective post–World War II campaign to unionize southern workers.

Oregon Trail Route of wagon trains bearing settlers from Independence, Missouri, to the Oregon Country in the 1840s through the 1860s.

Ostend Manifesto Memorandum written in 1854 from Ostend, Belgium, by the U.S. ministers to England, France, and Spain recommending purchase or seizure of Cuba in order to increase the United States' slaveholding territory.

Panic of 1819 Financial collapse brought on by sharply falling cotton prices, declining demand for American exports, and reckless western land speculation.

Panic of 1837 Beginning of major economic depression lasting about six years; touched off by a British financial crisis and made worse by falling cotton prices, credit and currency problems, and speculation in land, canals, and railroads.

Panic of 1857 Beginning of economic depression lasting about two years and brought on by falling grain prices and a weak financial system; the South was largely protected by international demand for its cotton.

Panic of 1873 Onset of severe six-year depression marked by bank failures and railroad and insurance bankruptcies.

Peace of Paris Signed on September 3, 1783, the treaty ending the Revolutionary War and recognizing American independence from Britain also established the border between Canada and the United States, fixed the western border at the Mississippi River, and ceded Florida to Spain.

Pendleton Civil Service Act (1883) Established the Civil Service Commission and marked the end of the spoils system.

Pentagon Papers Informal name for the Defense Department's secret history of the Vietnam conflict; leaked to the press by former official Daniel Ellsberg and published in the *New York Times* in 1971.

Philippine War American military campaign that suppressed the movement for Philippine independence after the Spanish-American War; America's death toll was over 4,000 and the Philippine's was far higher.

Pilgrims Puritan Separatists who broke completely with the Church of England and sailed to the New World aboard the *Mayflower*, founding Plymouth Colony on Cape Cod in 1620.

Pinckney's Treaty Treaty with Spain negotiated by Thomas Pinckney in 1795; established United States boundaries at the Mississippi River and the thirty-first parallel and allowed open transportation on the Mississippi.

Plantation An early word for a colony, a settlement "planted" from abroad among an alien population in Ireland or the New World. Later, a large agricultural enterprise that used unfree labor to produce a crop for the world market.

Planter In the antebellum South, the owner of a large farm worked by twenty or more slaves.

Platt Amendment (1901) Amendment to Cuban constitution that reserved the United States' right to intervene in Cuban affairs and forced newly independent Cuba to host American naval bases on the island.

***Plessy v. Ferguson* (1896)** U.S. Supreme Court decision supporting the legality of Jim Crow laws that permitted or required "separate but equal" facilities for blacks and whites.

Poll tax Tax that must be paid in order to be eligible to vote; used as an effective means of disenfranchising black citizens after Reconstruction, since they often could not afford even a modest fee.

Popular sovereignty Allowed settlers in a disputed territory to decide the slavery issue for themselves; program most closely associated with Senator Stephen A. Douglas of Illinois.

Populist Party Founded in 1892, it advocated a variety of reform issues, including free coinage of silver, income tax, postal savings, regulation of railroads, and direct election of U.S. senators.

Potsdam Conference Last meeting of the major Allied powers, the conference took place outside Berlin from July 17 to August 2, 1945; United States president Harry Truman, Soviet dictator Joseph Stalin, and British prime minister Clement Attlee finalized plans begun at Yalta.

Proclamation of Amnesty and Reconstruction President Lincoln's proposal for reconstruction, issued in 1863, allowed southern states to rejoin the Union if 10 percent of the 1860 electorate signed loyalty pledges, accepted emancipation, and had received presidential pardons.

Proclamation of 1763   Royal directive issued after the French and Indian War prohibiting settlement, surveys, and land grants west of the Appalachian Mountains; caused considerable resentment among colonists hoping to move west.

Progressive Party   Created when former president Theodore Roosevelt broke away from the Republican Party to run for president again in 1912; the party supported progressive reforms similar to the Democrats but stopped short of seeking to eliminate trusts. Also the name of party backing Robert La Follette for president in 1924.

Progressivism   Broad-based reform movement, 1900–1917, that sought governmental action in solving problems in many areas of American life, including education, public health, the economy, the environment, labor, transportation, and politics.

Proposition 13   Measure approved by California voters in 1978 prohibiting future increases in property taxes; marked beginning of "tax revolt" as major political impulse.

Public sphere   The world of political organization and debate in private associations and publications outside the control of government.

Pueblo Revolt   Uprising in 1680 in which Pueblo Indians temporarily drove Spanish colonists out of modern-day New Mexico.

Pullman Strike   Strike against the Pullman Palace Car Company in the company town of Pullman, Illinois, on May 11, 1894, by the American Railway Union under Eugene V. Debs; the strike was crushed by court injunctions and federal troops two months later.

Pure Food and Drug Act (1906)   First law to regulate manufacturing of food and medicines; prohibited dangerous additives and inaccurate labeling.

Puritans   English religious group that sought to purify the Church of England; founded the Massachusetts Bay Colony under John Winthrop in 1630.

Quakers (Society of Friends)   Religious group in England and America whose members believed all persons possessed the "inner light" or spirit of God; they were early proponents of abolition of slavery and equal rights for women.

Radical Republicans   Group within the Republican Party in the 1850s and 1860s that advocated strong resistance to the expansion of slavery, opposition to compromise with the South in the secession crisis of 1860–1861, emancipation and arming of black soldiers during the Civil War, and equal civil and political rights for blacks during Reconstruction.

Railroad Strike of 1877   Interstate strike, crushed by federal troops, which resulted in extensive property damage and many deaths.

Reaganomics   Popular name for President Ronald Reagan's philosophy of "supply side" economics, which combined tax cuts with an unregulated marketplace.

Reconstruction Act (1867)   Established temporary military governments in ten Confederate states—excepting Tennessee—and required that the states ratify the Fourteenth Amendment and permit freedmen to vote.

Reconstruction Finance Corporation   Federal program established in 1932 under President Herbert Hoover to loan money to banks and other institutions to help them avert bankruptcy.

Red Scare   Fear among many Americans after World War I of Communists in particular and noncitizens in general, a reaction to the Russian Revolution, mail bombs, strikes, and riots.

Redeemers   Conservative white Democrats, many of them planters or businessmen, who reclaimed control of the South following the end of Reconstruction.

Regulators   Groups of backcountry Carolina settlers who protested colonial policies.

Republican Party   Organized in 1854 by antislavery Whigs, Democrats, and Free Soilers in response to the passage of the Kansas-Nebraska Act; nominated John C. Frémont for president in 1856 and Abraham Lincoln in 1860; also the name of the party formed by Thomas Jefferson and James Madison in the 1790s.

Republicanism   Political theory in eighteenth-century England and America that celebrated active participation in public life by economically independent citizens as central to freedom.

Revolution of 1800   First time that an American political party surrendered power to the opposition party; Jefferson, a Republican, had defeated incumbent Adams, a Federalist, for president.

Right-to-work   State laws enacted to prevent imposition of the closed shop; any worker, whether or not a union member, could be hired.

***Roe v. Wade* (1973)**   U.S. Supreme Court decision requiring states to permit first-trimester abortions.

Roosevelt Corollary (1904)   President Theodore Roosevelt announced in what was essentially a corollary to the Monroe

Doctrine that the United States could intervene militarily to prevent interference from European powers in the Western Hemisphere.

Rough Riders   The first U.S. Volunteer Cavalry, led in battle in the Spanish-American War by Theodore Roosevelt; they were victorious in their only battle near Santiago, Cuba, and Roosevelt used the notoriety to aid his political career.

Santa Fe Trail   Beginning in the 1820s, a major trade route from St. Louis, Missouri, to Santa Fe, New Mexico Territory.

Saratoga, Battle of   Major defeat of British general John Burgoyne and more than 5,000 British troops at Saratoga, New York, on October 17, 1777.

Scalawags   Southern white Republicans—some former Unionists—who supported Reconstruction governments.

Schenck v. U.S. (1919)   U.S. Supreme Court decision upholding the wartime Espionage and Sedition Acts; in the opinion he wrote for the case, Justice Oliver Wendell Holmes set the now-familiar "clear and present danger" standard.

Scientific management   Management campaign to improve worker efficiency using measurements like "time and motion" studies to achieve greater productivity; introduced by Frederick Winslow Taylor in 1911.

Scopes Trial (1925)   Trial of John Scopes, Tennessee teacher accused of violating state law prohibiting teaching of the theory of evolution; it became a nationally celebrated confrontation between religious fundamentalism and civil liberties.

Scottsboro case (1931)   In overturning verdicts against nine black youths accused of raping two white women, the U.S. Supreme Court established precedents in *Powell v. Alabama* (1932), that adequate counsel must be appointed in capital cases, and in *Norris v. Alabama* (1935), that African-Americans cannot be excluded from juries.

Second Great Awakening   Religious revival movement of the early decades of the nineteenth century, in reaction to the growth of secularism and rationalist religion; began the predominance of the Baptist and Methodist churches.

Segregation   Policy of separating persons on the basis of race in schools, transportation, and other public facilities; *de facto* segregation refers to social customs that accomplish this, *de jure* segregation to laws requiring it.

Seneca Falls Convention   First women's rights meeting and the genesis of the women's suffrage movement; held in July 1848 in a church in Seneca Falls, New York, organized by Elizabeth Cady Stanton and Lucretia Coffin Mott.

"Separate but equal"   Principle underlying legal racial segregation, upheld in *Plessy v. Ferguson* (1896) and struck down in *Brown v. Board of Education* (1954).

Separation of Powers   Feature of the United States Constitution, sometimes called "checks and balances," in which power is divided between executive, legislative, and judicial branches of the national government so that no one can dominate the other two and endanger citizens' liberties.

Servicemen's Readjustment Act (1944)   The "GI Bill of Rights" provided money for education and other benefits to military personnel returning from World War II.

Settlement houses   Late-nineteenth-century movement to offer a broad array of social services in urban immigrant neighborhoods; Chicago's Hull House was one of hundreds of settlement houses that operated by the early twentieth century.

Seventeenth Amendment (1913)   Progressive reform that required U.S. senators to be elected directly by voters; previously, senators were chosen by state legislatures.

Shakers   Founded by Mother Ann Lee in England, the United Society of Believers in Christ's Second Appearing settled in Watervliet, New York, in 1774 and subsequently established eighteen additional communes in the Northeast, Indiana, and Kentucky.

Sharecropping   Type of farm tenancy that developed after the Civil War in which landless workers—often former slaves—farmed land in exchange for farm supplies and a share of the crop.

Shays's Rebellion (1787)   Massachusetts farmer Daniel Shays and 1,200 compatriots, seeking debt relief through issuance of paper currency and lower taxes, attempted to prevent courts from seizing property from indebted farmers.

Sherman Antitrust Act (1890)   First law to restrict monopolistic trusts and business combinations; extended by the Clayton Antitrust Act of 1914.

Sherman Silver Purchase Act (1890)   In replacing and extending the provisions of the Bland-Allison Act of 1878, it increased the amount of silver periodically bought for coinage.

Single tax   Concept of taxing only landowners as a remedy for poverty, promulgated by Henry George in *Progress and Poverty* (1879).

Sit-down strikes   Tactic adopted by labor unions in the mid- and late 1930s, whereby striking workers refused to leave factories, making production impossible; proved highly effective in the organizing drive of the Congress of Industrial Organizations.

Sit-ins   Tactic adopted by young civil rights activists, beginning in 1960, of demanding service at lunch counters or public accommodations and refusing to leave if denied access; marked the beginning of the most militant phase of the civil rights struggle.

Sixteenth Amendment (1913)   Legalized the federal income tax.

Smith v. Allwright (1944)   U.S. Supreme Court decision that outlawed all-white Democratic Party primaries in Texas.

Social Darwinism   Application of Charles Darwin's theory of natural selection to society; used the concept of the "survival of the fittest" to justify class distinctions and to explain poverty.

Social Gospel   Preached by liberal Protestant clergymen in the late nineteenth and early twentieth centuries; advocated the application of Christian principles to social problems generated by industrialization.

Social Security Act (1935)   Created the Social Security system with provisions for a retirement pension, unemployment insurance, disability insurance, and public assistance (welfare).

Socialist Party   Political party demanding public ownership of major economic enterprises in the United States as well as reforms like recognition of labor unions and women's suffrage; reached peak of influence in 1912 when presidential candidate Eugene V. Debs received over 900,000 votes.

Sons of Liberty   Organizations formed by Samuel Adams, John Hancock, and other radicals in response to the Stamp Act.

South Carolina Exposition and Protest   Written in 1828 by Vice-President John C. Calhoun of South Carolina to protest the so-called Tariff of Abominations, which seemed to favor northern industry; introduced the concept of state interposition and became the basis for South Carolina's Nullification Doctrine of 1833.

Southeast Asia Treaty Organization (SEATO)   Pact among mostly Western nations signed in 1954; designed to deter Communist expansion and cited as a justification for U.S. involvement in Vietnam.

Southern Christian Leadership Conference (SCLC)   Civil rights organization founded in 1957 by the Reverend Martin Luther King Jr., and other civil rights leaders.

Spoils system   The term—meaning the filling of federal government jobs with persons loyal to the party of the president—originated in Andrew Jackson's first term.

Sputnik   First artificial satellite to orbit the earth; launched October 4, 1957, by the Soviet Union.

Stalwarts   Conservative Republican Party faction during the presidency of Rutherford B. Hayes, 1877–1881; led by Senator Roscoe B. Conkling of New York, Stalwarts opposed civil service reform and favored a third term for President Ulysses S. Grant.

Stamp Act (1765)   Parliament required that revenue stamps be affixed to all colonial printed matter, documents, and playing cards; the Stamp Act Congress met to formulate a response, and the act was repealed the following year.

Standard Oil Company   Founded in 1870 by John D. Rockefeller in Cleveland, Ohio, it soon grew into the nation's first industry-dominating trust; the Sherman Antitrust Act (1890) was enacted in part to combat abuses by Standard Oil.

Staple crop   Important cash crop, for example, cotton or tobacco.

Steamboats   Paddlewheelers that could travel both up- and down-river in deep or shallow waters; they became commercially viable early in the nineteenth century and soon developed into America's first inland freight and passenger service network.

Strategic Defense Initiative ("Star Wars")   Defense Department's plan during the Reagan administration to build a system to destroy incoming missiles in space.

Student Nonviolent Coordinating Committee (SNCC)   Founded in 1960 to coordinate civil rights sit-ins and other forms of grassroots protest.

Students for a Democratic Society (SDS)   Major organization of the New Left, founded at the University of Michigan in 1960 by Tom Hayden and Al Haber.

Sugar Act (Revenue Act of 1764)   Parliament's tax on refined sugar and many other colonial products.

Taft-Hartley Act (1947)   Passed over President Harry Truman's veto, the law contained a number of provisions to weaken labor unions, including the banning of closed shops.

Tariff   Federal tax on imported goods.

Tariff of Abominations (Tariff of 1828)   Taxed imported goods at a very high rate; aroused strong opposition in the South.

Tariff of 1816   First true protective tariff, intended to protect certain American goods against foreign competition.

Tax Reform Act (1986)   Lowered federal income tax rates to 1920s levels and eliminated many loopholes.

Teapot Dome   Harding administration scandal in which Secretary of the Interior Albert B. Fall profited from secret leasing to private oil companies of government oil reserves at Teapot Dome, Wyoming, and Elk Hills, California.

Tennessee Valley Authority   Created in 1933 to control flooding in the Tennessee River valley, provide work for the region's unemployed, and produce inexpensive electric power for the region.

Tenure of Office Act (1867)   Required the president to obtain Senate approval to remove any official whose appointment had also required Senate approval; President Andrew Johnson's violation of the law by firing Secretary of War Edwin Stanton led to Johnson's impeachment.

Tet Offensive   Surprise attack by the Viet Cong and North Vietnamese during the Vietnamese New Year of 1968; turned American public opinion strongly against the war in Vietnam.

Thirteenth Amendment   Constitutional amendment adopted in 1865 that irrevocably abolished slavery throughout the United States.

Three Mile Island   Nuclear power plant near Harrisburg, Pennsylvania, site of 1979 accident that released radioactive steam into the air; public reaction ended the nuclear power industry's expansion.

Title IX   Part of the Educational Amendments Act of 1972 that banned gender discrimination in higher education.

Tonkin Gulf Resolution (1964)   Passed by Congress in reaction to supposedly unprovoked attacks on American warships off the coast of North Vietnam; it gave the president unlimited authority to defend U.S. forces and members of SEATO.

Townshend Acts (1767)   Parliamentary measures (named for the chancellor of the Exchequer) that taxed tea and other commodities, and established a Board of Customs Commissioners and colonial vice-admiralty courts.

Trail of Tears   Cherokees' own term for their forced removal, 1838–1839, from the Southeast to Indian lands (later Oklahoma); of 15,000 forced to march, 4,000 died on the way.

Transcendentalism   Philosophy of a small group of mid-nineteenth-century New England writers and thinkers, including Ralph Waldo Emerson, Henry David Thoreau, and Margaret Fuller; they stressed personal and intellectual self-reliance.

Transcontinental railroad   First line across the continent from Omaha, Nebraska, to Sacramento, California, established in 1869 with the linkage of the Union Pacific and Central Pacific railroads at Promontory, Utah.

Truman Doctrine   President Harry S. Truman's program announced in 1947 of aid to European countries—particularly Greece and Turkey—threatened by communism.

Trust   Companies combined to limit competition.

Twenty-first Amendment (1933)   Repealed the prohibition of the manufacture, sale, and transportation of alcoholic beverages, effectively nullifying the Eighteenth Amendment.

Twenty-second Amendment (1951)   Limited presidents to two full terms of office or two terms plus two years of an assumed term; passed in reaction to President Franklin D. Roosevelt's unprecedented four elected terms.

Twenty-sixth Amendment (1971)   Lowered the voting age from twenty-one to eighteen.

U.S.S. *Maine*   Battleship that exploded in Havana Harbor on February 15, 1898, resulting in 266 deaths; the American public, assuming that the Spanish had mined the ship, clamored for war, and the Spanish-American War was declared two months later.

Uncle Tom's Cabin   Harriet Beecher Stowe's 1852 antislavery novel popularized the abolitionist position.

Underground Railroad   Operating in the decades before the Civil War, the "railroad" was a clandestine system of routes and safehouses through which slaves were led to freedom in the North.

Understanding clause   Added to southern state constitutions in the late nineteenth century, it allowed illiterate whites to circumvent literacy tests for voting by demonstrating that they understood a passage in the Constitution; black citizens would be judged by white registrars to have failed.

Unitarianism   Late-eighteenth-century liberal offshoot of the New England Congregationalist Church; rejecting the Trinity, Unitarianism professed the oneness of God and the goodness of rational man.

United Farm Workers Union for the predominantly Mexican-American migrant laborers of the Southwest, organized by César Chavez in 1962.

United Nations Organization of nations to maintain world peace, established in 1945 and headquartered in New York.

Universal Negro Improvement Association Black nationalist movement active in the United States from 1916 to 1923, led by Marcus Garvey.

V-E Day May 8, 1945, the day World War II officially ended in Europe.

Vertical integration Company's avoidance of middlemen by producing its own supplies and providing for distribution of its product.

Veto President's constitutional power to reject legislation passed by Congress; a two-thirds vote in both houses of Congress can override a veto.

Vicksburg, Battle of The fall of Vicksburg, Mississippi, to General Ulysses S. Grant's army on July 4, 1863, after two months of siege was a turning point in the war because it gave the Union control of the Mississippi River.

Vietnam War Longest war in which the United States has been involved; began with giving American financial assistance to France, who sought to maintain control over Vietnam colony; moved to dispatching advisers to bolster the government of South Vietnam; and finally sent over 500,000 American soldiers by the mid-1960s; resulted in massive antiwar movement, eventual American withdrawal, and communist victory in 1975; only war the United States has lost.

Virginia and Kentucky Resolutions (1798–1799) Passed by the Virginia and the Kentucky legislatures; written by James Madison and Thomas Jefferson in response to the Alien and Sedition Acts, the resolutions advanced the state-compact theory of the Constitution. Virginia's resolution called on the federal courts to protect free speech. Jefferson's draft for Kentucky stated that a state could nullify federal law, but this was deleted.

Virginia and New Jersey Plans Differing opinions of delegations to the Constitutional Convention: New Jersey wanted one legislative body with equal representation for each state; Virginia's plan called for a strong central government and a two-house legislature apportioned by population.

Volstead Act (1919) Enforced the Prohibition amendment, beginning January 1920.

Voting Rights Act of 1965 Passed in the wake of Martin Luther King Jr.'s, Selma to Montgomery March, it authorized federal protection of the right to vote and permitted federal enforcement of minority voting rights in individual counties, mostly in the South.

Wabash Railroad v. Illinois (1886) Reversing the U.S. Supreme Court's ruling in *Munn v. Illinois*, the decision disallowed state regulation of interstate commerce.

Wade-Davis Bill (1864) Radical Republicans' plan for reconstruction that required loyalty oaths, abolition of slavery, repudiation of war debts, and denial of political rights to high-ranking Confederate officials; President Lincoln refused to sign the bill.

Wagner Act (National Labor Relations Act of 1935) Established the National Labor Relations Board and facilitated unionization by regulating employment and bargaining practices.

War Industries Board Run by financier Bernard Baruch, the board planned production and allocation of war materiel, supervised purchasing, and fixed prices, 1917–1919.

War of 1812 Fought with Britain, 1812–1814, over issues that included impressment of American sailors, interference with shipping, and collusion with Northwest Territory Indians; settled by the Treaty of Ghent in 1814.

War on Poverty Announced by President Lyndon B. Johnson in his 1964 State of the Union address; under the Economic Opportunity Bill signed later that year, Head Start, VISTA, and the Jobs Corps were created, and programs were created for students, farmers, and businesses in efforts to eliminate poverty.

War Powers Act Law passed in 1973, reflecting growing opposition to American involvement in Vietnam War; required congressional approval before president sent troops abroad.

War Production Board Created in 1942 to coordinate industrial efforts in World War II; similar to the War Industries Board in World War I.

Warren Court The U.S. Supreme Court under Chief Justice Earl Warren, 1953–1969, decided such landmark cases as *Brown v. Board of Education* (school desegregation), *Baker v. Carr* (legislative redistricting), and *Gideon v. Wainwright* and *Miranda v. Arizona* (rights of criminal defendants).

Washington Armaments Conference Leaders of nine world powers met in 1921–1922 to discuss the naval race; resulting treaties limited to a specific ratio the carrier and battleship tonnage of each nation (Five-Power Naval Treaty), formally ratified the Open Door to China (Nine-Power Treaty), and agreed to respect each other's Pacific territories (Four-Power Treaty).

Watergate　Washington office and apartment complex that lent its name to the 1972–1974 scandal of the Nixon administration; when his knowledge of the break-in at the Watergate and subsequent coverup was revealed, Nixon resigned the presidency under threat of impeachment.

Webster-Hayne debate　U.S. Senate debate of January 1830 between Daniel Webster of Massachusetts and Robert Hayne of South Carolina over nullification and states' rights.

Whig Party　Founded in 1834 to unite factions opposed to President Andrew Jackson, the party favored federal responsibility for internal improvements; the party ceased to exist by the late 1850s, when party members divided over the slavery issue.

Whiskey Rebellion　Violent protest by western Pennsylvania farmers against the federal excise tax on whiskey, 1794.

Wilmot Proviso　Proposal to prohibit slavery in any land acquired in the Mexican War, but southern senators, led by John C. Calhoun of South Carolina, defeated the measure in 1846 and 1847.

Women's Christian Temperance Union　Largest female reform society of the late nineteenth century; it moved from opposing sale of liquor to demanding the right to vote for women.

Works Progress Administration (WPA)　Part of the Second New Deal, it provided jobs for millions of the unemployed on construction and arts projects.

Wounded Knee, Battle of　Last incident of the Indian Wars took place in 1890 in the Dakota Territory, where the U.S. Cavalry killed over 200 Sioux men, women, and children.

Writs of assistance　One of the colonies' main complaints against Britain, the writs allowed unlimited search warrants without cause to look for evidence of smuggling.

XYZ affair　French foreign minister Tallyrand's three anonymous agents demanded payments to stop French plundering of American ships in 1797; refusal to pay the bribe was followed by two years of undeclared sea war with France (1798–1800).

Yalta conference　Meeting of Franklin D. Roosevelt, Winston Churchill, and Joseph Stalin at a Crimean resort to discuss the postwar world on February 4–11, 1945; Joseph Stalin claimed large areas in eastern Europe for Soviet domination.

Yellow journalism　Sensationalism in newspaper publishing that reached a peak in the circulation war between Joseph Pulitzer's *New York World* and William Randolph Hearst's *New York Journal* in the 1890s; the papers' accounts of events in Havana Harbor in 1898 led directly to the Spanish-American War.

Yeoman farmers　Small landowners (the majority of white families in the Old South) who farmed their own land and usually did not own slaves.

Yick Wo v. Hopkins　Supreme Court decision in 1886 overturning San Francisco law that, as enforced, discriminated against Chinese-owned laundries; established principle that equal protection of the law embodied in Fourteenth Amendment applied to all Americans, not just former slaves.

Yorktown, Battle of　Last battle of the Revolutionary War; General Lord Charles Cornwallis along with over 7,000 British troops surrendered at Yorktown, Virginia, on October 17, 1781.

Young Americans for Freedom　Organization of conservative students founded in 1960; played major role in 1964 presidential campaign of Barry Goldwater and in rebirth of conservatism in the 1960s.

Zimmermann Telegram　From the German foreign secretary to the German minister in Mexico, February 1917, instructing him to offer to recover Texas, New Mexico, and Arizona for Mexico if it would fight the United States to divert attention from Germany in the event that the United States joined the war.

CREDITS

PHOTOS

Half Title Courtesy of the Massachusetts Historical Society. Banner, William Lloyd Garrison (1805–1879) "Proclaim Liberty Throughout all the Land unto all the inhabitants thereof." MHS image #332; **Title Page** Reproduced from the collections of the Library of Congress, Prints & Photographs Division, P&P LC-USZC2-3794; **Title Page** American Social History Project, NY; **Title Page** George Eastman House; **Title Page** Cecil J. Williams; **546–547** Chicago Historical Society; **549** Reproduced from the collections of the Library of Congress, Prints & Photographs Division, LC-USZC4-1733; **550 (top)** Courtesy of the New-York Historical Society, New York City; **550 (bottom)** Photographic History Collection, National Museum of American History, Smithsonian Institution; **553** American Social History Project, New York; **554** © Corbis; **555** Courtesy of the New-York Historical Society, New York City; **559** Georgia Department of Archives and History; **561** Frank Leslie's Illustrated Newspaper, January 19, 1867; **562** Reproduction from the Collections of the Library of Congress LC-U5Z62-57937; **563** Museum of American Political Life, University of Hartford; **564** Reproduced from the Library of Congress Rare Book and Special Collections Division, LC-USZ62-40764; **565** Manuscripts, Archives & Rare Books Division, Schomburg Center for Research in Black Culture, The New York Public Library, Astor, Lenox and Tilden Foundations; **566** Chicago Historical Society; **567** The Library of Congress; **568** American Social History Project, New York; **570** The Library of Congress; **571 (top)** Harper's Weekly, November 16, 1867; **571 (bottom)** Reproduction from the Collections of the Library of Congress, LC-USZ62 33248; **572** American Social History Project, New York; **574** Cook Collection, Valentine Richmond History Center; **575** Reproduction from the collections of the Library of Congress, Prints & Photographs Division, P&P LC-USZ62-8788; **576** Alabama Department of Archives and History, Montgomery, Alabama; **577 (top)** Collection of Greg French; **577 (bottom)** Stern Collection of Licolniana, Rare Book and Special Collections, LOC, Portfolio 4, #31; **578** Fine Arts Museums of San Francisco, Gift of Joseph Martin Jr., 1994.120.4; **579 (top left)** American Social History Project, New York; **579 (top right)** © Corbis; **579 (bottom)** American Antiquarian Society; **581** American Social History Project, New York; **586 (top)** Metropolitan Museum of Art, Rogers Fund, 1948. (48.80) Photograph, all rights reserved, The Metropolitan Museum of Art; **586 (bottom)** Ed

Sullivan / Museum of American Political Life; **587 (top)** Library of Congress, Prints & Photographs Division, LC-USZ62-22260; **587 (bottom)** Library of Congress; **588–598** Thomas Pollock Anshutz, *The Ironworker's Noontime*, 1880, oil on canvas 17 × 23 7/8 (43.2 × 60.6 cm), Fine Arts Museums of San Francisco, Gift of Mr. And Mrs. John D. Rockefeller 3rd, 1979.7.4; **590** Reproduction from the collections of the Library of Congress, Prints & Photographs Division, LC-USZ62-8788; **591** © Deutsches Historiches Museum, Unter den Linden 2, 0-1086 Berlin; **592** Reproduction from the collections of the Library of Congress, Prints & Photographs Division, LC-USZC4-11235; **594 (top)** Science, Industry & Business Library, The New York Public Library; Astor, Lenox, and Tilden Foundations; **594 (bottom)** The Granger Collection, NY; **596** Chicago Historical Society; **598** Reproduction from the collections of the Library of Congress, Prints & Photographs Division, LC-USZC4-435; **600 (top)** Reproduction from the collections of the Library of Congress, Prints & Photographs Division, LC-USZC4-4624; **600 (bottom)** Courtesy of the New-York Historical Society, New York City; **601 (top)** © Bettmann/Corbis; **601 (bottom)** Museum of the City of New York, The Jacob Riis Collection (#108); **602** Nebraska Historical Society; **604** California State Library; **605** Yale Collection of Western Americana, Beinecke Rare Book and Manuscript Library; **606** Courtesy of the New-York Historical Society, New York City; **607** The Metropolitan Museum of Art, Rogers Fund, 1907 (07.123). Image © 1985 The Metropolitan Museum of Art; **608** © Bettmann/Corbis; **609** Smithsonian, National Anthropological Archives; **613 (top left)** Smithsonian, National Anthropological Archives; **613 (top right)** Smithsonian, National Anthropological Archives; **613 (bottom)** Oklahoma Historical Society; **614** Library of Congress; **615** Department of the Interior; **616** Library of Congress, Prints & Photographs Division, LC-USZC4-494; **619** Museum of the City of New York; **622** Metropolitan Museum of Art, Rogers Fund, 1948. (48.80) Photograph, all rights reserved, The Metropolitan Museum of Art; **624** Scribner's Magazine, July 1895; **625 (top)** © Corbis; **625 (bottom)** © Bettmann/Corbis; **627** © Bettmann/Corbis; **629** © Bettmann/Corbis; **630** Wisconsin Historical Society, Whi-47662; **634–635** Frederic Remington Art Museum; **637** Keystone-Mast Collection, UCR/California Museum of Photography, University of California, Riverside. "General View of Blast Furnaces, Homestead, Pennsylvania" Image # WX13101; **638** Kansas State Historical Society; **639** Museum of American

Political Life; **640** People's Party Paper 25 February 1892; **642** Library of Congress, Prints & Photographs Division, LC-USZ62-9803; **643** Courtesy of Picture History; **644** Library of Congress, Prints & Photographs Division, LC-USZC4-9712; **645** National Museum of American History, Smithsonian Institution, Behring Center; **646** Florida State Archives; **647** Library of Congress, Prints & Photographs Division, LC-USZ62-74043; **648 (top)** Library of Congress; **648 (bottom)** Kansas State Historical Society; **649** Library of Congress Prints and Photographs Division, Historic American Building Survey Field Records, HABS FN-6, #KS-49-12; **653** Library of Congress, Prints & Photographs Division, LC-USZ-62-8660; **654** Judge Magazine; **655** This item is reproduced by permission of The Huntington Library, San Marino, California; **658** University of Washington Libraries, Special Collections, #1678; **659** Bettmann/Corbis; **661** Library of Congress, LC-USZ62-683; **663** Puck Magazine, Bernice Bishop Museum Archives, Honolulu, XS 30.782; **664** Library of Congress, Prints & Photographs Division, Minstrel Poster Collection, LC-USZ62-24126; **668** Library of Congress LC-USZ62-80332; **669** Library of Congress, Prints & Photographs Division, LC-USZCZ-1025; **670** American Social History Project, NY; **671** © David J. & Janice L. Frent Collection/Corbis; **xviii, 674–675** Library of Congress, Prints & Photographs Division, Detroit Publishing Company Photograph Collection, LC USZC4-1584; **677** Brown Brothers; **678** The J. Paul Getty Museum, Los Angeles, © Estate of Georgia O'Keeffe, © 2004 The Georgia O'Keeffe Foundation/Artists Rights Society (ARS), New York; **679 (top)** Museum of the City of New York, The Byron Collection; **679 (bottom)** The Phillips Collection, Washington, DC; **680 (left)** Bettmann/Corbis; **680 (right)** Bettmann/Corbis; **682 (top)** World Magazine; **682 (bottom)** George Eastman House; **684 (top)** Library of Congress, Prints & Photographs Division, LC-USZ62-97491; **684 (bottom)** Brooklyn Museum; **685 (top)** Museum of the City of New York, The Byron Collection; **685 (bottom)** Library of Congress, Prints & Photographs Division, LC-USZ62-70774; **686** John Sloan, cover of *The Masses*, July 1913; **687** Keystone-Mast Collection, UCR/California Museum of Photography, University of California, Riverside. "Upholstery Department, Ford Motor Company, Michigan" image # X12063; **688 (top)** © Bettmann/Corbis; **688 (bottom)** Reproduced from the Collections of the Library of Congress, LC USZ6-620; **690** © Corbis; **694** Walter P. Reuther Library, Wayne State University; **695 (top)** Brown Brothers; **695 (bottom)** Reproduced from the

TEXT, TABLES, AND FIGURES

(Washington, D.C., 1975) 131; **686** (Table 18.4) U.S. Bureau of the Census, *Historical Statistics of the United States* (Washington, D.C., 1975) 139; **687** (Table 18.5) U.S. Bureau of the Census, *Historical Statistics of the United States* (Washington, D.C., 1975) 716; **747** (Table 19.1) Robert B. Grant, *The Black Man Comes to the City* (Chicago, 1972), 28–30; **774** André Siegfried, "The Gulf Between" excerpt from *The Atlantic Monthly*, Vol. 141, 289–95; **787** (Table 20.1) Mae M. Ngai, "The Architecture of Race in American Immigration Law: A Reexamination of the Immigration Act of 1924, *Journal of American History 86* (June 1999), 25; **823** John Steinbeck, "The Harvest Gypsies: On the Road to the Grapes of Wrath" excerpt from *America and Americans and Selected Nonfiction* (New York: Heyday Boooks, 1988); **858** (Table 22.1) U.S. Bureau of the Census, *Historical Statistics of the United States, Colonial Times to 1970* (Washington, D.C., 1970), 176–77; **915** Copyright © 1947 by *Harper's Magazine*, all rights reserved, reproduced from the September issue by special permission; **952** Copyright 1952, 1953, by David E. Lilienthal. Copyright renewed © 1980 by David E. Lilienthal & 1981 by David E. Lilienthal, Jr. Reprinted by permission of HarperCollins Pub-

lishers; **953** Reprinted by arrangement with The Heirs to the Estate of Martin Luther King Jr., c/o Writers House as agent for the proprietor, New York, NY. Copyright 1969 the Estate of Martin Luther King Jr., copyright renewed 1997 Coretta Scott King; **981** (Figure 25.1) *Congressional Quarterly, Civil Rights: A Progress Report* (1971), 46; **988** "The Sharon Statement" by Young Americans for Freedom, from the *National Review*, September 24, 1960, 173; **989** Used by permission of Tom Hayden; **1015** (Table 26.1) U.S. Bureau of the Census, *Statistical Abstract of the United States* (Washington, D.C., 1982); **1034** The Redstockings Manifesto was issued in New York City on July 7, 1969. It first appeared as a mimeographed flyer, designed for distribution at women's liberation events. Further information about the Manifesto and other materials from the 1960s rebirth years of feminism is available from the Redstockings Women's Liberation Archives for Action at www.redstockings.org; **1035** Phyllis Schlafly, "The Fraud of the Equal Rights Amendment," *The Phyllis Schlafly Report*, Vol. 5, February 1972. Reprinted with permission of Phyllis Schlafly; **1068** Puwat Charukamnoetkanok, "Triple Identity: My Experience as an Immigrant in America" (1990)

reproduced with permission; **1069** Used by permission of Global Exchange; **1070** (Table 27.1) *2001 Statistical Yearbook of the Immigration and Naturalization Service* (Washington, D.C., 2002), 6–9; **1075** (Table 27.2) Lizabeth Cohen, *A Consumer's Republic: The Politics of Mass Consumption in Postwar America* (New York, 2003) 222; **1076** (Figure 27.4) U.S. Census Bureau; **A29** Reprinted by arrangement with The Heirs to the Estate of Martin Luther King Jr., c/o Writers House as agent for the proprietor, New York, NY. Copyright 1969 the Estate of Martin Luther King Jr., copyright renewed 1997 Coretta Scott King; **A34** U.S. National Archives and Records Administration; **A44** *Historical Statistics of the United States* (1975); *Statistical Abstract of the United States* (1991, 1996); Population Estimates Program, Population Division, U.S. Census Bureau, April 2001.

Every effort has been made to contact the copyright holder of each of the selections. Rights holders of any selections not credited should contact Permissions Department, W. W. Norton & Company, Inc., 500 Fifth Avenue, New York, NY 10110, in order for a correction to be made in the next reprinting of our work.

Page numbers in *italics* refer to illustrations.

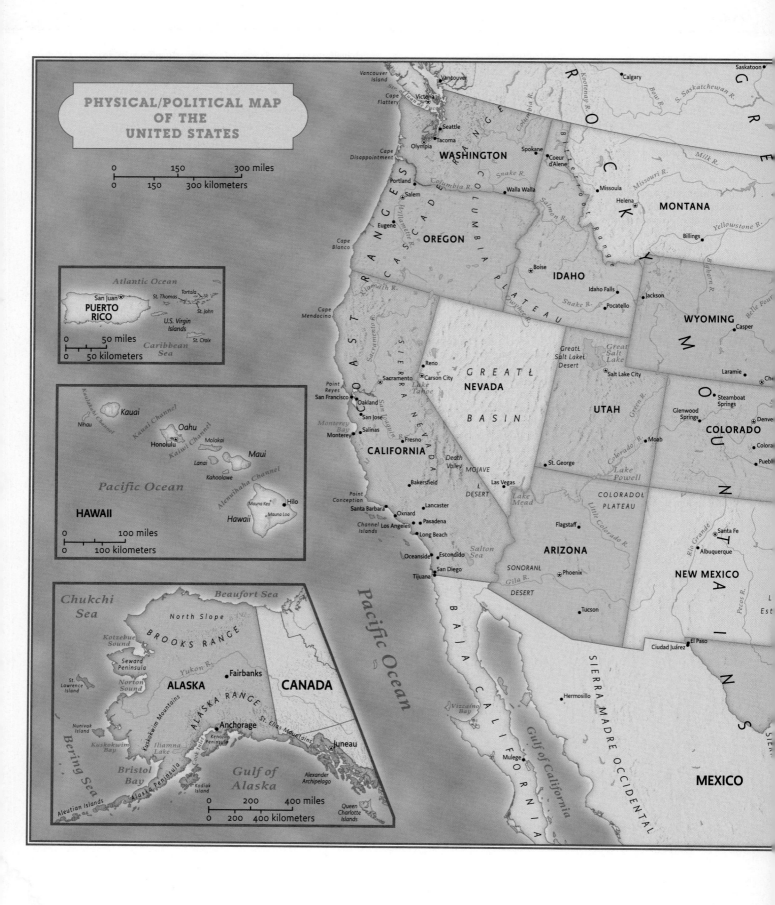

PHYSICAL/POLITICAL MAP OF THE UNITED STATES

0   150   300 miles
0   150   300 kilometers

PUERTO RICO
Atlantic Ocean
San Juan
St. Thomas   Tortola
St. John
U.S. Virgin
Islands
St. Croix
Caribbean
Sea
0   50 miles
0   50 kilometers

HAWAII
Kauai
Niihau   Kauai Channel
Oahu
Honolulu   Molokai
Lanai   Maui
Kahoolawe
Kaiwi Channel
Alenuihaha Channel
Mauna Kea
Mauna Loa
Hilo
Hawaii
Pacific Ocean
0   100 miles
0   100 kilometers

ALASKA
Chukchi
Sea
Beaufort Sea
North Slope
BROOKS RANGE
Kotzebue
Sound
Seward
Peninsula
Norton
Sound
St.
Lawrence
Island
Yukon R.
Fairbanks
ALASKA
CANADA
Nunivak
Island
Kuskokwim Mountains
Kuskokwim
Bay
Iliamna
Lake
ALASKA RANGE
Anchorage
St. Elias Mountains
Juneau
Bering
Sea
Bristol
Bay
Alaska Peninsula
Kodiak
Island
Kenai
Peninsula
Cook Inlet
Gulf of
Alaska
Alexander
Archipelago
Aleutian Islands
Queen
Charlotte
Islands
0   200   400 miles
0   200   400 kilometers

Vancouver
Island
Vancouver
Cape
Flattery
Victoria
Seattle
Tacoma
Olympia
WASHINGTON
Spokane
Coeur
d'Alene
Cape
Disappointment
Portland
Salem
Columbia R.
Walla Walla
Snake R.
Missoula
Helena
MONTANA
Billings
Yellowstone R.
Milk R.
Missouri R.
Calgary
Bow R.
S. Saskatchewan R.
Saskatoon
ROCKY
GRE
Eugene
CASCADE RANGE
OREGON
COLUMBIA PLATEAU
Boise
IDAHO
Idaho Falls
Pocatello
Snake R.
Jackson
WYOMING
Casper
Belle Four
Bighorn R.
Bitterroot Range
Salmon R.
Cape
Blanco
COAST RANGES
Klamath R.
Cape
Mendocino
Sacramento R.
Reno
Sacramento
Carson City
Lake
Tahoe
GREAT
NEVADA
BASIN
Great
Salt Lake
Desert
Great
Salt
Lake
Salt Lake City
UTAH
Laramie
Steamboat
Springs
Glenwood
Springs
COLORADO
Denver
M
O
U
N
T
Point
Reyes
San Francisco
Oakland
San Jose
Monterey
Bay
Salinas
Monterey
SIERRA NEVADA
San Joaquin R.
Fresno
CALIFORNIA
Death
Valley
MOJAVE
DESERT
Bakersfield
Las Vegas
St. George
Green R.
Colorado R.
Moab
Lake
Powell
COLORADO
PLATEAU
Little Colorado R.
Colora
Pueblo
Point
Conception
Santa Barbara
Oxnard
Pasadena
Lancaster
Los Angeles
Long Beach
Channel
Islands
Oceanside
Escondido
San Diego
Tijuana
Salton
Sea
Lake
Mead
SONORAN
DESERT
Gila R.
Flagstaff
ARIZONA
Phoenix
Tucson
NEW MEXICO
Santa Fe
Albuquerque
Rio Grande
Ciudad Juárez
El Paso
Pecos R.
Est
SIERRA MADRE OCCIDENTAL
Hermosillo
BAJA CALIFORNIA
Vizcaíno
Bay
Mulege
Gulf of
California
MEXICO
SIER
Pacific Ocean

POLITICAL MAP of the WORLD

Scale at equator

0 — 750 — 1,500 miles
0 — 750 — 1,500 kilometers

Arctic Ocean

Ellesmere Island

Queen Elizabeth Islands

Greenland (Denmark)

Banks Island

Baffin Bay

Beaufort Sea

Amundsen Gulf

Victoria Island

Baffin Island

Baffin Strait

Chukchi Sea

RUSSIA

Alaska (U.S.)

Foxe Basin

Denmark Strait

ICELAND

Reykjavik

Jan Ma (No

Bering Sea

Gulf of Alaska

Hudson Strait

Hudson Bay

Labrador Sea

IRELAND

Celtic Sea

English

Aleutian Islands

CANADA

North Atlantic Ocean

North Pacific Ocean

Ottawa ·Montréal

Toronto·

PORTUGAL

Lisbon·

Chicago·

New York

Azores (Por.)

UNITED STATES

Washington, D.C.

Madeira Islands (Por.)

Rabat

San Francisco

MOROCCO

Los Angeles·

Bermuda (U.K.)

Canary Islands (Sp.)

Western Sahara (Mor.)

Dallas ·

Hawaii (U.S.)

Gulf of Mexico

Nassau

BAHAMAS

Nouakchott·

MAURITANIA

MEXICO

Havana·

CUBA

HAITI

DOMINICAN REPUBLIC

Puerto Rico (U.S.)

ST. KITTS AND NEVIS

CAPE VERDE

SENEGAL

Mexico City·

BELIZE

DOMINICA

GAMBIA

Kiritimati (Kiribati)

GUATEMALA

JAMAICA

ST. LUCIA

ST. VINCENT AND THE GRENADINES

GUINEA-BISSAU

GUINEA

EL SALVADOR

Caribbean Sea

BARBADOS

SIERRA LEONE

CÔTE D'IVO

HONDURAS

TRINIDAD AND TOBAGO

LIBERIA

Ivo Coas

NICARAGUA

Caracas·

SÃO

Phoenix Islands

COSTA RICA

VENEZUELA

GUYANA

KIRIBATI

PANAMA

Bogotá

·

Galapagos Islands (Ecuador)

COLOMBIA

French Guiana (Fr.)

Ascension (U.

Marquesas Islands (Fr.)

Quito·

ECUADOR

SURINAME

SAMOA

South Pacific Ocean

PERU

BRAZIL

Apia·

Pago Pago

Lima·

FIJI

Papeete·

Cook Islands

French Polynesia (Fr.)

La Paz

·Brasília

S (

TONGA

Nuku'alofa·

BOLIVIA

Sucre·

Pitcairn Islands (U.K.)

PARAGUAY

Rio de Janeiro·

South Atlant Ocean

·Adamstown

Easter Island (Chile)

Asunción·

Tristan Da Group (U.

Juan Fernandez Archipelago (Chile)

Santiago·

URUGUAY

Buenos Aires·

Montevideo·

CHILE

ARGENTINA

S (

THE POLES

Atlantic Ocean

Southern Ocean

Pacific Ocean

SOUTH AMERICA

ANTARCTICA

Pacific Ocean

Southern Ocean

Indian Ocean

Pacific Ocean

NORTH AMERICA

Arctic Ocean

ASIA

Atlantic Ocean

EUROPE

0 — 1,500 miles
0 — 1,500 kilometers

Falkland Islands (U.K.)

South Georgia

South Sandwich Islands

Scotia Sea

South Shetland Islands

South Orkney Islands

Southern